Center for Basque Studies
Conference Papers Series, No. 3

Voicing the Moment

Improvised Oral Poetry and Basque Tradition

EDITED BY

Samuel G. Armistead and Joseba Zulaika

Center for Basque Studies
University of Nevada, Reno
Reno, Nevada

This book was published with generous financial support from the Basque Government.

Center for Basque Studies
Conference Papers Series, No. 3
Series Editors: Joseba Zulaika and Cameron J. Watson

Center for Basque Studies
University of Nevada, Reno
Reno, Nevada 89557
http://basque.unr.edu

Cover and Series design © 2005 by Jose Luis Agote.
Cover photograph by de César Lera. Background photograph by Juantxo Egaña.

Library of Congress Cataloging-in-Publication Data

Voicing the moment : improvised oral poetry and Basque tradition / edited by Samuel G.
Armistead and Joseba Zulaika.
    p. cm. -- (Center for Basque Studies conference papers series ; no. 3)
    "The first international symposium on Basque orally improvised poetry was held in
Reno (Nevada), on May 16-17, 2003, under the auspices of the Center for Basque Studies
at the University of Nevada, Reno"--Pref.
    Includes bibliographical references (p.) and index.
    ISBN 1-877802-56-5 -- ISBN 1-877802-55-7 (pbk.)
  1. Folk poetry, Basque--History and criticism. 2. Folk poetry,
Spanish--History and criticism. 3. Improvisation (Music) I. Armistead,
Samuel G., 1927- II. Zulaika, Joseba. III. University of Nevada, Reno.
Center for Basque Studies. IV. Title. V. Series.

    PH5290.V65 2005
    398.2-dc22

2005013593

CONTENTS

Acknowledgments

The international symposium on which this volume is based was underwritten by the Bernard and Lucie Marie Bidart Fund, through the guidance and support of Mike and Jeannette Bidart. For many years Mike has shown not only that he is a first class lawyer, but that his passion for Basque songs, accordion, and *bertsolaritza* are equally unparalleled. All we lovers of orally improvised poetry are indebted to him for the initial idea and the financial support of the entire project. *Esker anitz!*

The symposium also received a generous grant from the Program for Cultural Cooperation – Spanish Ministry of Education, Culture and Sports and United States Universities.

Finally, we thank Karen Olson, at the University of California, Davis, Jill Berner, at the Center for Basque Studies, and in particular Cameron Watson for skillfully shepherding the manuscript and its various authors though the editorial process. We would also like to thank Kate Camino for her indispensable help.

Preface

The first International Symposium on Basque orally improvised poetry was held in Reno (Nevada), on May16-17, 2003, under the auspices of the Center for Basque Studies at the University of Nevada, Reno. Papers read at the conference included, on one hand, contributions from a number of scholars involved in the study of oral theory and Hispanic and extra-Hispanic improvised poetry and, on the other, papers in which leading practitioners of *bertsolaritza* studied, evaluated, and characterized their own poetic art and its techniques. We believe that such a happy combination of diverse perspectives may constitute a significant addition to the growing body of scholarship concerning orally improvised poetry, in theory and in practice. As a fitting prologue to the present volume, Antonio Zavala describes his own heroic, single-handed, life-long commitment to documenting, evaluating, and vindicating *bertso* poetry as an authentic –indeed *the* authentic– expression of the Basque cultural heritage. We have divided our edition of the proceedings into five segments: I. The Theoretical/ Comparative Frame; II. The Iberian Context; III. *Bertsolariak*: Histories; IV. New Theories; and V. Music.

In a survey of improvised oral poetry in the Hispanic tradition, S. G. Armistead documents a variety of Mediterranean and Near Eastern cultural currents that may have contributed to the origins of oral improvisation in the Hispanic tradition, pointing to Latin, Hispano-Arabic, and early Castilian invective poetry, as early antecedents to modern forms of oral improvisation. Maximiano Trapero identifies and documents, within a world-wide context, the diverse regional subtraditions of modern improvised poetry in Spain: Basque *bertsolaritza*, Murcian and Alpujarreño *trovos*, the Balearic *glosat*, the Galician *regueifa*, and the Canarian *punto cubano*. John Miles Foley looks at oral traditions from a wide-ranging, trimillenial comparative perspective. Asking two challenging questions: "What does an oral bard really do?" and "What is a *word* in oral tradition?", in search of answers, Foley studies the performance and the poetry of Tibetan paper-singers and South Slavic *guslari*. As Foley shows, Gutenberg's printing press came into existence only on day 363 of Homo Sapiens' Species-Year and essentially throughout human existence, "oral poetry has been the major medium for communication of cultural knowledge." From the perspective of Basque *bertsolaritza*, John Zemke studies Biblical and Medieval Hebrew improvised debate poetry and its representation in literature as a "*fictive* poetic contest," Zemke discovers the same phenomenon in Provençal *tenso* poetry, in Galician Portuguese

Joxerra Garzia and Samuel G. Armistead, participants in the first International Symposium on Basque orally improvised poetry, Reno, 2003.
By permission of *Bertsolari Aldizkaria*.

cantigas de maldizer, in medieval Pan-European debate poetry (clerk-knight, water-wine, body-soul), in Juan Ruiz's *Libro de buen amor*, and in the *pregunta-respuesta* poems of Castilian *cancionero* court poetry.

Within the context of Iberian improvising tradition, James W. Fernandez discusses the phenomenon from an anthropologist's point of view, drawing examples from his own field work with Spanish Cantabrian versifiers and West African Fang sermonizers. William A. Christian has likewise done extensive field work in Cantabria (especially in Polaciones) and here he documents the flourishing and the decline of local improvised verse, its various functions in the area's traditional life, and also the existence of various other forms of oral poetry in the Polaciones tradition. James T. Monroe characterizes the multisecular Arabic tradition of invective *hijā'* poetry. This often brutally insulting and not infrequently obscene genre can already be documented in pre-Islamic times, while Saudi and Iraqi poets (or, in the latter case, rather their Yemeni surrogates) still continued to berate, in the most insulting terms, each other and their respective nations, by radio during the 1991 Gulf War. Monroe has discovered an early and notably important Hispano-Arabic text, dating from 912, which indisputably was improvised and which also embodies the earliest known example of a poetic text in Colloquial Andalusian Arabic. Recognizing many traditional features in Ibn Quzmān's Hispano-Arabic *zajals*, Monroe relates his poetry to a multisecular tradition of scurrilous songs. In the context of *bertso* poetry, Wifredo de Ràfols studies in depth Federico García Lorca's *Romance sonámbulo* ("Verde que te quiero verde"). Stressing Lorca's essential connection with and love of traditional poetry (in the words of Jorge Guillén: "... en Federico renacía el bardo anterior a la imprenta"), de Ràfols discovers multiple and previously unnoticed affinities between Lorca's brilliant poem, the traditional *Romancero*, and other genres of Spanish traditional poetry.

Diverse aspects of the history of *bertsolaritza* poetry are addressed in section III. Gorka Aulestia discusses in detail the genre's history in relation to the Basque Cultural Renaissance, to more recent developments, and to the current triumph of *bertsolarismo*, identifying and perceptively characterizing, at the same time, crucially important figures —poets, singers, and scholars— who have played significant roles in encouraging the cultivation of the genre. Aulestia's paper closes with useful comparative observations concerning the existence, in a world-wide perspective, of improvised poetry in other languages and cultures. Kepa Fernández de Larrinoa has done extensive field work in Zuberoa (Soule), concerning a complex polygeneric traditional form known as *Maskarada*, which combines drama, dance, and both memorized and improvised poetic performances. In tone, the *Maskarada* is obscene, parodic, transgressive, subversive, and multilingual (Basque, Occitan, French, Spanish) and seeks to undermine and devalue normally accepted symbols of social and political power. Traveling from village to village in Zuberoa, the *maskarakaiak* ("visiting performers") present their dance-play-recitations, also allowing, however, for input from the host village's performers. As Larrinoa demonstrates, the result is an extremely complex and intensely interesting folk literary phenomenon. Joxe Mallea-Olaetxe recalls childhood experiences in Bizkaia with Basque traditional narrative songs sung by his family and a crucial later conversation with his *bertsolari* friend, Jesus Goñi, concerning the current status of *bertsolaritza* in the American Northwest. Addressing an impressive number of topics and a wide variety of cultural problems, *bertso*

Arabic		Transcription	
أ	أَلِف	a	ʾalif
ب	بَاء	b	bāʾ
ت	تَاء	t	tāʾ
ث	ثَاء	ṯ	ṯāʾ
ج	جِيم	ǧ	ǧīm
ح	حَاء	ḥ	ḥāʾ
خ	خَاء	ḫ	ḫāʾ
د	دَال	d	dāl
ذ	ذَال	ḏ	ḏāl
ر	رَاء	r	rāʾ
ز	زَاي	z	zāī
س	سِين	s	sīn
ش	شِين	š	šīn
ص	صَاد	ṣ	ṣād
ض	ضَاد	ḍ	ḍād
ط	طَاء	ṭ	ṭāʾ
ظ	ظَاء	ẓ	ẓāʾ
ع	غَين	ʿ	ʿayn
غ	غَين	ġ	ġayn
ف	فَاء	f	fāʾ
ق	قَاف	q	qāf
ك	كَاف	k	kāf
ل	لَام	l	lām
م	مِيم	m	mīm
ن	نُون	n	nūn
ه	هَاء	h	hāʾ
و	وَاو	w	wāw
ي	يَاء	y	yāʾ

A transcription table for Arabic text. Several authors in the present volume will use these diacritics as a means of transliterating Arabic words and text into the Latin script.

singing would still seem to enjoy great popularity among Basques in the American West. But poignant *bertsos* composed by Jesus Goñi, about his difficult decision finally to leave the traditional world of sheepherding and move to a new life in an urban context, bespeak the profound problems of acculturation which must assail even the first-generation immigrant, his culture, his language, and his song tradition: "At a corner of the ranch, / I see the dog and the horse, / while waiting for me on the road / are the girl and the car." Addressing the vast cultural distance between his father's life and his own career as a university professor, Joseba Zulaika concludes that "we obviously belong to different worlds." Yet recalling how his father had formed and treasured his own richly diverse collection of *bertso* booklets and pamphlets and how, even alone, he was accustomed to sing them for his own enjoyment or sometimes also for anyone else who happened to be listening, Zulaika discovers a profound generational kinship by which any and all cultural differences fall away and are bridged, to reaffirm the shared common ground of a beloved tradition.

Under theoretical approaches, Linda White discusses whether or not formulaic theories can even be applied to Basque improvised poetry. Unlike the South Slavic *guslar* —a true singer of tales— who retells, in improvised form, a traditional narrative, with which both he and his audience are already well-acquainted, the Basque *bertsolari*, who is concerned with very modern, contemporary events and problems, is not recreating or retelling anything. His song is a total improvisation: "*Bertsolariak*, and Basque scholars who study them, believe that each verse is unique and no patterns are repeated or followed." White asks, however, if perhaps an examination of *bertsoak* might not reveal repetitive formulaic patterns. After studying thirty-six *bertsoak* created during *txapelketa* events held in 1997, White did not find "any favoritism with regard to specific bare words or phrases," yet "nouns, verbs and the inessive case were the clear favorites for use in rhyming." She concludes —tentatively— given the limited amount of material analyzed: "a case can be made that the postpositional structure of the language serves as an oral formulaic guide with regard to rhyme, ... [but such] similarities are not what others in the field intend when they speak of oral formulas."

Joxerra Garzia proposes a theoretic framework for improvised *bertsolaritza*, pointing out that "current analytical models are . . . . inadequate in explaining its extemporary nature." Garzia identifies an unfortunate "general tendency to judge and analyze works of oral art within the parameters of written culture." He offers a detailed account of the recent history and development of *bertsolaritza* and its evolving performance contexts, going on to stress that "orality and writing are not two mutually exclusive realities as the oralists would have it. Rather, they live together, at least in modern societies, in continuous interaction." He suggests that a possible frame for the study of improvised *bertsoak* may be discovered in the study of classical rhetoric. Garzia concludes by identifying a "progressive impoverishment of discourse" characterizing contemporary culture and hails the rhetorical skills inherent in the art of *bertsolaritza* as a possible corrective.

Jon Sarasua describes and characterizes present-day *bertsolaritza*, pointing to its five major manifestations: as a spectacle or as a public performance; as a contest; as infor-

Several participants in the first International Symposium on Basque orally improvised poetry, Lake Tahoe, Nevada, 2003. Andoni Egaña, Jon Sarasua, Joseba Zulaika, Joxerra Garzia, and Maximiano Trapero. By permission of *Bertsolari Aldizkaria*.

mal group entertainment; as a pedagogical exercise; and as a media sub-genre. Sarasua identifies three keys to the genre's future development: "attitudes of self-confidence, a determination to maintain transmission from generation to generation, and organizational self-management." He stresses four fundamental factors crucial to the future life and development of *bertsolaritza*: transmission, dissemination, archiving and research, and an awareness of territoriality. Sarasua closes by pointing out the crucial role being played by the Bertsozale Elkartea (Association of Friends of *Bertsolaritza*).

Andoni Egaña explores the process by which improvised *bertsoak* are created. This is "one of the few cultural expressions wherein the moment of artistic creation and that of its exposition to the public are one and the same." He discusses melodies, meters, and rhyme, and goes on to describe the principal strategies used in constructing improvised *bertsoak*. A basic and frequently used strategy is to compose first the *bertso*'s conclusion – its punch line. The singer's major goal is to establish and maintain an unbroken connection with the audience, to keep the listeners "glued" to the *bertso*. Egaña then reconstructs the hypothetical mental processes of a *bertsolari* faced with the challenge of improvising her/his *bertso* on a previously imposed topic. Egaña uncovers various exceptions to the strategy of composing the punch line first. For Egaña, the "soul of *bertsolaritza*" is the improvised oral confrontation, in which "one *bertsolari* faces another and they weave a performance of a greater or lesser number of *bertsoak* between the two of them."

Israel J. Katz concludes the conference proceedings with a study of *bertso* music. After tracing and documenting the early history of musicological scholarship on Basque traditional poetry (pioneers: Humboldt, Iztueta, Albéniz, Sallaberry), describing later developments (Arizmendi, Bordes, Manterola, Azkue, Barandiaran, et al.), followed by the public reemergence of *bertsolaritza,* after the Franco regime's failed attempt to crush the Basque language, popular culture, and traditional poetry, Katz goes on to transcribe and study six examples of *bertso* music. Three appendices list further data on *bertso* singing.

Samuel G. Armistead

Joseba Zulaika

Prologue

ANTONIO ZAVALA

How did I ever embark on this adventure? I was born in Tolosa (Gipuzkoa), a town that at that time had recently become bilingual, with our generation being the first to speak Spanish. My Basque literary baggage was limited to a few songs, together with a profusion of studies and readings in Spanish, so it wasn't the environment that motivated me.

The first time I heard a *bertsolari* perform was in Aduna, a town between Donostia (San Sebastián) and Tolosa. However, what influenced me even more at the time were the vendors selling *bertso-paperak*, poems printed on sheets of paper. These vendors continued to show up, every Saturday, in the Tolosa marketplace until the mid 1950s. There, at the old Castile gate, beside the Piarist school which had been a historical meeting place of Gipuzkoa's autonomous council, they hawked their wares; that is, they sang them. On one occasion a Piarist father, tired of the chanting, instructed one of his students to go and tell these singers to stop singing so he could conduct his class in peace. The boy ran outside, went up to the vendor, and said to him: "*Orko apaiz batek esan du oso ondo kantatzen dezula; eta ea gertuago jarriko zeran, obeto entzuteko*" ("One of our priests says you sing very well, and maybe you could move closer so we can hear you better"). I used to see those vendors when I got out of school at noon but never stopped to listen to them more carefully. Yet the image of the vendor, standing in the center of a circle of listeners hawking his papers, stuck in my memory. It was, in effect, the end of a thread I would later start to pull, having no idea what ball of yarn I would come up with.

Other things conspired to arouse my interest in the Basque-speaking world: excursions into the mountains, my years in Loiola (Loyola), a valley in Gipuzkoa where only Basque was spoken, and the reading of Basque books. From Oña (Castile) I wrote home asking that if anyone saw those vendors selling sheets of poetry in the marketplace, to buy one and send it to me. I then attended school in Javier (Navarre) where a student I met kept talking about all the sheets of poetry in his house. One year, just before leaving for Christmas vacation, I asked him to bring those papers back after the break for me to take a look at. When the buses arrived on the day after Epiphany, someone shouted to me: "*Ekarri ditut!*" ("I've brought them!"). That shout, beside Javier castle on January 7, 1954, was like a starting-gun that would eventually propel me toward my future task. There were about thirty sheets of paper in that batch, which immediately provoked a question: namely, if there was this much in a single home, how much more might there be throughout the entire Basque Country? Now it seemed well worth the trouble to try and collect it.

I started out by using the mail. I wrote off to where I thought there might be someone who had such papers or knew about their whereabouts. Some replied, others didn't. Then, in the summer I ventured out from Loiola or Donostia, and traveled from village to village and town to town. In many ways it was like going hunting, and indeed it produced the same feelings. For example, from a place where I expected good results, I'd often come back empty handed; and vice versa. How many archives and homes did I visit during this time? How many miles did I travel? I wouldn't know. But what did that matter to me, in my twenties? Recalling this now makes me feel quite nostalgic.

I didn't just collect *bertso-paperak* or sheets, of course. I also transcribed strophes that older people dictated to me if there was no written version. When an author or a genre began to pile up, I would just open a new file. I was a collector of something few people cared about and as such, I had no competition. For at that time puritanical *Sabiniano*[1] criteria still prevailed, by which popular poetry, expressed not in an ideal *Euskara* (the Basque language) people dreamed about but in the real Basque people used, had no value. There were, however, a few others who were also beginning the task of compilation: José Manterola and Gregorio Múgica from Donostia; father José Ignacio Arana, from Loiola; the Adurriaga brothers from Tolosa; Enrique Elicechea from Errenteria (Gipuzkoa); and Luis Dassance, from Uztaritze in Lapurdi (the northern Basque Country). There were collections I heard about, but which for one reason or another had disappeared: for example, one from the López-Mendizabal publishing house, another from the Muguerza publishing house, both in Tolosa; another very likely collection belonging to the priest Pedro Miguel de Urruzuno, from Mendaro (Gipuzkoa); still another was that of José Ariztimuño or "Aitzol," compiled in the 1930s during the years of the Second Republic and about which Gorka Aulestia has written extensively (Aulestia 1995 and 2003).

This was all new to me then, as I had entered unknown territory, with no knowledge of what was in store for me or any names other than Bilintx (Indalecio Bizkarrondo), Pello Mari Otaño, Ramos Azkarate, and Pello Errota. However, many others soon came to my attention: Xenpelar (Francisco Petrirena) and his classic *Bertso berriak Xenpelarrek jarriak* ("New Verses Composed by Xenpelar"), Txirrita (Joxe Manuel Lujanbio), Altzoko Imaz, Udarregi (Juan José Alkain), Gaztelu (Juan Ignacio Goikoetxea), Fermin Imaz, Lezo, the Zapirain and Zabaleta brothers, Zubizarreta, Ramón Artola, Paulo Yanzi, Iturzaeta, and Mendaro Txirristaka (Eusebio Mugertza). I also heard about Jean Baptiste Elizanburu, Ibarrart, Joanes Oxalde, Etxahun (Pierre Topet), from the other side of the river

---

1. From Sabino de Arana y Goiri (1865–1903), the founder of Basque nationalism.

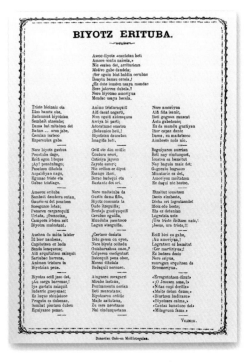

Bertso-paperak. The traditional recorded, written form of improvised, oral poetry in Basque.
By permission of the Xenpelar Dokumentazio Zentroa, Donostia.

Bidasoa in Iparralde or the northern Basque Country. I was amazed at the variety of topics treated: the lives of saints, such as Santa Bárbara by Xenpelar or Santa Genoveva by Zapirain; popular missions; compositions related to the Marian sanctuaries: Arantzazu, Itziar, and Izaskun; and poems about the exploits of fishing boats from Orio, Pasaia (Pasajes), and Ondarroa, about which I have just published a collection of more than seventeen hundred stanzas. In the prologue to this collection I recall the vendor of *bertso-paperak* who, one Sunday morning in September 1941, planted himself in the doorway of the parish church in Tolosa and began to sing (I might even have heard him from my bed) stanzas in honor of the Hondarribi rowing crew which had just won the Donostia regatta.

There were also compositions about various traditional Basque sports: for example, wagers on competitions between *aizkolariak* ("woodchoppers"), *arri-jasotzailleak* ("stone lifters"), and bar throwers, as well those on *pelota* ("Basque handball") matches and ox pulls. Others addressed numerous conflicts from the war of the Convention (between Spain and France), the Spanish-American war, Spain's colonial wars in North Africa, World War One, and the Spanish Civil War. During the two nineteenth-century Carlist wars in Spain (which were principally fought in the Basque provinces), both sides fought not only with guns, but also with verse, in order to win over the people.

There was also a great deal of verse dedicated to matters of the heart. Sometimes, if a young man was jilted by his girl, if her love turned to hate, he would go and explain the situation to a *bertsolari* in his own way. The latter would then write a few stanzas denigrating the poor girl, take the young man's money and the *bertso-papera* would be printed and distributed. Sometimes the girl would respond or her father would sue the boy. I have a copy of one such verdict, and have published two volumes with strophes on this genre, though without the names of persons and places, so we have the accounts of the sins but not the names of the sinners.

Other compositions typically describe the relations between a *morroi* ("servant") and *nagusi* ("master"), the poverty of life, or hunger because life in the Basque Country has not exactly been idyllic. This led to the hemorrhage of emigration, as expressed, for example, by Patxi Bakallo, José Mendiague, or Pedro María Otaño. Indeed, some sheets concerning this theme were published in Buenos Aires. Others are about shipwrecks, northwesterly gale winds, and whales. For example, in 1878 some Zarautz (Gipuzkoa) whalers injured a whale but it was taken away from them by some other whalers from the neighboring town of Getaria. This lead to a trial to determine who the rightful owners were, while in the meantime, days went by and the whale rotted. Farm workers talk, for example, about a deal struck over a cow or a strike by dairy workers. And just like fishermen, they describe not so much their routine daily lives but things that interrupt its monotony. This is similar to what happens in the epistolary genre, where one doesn't communicate what one thinks the recipients know but rather what they don't know.

There are other topics, of course, but the above mentioned themes serve to show that in popular poetry our people reveal their whole life and soul. And they do this with the sincerity of people who are not aware that they are testifying, and a certain naturalness of expression that is akin to those people who, for example, aren't aware they are being photographed.

Early on, these compositions were committed to people's memory or written down on paper. This produced the handwritten evidence that appears from time to time in the archives. However the great step forward, namely the printing of these verses, seems to have taken place towards the end of the eighteenth century. This method became more and more popular, and was already quite common, for example, by the time of the first Carlist war (1833–1839). Thereafter, over many decades, an eternal spring bloomed in our land, because, no matter the month, leaves (or sheets) sprouted constantly; sheets of popular poetry that is, the *bertso-paperak*, which were sold in marketplaces and on pilgrimages.

How many hundreds of compositions were printed during this period? If what's been preserved is substantial, far more must have been lost. Sometimes I think our people have been afflicted (or blessed) with a veritable *bertso*-mania. Without doubt, though, this was dealt a serious blow during the bitter Spanish Civil War (1936–1939), although even during the conflict we kept writing verse. And after the war, during the Franco dictatorship (1939–1975), the old tree sprouted new shoots, for there were always those who managed to side-step censorship, like matadors. The decision to allow the publication and sale of *bertso-paperak* must have depended, I believe, on local authorities. Indeed, there are sheets dating from the 1950s and even the 1960s although it was at this time that, after a century and a half of life, the *bertso-paperak* or printed sheets of popular poetry died.

However, the *bertso* phenomenon continued producing fruit in a different way. Specifically, newspapers and magazines at this time were enriched by the compositions of new poets: Basarri (Ignacio Eizmendi), Machain, Kalonje, Salaberria, Olea, Ibaiertz, Manterola, Ataño, Izazpi, Iraola, Mujika, Santi Zabala, Lertxundi, and many others. In this way thousands of strophes, generally of high quality, were published during the next three decades. Yet ultimately this new flowering also declined and popular Basque poetry is no longer published. Poetry contests are organized and prizes are awarded, but the poems aren't published or it remains difficult to access them. Can it be because those running the media don't like the genre? Or are the people quenching their thirst from another source?

Because that's what the people sought in popular poetry: to quench their aesthetic-literary thirst. In other words, the mission that typically literature or the press fulfills in other matters was carried out among us by these simple poetic manifestations, which were born as small, humble wildflowers. My work of gathering this poetic work, which led me to knock on so many doors, was by this time becoming known. So it was that after two and a half years, in September 1956, when the collected materials were already substantial, I was invited to present a paper at a conference of Basque studies in Arantzazu (Gipuzkoa), the first since the Spanish Civil War. In retrospect, I can see now that that this presentation was a public declaration of intentions and projects that gave a certain official character to my work.

By the 1960s it was clear to me that the time had come to start publishing my findings; for returning to the people what I had received from them. As a result, in 1961 I started a book series entitled *Auspoa*, meaning "bellows," because a bellows is used to do what we wanted to do: namely, to revive a flame. This collection currently consists of 238 titles, in addition to twenty large volumes, and its content can be divided in two parts: one in verse, the other in prose.

In the first part appear the biographies and poems of old *bertsolariak*, whom I have already mentioned, together with numerous compositions by contemporary *bertsolariak*. For example, one can consult the work of Basarri, Uztapide, Xalbador, Mattin, Lasarte, Enbeita, Olea, Arozamena, Lexoti, Arrosagaray, Salaberría, Pujana, Ernani-Txikia, Aierbe, Tximela, Mujika, Etxebarria, Aiesta, Lertxundi, Zendoia, Kalonje, Ataño, Txomin Garmendia, Azpillaga, Joxe Lizaso, Intxausti, Matxain, and Mugartegi; quite a few of whom have already died.

The second part, the books in prose, was put together slowly. On the one hand, I began to observe, as I chatted with ordinary men and women, that there were excellent narrators among them. On the other, I sought to accompany the publication of the verse with an explanation of the purposes that motivated them. For this task I got information from the children, relatives or friends of the author, as well as from history books, in the case of sheets related to politics or wars. While these events were happening, poems were created for an audience that already knew about the context; therefore we, less aware of exactly what was happening at the time they were created, might end up unaware of how things were really progressing.

That information sometimes turned out to be more interesting than the poems themselves. With time it became clear to me that there existed here a narrative, traditional and ancient art, handed down from elders and practiced privately (usually in the kitchen) at home and publicly in the village tavern. Why not, I thought, put those oral narrations in print? This is precisely what I did with the case of the *bertsolari* Joxe Manuel Lujanbio, or Txirrita (1860–1936). People who had known him were still alive and I began transcribing their testimonies, together with anecdotes and events recounted by his nephew, who had lived with his uncle for sixteen years. This was followed in 1963 by the book *Pello Errotaren bizitza bere alabak kontatua* ("The Life of Pello Errota Narrated by his Daughter"); he was ninety-three at the time.

In 1964 came the war memoirs of Sebastián Salaberría and the autobiography of Jose Ramon Subillaga, followed a few years later (in 1975) by that of Uztapide: *Lengo egunak gogoan* ("The Memory of Past Days"). There followed the books about Alkain, Irazusta, Arrizabalo, Erauskin, as well as those of the inexhaustible Ataño, Otxiki, Txomin Garmendia, Aierbe, Echebarne, Etxaburu, Azpiroz, Ibaiertz, Barandiaran, Beñat Karrika, Pujana, Lertxundi, Lasarte, Zinkunegi, Mujika, Etxebarria, Olea, Aiesta, Zendoia, Kosme Lizaso, Gerrikagoitia, and Larre.

These books are a testimony to both the lives and the world of their authors. At times, the author puts together a novel from his experiences, which also ends up being a way of bearing witness. They are books with a dual purpose: namely that of both the author, who remembers his life and of yours truly. For I see myself like the godfather of the child and, of course, the scribe of the work, who seeks, as he draws the likeness of a specific man, to paint at the same time a portrait of the entire community or town to which that individual belongs.

Father Francisco Apalategui, a professor of history for many years, was a pioneer in this genre. During the 1920s he began to interview veterans of the second Carlist war (1873–1876) from both sides, in order to transcribe their testimony in the language of the interviewee. In other words, he did this as a way of relating the history of the struggle, not from the top down, observing the events through the eyes of the leaders, but from the bottom up, through the eyes of the people. He eventually filled four notebooks, the publication of which I am now undertaking. These anecdotes are so rich that it's as if we weren't reading, but rather seeing and hearing what happened.

What Father Apalategui did, using the means available during that time and involving an armed conflict, I seek to accomplish now using modern methods and by broadening the scope to all aspects of the subjects' lives, in peace as well as war. I do not approach the people with a questionnaire as I believe such an approach distorts their life experiences. Rather, I let my informants speak freely. The framing can come later, just as grammar emerges from the spontaneous life of languages, or maps from geography. This popular language is very important among us because it presents Basque thought through *Euskara* or the Basque language, and there are fewer and fewer who do it this way, given the pressure from neighboring languages.

But it would be wrong to think that good narrators are exclusive to the Basque world, for I found them as well in the different provinces of Spain. Indeed, I came to see that there, too, were the products of a potentially rich mine although I remained reluctant to involve myself in new adventures. That was until one afternoon, when, after correcting the proofs of the book on the *Donostiarra* poet Bilintx, I decided to get some fresh air and visit the gothic hermitage of San Zoilo in Cáseda (Navarre). Here, flocks of sheep being herded from the Pyrenees to the La Bardena region of southern Navarre sleep at night. On the road I met an old man, Humbelino Ayape, who broke down my former resistance to studying verse outside the Basque-speaking world with all the interesting things he told me in that short time. My relationship with him ultimately led to four volumes entitled *Las tardes de la Bardena* ("Afternoons in La Bardena"). *La última trova* ("The Last Treasure"), by the Cantabrian Indalecio Zaballa, saw the light of day even earlier. Next came three by Hilario Jarne, from upper Aragón, entitled *Junto al fogaril de Atarés* ("By the Fire in Atarés"); and *El pastor del páramo* ("The Shepherd of the Wasteland") by Justo Peña from Burgos. The rest allow us to breathe the air of Asturias, Jaén, León, Burgos, Extremadura, Navarre, or the smell of gunpowder from the civil war.

Altogether, there are twenty-five volumes in this series. Previously I would go looking for informants; now, a number of them approached me with manuscript in hand. Perhaps my initiative was a wake-up call at a critical moment. Because I have met a few, but I am sure there must be many more grandfathers now, who, aware of having grown up in a world very different to this one, will decide to leave some proof and written testimony of their youth. On gathering such narratives, the work accomplished has not been two-sided, in other words one for each language, but rather a single work in two languages. For when botanists study and collect the flora of one region, they won't stop doing it just because they move to another.

It may be that I overvalue this genre, because of course there's great charm in hearing a good story from the lips of a shepherd, accompanied by the clanging of bells, while looking out over the snowy peaks of the Pyrenees or the vast spaces of the Castilian *meseta*. So I continue on, always wondering if I do what I do, not for its own merit but because it gives me pleasure. Another thing I can't figure out is whether my work consists of history, anthropology, ethnology, philology, or literature. Perhaps there's an element of each of these disciplines, but this is something that doesn't worry me and, indeed, that almost gives me pleasure. It's obvious that the existing source is far from being exhausted, and that the spring continues to flow. Earlier I thought that this work would take me a few years to complete and that I would have to come up with a new task for later on. That is, before I was looking for work to fill my time, but now I would like to find the time to do my work.

I referred earlier to the change the world has undergone. I am in the habit of saying that the environment in which today's older people were raised, especially those from the countryside, looked more like the Middle Ages than the information era in which their grandchildren are growing up. Between these two generations there's more distance than there was between many generations earlier. Yet this mutation doesn't just affect the circumstances, but also the very essence of things. I at least can verify that, after almost fifty years of dedication to the matter, this has changed to the point of being totally different. In other words, I see now that the mentality with which one creates and receives popular literature is different.

Before, this was a need for the masses. What it expressed shaped the mentality of the people, just as that of an educated person is shaped by the sediment received from reading books. In our homes, the names Xenpelar, Txirrita, or Pedro María Otaño have the same resonance as world famous authors have elsewhere. What the skill of those authors represents for the educated person was what that of the *bertsolariak* meant to our people, who regarded them not only as teachers but almost as prophets. That's the way it was for generations. When did this influence begin to diminish? In the history of all peoples, there is a time when everything is popular culture; then, this coexists with culture acquired in classrooms. However, the latter then begins to gain influence until finally it becomes the only culture.

The same thing happens in other areas such as craftsmanship, for example. This was a skill that in the beginning provided everyone with utensils and tools. Then came competition from industry, which ended up monopolizing everything. Yet the products of manual or mental craftsmanship don't entirely disappear, because among those people educated according to modern precepts, there are always a few, perhaps a bit romantic or nostalgic, who might not exactly believe that the past was perfect, but who suspect that modern times may not be any better either.

So they come up with the idea of salvaging everything of value from the sinking ship. This is the work we so-called folklorists are engaged in; preserving in books what was formerly considered life in the minds and on the lips of the people. In the same way, others collect the utensils used by these same people –the beds they were born in and where they slept and died; the clothes they wore; the pots they cooked in and the dishes from which they ate; or the tools with which they worked– and carefully preserve them in museums. Sometimes I think there's something book-like about museums; and books, at least the ones that I and others like me publish, are much like museums. There's an infinity of things that we value first for the utility they provide; and afterwards, out of gratitude, for the service they once rendered us. At first we need them for living, but later they live on, or are maintained, thanks to us.

But at this moment a radical change is taking place. Those objects still have the same components, but they signify something different. What was once a resource or a tool for life has now become an adornment. Currently, then, in our houses (and elsewhere) we view what was, in our childhood, a utensil for everyday life as decoration: yokes end up as hanging frames; the wheels from carts are hung as chandeliers in churches; mortars rest on chests of drawers; and horseshoes are transformed into coat hangers. Similarly, ethnographic museums are created for all the tools that have fallen into disuse and in church towers, bells no longer ring out their distinctive sounds, but remain silent and are replaced by a carillon.

The old customs, too, which were once the life and soul of the people, have become spectacle, merely another ornament or decoration. In village festivals, representations of weddings or pilgrimages are organized in this manner, sometimes resulting even more showy than authentic ones from past times. In the same way, imitations of ancient ironmongery, fabricated today not for use but to be sold to tourists and as gifts for display, may be of even higher quality than authentic ironwork. The law of change is formulated in an old quatrain: "At the door of the mill / I started to consider / the turns the stone makes / and those still to be made." And one day while I was taking a walk, I came to a sudden stop, because right in front of me was a millstone converted into a garden table.

In folkloric demonstrations the same thing happens. When a group performs a traditional dance for us today, they'll do it much better than their grandparents and great grandparents. However, back then that dance was life. Today it's spectacle. The *txistulariak* (Basque flute players) or *trikitilariak* (small accordion players) of today probably play their instruments better than those of the past. But while older generations did so in a plaza full of young men and women dancing, the modern ones do it in a hall, without any-one moving a foot or rising from their seats.

Public psychology has changed. In the past people loved those melodies because they provided the pleasure of dancing. So the notes would enter their hearts through their ears and reach down to their feet, injecting everyone with rhythm and movement. Today they are listened to as pleasure, while we try to guess, in the case of a competition, who will win the prize. Those pieces were valued previously for their capacity to make you dance, but now, it's for their musical quality. Or in other words, and as I said before, what was once life has now become spectacle.

With popular poetry the same thing has happened: namely, it used to be life. It was life for that boy, who as an old man told me the story about the time he declared his love to a girl in stanzas written on a piece of paper, which he left, held down by a stone, on the path down which she would walk, while he, hidden behind some bushes, watched to see if she would pick it up; or when, after the last public execution in Gipuzkoa (as pun-ishment for the Muatz parricide) the *bertsolari* Zubizarreta, from Azkoitia, composed some verses related to the case and came to the market in Azpeitia. He began to sing them to a mother who had one grown-up son and another who was twelve years old. That twelve-year old, as an old man, told me how Zubizarreta sold the several thousand pages that he had had printed. And there was a time when, as in the nineteenth-century Carlist wars, one side published a sheet of verses commenting on a battle or other event, and the other side quickly responded by putting out another sheet giving their version.

Life was when, after some altercation, the *bertsolari* Xenpelar was warned one night that on the road back to his house some men were waiting for him, intent on giving him a beating. However he didn't change his route, but instead, on approaching the place where he knew they would be waiting, he sang three strophes explaining the facts as he saw them, converting his enemies into friends. Life was when, on June 11, 1967 in the national *bertsolari* championship competition, on hearing the decision of the jury to advance Xalbador and leave others behind, part of the audience jeered that lasted five and a half minutes; until finally Xalbador managed to make himself heard, singing a strophe that transformed the protests into thunderous applause. That day the mutation was inverse: for a championship, which is normally part spectacle and part theater, was converted momentarily into reality and life. I could offer many other such examples and I say that they were life, or perhaps better, elements for life.

It's easy for today's strophes, many of them at least, to be better than those of the past. But they are sung in an enclosed space, before a seated public that wants to see who does it best, or at a round table performance for people who have just enjoyed a good meal. So it's an art or a spectacle. And even if they don't think of it this way, the *txistu-lariak*, *trikitilariak*, and *bertsolariak* are undoubtedly conscious of this. Something similar occurs with regional costumes. Our grandparents wore them every day because they were their normal dress; they were part of life. And now they are kept in a closet and only now and then, in Basque pilgrimages honoring patron saints, for example, do people bring them out to imitate their ancestors; in other words, to play a role. All in all, it may be that everything I am saying is merely another way of expressing my nostalgia and sense of loss, although this is a very human sentiment that shouldn't be at all embarrassing.

Nor are my books exempt from this emotion. When they started coming out, they appealed to two kinds of reader: one popular, the other educated. The popular or traditional reader bought them to read at home, as they had previously done with the *bertso-paperak* they bought in the market; and the educated public took spiritual nourishment from them as defenders or students of the Basque language. Now, after all these years, I have to face a truth that isn't much to my liking: that, while the second type of reader has remained steady or even increased in number, the first has gradually diminished and nearly disappeared. That is to say, people are no longer the same. So my books will still be found on bookshelves, but they won't have the good fortune that Xalbador sought for his:

Harmairu xokoetan ez gorde nehola,	Don't keep it in a corner of your closet,
zikint beldurrez edo nik dakita nola;	afraid it might get dirty or for some other reason.
Etzaio zikinduko dakarren eskola,	What's in it can't be dirtied,
kez beltzaturik ere ez izan axola,	nor should you worry if smoke blackens its cover,
sukaldeko solasen guardian dagola.	as long as you're attentive to what's said in the kitchen.

In fact, on several recent occasions when I have been in someone's house and asked if they had any poetry, and the answer is yes, they have brought out one of the books from our series, not only covered with soot, but also with grease stains and signs of having been read a lot.

Yet those first volumes were pocket books of reduced size and specifically made that way so they would be easy to read. With the passing of years, and wanting to adapt ourselves to the demands of the market, we've doubled their size. That has allowed us to arrange the strophes in two columns, more than doubling the number that would fit on a page. In this way we have published several books with more than a thousand strophes, which in *Euskara* generally consist of eight or ten verses. And in one case, in the book *Jesusen bizitza* ("The Life of Jesus") by Antaño, there were 2, 202 strophes. But in doing this, and without really noticing the change, we've gone from producing books for reading to making books for storage. In other words, I mean that the evolution I have been referring to has affected us as well: we no longer offer books to fulfill some everyday or popular need; instead we make books, not necessarily for mere ornamentation, but that are principally meant for scholars; books for bookshelves.

I hope no one will misinterpret my comments by taking them as words of condemnation of anyone or anything. I have always had high regard for the work of modern *bertsolariak* and others who promote popular artistic demonstrations. I hope they will continue as long as they have listeners. What constitutes and informs a people are the cultural elements they share: their myths, legends, customs, dances, songs, sports, literature, and poetry.

As regards popular Basque poetry one might say that it was born under a bad star. When the regular people (and the majority) admired and almost overvalued it, the educated classes scorned and rejected it. Now the latter are the ones who appreciate it and study it, but do the masses support it in the same way? As I mentioned before, the masses have undergone many changes since I initiated this project almost fifty years ago; that is, after a lifetime dedicated to gathering and preserving something that I feared would be lost. However, I don't want you to think I am a man who has sacrificed himself for a cause, for the truth is, aside from certain insignificant and fleeting annoyances, this work has made me happy for all these years.

More than once I have reproached myself for failing to formulate theories, interpretations, or analyses regarding the materials I have been presenting. The reason for this may be, at least in part, because it's a field in which I don't move all that comfortably; and also, because I believe it's more urgent to publish the materials that exist. I felt that this could not wait, while that could, and I left it for later. Now I realize that I'll never do it and this remains, then, for others to do.

This urgency and lack of time has also prevented me from reading and learning about all the good work that has been written on these topics in other languages and countries. So when I venture to offer my modest theoretical ideas, as I have today in regard to the change in Basque oral poetry from an element of life to an object of adornment, I can only fear that, at best, I am discovering the Mediterranean. If that's what I have donehere, I beg your indulgence. And many thanks for that and for your attention.

Part I:

THE THEORETICAL/COMPARATIVE FRAME

Improvised Poetry in the Hispanic Tradition

SAMUEL G. ARMISTEAD

Over a decade ago, I wrote a preliminary survey of orally improvised poetry in the Hispanic tradition, which Professor Maximiano Trapero was generous enough to publish in the Proceedings of the International Symposium, held in Las Palmas de Gran Canaria, in December 1992: *La décima popular en la tradición hispánica* (1994a).[1] Much invaluable work, by many different scholars, has been carried out and published since that time. All the same, I believe it may perhaps not be without value to offer, in the present context, an English version of my earlier paper, partially updated –where required– with certain essential references to more recent work, especially, but not exclusively, in Professor Trapero's splendid *Actas del VI Encuentro-Festival Iberoamericano de la Décima y el Verso Improvisado* (2000) (co-edited with Eladio Santana Martel and Carmen Márquez Montes) and his outstanding book, *La décima. Su historia, su geografía, sus manifestaciones* (2001b).

The singing of improvised oral poetry, in which composition and recitation are simultaneous and inseparable, was, until relatively recent times, a widely known cus-

---

1. The Spanish version of the present paper appeared in Armistead (1994a). The original Spanish and Portuguese texts of works quoted here in English can be read in the Spanish version. Certain references present in the Spanish version have been omitted from the present English translation, so, ideally, both texts should be taken into account. Without the least pretense of exhausting bibliographic references, I indicate some crucially important updating references, especially, but not exclusively, from Trapero, Santana Martel and Márquez Montes, eds. (2000), and Trapero (2001b). In 1996, I published a survey, for Spanish readers, of Parry-Lord scholarship and the theory of oral composition. For this, see Armistead (1996). Needless to say, a Spanish translation of Albert Lord's *Singer of Tales* is a much needed desideratum. Note now the 2nd ed., ed. by Mitchell and Nagy (Lord 2nd ed. 2000). As an indispensable supplement to the geographic perspective of the present paper, López Lemus' and Trapero's article (2001) must be taken into account. Two indispensable articles by Pedrosa (2000a and 2000b), supplement –with the admirable erudition characteristic of Pedrosa's works– the preliminary data offered in the Spanish version of this paper. I am indebted to a number of friends and colleagues for their generosity and erudition: Gorka Aulestia, Wilfrido Corral, Manuel da Costa Fontes, José Criado Fernández, Eduardo Dias, Joseph J. Duggan, Margit Frenk, Zunilda Gertel, Jesús Guanche, Yvette Jiménez de Báez, Israel J. Katz, Rafael Lapesa, María Teresa Linares Savio, James T. Monroe, Fernando Nava, Ward Parks, José Manuel Pedrosa, Rosa Alicia Ramos, Carmen María Sáenz-Coopat, Antonio Sánchez Romeralo, Robert M. Scari, Candace Slater, David Traill, Maximiano Trapero and Joseba Zulaika. They have contributed invaluable insights and, in several cases, have added significantly to bibliographic and geographic coverage.

tom in many areas of the Hispanic world and, in some cases, it has vigorously survived even down to the present day. Such poetry, often involving verbal dueling and mordant invective, has been cultivated by Hispanic peoples for many centuries.[2] Its origins remain obscure, but they undoubtedly involve a variety of Mediterranean and Near Eastern cultural currents, whose influence has contributed to the formation of a distinctive Hispanic heritage. From the early 1500s, we have several instances of improvised poetic dueling exemplified in Spanish plays – and in passages of an authentically popular tone, involving the participation of specifically peasant characters. In these poetic contests, known as *echarse pullas*, "one person wished all sorts of misfortunes, for the most part obscene, upon another, who replied in a similar strain."[3] According to contemporary testimony, the custom of exchanging *pullas* could be engaged in at weddings, while traveling, or in connection with certain agricultural activities, such as harvesting or gathering grapes.[4] In his erudite dialogue, *Días geniales o lúdicos* (completed around 1618), the formidable Golden Age scholar, Rodrigo Caro, convincingly connects the custom of *echarse pullas* –which he calls *darse grita* ("shouting at one another")– with a passage from Horace's *Epistolae* (Horace 1970: 408–409; Epistle II: I, vv. 145–146): "Fescennina per hunc inventa licentia morem, versibus alternis opprobria rustica ludit." ("Through this custom came into use the Fescennine license, which in alternate verses poured forth rustic taunts").[5] He then offers a Spanish verse translation: "Este rito licencioso / inventó los fesceninos, / y unos a otros se echan coplas, / pullas con rústicos dichos" ("This bawdy ritual / was invented by the Fescennians, / hurling couplets at each other, / *pullas* in rustic diction") (Caro 1978: Vol. 2, 96; *Diálogo Quinto*, ¶ II).[6]

Invective poetry, much of it –originally at least– orally composed and some of it undoubtedly improvised on the spot and at need, is surely of very ancient origin and is

---

2. Naturally, we will not be concerned here with such essentially learned forms as the medieval debates (*Clérigo y caballero, Alma y cuerpo, Agua y vino*, for example) or the Provençal *tenso* and its Castilian offspring in fifteenth-century *cancioneros*. For the former see, among many possible sources, Pérez Priego (1993) and Holmes (1962: 314); for the latter, see especially Cummins (1965) and Brooks' doctoral study (1990). For medieval debates and other forms of essentially written forms of improvisation, see John Zemke's contribution to the present volume.

3. For *echarse pullas*, see Crawford (1915). The etymology of *pullas* is uncertain; probably or at least possibly, it is from *púas* ("spikes" or "barbs") because of the verses' acrimonious character. Crawford reproduces a characteristic text and lists various additional examples. Corominas and Pascual provide still others and connect *echarse pullas* with the words *repullar* and *repullón*, already used in the early fifteenth century by Alfonso Alvarez de Villasandino. See Corominas and Pascual (vol. 4: 691–693; s.v. *pulla*). See also the various instances cited in Walter Schmid (1951: s.vv.). Note also a semantic parallel in the Colombian word *piquería* (see below).

4. The verses cited by Crawford from Diego de Avila's *Egloga ynterlocutoria* (before 1511) are delivered in the context of a rustic wedding. Covarrubias mentions travelers (*caminantes*), harvesting (*tiempo de siega*), and grape gathering (*vendimias*) (1943: s.v. *pulla*). See also Crawford (1915: 154, 158).

5. See also the useful notes in Edward P. Morris' ed. (Horace 1974: 150–151)

6. See also Crawford (1915: 153–154). The identity of the Fescennians and the origin of their name is subject to debate, but see Crawford (1915: 151–153, 158) and Morris' ed. (Horace 1974: 150–151n145). The relationship of *pullas* both to agriculture and to wedding festivities inevitably suggests a vast and millennial panorama involving the connections between fertility and obscenity in popular belief. See, for example, Randolph (1953: 333–339) and various additional sources cited in Armistead and Silverman (1979: 109–111 and 1982: 116 and n16).

probably world-wide in its distribution.[7] There can, however, be little doubt that Hispanic verbal dueling is ultimately connected in direct oral tradition to Horace's *opprobria rustica* and to an ancient Pan-Mediterranean heritage of poetic competition. Yet in Iberia, in particular, another historical factor also needs to be taken into account. James T. Monroe has identified, as the earliest known poetic evidence in Colloquial Hispano-Arabic, a verbal duel that inevitably calls to mind precisely the type of spontaneously composed oral poetry we are concerned with here. The text in question figures in a recently discovered manuscript of Ibn Hayyān's chronicle, *Kitāb al-Muqtabis*. In the year 912, the future Caliph, ᶜAbd al-Rahmān II, al-Nāsir, conquered some fortresses in the Alpujarras Mountains that had sided with the Hispano-Arab (or Mozarab) rebel ᶜUmar Ibn Hafsūn.[8] The incident which concerns us here is said to have occurred during the siege of one of those strongholds. It involves an acrimonious poetic exchange between one of the rebels who hurls down a poetic challenge from inside the fortress, to which a muleteer instantaneously responds, with a poetically improvised answer (Monroe 1989: 48).[9] As Monroe observes, "the verbal duel between the insolent rebel atop the fortress and the Caliph's loyal muleteer constitutes the earliest known poetic text in vernacular Hispano-Arabic. It thus plays a role in Andalusian letters akin to that enjoyed by the Oath of Strasbourg in Romance" (1989: 48). Given the twofold heritage –Romanic and Islamic– of Hispanic culture, Ibn Hayyān's striking account of Hispano-Arabic poetic dueling deserves our attention, as a possible, and indeed a crucially significant, antecedent in any discussion of improvised oral poetry in the Iberian tradition.

---

7. See, for example, Elliot (1960), who studies Greek, Arabic, Old Irish, and Latin satire, and Ward (1973a), who takes up Greek, Old Irish, Old Norse, and Indic instances. See also Ward's more extensive coverage (1973b). Crawford describes, among the Eskimos, "a formal contest . . . . which consists of heaping insulting terms upon each other until one of the contestants is exhausted" (1915: 157). Note also that, just like the early Spanish *pullas*, the Eskimo songs of derision "are sometimes exchanged between two friends without necessarily impairing their friendship" (Finnegan, ed. 1978: 227; examples 248–250). In regard to some of the *pullas* he records, Crawford observes: "the two lackeys begin their game without further formality and engage in a tongue-lashing which extends through fifteen stanzas and ends without enmity." Or again: "They proceed to wish each other all sorts of misfortunes in the most indecent terms until they finally call quits, apparently without animosity on either side" (1915: 160–161). Horace's use of the word *amabiliter* (v. 148) is significant in this regard: Though abusive, he believes that the Fescennine songs were originally performed in a "friendly" manner (Horace 1974: 151). I cannot resist recalling here a delicious incident described by Wilfred Thesiger: During one of his explorations of the Empty Quarter, two of his Bedouin companions spent an entire day wrangling –endlessly and insultingly– about the respective merits of their grandfathers. When, on the following day, they again took up the same debate, Thesiger, now wearied beyond all endurance, made bold to protest: "They looked at me in surprise and said: 'But it passes the time'" (1980:252). Note also Parks (1990).

8. Concerning Ibn Hafsūn, see Dozy (1913: 316–323 et alibi) and Armistead (2003).

9. The verses recorded by Ibn Hayyān exemplify the Arabic *hijā'* tradition of improvised invective, diatribe, and insult in verse. See the authoritative entry by Pellat (1971); also Elliott (1960: 15–18). On modern Arabian improvised invective, see Sowayan (1985 and 1989). In rival radio and television broadcasts, *hijā'* poetry was brought into play in the 1991 Gulf War, with Iraqis and Saudis trading poetic insults on a daily basis (Ya'ari and Friedman 1991). For more on *hijā'* poetry, see Van Gelder (1988). The confrontational dialogue between potential antagonists –one on a castle wall and the other below– is, incidentally, one of the classic commonplaces in Hispanic ballads. Compare, among others, the ballads *Afuera, afuera, Rodrigo*; *Aviso del zamorano*; *Búcar sobre Valencia*; *Alora la bien cercada*; *Gaiferos y Melisenda*; *Gaiferos sale de cautividad*; *Muerte de don Beltrán* (Wolf and Hofmann 1856: nos. 37, 44–45, 55, 79, 173, 174, 185, 185a). Note also Armistead and Monroe (1983–1984: 233, 238n9). Concerning Ibn Hayyān's text, see especially James T. Monroe's contribution to the present volume.

Concerning improvised poetry in modern Castilian-speaking areas of Spain, I can, at the moment, document the practice in Santander, Murcia, Almería, and Granada. We have a detailed account of popular gatherings (*veladas de trovos*), at which competitively improvised poetry was still sung, in the form of *quintillas* and *décimas*, at Cartagena, in the 1950s, though, at that time, the custom's situation could already be characterized as "precarious" (García Cotorruelo 1959: 131–143).[10] I recently collected some examples of originally improvised *quintillas* remembered by a Granada informant in Madrid, thanks to the generous help of my friend, José Manuel Pedrosa.

In his comprehensive work on the *Lírica tradicional canaria*, Maximiano Trapero alludes to popular poets in the Canary Islands, who, "despite being semi-illiterate, compose their *décimas* with such ease that they seem to have been born with that special talent, because, to improvise and create ten-verse strophes with a fixed rhyme-scheme would seem to be a task more suitable to reflection than to spontaneity" (1990: 205).[11] Competitive improvisation of *décimas* is still very much alive in the Canarian tradition, particularly on La Palma and La Gomera, islands which have a large population of Canarians (and their descendants), who, having emigrated to Cuba in the nineteenth century, subsequently returned to their native islands, bringing with them a dynamic tradition of improvised *puntos cubanos*. The present-day Canarian improvised *décima* would, ultimately, then, seem to be an offshoot of the Cuban *décima* tradition. As in most sub-traditions of improvised poetry, the Canarian repertoire involves, as an essential part of its artistry, highly competitive improvisation in which the singers seek to defeat their rivals, often resorting to the direst threats and the gravest insults. Here is a *contrapunto* between two singers, Bernardo Gutiérrez and Francisco Arteaga, one from the Island of La Palma, the other from La Gomera. But, as is usually the rule, it's all in good fun and, at the end of the session, both singers remain on good terms, stating that it has been a great honor to compete with the other and expressing their hope that another encounter can be arranged (Gutiérrez and Arteaga 1992):

B.G.:	Gomero, tú no te salvas	B.G.:	*Gomero*, you won't escape
2	en ninguna condición.	2	under any circumstances.
	Si tienes preparación,		If you are ready,
4	agárrate de la suerte:	4	accept your fate:
	Vas a llevar una muerte		You will have to suffer death
6	como se deb' al ratón.	6	such as only a mouse would deserve.
	(Guitar)		(Guitar)
F.A.:	Es para mí un compromiso	F.A.:	For me it's a problem

---

10. See now also Bonmatí Limorte (2000). For improvised poetry in Santander, see Christian (2000). Maximiano Trapero's contribution to the present volume extensively supplements and updates the data I offer here. Note also James W. Fernández's and William A. Christian's contributions to this volume.

11. For improvised oral poetry competitively performed by Canarian men and women at weddings and on other festive occasions, see Millares and Millares (1926: 182–183; s.v. *truján*). The Canarian scene described by the Millares is strikingly similar to the Argentinian episode evoked by Güiraldes in *Don Segundo Sombra*. The situation of the improvised *décima* in the Canary Islands is explored in detail in Trapero (1994a, 1996 and 2000).

8	tenerte que maltratar-a	8	to mistreat you like this,
	Es para mí un compromiso		For me it's a problem
10	tenerte que maltratar-a	10	to mistreat you like this.
	pero no te va a quedar-a		but you're not going to have
12	otro remedio que esto.	12	any other way to escape.
	(Guitar)		(Guitar)
	Porque tu campo analiza		Just try to understand the bad fix you're in:
14	que mueras muerto, mañero,	14	You're going to die, you old rogue,
	y si por ser te opusiero,		and, if I were to stand up to you,
16	yo voy a perder mi rumbo.	16	I'd lose my self control.
	Despídete d'este mundo,		Say goodbye to this world,
18	maldito viejo embustero.	18	you damned lying old man.
	(Guitar)		(Guitar)
B.G.:	Y aunque tú me mires viejo,	B.G.:	Though you may think I'm old,
20	yo no me lo creo así.	20	I don't see it that way.
	Aunque tú me mires viejo,		Though you may think I'm old,
22	yo no me lo creo así.	22	I don't see it that way.
	Antes de irme de aquí,		And before I depart from here,
24	yo con vida no te dejo.	24	I won't leave you alive.

There are numerous testimonies to similar practices from all over Ibero-America. Proceeding from north to south, I will start with the isolated Spanish-speaking *Isleño* enclave in St. Bernard Parish (Louisiana), where I have been doing field work since 1975. Improvised oral poetry, together with previously memorized compositions, was undoubtedly cultivated by the *Isleños* of earlier generations, among whom orally performed poetry was held in the highest esteem. The capacity to improvise an instantaneous poetic rejoinder assured the singer of enthusiastic public acclaim and great prestige within the community. Regarding the coexistence of improvised and memorized traditional poetry among the *Isleños*, my friend, Mr. Irvan Pérez, of Poydras, St. Bernard Parish –a fluent speaker of *Isleño* Spanish, an expert on all aspects of *Isleño* folk culture, and an accomplished traditional singer in his own right– expressed himself in the following terms: "They'd go and either sing one to the other, you know, recite as they go along, make up, or they'd go ahead and sing the old songs that they knew" (Pérez 1976).[12]

Clearly two different types of poetry are being identified here. On one hand, we have memorized traditional poetry, *romances, coplas, décimas*, and so forth (that is: "the old songs that they knew") and, on the other, some sort of improvised poetic competition ("sing one to the other," "recite as they go along, make up"). Another of my informants, Mrs. Julia Melerine Schiel, of Chalmette, St. Bernard Parish, provided a description of just such poetic dueling and remembered verbatim the mordantly sarcastic verses involved in that exchange, which became famous in the *Isleño* community (Armistead 1992: 83).

---

12. In my book (1992: 83–86), I discuss the existence of *Isleño* improvised poetry. Although *Isleño* folksongs are known as *décimas*, the form is not that of the classic Spanish ten-verse *décima*, but rather consists of anisosyllabic (usually eight-syllable) assonant couplets, similar to those of the *corrido* of Mexico and the American Southwest (Armistead 1992: 12–27).

In the late nineteenth century, ten-verse *décimas* were competitively improvised along the Texas-Mexican border. According to Américo Paredes (1966: 157), "the satirical *déci-ma* was not so much a jibe as a song-making challenge. The victim was supposed to answer and he would acquit himself very well indeed if he was able to reply in a gloss of four *décimas* based on the same *planta* (initial quatrain) used by his challenger."[13] Similar types of poetic competition were also popular in Cuba in the mid-nineteenth century. Here is an eye-witness account from 1839:

> The innumerable *décimas* exchanged by the three improvisers were highly original: some were addressed to us, affectionately showering us with exaggerated and childish praise. Most of the songs were full of the same amorous metaphysics to be found in our classical authors and generally there was a most agreeable tone to these spontaneous compositions. Curiously, these three peasants kept up a strange versified conversation among themselves, constantly answering each other, in a contest of poetic creativity (Lukin 1978: 70).[14]

And the competitive improvisation of *décimas* in Cuba continues to be very much alive down to the present day.

In Santo Domingo a now obsolete form of improvised poetry, known as the *me-diatuna*, used to be performed. The singers were known as *tuneros*. According to an eighty-year-old informant interviewed by Juan Francisco García (1946: 11), "some years before" 1946:

> The *mediatuna* formed an essential part of the musical program of the major festivals cele-brated in Santiago de los Caballeros and it was a sort of tourney or lyrico-musical contest which lasted several days and the winner would be the one who kept on singing alone after having exhausted the literary repertoire of his competitors.[15]

It is not clear solely from this description whether the competitors' "material literario" was improvised or memorized, but Juan Francisco García goes on to specify a well known form, familiar to anyone who has worked with Spanish American oral poetry:

> The tune of the *mediatuna* at that time was always the same and it was subordinated to the text. The latter consisted of a quatrain, called the *pie* ("foot," "basis"), and of a series of *déci-mas* (ten-line strophes), whose last lines had to be, successively, one of the four verses of the

---

13. Concerning the ten-verse *décima* form, see Armistead (1992: 12–13n2; 18–20). For the *décima* in Mexico, see, among other papers, Nava López (1994). For *bombas* improvised in Mexico and in many other areas of the Hispanic world, see Pedrosa (2001).

14. For more on *décimas* in Cuba, see, among other communications, Linares Savio (1994) and López Lemus (2000). A fundamentally important theoretical approach to Pan-Hispanic improvised poetry –initially based on the author's first-hand experience as a Cuban *repentista*– is found in Díaz-Pimienta (1998).

15. On improvised poetry in Santo Domingo, see Juan Francisco García (1946: 11). In the same journal, Manuel Jesús Javier García (1946) publishes a poetic duel between two young *campesinos*, Pedro and Juliana. The verses seem authentic enough, but no information is provided concerning source or context. The quatrains are anisosyllabic (between 5 and 7 syl-lables). The entire piece smacks more of *costumbrismo* than of authentic scholarship, but it still may, to some degree, be taken as a witness to popular usage, especially when compared with other instances that concern us here.

pie. The text concerned various matters. Thus *mediatunas* were sung about love, jealousy, religious themes, in competition, etc.

We have here, of course, the well known *décima-as-glosa*, which could be memorized or improvised, but, unless the tradition had become totally reduced to a fossilized ritual, the performance, in competition, of songs having such strictly prescribed formal characteristics –and a considerable diversity of not altogether predictable subject matter– must have involved a certain amount of improvisation, if not, at very least, a large memorized repertoire, upon which the singers were able to draw at will and with considerable mental agility. In Puerto Rico, similar competitions involving the same *décima* form have survived down to the present day, as is attested by extensive field work carried out by Pedro Escabí (1970) and in crucially important materials now edited by Maximiano Trapero. Escabí (1970: 176–177) describes the typical scenario:

> Two singers become involved in a debate: One suggests a topic in the form of a challenge and the other answers instantaneously. . . . .The ease with which they are able to improvise and sing, accompanied by a tune which is perfectly adapted to the verses' metrics, is incredible.[16]

For Venezuela, we have an early description by José Eustaquio Machado, from which it becomes clear that certain *cantaores* from the Venezuelan Llanos (*llaneros*) would get together to improvise oral poetry in competition (*contrapuntearse*), before an audience, which then took sides and responded to each singer with its applause or its mockery. The form used would seem to have been quatrains (*coplas*) rather than *décimas* (Machado 1922: 19).[17] In his 1992 Symposium concerning traditional improvised *décimas*, Maximiano Trapero made it possible for us to hear splendid performances of *décimas* from the Island of Margarita.

In Colombia, the art of improvised performance seems to be in radical decline, if not on the verge of extinction. George List's (1983: 343) perceptive analysis of the current status of oral *décimas* in the coastal village of Evitar is revealing:

> Those who can compose poetry are held in high esteem, but even greater prestige redounds to those who can improvise poetry in song form. Since the *décima* is the most complex poetic form in traditional use by the *costeño*, the ability to improvise a *décima* carries the maximum of social prestige . . . .Contests between *decimeros*, known as *piquerías* (from the verb *picar*, "to bite"), are also traditional in the region. In a *piquería* two or more *decimeros* vie for the plaudits of their auditors by improvising on a given theme. Experienced *decimeros* usually have a fund of *décimas* concerning common themes which they utilize as a whole or with

---

16. See also Escabí and Escabí (1976). Trapero (1994 and 1996) includes rich additional materials.

17. In Machado's pamphlet (1926), there is a slightly more detailed description, which also includes some phrases from Machado (1919: 21–22), but it remains unclear, in the pamphlet, when Machado is referring to *gauchos* and when to *llaneros*. For additional materials on Venezuela, see now Trapero (1994b and 1996) and Trapero, Santana Martel and Márquez Montes (2000).

some improvised changes in a *piquería* . . . . Upon inquiring in Evitar, we were told that *piquerías* had taken place in the village in the past, but not in recent times. There were few *decimeros* now, since most of the younger men had little interest in learning to perform *décimas*. A further reason was given by Simón Herrera, the youngest of the men who performed *décimas* for us. He stated that he did not know a sufficient number of *décimas* to engage in a *piquería* . . . .This statement offers some corroboration of my belief that even in a *piquería* a *decimero* is primarily performing from memory rather than improvising.

List's observations suggest the probable coexistence –in this particular tradition at least– of both improvised and memorized components, not only at a terminal stage, such as is described by List, but also very possibly even during earlier generations, when orally improvised poetry was at its apogee in many areas of Spanish America.[18]

A report from Panamá, referring to the late 1940s or early 1950s, clearly reflects a similar situation, in which "improvisation" –placed in quotes by the authors and characterized as less frequent than in other areas– would definitely seem to be on the way out. Panamanian *duelos y porfías* (poetic duels and competitions) now seem to take place in a rather formalized public setting. Manuel Zárate and Dora Pérez (1953: 29) observe:

> The singers must respond in *décimas* to the questions or problems posed by their adversaries, using the same type of strophe . . . . Sometimes the competition is interspersed with or concluded by "improvisations," which, because of their difficult or unusual character, evoke from the audience the greatest enthusiasm and admiration. We know that this feature of the competitions is more frequent in other countries of America than in our own.[19]

Ecuadorian *cantores* or *puetas* correspond, in general terms, to the Argentine *payadores* and Brazilian *cantadores*. Their improvised songs take various forms. One is the *tema*, where, like the Chilean *paya*, one singer poses a versified problem, to which his antagonist must instantaneously supply a poetic answer:

> *Temas* are a type of riddle or paradox, which they present to each other to be solved and which generally begin with a rather ironic compliment, a word of flattery or praise, regard-

---

18. Compare the observations, in regard to the Homeric epic, by Russo –calling himself a "modified oralist"– who evokes an analogous situation: "I would not characterize Homeric poetry as essentially composed in the act of performance, although I have tried to point out segments whose form must have been achieved in performance. I believe that much of the composing goes on the poet's head, between and before performances, and that the very act of performing a song often constitutes a process that is tantamount to practice, and inevitably brings about a condition that we might fairly call memorization, at least for some of the text" (1987: 549–565). The evidence for completely improvised poetry is, however, overwhelming and indisputable for many traditions; albeit, an interplay of memorized and orally composed segments, such as we have in Hispano-American *repentista* poetry, might suggest a possible –if partial and always tentative– explanation of the significant differences in formulaic density between, for example, Homeric and South Slavic epic poetry, on one hand, and, on the other, oral epics such as the *Cantar de Mio Cid* and the *Chanson de Roland*, that developed in Western Europe – always taking into account, of course, the fundamental differences between epic poetry and poetic dueling. See Menéndez Pidal (1965–1966). Note also Valenciano (1992). The Columbian term, *piquería*, occupying a semantic field including "bite," "sting," and "stick," adds support to Corominas' contention (Corominas and Pscual 1980–1991: vol. 4, 691–693) that the Spanish *pulla* (in *echarse pullas*) may have originated as *púa* "point," "spike," "barb," or "spur."

19. For *bombas* improvised in El Salvador, see the texts brought together by Espinosa (1934). Note also Pedrosa (2001).

ing the talent and wisdom of the contender who is to find the solution (Carvalho-Neto 1964: 396–397, s.v. *tema*).[20]

Another improvised Ecuadorian genre is the familiar *contrapunto*, in which, here at least, one *cantor* sings the first three verses of a quatrain (*copla*) and his opponent must supply the fourth:

> Famous singers (*mentaos*) . . . . would agree to meet at a festival in such and such a town. Once they had settled in with their supporters and the *contrapunto* had been started, the audience preferred such a spectacle to all others; bets were placed and the competition could go on from dusk to dusk and by turns during every day of the festival, one pair of rivals consecutively replacing the others (Chávez Franco 1930: 632–633; rpt. in Carvalho-Neto 1964b: 125).[21]

For the traditional improvisation of *décimas* in Peru, we can count now on the detailed exploration of all aspects of the problem by Nicomedes Santa Cruz, who tells us of the "long agony experienced by the *décima* since approximately half a century ago" (Santa Cruz 1982: 77). It is clear, from the numerous testimonies brought together by Santa Cruz, that the competitive improvisation of *décimas* enjoyed great popularity in Peru in earlier times.

With Chilean *payadores,* we feel quite at home. We are now moving into already familiar territory, according to the following description by Ramón A. Laval (1916: 144):

> *Pallas* are dialogues improvised by two popular poets, where, generally, they pose to each other difficult to solve problems, which they must immediately solve or in which they insult one another, at first rather gently, but gradually the argument becomes more and more severe, until the encounter ends in discord.[22]

One has the impression that Chilean *payadas* are now a thing of the past. Already in 1911, *El Niño* Pérez was Laval's only informant in Carahue capable of exemplifying the genre. In the verses reproduced by Laval, *El Niño* is recalling part of an exchange of *décimas:* The challenger provides a quatrain in *abba* and his rival delivers a *glosa* of ten primarily octosyllabic verses in one of the most frequently used *décima* patterns: *abba-ac-cddc*. On the other hand, the famous *payada* between Javier de la Rosa and Taguada the Indian is in octosyllabic assonant *coplas*.[23]

The Argentine *payadores* were, without doubt, the most famous of Spanish American oral poets. José Hernández immortalized the *payador* and his artistry in creating the famous encounter between Martín Fierro and *El Moreno* (Hernández, 6th ed. 1979: vv. 3913–3916):

20. Note now also Hidalgo's splendid book (1990; rpt. 1995).

21. See also Carvalho-Neto (1964a: 114–115, 137, 187; s.vv. *cantor, contrapunto,* and *desafío*).

22. For additional pertinent publications, see Simmons (1963: nos. 122, 613, 622, 699). Note also the descriptions in Santamaría (1942: s.vv. *contrapunto, paya, payada, payador*). For Chile, see now also Contreras Oyarzún (2000).

23. For the famous *payada* of Javier de la Rosa and Taguada el Indio, see Dölz-Blackburn (1984: 84–87). For more bibliography on this famous contest, see Slater (1989: 11n 21).

Tomó Fierro la guitarra,	Fierro took his guitar
pues siempre se hall dispuesto,	which he was always ready to do,
y ansí cantaron los dos	and so both of them sang
en medio de un gran silencio.[24]	and everyone listened in silence.

In *Don Segundo Sombra*, Ricardo Güiraldes recreates an example of *coplas* improvised during a popular dance (1926; rpt. 1988 ch. 11). The boy addresses the girl he is dancing with:

Uno, dos, tres, cuatro	One, two, three, four,
si no me querés me mato.	if you don't love me, I'll kill myself.

To which the girl instantly replies:

Uno, dos, tres,	One, two, three,
matáte si querés.	kill yourself if you want.

The great Argentine folklorist, Juan Alfonso Carrizo, learned popular dances and learned how to improvise oral poetry, as a technique to facilitate his field work in rural Argentina. Carrizo was, to say the least, quite obese, weighing in at 130 kilos (around 270 lbs.). While dancing a traditional *gato*, with an attractive Indian girl, he improvised a poem in her honor, which however, seems not to have pleased her at all. She instantly responded with the following verses:

De Tolombón hi venío,	I have come from Tolombón,
en un caballo lobuno,	riding on a gray horse:
hi visto animales gordos,	I've seen plenty of fat creatures,
pero como Vd. ninguno.[25]	but none as fat as you.

Mario López de Osornio's characterization of the Argentine *payador* embodies various features with which we are now largely acquainted (1945: 52):

> The *payador* was something more than a mere improviser, since, in addition to knowing how to improvise, he knew how to sing, how to declaim and strum the guitar. The word *payador* comes from Quechua, *paya/palla* 'to pick up from the ground,' as if, in metaphorical terms,

---

24. The *desafío* runs from v. 3917 to v. 4522. Becco, the editor, (Hernández, 6th ed. 1979: 407n467) is informative concerning *payadores* and the connotations of the term *contrapunto*. Nowhere else in Latin America have the improvisation and the improvisor of oral poetry achieved such a cultural resonance, such a transcendental importance in national mythology, as in Argentina. The *payador* and his poetry –or at least its learned recreation, as in *Martín Fierro* (1872–1879)– have come to occupy a position in national ideology similar, perhaps, to that of the *Chanson de Roland* in France or the *Cantar de Mío Cid* in Spain. Elias Lönnrot's Finnish *Kalevala* might be an even closer analogy, though in the *Kalevala* we have an assemblage and adaptation of actual ballads collected from oral tradition, while, in *Martín Fierro*, Hernández recreates, from his own inspiration, the gaucho's world and an authentic imitation of the *payador*'s art. In any event, improvised poetry has attracted the attention of Argentine literary giants, such as Lugones (1916) and Borges (1950), as well as many other, lesser writers. In regard to another form of Argentine improvised poetry, we should bear in mind the piquant anisosyllabic verses exchanged by dancing couples, as in a traditionally authentic episode genially recreated by Güiraldes (1926; rpt. 1988 ch. 11).

25. Carrizo's improvised exchange ("gato con relación") with the beautiful Indian girl is related in his book (1933: xxxii–xxxiv). Janet Casaverde (2000) studies the tradition of improvised poetry among indigenous groups in northern Argentina.

it was the act of lifting from the ground the gauntlet, the challenge made to a *payador* to answer some question, in verse and with musical accompaniment. Sometimes, versified *contrapunto* dialogues would be struck up, giving each other reciprocal problems and testing the skill and mental agility of each singer, so as to save their respective prestige.[26]

Argentine *payadores* used a number of different forms: *sextinas* and *octavillas*, as well as *coplas* and *décimas*. Hernández has Martín Fierro and *El Moreno* using the popular six-verse octosyllabic *sextina*.

Returning now to non-Castilian-speaking areas of the Iberian Peninsula, I must mention, at this point, James W. Fernandez's pathfinding and abundant work on Asturias (see especially Fernandez 1986a). Evidence of orally improvised poetry in the Galician-Portuguese linguistic domain and its overseas extensions is abundant and widely distributed. In Galicia itself, improvised verses were sung as part of traditional wedding celebrations: "The young men get together at the door of those who are about to be married, and with them everyone from the surrounding villages; the best singers begin to improvise verses, claiming for themselves the *regueifa*, which is a large loaf of bread" (Pérez Ballesteros 1885: xxxviii–xxxix).[27]

Another type of supposedly improvised Galician poetry is known as *enchoyadas*: "Contests between young men singing improvised quatrains (*coplas*) are called *enchoyadas*. Generally they are linked together, in that one of the opponents uses, as the first verse of his *copla*, the last verse of his competitor" (Pérez Ballesteros 1885: 81n1).[28]

The form used in both these cases is an octosyllabic quatrain, with assonant rhyme in the second and fourth verses, although instances of rhyme schemes in *abab*, and others, are also in evidence. In regard to the allegedly improvised character of these genres, Pérez Ballesteros' warning needs to be taken into account (1885: I, 91–92): "The songs of *cantadeiras* or *enchoyadas* are sung, as has been said, in a sort of competition or dispute between improvisers; however, generally, verses that are very widely known among the rural people are considered to be improvisations."

---

26. Morínigo expresses well reasoned doubts about the Quechuan origin of *payada, payador, payar* (1966: s.vv.). There is an extensive bibliography concerning Argentine *payadores*: Olivera-Williams (1986) is a fundamental starting point. Note also Fuente (1986); Aretz, (1954: 78–86); Guerrero Cárpena (1946); Usandivaras and Usandivaras (1953: 259–267). For additional references, see Simmons (1963: nos. 137, 249, 250, 359, 361). There were also *payadores* in Uruguay and Bolivia (Simmons: nos. 436, 438, 455). See Abel Zabala (2000).

27. For Galicia, see Pérez Ballesteros (1885), Braga (1868), and a facsimile ed. of Pérez Ballesteros' *Cancionero* (1979). Concerning the *regueifa*, see also Otero Pedrayo (1979–1980: II, 718–719, 546, 566, 718–719, 774; on improvised poetry and *desafíos*: 537–542, 554, 557–559). The word *regueifa* is from Arabic *raghîf*, pl. *arghifa* ("flat loaf of bread," "roll," or "bun"). See Dozy and Engelmann (1869: 330), and now, Corriente (1999: s.v. *regaifa*). *Regueifa* can also refer to a type of traditional Galician dance (Taboada Chivite 1972: 193). Crawford contrasts the aggressive character of Castilian *pullas* with the less belligerent Galician songs, which "do not concern us here, since they are not primarily abusive" (1915: 161n39). See now also Blanco (2000).

28. Concerning Galician *enchoyadas*, see Pérez Ballesteros (1885: 81n1). In Galician, *enchoyar* (=Sp. *enamorar*) means "to court," or "to flirt," as when a young couple begins "conversing" (*parolar*), with a view to future engagement (Carré Alvarellos 1951: s.v.; Crespo Pozo 1963: s.v. *enamorado* 'enchoiado'). I do not know the etymology. Xoaquín Lorenzo Fernández discusses some of the formulaic components and techniques used in the composition of various types of Galician improvised poetry, and edits a substantial number of examples (1973: 13, 16, 19, 24–25, 171–185).

For Continental Portugal there is substantial evidence. Challenging songs (*cantigas ao desafío*) are well known in the Trás-os-Montes region, where various genres of the local song tradition are notably archaic in character:

> *Desafíos* are generally performed to music, among two or more contenders, either with an impromptu character revealed in its improvised inspiration –and in that case the quatrains are not so perfect– or as separate memorized compositions suitable for answering back (*despiques*), which are more frequent (Borges de Castro 1983: 7).[29]

Once again, we note here the coexistence of both improvised and memorized materials in the oral tradition.

Improvised poetry exists (or existed) in other regions of continental Portugal as well: Manuel Viegas Guerreiro reports on the impressive improvisatorial talents of "Pôtra," an illiterate shepherd from the vicinity of Beja (Baixo Alentejo). The form used in this case is a predominantly octosyllabic *décima* with the rhyme scheme: *abba-ac-cdde* (Viegas Guerreiro 1978: 20).

In contrast to a rather pessimistic prognosis for improvised poetry on the continent, similar songs seem to be alive and well in the Portuguese Atlantic islands. *Desafíos* are still enthusiastically cultivated on Terceira and Azorean *cantadores* even visit California to compete with local singers in improvising quatrains (*quadras*).[30] From an earlier time, Théophilo Braga edited a number of *despiques* from São Jorge, in which a man and a woman "converse" in improvised octosyllabic assonant quatrains. Here we may note, in certain cases, a pattern similar to the Galician *enchoyadas*: The first verse of the answer picks up the thematic word of the preceding *quadra*'s last verse (Braga 1868: 119–138). Though I do not have published documentation, my friend and colleague, Manuel da Costa Fontes, assures me that *desafíos* are or at least were also cultivated in Madeira.

For the Cape Verde Islands, Elsie Clews Parsons published some highly aggressive, indeed abusive, improvised verses in the local Portuguese Creole – recalling perhaps the

---

29. The brief introduction is followed by 266 examples of *desafíos*. The form, octosyllabic assonant quatrains (*quadras*), is the same as that we have just seen in Galicia. Borges de Castro's booklet is actually an attempt to interest "young singers" in cultivating the *desafío* genre (Borges de Castro 1983: 5, 8). As an indication of the present perilous status of such poetry –even in this most conservative of Portuguese regions– Borges de Castro inveighs against the threat posed by record players: "The irritating plague of record players is the death of the popular tradition; they become insufferable because of the excessive noise – which disaffects many people" (1983: 8). However many people may –or may not– be turned off by the high decibel music of blaring rock bands, the future of Trasmontanian improvised poetry would seem to be very bleak indeed and beyond the help of any such well-intentioned initiatives as Borges de Castro's. Costa Fontes has published various *cantigas ao desafío* composed by the aged *cantador*, Manuel António Gonçalves, of Sacóias (Bragança). Some of these compositions are in *quadras*, but there are other strophic arrangements as well and, in one case, there is a *quadra* glossed in four *décimas* (Costa Fontes 1987: II, nos. 1668–1672). No. 1673 is also a *cantiga ao desafío*, but composed by a different informant. Leite de Vasconcellos alludes briefly to a Portuguese tradition of professionally singing *desafíos* ("medeante certo salário"), but does not specify the regions or the popular festivals when such singing took place ("a diferentes terras por occasião de festas, etc.") (1882: 248–249; 2d ed. by Viegas Guerreiro 1987: 278). For more on Portugal, see Lima (2000 and 2001).

30. Frederico Lopes (alias João Ilhéu) (1980) devotes a whole chapter to *desafíos* (ch. 10: 351–362). I have not seen the book itself, but I rely on Pereira de Brito's substantial review (1980–1986). For Azorean *desafío* singers in America, see the crucial data provided by Costa Fontes (1980: xxxv, xxxviii, xli). Note also his article (1991: 120 and 131n18).

early Castilian *pullas*. She observes (Parsons 1923: II, 212–213) that, in "such songs, I am told, two persons may sing against each other an entire evening."[31]

Improvised poetry is still vigorously cultivated in Brazil, particularly in the northeast, by "poet-improvisers known as *cantadores* or *repentistas*, famous throughout the backlands for their on-the-spot compositions and spirited exchanges in verse" (Slater 1989: 9–10 and n19).[32] The prevailing form is usually a type of *sextilla*, six verses of seven syllables, having a consonantal rhyme scheme in *abcbdb*. In these Brazilian *repentistas*, it is as if some close relative of the Argentine *payadores* had miraculously survived down to our own time. Any exhaustive survey –a much-needed desideratum– for which the present prologue offers only the most cursory and undoubtedly still lacunous outline, must obviously begin with such still living traditions as those of Brazil and the Portuguese Atlantic islands, together with Mexico, Cuba, Puerto Rico and the Canary Islands.[33]

As we have just seen, improvised oral poetry is today either recently extinct or in terminal decline in various areas of the Spanish- and Portuguese-speaking world, with Brazil, the Azores, the Canary Islands, México, Cuba, and Puerto Rico among the notable exceptions. At the same time, such a crucially important, intensely interesting phenomenon –seemingly shunted aside by our exclusive fascination with the *Romancero*'s richly multisecular Pan-Hispanic traditionality– has, until recently, not been subjected to an in-depth comparative inquiry.[34]

In the face of such a situation, the vigorous survival of Basque *bertsolari* poetry is nothing less than inspirational. Thanks to the distinctive cultural situation of the Basque people and their devotion to Basque culture, language and poetry, *bertsolari* improvisation has not only managed to survive, in health and vigor, down to our own time –and indeed to survive, as few other oral traditions have been able to survive– the perilous transition into a world of the mass media, of radios, televisions, cassette recorders, CDs and so forth.

---

31. All the materials published by Parsons were collected from Cape Verdean immigrants in New England (Parsons 1923: I, xi). The "verses" are anisosyllabic and unrhymed. Outside a Hispanic context, the Cape Verdean songs are reminiscent of the insulting verses known, in the English Creole Taki-Taki of Surinam, as *lobi singi*, which, however, though "improvised," are one-sided and do not involve poetic dueling (Herskovits and Herskovits 1969: 23–32).

32. Slater (1989) exemplifies the very substantial scholarly literature devoted to the *repentistas*. Note, for example, Suassuna (1962 and 1974); Câmara Cascudo (1978: 359–364 et alibi); and Motta (1921). Suassuna's contributions attest to a major writer's keen interest and esteem for the artistic creativity of *repentista* poetry.

33. For improvised poetry in the Catalan domain, note Amades, who designates all the Catalan *cobles* (quatrains) in his monumental work (1951: 813–934), as "cançons improvisades." Such a conclusion, seemingly based on Amades' unsubstantiated deductions –echoing nineteenth-century Romantic theories about the origins of oral poetry– is difficult to accept. He gives no details concerning the supposed contemporary circumstances of such improvisations. But see now Sbert i Garau (2000). For Catalan improvised poetry see also the contributions of Maximiano Trapero and Gorka Aulestia in the present volume.

34. The Hispanic ballad tradition –one of my own fields of long-standing activity– is eminently deserving of in-depth study and merits our on-going attention, but there can be little doubt that other folk literary genres have, until now, been shortchanged in favor of the *Romancero*. See my article (1993: 360). Compare Durand's remarks (1979: 164–165), as well as those of Haboucha (1982), and now also my preface to Beatrice Schmid et al. (2003: 7–13).

The 1986 Txapelketa Nagusia or National *Bertsolaritza* Championship. In the contemporary Basque Country, thousands attend this event, held, throughout the course of one day, every four years.
Photo by Juantxo Egaña. By permission of the Xenpelar Dokumentazio Zentroa, Donostia.

At a time when the study of orally composed poetry is acquiring ever greater refinement and critical cogency, in a rich panoply of multi-cultural scholarly contributions,[35] we now also have pathfinding new explorations of *bertsolari* poetry written by Basque authors – all personally very close to the practice and performance of *bertsolaritza*, and, in some cases, these writers are also expert poets and improvisers in their own right. I am referring, of course, to the recent books and articles by Gorka Aulestia, by Kepa Fernandez Larrinoa, and by the co-authors Joxerra Garzia, Jon Sarasua, Xabier Payá, and Andoni Egaña.[36] All of us who work in oral literature, be it in a Hispanic or in a broadly comparative perspective, owe these authors an unlimited debt of gratitude for such splendid, pathfinding studies. These publications make available to us a rich and previously unknown poetic tradition, which otherwise, for obvious linguistic reasons, would have remained a closed book to almost all of us. We are immeasurably enriched by their work.

---

35. Especially the work of John Miles Foley. See two of his particularly groundbreaking books (1990a and 2002). For the vast geographic scope of oralist studies see Foley (1985). Similarly, Foley (1988 and 1995) is also obligatory reading; and see also Foley (1990b and 1998).

36. Indispensable sources for the study of *bertsolaritza* are Aulestia (1990 and 1995); and Garzia, Sarasua, and Egaña (2001). Note also Garzia (2000b) and Sarasua (2000).

In addition to welcoming all the distinguished contributors to our Symposium, I want to welcome and to thank, in very special terms, the famous and much admired *bertsolari-ak*, who have enriched the perspectives of this meeting with their distinguished presence and with the unique art of their improvisations. Thanks from all of us go to Jesus Arri-ada, Johnny Curutchet, Andoni Egaña, Martin Goicoechea, Jesus Goñi, and Jon Sarasua. In the present context, you are, in every sense, the experts and we –the academics– are here only as humble disciples, in search of acquiring a better understanding of your splen-did poetic art. My only regret, at the present moment, is my incapacity adequately to express these sentiments of welcome and of thanks, as they should be expressed, in the Basque language: *Eskerrik asko ta ongi-etorri!*

Improvised Oral Poetry in Spain

Maximiano Trapero

Improvised Poetry: An Ancient and Universal Phenomenon

On several other occasions I have observed that improvised poetry is an ancient, as well as a universal, phenomenon. Such an assertion calls to mind a most general reality that soon forces one, by its very nature, to practically conclude the following: all peoples with a degree of independence, measured through the "civilization" that each has achieved,[1] possess a popular poetic heritage. Another dimension altogether is really grasping what the specific characteristics of each of these cultural legacies are, for poetic improvisation is one of the most spontaneous and primordial signs of all civilization. Indeed, beyond merely stating this fact, and although it once again seems obvious, it would be difficult to imagine any kind of popular culture that has been historically shaped through a maternal language, where some form of improvised oral poetry has not been developed, however simple it may have been.

Naturally, for those of us whose spiritual outlook has been molded by what we call "western culture," saying that poetic improvisation is very old is somewhat obvious, given that it appears in full in one of the first cultural, and at the same time crowning, statements of this western culture. When we read the *Odyssey*, the fact that at every banquet there is an indispensable character, the *aedo* (bard), whom everyone looks at and who becomes the center of attention, is striking. This is an admired and lovable character that always remains above any argument or debate. The *aedos* were professional bards that would either stroll from town to town or respond to royal petitions to perform at court; singing poets who, through a formulaic language whose technique they fully mastered, were capable of improvising verse about the great achievements of ancient heroes. From

---

1. As has been stated, as regards poetry, countries are neither more nor less developed than one another and even less do "third world" countries exist; on the contrary, there are countries catalogued according to the latter socio-political category which possess a poetic "potential" that is far superior to that of their "developed" neighbors.

the story of Homer, the names of Phemius, *aedo* at the palace of Ulysses in Ithaca, who sang the mournful return of the Acheans (*Odyssey* I, 326ff.) and that of Demodocus, *aedo* of the palace of Alcinous, king of the Phaeacians, whom the Muse persuaded to sing about how Achilles and Odysseus quarreled (*Odyssey* VIII, 73ff), have gone down in history. And on closer inspection one can see that Homer himself was an *aedo*, the model of an epic poet capable of recreating a complete ancient Hellenic world, the greatest minstrel of all time.

The example of Homeric minstrels represents one kind of individual poetic improvisation. However, the early texts of Greek and Roman literature are full of another kind of improvised oral poetry that is even more complex, namely one that pits two characters against one another. This even has a specific name, *amebic verse*, through which the contestants sing both alternately and competitively, abiding by certain rules and hoping to claim a victory that must be judged by a neutral man who performs the task of a jury. And if those who sing in both the *Iliad* (I, 604) and the *Odyssey* (XXIV, 60) are the Muses, in Virgil's *The Bucolics* (III) they are now two flesh and bone shepherds, Menalcas and Dametas, who compete with one another. As Menalcas says:

Do you want us to try alternately to see what each of us is capable of?

This poetic contest had certain rules: whoever started had the right to choose the subject and his opponent had to answer him, to such an extent that the latter always remained at the mercy of the former's chosen topic and subject to his "attacks"; yet the second one could both answer and counter attack at the same time, thereby giving rise to a duel of attack and counter attack that could go on until one of the contestant's strength (and reason) waned, or until both of them (as was the norm and indeed the case of Virgil's two aforementioned shepherds) declared himself the winner.

Subjects in ancient times were chosen without much effort: those of a philosophical nature were most common, with questions concerning difficult concepts that had to be answered instantly. However, those of a more bucolic nature, of love, interpreting destiny, the natural order, together with prophetic verses full of adages and popular sayings, as well as others of a moralist bent, were also common.

But Also a New and Local Phenomenon

We always knew that poetic oral improvisation was an ancient phenomenon. What we didn't know was that this phenomenon continued to live on, at least in unlikely ways. To tell the truth, the evidence of its survival became more obvious when a more a general understanding of both national and local popular cultures was encouraged. However, one thing seemed to unite all these cultures: their hidden or suppressed nature before formal research and the silence with which "academic" criticism treated them.

Only as a result of such general ignorance can one explain the intellectual commotion provoked by the discovery, by Milman Perry and Albert Bates Lord during the first half of the twentieth century, of the southern Slavic people's popular epic poetry (especially that of the Serbs, Bosnians and Croats, but also Macedonians). For the importance of

Parry's breakthrough was not only related to discovering a local poetic tradition, for all that this was indeed an extraordinary achievement. Rather, it resided in the repercussion of Lord's subsequent studies, where he proved (and demonstrated) that the "formulistic" resources of popular Slavic poetry functioned from a mechanistic base similar to that of Homeric poetry. In other words, just as Homeric verse was one example –although indeed a sublime one and of course the individual creation of a genius– of traditional poetry eight centuries before the birth of Christ, so he came to demonstrate that this way of creating poetry had not disappeared. Instead, it once again came to the attention of the rest of the world, in a Balkan region, twenty-eight centuries after those early Homeric landmarks.

Later, those works that followed the direction forged by Parry and Lord (Ong, Zumthor, Finnegan, Havelock, Armistead, Frenk, and Foley, for example), and which shaped the so-called "oral theory," highlighted more and more worldwide examples of improvised oral poetry. These cases were grounded firmly in living, functional and popular traditions, within other environments and among other peoples far removed from those of the South Slavs: in the Fiji Islands, Turkey, Cyprus, Greece, Crete, Wales, Russia, Japan, Africa (among both the Bedouin of the southern Sahara and the Berbers of the High Atlas Mountains), together with other examples. And soon it became demonstrably clear that the Yugoslavian *guslari* were not miraculous survivors of another age, exclusively isolated in their southern Balkan outpost. Instead, parallel figures of the Slav bards (and comparable to the mythical Montenegrin *guslar*, Avdo Medjedovic) could be found, for example, among the Sardinian *cantadori*, Cretan *pytaris* or Maltese singers of *spiritu pronto*. Similarities could also be found with Basque *bertsolariak*, Balearic *glosadores*, Andalusian *troveros*, and the *verseadores* of the Canary Islands, to cite some of the Hispanic examples; or with Argentinian, Uruguayan and Chilean *payadores*, Venezuelan *galeronistas*, Cuban *decimistas*, Mexican *troveros*, or the *repentistas* of any Latin American country. These bards are to be found, above all, in Latin America where, in my opinion, the most impressive improvised oral poetry movement in the world thrives (at least in my own "known world"). Indeed as José Martí, who was especially familiar with the *repentística* tradition ("improvisational oral poetry") of his native Cuba and Latin America, observed at the end of the nineteenth century: "Why read Homer in Greek when he's alive and well, guitar on shoulder, wandering through the deserts of Latin America?"

And now everyone, even framed by a particular cultural boundary, has a wealth of opportunities to discover other worlds of improvised oral poetry that were, until comparatively recently, close and yet ignored. In my case, this initially happened with several kinds of improvised poetry that exist in the Canary Islands and later, little by little, with the various improvisational genres practiced in the Iberian Peninsula, both in Spain and in Portugal. More recently, I have discovered the spectrum of improvisational poetry in the Mediterranean basin within a complex and diverse framework of countries, languages and peoples. And at the same time, I discovered "another world," that splendid reality that is the spectrum of improvised oral poetry in Latin America.

One literary character and one book in particular embody *par excellence* this kind of poetry in Latin America and, therefore, throughout Hispanic literature: *Martín Fierro* by José Hernández, a late nineteenth-century Argentinian author that immortalized, in the form of an epic poem, the image of the *gaucho*. In this epic tale, the *gaucho* emerged as both rebellious and quarrelsome, minstrel and outlaw, but this was also as an accurate reflection of the thoughts and feelings of an individual who came into the world with only a pair of hands with which to work and a sense of himself as a "man." As a *gaucho* and as a consequence of the geographical setting for these exploits, Martín Fierro had to be Argentinian. However, as regards his poetic qualities, he might also have been Chilean, Peruvian, Venezuelan or Cuban: in other words, Latin American. In fact, *Martín Fierro* became a "classic" for ordinary people and extensive parts of the story, mostly those episodes that deal with poetic debates between Fierro and El Moreno, passed into orality being repeated and transmitted through generations, not only in Argentina, but throughout the Hispanic world. The point here, of course, is that the troubadour Martín Fierro does not merely represent a piece of literary fiction invented by Hernández; he is a person who is as real as life itself, and so representative of those aforementioned areas and cultures that he didn't require any literary embellishment:

Yo no soy cantor letrao,	I'm no learned singer,
mas si me pongo a cantar,	but if I begin to sing,
no tengo cuándo acabar	I don't know how to stop
y me envejezco cantando;	and I sing until I get old;
las coplas me van brotando	verses pour out of me
como agua de manantial.	like water from a spring.

(*Martín Fierro*, I, vv. 49–54)

The Absent Tradition of the "Academy"

When one thinks about poetry today, one immediately associates it with writing, with *littera* (from which 'literature' or "that which is written" derives). However the history of humanity and its culture –and, it should be remembered, of its literature– began long before western man's cultural behavior made writing a normal practice. Indeed, this was still the case when this cultural behavior became collective, that is, when it became common or normal throughout society. Written poetry is an extremely modern phenomenon, almost dating to our own lifetimes. On the other hand, when one examines the origins of literary history and the beginnings of poetry, one finds a single word that is an all-embracing definition of the tradition: oral. What better way is there to define the first two examples of poetry in the Spanish language, the *jarchas* and the *cantares de gesta* –one, lyrical poetry, the other, epic poetry– than by orality? And while the further one looks, and the narrower the spectrum becomes, so the oral realm appears stronger and stronger. This argument could be turned around to contend that the closer poetry is to orality, the closer it is to its origins and natural roots.

No first-hand account of this former genre of improvised, oral poetry exists outside of what literature (by an author and written down) can furnish, but such contributions are so many and so diverse that they remain unmistakable testimonies. Initially, the medieval literary genre of *debates* (also known as "*recuesta*," "*tensó*" or "*partiment*") became famous, with Provençal troubadours taking the genre to its highest levels and spreading it throughout Europe. The debate might bring forth real, flesh and bone, people or instead concern abstract, allegorical beings, to which human conditions were ascribed. This all took place in a context of opposites: male/female, love/dislike, noble/priest, wine/water, winter/summer, rich/poor and so on.

Within Spanish literature no original testimony survives to confirm that these "debates" were indeed oral, but no-one says they were not; further still, the texts that we do have concerning this genre (for example, "La disputa del alma y el cuerpo" or "The Dispute of Soul and Body"; "La razón de amor" or "Love's Reason"; "Los denuestos del agua y el vino" or "Insults of Water and Wine"; and "La disputa de Elena y María" or "The disagreement of Elena y María) display characteristics which are very close to those of orality. And the medieval debate did not become extinct after the Middle Ages: The popularity of such literary debates (of the written not oral variety) has continued to this day. Indeed, from this popularity one might credit the seemingly infinite volumes in the genre that, until quite recently, were sold in towns and city squares throughout Spain and Latin America.

In classic Spanish theatre there exist several examples of these challenges, which are termed *echarse pullas* ("hurling insults"). For example, in Rodrigo Caro's celebrated seventeenth-century work, *Días geniales o lúdicos* ("Pleasant or Playful Days"), there is clear evidence of this. Already at that time, this kind of improvised oral poetry was associated with "rustic folk." And the modern oral tradition continues to confirm this image, since it remains an exclusively popular and, more often than not, rural form.

This popular, oral dimension is perhaps the reason why the "academy" and its researchers so often overlooked improvised oral poetry. It would appear that oral poetry was considered "less important" and unworthy of "scientific" treatment by such erudite and qualified people. What an injustice against popular poetry and what a pitiful void in such research! Within the improvised oral poetry that today takes place all over the globe, and especially in the Hispanic world, the spirit of medieval minstrels and troubadours lives on. These were the people who created the first spoken (and later written) literature in Castilian and, without losing an ounce of their original function, it now also remains the legitimate and natural wish of many peoples, at the same time, to understand, to recreate and, through what they possess in the *canturías* ("musical songs"), to have access to this cultural world:

Es poesía la ciencia	Poetry is the science
que enseña a expresar lo hermoso	which shows how to convey beauty,
en el lenguaje glorioso	in the glorious language
de la medida y cadencia.	of cadence and perfect form.

Es poesía elocuencia,	Poetry is eloquence,
encantamiento cristiano,	Christian enchantment,
germen que el cerebro humano	seed which the human mind
engalana sin esfuerzo	effortlessly adorns
y es el bello arte del verso	and it is the beautiful art of verse,
igual agudo que llano.	both sharp and simple.

This *décima* ("ten-line stanza") belongs to a famous debate, dating from the beginning of the twentieth century, between a pair of Cuban improvisers, Limendoux and Santana, two pure representatives of what the *décima* and *canturía* meant in Cuban culture. I have witnessed, on more than one occasion, hundreds of Cuban peasants absorbed by and engrossed for hours in a flood of verse that the most "intellectual" improvisational poets of their country have been able to offer them on days when they have been able to take some time off work. For them the *canturía* is their only non work-related activity; indeed they live it so intensely that they refer to their favorite poets as if they were idols; and their poet does not speak to them about politics or the domestic economy, nor about the weather forecast; he speaks to them about love, about loss or about memory, about the dreams of man, about abstract subtle subjects, and he does so using the most exquisite similes and metaphors; and Cuban peasants –the *guajiros*– understand, are overcome by emotion and vociferate the best poetic rewards of a *repentista* ("improvisational oral poet").

Spanish Popular Poetry

Spanish popular poetry has always appeared in two forms: the *romancero* and the *cancionero*. In the first form, which belongs to the epic or narrative genre, the same meter has always been used: the romance meter. This is typically a long series of eight-syllable verses, with an assonant rhyme every two lines. For example, consider the *romance*, "El caballero burlado" ("The Baffled Knight"):

A cazar va el cazador,	The hunter's going to hunt
a cazar como solía,	to hunt as he always did,
los perros lleva cansados	his hounds were exhausted
y la jurona perdida.	And he had lost his ferret.
Se sentaba a descansar	He sat down to rest
al pie de un haya que había…	at the foot of a beech tree…

In the second lyrical form, a variety of meters have been used: *jarchas* (verses in Hispanic Romance cited in Medieval Arabic and Hebrew poems), the *zéjel* (Castilian strophic poetry), the *villancico* (early Castilian lyric poetry), the *dístico* ("distich"), *letrillas* ("short verses"), the *canción* ("song"), the *seguidilla* (alternate five and seven syllable verses), the *cuarteta* ("quatrain"), and the *copla* ("verse"), to mention but a few. For example:

Por el aire va que vuela	The flower of the Indian cress
la flor de la marañuela.	goes flying through the air.

or

Dicen que no nos queremos	They say that we don't love each another
porque no nos ven hablar;	because they never see us talk;
a tu corazón y al mío	they should only ask
deberían preguntar.	your heart and mine.

These two genres, epic and lyric, which emerged during the Middle Ages and have been in continual use down to this day, nourished, through two parallel mechanisms, what came to be known as Spanish *traditional poetry*: the conservation (and recreation) of ancient texts and the creation of new texts that followed earlier models, since popular inspiration has never ceased to think up poetry. And these two genres continue to survive, to greater or lesser degrees, according to the different regions where they exist, throughout the Spanish-speaking world, both in peninsular as well as insular Spain, together with Latin American lands and countries.

Being "traditional" does not necessarily mean that the text is rigid, as is the case of a text fixed by literature. The laws which govern all oral literary genres revolve around two simultaneous procedures: repetition and renewal. Menéndez Pidal observed that it was, "poetry [or literature] that lives through variation." This was and, in my opinion still is, the best definition that one can make of such poetry. However, it is unquestionably the first form, namely that of repetition, that predominates in the aforementioned transmission; for that reason certain Hispanic oral genres like, for example, the *romances*, have remained in the collective memory of diverse peoples for five, six and even seven centuries, with extremely important differential variables but maintaining an essential thematic identity. Consequently, one might rightly term this kind of poetry as "memorial poetry." This contrasts with another type of poetry, that, although surviving through a tradition of forms, functions, uses and even meaning, is still "improvised poetry."

This first "memorial" kind of poetry is always collective in nature, belonging to and representing a specific group: it is the poetry (or literature) of an entire people. Take the *romance* of *Delgadina*, for example: there are thousands of different individual oral versions of this tale that have emerged throughout the Spanish-speaking world (as well as in Portuguese, Galician, Catalan and Judeo-Spanish). The story represents, at a general symbolic level, an incestuous relationship between a father and a daughter, which the "official" culture of these peoples condemns for going "against nature"; but if one considers it from a less generalized point of view, one might draw attention to the fact that this *romance* text also changes according to the emphasis, in greater or lesser degrees, accorded diverse aspects of the story. This emphasis changes according to the particular country or folkloric region from where this universal story emerges. As such, some cultures may emphasize, for example, the cruelty of the mother and the sisters of the unlucky maiden, when they deny her access to water, the harsh nature of the prisons where she is kept, or the miraculous help that arrives from heaven at the end of the story.

Alexis Diaz Pimienta and Tomasita Quiala, Las Palmas, Canary Islands, Spain, 1998. The poet, writer and theorist, Diaz Pimienta, performs with the great *decimista*, Quiala.
By permission of the Xenpelar Dokumentazio Zentroa, Donostia.

On the contrary, improvised oral poetry always demonstrates an individual quality, the natural result of a collective tradition that emerges according to the specific conditions of a certain place and the differential qualities of a particular community, but also always attributable to the individual character of each singer. As such, Tomasita Quiala's poetry, for example, is unquestionably a form of improvisation known as *punto cubano*; that is, improvised oral poetry in *décimas* or ten-line stanzas, abiding by the musical and instrumental rules which accompany it, as well as complying with the particular Cuban "rules" (at least those that tend to dominate), as regards improvised oral poetry. This might be contrasted with the *trovo* (a particular kind of improvisational style) of Miguel "Candiota," an improvised oral poetry in *quintillas* ("five-line stanzas") and sung according to the structure and form of *malagueñas* or *fandangos* from the Las Alpujarras region of Andalusia. And one might again contrast these two with Andoni Egaña's poetry or *bertsolaritza*; that is, improvised poetry in the Basque language, where he can choose from a variety of meters and where he must also follow a song pattern, either based on a traditional melody or another one that the poets themselves might make up at that moment, but which must be sung without instrumental accompaniment or *a capella*. Each of these three poets sings in the "style" of the folkloric region to which he or she belongs and abides by the "laws" that in each of these regions have been developed over time; in other words, within either a local or a national tradition. Here the individual performance, as with all those that emerge from a traditional culture, draws from the dominant characteristics of the common tradition of each people. However, Tomasita Quiala's poetry remains noticeably distinct from other Cuban *repentistas*, in the same way that Miguel "Candiota" differs from other *troveros* of Las Alpujarras, or Andoni Egaña from other Basque *bertsolariak*. Each one of them, in so far as they are three undeniable "figures" of improvised oral poetry in their respective folkloric regions, might have a number of loyal followers among the general public, as well as imitators among other improvisers themselves, but this would be only because of their differential "I" status, an individual subject emerging from collective poetic production.

Forms of Improvised Oral Poetry in Spain

To tell the truth, I am not familiar with the details of every example of improvised oral poetry that exists in Spain as regards their particular qualities, current relevance, and so on. This is because, if popular poetry in general has been a secondary line of investigation within the general study of and research on popular culture, improvised oral poetry has indeed been, as Samuel G. Armistead (1994a: 42) has observed, very much the "dark side" or "black sheep" of popular literature. Only in recent years, and thanks in the main to the sensitivity of new ways of thinking on the subject by cultural teachers and researchers in their respective regions, have we begun to comprehend the full spectrum of improvised oral poetry practiced in Spain.

Here I will examine only what I consider to be the most important varieties of improvised oral poetry, exploring also the social repercussions that they have had in their respective regions and the degree of energy with which they continue to operate, namely: *bertsolaritza* in the Basque Country, the *trovo* in parts of Murcia and Andalusia, the *glosat* in the Balearic Islands, the *regueifa* in Galicia, and the *punto cubano* in the Canary Islands.

There are other varieties of improvised oral poetry in other regions of Spain, which, however, I would like to mention: *cantar al picadillo* ("popular humorous verse contests") in the western mountains of Santander (Christian 1998 and 2000), *chacarrá* (another kind of sung improvisation) in the Campo de Gibraltar, Cádiz (Ruiz Fernández 2000), quatrains and *ovillejos* ("eight-syllable verses") in Brihuela and other towns of La Alcarria, Guadalajara (Caballero Barriopedro 1996), *corrandes* ("improvised verses") in the provinces of Lleida and Tarragona (Catalonia), together with several other improvisational forms in parts of the Community of Valencia (Santapola, Elche, and Orihuela for example) and Andalusia (in the Genil basin where the provinces of Málaga, Córdoba and Granada meet, as well as in the northern part of Almería), apart from the Las Alpujarras area, which I will examine in more detail.

Bertsolaritza in the Basque Country

In all likelihood, the most well-known phenomenon of poetic improvisation in Spain is that of the Basque Country, where it is termed *bertsolaritza* and its performers are *bertsolariak*. It dates from time immemorial and is still widely practiced. One might even go further by arguing that Basque *bertsolaritza* is currently experiencing the apogee of its legendary history.

Moreover, Basque *bertsolaritza* has benefited, more than any other kind of Spanish or Latin American variety in general, from numerous and varied studies, among which I will mention here only those written in or translated into Spanish: The range of studies includes the early works of Michelena (1960), Lekuona (1965), Zavala (1996b and 2000) and Aulestia (1990) to later ones by Egaña (1996), Garzia (2000b) and Sarasua (2000), culminating in an essential study by the latter three authors together (Garzia, Sarasua and Egaña 2001),[2] together with all kinds of works and articles, some informative, others analytical, and additionally two large collections of *bertsoak* ("strophes")[3] by the most famous *bertsolariak*. The first of these was compiled through the diligence and work of Antonio Zavala, the principle figure in charge of these editions, and the great love of Basque culture by Joaquín Satrústegui, managing director of the Sendoa publishing house, where the first collection was published. The second was published by the Basque Country Association of *Bertsolaritza* Followers (*Euskal Herriko Bertsozaleen Elkartea*, with its headquarters at Igeldo Pasealekua, 25, 20008 Donostia), which, since 1988, has edited an annual anthology under the generic title *Bapatean*, recording the improvised *bertsoak* of various competitions held throughout the Basque Country.

My knowledge of Basque *bertsolaritza* originated in reading the aforementioned bibliography together with what I would argue was the far superior and live experience of attending the final, in 1997, of the National *Bertsolaritza* Championship. An experience like that, at the high point of *bertsolaritza*, stretched out throughout the day, to last eight hours, allowing me, not only to get inside this world to a great extent, but also to check the sociological environment in which this phenomenon thrives. This energy is clearly based on a social support which, in this case, goes far beyond mere enthusiasm, to reach a level of identifying with one of the most outstanding demonstrations of Basque culture (Trapero 1998).

This, in the first instance, is what I would most like to highlight: the identification of *bertsolaritza* with native Basque culture. In certain cultural circles there are those who maintain that the survival of *Euskara* (the Basque language), which experienced historical moments of great weakness and fragmentation, is due, at least in part, to the existence

---

2. Andoni Egaña and Jon Sarasua have, moreover, written an extremely interesting book, whose argument appears in the form of a conversational reflection, in the style of a two-way correspondence, about the *bertsolaritza* phenomenon and the circumstances surrounding the lives and thoughts of the *bertsolariak*. The book, originally written and published in Basque (*Zozoak beleari*, Irun: Alberdania, 1997) was translated by the authors themselves into Spanish, under the title *El mirlo le dijo al cuervo* (The Blackbird said to the Crow), but it remains as yet unpublished.

3. In Basque *bertso* (*bertsoak* in plural) means "strophe," while each verse is termed a *line*.

of so many anonymous *bertsolariak*, who, by always singing in *Euskara*, maintained a loyal support throughout the smallest villages and towns of the Basque valleys.

And this is also one of the principal, if not the most important, characteristics of *bertsolaritza*: that one always sings in *Euskara*. And it is not only the language, but also the music: *bertsolariak* always sing their improvisations *a capella*, without any instrumentation and, as such, they use infinite melodies, finding room in each case for a type of *bertso* ("verse," "strophe") that they have chosen for their improvisation, to such an extent that the repertoire of melodies that an individual *bertsolari* can call upon is enormous. I don't mean that a *bertsolari* can't create *ex profeso* a melody to improvise with, but it is true that the great majority use already existent melodies, while of course adapting them to the variation and taste of the singer. Thus, that wealth of music employed in *bertsolaritza* is also traditional Basque folk music which can be used for many other popular and collective songs: one more way of getting to the heart of an art that is quintessentially individual, *bertsolaritza*, through a collective tradition, namely music. This explains –something that I found very striking– the fact that, when a *bertsolari* performs in a championship and gets to the end of the *bertso*, repeating the last two verses, these are collectively sung together by the public, as they too are experts in the melodies. And the Basque love of music is well-known, as their choirs and attachment to singing in choral groups is legendary, and it goes without saying that Basque music is full of beautiful melodies.

Added to the infinite musical range *bertsolaritza* also shares a great variety of improvisational forms, both through the type of strophe and versifying chosen and through the type of performance imposed on the *bertsolariak*. The particularly special characteristics of the Basque language also mean that there are distinctive versifying laws which roughly correspond to the following strophes in Spanish: quatrains, six-, eight- and ten-line stanzas (though not *espinelas*, another kind of *décima*) up to and including strophes of twelve and fourteen verses, with a quite varied rhyming system that sometimes becomes so complicated as to test the individual *bertsolari*. However, one of the most frequently used strophes is that of ten verses, although not with the same rhyme as that of the *espinela* (*abbc:cd:deed*), but rather with that of a *romance*, assonating each pair of verses. The most typical verse is that of eight syllables, although certain anisoyllabic combinations (8/6, 10/8, or 6/4) are also common.

As regards the types of improvisation performed, it depends to a large extent on the type of performance itself: in spontaneous (or even planned) performances in front of an audience, duels between *bertsolariak*, where they either sing about an open or a predetermined subject, tend to predominate. In competition performances (and even sometimes spontaneous situations), *bertsolariak* tend to perform alone and according to a wide variety of forms: solitary improvisation, two or three strophes of a set theme (with, for example, subjects like solitude, the moon, faith, Monday, a letter, and so on), defining a word without being able to say it (for example, kitchen, brush, head, forest, and so on), finishing a *bertso* after hearing one or two previously set strophes (a kind of initial "forcing of the issue") and also in a designated metric structure. Within all these varieties, one not only assesses the poets' virtuosity, but also –and to a great extent– their ideology. When I use the term 'ideology' here, I mean it in an intellectual rather than political sense; that is, their ability to develop an argument, their ingenuity and speed of response, and the originality of their thoughts, to such an extent that the successful *bertsolari* is also, in many ways, an ideologue or an intellectual leader of the Basque people.

Basque *bertsolaritza*, as I said before, is experiencing one of its strongest moments, being enormously popular and, what is even more rare and undeniably prestigious (especially when compared to other regions where some kind of poetic improvisation is performed), two other points distinguish contemporary *bertsolaritza* in the Basque Country:

1. It is now an urban phenomenon (without giving up its rural dimension) and is sociologically refined; today *bertsolariak* regularly perform in cities and in large population centers, and those who make up their audience come from a variety of backgrounds, not only the humble folk of previous times.

2. Today it is also a youth phenomenon, rather than the preserve of older people: the predominant age among contemporary *bertsolariak* ranges between eighteen and thirty; and moreover it is a phenomenon of university-educated young people: of the eight finalists in the aforementioned National *Bertsolaritza* Championship in 1997, seven of those had attended or were attending university, and four had degrees.

The creation of the Basque Country Association of *Bertsolaritza* Followers (*Euskal Herriko Bertsozaleen Elkartea*) was especially important in aiding this generational renovation and the major change in *bertsolaritza*'s sociological substratum. This occurred through the association's organization of regional, provincial and national *bertsolaritza* "championships," coordinating the performances of *bertsolariak*, promoting a love of *bertsolaritza* in the *ikastolak* (schools where instruction is carried out in the Basque language), creating schools and workshops where basic improvisational techniques are taught, and achieving an informative infrastructure which successfully disseminates news through to ordinary public opinion, using the basic media (press, radio and television). Moreover, this association also publishes the "records" of the latest national and provincial *bertsolaritza* championships. All this makes Basque *bertsolaritza* –as I said at the beginning– the most important variety of contemporary poetic improvisation in Spain and quite likely in the world.

The *Trovo* in Murcia and the Campo de Cartagena

Another of the most important types of improvised oral poetry in Spain is found in the region of Murcia, and more specifically in the municipalities of Cartagena and La Unión (typically referred to as the "Campo de Cartagena"). This is the result of the recognition and acceptance of its condition as a social phenomenon, as well as the high standards with which it is performed, although it does not nowadays display that touch of criticism and social condemnation that it possessed in former times.

The bibliography surrounding Murcian *trovo* is neither abundant nor especially old, but it is interesting: There is a historical account by the contemporary *trovero* Ángel Roca in *Historia del trovo* (2000), but the best general examination that I know of is that of Bon-mattí Limorte (2000); there are also studies and anthologies of famous Murcian *troveros*, such as those dedicated to "El Minero" and Castillo by Mouzo Pagán (1966 and 1995).

The typical improvisational form is the *trovo*, with the improvisers known as *troveros*. The dominant metric structure is the *quintilla* or five-line stanza (*ababa*, with some varia-tions in rhyme), generally assonant, sung in *malagueña* style and close to *flamenco* (termed *malagueña trovera* or, simply, *cante del trovo*), and accompanied by a guitar played flamenco-style, with long and elaborate interludes. To mark the rhythm of the text's *quintilla* to the structure of the music's six thirds, the first verse is always repeated, thereby raising the public's expectation and allowing the *trovero* more time to improvise a verse.

Other forms are also used in the Murcia region to improvise, from the quatrain up to the *décima* or ten-line stanza (which is termed *guajira*). This has been a recent innova-tion and stems from the influence of some *troveros* who migrated to Cuba and returned bringing with them the typical Latin American strophe, but one should underscore the fact that the basic Murcian *trovo* is performed in five-line stanzas. However, there is one spe-cial form of *trovo par excellence*, and one which becomes the principal test when it's a ques-tion of evaluating the *trovero*'s approach, which is the *glosa* in five-line stanzas of a set quat-rain, in such a way that the four *quintillas* which the poet must improvise must be completed, not only on the understanding of finishing each of the quatrain's verses, but that they should also respect their rhyme. Thus, if the quatrain is alternate (*abab*), so should the five-line stanzas also be alternate (*ababa*), and if they are inclusive (*abba*), so must the five-line stanzas also be inclusive (*abbab* or *abaab*).

Another distinctive and curious way of improvising in Murcia is what might be termed "the dictated form": when a *trovero* is a poet, but not a singer, he dictates the vers-es to somebody else, who in turn sings them, in such a way that it becomes a shared per-formance, as poet and singer act in unison and together receive the public's applause.

Contemporary Murcian *trovo*, both in terms of obligatory metric questions and the-matic content, is to a large extent governed by the "laws" established by the most famous *trovero* of all time, José María Marín (1865–1936). Marín invented a series of recom-mendations to elevate the poetic nature of the *trovo* which, owing to his undeniable pres-tige, subsequently became "laws".

The Murcian *trovo* is also currently experiencing a wonderful moment, since it is not only popular with a loyal following, but also enjoys the support of regional and local cul-tural institutions. These institutions support a number of initiatives to promote the *trovo*, either at a local level or at national and international meetings and competitions of impro-vised poetry. And as an example of its popularity in attracting people, there exists a National *Trovo* Competition, organized by the Cartagena City Hall, which has been held annually since 1977.

Finally, one should not confuse the Murcian *trovo* with the *trovo* of Las Alpujarras (and even less with that of the Genil poets), since, although they are closely related and there is at present a strong relationship between their respective *troveros*, there are also note-worthy differences, especially in musical aspects.

The *Trovo* of Las Alpujarras

Las Alpujarras is a historical region of eastern Andalusia, descending from the foothills of the Sierra Nevada Mountains to the shores of the Mediterranean, and is divided between the provinces of Granada and Almería. It is, therefore, an extremely mountain-ous region, with traditionally difficult communications and an impoverished economy that has been almost entirely agricultural. Furthermore, from around the middle of the twen-tieth century, it began to suffer severe depopulation with, in the main, people descending to the lowlands to work in the hothouse cultivation industry on the coast of Almería. As a result today the Las Alpujarras *trovo* movement and the most famous *trovos alpujarreños* are mostly found in the hothouse El Ejido region.

José Criado (1993 and 1994) is the most renowned expert on the *trovo alpujarreño*, but the works of Checa (1992) and Fernández Manzano et al. (1992) are also interesting, and there is, moreover, a good *trovo* anthology under the direction of Criado and Ramos Moya (1992).

The typical form of *alpujarreña* improvisation is comparable to that of Murcia; the art is known as *trovo* and its practitioners are *troveros*. They improvise *quintillas* or five-line stan-za strophes, usually with an assonant rhyme (*ababa*). What changes here is the *trovo*'s music and instrumentation. The song is a *fandango* and the instruments used are the vio-lin and the guitar (and on some occasions, the lute and castanets). The most typical way of performing is that of alternating between two *troveros*, usually in the form of a contest. *Tanda* or *velada de trovo* ("a *trovo* group or evening") is the term used to describe this per-formance. It is essentially sung, but there are numerous recital interventions, mostly at the beginning, by way of introduction, and at the end, both as a send-off and as a means by which the musicians can take a rest.

The frame of mind with which the *troveros alpujarreños* sing is very tense, almost at a breaking point. This is the most striking characteristic of their songs, full of *melismas* ("short melismatic improvisations") and an extraordinary expressivity, with undeniable roots in *flamenco*. Each *trovero* begins his turn by shouting *rajao* (a kind of exclamation), to work themselves up, and each singer manages to achieve truly incredible moments of dra-matic expressivity.

More recently, some *troveros alpujarreños* have taken to singing *décimas* or ten-line stan-zas (known as *guajiras*), which they undertake in an expert way, though this has come about more through the influence of Murcia (and more lately through their new rela-tionships with Cuban *repentistas*). Proof that the ten-line stanza was not the typical form performed in Las Alpujarras is that they sing it (or rather recite or chant it) without any musical accompaniment. One example is this magnificent *décima* that Candiota recited, improvising at the Sixth Las Palmas Festival-Meeting:

Décima, mi paisana,	A ten-line stanza, my compatriot,
andaluza como yo,	Andalusian like me,
¿qué viento te trasplantó	which wind uprooted you
a la selva americana?	to the Latin American jungle?
No pude, querida hermana,	I could not, dear sister,
en mis tiempos conocerte,	during my time get to know you,
pero esta noche por suerte	but fortunately tonight
conmigo vas caminando,	you walk along beside me,
cuando me voy acercando	as I get closer and closer
al teatro de la muerte.	to the theater of death.

The *Glosat* of the Balearic Islands

The diversity of poetic improvisation in the Balearic Islands, both in terms of metric and musical form, is particularly striking. In fact the three islands only coincide in three ways: the name of the improvisers (they are termed *glosadores* and their improvisational art is *glosat*, and if they compete against one another it's known as *glosat de picat*), in the position of those seated while they improvise (as in the manner of a relaxed and agreeable conversation), and the use of their native language, insular *Català* (Catalan): *Mallorquí* or *Menorquí* according to whether they come from Mallorca or Menorca (or *Eivissenc*, if they are from Ibiza).

They always sing octosyllabic verses (as in almost all improvisational forms in Spain and Latin America), but without having a set or single strophic structure. As a general rule the *glosadores* of Ibiza perform in assonant quatrains (*abcb*), those of Mallorca in quatrains (*abba*) (or double quatrains which become false *octavillas* or eight-line stanzas: *abba, abba*), and those of Menorca in assonant *septillas* or seven-line stanzas (*abba:bab* or *abab:bcb*), but through developing the *glosat*, they may become *octavillas*, (non-*espinela*) *décimas*, and up to strophes of twelve verses.

From all of these different options, I believe the best form is that of Menorca, both for the music with which they sing (accompanied by a single guitar playing a beautiful, solemn, almost ritual and entirely "Mediterranean" melody) and for the stance they adopt in their performance (seated, still, almost motionless apart from their hand actions), as well as their poetic art and the vitality with which they perform.

Sbert i Garau (2000) offers a wide-ranging and general study of improvised oral poetry in the Balearic Islands, and as an example of the work being undertaken in the schools of Mallorca to promote the art of *glosat*, see Munar's *Manual* (2001).

The *Regueifa* of Galicia

Among various improvisational forms in Galicia, the most typical, extensive and, at the same time, most assiduously practiced, is that termed *regueifa*. The name is related to its origins: it was a dispute in verse and sung between several opponents as a way of obtaining wedding bread that was offered to those, who, without being invited to the wedding in question, used to approach the door of the banquet hall, where the reception was being held, in search of food. The wedding bread (really a large cake) was known as *regueifa* and, through metonymy, the improvised songs came to be known by the same name.

Today this custom is still practiced, mainly in smaller villages, but improvised song in Galicia has also diversified, as have its functions. It is still termed *regueifa* in the Bergantiños region, in the western part of the Corunna province; in eastern parts of Lugo province, it is known as *brinda, beringo* or *loia*; while in the southern part of Ourense province, towards the border area with Portugal, it is known as *cantigas ao desafío*. Its performers are termed *regueiferos* or *brindeiros* ("those who make a toast"), as that, effectively, is their principal function nowadays, namely to make toasts at celebrations and ceremonies to which they are invited.

The metric structure is the same throughout the region: the quatrain with an assonant rhyme in pairs of verses: the simple and very Spanish *copla* (*abcb*). Another typical characteristic is the use of *Galego* (the Galician language) in these songs and the singing style, a monotonous melody, *a capella*, without instrumentation (in former times they used bagpipes and tambourines), although with significant differences according to the regions.

The most striking aspects of the *regueifa* are the speed with which it is sung, the spontaneity of the improvisation and the ingenuity of the responses, more than the literary standards associated with other forms of improvisation in the Hispanic world.

Various authors have explored the different improvisational forms used in Galicia, with the works of Lisón (1974) and Blanco (2000) being particularly important.

The *Décima* and *Punto Cubano* of the Canary Islands

What makes the kind of poetic improvisation found in the Canary Islands stand out from the rest of the Spanish regions is the use of the *espinela décima* (*abba:ac.cddc*), a strophe born as a fashion of the late sixteenth century and transformed, from the eighteenth century onwards, into one of the most important examples of popular literature in the Hispanic world (including both Spain and Portugal). And here another differentiating characteristic emerges: the Canary Islands lie halfway between the Iberian Peninsula and Ibero-America; and this, as a geographical reality, results in a natural connection, in some cultural matters at least, between the Canary Islands and Latin America. For example, here, through use of the *décima*, the Canary Islands are closer to Latin America than to Spain. Today, both in Spanish- and Portuguese-speaking Latin America, improvised oral poetry is a much more sociologically (and literarily) important and widespread phenomenon of popular culture than in Spain (with the only possible exception of the Basque Country), as well as those of other countries that I am familiar with. And poetic improvisation throughout Latin America is performed in ten-line stanzas.

Not only do academic studies discuss and write about the origins of the *décima* (Clotelle Clarke 1936; Cossío 1944; López Lemus 1999 and 2003; Trapero 2000; and Orta Ruiz and Trapero 2001, among others), but it is also a recurring theme among the *decimistas* ("ten-line stanza improvisers") themselves. I believe that absolutely every *decimista* in Spain and Latin America must have improvised something about this fact at some time: it would certainly be worth investigating this, since among other things it would demonstrate how, in regard to one single theme, for all the many times that it could be repeated, improvisation is always capable of finding a differential nuance, an original word or idea, never before felt or uttered. This has always seemed most striking to me and I have always been interested in collecting ten-line stanzas that discuss this subject: no *decimista* doesn't know, nor misses an opportunity to mention in their verses, that its creator was Vicente Espinel; by way of a brief biography, they state that Espinel was an Andalusian from Málaga province, born in the town of Ronda, and they even add the year of his birth (1550), the year in which the *décima* was created (1591), and the book title which gave rise to it (*Diversas rimas; "Diverse Rhymes"*). I have even heard it said that his discovery took place at night, during a full moon, but that is already a metaphor. All *décimas* are incredible as regards their content and beauty of expression, as in the following example by the Cuban Jesusito Rodríguez, who said during the *Decimista* Festival of Las Palmas in 1992:

> Málaga, mano de miel,   Malaga, honeyed hand,
> nueve lunas esperó   awaited nine moons
> y en una estrella le abrió   and a star opened
> las pupilas a Espinel.   Espinel's eyes.

I will now cite in full one of the most beautiful and certainly the most famous of all *décimas*, by the Cuban Jesús Orta Ruiz or "Indio Naborí," recognized by everyone as the best *decimista* of the twentieth century, where he speaks of his Spanish birth and Latin American upbringing:

> Viajera peninsular,   Peninsular traveler,
> ¡cómo te has aplatanado!,   how native you have become!
> ¿qué sinsonte enamorado   Which enamored mockingbird
> te dio cita en el palmar?   met you in the palm grove?
> Dejaste viña y pomar,   You gave up vineyard and apple orchard,
> soñando caña y café,   dreaming about sugar cane and coffee,
> y tu alma española fue   and your Spanish soul was
> canción de arado y guataca   a song of plough and a shovel
> cuando al vaivén de una hamaca   when to the rocking of a hammock
> te diste a «El Cucalambé».   you fell into "El Cucalambé".

It is true that the *décima* is not only used in the Canary Islands to improvise with, since it has also become –as in Latin America– an expression of popular poetry of the traditional sort (next to the *cancionero* and the *romancero*). It is also true that in the Canary

Islands other metric forms are used in improvisational poetry (such as the *meda* on the island of El Hierro and *ranchos de ánimas* in Gran Canaria), but in all cases the ten-line stanza remains the most typical form.

The most typical way of expressing the *décima* in the Canary Islands is through the *punto cubano* ("Cuban pitch"), as in Cuba: a kind of chanted recital that each singer speeds up, slows down, or embellishes, according to their own styles, together with generous musical interludes on the instruments which accompany them, the guitar and the lute (sometimes also with harpsichords). The *decimistas* are known as *versadores* or *verseadores* ("versifiers") and their art is termed *poesía* ("poetry").

Punto cubano (improvised and sung *décimas*) was very common throughout the Canary Islands archipelago and on all its islands one could find famous and popular *verseadores*, but the truth now is that only on one island, La Palma, is the *punto cubano* still vigorous and strong, with a number of performances and meetings, either during popular local *fiestas*, where it takes place on a stage, or in the more intimate setting of a get-together by a group of friends, in a *bodega* or on private property. However I should add a note of hope. On the one hand there are the frequent visits to the Canary Islands of Cuban *repentistas*, all of them exceptional, with many performances throughout the archipelago and, on the other, the numerous holding of colloquiums, symposiums and festivals about the *décima*, which have encouraged a very favorable reaction towards the performing of *puntos cubanos*, leading to the emergence of new, young *verseadores* possessing extraordinary qualities, all of which indicates an interesting resurgence of the ten-line stanza in the Canary Islands.

Lately several studies have emerged on the *décima* in the Canary Islands (Martín Teixé 1999; Rodríguez Ramírez 1994; Siemens Hernández 1994; and Trapero 1994a) together with various anthologies, sometimes in the improvised variety and others in written form, about and by popular authors in the Canary Islands (González Ortega 1994; Hernández 1994; Martín Teixé 1992; Martín Teixé and López Isla 1994; Noda Gómez 1993). These all have served as a tremendous stimulus for the Meetings-Festivals that took place about the *décima* and improvised verse in Las Palmas de Gran Canaria in 1992 and 1998 (the "records" of which are collected in Trapero 1994b and Trapero, Santana Martel and Márquez Montes 2000).

The bibliography, both from a general perspective and in studies of specific countries, is much more abundant as regards the Latin American *décima*: most work has been done on Cuba (Díaz-Pimienta 1995; Feijóo 1961; Guanche 1994; Linares 1994, 1995, 1999a and 1999b; López Lemus 1995a, 1995b and 1997, for example), but also on Chile (Dannemann 2000), Ecuador (Hidalgo 1990; rpt. 1995), Puerto Rico (Jiménez de Báez 1964; Córdova Iturregui 1994), Mexico (Jiménez de Báez 1992 and 1994; Mendoza 1957; and Nava López 1994), Argentina and Uruguay (Abel Zabala 2000), and so on. Apart from these works, see also the "records" of conferences and festivals about the *décima* and improvised verse held recently in Las Tunas, Cuba (*La décima popular en Iberoamérica* 1995 and Hernández Menéndez 1999).

Jesús Orta Ruiz, "Indio Naborí," and Andoni Egaña, Veracruz, Mexico, 1996. *Decimista* and *bertsolari* traditions come together in a meeting of their most renowned contemporary exponents.
By permission of the Xenpelar Dokumentazio Zentroa, Donostia.

There is one author on *décimas*, who, as both improviser and expert researcher in the field, stands out. He is the Cuban Jesús Orta Ruiz, or "Indio Naborí" (Orta Ruiz 1980, 1999; Orta Ruiz and Valiente 1997). The most important work on the improvisational genre in ten-line stanzas is that of Díaz-Pimienta (1998). And on the *décima* in general, as a form of popular poetry, see the work of Armistead (1994a and 1996), López Lemus (1999 and 2003), Orta Ruiz (1991), Pérez Vidal (1965), and Trapero (1996 and Trapero, Santana Martel and Márquez Montes 2000). A recent wide-ranging perspective on the history, geography and diverse manifestations of the ten-line stanza can be found in Trapero (2001b), with articles by Orta Ruiz, López Lemus, Díaz-Pimienta, Linares, Lima, Leyva and Trapero.

General and Final Characteristics

In Spain (and this must be a universal characteristic) poetic improvisation takes place in the native language of each region: in the Basque Country in *Euskara*; in Galicia in *Galego*; in the Balearic Islands in *Mallorquí* or *Menorquí*; in Catalonia in *Català*; in the Valencian Region in *Valencià* or Castilian, according to the area; and in the Canary Islands, Las Alpujarras, Murcia and the rest of the places, in Castilian.

The names that these improvisers are known by (in the same way as their art) are also peculiar to each region: *bertsolariak* in the Basque Country, *troveros* in Murcia and Las Alpujarras, *poetas* in the Genil basin, *glosadors* in the Balearic Islands, *regueifeiros* and *brindeiros* in Galicia, *versadores* or *verseadores* in the Canary Islands, *corrandistas* in Catalonia, and so on.

The typical metric structure of each improvisational form is also peculiar to each region: in the Canary Islands the *espinela* ten-line stanza is used; in Las Alpujarras, Murcia and the Genil basin, it is the five-line stanza; in Galicia and Catalonia it is the quatrain; in the Balearic Islands, it is the seven-line stanza, with some variations; and in the Basque Country there are a great number of different forms.

However, the eight-syllable verse is common to all (the typical form running throughout Spanish and Latin American popular poetry), as is the rhyme system which is predominantly assonant, although it is adapted to the typical strophe of each region.

The musical element is also quite a common characteristic to all forms: poetic improvisation in Spain is always performed by singing and, with the exception of the Basque Country (and now also Galicia and the Genil basin), always with musical accompaniment, even though this is done in quite a variety of ways: in the Balearic Islands and Murcia a lone guitar is used, although with quite a different "touch" in each case; in the Canary Islands both the guitar and the lute are used (with the appearance, sometimes, of the harpsichord); and in Las Alpujarras the guitar and the violin are used (as are sometimes also the lute and castanets).

Ultimately, each one of these musical demonstrations, although backed by improvised oral poetry, has turned into a folkloric genre specific to each region: the *punto cubano* in the Canary Islands, the *trovo* through *malagueñas* in Murcia, *fandangos* in Las Alpujarras, *fandangos verdiales* in the Genil basin, *regueifa* in Galicia, *glosat* music in the Balearic Islands, the *cant d'albaes* in Valencia, and through the innumerable repertoire of (incredibly beautiful) melodies in the Basque Country.

Comparative Oral Traditions

JOHN MILES FOLEY

Introduction

Let me begin by sketching a map for the journey we will be taking in this paper. Our goal is to examine the place and role of oral traditions in the world's verbal art, and our "pathway" or *oimê* –and here I use the term employed by the ancient Greek oral poet Homer for the mental journey undertaken by a singer as he or she makes the song– will bring us to six continents over a time period of some three thousand years. Of course, since oral poetry dwarfs written poetry in both amount and variety, the most we can provide is a realistic spectrum of examples; an exhaustive demonstration of oral tradition's worldwide diversity and history lies far beyond our reach, not only because of its inherent variety, but also because its existence long predates the invention of writing and other recording technologies. But along the way, we can at least consider some real-life instances of oral poetry, which collectively should help to create an international context and a background for the phenomenon of Basque oral improvisation.[1]

Two Questions

To start, then, I pose two simple but deceptively challenging questions: (1) What does an oral bard really do? and (2) What is a "word" in oral tradition? For the first question, I offer as evidence the oral epic performance of a Tibetan "paper-singer," Grags-pa seng-ge, who composes his long narrative poetry over many hours while holding a sheet of white paper directly in front of his eyes at about arm's length.[2] Our first instinct, as high-

---

1. Parts of this discussion are drawn from my *How to Read an Oral Poem* (Foley 2002), which features an internet E-companion at www.oraltradition.org/hrop/. Readers who consult this electronic resource can view and listen to video and audio performances of various oral traditions, as well as browse through an annotated version of the book's bibliography. Also available at the web site are a video of Chinese Suzhou storytelling, an E-companion to Mark Bender's *Plum and Bamboo* (2003); and a sound-file of the 1030-line performance of Halil Bajgorić's *The Wedding of Mustajbey's Son Bećirbey*, a South Slavic oral epic. See further, Foley (2004).

2. A photograph of Grags-pa seng-ge is available on the cover of Foley (2002) and at www.oraltradition.org.

Grags-pa seng-ge, a Tibetan paper-singer. Holding a sheet of paper directly in front of his eyes, this oral poet "sees" the action of his story as a direct projection, much like a film projected on a screen. The paper is blank and he is nonliterate. Photo by Yang Enhong, Chinese Academy of Social Sciences.

ly literate people and voracious consumers of textual materials, is to understand him as actually reading something from the paper, whether we imagine to include lines of poetry, notes, or some other mnemonic device. But that expectation is quickly dashed once we realize that the sheet is absolutely blank. What is more, if there is no white paper available, these bards use a piece of newspaper. It doesn't matter, because they are illiterate. When asked what role the white sheet plays in his performance, Grags-pa seng-ge responded that he sees the action of his story "projected" (like a film, it seems) on the surface of the paper, and it is that audiovisual action –rather than the silent coding of a text– that he is gazing at so intently.

I offer this example of the paper-singer Grags-pa seng-ge as evidence for the inadequacy of our usual categories for understanding the dynamics and diversity of oral traditions. We customarily assume that anything held before the eyes must necessarily be the central resource for the performance; if the singer is looking at a textual surface, we reason (based on our text-based culture) then it must necessarily serve as his inspiration, something he cannot perform without. But oral tradition reverses the usual hierarchy: for the paper-singer, it is the performed story that is primary, while the sheet of paper is merely a "screen" for projection of the story's action. This instance of oral poetry graphically reveals how non-universal our categories are, how we must be ready to question and revise even our most fundamental assumptions about how an oral poet makes a poem.

The second question –What is a "word" in oral tradition?– may initially seem too obvious to worry over, but a few observations will help us realize that this concept also deserves reexamination. Consider the options that our print-based culture presents us. Some of us might resort to defining a "word" as a textual unit, a sequence of letters bounded on both sides by white space (like the words you are reading now). But what about ancient and medieval manuscripts, which join such units together, or subdivide them, according to a different logic? And that is to say nothing of living oral traditions, which in their original form use neither printing nor manuscript writing. Others of us might choose a second option: to define a "word" as a lexical unit, an entry in a dictionary, but once again this is a post-Gutenberg definition that cannot be applied to oral poetry. As a third possibility, we might consider the linguistic definition of a "word" as a morphemic unit, that is, the smallest possible unit of lexical meaning, which can in turn undergo further change by adding inflections, shifting internally, or exhibiting some other sort of morphology. But even the linguistic concept of the morpheme will fail to match what oral bards themselves say about their "words." All three of these options are handicapped by interference from cognitive categories based on literacy.

For an insider's viewpoint, let's ask some experts, South Slavic *guslari* (epic singers), about their concept of the "word" or *reč* within their oral tradition. Here is an excerpt from the *guslar* Mujo Kukuruzović's conversation with Nikola Vujnović, Milman Parry and Albert Lord's native interpreter and assistant, during their 1933–35 fieldwork in the former Yugoslavia:

> *Nikola:* Let's consider this: "Vino pije lički Mustajbeže" ["Mustajbey of the Lika was drinking wine"]. Is this a single *reč*? *Mujo:* Yes. *N:* But how? It can't be *one*: "Vino pije lički Mustajbeže." *M:* In writing it can't be one. *N:* There are four *reči* here. *M:* In writing it can't be one. But here, let's say we're at my house and I pick up the *gusle* –"Pije vino lički Mustajbeže"– that's a single *reč* on the *gusle* for me. *N:* And the second *reč*? *M:* And the second *reč* –"Na Ribniku u pjanoj mehani" ["At Ribnik in a drinking tavern"]– there. *N:* And the third *reč*? *M:* Eh, here it is: "Oko njega trides' agalara, / Sve je sijo jaran do jarana" ["Around him thirty chieftains, / The comrades all beamed at one another"].

And now from another of Vujnović's interviews, this time with the *guslar* Ibro Bašić from the same general region of Stolac in central Hercegovina:

> *Nikola:* But what is a *reč*? What is a *reč*? Tell me. *Ibro:* An utterance. *N:* An utterance? *I:* Yes, an utterance; that's a *reč*, just like when I say to you now, "Is that a book, Nikola?" "Is that a coffeepot, Nikola?" There you go, that's a *reč*. *N:* What is, let's say, a single *reč* in a song? Tell me a single *reč* from a song. *I:* This is one, like this, let's say; this is a *reč*: "Mujo of Kladuša arose early, / At the top of the slender, well-built tower" ("Podranijo od Kladuše Mujo, / Na vrh tanke načinjene kule"). *N:* But these are poetic lines (*stihovi*). *I:* Eh, yes, that's how it goes with us; it's otherwise with you, but that's how it's said with us. *N:* Aha!

What quickly becomes apparent is that *within the oral tradition* a "word" is a speech-act, a unit of utterance, an atom of composition and expression. As such, it is never what we literate users of texts mean by words. For a South Slavic *guslar*, a single "word" is never smaller than a phrase, and it can be a whole poetic line, a scene or speech, and even the whole epic story. Likewise, the ancient Greek oral poet Homer describes an *epos* (literally, "word") that is always a speech or story, rather than a collection of dictionary entries. And the Old English poets of *Beowulf* and other oral-derived poems likewise speak of a *word* as an entire unit of utterance. Examples abound from international oral traditions, and include the Mongolian concept of a "mouth-word," once again much larger than the typographical units you are reading. The lesson is simple but profound: in the realm of oral tradition, the vehicle for expression –the "sound-byte"– is a unit appropriate to the medium. The conventions of textual representation mean nothing; "words" as speech-acts are what matter.

How Old is "Literature"?

With answers to these first two questions in hand, we now turn to a third – "How old is "literature"? Of course, the conventional assumption is that verbal art begins with ancient traditions such as Mesopotamian, Indian, and Greek, and that European literature is built upon that foundation. But such ideas mask the true history of verbal art, which begins much earlier than the various technologies of writing. The culturally sanctioned media of manuscript and print are latter-day inventions.

In revising our grasp of the history of verbal art, I start by noting the etymology of the term "literature," ultimately from classical Latin *littera* ("letter") via medieval Latin *litteratus* ("a lettered individual"). By definition, then, literature as we customarily conceive of it can arise no earlier than letters. This observation then raises the question of how old letters, or scripts of any kind, might be. Below, Table 1 summarizes the history of media by providing an approximate date for the invention of each medium; in assembling the table, I have chosen both to give the actual historical reference (for example, 8000 BCE) and then to convert each date for placement on the calendar of our existence as the species homo sapiens (as an example, day 328 of 365 = November 22 of our "species-year"). This system of representation should help us to understand the historical depth involved, and specifically to appreciate how recent an invention writing really is.

Table 1: Media Events in Homo Sapiens' Species-Year

Invention	Date	Day	Species-date
Numeracy (Middle Eastern tokens)	8000 BCE	328	November 22
Pre-writing (Vinča signs, Balkans)	5300 BCE	338	December 2
Egyptian script traditions	3200 BCE	346	December 10
Mesopotamian cuneiform	3100 BCE	346	December 10
Semitic scripts	2000 BCE	350	December 14
Greek alphabet	775 BCE	355	December 19
Mayan & Mesoamerican scripts	500 BCE	356	December 20
Alexandrian Library	fl. 250 BCE	357	December 21
Chinese printing technology	750 CE	360	December 24
Gutenberg's printing press	1450 CE	363	December 27
Cherokee script (Sequoyah)	1821 CE	365	New Years Eve, 8 am
Typewriter (C. L. Scholes)	1867 CE	365	New Years Eve, noon
Internet	fl. 1997 CE	365	New Years Eve, 11:44 pm

A few features of this table stand out. First, note that Homo sapiens spends almost eleven months or about ninety percent of its species-year wholly without writing. During that period oral tradition wasn't simply one of a number of competing communications media; it was the only such technology. Stories were told, laws were made, history was compiled and transmitted, and all of the other verbal traffic associated with cultural formation and maintenance was carried on without texts of any kind, and oral traditions were the sole vehicle. Second, even the most ancient scripts –Egyptian, Mesopotamian, Semitic, Greek– arise only in mid-December. This means that the works we customarily understand as the very origin of verbal art (*Gilgamesh*, the *Odyssey*, and so on) were not fixed in writing until about ninety-five percent of the way through our species-year. Third, it becomes obvious that the media we most depend upon –and have a hard time imagining culture without– entered the picture just a few species-days ago: printing on December 24–27, and the all-powerful internet only sixteen minutes before the end of our calendar year. Most crucially, for this entire twelve-month period, from the beginning of Homo sapiens' life-span until this very moment in late 2003, oral tradition has been the major medium for communication and transmission of cultural knowledge. Even with the advent of other media in the final two weeks of the year, the ongoing vehicle has always been oral tradition.

Along with this revision of our media history, a few other adjustments must be made. Even when literacy of any sort arose in the ancient and medieval worlds, it was seldom if ever used as a means to record verbal art. Initially, writing was employed to keep track of commercial activities or to record ownership and holdings, and only later was it pressed into service to fossilize oral traditional performances. Indeed, comparative investigation shows that the commission of oral epics to written form has almost always resulted from the intervention of an outsider to the culture, someone external to the process that develops a reason for transferring the epic from its native medium to the new medium.[3] And even when it is transferred, two related questions present themselves. The first of these –Who can read it?– speaks to the reality that reading skills were limited to very few in the ancient and medieval worlds. Scribes handled the job of creating and reading texts, and literacy was hardly a general phenomenon in any sector of the ancient or medieval societies. The second question –How user-friendly were the texts?– addresses a reality we usually ignore by anachronistically impressing our modern situation of mass paperback books with a mass readership back onto ancient Greece and medieval Europe. Consider, for example, the fact that a single book of the *Iliad* or *Odyssey* –one twenty-fourth of either epic– required a twenty-foot scroll to contain it at the time of the Alexandrian Library. Along with the problem of having very few people who could read the alphabetic script, then, there is the additional challenge of the awkwardness of the written medium during these stages. It could be neither read nor duplicated without an enormous expenditure of time and energy, and there was almost no one qualified to do either job. "Textuality" in these early days of literacy was entirely different from what we take for granted in the modern world.

How Widespread Are Oral Traditions in the Ancient and Medieval Worlds?

Given such realities about "literature," we next ask about the provenience of oral traditions in the ancient and medieval worlds. Most centrally, as the table above indicates, all cultures' verbal arts began with oral tradition. From that basic fact we can derive the proposition that textual strategies of all sorts have their roots in non-textual expression. For example, many of the rhetorical figures of classical and medieval literature are traceable to compositional and mnemonic patterns that served the performance of oral traditions. Then, too, recent research has demonstrated that oral traditions and written literature are best understood not as a Great Divide of orality versus literacy, but as a spectrum or continuum with innumerable different forms that depend upon the special circumstances of different cultures and genres.

Merely as a suggestion of the richness of surviving oral-derived works –that is, *verbal art with roots in oral tradition*– consider the following (hardly exhaustive) roster: the Old and New Testaments of the Judeo-Christian Bible, *Gilgamesh* (Sumerian), *Iliad* and *Odyssey* (ancient Greek), the *Mahabharata* and *Ramayana* (Sanskrit), *Beowulf* (Anglo-Saxon), the *Song of Roland* (Old French), the *Poem of the Cid* (medieval Spanish), the *Nibelungenlied* (Middle High German), and the *Mabinogion* (medieval Welsh). Beyond the simple recognition of the amount and diversity of oral-derived works, scholars are now beginning to explore the implications for understanding these many and various instances of oral traditions that survive only as texts. For example, in her book *Oral World and Written Word* (1996), Susan Niditch has shown how ancient Israelite texts depend on an oral economy of language,[4] while Werner Kelber has demonstrated the crucial importance of the oral roots of the

---

3. On this conversion of oral epics to books, see Honko (2000).
4. See also Niditch (1995) and Jaffee (2001).

New Testament in *The Oral and the Written Gospel* (1997). Likewise, the oral traditional background of medieval Spanish works has been explored by many researchers (see Zemke 1998 for an overview), as have the oral traditional language and background of *Beowulf* (see O'Keeffe 1997) and the Homeric poems (for example, Foley 1999). From a comparative perspective, studies in oral tradition have reached an exciting point: not only are we becoming more aware of oral-derived texts from the ancient and medieval worlds, but we are starting to understand how a text's roots in oral tradition can affect how we understand it. Of course, we can never be precise about such works' actual relationship to oral tradition (since it is no longer possible to experience these traditions directly), and we should avoid the temptation to craft positivist hypotheses as substitutions for factual, first-hand knowledge. But at the same time, it becomes ever more urgent for us to take account of these still-nourishing roots and to interpret oral-derived works accordingly.

How Widespread Are Oral Traditions in the Modern World?

Since it is well established that many of our most cherished texts derive from prior and contemporary oral traditions, we may go on to ask about the prevalence of still-living oral traditions in the modern world as we enter the third millennium. Is oral tradition still a common medium and technology? Again some unexamined assumptions await our attention. With the advent –at least in certain segments of the world's population– of high-speed printing and electronic communication, many have presumed that oral traditions are universally dying out, that the new media have largely displaced the age-old technology.

In fact, nothing could be further from the truth. Even in the most high-tech societies, oral traditional genres exist alongside books, newspapers, and the internet. And in those parts of the world where computers and mass-paperback publication have not made as much of an inroad, oral tradition remains the principal communications medium. Consider the example of China, the world's most populous nation, which includes among its ethnic groups fifty-five officially designated minorities (and many more that are unofficial). According to the director of the Ethnic Minorities' Literature division of the Chinese Academy of Social Sciences in Beijing, which has recently founded an Oral Traditions Center, only about thirty of these groups possess a writing system. Nonetheless, all fifty-five can boast thriving oral traditions.[5]

Similarly, the African continent is home to hundreds of active and vital oral traditions, including epic, praise-poetry, folktale, oral history, folk drama, and many other genres.[6] From India we have a striking example of oral tradition and its social dynamics in Gopala Naika's performance of the *Siri Epic* (Honko et al. 1998). In this latter case, the mythology surrounding this story of a female hero involves many linked genres such as drama,

5. Chao Gejin, personal communication. For examples and analyses of these oral traditions, see Chao (2001).
6. For epic, see Johnson (1997); for praise-poetry, see Opland (1998).

work songs, folktales, and the like. Standing at the center of the social and religious organization, the myth of Siri permeates ritual and everyday activities alike.[7] Still more examples of extant oral traditions, many of them playing important social roles, are available
among many Native American and African American ethnic groups. The Mayan peoples
of Guatemala, for instance, have long cultivated oral stories conveying the miraculous
exploits of Brother Peter (Hermano Pedro) in both Spanish and Kaqchikel,[8] while the non-
commercialized varieties of rap and hip hop music exist as an ongoing oral tradition (Pihel
1996). Everywhere one looks, whether in third-world or high-tech societies, oral tradition
remains central to human communication. On a per capita basis, there is little doubt that
–notwithstanding the culturally egocentric models of books and electronics that we scholars tend to employ– oral tradition is still the major communications technology for our
species.

Orality Intersects with Literacy

If comparative research has taught us anything, it is that the so-called Great Divide model
of orality versus literacy obscures more than it explains. Whether in the ancient and
medieval contexts or in the modern world, intersections of oral traditions and texts are
much more the rule than the exception. To be explicit, we have learned that orality and
literacy are not at all airtight categories: they can and do coexist in the very same culture and society, and even in the very same person.

   In order to understand how these interfaces can occur, we need a more diagnostic
model for oral traditions against the background of other media. Linguistic anthropology has provided the concept of *registers*, that is, ways of speaking or writing that are linked
to specific social situations.[9] We can grasp the central idea of registers of language by
thinking through the following experiment. Imagine that you wish to convey the very
same political observation to three different audiences: a group of children, your father
or mother, and a colleague. Try as you might, the three "performances" will not be identical. You will make adjustments in your *way of speaking* for each audience – simplifying in
one case, deleting off-color language in another, adding details and examples in a third.
Each description will contain roughly the same information, of course, but each will also
be calibrated for the person or group you are addressing. Moreover, in order to be effective communicators to multiple audiences, we need not just one but a repertoire of registers, a menu of ways of speaking.

   Registers in oral poetry work similarly. Each type of speech-act –whether it be *bertsolaritza*, Homeric epic, or verbal magic from the former Yugoslavia– has its own rules
for composition (the performer's job) and reception (the audience's job), and each regis-

---

7. See further Foley (2002: 171-77) and Honko (1998).
8. See Foley (2002: 153-55) and Canales and Morrissey (1996).
9. On registers, see further Foley (2002: 95-108) as well as Hymes (1989 and 1994).

ter is markedly different from the everyday discourse of informal talk. Within a given oral tradition, as we shall see below in regard to the ecology of South Slavic genres, each kind of oral poetry employs its own channel of communication. Once we realize that overall linguistic competence consists not simply of knowledge of the general, standard language, but fluency in a wide range of registers, then it is easier to understand how cultures and individuals can and do command both oral and written modes of expression. Consider the professor from North Carolina, who holds a Ph.D. degree and yet is a primary performer of "Jack" folktales, or the many highly literate inner-city "slam poets" in North America who publish their poetry exclusively through oral performance.[10] Individuals can be competent in a spectrum of oral and written registers, and oral traditions can be preserved alongside writing and print, and even *within* writing and print. It's simply a matter of fluency.

A Realistic Model for Oral Poetry

So far we have aimed at establishing two fundamental facts about the nature and provenience of oral poetry: (1) it dwarfs written literature in both amount and variety, and (2) it does not submit to a "binary" definition of oral versus written, illiterate versus literate, and so forth. In other words, oral poetry is a much larger, more complex, and more heterogeneous body of verbal art than we have often been willing to admit. From a practical point of view, it is well to remember that "written poetry" or "written tradition" –the usual subject of college and university courses in verbal art across many departments and programs– is itself tremendously various and complex; in no way does it constitute a single, monolithic collection of works. And if oral poetry dwarfs even that body of verbal art, and further if oral traditions cannot be effectively described as its opposite, then forcing works as different as the *Odyssey, bertsolaritza*, Chinese storytelling, and Native American folktales into a single category will prove impossible. The differences seem to outweigh the similarities.

But we can gain some genuine insight into the nature of oral poetry, as well as provide a framework for meaningful analogies and comparisons, by focusing not on the content or form of the various traditions but on *how they are created, transmitted, and received*. That is, we can best understand each oral poetry –and the place of each instance within the worldwide phenomenon of oral tradition– by concentrating on three basic parameters of its medium: composition, performance, and reception.[11] Table 2 below represents four categories of oral poetry defined according to these three features:

---

10. On Professor Leonard Roberts, see Foley (2002: 26); on slam poetry, Foley (2002: 3-5, 156-65).
11. For a full explanation of this model, see Foley (2002: 38-53).

Table 2: Categories of Oral Poetry

	Composition	Performance	Reception	Example
#1. Oral performance	Oral	Oral	Aural	*bertsolaritza*, South Slavic epic
#2. Voiced texts	Written	Oral	Aural	slam poetry (North America)
#3. Voices from the past	O/W	O/W	A/W	Homer's *Odyssey*
#4. Written oral poems	Written	Written	Written	*Kalevala* (Finland)

Each of the four categories is flexible enough to contain many different kinds of oral poetry. For example, *Oral performance* can accommodate traditions as various as *bertsolaritza*, the South Slavic epic, or South African praise-poetry. All that is necessary for inclusion in this first category is that the poem be composed orally, performed orally before an audience, and received aurally by that audience. Many hundreds of traditional genres, otherwise quite distinctive from one another, answer these three criteria. Correspondingly, the next category of *Voiced texts* includes those works of verbal art that are composed in writing but then performed orally for aural reception by an audience. North American slam poetry, an oral tradition that begins when the author composes a text, but which reaches "publication" only via oral performance, is one instance of this type. Somali oral poems, customarily composed via memorization in advance of performance (by creating a fixed mental text the poets are effectively using written composition), furnish another example; even though they are fixed texts, these poems reach their intended audience exclusively via oral-aural performance. Other examples include ballads, which move in and out of oral tradition, and many forms of popular music.

Category #3, *Voices from the past*, is intended to contain the numerous ancient and medieval works that certainly originate in oral traditions, but now survive only in manuscript form. These are the works that we called "oral-derived" above, and include, for instance, the *Odyssey*, *Beowulf*, and the *Poema de Mio Cid*. On the one hand, it would be wrong to classify them along with *Oral performances* (category #1) or *Voiced texts* (#2), since we cannot be absolutely sure which of these oral-derived works were actually composed orally (and then transcribed), performed orally (whether with or without the support of texts), or received aurally. Some ancient and medieval poets may have mastered the special language of oral poetry so thoroughly that they could use it to create in writing, some performances may have been based on texts while others were re-creations without texts, and some of these works may have been presented live before an audience while others were read silently (or aloud) by a single individual. Given the partial nature of the evidence, it seems safest to assume that all three parameters –composition, performance, and reception– could involve either orality, literacy, or a combination of both. In this way we can treat oral-derived works as the hybrids they undoubtedly were, according them their status as oral poetry without asserting hypotheses that we will never be able to verify.

The fourth category, *Written oral poems*, is meant as a classification for works that are produced in writing, transmitted as texts, and read from books. But although every aspect of their existence owes a debt to writing, these works also use the special language of oral poetry. Thus we can read them effectively only when we take into account their genesis in an oral tradition. Consider the example of Bishop Njegoš, a nineteenth-century cleric and scholar who was extremely well educated in the literature of his day. Nonetheless, as a boy in a Montenegrin village, he had learned the specialized language of the South Slavic oral epic, and it was this register that he used to compose his poetry. Because Njegoš was in effect "singing on the page," communicating via texts but in an oral poetic language with a recognizable structure and built-in idiomatic implications, he was for all practical purposes a "writing oral poet." His works owed their composition, performance, and reception to the technology of literacy and publication, but they owed their structure and meaning to a tradition of oral poetry.[12] Similarly, a highly literate physician, Elias Lönnrot, collected small poems from Finnish oral tradition and wove them into his composite epic, the *Kalevala*. Because in the process of assembling small parts into a single large whole he also personally composed brief sections to help the pieces fit together, Lönnrot has sometimes been accused of falsifying the oral tradition. But from another perspective, he had learned the traditional register so thoroughly that he too could "sing on the page." From that point of view his *Kalevala* is also a written oral poem.[13]

How Does Oral Poetry Work within a Real Society?

Let us now focus our investigation more closely and move from general observations about oral tradition to a specific case study: the oral poetry of the former Yugoslavia.[14] A few preliminary remarks will assist our inquiry.

First, the simple answer to how oral poetry works within a real society is *pluralistically* and *functionally*. That is, even within a single, well-defined group one very often finds more than one kind of oral poetry. Just as any speaker of a language is fluent in many different registers, so societies can cultivate more than one genre of oral tradition; and that reality means in turn that we cannot base our idea of a culture's oral traditions on any single genre. As for function, we should be prepared to consider other roles for oral poetry in addition to those that written literature usually plays. Along with the classical functions of entertainment and instruction, oral poetry also supports the performance of rituals, contests, healing remedies, genealogies, laments, and myriad other activities. In that respect it is a much more utilitarian form of verbal art than is the more narrowly functional written literature.

Given a communications medium and technology that is so inherently pluralistic and functional, I propose the *ecology* or *ecosystem* as the most apposite model for an oral poet-

---

12. For more on Bishop Njegoš, see Foley (2002: 50-51).

13. On the *Kalevala* as oral poetry, see Foley (2002: 51-52) and DuBois (1995).

14. I choose this set of examples because of my longstanding familiarity with many of the genres, both through fieldwork in Serbia and through examination of archival materials at the Milman Parry Collection of Oral Literature at Harvard University. See further Foley (2002: 188-218 and 2004); some of these genres are available for listening at the web site of the Center for Studies in Oral Tradition at the University of Missouri-Columbia: www.oraltradition.org/hrop/eighth_word.asp.

ry. A society that produces (and actively uses) various different genres is participating in
an ecology of oral poetry, wherein different "species" coexist and interact according to specific "environmental rules." For example, certain types of oral tradition may be assigned
to females and others to males, some forms may be performed in groups or singly, while
others may or may not require special costuming or musical instruments. Whatever the
case, each species of verbal art will be unique – composed within a particular register of
the language different both from the everyday language as well as from the unique registers of other oral genres. To understand the whole array of traditional forms it will be
necessary to study them individually, paying attention to their specific qualities and attributes and observing how they interact. Only then can we move from one-dimensional
description to a grasp of the entire interactive ecosystem of different oral-poetic species.

During fieldwork in rural Serbia in the 1970s and 1980s, our research team (cultural anthropologist Joel Halpern, linguistic anthropologist Barbara Kerewsky Halpern, and
myself) discovered seven clearly differentiated genres of oral tradition. I list the first six in
Table 3 immediately below, citing the genre, the performer(s), and the form for each type
of speech-act.[15]

Table 3: Genres of Oral Tradition

Genre	Performer(s)	Form
epic (*epske pjesme*)	older men	decasyllable
lyric (*lirske pjesme*)	women of any age	octosyllable
genealogy (*pričanje*)	older men	decasyllable
lament (*tužbalice*)	women of any age	octosyllable
charms (*bajanje*)	older women	octosyllable
folktale (*basme*)	men of any age	prose

Certain rules governing the ecology of oral tradition in this area make themselves
readily apparent. One is the metrical shape of the registers involved in the various genres: women exclusively use the eight-syllable poetic line, a balanced meter of four plus four
syllables with a midline caesura, while men use the ten-syllable line, which consists of two
parts (four plus six syllables) with a caesura in between. The only prose genre, that of
folktale, is performed by men.[16] Secondly, we see that women are responsible –again, without exception– for many kinds of lyrics, for funeral laments, and for magical charms
designed to heal various maladies. Men, on the other hand, are solely responsible for epic,
genealogy, and folktale. Assignment of poetic species by gender is a powerful "environmental" rule within the overall ecosystem.

But the internal organization of oral poetry in central Serbia does not end there.
Within the genres assigned to each gender there are additional rules for composition and

---

15. For audio and textual examples of many of these genres, visit www.oraltradition.org/hrop/eighth_word.asp.

16. It is worth adding here that decasyllabic poetic lines (verses construed according to the men's meter) occasionally
appear in these prose stories.

expression. For example, lyric poems are themselves a system: some are performed by groups of women, some by individuals; some poems are love songs, others are associated with particular non-calendrical rituals, such as weddings. And, although magical charms are learned by young girls from their grandmothers, these oral-poetic remedies can be put into practice only by post-menopausal females. This pattern of learning versus actual usage means a gap of perhaps thirty-five years or more between internalization and performance. On the men's side, genealogies are the province of patriarchs, senior members of *zadruge* (or "extended families"), and not of younger men, while epics can theoretically be sung by a male of any age.

As for interactivity among the various species that populate this ecosystem, the primary criterion is the octosyllabic versus decasyllabic formats. Phraseology that is made and re-made according to one of these meters can be translated to the other only with difficulty. If there is to be any interchange among genres, then, it must take place within either the set of female types or the set of male types of oral poetry (that is, among the genres of lyric, lament, and charm or between those of epic and genealogy). Although we do encounter some crossover within each of these two groups, the secondary criterion of function limits their interactivity. In other words, the female genres may share a common metrical pattern, but the distinctiveness of their social contributions makes their registers idiosyncratic. The primary purpose of magical charms is to banish disease and restore health, and that is a goal quite distinct from the many different functions of lyric or funeral lament. Similarly, although epic and genealogy have a decasyllabic format in common, the long narratives of mythic and semi-historical figures and events differ radically from the much briefer recounting of family lineage.[17] The different species function differently, while collectively they serve the society in many ways – from the recording of personal and ethnic history and identity, through the support of rituals important to the village, to medical intervention and group counseling of the community after a loss of one of their members. Far from mere entertainment and instruction, oral poetry is a vital, diverse, and multi-functional phenomenon that nourishes and protects the people who practice it.

As a demonstration of how rule-governed improvisation can enter the picture, I adduce the seventh genre we located in the village repertoire. There was no evidence that this momentary creation –which nonetheless depended on longstanding fluency in composition and reception– represented a formal genre in the village. Quite the contrary: it was an immediate, idiomatic response to an unprecedented situation, illustrating both the flexibility of oral poetry and its pattern-dependent resources.

Here is the example in context. We were finishing up an interview of Milutin Milojević, an epic singer (*guslar*), in his home village of Velika Ivanča, Serbia. In response to having his photograph taken as part of our documentation, Milojević, who had never seen a

---

17. Such semi-independence among genres is not the case in the Anglo-Saxon ecology of oral poetic genres, in which all types of poetry follow a single metrical scheme and the sharing of phraseology among registers is very common. See further Foley (2003) for comparison of South Slavic, Anglo-Saxon, and ancient Greek poetic ecologies.

camera, spontaneously composed the following four decasyllabic verses in two rhymed couplets:

Ja od Boga imam dobrog dara,	Yes, from God I have a fine gift,
Evo mene mojega slikara;	Here is my photographer;
Kogod 'oće, ko me lepo čuje,	Whoever wishes, whoever hears me [sing] well,
On mene lepo nek' slikuje.	Let him take my picture well.

Although confronted by a situation entirely new to him, Milojević was able to craft decasyllabic lines based loosely on the patterns he used in his singing of epic narratives. From one point of view, his performance was indeed an improvisation, since it responded immediately to an experience he had not had before. From another perspective, however, he was drawing from the resources of his epic register –his epic *way of speaking*– to compose this "new" poem. Clearly, it was his fluency in the epic register that supported his compositional dexterity; he could say something unprecedented precisely because he knew the specialized language so thoroughly. In that respect, improvisation amounts to creativity within a traditional medium.

Oral Poetry on the Page and Beyond

As a coda to this discussion, I offer an example of oral poetry that can be read and re-experienced as *Oral performance*: the *guslar* Halil Bajgorić's performance of *The Wedding of Mustajbey's Son Bećirbey*, recorded on June 13, 1935, by Milman Parry and Albert Lord in the central Hercegovinian village of Dabrica in Bosnia.[18] The *guslar* is accompanying himself on the *gusle*, a single-stringed, lute-like instrument that he bows as he sings. In order to recover as much of the reality of this oral poem as possible, you may listen to the original acoustic recording of the performance at www.oraltradition.org/performances/zbm. Here is the original-language text and an English translation of the first 49 lines of the 1030-line song:

Instrumental introduction (29 secs.)   1/0:00

wOj! Rano rani Djerdelez Alija,	0:30	Oj! Djerdelez Alija arose early,
vEj! Alija, careva gazija,		Ej! Alija, the tsar's hero,
Na Visoko više Sarajeva,		Near Visoko above Sarajevo,
Prije zore vi bijela dana –		Before dawn and the white day –
Još do zore dva puna savata,	5	Even two full hours before dawn,
Dok se svane vi sunce vograne		When day breaks and the sun rises
hI danica da pomoli lice.		And the morning star shows its face.
Kad je momak dobro vuranijo,		When the young man got himself up,
vU vodžaku vatru naložijo		He kindled a fire in the hearth
vA vuz vatru dževzu pristavijo;	10	And on the fire he put his coffeepot;
Dok je momak kavu zgotovijo,		After Alija brewed the coffee,
hI jednu, dvije sebi natočijo –		One, then two cups he poured himself –

---

18. For an edition and translation of this performance, see Foley (2004).

hI jednu, dvije, tu ćejifa nije,	One, then two, he felt no spark,
Tri, četiri, ćejif ugrabijo,	Three, then four, the spark seized him,
Sedam, osam, dok mu dosta bilo. 15	Seven, then eight, until he had enough.
*v*U bećara nema hizmećara,	A bachelor has no maidservant,
Jer Alija nidje nikog nema,	And indeed Alija had no one anywhere,
Samo sebe *j*i svoga dorata.	Just himself and his bay horse.
Skoči momak na noge lagane,	The young man jumped to his light feet,
Pa poteče ni*s* kulu bijelu, 20	Then hurried down the white tower,
Strča momak u tople podrume,	Into the warm stables the young man ran,
Do dorata konja kosatoga.	To his long-maned bay horse.
Svog dorata *v*od jasala jami,	He brought his horse out of the manger,
Vodi konja, do pod hajat sveza.	Led it out and tied it below the eave.
čula svali, metnu timar gor*i*, 25	He threw off the blanket, pressed the curry-comb on top,
Stade *v*aga češ'ati zlatala.	He began to comb the golden one.
*v*A dok dobra konja timarijo,	And after he groomed his fine steed,
*v*U sundjer mu vodu pokupijo	He collected water in a sponge
*v*A dj*i*bretom dlaku *v*otvorijo.	And spread his horse's coat with a goatskin pouch.
ćebe preže, bojno sedlo ba*ć*, 30	He hitched up the blanket, threw on the war saddle,
*v*A po sedlu četiri kolana	And on the saddle four girths
*h*I peticu svilenu kanicu;	And a fifth of silken thread;
Sve zapuči na jednu sponicu,	He fastened them all with a single clasp,
Kad ga steže da ga ne preteže.	Then tightened the saddle to balance it.
Založi ga djemo' studenijem, 35	Then he warmed up his mount with a cold snaffle-bit,
Spuči konju pucu pod vilicu;	Attached it with a button below the jaw;
Zlat'u re*ɟ*mu za *vu*ɟ*i zaba*ć*,	He threw a golden chain behind the horse's ears
Dva dizgina na dva rama tura,	And two reins over its two shoulders,
Pjetericu metnu uz vilicu.	Placed a riding bit in its jaw.
Sam se *š*ede dorat okretati 40	Alone the bay horse began to prance
Po avliji *j*i tamo *vi j*amo,	Through the courtyard back and forth,
*P*rez kandžije *hi p*rez binjadžije.	Without a whip and without a rider.
Kako dorat potkočijo glavu! –	How proudly the bay horse bore his head! –
K'o *vu* brdu piš*ki* čobanica	Like a careless young shepherdess up on a mountain
*v*U kukulju, *vu* šarenu gunju, 45	Clothed in her hood, in her motley jacket,
Još kojoj je *v*osamn'es' godina, 2/4:03	Only eighteen years of age
Još koja je jedina *vu* mame;	And her mother's only daughter;
Pa joj mama meće *vu*žinicu	Her mother put up a small snack for her
Da joj nj*e* bi *š*ćerka *v*ogladnila.	So her little girl wouldn't go hungry.

Compositional features of the bard's craft include a highly patterned language consisting of *formulaic structure* (recurrent phrases), *typical scenes* (recurrent scenes), and *story-patterns* (recurrent tale-types). Virtually every line in this song can be located, with minimal variation, in other songs by Bajgorić and his fellow singers, as can typical scenes such as the scene of "Readying the Hero's Horse" in lines 17–49.[19] The entire song follows the

---

19. For additional instances of this typical scene, see Foley (1991: 67, 125-27 and 2004).

story-pattern of a wedding, which conventionally involves the assembly of a large and magnificent wedding party/army, the rescue of a kidnapped maiden by means of a great battle, and a culminating marriage ceremony. Moreover, each of these structural features is a traditional "word," a unit of utterance in the singers' specialized language or register. Research on such "words" indicates that they serve two important purposes in this species of oral poetry: they provide a ready *structure* for the performance, and they carry *idiomatic implications* well beyond their literal meanings. In effect, the *guslar* –or any other oral poet in any genre– has at his or her disposal a highly coded register that both supports composition and guides audience reception.[20]

Summary

To conclude, I will review some of the fundamental ideas developed above by citing a series of homemade proverbs, which I have coined to promote easy recall of important concepts.[21] Each proverb will be followed by a few sentences of explanation.

1. "*Oral poetry works like language, only more so.*" It is easy to forget that oral poetry is neither an item nor a text, but a living language that is subject to rule-governed change. The major difference, in comparison to everyday language, is that the specialized registers of oral poetry are characterized by greater structure and more highly coded idiomatic meaning. Idiom is the "more so" in this proverb.

2. "*Performance is the enabling event; tradition is the context for that event.*" The mere fact of performance means that a speaker must be understood differently, and that an audience must adjust its reception to understand him or her accordingly. Tradition is the background or referent for the event; it "fills in the blanks" of each performance by relating what is happening in this performance to the audience's larger experience.

3. "*The art of oral poetry emerges through rather than in spite of its special language.*" Special ways of speaking (and the recurrence that accompanies them) do not constrain the performer. Because registers act as familiar cues for traditional meaning, they are more expressive than everyday language can ever be.

4. "*Composition and reception are two sides of the same coin.*" In order for an audience to understand an oral poem, they must receive the transmission according to the same expressive rules that the performer used in composing it. Performer and audience must speak the same register.

5. "*Oral poetry is a very plural noun.*" Because it dwarfs written literature and consists of so many different varieties within the four categories of *Oral performance, Voiced texts, Voices from the past,* and *Written oral poetry,* we cannot define oral tradition as simply the

---

20. For further explanation of these structural and idiomatic aspects of oral traditional registers, see Foley (1990, 1991, 1995 and 2002: 109-24).

21. These and other proverbs are discussed at length in Foley (2002: 125-45).

opposite of texts. We must be prepared to engage it in its full complexity, examining each ecosystem and each individual species on its own terms as well as by analogy.

6. *"True diversity demands diversity in frame of reference."* Given the inherent variety of oral poetry, we need to develop a repertoire of approaches for dealing with its complexities. The three most commonly used approaches –Performance Theory, Ethnopoetics, and Immanent Art– share a concern with the special economy of language and performance (including performance on the page),[22] and provide a suitably diverse set of perspectives on a challenging phenomenon.

---

22. On the common aims of these three approaches, see Foley (1995: 1-28 and 2002: 79-124).

Improvisation, Inspiration and Basque Verbal Contest: Identity in Performance

JOHN ZEMKE

Among modes of the verbal arts extemporaneous improvisation may be said to resemble prophetic speech in the sense that "it is the very nature of true prophetism to be spontaneous" (McCurdy 1906–07: 213).[1] Albert Lord offers a key insight in the final chapter of *The Singer of Tales*: "The traditional oral epic singer is not an artist; he is a seer. The patterns of thought that he has inherited came into being to serve not *art* but religion in its most basic sense" (1968: 22). These considerations raise the question of whether the contemporary Basque audience views the improvisational content and delivery of *bertso-*

---

1. In a welcome introduction to *bertsolaritza* for non-Basque readers, Gorka Aulestia insists improvisation "is the most distinctive characteristic of bertsolaritza" (1995: 32), alternatively, "improvisation is what bertsolaritza is all about" (1995: 33), and emphasizes that "swift spontaneity is especially demanded in bertsolaritza, where the artist is given no more than a few seconds to improvise and to answer an opponent" (1995: 15). Aulestia underscores the special status accorded the performing *bertsolari*, who "is allowed to say things he would not be able to say in ordinary conversation . . . . This oral literary art provides an escape from social repression" (1995: 39). Continuity in the socially authorized status of the *bertsolari* is exemplified by Fernando Amezketarra (1764-1823), whose "verses addressed the economic difficulties faced by laborers and their desires to overcome them" (Aulestia 1995: 73). That modern *berstolaritza* is a mechanism for reflecting on social conflict and a possible mechanism for addressing obdurate tensions and anxieties is made clear by a review of the themes assigned to *bertsolariak*, for instance "The Debate about Wind Farms" (Garzia, Sarasua and Egaña 2001: 125-26); for additional examples, see Garzia, Sarasua and Egaña (2001: 58-60). That sample contrasts markedly with the themes Caro Baroja mentions in his appraisal from more than one-half century ago of *bertsolaritza* in village life: "Sobre un tema conocido bastante ramplón . . . . dos 'bertsolaris' comienzan a improvisar coplas en las que se aluden mutuamente entablando un pugilato de agudezas. El primero le achaca al otro el vicio de la gula, en cambio el segundo le replica reprochándole su excesivo amor a las faldas siendo un hombre ya maduro, por ejemplo. Sobres cuestiones semejantes van haciendo una retahíla interminable de versos más de una vez cojos o sobrados . . . . para ensartar una serie de consideraciones rimadas más o menos ingeniosas" (1944: 232). The comparison points up the ductile nature of *bertsolaritza* and its accommodation of vital contemporary themes: "sociopolitical and cultural themes are the most common today and are of great interest to this minority nation in the process of recovering its autochthonous values" (Aulestia 1995: 19).

laritza as a prophetic mode of speech.[2] The *bertsolari* performs voluntarily, unlike the prophet,[3] and disavows divine diction, but this does not preclude the audience from attributing the source of the *bertsolari*'s improvised poetry to inspiration.[4] Musical genres that rely upon improvisation –American Jazz, Arabic and Turkish *maqām*, Indian art music or Iranian music, among others– cultivate audiences whose aesthetic judgment of a performance rests upon the dual premises of individual creativity within generic paradigms and the flow of musical content from an ultimately supra-individual wellspring.[5] Improvisation tests the ability to turn the unexpected to advantage –the human experience in microcosm– and creates circumstances under which the verbal artist wrests control over the inexorable advance of time by marking, however temporarily, its cadence. Composition *ex temporare* is fraught with risk: failure of artistic competence for the performer and frustrated expectations for the audience.

The above considerations may be more relevant to *txapelektak*,[6] the large scale public contests[7] between *bertsolariak*, than other modalities of *bertsolaritza*. *Txapelketak* reflect the general features of poetic competitions elaborated by Earl Miner (1993: 925):

> Western poetic contests are formal, agonistic exchanges in verse that display some or all of the following characteristics: (1) two or more poet contestants, (2) physically present to each other, (3) in a public setting before witnesses, (4) engage in a verbal duel or debate that (5) treats a conventionalized or pre-stipulated subject matter (often of an *ad hominem* variety),

---

2. The origins of *bertsolaritza*, and the ebb and flow of its social vitality, is a matter of some conjecture, for a review see Aulestia (1995: 65–71). As a product of "popular, oral" culture *bertsolaritza* garnered scant attention from literary historians until the late twentieth century. Villasante, for example, notes the inseparability of oral and literary verbal cultures but excludes the former from consideration: "Queda propiamente fuera del ámbito de éste [el presente estudio] la literatura popular u oral, los cantares antiguos épicos o líricos, el folklore, el bertsolarismo, el teatro popular suletino, aunque en el libro no deja de haber indicaciones sobre casi todos estos puntos" (1961: 20).

3. The English term "prophet" is derived from the Greek Septuagint translation of Classical Hebrew *navi*, "spokesman."

4. The roles assigned "inspiration" in Western literary thought from Homer through Romanticism and Freudian psychology are reviewed by Brogan (1993). A summary of the aesthetic links between musical creativity and inspiration is supplied by Reimer and Wright (1992: 254–55). Aulestia seems to allude to inspiration in a description of the great nineteenth-century *bertsolari* Indalecio Bizkarrondo (1831–1876): "Verses came to him like song to a bird" (1995: 84). The same scholar underscores the audience's role as co-creator, and the collective quality of oral performance: "As we probe more deeply into the characteristics of oral literature we find that the actual author is a collective and anonymous entity: the community" (1995: 13).

5. For a review of pertinent concepts, practices, and relevant bibliography on musical forms rooted in improvisation, see "Improvisation" in *The New Grove Dictionary of Music and Musicians* (2001:12: 96ff).

6. Public contests between *bertsolariak*, see Aulestia (1995: 45–46); for select analogues, see Aulestia (1995: 126–36). For exhaustive listings of analogue forms of improvisational poetry see the respective articles by Samuel G. Armistead, John Miles Foley and Maximiano Trapero in this volume.

7. In this regard, Ong observes that "verbal contest is a massive and seemingly universal phenomenon in early cultures across the world" (1981: 27). Additionally, he supplies an instructive etymology of the term "contest," indicating that the "agonistic situation" requires an audience: "'Contest' comes from the Old French *conteste*, which in turn derives from the Latin *contestari*. *Testis* means a witness and derives from the Proto-Indo-European root *trei* ("three") compounded with *stā* ("stand"), to the form . . . . *tri-st-i*, meaning a third person standing by, as in a dispute between others. Thus a *testis* or witness, a 'third stander', implies an agonistic situation between two persons, which the *testis* or third person reports from outside" (1981:45). In the arena of *bertsolaritza* the audience is, nevertheless, a participant, and not a disinterested witness as is the case, for instance, of a notary public.

(6) undertaken for the sake of a prize, material or spiritual, and (7) resolved through appeal to external judgment . . . . Indeed, the poetic contest itself is not a genre at all but rather the verbal expression of a general mode of human interaction–the aggressive and agonistic–whose roots extend deep into biology and psychology.

For artist and audience of such contests, the aesthetic stakes are heightened by the nature of the event: a verbal high-wire confrontation between performers, a contest made more intense by "the unique and emergent quality of the oral text, composed in performance."[8] In the light of its chief hallmark, spontaneity, of a putative perception that the *bertsolariak* draw content from a recondite supra-individual source, and, the contemporary social issues infused into the genre, *bertsolaritza* may socially and culturally be seen as a kind of prophetic speech.[9] In fine, the question is whether *bertsolariak* in the performance arena are viewed by their audience as social and cultural prophets, an implication suggested by the report that "the bertsolari himself has often been equated with Basque patriotism" (White 2001: 19).[10]

The prophetic aura illuminating extemporaneous verbal composition constitutes a powerful aesthetic motivation for *fictive* improvisation in literary debate genres, particularly among societies that historically practiced or continue to practice improvisational poetry. That improvisation is an essential quality of poetic debate finds illustration in the persistence in erudite literary debate poems of *fictive* improvisation. Whether the improvising cue is given in the mise-en-scène, in the course of the declamation, or remains simply implicit, the appeal to improvisation serves as an index to a poetic tradition, and by invoking that index the poet endeavors to place a temporal verbal creation under the aegis of extemporaneousness gaining the immediacy of emergent creation.[11] The erudite poetry anthologized in the balance of this paper presents iterations of the intimate link between

---

8. Thus Richard Bauman describes one of Albert Lord's crucial insights into oral tradition (Bauman 1977: 39). John Miles Foley recalls that a fundamental feature of verbal improvisation is its emergent quality: the audience is present at and witness to the unfolding act of creation (personal communication, October 15, 2003). Aulestia describes the relationship between the audience and the *bertsolari*'s verses as being "a river that flows by the listener only once and can never return to its origin" (1995: 20).

9. On the shifting nature of such social expectations, see Garzia, Sarasua and Egaña (2001:15–28, 35–47). Many forms of oral tradition serve as mechanisms for affirming identity, solidarity, and self-recognition in a social setting. For examples among school children, see Opie and Opie (1959: 344–46); for instances in *bertsolaritza*, see Garzia, Sarasua and Egaña (2001: 37). The concurrent expansion of enthusiasm for *bertsolaritza* with developments in the social and political life of its audience seems not to be mere coincidence. In a penetrating study of verbal contest among blacks in urban America, Roger Abrahams elaborates the social functions of verbal dueling: "Contest does not exist for itself; it is a mechanism for the dramatic dialectic expression of specific psychic problems, generally brought about by the inherent conflict of the individual living (or trying to live) in society" (1963: 41). That an improvising poet temporarily enjoins social taboo is borne out by Adnan Haydar's assessment of the contemporary Lebanese *zajal* genre, improvised sung poetic contests: "within the medium of verbal dueling, radical statements, political dissent, and social criticism are sanctioned, encouraged, and held up as models for corrective social and political measures" (1989: 189).

10. Linda White offers a compelling review of the association between *bertsolaritza* and Basque nationalism. See White (2001).

11. For a specific illustration of the general phenomenon of indices, see Foley's discussion of the Tibetan paper-singer Grags-pa seng-ge and the Gesar epic cycle (2002: 1–3). For other implications of indices for oral tradition, see Foley's remarks on "tradition-dependence" (1990b: 16–19).

Bertsolari facing audience. Prior to starting an improvised *bertso*, a tense silence comes across the auditorium. Success or failure is seconds away.
By permission of the Xenpelar Dokumentazio Zentroa, Donostia.

oral improvisation and the emergent quality of poetry: invocation of the former compels the presence of the latter in the declamation of the poem. Drawn from diverse languages and eras, the sample texts point to an awareness or consensus among the erudite that, in extemporaneous poetic creation, the emergent quality of performance is superlative.[12]

Fictive Poetic Contests: Representative Texts

The most ancient examples of improvisational poetic debates discussed here come from the Hebrew Bible. Job 3–31 comprises several sets of poetic complaint-response patterns between Job, Eliphaz, Bildad, and Zophar, while Job 33–37 airs Elihu's reply and Job 38–42 the Lord's reply. Putative improvised poems include Genesis 49.2–27, Jacob's blessings on his sons, and Exodus 15.1–18, Moses' song at the Sea of Reeds. The king of the

---

12. Among the many traditions of improvisational poetry unaccounted for here, the wealth of contemporary Arabic varieties represent a highly promising set of parallels for comparative study. For an introduction, see the collected articles in *Oral Tradition* 4 (1989), "Arabic Oral Traditions," especially those of Haydar, Sbait, and Sowayan. For a full treatment of sung poetic improvisational genres among Palestinians, see Sbait (1982).

Moabites, Balak, directs Balaam to curse the Israelites at Numbers 22.6, though the prophet instead pronounces a blessing. Goliath's taunting of David, and the latter's retort before entering into combat are found at 1 Samuel 17.10 and 17.43–46.

Several millennia later, on the far western reaches of the Mediterranean, improvisational poetry was highly prized among medieval Andalusian Hebrew poets.[13] Skilled improvisers were challenged to compose one or more variations employing the same metrical and rhythmic patterns of the set poem. The first great Hebrew poet of the period, Samuel the Nagid (Ismail ibn Nagrelʿa) (993 Córdoba – 1055/56 Granada), vizier and commander-in-chief of the kingdom of Granada, was renowned for his ability to improvise, and on one occasion improvised a battlefield poem in lieu of the evening prayer, for which there was no time (Schirmann 1954: 246). The riddle-poem reproduced below is the third of fifteen variations Samuel the Nagid improvised on an Arabic epigram during a *majlis* ("session," "council," "salon"). The composite superscription describes the situation (Cole 1996: 12, 167):

> And he mentioned being at his house where one of the poets recited a poem about a bowl of fine and beautiful apples which were brought before him. One of the company translated the poem into Hebrew. And then they implored him to respond with a version of his own, and he improvised the following:

> > I, when you notice,
> > am cast in gold:
> > the bite of the ignorant
> > frightens me.

During the Andalusian period, professional poets competed in sessions of poetry and improvisation. Another Hebrew poet, Judah Halevi (ca. 1075 Tudela – July, 1141 Egypt) entered onto the Andalusian scene at a literary séance in Córdoba, where the gathered poets had failed to extemporize a suitable contrafactum of a *muwashshaḥ* ("girdle-poem"). Pressed to try his hand, Halevi succeeded in improvising a contrafactum on the model prosodic pattern.

Judah al-Ḥarizi (ca.1170 Toledo – after 1235) composed the *Taḥkemoni* (after 1216) in rhymed prose on the pattern of the fifty Arabic *maqāmāt* ("gates") written by Abu Muhammad al-Qāsim al-Ḥariri of Basra (1054–1122). The thirty-second "gate" of the *Taḥkemoni* depicts an improvised poetic contest between a youth and an old man, who trade poems on the pen, the letter, the sword, and so forth; the excerpt highlights the technique of shared composition and the aesthetic appeal of *fictive* improvisation (Reichert 1965–1973: Vol. 2, 171–72):

---

13. The arabicized Hebrew poets of al-Andalus drew their models from the standard Arabic genres. Zwettler (1978) studies the oral tradition of classical Arabic poetry. Monroe (1972) reviews the question of oral composition in pre-Islamic poetry. For modern Arabic improvisational poetry, see n.12 *supra*. For the literary theory of classical Arabic *irtidjāl*, "improvising, extemporizing a poem or a speech," see Bonebakker (1978). For Arabic invective poetry, *hidjāʾ*, see respectively Charles Pellat (1971) and Van Gelder (1988).

A youth who musters skill in poetry, and a sage invincible in repartee. Heman, the Ezrahite speaks: In the days of my youthful vigor, I was *once* in the presence of sages . . . . Then one of the select company drew near unto him . . . . "come, now, and let us run together in the art of poetry. Let us divide two stanzas between us. I will build one stanza and lay the foundation. You will compose the second stanza with a metaphor that will complete its theme. If you fulfill this condition, you will find your request and you will see your desire. Said the Old Man: "The thing that you have spoken is good" . . . . Then the Young Man drew near and spoke concerning.

The Pen

How precious is the scribe's pen, shimmering green and bright, pleasant and beloved; Against heroes it storms; and it loves to enter the battle of diction.

Said the Sage: It is like a golden scepter. Its lines are as flaming rows in which are grace and love, heat and storm.

Then the Youth improvised and said: The scribe's quill races on the scroll, And traces a jet-black row upon the white.

Said the Sage: Like a serpent that slithers through the dust, And leaves behind an up-raised path in sight.[14]

At a cultural and geographical remove from al-Andalus, William Fitz Stephen (d. 1190) reports in *Discriptio nobilissimae civitatis Londoniae* on improvised street debates between London schoolboys which recall the medieval English debate poem, *The Owl and the Nightingale* (ca. 1198–1216), typical of the intellectual renaissance of the twelfth century (Fitz Stephen 1990: 51–52):

> Boys of different schools strive one against another in verse to contend concerning the principles of the art of grammar or the rules governing the use of past or future. There are others who employ the old wit of the cross-roads in epigrams, rhymes and metre; with "Fescennine License," they lacerate their comrades outspokenly, though mentioning no names; they hurl "abuse and gibes," they touch the foibles of their comrades, perchance even of their elders with Socratic wit, not to say "bite more keenly even than Theon's tooth," in their "bold dithyrambs." Their hearers "ready to laugh their fill," "with wrinkling nose" repeat the loud guffaw.

A philosophical debate on nominalist versus realist positions on the nature of language occupies a *tenso* between Aimeric de Peguilhan (fl. 1190–1225), Toulouse, who visited courts in Castile, Aragón, and northern Italy (Dante, *De vulgari Eloquentia* 2.6) and Albert de Sestaron (1194–1221), a Provençal troubadour.[15] The excerpt implies fictive improvisation between the debating troubadours (Bossy 1987: 156–61, 190–91):

---

14. The poets continue improvising and exchange verses on: The Letter, The Sword, The Coat of Mail, The Horse, The Torch, A Bundle of Myrrh, The Wine, The Falcon, The Wolf, The Lightning, Waters of the Streams, Pomegranates, Nuts, The Harp, The Moon, The Citron, and The Lamp.

15 Samuel G. Armistead graciously called my attention to *l'ensenhamen* of Guiraut de Cabrera (ca. 1150), a veritable inventory of medieval French *romans*, *fablauix*, and *chanson de geste* which censures the ignorance of a *jongleur* identified only as "Cabra," whose negligent repertory is a disgrace to his office.

1. Amics Albertz, tenzos soven
    Fan assatz tuit li trobador,
    E partisson razon d'amor
    E d'als, qan lur platz, eissamen.
    Mas ieu faz zo q'anc om non fes,
    Tenzon d'aizo qi res non es;
    Q'a razon prom respondrias,
    Mas al nien vueil respondatz;
    Et er la tenzos de non-re.

    Friend Albert, it is common enough
    To see poets turning out verse debates
    And contending on questions of love
    Or whatever else suits your fancy.
    But I'll undertake what no one yet has done:
    A debate on a non-existing thing.
    Given a topic, you'd spin an apt reply,
    But I want you to respond to a pure blank,
    So our's will be a debate about nothing.

2. N'Aimerics, pueis del dreg nien
    Mi voletz far respondedor,
    Non voil autre razonador
    Mas mi meteus. Mon eiscien,
    Be.m par q'a razon respondes
    Qi respon zo qe res non es.
    Us nienz es d'autre compraz.
    Per q'al nien don m'apellatz,
    Respondrai com? Calarai me!

    . . . .

    Sir Aimeric, since you wish to turn me
    Into one who responds to nothing,
    I want to face no other pleader
    Than myself. It seems to me
    That the right rejoinder would be
    To offer in reply what's non-existent
    One blank squarely balances another.
    Seeing as you challenge me to nothing,
    How shall I reply? I'll keep silent!

    . . . .

7. Albertz, zo q'eu vos dic vers es:
    Doncs dic eu qe om ve non-res,
    Qar s'un flum d'un pont fort gardatz
    L'ueil vos diran q'ades anatz
    e l'aiga can cor s'i rete.

    Albert, what I tell you is true:
    I say a non-existent thing can be seen:
    For if you stare at a stream from a bridge
    Your eyes will tell you that you're drifting
    While the water is holding still.

8. N'aimerics, non es mals ni bes,
    Aizo de qe-us es entremes,
    Q'atrestam petit essegatz
    Com molinz q'a roda de latz,
    Qe's mou tot jorn e non vai re.

    Sir Aimeric, what you undertook
    Is neither good nor ill,
    For you'll accomplish as little
    As the mill flanked by a wheel
    That turns all day yet goes nowhere.

Medieval Galician-Portuguese poets produced vast quantities of invective and *ad hominem* attacks in the genre of the *Cantiga de maldizer*. Many of the poems are far more scabrous than the light repartee in the following example of implicitly improvised dialogue between the poets Lourenço (fl. 1250–1275) and Joan Váasquez (fl. 1250–1275) (Rodrigues Lapa 1970: 412; my translation):

1. Joan Vaásquez, moiro por saber
    de vós por que leixestes o trobar
    ou se foi el vós primeiro leixar,
    ca vedes o que ouço a todos dizer:
    ca o trobar acordou-s'en atal:
    que'estava vosco en pecado mortal
    e leixar[r] vos [foi], por se non perder.

    Joan Vaásquez, I'm dying to learn
    from you why you quit poetry
    or did Poetry quit you first,
    You know I hear everyone saying:
    Poetry woke up and saw
    she was living with you in mortal sin
    and left you to save herself.

2. Lourenço, tu vẽ es por aprender
   de min, e eu non cho quero negar:
   eu trobo ben quando quero trobar,
   pero non o quero sempre fazer;
   mais di-m ti, que trobas desigual:
   se te deitan poren de Portugal,
   ou mataste omen ou roubaste aver?

Lourenço, you've come to learn something
from me, and I won't deny you:
I make fine poetry when I want to,
but I don't always want to;
worse than me you, whose verses don't scan:
is that why they kicked you out of Portugal,
or did you kill a man or steal property?

3. Joan Vaásquez, nunca roubei ren
   nen matei omen, nen ar mereci
   por que mi deitassen, mais vĩi aqui
   por gaar algo, e iguar-mi ben
   con o trobar vosso; mais [eu] estou
   que se perdia con vosqu'e quitou-
   se de vós; e non trobades poren.

Joan Vaásquez, I never stole naught
nor killed a man, nor anything deserving
exile, rather I came here
to earn something, and measure up
against your poetry; but I think
Poetry was lost with you and she
left you with nothing to sing about.

A brief excerpt from the anonymous Leonese debate poem *Elena y María* (last third of the thirteenth century) is noteworthy for its visual staging of metalinguistic features of debate[16] (Bossy 1987: 78–81):

    Elena la cato
    de su palabra la son sano
    gravemientre le rrespuso.
10. Agora oyd commo fabro:
    "Calla, Maria, por que dizes tal follia?
    Esa palabra que fabreste
    al mio amigo denosteste,

Elena looked at her;
She scoffed at her word
And gave her a sharp reply
Listen now to what she said:
"Be silent, Maria, why do you speak so foolishly?
Those words you uttered
were slurs against my lover,

The social reality of such verbal altercations is addressed by the legislation drafted during the reign of Alfonso X, the Learned (1252–1284), in *Las Siete Partidas* (1256–1263/65) (Partida. vii, ley 3, título. 9, my translation): "que ningun ome non fuese osado de cantar cantiga nin decir rimas nin dictados que fuesen fechos por deshonra e por denuesto de otro" ("no person shall sing a song nor recite rhymes or sayings that dishonor or slur another person").

The fifteenth-century *pregunta-respuesta* served as a courtly amusement, especially during the reign of Juan II (1406–1454).[17] Alfonso Álvarez Villasandino (ca. 1340–1425) com-

---

16. See also Menéndez Pidal (1914). For studies of the Latin and European debate traditions, see Steinschneider (1908) and Walther (1920). Curiously, the *Libro de buen amor* of Juan Ruiz (fl. 1325–1350), the quintessential Castilian anthology of medieval poetic forms, is staged as a sustained series of improvised poetic debates between the fictional characters. The debate between the Greeks and the Romans (Blecua 1992: 21–25), or the well known *serranilla* (*pastourelle*) exchanges between the archpriest and the mountain girls (Blecua 1992: 233–34) should not obscure the preponderant narrative key of *fictive* improvisational debate.

17. For a study of themes and rhetorical devices in the *preguntas* in the *Cancionero de Baena*, see Labrador Herraiz (1974). Cummins examines the relationship between Provençal debate forms and the Castilian *pregunta-respuesta* (1963 and 1965). For an exhaustive study of the Castilian *pregunta-respuesta*, see now Chas Aguión (2000).

Imanol Lazkano, Jose Miguel Iztueta, "Lazkao Txiki," and Sebastian Lizaso, Day of the *Bertsolari*, Donostia, Basque Country, 1983. The performance of a *bertsolari* rests on his or her confidence. This confidence, and the improvisation it inspires, is capable of moving the collective emotions of an audience and may even be prophetic. By permission of *Sendoa*.

posed more than one hundred poems collected in the *Cancionero de Baena* (ca. 1430), about his opponent, the Bachiller, nothing is known. This example of a fictive improvisation raises the question of the apparent paradoxical movement of the heavens to which the respondent answers with reference to the Creator's incommensurable knowledge and his own slight formal training (Dutton and González Cuenca 1993: 116–117, my translation):

Pregunta del dicho Bachiller contra Alfonso Álvarez [Villasandino]

1. Señor, non tomedes enojo nin saña
   por vos preguntar quien poco depriso,
   que bien sé que sodes cortés e enviso
   e muy bien criado de noble compaña;
   porque yo veo cosa muy estraña
   en razón del çielo e de su espera,
   que siempre se muda de una manera:
   dezid quién la muda, siendo tamaña.

   Sire, take no offense or anger
   if one who has learned little asks you,
   for I know you are courtly and wise
   and well trained in noble company;
   I see a marvelous thing
   concerning the heaven and its sphere,
   that changes ever in one way:
   being so large, tell, who moves it?

2. Ca non se mueve d'allí do es puesta
   desque fue criada del Primer Moviente;
   maguer faze curso tan súbitamente,
   a parte adversa jamás non acuesta.
   A esto me dad, señor, la respuesta
   por los almanaques de filosofía,
   o por vuestra bondat o por cortesía.

   It doesn't move from where it is placed
   since it was created by the First Mover;
   though quickly traveling its course,
   it never arrives at a proximate place.
   On this, Sire, give me your answer
   from the philosopher's almanacs,
   or from your goodness or your courtesy.

3. Ruégovos mucho, por amor de mí,
   que esta demanda que vos fago aquí
   me sea por vos con razón espuesta.

   I beg you, for love of me,
   that this request I make here
   be answered by you with reason expounded.

Respuesta de Alfonso Álvarez contra el Bachiller

1. Non siento tal lego, amigo, en España
   que vos declarasse luego emproviso
   las obras del çielo nin Dios por qué quiso
   criar la Natura por fuerça o por maña.
   A esto respondo, como por fazaña,
   que es un secreto d'escura carrera
   del Alto sin fin, sin cuento e sin era,
   e quien de ál enfinge creo que se engaña.

   I never heard, friend, of a layman in Spain
   who improvised on the spot an explanation
   of the workings of the heavens or why God
   created Nature, by obligation or by skill.
   To that I answer, as a heroic deed,
   that it is a secret of unknown ways
   of the Highest without end, measure or age,
   and who pretends otherwise deludes himself.

2. Amigo, ya tengo mi razón propuesta:
   que este secreto es del que non miente
   e sobre Natura impera viviente,
   potestad divina, luz clara e apuesta.
   Quien ál me demanda su saber denuesta,
   que yo non entiendo qué's astrología,
   nin sus almanaques, mas por poetría
   faré mi razón limada compuesta.

   Friend, I have now my reason proposed:
   the secret belongs to the one who does not lie,
   and over Nature rules alive,
   divine power, clear and fine light.
   Who asks me more abuses his knowledge,
   for I know no astrology,
   nor astrological table, but for poetry
   I'll compose my polished reason.

3. Amigo señor, yo nunca aprendí
   ninguna çiençia, salvo que oí
   tañer e dançar d'oçida e traspuesta.

   Dear friend, I never learned
   any science, except I heard
   the playing and dancing to the trumpet.

The foregoing examples of *fictive* improvisational debate poems rehearse and stake claim to an identity, whether of a people, an individual, a class, a philosophy, or a profession. That *bertsolaritza* is a poetic phenomenon that makes a social claim to Basque identity is clear from the work done by Aulestia, Garzia, Sarasua and Egaña, and White. James Fernandez sheds further light on the linkage of cultural identity with verbal art (1986a: 93):

> learning culture is the learning of a set of dimensions of discrimination against which to judge our experiences in respect to some basic interests we have in them: their admissibility, desirability, belongingness, solidarity, trustworthiness, dominance, subordinance, etc. Poetry, particularly the variety of spontaneous folk poetry we have before us here, is a vehicle for "discriminating" in striking, though indirect, ways. It is a vehicle primarily for evoking affective response, for pungently changing the quality of its subjects –the consequences of poetic discrimination– by apt use of those prime vehicles of our understanding, metaphor and metonym. These act movingly on subjects by linking them in untoward ways to untoward subjects.

It is in this sense, then, that Basque verbal contest may be seen as a performance of Basque identity, with ample consideration for the "emergent" quality of performance, and that the *bertsolariak* may be regarded as seers, spokespersons, for a unique social collective.

Part II:

THE IBERIAN CONTEXT

Playfulness and Planfulness: Improvisation and Revitalization in Culture

JAMES W. FERNANDEZ

> Habitus: "the durably installed, generative principle of regulated improvisation."
>
> Pierre Bourdieu

First Things First, An Anthropological View of Improvisation: An Improvisational Animal Evolving Towards Regulation?

As the epigraph from Bourdieu indicates, improvisation is a constant in the human condition, if not in Darwinian survival itself.[1] We are improvising animals, and perhaps it might be forgiven an anthropologist, as one anchored in the study of human nature in all its manifestations, to suggest why that should be. This is to understand the anthropologist's task as ultimately that of pointing out some fundamental things about the human condition itself that constitute, as we say, "the conditions of possibility" of a given idea or a given behavior, in this case improvisation. I recognize that it is not mainly the *cultural* anthropologist's task to account for the durably installed, not to say hard wired propensities, of our human nature in culture. Rather, it is our challenge to understand the particular cultural conditions that produce certain kinds of quite variable behavior, such as competitive versifying in some cultures yet not in others. Without embarking, like some eighteenth-century Scottish Philosopher, on a treatise about improvisation and human nature, however, let me suggest some parameters of our human condition that enable us to be improvisational creatures.

---

1. In the sense that there is no teleological guarantee of survival for any animal species. When the conditions and the niche to which any animal is suitably adapted changes, survival depends on improvising heretofore unpracticed behaviors that have survival value in the changed conditions.

First there is our remarkable dexterity which gives us both power and precision in manipulating the things of the world; a set of capabilities that have enabled us over the course of human evolution, and as we work in the transient and often changing material world, to make remarkable and enduring improvisations (Napier 1993). Monkeying around with the environment became tinkering and tinkering became inventing and this has long since been an admired and adaptive capacity in our culture. To be sure, there is cultural difference in the admiration for and cultivation of that capacity, and probably attitudes toward improvisation itself. Indeed, Unamuno's famous phrase "*que inventen ellos*" ("let them invent") is indicative of that. Secondly there is the openness of our language systems. There are three things that such openness has brought us in language use: *productivity*; that is, "we freely emit utterances that we have never said or heard before while being usually understood"; *displacement*; that is, "we speak freely of things that are out of sight or in the past or future – or even non-existent" (Hockett 1960; Hockett and Ascher 1964: 139); and finally we employ *duality of patterning* which separates a sound system from a meaning system that enables our productivity. In other words, it enables the generation of new meanings with remarkable creativity. These three capacities are, essentially, the constitutive features of our improvisational capacity. The vast lexicons of individual languages, our dictionaries which might be called the legacies of countless improvisations, demonstrate this.

And finally, if culture is defined as awareness of choice and the possibility of making choices in behavior, and cultural evolution is seen as incremental in respect to that awareness of available choices, then it follows that cultural evolution has meant increases in improvisational possibility; improvisation in this sense defined as being able to substitute for an accustomed choice a previously untried or unexpected or unaccustomed one and being able to transmit that improvisation from generation to generation as tradition (See Bonner 1980). Pronounced possibility of choice and traditional transmission is certainly the human condition and is a fundamental "condition of possibility" of the relatively constant improvisation we find among us humans

I want to repeat that I only emphasize these "conditions of the possibility of improvisation," characteristic of the human condition, to help us understand in the most fundamental terms why "improvisation" in communicative interaction should be felt to be so interesting and usually admirable. It is because it is seen or felt as the realization of something, a fundamentally human capability. Yet of course, while it may be felt as fundamentally human and as the epigraph from Bourdieu also suggests, it does not exist without regulation. And the regulation of improvisation in cultures is in important ways variable and influencing in the conditions of possibility of its presence. In other words, the anxieties attendant to improvisation are variable. Indeed, since cultural evolution is also the evolution of an increasingly complex and orderly organization of life –which is to say increasing regulation of our interactive relations, of planning one's work and working one's plan as it were– it may seem more understandable why improvisation has often enough received

Patxi Etxeberria, Txomin Garmendia, Bautista Madariaga, Jose Miguel Iztueta, "Lazkao Txiki," seated, and Santi Zabala, "Lexo," performing. The introspective nature of the performers reveals the concentration needed to undertake the fundamentally human ability to improvise.
By permission of *Sendoa*.

a bad name. But here also in the escape that improvisation offers from the reiterated and the regulated for we can understand its, in this case, subversive attractions.

If we see cultural evolution, as we must, in terms also of increasing organization, that is to say regulation, of our time in the sense of making, in various organized ways, foregone commitments of that time, then, further, we might also begin to understand how improvisation, however fundamentally a human condition, may yet also become more and more an improvident violation of these anticipated commitments. This is evident in the etymology of the word itself: *im* ("not") *provisus* ("foreseen"). In other words it is an unforeseen and hence surprising activity. And insofar as organization in social life is always a provident and increasingly foregone organization of our time, we can see the etymological intelligence in the cognate term for improvisation, extemporaneous; namely, an activity which stands somehow "out of time" or *ex* ("out of") *tempus* ("time"). Once again that unforeseenness and out-of-timeness is an important part of the attraction of the improvised and the extemporaneous. On the other hand, in thus beginning my paper and since we have in anthropology very considerable organized knowledge about our cultural evolution over time (as the references attest), I have wanted to avoid improvisation and the extemporaneous in launching my field materials relevant to the topic!

If there is still in the reader a resistance to this argument that humans are extemporaneous animals we may wish to consider two additional arguments. The first comes from observations of play in childhood which, although increasingly "*parentified*" in our increasingly regulated world, is still remarkably improvisational (Cf. Sawyer 1997: chs. 2 and 8). Young children, pretty much left to their own devices, prove quite capable by themselves and with others of considerable improvisation within the rules necessarily governing their activities. And this improvisational possibility is no doubt an important part of the fun that children derive from their play and the playfulness that it allows! Just as, independent of the pleasure we have of learning about an absorbing institution of the Basques in taking up our topic here, it is part of the fun we have in this colloquium in taking up the topic of improvisation.

The second argument comes from the annals of pragmatic philosophy in its two most important twentieth-century practitioners: Wittgenstein and Rorty. The former with his ludic insistence on the never-ending possibilities of "language games" in communicative interaction (Wittgenstein 1966: 8 qtd. in Lurie 1991: 226) and the latter with his preoccupations with the contingencies that arise to challenge human solidarity, and which must be answered by our improvisational capacity (Rorty 1989). Both philosophers seek to rescue us and our creativity from timidity and the dead weight of convention and philosophical "decidedness." Both, by denying fixedness, final metaphysical regulation and final truths, seek to instill a pragmatic openness or playfulness, which is to say a sense of improvisational possibility. Both could be said to adhere to the view that man is centrally, if he would only realize it, an "improvisational animal."

Displaced Understanding: The Everyday Poetics of Improvisation

For Rorty an important part of this pragmatic capacity for improvisation lies in our competence through convincing narrative to coin, in the presence of confusion, nescience and misunderstanding, new narrative figurations or tropes of understanding. Such tropes for him are "instruments of moral and intellectual progress" (1987: 296 qtd. in Lurie 1991: 229). Insofar as one is concerned with human solidarity as the main project of our (or one's) humanity, ethnographic narrative of other ways of life is taken by Rorty to be one of the prime methods of extending understanding and creating the possibility of wider solidarity.[2]

This philosophical concern, insofar as it points to a study of convention and the possibility of creative escape from convention, is akin to this anthropologist's interest in both religious and social-political revitalization movements, and their dynamic relation to convention. That is to say, revitalization movements are always to some degree or another

---

2. See Rorty (1989: ch. 2). In this collection Rorty writes that there are two main projects to which men appeal to justify their lives: that of contributing to human solidarity and that of contributing to the discovery of truth. See also Wittgenstein's interest in ethnographic narrative as offering a perspective on, and an opening up of, the chains of convention in his reading of Frazer's *Golden Bough*.

and initially break-away movements from more conventional religious and social allegiances. And in this separating impulse lies their vitality as far as their membership is concerned. As a result we find in them a considerable degree of improvisation in which adepts can at the least take pride and at most feel they offer greater and more vital contact with reality. More than that, however, I think we have to understand this improvisation in terms of displacement.

I will discuss examples of these various movements or displacements below but I would like here to refer to a few specifics of resourceful revitalization understood in figurative terms, and further as displacement from commonplaces, which as I say is one important way of understanding improvisation. We have, of course, to understand displacement in modern trope theory; not in an Aristotelian way (namely, in terms of the organization of categories by necessary and sufficient defining features) but in Wittgensteinian terms of relations of family resemblance or proto typicality. That is to say further, that a category will contain members with relatively few distinct features in common, yet whose members will be related to each other by resemblance in some respect to the prototype. Such tropes play along the lines of these resemblances extending, for example, the prototype of the father –basically the biological and jural father– to include political leaders, priests, deities and even geography (the Fatherland). There is something elementally improvisational in these extensions or displacements of a prototype, for they enable us to contemplate by extended category a rather different membership than would be allowed by strict observance of the given and conventional defining features of a category. We might say, in light of this Wittgensteinian rather than Aristotelian notion of the categorical logic of inclusion and exclusion, that improvisation is very much related to relocation or displacement and extension of proto typicality. Furthermore the dynamic of the prototype is, by its very nature, more improvisational in its "displacement potential" than the primary dynamic of inclusiveness and exclusiveness characteristic of Aristotelian categories.

In the Wittgensteinian view, the frequency of, or the need for displacement (namely, improvisation in "communicative understanding") is constant because of the unsettled nature of family resemblances and of the prototype itself. The "word games" we constantly play are in that sense inveterate. The logic of Aristotelian categorization, on the other hand, drives the thinker to placement rather than displacement, to the clearest possible specification of defining features for purposes of secure placement, which is of very definite inclusion or exclusion. Despite the philosophers' attempt to tie us down to permanent forms, this displacement or improvisation is constant and has been constant in thinking since time immemorial because of the essential uncertainty of categorical belonging. Despite Aristotle's effort in his theory of *the Categories* to defeat that uncertainty, his attention to the vagaries and creativity of human communication in his *Rhetoric* and *the Poetics* displays an awareness of the constancy of displacement and improvisational possibility. Many of the displacements present for Aristotle in these works have long since become conventional and we hardly notice them if we notice them at all. Their original improvisational creativity has long been lost although it is always possible to reinvigorate or revitalize it.[3]

Since we are here engaged in a display of rather abstract theorizing, let us take the abstract idea of theorizing itself and consider some ways in which our understanding has been displaced in understanding it. Basically we might argue that the abstract notion of theorizing has been understood by reference to the prototypical activity of putting things together into a structure or pulling things apart from a structure. Put simply, to theorize is to build up or take apart a structure. The trope of structure gives us a fairly secure grasp of the abstraction "theory" but not much effective and affective "experiential understanding," perhaps because the trope has become conventional, embedded and almost entirely moribund.

As pointed out by cognitive linguists (see for example Lakoff and Johnson 1999) any trope of convention, such as "theory as structure," contains implicated and frequently used sub-parts so that we generally speak about the "foundation" of a theory, for example, or the pro-positions by which we are oriented within it. However, as is also observed, there are normally unused parts of any metaphoric extension: the roofs, internal rooms, staircases, hallways, internal plumbing, and so on. While what we may call a base level understanding of a conventional figurative expression may derive from some grasp of the sense that theorizing is structuring or restructuring, creative improvisation is always possible and involves making use of the conventionally unused parts of an established but conventionally understood figure of understanding. As an example of this kind of improvisation take the following play upon the notion of theory as structure:

> "His theory has thousands of little rooms and long, winding and windy corridors" (Lakoff and Johnson 1999).

> "His theories are baroque self indulgent structures lacking classical rigor and cleanliness of line" or "His theories are frightful Gothic structures covered with Gargoyles" (Lakoff and Johnson 1999, with a little help from their friend).

> "It's a drafty theory he is developing there!"

> "His theory of language structure is a charnel house containing only the bare bones of human communication."

Cognitive linguists distinguish two different kinds of imaginative or improvisational extension –by extension and exploration– of a conventional figuration of our thought, which lie beyond or outside the conventionally used parts of the trope:

---

3. See the discussion in Fernandez (1989). While agreeing with Keesing's main criticism that anthropologists have a tendency to read creative meaningfulness into what are conventional texts to the people they study, I am interested in pointing out (i) the original creative displacement that occurred in the given moribund figure of speech; in this case, the notion of "*solutions* to problems" and (ii) the always possible revitalization of a moribund figure as in the bumper sticker "Chemists Have the Solutions."

1. Extensions of the used part of a metaphor: "These facts are the bricks and mortar of my theory."
2. Instances in which an unused and unexpected part of the conventional metaphor is explored: "His theory has thousands of little rooms and long, winding and windy corridors."

There are enlivening consequences for theoretical argument, to be sure, in these extensions and explorations. Yet there are also enlivening possibilities in the coinage of a new and quite novel metaphor, and enlivening as regards the usual way that the abstraction "theory" is conventionally conceived: "Classical theories are patriarchs who father many children, most of whom who fight incessantly among themselves with much emotional involvement." What we have here is creative; that is, an aptly improvisational displacement of our understanding. It is also revitalizing to our understanding and, in terms of communicative interaction, this is a fundamental kind of revitalization. I might add that being present at these improvisational coinages is one of the pleasures of ethnographic fieldwork, which is to say they can also be revitalizing to the ethnographer in his or her task.

So let me begin to think about improvisation by considering this particular "play of tropes"; a deep-rooted if not chronic interest of mine (if not quite yet "a durably installed generative principle of regulated improvisation") by which, through always originally improvisational metaphoric and metonymic manipulations, we assign categories and hence identities to significant others. The Russian linguist Roman Jacobson (1960) suggests that these aleatory associations of congruity and similitude in the various contexts of our associative co-presence with other persons, things and events in the passage of our daily lives, regularly provide opportunities for an improvised sense of relations that becomes an enduring possibility of displaced identity. It is a kind of imaginative play that is basic to the poetics of everyday life. I have previously treated this topic of metonymic representation and misrepresentation by which, improvising on some semblance or another, we take the part for the whole or the whole for the part (Fernandez 1998).

Instances of this kind of revitalizing displacement are numerous in my fieldwork. But let me begin with a once creative and now conventional displacement which should be very much in our minds here in the American West and at the Center for Basque Studies in Reno, where the historic presence of the Basque sheepherder in the mountain states has been such a fundamental influence in the foundation and development of a center dedicated to Basque-related themes. Let us recall the poetics of that calling which are particularly accessible through the Spanish word *pastor* ("shepherd"), though now almost entirely moribund and conventional in the English-language concept of "Protestant pastor and pastorate." It was Jesus' (the Good Shepherd after all) poetic improvisation in the Bible, *Ego Sum Pastor bonus*, that set in motion a whole field of associations, a metonymic (contiguity) and metaphoric (similarity) play especially apt for the ancient herding societies of the Middle East, that surely suggests a likeness between religious leaders and sheepherders or pastors, ever watchful and mindful of the well-being of their flocks, otherwise understood to be members of the Christian church. The Basque sheepherder has served as a vehicle for, and energized a whole center of activity thereby revitalizing a sense of relationship between past and present here in Nevada and between a United States-based diaspora and a European homeland. Yet the sheepherder in general has also been a widespread vehicle for revitalizing the sense of religious relationships. The notion of a pastor and a pastorate may now be entirely conventional for established religions, but the concept of a vital relationship between the Basque sheepherder and the Center for Basque studies is surely not! For the center has assumed, particularly through the prophetic figure of its director (if I may coin anew the phrase) a pastoral, good shepherd, image; a responsibility towards both a heritage here in the United States, and in the *Vascongadas* (the Basque Country), of that dispersed flock of, for want of a better identification, sheepherders!

A further example of the improvisational use of an accidental series of associations that recently intrigued me arose in a newspaper article discussing the relation to Spanish politics of the sinking of the tanker, the Prestige, off the coast of Galicia in 2002 and the crude oil spill which subsequently affected much of the Cantabrian coast. This sea-carried and current-driven thick crude oil, almost tar-like in consistency and termed *chapapote* (in Galician) or *galipote* (in Asturian) was quickly improvised into a convenient referent to the many long years of the Franco regime (1939–75) and its lingering presence in the present-day *Partido Popular* or Conservative Party. The improvisation called attention to a sticky and difficult-to-clean lingering political presence adhering to and soiling all citizens. It was and still is a detectable presence in the Spanish polity, the columnist argued, despite the present assumption of democratic citizenship. "Every year as we commemorate the deaths of the civil war," the author writes, "let us demand of our politicians that they redouble their efforts to liberate us from this '*chapapote franquista.*'" (Sánchez Rodilla 2003). So much for a very resonant improvisation.

Similarly, in the Oviedo newspaper, *La Nueva España*, in February 2003 a columnist and Asturian nationalist long associated with the revival and oficialization of the Asturian language takes the opportunity to chide the press and public for using the Galician term *chapapote* or the Yankee word *fuel* rather than the perfectly respectable Asturian word *galipote*, to denote a crude oil discharge from tankers cleaning their tanks and long known on Cantabrian beaches. He also takes the opportunity to refer to the Castilian language, long dominant over Asturian in the province, as a *galipote* that has become stuck to and contaminated Asturian linguistic habits (Sánchez Vicente 2003).

The most extended improvisation on this oil slick theme, however, comes in a column discussing the president of the Galician Autonomous Community, Manual Fraga Iribarne, a long-standing and popular conservative politician, still in power but now an old man and in evident decline, who got his start as a minister and ambassador in the Franco regime. According to the columnist, the Prestige continues to discharge crude into the sea and the Conservative Party is sink-ing as well. Fraga voyages in this boat making *trompicones* ["slip-ups"] from the bridge and from his cabin. He wishes to reach land and find serenity. But his testament will not reach land. The *galipote* creates a black sea all around him, while his bones tell him it is time to put an end to this long political career characterized by authoritarianism and collaboration with a long dictatorship. Because his world has become *viscoso* ["viscose"] like the fuel lay-ing a dead hand upon the maritime landscape, once sweet and magical, his own fossiliza-tion has come on him suddenly and unexpectedly (Arias Arguelles-Meres 2003).

These improvisations, taking advantage of the contingencies of everyday life and which lend vitality and interest to that life are, of course, of fundamental interest to the anthropologist for the very vitality they lend to that life and its "communicative interac-tion." Indeed, the argument here is in great part that improvisation has revitalizing con-sequences in culture. And it is our responsibility to be alert to such consequences and to give an account of them in as accurate a way as possible, which is to say a thick descrip-tion not only of the structure, but of the feeling and tone of daily life!

In the Presence of Improvisation: African Sermonizers and Cantabrian Versifiers

Testimonies to Eternity

In the previous section I principally took advantage of the media to detect and keep track of the improvisational dimension in local cultures. However, any alert field-working anthro-pology puts one, as I have suggested, in the presence of improvisation of one kind or another on an almost daily basis. I ought to repeat that I have always been, because of my enduring interest in cultural revitalization, centrally interested in improvisational moments because of their revelatory nature and revitalizing consequences.

I want to specifically compare here my experience with African Sermonizers and Cantabrian Versifiers. In the first case we are speaking about the role of improvisation in enabling and confirming religious movement and in the second about the presence of poetic *repartee* and *retort* as an enlivening part of village life. In neither case would I go so far as to speak of competitive improvisation as we know it in the case of Basque *bertso-lariak* but they are, I think, instructive related phenomena. We were certainly in the pres-ence of the poetic impulse in our Asturian work. My wife and co-worker, Renate Lellep, in her first year of research in several agro-pastoral mining villages was continuously and voluntarily supplied with verse of various kinds such as *trovas, cantares, romances* and so on. However, their improvisational character is not to be assumed and has to be defined.

Though my main work in Africa has focused on religious movement and revitaliza-tion, I also ought to say that I spent quality time among Fang where I conducted my longest (more than two years) research in the men's council house. I was especially inter-ested in the vitalities of this institution where ready repartee and retort were the order of the day in the discussions, debates and moots that daily went on there. There, the capacity for improvised argument both in accusatory and counter statements was widely admired. And the debates and moots of this institution would be an excellent subject matter for anyone interested in an extended analysis of that kind of improvisation, which is to say the improvisation of repartee and retort.[4] Likewise, the village *juntas* or monthly reunions of *vecinos* ("neighbors") in Cantabrian villages after Franco would reveal to us plenty of examples of *repentismo* ("improvisation") and *ocurrencia* ("witticism") in argument that was much appreciated, admired and indeed central to the liveliness of these sessions.

But let me here compare African sermonizers and Cantabrian versifiers, who have both been more specific objects of my interest. In the first case we are speaking about the role of improvisation in enabling and confirming religious movement through the demonstration of religious presence; in the second, about presence of mind amidst the jocular antagonisms of village and inner village life. I have been principally interested in the imaginative figurations introduced in these sermons or verses, and hence in understanding improvisation in the sense of "an argument of images" (See for example Fernandez 1986b).

The sermonizers of the African religions studied, most usually but not always the leaders of their particular cult or sect, could hardly employ the word improvisation because of its implications (in English usage at least) of the temporary and contrived. Their sermons were felt to be testimonies confirming eternal verities and of those things which existed out of time. More properly they could be described as ex-temporary in the sense described above. So rather than improvisation, the term extemporary or *extemporaries* would more properly describe them. In most cases the sermonizer closeted himself in such as way as to produce a vision about which he could sermonize. A particularly dramatic, if not classic, example could be found in the sermonizers of the Bwiti religion who closeted themselves in a grave-like chamber dug out under an altar. There they meditated for several hours, aided by the mental effects of a small dose of the psycho reactive plant *eboga*. At midnight the sermonizer would arise, climb out of the pit and deliver his sermon extemporaneously in a quiet and removed tone of voice. These sermons were extemporaneous in the sense that (i) They had their origin in a mildly removed or alienated psychoactive state produced by the alkaloid stimulant *ibogaine* (ii) The sermon's words were thought to have been conveyed to the sermonizer from ancestors living in a different time dimension in the world of the dead and (iii) They were attempts to convince the listeners of the reality of that extemporaneous, in many respects pre-colonial, world and to invite them, through ritual, into it. In short, a different time dimension was referenced and projected.

The tropological approach that I customarily follow also suggests an extemporaneous or "other world analysis" (Cf. Levin 1977 and 1988). This follows an enduring argument in metaphor theory which maintains that metaphors are not simply re-statements

---

4. For a discussion of the sources of Fang argumentativeness and attempts to understand its particular imaginative vitalities see the numerous headings in the index under "Argument and Argumentativeness" in Fernandez (1982: 680).

of a pervasive literal reality but are in fact "displacements" which actually bring other worlds into being within the imagination. Indeed, the objective of the African religious leaders and sermonizers I studied was the invigoration or re-invigoration of either a spiritual world lost or abandoned during colonial times, and under the evangelical pressure of missionaries and administrators, or the discovery and entry into a spiritual world promulgated by missionary evangelization but never fully grasped under missionary pressure.

Of course, it was not by word alone that these revitalized worlds were brought into being but also by image-rich ritual activity. Just the same the sermons themselves were efficacious verbal instruments of world creation. I believe, as I say, that the word "ex-temporality" is the right one to describe what is achieved in these sermons. Yet if improvisation is to be employed as our referent term what we find is nothing less than "world improvisation." It may be more accurate, of course, to point out that these were usually syncretized worlds attempting to bring together in some convincing way that was not subservient to either a traditional religious world of ancestor worship, or adherence to a new Christian world of missionary evangelization. That is to say, these sermons sought to convincingly displace their membership from the conflicted colonial situation.

I examined a selection of these sermons to show how they obtained the power of world revelation, if we can call it that, by a syncretic argument of both indigenous and Christian images. Though the sermons themselves must be seen as extemporary in the sense given, in the images produced we can see improvisation for the purpose of "capturing the imagination" of the congregation. For example the "straight and narrow" path of Christian evangelization was taken and syncretized with a forest path image, to produce a path of birth and death enriched at every turn by local nature images which interwove a whole world of understanding. This constant syncretism in the argument of images, I would suggest, was truly improvisational and was admired as such (See Fernandez 1982 ch.19).

Testimonies to Locality: "Nuestros improvisadores asturianos" ("Our Asturian Improvisers") (Jovellanos)

But let me turn from the extemporaneous and the improvisational in African sermonizing to the ever presence of the poetic in our Asturian villages and villagers. As I say, this poetic culture was thrust upon us from practically our (my wife's actually) first moments of fieldwork in the 1960s as something vitally important that we should know about village life: *romances*, long poems of several hundred lines about the Moroccan Wars, and above all *troves* or *trovas* and *cantares*, the preferred local terms.[5] Our notebooks are full of these which practically all arose, it was said, competitively (*de picadillo*) in response to various

---

5. I ought to say that we probably missed an opportunity, in our concentration on collecting topical and contemporary verse of various kinds, to record "romances of the Golden Age" (*romances del Siglo de Oro*), one of the treasures of the folklorist's profession and which were surely present in the heads of some of the elders in the mid sixties. Fortunately, all was not lost and we have the admirable collections of these *romances* by Jesús Suárez López (1997 and 1998), including, in the former book, several from the parish (El Pino, Aller) where we worked.

village events or actions: these included courtship rounds (*rondas*), during competitive moments in the weekly dances (*bailes*), and especially at weddings (*bodas*), where competitive, often jocularly hostile verses (*agresividad en comensalidad* or "friendly aggressiveness," as Carmelo Lisón has called them) were the order of the day, particularly if the wedding families came from different villages or parishes.[6] Many *cuartetas* ("quatrains") spring up in the joking challenge between strong-willed personalities, as in the exchange credited to Jesusa given below.

Many if not most of these interactive verses were, as we say, mischievous, socially sardonic and put-downish; even in some cases mildly malicious. The claim was often made that these verses –mostly four line couplets with a second and last line rhyme scheme (*cuartetas*), though they could be twice or three times as long– were composed on the spot in response to one event or challenge or another, though our considered view is that they were usually pondered a while (indeed from several hours to over-night or even longer) before being brought forth. We do not have much evidence of more or less immediate responses in our fieldwork days; that is, of direct competitive interaction as is the case of the Basque *bertsolariak*.[7] It was said, however, that this rapid responsive improvisation was much more the case in former days and early on several villagers (mentioned below) were pointed out to us that were still adept at improvisation.

The verse and the versifiers in which the villagers took most pride were of two sorts: those who were thought capable of reciting long *trovas*, such as *romances* learned from others and dedicated to patriotic, provincial or religious themes; and those who more or less spontaneously could compose *trovas* or *cantares* upon local themes. One year we became lost for more than three hours in the frequent mountain mists of the uplands of Asturias and finally managed to come upon a *majada* ("sheepfold") with a *cabaña*, where we found two village brothers who had emigrated to the New World (to Miami and Canada in this case), but who returned every summer with their families and children so as not to lose the traditions or speech ways for the next generation. While cups of hot tea were handed out we spent several hours with them as they sought to recite from memory, with some stops and starts, a 102-line poem or *trova* entitled "El Cuañy-on de los Rancones." It was about the escape from bombardment into a cave of a local extended family during the Spanish Civil War (1936–39) and featured the idiosyncrasies of the various family members. It was originally composed, so they said, by their father without pen or pencil, a man well-known for *sacando trovas* (pulling out *trovas*). They also

---

6. See here the ample selection of this confrontational wedding verse culled from the archives by William Christian.

7. I did, however, gather one bit of evidence myself. One morning on the day before the local Patronal Fiesta I passed an old friend seated on a *mentidero* in a nearby village where I rented a study space. Walking down to his village I had thought up a simple *cantar* for him (without pen and paper I might add): "Hoy Sabado, preciso es/ pa todos ayunar/Pa que mañana ye fiesta/Comemos panchón a fartucar." When I returned two hours later Jaime, still on his bench, and without pen and pencil, had improvised (*discurrido de la cabeza*) the following response: "Le dejo aqui invitao/A comer conmigo panchón/Lo que produce la tierra/Ye de la luna? Non!/Y nesto no lo traigan/Los Americanos participación!"

shared several humorous *cuartetas* of his gently mocking the local schoolteacher of their youth, Don Florencio.[8]

Most frequently heard or volunteered were locally improvised *cantares* of love and of comment on local authority figures. The former could be recited by most everyone in apt social moments, for example during the preparation of the fiesta sweet bread (*panchon*) and formerly during corn husking and chestnut husking (*esfoyaza* and *amaguestu*). These recitations of *coplas* ("verses") or *cantares* were an important part of the pleasure of such events. From dozens of these collected let me give some favorites. I ought to say that many in our collection are relatively common place, being made up of *frases trilladas ya hechas* ("previously thought up well-known phrases"). Indeed, they were and maybe still are widely collectible in the north of Spain. Among the more original in our view are the following:

¡Cuando paso por tu casa,	When I go by your house,
porto pan y toy comiendo,	I take bread and pretend to eat,
pa que nun digan los tus padres	so your parents won't say
con que verte me mantengo!	I survive by watching you!
¡El amor ye un cuchillo	Love is like a knife
que por los güeyos se mete	that enters through the eyes
y en llegar al corazón	and, when it reaches the heart,
da puñeladas de muerte!	it stabs you to death!
Oí que tu moza echó	I heard that your girl
un gran peo na misa.	farted loudly during mass.
¡Ante tanta devoción,	Such reverent devotion
nun pues facer caso omiso!	cannot be overlooked!
Anoche me detuve a tu puerta;	Last night, I stopped at your door;
tres veces pique el candao.	three times I knocked at the latch.
Tú pa tener amores,	For someone who's interested in love,
tienes el sueñu pesao.	you're a pretty sound sleeper.
Entre Petra que se pinta	Between Petra who uses make-up
y Susana que se lava,	and Susan who takes a bath,
me dijo la madre mía	my mother told me
¡con Susana mejor me taba!	I'd be better off with Susan!

Or as a transition to our next versifier the following comment, in original rhyme, on the local priest who was a bird lover and for some months kept a pet crow!

8. Don Florencio was famous for a dirty old *boina* (beret) he constantly wore. Their father rhymed, "La boina de Florencio/Tiene brillo de charol! Y cuando sale al recreo,/Brilla mas que el mismo sol!" (Florencio's beret / shines like patent leather; / when he goes out for a good time, / it's brighter than the sun!). And then their cousin immediately (they said) retorted, "La boina del Florencio/La van a someter a prueba/a ver si puede extraer/ aceite, cebu y mantega!" (They're going to put / Florencio's beret to a test, / to see if they can extract / olive oil, fat and lard!).

¡El señor cura cría cuérigo!	Our priest keeps a pet crow!
¡Dos cuérigos felices!	Two happy crows!
Pero malo de sostener,	But hard to sustain,
entre nosotros feligreses,	among those of our parish.
¡Bastante tenemos a mantener!	We've got enough to maintain.

Many villagers were adept in those years at *corriendo o discurriendo cantares o coplas* ("running with or thinking up *cantares* or *coplas*") in such a manner, and most can remember many *cantares*. Many, perhaps the majority, had become common property and their authors had been forgotten. Those who were remembered and with whom we worked were notable, perhaps, because they were reputed to rapidly (*de repente*) *discurrir* ("think up") o *andar* ("employ") longer pieces of several stanzas. During our years there two of the best known for this rapid thinking-up were Eladio Díaz, a man of little schooling and not much given to reading and writing but quite adept in *sacando un trove* ("coming up with a verse") rather quickly after some incident or scandal; and Jesusa del Crucero (Tejón Castañón), a poor (*pobre de solemnidad de hecho*), barely literate spinster with a very quick capacity of retort and a respected, even dreaded, facility for making pointed comment in verse on fellow villagers!

One of Eladio's favorite subjects was the local priest, Don Francisco, who lived with and was protectively cared for by his sister. When the priest fell into the river while fishing, the next day Eladio circulated reciting to friends and relatives:

El señor cura fue a pescar	Our priest went out fishing
¡y cayó nel ríu!	and fell in the river.
Lo tuvieron que a sacar	They had to fish him out,
¡aterrado del fríu!	terrified with cold!
Esperanza se enteró	Esperanza found out
que cayóse nel río.	that he fell in the river.
corriendo se fue a buscar:	She ran to look for him:
–¡Aye! ¿Onde está mi hermano?	"Oh, where's my brother?
¡Aye! ¿Onde está el dios mío?	Oh, where's my lord?"
¡Tranquila, Esperanza,	Calm down, Esperanza!
hay que esperar!	You've got to wait.
¡A San Estéban de Pravia	He'll end up down there
es donde va a parar	in San Esteban de Pravia,
todo que arrastra el río	like everything else the river drags along
antes que entra nel mar!	as it flows into the sea!

And when a woman well-known as a Vista Santos fell asleep in mass and as a consequence was locked in the church, Eladio quickly circulated with the following set of *estrofas* ("strophes"):

En combinación con Fe,
quedaste en la iglesia escondía.
¡Para robar a los Santos
lo que en los cepos tenía!

Together with Faith,
you stayed hidden in church,
to steal from the poorbox
the money for the Saints!

El cura, cuando sintió,
las campanas repicar,
corriendo a fuera de la iglesia
¿qué milagro puede pasar?
Que las campanas quedaban solas
y saltaron a tocar.
¡Y descubrieron a María
con los cepos de par en par!

Our priest, when he heard
all the bells were ringing,
he ran to the church:
What sort of miracle is this?
There was nobody there,
but the bells were all ringing.
Then they found María
with the alms boxes all open!

–Perdóname Señor Cura,
que nada pude llevar.
¡Los cepos están vacíos,
y no le pude robar!

"Forgive me, Reverend Priest,
I couldn't take a thing.
The boxes are all empty
and I couldn't steal a thing!"

Yet Eladio's verse also touched on local customs and cautionary advice concerning them. In one example, concerning the marriage of a young relative to a woman (*mayorazas*) with *una buena herencia* ("a good inheritance"), he composed:

Muchas mayorazas hay
en este rico lugar:
Una Lola de Barso
¿Por qué no la fuiste a buscar?

There're plenty of rich girls
in our fine village:
Why'd you have to go
for a Lola from Barso?

¿Pienses que mejor sería
haberte casado con Lola?
¿Y llevála pa casa
y no quedarte sola?

Did you think it'd be better
to have married Lola
and bring her back home
than keep living alone?

¡Poco te valió te digo
el casar con mayoraza!
¡Que a la hora de casar
a ti te llevaron de casa!

It did you little good
to marry a rich girl!
Just as soon as you married,
they made you leave home!

And of course, as is frequently remarked, there could be something quite *brutal* in the cloacal-sexual sense of some of this aggressive verse. Ethnographic science requires me to register here one of Eladio's more combative *coplas*, directed towards the other *barrio* (*el barrio de abaxo*) in the village. After he recited it to me, he put his hand to his forehead with a half embarrassed smile and a cackle, saying *he, he, he, terrible, terrible. ¡Qué feo! ¿Verdá? Avergonzoso, ¿no?* ("Ha, ha, ha, awful, awful. How nasty, right? Shameful, don't you think?") Improvisation doesn't always lead us down a *buen camino* ("good path")!

Esos del barrio de abaxo
son un pecio de pendangas.
¡Cuando hicieron las casadietas
todos salieron blandas!

Those people from the Lower Town
are all a bunch of fools.
When they fried the Christmas cookies
they all turned out soft!

La Santa María de Manolón,
ella que fornaba primera;
el día de la comunidá,
era ella la cocinera.
¡Pero aquel día por mayor
andaba de ganadera!
¡Y no va una que reír
a tanta tropera!

That lady, "Holy Mary," from Manolón,
She was first to bake the bread;
she did all the cooking
for all the neighborhood.
But that day especially
she was herding the cows.
One couldn't help but laugh
at such a big herd!

Esos del barrio de abaxo,
los que andan a la mina,
¡En casa del Ramón de Fernandu,
mearon na cocina!
¡Qué ha sido, no lo sé,
perque no estuve presente,
pero creo que mearon
y que cagaron caliente!

Those people from the Lower Town,
the ones who work the mine,
in Ramón de Fernandu's house,
they pissed in the kitchen!
I don't know what happened,
'cause I wasn't there,
but I believe that they pissed
and they took a good shit too!

The best known versifier in the village was Ceferino Suárez, whose extensive and often lengthy poetry and quick wit I have elsewhere treated (Fernandez 1976–1977). This was a man who was quite literate, had spent a number of years in Cuba and who wrote poetry on a wide variety of topics, though usually on village fads and foibles. He was also said to be quick in poetic repartee and verses of his composed quickly in challenging encounters were often quoted, which I comment on in the aforementioned article. As Ceferino was a quite literate, though mostly self educated and worldly man, and one whose verses almost always had a more complicatedly playful thought-out quality, I was never able to fully credit the *repentismo* reputed to him. Indeed the exchanges of jocular insults between villagers or between villages in respect to bodily appearance and cleanliness, in which Ceferino offered some memorable retorts or took the leading role for his village, were probably composed over some hours or even a day's time (previously or afterwards), and were not immediately in response as many villagers claimed. But we cannot be sure, for the custom of jocularly aggressive poetic exchanges during wedding banquets, where some of his famous retorts may have occurred, was largely in abeyance and we could not confirm it.

Jesusa, the barely literate spinster and among the poorest people in the village, was on the contrary an undoubted quick wit fully capable of *de repente* ("sudden") retort, though we have no record of a directly responsive stand-off between her and another, even though victims of her poetic aggressions were numerous. As I have treated her poetry elsewhere, I will only give one example of her quick poetic wit. On returning home from digging potatoes in her one small meager field, a handicapped veteran taking the sun taunted that meagerness with a *cuarteta* as she passed him.

¡Las tierras de Mamedián	Over in Mamedián,
salen caras las patatas!	potatoes cost a lot!
Vale más preparar el viaje	It's better to pack your bags
y embárcate pa Caracas.	and leave for Caracas.

Jesusa is said, by witnesses present, to have snapped back immediately:

Tú pa Caracas nun vas,	You're not going to Caracas;
perque vas de mala gana.	you really don't want to go.
¡Nun quieres perder la paga	You don't want to lose
de la mutilada en España!	your pension money in Spain.

That we were in the presence in some way of poetic improvisation here cannot be doubted. The villagers recognized and admired it although they had a different vocabulary of appreciation, using such action terms as *correr versos, discurrir cantares, sacar trovas*; and in those terms, "to run with verse," "to inventively versify along with the flow of things," "to pull out verse from who knows where," recognizing the relative immediacy and emergent quality of the verse as responsive to ongoing social interaction.[9] Even Jovellanos, as can be seen from the title to this section, recognized its characterizing and important presence in Asturian village life in the eighteenth century. But while some of this still goes on, it is doubtful that any anthropologist arriving in these selfsame villages today would be presented proudly with local verse of various genres, and recommended to local versifiers, as we were when we started our fieldwork in the mid 1960s. It was a time of poetic presence in Asturias. As William Christian observes in his own study of improvised verse in the western mountains of Cantabria, even at the time of his original fieldwork in the late 1960s this genre was in decline and he was obliged mostly to work the archives and memories of the very elderly to salvage this poetic practice. This, as he so well says, once very quotidian verse of almost effortless and casual deployment and usually anonymous in creation, was just another to-be-expected ability regularly found among villagers (*una destreza más*), like that of having a special mastery in the scything of grass, or a special touch in caring for cattle, or a gift for distracting a crying child (2000: 405).

What has happened? Before we conclude with some observations on that question in the context of our general treatment of improvisation let me turn finally to the well-known *monólogo Asturiano* ("Asturian monologue"), a genre which became very popular and commercialized in the mid last century up to the present. It is a genre whose recitation by talented persons has sometimes been treated as another example of *nuestros impro-*

---

9. One is reminded here of Benjamin's use of the German word *Erfahrung*, the experience gained by ongoing interaction with others, rather than *Erlebnis*, or stable settled acquired experience. There is, indeed, a sense of motion in the presence of others that is captured in the Asturian Spanish phrasings. See Jack Zipes' (1997) discussions of Benjamin's active, motivated and emotional usage of the term to capture the experience shared in genuine, endlessly emergent storytelling.

visadores Asturianos ("our Asturian improvisers"). But in fact, it is a continuation and popularization of the European minstrel or troubadour (*juglar*) tradition which has been especially strongly preserved in Asturias.[10] The minstrel *monologista* is not to be confounded with the true *improvisador*, because he or she composes a verse that will be "ministered" to an audience *mucho de antemano* ("well in advance"). Nevertheless these wandering minstrel *monologistas* will always try to make their sung soliloquies relate in some way to their local audiences, and thus are improvisational to that extent.

Let me make reference to several *monólogos* sung-chanted by the *monologista*, Pin de la Cotolla, invited and paid to sing-recite during the first evening of the *patronal* ("saint's day") festival of Nuestra Virgen del Carmen (or *El Día de Carmín*), in Felechosa, Alto Aller, Asturias, at the end of August 1984. The favorite for the crowd was *Xuacu el Oso*, about a powerful but simple minded youth whom his cousin had convinced to dress in a bear skin so as to be sold at a good price to a *rico Señor,* from whom he could later easily escape and keep the money. The *señor* had a small private zoo and wished to add another bear, or so he said. But as it turned out, he wished to mate Xuacu with a very large white bear that he already possessed. Xuacu couldn't escape his obligation and was placed in the cage with the large white bear, which lumbered towards him with evident suspicious and menacing curiosity.

El blanco…,	Then the big white bear, …
por ver si el otro rendía,	to see if the other would yield,
pegó un bufido tremendo	gave a tremendous roar
y encrespóse y más tovía.	and became even more furious.
Ai, por Dios, el blancu	Oh, in God's name, that white bear,
alzó les pates p'arriba.	lifted up its paws.
Y entós el probe Xuacu,	And then poor Xuacu,
al ver ya que lu comía,	seeing it would devour him,
dobla les manos nel suelu	kneeling, folded his hands
y diz con voz decayía:	and said in a feeble voice:
–¡Ai! ¡Xuaquín ahora te zampen,	"Oh, Xuaquín, now you'll be devoured,
Ave María Puríssima!–	Holy Immaculate Mary!"
Y diz tóo seriu el blancu:	And the white bear, in a serious voice,
–¡En Sin Pecado Concebía!–	answers: "Conceived without sin!"

Now the choice of this widely appreciated monologue was entirely appropriate for the parish of El Pino and Felechosa. For in the nineteenth and early twentieth centuries it had supported a hunting lodge where the provincial landed gentry hunted bears and, indeed, though long ago hunted out of existence in those mountains, there was a statue to an *Oso*

---

10. It is interesting to note the word most used in Asturias, and the north of Spain in general, for these improvised verses, *trovas*, and its relation to the word *troubadour* and the etymology of that term: namely, from the Medieval French *trouver* and the Latin *tropare*, meaning to come across or find something, and thus to invent (cf. also the word "contrive," which comes from *con-trouver)* or find in verse. This interesting etymological connection should not, however, lead us to confuse our *"trova-dores"* with the wandering minstrel, if only because our *improvisadores asturianos* are very much socially situated. They may have wandered once, but their improvisations are very much now rooted in local circumstance!

Pardino Cantábrico (a female bear and her cub) in the town square in which the monologue was delivered. So the *monologista*, who knew many monologues, was careful to select an especially meaningful one. And this was, for the locals, an example of apt and appreciated improvisation on his part. Such constant adjustment of, or very minor improvisation in, an established oral narrative is well known to the folklorist whether it be a matter of the singers of Balkan epics, the Massada legends retold in Israel or by any psychological study of the repetitions of a story told in one ear and passed on by word of mouth to another! Each person and each context acts as both a filter and a source of minor adjustments in any minstrelsy. There is always an element of improvisation, however slight, in any oral narrative. And it is something that the age of mechanical reproduction should not allow us to forget. Furthermore, these minor emergent improvisations furnish oral narrative with an important part something of its charm and vitality.

The other two *monólogos* (also *diba a la medula de la xente local*) were: "El Cazaor de Gochos," about a hunter who mistook a pig for a bear; and "Pachin, el Luna-nauta," who, on buying a tin of snails noted a reference to *baño María* ("*bain marie*" or "double saucepan") in the cooking instructions; but since he did not know any Marías in his village who had a *baño* ("bathtub") or whom he could approach for its use, he heated the can directly on a stove, such that it eventually blew up and some of these snails reached the moon. In these monologues the *minstral monologista* substituted local county place names for the events described. We can see in the "Luna-nauta" monologue the influence of contemporary events. This is a frequent recourse, such as in the very popular "Un Asturianu en Madri," where often recent noteworthy events in the capital will be added to the typical country bumpkin adventures in this recitation. As with the *bertsolariak* there has been a very significant expansion over the decades in the themes treated.[11]

Just to give a sense of what the *monólogo* has become, before concluding, and in order to bring this essay into the context of the twenty-first century, let me give my readers the following e-mail and internet addresses to consult: pnuntris@netcom.es and http://astur-shop.com/. Here, tapes and books of recent and current *monólogos* are for sale and one can actually engage the services of a *monologista* for a wedding, family, village or business celebration. The e-mail address puts the web-surfer in contact with NunTris S.L., which specializes in the "*recuperación y divulgación*" ("recovery and dissemination") of the dying oral tradition, and particularly in sponsoring visits to schools and celebrations of dramatic presentations from the traditional but now disappeared itinerant *comedias de los Guirrios*, as well as more generally from the *monologista* repertoire. Asturshop features the following monologues: "El despelote de pachu," "Los concursos de la tele," "Xuacu el osu," "Un Asturianu en Madrid," "Enguedeyos de estos tiempos," "El sesenta y nueve," and "Cuento asturianu." With such story telling provided over the internet and by e-mail, and so eas-

---

11. Garzia, Sarasua and Egaña testify to the increased heterogeneity of themes with which the singers have been confronted in *bertsolaritza* since 1980, and the importance of studying the impact of this diversification on the singers and the verse (2001: 140–144, 186–187, 231–235).

ily accessible and overwhelmingly present, why improvise anything for oneself in village life? It's already canned and ready to eat! You just have to know how to heat it up in a *baño María* and you can then open it to your entire satisfaction!

Conclusion: Improvisation, Dislocation and Revitalization

Bertsolaritza is such a captivating cultural practice, so demonstrative of what our improvisational capacities can be, that one would like to include alongside it an equivalent Asturian practice. The Basques are in many ways a challenging people who also regularly challenge themselves, whether we are talking about axemanship, lifting or dragging heavy weights, rowing down rivers or across sounds, arm or body wrestling, climbing the most daunting mountains, cycling the most treacherous roads, or reciting improvised verse, as we so well know by now. And they challenge others too. There is friendly competition in the air when you are with Basques. And, of course, one would like to offer something from Asturias to compete forthrightly with *bertsolaritza*. Alas, and though I resist having to contribute another modicum of luster to the already substantial "Basque mystique," I have to capitulate. There is nothing like Basque *bertsolaritza* in Asturias now and there probably never was, though there is an echo of it in the competitive versifying that once went on at weddings and at *patronal* festivals. Though we were provided in our time in the field with much verse, some of which was said to have been spontaneous, and though we were invited and attended our share of weddings and *espichas*,[12] unfortunately your ethnographers never had the opportunity to witness or directly confirm improvisational verse of the spontaneous kind we know and have come to appreciate even more among the Basques.

Of course there was considerable improvisational verse of a kind, and I have given examples of it. However, we have little good evidence of any institution like the *bertsolariak*. And I suppose that recognizing, from the first, my eventual capitulation on this count of co-equal comparison between *los Asturianos* and our friends and co-*norteños* ("northerners"), *los Vascos*, I adopted a tactic of zooming out and enlarging our subject, as an anthropologist is privileged to do, to reflect on the place of improvisation itself in social life and human evolution. I argued first that we are, or evolution has made us, "improvisational animals." From this assertion we moved on to see improvisation, in the "argument of images," as constantly present in communicative interaction in Asturias as elsewhere. And finally we zoomed in and focused on field materials that show the degree to which the Asturian villagers we know engage in such improvisation.

In generalizing about the central place of improvisation in the human condition I have had the advantage of employing Bourdieu's lucubrations on the *habitus* in communicative interaction, as seen in our epigraph. Furthermore, I have also had the benefit of a robust literature in the social sciences. In recent decades, this literature has sought to escape the

---

12. The *espicha* is a gathering that takes place in the *llagar* or cider cellar for the first tasting of the new cider. It is said to be a time for jousting in verse.

static ontologies, constrictions and regulations of human possibility present in the straight-jacket of such Platonic theories as structural functionalism with its tendency to create "cultural dopes" or automatons of structural requirement and cultural constraint creatures, in short, conforming to code! There is now a large body of literature seeking to expand our understanding to the place of contingency in ongoing life. And the whole theme of our conference, it seems to me, shines all the more in the reflected light of that recent interest in contingency and how it is managed, indeed institutionalized, so impressively among Basques in their versifying. For if there is anything that characterizes the situation of the *bertsolariak* it is their regular confrontation with contingency.

The even more impressive thing, of course, is how the Basques have managed to continue to foster and institutionalize these so-human improvisational moments, in the presence of "mechanical reproduction" and the avaricious commercialization of story telling by those for whom business is the bottom line.[13] The Asturians have institutionalized their deep song, the Asturian *"tona'a"* and their tradition of monologue recitation in annual festivals and competitions. And there is sometimes a competitive (in the *bertsolaritza* sense) element to these, but, as I say, there is nothing *as* challengingly improvisational and directly illuminating about the human capacity to deal with contingency.

When we who work in Asturias, for example, ask the question of what has happened to all the oral poetry of village life and all the improvisation that once seemed to come forth so naturally there, or at least came forth to us in our first field trip, we embark on a more general question. This is a question that has been abundantly treated in the literature during the last half century, from Robert Redfield's anthropological work in the 1950s where he spoke about the civilizational process; and an evolutionary passage through levels of dislocation from that closed "human whole" of the Little Community, to its subsequent integration into higher levels of belonging, to the part-whole peasant world and the dominating, expansive cultural and commercial role of cities which acted to absorb these parts into the whole. And we have Peter Lazlett's *The World We Have Lost* in the 1960s and 1970s, Kenneth Boulding's *The Great Transition* in the same period, not to mention Karl Polyani's *The Great Transformation*.

Folklorists, above all perhaps, have been aware of this great transition, transformation or evolution –dislocation really– from endocentric, whole societies to exocentric part-whole societies (or from kinship societies to associational societies) and its effects on folklore, the transformation of folklore into urban legend and its general commercialization. And, of course, the theory globalization has carried us much further in our notions of that whole of which we are a part. Accessing the Internet we find any number of commercial associations peddling back, as it were, to Asturians and other Spaniards their canned minstrel wares – though you can arrange for a real *monologista*, if you wish, who will come to you more or less on cue like a singing telegram. Walter Ong is among those

---

13. See here the abundant work of Jack Zipes (1997 and 2001) seeking to subvert the avalanche of commercially "interested" (that is profit-minded) use of folklore.

who have written most comprehensively on the lost oral world of *noetic* activity un-buttressed and unsupported by all the distracting and dampening technology of "mechanical reproduction," as Benjamin terms it in *The Storyteller*. Ong was referring to the interpersonally isolating and alienating influences of what he calls the "chiropractic" world with an air of disparagement.

I am not, however, going to rehearse in conclusion here all that literature of the "great transformation," transition, lost worlds and new worlds, little communities gone and urbanity and worldliness gained, of *noesis* demeaned and denied. Rather, I am going to stick to the anthropologist's last by returning to that very general theme provoked by *bert-solaritza* improvisation: revitalization and the relation of that process to just one aspect of the "great transformation," namely dislocation! The human condition is such that human relations must constantly be revitalized. I have argued here, perhaps in too *soto voce* a way, that an important kind of vitality and re-vitalization for the *habitus* of everyday life lies in the possibility of being able to realize our improvisational capacities. There is, of course, a satisfaction and a necessity for a rule-making creature in being able to follow rules and regulations. But it can be argued that we realize ourselves most vitally by facing down the recurrent contingencies of the human condition through improvisation and by thus bringing contingency to emergent order. Here too there is an important literature: Victor Turner's work, for example, on the improvisational moments in *communitas* celebrations, in which a revitalizing and transitional shift from the heavy overburden of *societas* is achieved in the presence of wayward *significata*, while still a new revitalized relation to its structures is consequently prepared. Yet here too there is a whole literature on the important place of improvisation in time-out and recreational activities.

However, rather than engaging any further these literatures, let me just end on a simple observation. Our ethnographic work on the improvisational verse in our villages, some of which I reference here, offered us, at the time, compelling moments of real emergent vitality and pleasure. And this was so for all parties concerned. It was a vital, indeed revitalizing, kind of inquiry and a pleasurable part of our fieldwork. Naturally it was, in part, a result of the sly humor. But mostly it was an emergent sense of the interactive vitality of human relationships that it revealed, even in their sardonic, satiric or derisive aspects. In recent years, however, these poetic moments have been in abeyance and mainly because of dislocation. It is a well known argument in folklore studies that, as in real estate dealings, genuine story telling and versifying is always located. It is always integrally a part of the interactive social and cultural situation, the community out of which it emerges and out of which develops its scenarios (See Kroeber 1990). And this is certainly the case with the improvisational verse considered here, which was more or less vis-a-vis, *cara-a-cara* ("face-to-face"), and an integral part of the located interactions of village life.

We know most of the reasons of the ensuing dislocation in modern life. In the several villages of our specific parish locality the main causes have been the increasing availability of work elsewhere in the mines, the migration of young people and their families to the cities, and an increasing catering to transitory summer visitors and to tourism in general. These are all challenges to community. Modernization, urbanization and globalization are all names we use for these processes and for the various forms of dislocation. Various critical theories of the last several centuries, whether utopian socialism (Fourier), political economy socialism (Marx), or the Frankfurt School of critical theory, have all sought community or communitarian revitalization to combat the alienation, distanciation, globalization and the other dislocations and alienations of the individual from his or her own located self, by re-establishing his or her creative personhood in community.

With all that in mind we get a better understanding of the achievement and the vulnerability of the improvisational verse we consider. It must lie in its capacity, amidst all the dislocations of the modern world, to restore locality by recapturing, at once, the primary interpersonal contingency of the human situation *and* its particular possibility of regulation through improvisation. That is something that I think that the Basques have achieved by institutionalizing, in this interesting poetic way, community as interactive locality. Of course, there have been many other attempts to preserve and restore the institution. The world wide web has a collection of sites[14] where you can learn improvisational acting and in Chicago, as in many places in the United States and Europe, a very popular kind of theater put on by the Second City Repertory Theater Group are the "Impros," a late, post-play session of an hour or so where the audience tosses out a theme to be improvised by the group. Yet among the Basques it is not an after thought. Among other efforts, it is a way of at once adapting to modernity while resisting dislocation of community in an increasingly more dislocated world. Of course, there is a downside, a fierce side to that intense commitment to community as we are all aware. But here the impetus to our inquiry and our subject matter has been a very gratifying celebration among the Basques of both the human condition in all its regulated improvised quality, together with a celebration of the pleasures and pains of their life in community! The gratifying experience I have had here in Reno among *bertsolariak* and students of their estimable art gives an anthropological student of culture and the human condition, like me, and especially a student of Asturian culture, much meditative and companionable pleasure.

---

14. For example, see http://www.learnimprov.com.

The Sting in the Tail: The Flourishing and Decline of Improvised Verse in the Mountains of Cantabria[1]

WILLIAM A. CHRISTIAN JR.

The valley of Polaciones (Cantabria) has long been singled out as a fertile ground for verse. The literary historian José María de Cossío has written, "Polaciones is a reliquary of traditions and an open chest in which the remains of traditional poetry that still remain in Spanish show a vitality and are remembered with a precision worthy of note" (1960: 61). In the early 1930s Cossío and Tomás Maza Solano collected many *romances* there, and others have collected more since. Three compact discs have been made with recordings of the valley *romances* and songs.[2] Performers from the valley like the late Pedro Lamadrid and Antonio Morante are well known in the Cantabria. In the late 1960s, when I was preparing my thesis on the adjacent valley of Tudanca, Cossío told me about the skill of women and men in Polaciones in improvising verse, showing me his privately circulated book, *Cantares Cazurros* (1942). This was a fifty-copy edition of some of the best-known verse quips of Polaciones' most famous improviser, Juan José Alonso Morante – Tío Juan José de Callecedo (1822–1901). In the introduction, Cossío gave a blunt assessment of the culture of Polaciones that gave rise to the "monstrous flowering" of Tío Juan José's improvisations (1942: 15–17):

> The valley of Polaciones is located south of this valley of Tudanca, and hence even higher up and more protected by forests, mountain peaks, and fog . . . . In Polaciones all passions and cupidity run wild and are as well known to the honorable people who reject them as to the less scrupulous who practice them. It cannot be said that their habits violate any law, since they know no laws and have never taken any of them into account. The diversions and recreations of the young people are so absolutely brutal and shameless that they seem

1. I gratefully acknowledge the help of José Ramón Rodríguez, Enrique Molleda, Rafael Gómez de Tudanca, José Manuel Pedrosa, Maximiano Trapero, the late José María de Cossío, Angel Molleda, María Rábago, Antonio Morante, Luis Gómez, Rosa García and Aurora Morante.

2. By José Manuel Fraile Gil. See, for example, Fraile Gil (1997). Two more are forthcoming.

to antedate any moral principle, including modesty. A band of youths at the high point of their diversion would be a demonic spectacle were it not that its primitive quality gives their malice the character of absolute ignorance of any moral law.

Cossío was writing shortly after the end of the Civil War, in which in Polaciones, close to the front lines in the Cantabrian Mountains, about fifteen men were executed by the local Republican authorities, and seven when the Franco forces took control. Arcadia this was not. But contrary to what one might expect from Cossío's description, many of Polaciones' inhabitants were well traveled. Some of the men had spent periods in Mexico or Cuba, and those who came back with savings invested it in property in the cities or farmland in Castile. Rents from the tenant farms in southern Palencia were paid in grain, and before the war the valley had a score of water-powered mills in operation and in the postwar period produced considerable black market flour and bread. Herdsmen in the valley complemented their farming by working ox teams in the spring and fall hauling ore from high mountain mines in the valley of Liébana to the coast, or circulating across the north of Spain in the winter as timber jacks and sawyers.

Nevertheless, separated from Palencia to the south and Cantabria to the north by mountain passes, with long winters of relative inactivity, Polaciones was to a certain extent a world to itself with a culture of its own, one in which a particular style of verse improvisation flourished. Its elaboration was doubtless favored by the large number of villages –nine in all– in close contact and competition, for inter-village rivalry was one of the great themes of its verse contests and clashes.

Up until the 1970's, when the population declined sharply, the villages of Polaciones were each small theaters in which every inhabitant was a personality and every day a drama, so that the valley itself was one large theater complex. Especially prior to the Civil War, the high point of the year was carnival, in which male youths composed ribald and irreverent shows based on the year's events, often with elaborate props, and performed them successively in each village.

As in the surrounding valleys, customary or specially prepared verse (especially octosyllable quatrains with assonant abcb endings) dignified or enhanced most important collective occasions. These included the calendrical liturgical cycle in church and out of it – the presentation of a decorated bough at Christmas, door-to-door youth questing for *aguinaldos* ("bonuses") at Epiphany and *marzas* at the spring equinox, special prayers in Holy Week, novenas, mission hymns, and ritual dances to the patron saints. They also marked programmed breaks in the daily routine like the *rondas*, nocturnal serenades, whether amorous or insulting, by boys of girls, evening dances with tambourine or the two string *rabel* or *bandurria*, spinning circles, weddings, the arrival or departure of the bishop, missionaries, or other dignitaries, the inauguration of public works, the autumn descent of cows from upper pastures, and the first mass of a locally-born priest. Or, in the form of *trovas* or carnival *comparsas* ("groups" or "processions"), they celebrated, chronicled, or criticized people or events worth remembering such as unusual courtships, logging expeditions, practical jokes by village youth, sagas of emigration, mishaps of herdsmen, feats of wolf or bear hunts, or unusual moments in the slaughter of pigs. In these longer forms they were like local versions of the *romances* that these mountain people also can recite, whether ancient verses of the Carolingian cycle, or more recent accounts of despicable crimes (Christian 1998: passim.).

For several generations virtually everyone in these valleys has been literate, and for the more valued verses there has a continual back-and-forth from memory storage to written storage. Longer romances or *trovas* might be learned from written copies, the copies discarded, then dictated for someone else to learn, then the new copy discarded. *Pandereta* ("tambourine") dance songs would generally be learned by word of mouth, but then might be written down and kept in a scrapbook. I have seen handwritten scrapbooks of longer *trovas*, Holy Week prayers, healing prayers, and dance songs. Other occasional material is kept on the loose sheets used by those who sang it together.

One can distinguish between three kinds of verses in terms of how they have been preserved: those well codified, that were handed down, memorized, and often kept by at least one depositary in written form for their next reuse; those newly composed, usually in written form, before an expected occasion or after an unexpected event, often memorized and discarded; and those newly composed in the heat of the moment in oral improvisation, rarely transcribed, and passed on, if at all, almost exclusively by oral tradition.

Stimulated by the interest of Maximiano Trapero, I made trips to Polaciones and Tudanca to see what improvised verses people could recall in September 1998 and July 1999. While there are those who still remember medieval *romances*, *trovas* from the beginning of the twentieth century, and carnival *comparsas* from the 1930s, small scraps of improvisation in the memory of a few persons over seventy years old were all that were left of what, in Polaciones especially, was until recently a common and admired skill. The young adults who listened in on my sessions with their grandparents had nothing to offer from their generation. But these scraps, plus rare transcriptions saved by Cossío in the Tudanca Casona library or printed in *Cantares Cazurros*, provide a sense of the occasions in which verse improvisation and verse dueling occurred, the enduring pleasure that the remembered verses retain, and the reasons why the improvisations ultimately tend to be forgotten.

Unlike in Galicia, where there are now regional contests of improvised verses, or the País Vasco (Basque Country), where *bertsolaritza* has become almost an official component of national identity, in Cantabria verse improvisation is a skill that has not been recognized, encouraged, or taught in schools. There have long been regular radio programs of traditional verse and song, and regional exhibitions of *troveros*, but neither of live improvisation. From this survey of Polaciones, then, emerges a picture of a cultural form that flourished and declined without any intervention from political institutions or the media, a kind of natural history of a largely unrecognized species that is now almost extinct.

Improvisational skill in verse requires an intense exposure to verse. Jesús Orta Ruíz, "Indio Naborí," who many consider the Hispanic world's greatest living improviser, has described his saturation with verse growing up in rural Cuba: songs of his family members, RCA Victor records, verse in magazines, broadsides, on the radio, and later in books (See Orta Ruíz 2000). We have seen already how this condition applied as well to Polaciones and in general many of the nuclear settlements of northern Spain: daily life was saturated in verse, most of it memorized, and much of it composed. It was typical of the emigrants of the high valleys to the New World that they composed memories of their homeland in verse and that the verses remembered from their homeland condensed their culture of origin. Nostalgic, elegiac emigrant *trovas*, lovingly figuring the home landscape in quatrains are a recognized poetic form. The emigrant to Mexico, Eloy Vejo Velarde, interlards his memoirs with verses of his home village, Caloca, near Polaciones in Liébana. So do all of the men from this region whose autobiographies Antonio Zavala has recorded and published.

But while almost everyone in these valleys has a repertoire of verses they can recall and sing, a much smaller number has a facility for composing verses, and fewer still are able to improvise verses extemporaneously. The people I talked to in Polaciones quickly made the distinction between those who could *componer* ("compose") or *discurrir* ("think up") verses and those who had the wits –"*tenían cabeza*"– for sudden challenges or quick replies.

Another requirement was the appropriate occasion. We can deduce kinds of occasions from the fragments of improvisations that are still remembered.

Occasions: Subversion of Formality

When I was collecting improvised verses in July 1999, the Bishop of Santander visited the valley of Tudanca. The women of the valley practiced and presented ceremonial verses (*picayos*) adapted by Laura Toribio of Sarceda from those of previous occasions.

On this occasion everything went as planned, but in the past such a visit would have been an opportunity for someone to step out of line and throw in something unexpected, possibly invented on the spot. Laura Toribio's great grandfather, Tío Ladio Toribio (approx. 1835–1933), was a wit immortalized by José María de Pereda in the novel *Peñas Arriba* and is still remembered fondly in the valley. In 1923, when he was eighty-eight years old, a Santander newspaper reported his greeting of the new priest in Sarceda, Angel de Cosío:[3]

Señor Cura de Cosío,	Reverend Pastor De Cosío,
yo le doy la bienvenida:	I welcome you:
y cuente que la primera defunción	You can count on the first demise here
creo que será la mía.	being mine, I think.

A similar greeting by Tío Juan José on the occasion of the pastoral visit of the bishop of Palencia to Polaciones in the late nineteenth century is still widely repeated (Cossío 1942: 35):

---

3. *Diario Montañés*, April 14, 1923: 1. Age at death from Laura Toribio, personal interview, Sarceda, May 11, 2003.

Ilustrísimo señor,	Most illustrious lord,
compadézcase usté al ver,	take pity at the sight
en esta triste montaña,	in these sad mountains
soltera tanta mujer.	of so many women unmarried.

Of course one does not know whether these verses were extemporaneous or prepared, since the occasion itself was not unexpected. Had the clergy replied in verse, we would be sure that they were improvising. On these occasions, however, no verse reply is expected, for the humor is directed not at the clergy, but at the singers or their communities.

Occasions: The Sting in the Tail

In *The Art of Bertsolaritza*, Garzia, Sarasua and Egaña (2001: 103–104) refer to the general strategy of Basque verse improvisation as "the sting in the tail," referring to the crucial last two lines of the verses, which carry the most impact and are thus composed first. Their metaphor, in a rather different sense, also fits one broad strategy of verse improvisation of the Cantabrian Mountains: to sting a potential opponent in his or her most defenseless parts. Many improvised verses among those now remembered arose when a weakness was visible and particularly available.

Aurora Morante (b. Tresabuela 1907) remembers a verse inspired by the sight of two remarkable youths working together (1997): "One had very big ears, and the other hair that was completely white, although he was young. They came down with a cart belonging to Tomasa of Lombraña. Marina, when they arrived, sang":

Los que vienen con el carro	Those coming with the cart
los conocimos de lejos:	we recognized from afar:
a Fidel por las orejas	Fidel by his ears
y a Vicente por el pelo.	and Vicente by his hair.

One day Abel Fernández saw from an upper window that a certain man was leaving his village in Polaciones for the upper pastures. This man had fathered a son with a woman, but had not married her, and this was the day the son was to be married. Abel, who was a cousin of the bride, stepped out on the balcony and sang to him (García Fernández 1999; Morante 1998):

¿Dónde vas, pobre infeliz?	Where are you off to, poor wretch?
¿A dónde vas, Macareno?	Where are your going, Macareno?
Si hoy se casa tu hijo,	Today your son will be wed
tú te vas vaquero al puerto.	and you're off to your cows in the mountains.

The grandfather of Luis Gómez (b. Salceda 1920) hauled ore from the mines in Liébana. One time at Andara, standing between two merchants weighing grain for his oxen, he sang (Gómez Lombraña 1999):

En el monte murió Cristo	Christ died on the cross
en medio de dos ladrones;	between two thieves;
Yo me veo como él	I see myself like him
en algunas ocasiones.	at times.

The challenge to El Conejo ("The Rabbit"), a young man from a prosperous house in Lombraña who had just married one of the poorest girls in Uznayo, points up the importance, in those days, of marriage as an economic strategy (García 1999; Morante 1999):

Al Conejito de Lombraña	For Little Rabbit of Lombraña
Le vengo yo a suplicar:	I have a question:
¿Las riquezas de su padre	Where did the wealth of your father
dónde fueron a parar?	end up?
A casa de Felipón,	In the house of Big Felipe,
el mas pobre del lugar.	the poorest man in town.

Occasions: Stings That Provoke

The improvised attack was a act of public censure which surely stung and marked the delinquent father for life, since the verse is still remembered when he has long been laid to rest. No reply to this verse is recalled, and it is doubtful the father would have been up to it. And the grain merchants with heavy thumbs at Andara may well have not been improvisers. But big-eared Fidel, for instance, was very good-humored and composed carnival *comparsas*, and could have been expected to react, and The Rabbit was directly posed a question. Often stings in the tail call for, hope for, and intend to provoke replies, setting up a verse duel or sparring. In these valleys they call this provocative action to *picar* and the state of mutual arousal a *pique*. These words have close equivalents with similar connotations in English. The relevant definitions of *picar* in Spanish are, in order of their listing in the *Dictionary of the Royal Spanish Academy*: "to goad a bull by a picador;" "to bite or wound with beak [*pico* in Spanish] or mouth by certain animals" (for example, "to peck" or "to sting"); "to spur a horse"; "to anger, vex, irritate another with words or deeds" or in passive usage, "to be offended or angered or enraged because of some offensive or indecorous word or deed" (most directly apropos for our purpose); and "to follow an enemy in retreat, attacking the rearguard of its army" (namely, to harass). The French and Spanish term *pique* is carried into English, where in the *Oxford Concise Dictionary* "pique" is both verb and noun, meaning "to irritate, wound the pride of, ill-feeling, or enmity."

The common denominator of these meanings seems to involve the piercing of a surface with a sharp instrument in a painful place, as with the English verb "prick": the peck of a bird, the sting of a bee, the bite of a spur, the goad of an ox, the harassment of an army's flank. In most of these situations there is an element of surprise: the aggression is unexpected and sudden, or unexpectedly painful. In most of these situations the result is arousal and quick reaction.

Various alternatives are open to those *picado* or piqued by verses who feel impelled to reply. First of all of these is the preemptive strike. When Tío Juan José de Callecedo married for a second time he was elderly and his wife was young. When the neighborhood youth came to hold a charivari he went out and banged a pan along with the best of them. And when a group of friends, including the priest, called on him, he headed off what he thought would be gibes about his potency by singing from inside (Cossío 1942: 37):

Que se vuelvan los señores	Go away you people
que están a mi puerta ahora,	now at my door,
que yo estoy en el pajar	for I'm now in the hayloft
fornicando con la novia.	fornicating with my bride.

Another alternative is disarming humorous distraction. When one José in Polaciones was provoked with a verse about being left by his fiancée, he shrugged it off with enough style to be remembered by Rosa (García Fernández 1999) and by Aurora (Morante 1999) in Uznayo:

Taunt:

Ese que llaman José	That José,
ahora le dejó la novia;	now that his girlfriend's left him,
no sé qué tal le irá	I'm not sure how easily
para poder encontrar otra.	he'll find another.

"They were teasing him, of course." ("*Le picaban, claro*"):

Response:

Lo que sobran son mujeres,	There's a surplus of women,
para cada hombre, tres;	three for every man;
por eso no me apuro,	that's why I'm not worried,
porque hay donde escoger.	there's plenty to choose from.
Mañana voy pa abajo	Tomorrow I'm going
voy por la Peña Bejo;	down in the valley;
si no la encuentro en Tudanca,	If I don't find one in Tudanca,
me voy a Muñorrodero.	I'll go on to Muñorrodero.

The most common response, however, was reprisal.

Luis Gómez's father, Eloy, had two distinctive possessions: a wool cape made for him by his wife and a book of *adivinas* or charms for finding lost objects, given to him by a man in Uznayo. One Sunday on his way to mass, Eloy was challenged in verse by a woman who did not attend mass and whom he considered a witch. In his response, Eloy referred to the town in Burgos, Cernégula, where witches were supposed to gather at night.

Challenge by neighbor woman:

El libro de adivinas	The book of charms
y el capotón que encontrasteis,	and the big cape that you found,
buenos ratos pasarías;	you must have had a good time;
¿dónde los arrebañasteis?	where did you filch them?

Response by Eloy Gómez:

En los profundos infiernos,	In deepest hell
allí existe tu familia;	dwells your family;
allí rebañé el capote	there I stole the cape
y el libro de las adivinas.	and the book of charms.

El capote le encontré	The cape I found
en medio de la carretera	on the highway
y el libro me dió Chosqui,	and Chosqui, the brother-in-law of The Skinflint,
cuñado de La Pesetera.	gave me the book.

En algún rincón de casa	In some corner of the house
encontrarás los pucheros;	you will find the pots [for witch's ointment];
cuando vayas a Cernégula	when you go to Cernégula
que adviertes con los senderos.	don't lose your way.

Aurora Morante (1999) recalled an exchange that earned a neighbor in Uznayo the nickname Patucas, or Little Feet: "There was one fellow here in the town who was very shortsighted –he was Emilia's brother– and he liked to do carpentry. And he was able to make a large wooden chest. People would find out about things right away, and a brother of Aurelia (Oliva's mother), who was bald, very bald (he never took off his beret in order not to show his baldness), sang to him":

Attack on Aurelia's brother:

Eres ciego, ciego rato;	You are blind, stone blind,
eres ciego que no ves:	you cannot see at all;
porque hicistes un armario	because you made a dresser
con los pies en el revés.	with the feet on backwards.

"Right away he replied":
Response by Emilia's brother:

La que se casa con calvo	A woman who marries a baldy
tiene penitencia entera:	has complete penance:
tiene cruz y calvario,	cross, calvary,
y a la noche calavera.	and, at night, a skull.[4]

---

4. This response might well be a non-invented, already known verse, but even in that case the beauty lies in coming up with it at the right moment.

Around 1830 a young woman in Sarceda was taunted at the village dance for being the daughter of a shepherd, a position inferior to a cattle owner; her family handed down her reply and her descendant, Isidro Narváez (b. San Sebastián de Garabandal 1912), having heard it from his great-grandmother, later recalled it (1969):

Soy hija de un ovejero,	I am the daughter of a shepherd,
Cristo también las guardó;	Christ kept them too;
tu padre por las tabernas	your father in taverns
gastó lo que no pagó.	did not pay for what he drank.

The most famous, even paradigmatic, sequence of attack and defense is known to all in Polaciones, because it is a matter of valley pride. The attack took place on alien territory in Camasobres in the valley of Pernía to the south, and the response was a defense of the entire valley. Opinions vary as to whether it took place upon the arrival of Purriegos for a wedding or in a train of hauling wagons (Cossío 1942: 22; Morante 1998): Attack in Camasobres, Nineteenth century:

Asomarse a la ventana,	Look out the window,
abrid puertas y balcones,	open doors and balconies,
veréis ir en ringlera	see lined up
los tochos de Polaciones.	the dolts of Polaciones.

Response [of Tío Juan José, according to Cossío]:

Del valle de Polaciones	From the valley of Polaciones
sacó el rey sus consejeros;	the king chose his advisors;
del condado de Pernía	from the county of Pernía
pastores y borregueros.	his shepherds and sheep drivers.

Weddings

Most of the above examples took place in the public arena, "*la calle*," when the mood or the whim struck someone to let fly. But as in Galicia and Asturias the wedding banquet was a context in which verse dueling was totally expected and avidly awaited. In Polaciones weddings of all but the poorest inhabitants were enveloped in verse: verse when leaving the bride's house, verse directed to members of the wedding procession in the hope of money (later spent on a youth *chocolatada* the next day); verse calling the priest at the church entrance; verse leaving the church; verse demanding tobacco from the groom leaving the church; verse on arrival at the groom's house; and verse from the male youths of the town of the bride or groom or both when they arrived with a decorated hen at the wedding banquet. These verses were fairly standard and prepared in advance. They might be read from rough copies, like that depicted in this photograph of the young men's demand for tobacco in Uznayo in 1982.

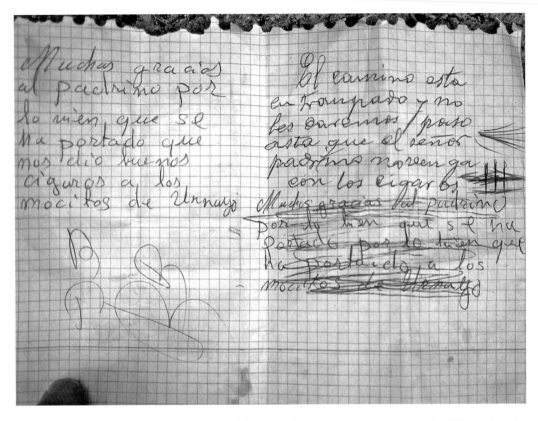

Verses to demand tobacco at a wedding, Polaciones. These quatrains were composed by male youths of Uznayo blocking a wedding procession to demand tobacco from the best man. Written down so the youths could sing them together, they would normally be discarded afterwards. Verses saved by Julio Movellán, Uznayo; photo W. Christian July 17, 1999.

Occasionally, as with the reception of priests and bishops, the verses sung in the protocol portions of the ceremony were sufficiently innovative to be memorable, as with Vicente el Pellejero, from the small village of San Mamés, who formed a youth group of one when he presented the hen at a wedding (García Fernández 1999):

Aquí tienes a la puerta	Here at the door
los mozos de San Mamés.	you have the youths of San Mamés.
La cuadrilla no es muy grande,	The group is not very numerous:
que faltan dos para tres.	for there to be three, you'd need two more.

Interspersed with the formulaic verses, there might be spontaneous replies, from members of the wedding party, described at least from the mid-nineteenth century. But when the youths arrived with their hen, responses and sparring were expected. Once in the banquet there would be verse banter, usually between the groom's party and the bride's party, particularly if they were from different towns. A rare transcription of some of this verse survives from a Polaciones wedding in 1893.[5] Here it appears that the wedding party had a designated female versifier, *la doncella* or damsel, to respond to the youths with the hen; and that the male youth group and the female youth group delivered their verses through spokespersons; those, in Rosa García's words (1999), who had "better heads." The semiofficial wedding versifiers were referred to in the mid-twentieth century as *mayordomas*. The improvisations centered on rivalries and recent humorous encounters between inhabitants of the various towns involved in the wedding. This pattern was common to Polaciones and at least the higher villages in Liébana to the west. It survived in Polaciones into the mid-1990s, by then in restaurants, as wedding feasts were no longer held in private houses. When I observed it in 1969, the verses improvised were a collective enterprise, and many were concocted by skilled older poets, who passed them on orally to the singers. María Rábago (1998) described it succinctly: "In weddings there were two different kinds of verse: some songs that were prepared and were more or less the same in each wedding, and then some improvisers, two or three, women or men, who prepared the words and passed them to the singer, all in good spirit. If the guests were fancy, you were less daring." Two women in Liébana described similar wedding contests, as a thing in the past, to the folklorist José Manuel Pedrosa: "These songs were very spicy [or sharp or provocative – *picantes*]. Older women would say them to the boys, and others say them to us girls, and one in relation to the other. It was the best thing that happened in those days. You had to answer what they were saying, and we didn't know what the women were saying to the boys. And the other women would tell them, 'Now answer them with this!' And the others would say to us, 'Then answer them with that!' And it went on for a couple of hours, the time it took to eat" (Alicia Tejón Martínez and Caridad Campollo, qtd. in Pedrosa 1999: 170–171).[6]

The verse contests could unexpectedly veer and focus on a certain person, not unlike the sudden attacks we have seen on unsuspecting persons "in the street." Tío Juan José was a dangerous person to provoke. At one wedding this verse was sung to him, playing on the word *potra*, referring to his hernia, but which also means "a filly," and with double (or triple) meaning (Cossío 1942: 36):

Attack, Nineteenth century:

A mí me han dicho que tienes	They tell me you have
jaca, mula, yegua y potra,	a jennet, a mule, a mare, and a filly,
y que andabas a caballo	and when you go riding
cuándo en una, cuándo en otra.	you change from one to another.

---

5. It is in the Casona of Tudanca, and is partially transcribed in Christian (2000: 412–413), where the date is incorrectly given as 1892. Rosa García is the niece of the groom.

6. See also description in López Linage (1978: 260), who cites a Lebaniego who asserts these verses occurred especially in the weddings of the better off.

Response of tío Juan José:

La tu mujer me brindó	Your wife invited me
a comer el otro día,	to eat the other day;
ella te podrá decir,	she can tell you
la recua que yo traía.	the drove that I was driving.

The pleasure and piquancy of the verse debates were heightened when the bride and groom or the guests were from different villages, or even better, from different valleys, for then to the inevitable sexual innuendos could be added collective insults, sexual or otherwise, to entire villages or valleys, raising the stakes of the contest.

A number of men I spoke to in the senior citizens' center, Calle Alta, Santander in 1998 recalled the following quatrain was sung by Purriegos against Tudancos in a mixed wedding:

Attack:

De la Virgen de la Luz	We are all very devoted
todos somos muy devotos,	to the Virgin of the Light [a local shrine],
pero más son los tudancos	but the Tudancos are even more so
de morcillas y boronos.	to blood sausage and cornbread.

At a wedding in the Polaciones town of Puente-Pumar, about 1948, the three cooks or *mayordomas* sang the following to a wedding guest from Liébana, whose fiancée had decamped after all the wedding banns had been read:

Attack by mayordomas:

Fuiste novia quince días	You were a bride for fifteen days,
y pusiste los galones:	and you put on the badges;
vienes a correr los toros	now you come to run the bulls
al Valle de Polaciones.	in the valley of Polaciones.

The woman came weeping to Quintana (Antonio Morante), who knew that among the *mayordomas* was an unmarried mother and thought up this reply for the Lebaniega:

Response composed by Quintana:

Fuisteis monjas sin convento,	You were nuns without a convent,
casaditas sin marido,	spouses without husbands,
doncellitas sin honor,	damsels without honor,
y escucha lo que te digo.	and listen to what I say.

Quintana told me (Morante 1998), "that shut the women up; they didn't respond to that."

As in Galicia and the Basque Country, verse dueling could be the occasion for bets. Quintana (Morante 1998) recalled that after the wedding of the son of Marcos de Callecedo about 1941, the male youths of Uznayo and Tresabuela bet two *cántaros* ("pitchers") of wine and two bottles of cognac, and sang back and forth until four in the morning. Fragments of one-on-one competitions in taverns are recalled by older people in Rionansa and in Liébana. But as far as we know, these competitions were neither formalized nor publicized (Christian 2000: 407).[7] In his *Guipuzcoaco dantza gogoangarrien condaira edo historia, beren soñu zar eta itz neurtu edo versoaquin* (1824), Juan Ignacio de Iztueta described similar verse bets in Gipuzkoa, but it appears that even then the contests had more rules than in Cantabria: "The versifying is in octaves, or other measures, improvised and face to face. There are bets in money or kind, and the number of improvisers may be one against one, two against two, and four against four. The improvisers are normally shepherds, farmers, or charcoalers, all of them illiterate" (Iztueta 1824: XVII, 165, summarized in Estornés Zubizarreta 1988: 168).

The Decline of Verse Improvisation

The verse improvisations of Cantabria are at best dormant. Women and men skilled at creating them are still alive, but the context that produced them is virtually extinct. That context was a world in which the lives of one's neighbors were the chief, virtually the only, entertainment; a world in which personalities and eccentricities were savored. To some of their neighbors in adjacent valleys the attacks on differences in appearance, births out of wedlock, poverty, and impotence seemed uncouth and brutal. But running through the recollections of the older men and women I talked to were phrases like, "nobody was offended," "they took it in good humor," "it was part of the fun," or "we all looked forward to it." In 1942 Cossío wrote that the people of Polaciones knew no moral laws. One could also say that they had been able to maintain their own laws, were different measures for what could be said and done and what was considered an offense. Now, with grandchildren of these people who may be urban lawyers, one thinks twice about which verses one might want to print.

But perhaps the essential difference between the verses here and those of the present-day verse competitions in the Basque Country, Galicia and Murcia, is that without an extensive gloss and an explanation of context, the verses and their humor can mean little to outsiders. Every verse in Cossío's collection of Tío Juan José requires a prose prologue. The verses tend to include humorous nicknames that evoke known personalities and often require knowledge of kin relations. They are rarely "poetic" or metaphoric and are totally un-"literary." In these valleys it was not the words, not the verse form, not the literature, that counted. What counted instead were the personalities and the human relations that the words described and affected. With an exclusively local audience, these competitions had the luxury of being able to include specific people, local places, and local mini-events. They were not spoken into microphones, broadcast, videotaped or, with the excep-

---

7. Xavier Payá Ruiz (2003) reports this verse sung by his grandmother, María Inés Braceras Vadillo, b. April 17, 1916, in San Miguel de Aguayo (Campóo): "A cantar cantares nuevos /nadie me puede ganar / porque tengo un saco lleno / y un arca sin empezar."

tion of Cossío's bootleg edition, published, and so did not have to be depersonalized, generalized, diluted or politically-corrected for distant audiences.

By the same token their lifespan rarely extended beyond the memories of those who knew the persons involved. For the younger people present when Rosa, Aurora, Quintana and Luis recounted these verses, most of the quatrains were just as new as they were to me and required just as much explanation to be understood. Here we see the difference, not only with the public competition verses of the *bertsolariak* and the *regueifas*, but also with the ancient *romances*. The *romances* in these valleys are almost exclusively maintained in memory, yet they have survived virtually unscathed for centuries. This survival must be precisely due to the fact that they are self-sufficient and do not depend on local referents for their interest and attraction. They therefore do not have a built-in expiration date, unlike most of the *trovas*, *comparsas*, and improvised verse.

Another aspect of improvised verse that leads it to expire quickly is timing. Repeatedly, Aurora, Luis or Rosa would add phrases like, "he answered right away, in a flash." Often these verses are entertaining precisely because they are improvised. As verses composed, not invented on the spot, some of them would be rather ordinary. So part of what is going on in the recounting is the memory, not just of the verse, but also of its circumstance and delivery ("not bad for a sixteen-year-old"), and this knowledge too has an expiration date.

All of these are reasons for the evanescence of particular verses, but not for the current dormancy of the form and the practice. The younger people who listened in had no improvised verses from their generations to report for reasons that are social and economic, which must include the emptying out of the countryside and alternative means of entertainment, whether easier access to the city or the television in the kitchen. There are no youth groups. With few actors, and those few less in the street, these villages are no longer, or much less than they used to be, stages, and their inhabitants in the forty years I have known them, have gone from being larger-than-life personages to being more anonymous, everyday, citizens in a wider world.

Improvised Invective in Hispano-Arabic Poetry and Ibn Quzmān's "Zajal 87" (When Blond Meets Blonde)

JAMES T. MONROE

Arabic literature provides us with an unbroken, multisecular tradition of invective poetry known as *hijā'*. This tradition begins with the earliest poetry that has come down to us from pre-Islamic times, all of it both oral and formulaic (Monroe 1972; Zwettler 1978),[1] and it continues into the Umayyad period, at which time the poets al-Farazdaq and Jarīr (both died in 110/728) engaged in an extended poetic slanging-match, the details of which were compiled into a famous collection known as *al-Naqā'iḍ* /"poems that contradict one another"/. In this tradition, everything pertaining to the opponent was fair game. In particular, his womenfolk were often the target of ridicule. Thus, on many occasions Jarīr made disparaging sexual remarks about Ji'tin, the sister of al-Farazdaq, accusing her (without foundation, according to the commentators) of having been the victim of a gang rape. Here is one example of Jarīr's treatment of this subject:

> Your betrayal of Zubayr at Minà summed you up entirely, along with the rape of Ji'tin at Ḏāt Ḥarmala.
>
> Farazdaq spent the night looking out for himself, while Ji'tin's arse was being used like a highway.
>
> Where were those you imagined would not arrive to rape Ji'tin, O son of an abscessed mother?
>
> You surrendered Ji'tin, when she was dragged off by the foot, and the Minqarī pierced her with his skewer.
>
> Her arse sank to the ground as she cried out: "Help, Mujaši'!" while the crack of her hole squinted like an eye (Arabic text in Bevan 1905, I: 211–231, ll. 25–29).[2]

---

1. Not only was poetry oral-formulaic in this early period of Arabic literature, but in a recent and important study, the oral-formulaic nature of the Qur'ān has finally been brought out of the closet too (Dundes 2003).

2. The above, and all subsequent translations, are mine, unless otherwise indicated.

This tradition of invective poetry was introduced by the Arabs to al-Andalus, and references to it survive from the early period. It was largely composed in Classical Arabic, and following the Classical system of prosody. For example, the chronicler of the Andalusī Umayyads, Ibn Ḥayyān (376/987–467/1075), informs us that in the year 312/925, the Caliph of Córdoba ʿAbd al-Raḥmān III (r. 299/912–350/961) defeated and captured the rebel lord of Lorca, named ʿAbd al-Raḥmān ibn Waḍḍāḥ, whom the Caliph brought back with him as a hostage to Córdoba. The rebel was famous for the length of his beard, and for a large dog he brought with him on a chain, by which it was rumored that he used to have his enemies devoured. A Cordovan satirist said about him:

> Ibn Waḍḍāḥ came to Córdoba by daylight with his dog in front of him, but his dog can do us no harm;

> He came with his beard dragging along the ground, so that at times you could see him, and at times he was hidden within its midst.

> Seventy beards a day could emerge from what his alone produces, nor would they be short ones.

> In it, there is a load of wool and hair so abundant that, if it were to be woven, it would clothe the poor (Arabic text in Ibn Ḥayyān 1979: 196–197).

Very interestingly, after these four lines of invective, the chronicler ceases to quote any further from the poem, stating "what follows is too indecent to mention." Similarly, we are told about the Andalusī poet Ibn Ṣāra al-Šantarīnī (d. 517/1123) that he specialized in satirizing the notables of his time by writing love poems to their wives. Ibn Bassām (d. 541/1147), the compiler of Ibn Ṣāra's work puts it thusly:

> [Ibn Ṣāra al-Šantarīnī] expressed his impassioned love for well-guarded females, exposed them to notoriety, and used them as barbs which he hurled, in the form of insults concocted against the grandees of his time, with which he stigmatized the pride of their reputations, leaving them as a warning example to their descendants . . . . I have seen many pieces by him on *hijāʾ*, so numerous that they exceed the number of pebbles on the desert plain for, in [that genre], his arrow is accurate and his judgment effective. But I have [generally] kept [such poems] to myself and ignored them –even if I have very infrequently alluded to them, if only so that you may take note and be informed– for had I deemed it permissible for part of what he wrote in this genre to be recorded in this book [*Kitāb al-Daḥīra*], you would have realized that such of his compositions are an entirely covert, indirect insult and a defamatory thunderbolt. I have included a vast amount of [such poems], composed by him and by a large group [of other poets], in my other book entitled *Daḥīrat al-Daḥīra* [which has not survived], (Arabic text in Ibn Bassām 1978, II: 834–835).

If we turn from the Classical to the Andalusī Colloquial tradition, we once more find Ibn Ḥayyān reporting that, in the year 299/912, ʿAbd al-Raḥmān III conquered the fortresses of the Alpujarras in Granada, which were supporting the insurrection of the famous rebel 'Umar ibn Ḥafṣūn (d. 304/917). The chronicler proceeds to narrate the following incident that took place during the campaign:

> All the fortresses of the Alpujarras were also conquered, since they had joined forces with Ibn Ḥafṣūn, but ['Abd al-Raḥmān III] al-Nāṣir li-Dīn Allāh reduced them to submission during that campaign of his, for the signs of [divine] approval were clear, so that both his warlike and peaceful activities toward them were goodly and successful. One of the insolent fools in those haughty fortresses showered down blame and scorn upon him, saying: "*Ruddū ruddū aban ummuh fī fummuh*" ["Cast down, cast down, the son of his mother, onto his mouth"], but a muleteer in charge of the baggage who was in the ranks near [the Caliph], refuted [the fool, answering]: "*Wa-llāh lā naruddu-hā 'illā bi-rās aban ḥafṣūn fī ḥukmuh*" ["By God, we will not cast it (i.e., 'his mouth') down, save when the head of Ibn Ḥafṣūn is in his power"], (Arabic text in Ibn Ḥayyān 1979: 64).

This passage contains the earliest known poetic text in Colloquial Andalusī Arabic, and that text constitutes a satirical exchange. Whether it is also a proto-*zajal*, as has been claimed (Corriente 1989: 22), is a matter about which I have serious reservations. But this does lead us to the question of whether the colloquial *zajal*, known to us largely from the clearly literate poetry of Ibn Quzmān (d. 555/1160), could have (1) had an earlier oral, and largely undocumented stage, and (2) whether that stage may have served as a vehicle for invective, as it often did later on.

As far as the first question is concerned, Ibn Quzmān himself provides an answer in the prologue to his *Dīwān*, in which he expresses unusual scorn for the literary achievements of his immediate predecessors, despite the fact that these precursors were held in great esteem by the public of his time. Among the various defects of the poets he inveighs against, was one with which Ibn Quzmān was deeply concerned: They used occasional classical inflexions (*i'rāb*) in their colloquial poems, a practice that he proudly claims to have banned from his own production: "I stripped [the *zajal*] of the classical inflexions [used by my predecessors] for [classical inflexions] are the ugliest feature to appear in a *zajal*, and more unpleasant than the arrival of death (Corriente 1995: 17)." To this he adds: "The usage of colloquial wording within the classically inflected diction of *qaṣīdas* and *muwaššaḥs* is no uglier than the usage of classical inflexions in the *zajal* (Corriente 1995: 17)." As I have argued elsewhere, insofar as the use of *i'rāb* is viewed as a lapse from perfection, it is a clear indication that such poets were literate; that their lapses were literate ones and, therefore, that their poetry was not the product of oral composition (Monroe 1988 [*Irāb*], 1989). In contrast, truly illiterate poets could not have known the subtleties of literate, classical inflexions and, thus, could never have used them. Moreover, since Ibn Quzmān insists that the true, pure, and original *zajal* did not make use of *i'rāb*, we must conclude that that true, pure, and original *zajal* (today lost to us), must have been the product of an illiterate and oral milieu. As we now know, the colloquial *zajal* was a very ancient Andalusī genre; it was popular in origin and, at the outset, it flourished within a purely oral context. At some point, it began to attract the attention of learned poets who began to imitate it with greater or lesser success. One of these poets was Ibn Quzmān, whose poetry is practically all that is left to us of the tradition.

As to whether the early *zajal* served as a vehicle for invective, we can only state that, before the appearance of Ibn Quzmān, who has left us a *dīwān* containing 149 surviving *zajals* (a few pages of the manuscript have been lost), most of which are covertly satirical, we have little by which to go. Nonetheless, there are some early references to the *zajal* that suggest its obscene and scurrilous nature. For example, we have a copy, finished by a Mozarabic monk named Vicente, on Tuesday, October 17, 1046, of a manuscript entitled *Kitāb ʿAbd al-Malik al-Usquf* /"The Book of Bishop ʿAbd al-Malik'"/. A passage in this work states:

> It is not permitted for clergymen to attend performances or *zajals* in weddings and drinking parties; but rather, they must leave before the appearance of such musical performances and dancers, and withdraw from them (Arabic text in Monroe 1989: 45–46).

What was valid for Christians was just as valid for Muslims for, in his treatise on the regulation of markets (*ḥisba*), the inspector Ibn ʿAbd al-Raʾūf (*fl. ca.* 319/931) states:

> Those who go about the markets singing *zajals*, *azyād* [?], and other types [of song] are forbidden to do so when [people] are being summoned to Holy War, or when they are being exhorted to go to the Ḥijāz [in pilgrimage]. But [if] they exhort people to participate [in the above enterprises] in a seemly manner, there is no harm in it (Arabic text in Monroe 1989: 46–47).

If the singing of scurrilous songs in Colloquial Arabic offended Muslims as well as Christians, it was also a matter of great concern to Hispano-Jewish scholars for, in a passage on the subject, Moses Maimonides (529/1135–600/1204) comments on the scurrilousness of strophic songs in Arabic, Hebrew, and Romance:

> Know that poems composed in any language whatsoever, are only valued for their content, and that they follow the classifications of speech that we have established. I have explained this, even though it is self-evident, only because I have observed that, when certain religious scholars and learned men of our nation attend a wine party, a wedding, or the like, and someone begins to sing in Arabic, even though the subject of the poem is praise of courage or generosity, which belongs to the category of what is commendable, or praise of wine, they disapprove of it from every possible angle, nor do they consider listening to it to be permissible, whereas if the singer sings a *muwaššaḥ*[3] in Hebrew, it meets with neither disapproval nor disdain, even though such speech may contain what is forbidden or reprehensi-

---

3. The Arabic language was, and still is, manifested in both a classical and a colloquial form. The strophic form of poetry couched almost entirely in Classical Arabic (with the sole exception of its colloquial *ḫarja*) was the *muwaššaḥ*, whereas the strophic form couched entirely in Colloquial Arabic was the *zajal*. Insofar as Hebrew was, until very recently, an exclusively liturgical and literary, rather than a spoken language, it lacked a colloquial form, as a result of which, Hebrew writers made no distinction between the two literary forms under consideration, and referred to either, be they *muwaššaḥs* or *zajals*, with the same term, namely *muwaššaḥ*. The above passage is, thus, fully applicable to the *zajal*, the strophic form of which does exist in Hebrew.

ble. This is downright ignorance, for speech is not forbidden, permitted, recommended, or reproved, nor is its utterance commanded, on the basis of its language, but on the basis of its content instead. Thus, if the poem's subject is a virtue, its utterance is required, regardless of its language, whereas if its subject is a vice, it must be shunned, regardless of its language. Indeed, there is more to the matter, in my opinion, for if there are two *muwaššaḥs* on the same subject, namely one that arouses and praises the instinct of lust, and encourages the soul to [practice] it (despite the fact that [lust] is a vice, so that [the poem] will belong to the category of defect in character, as is explained by our words in Chapter Four), and if one of these two *muwaššaḥs* is in Hebrew, and the other is either in Arabic or is in Romance, why then, listening to, and uttering the one in Hebrew is the most reprehensible thing one can do in the eyes of the Holy Law, because of the excellence of the [Hebrew] language, for it is inappropriate to employ [Hebrew] in what is not excellent, especially if to this is added the use of a verse of the *Torah* or of the *Song of Songs* on the same subject, for then [the poem] departs from the category of the reprehensible, only to enter that of the forbidden and the prohibited, since the Holy Law itself forbids prophetic discourse from being applied to types of songs about vices and unworthy acts (Judeo-Arabic text in Monroe 1988–1989: 19).

From this passage we may infer that Maimonides too, attests to the existence of an obscene genre of poetry composed in Colloquial Andalusī Arabic, in Hebrew, and in Hispano-Romance.

Be that as it may, when we come to a period of greater documentation, as exemplified by the poetry of Ibn Quzmān, a curious feature stands out: The vast majority of Ibn Quzmān's *zajal*s are, ostensibly, panegyrical in nature, while, at the same time, the poet ridicules his patrons by placing his praise in the mouth of a literary persona who is presented as a ritual clown or buffoon. By so doing, the poet manages to be devastating in his criticism of society, while not offending the sensibility of his more sensitive patrons and critics. I tend to think that, in this respect, Ibn Quzmān represents a literate, as opposed to an oral, approach to satire. Whereas earlier, oral invective had been entirely direct in its approach, this new kind of invective, belonging to a written tradition, was more subtle and circumspect. We have thus gone full circle, from a direct, to an indirect, and even ironic form of satire. In what follows, let us explore a typical *zajal* by Ibn Quzmān in detail, to illustrate this point.

Like many other poems by Ibn Quzmān, his "*Zajal 87*" is a complex, artfully constructed masterpiece containing far deeper levels of meaning than are, on first inspection, apparent. It begins by telling us about an encounter between the poet and a married Berber woman, whom he attempts to seduce. She, however, manages to trick the poet by luring him to her neighborhood, where he is beaten and humilated by its inhabitants. At its end, the poem proceeds to praise an unidentified Andalusī notable. On a secondary level, the poem addresses a few issues that were crucial to medieval Andalusīs, who, at the time during which the poet was writing, were ruled by the Almoravids, a Berber dynasty from North Africa whom they despised for its lack of culture, but without whose presence in al-Andalus, they could not have defended themselves against the military onslaughts proceeding from the Christian North. In what follows, I will discuss the poem in light of the above remarks, in order to facilitate which, an edition and English translation of the Arabic text are first provided.

Edition and Translation:

0. kunnā ṣibyān wa-dārat al-aḥwāl
    wa-ltaḥaynā wa-ṣirnā ḍāba rijāl

    First we were boys but, as years went by,
    we grew beards, and have now become men.

1. kabarat laḥyatī fa-ṣirtu zaġal
    qisṭī miktāf ṣaḥīḥ qawī ka-l-baġal
    fī suwayʿah naʿmal lak alfi šuġal
    wa-law annuh rafʿ aṣ-ṣuḫū,r aṭ-ṭiqāl

    My beard grew, and I became a young brave;
    sturdy, broad-shouldered, healthy, strong as a mule.
    In an instant I could perform a thousand chores for you,
    to the point of lifting heavy stones.

2. ʿajabat-nī nufaysatī ʾayyām
    ḥattà kassartu šaʿrī fà l-hammām
    wa-ʿtadal min warā wa-min quddām
    wa-ḍaraytu wa-jā-nī minnu jalāl

    I was so charmed with my darling self at the time,
    that I had my hair curled at the public baths,
    so that it looked even, behind and in front:
    I made a habit of doing so, and became famous for it.

3. w-anā ʾan-nassī munḏu kunt labbās
    ṭiyābī lāḏ ʿalà baṭāyin lās
    wa-ġafāyir milāḥ ʿalà ʾajnās
    wa-ʿamāyim dabīq tasāwī māl

    As for me, ever since I became a dandy,
    I wore silken robes over satin linings,
    and handsome hooded cloaks of different kinds,
    as well as costly turbans from Dabīq.[4]

4. wa-nidaʿ man yuqūl safīh aw rašīd
    innamā namši jīd wa-nukul jīd
    wa-nahāran jadīd wa-rizqan jadīd
    wa-min al-yawm ilà ġadā ʾāmāl

    I ignored all advice, be it foolish or wise;
    I just lived well, and ate well:
    Every new day brought me a new dish,
    and hopes that tomorrow would be as good as today.

5. wa-kān akrayt duwayra min insān
    bi-rubāʿī sakantu fī-hā zamān
    ṯumma qāl-lī nirīd ṯalāṯ aṯmān
    wa-nizīduh wa-law ṭalab miṯqāl

    I once rented a charming house from a certain man,
    for a quarter *miṯqāl*,[5] and dwelt in it for a time,
    then he declared: "I want three-eighths of a *miṯqāl*."
    Had he demanded a whole *miṯqāl*, I would have paid it.

6. inna fī-hā ḥanīya amām as-sarīr
    wa-ʿuqāban malīḥ bi-janb al-bīr
    wa-quṣaybah ʿalay-hā bāban kabīr
    takšaf al-faḥṣ min ṯalāṯ amyāl

    In it, there was an alcove in front of the bed,
    a handsome winch at the rim of the well,
    and a belvedere with a large door,
    from which to admire the view for three miles around.

7. wa-r-rabaḍ lā šuyūḥ wa-lā ḥujāj
    wa-ʾarāmil milāḥ bi-lā ʾazwāj
    wa-yijū-nī ṭūl an-nahār ʿan ḥawāj
    wa-ašyātan las yanbaġī ʾan tuqāl

    No religious scholars, and no pilgrims in that neighborhood!
    Just pretty widows without husbands,
    who came to me all day long for certain needs of theirs,
    and for other matters that shall go unmentioned.

---

4. An unidentified location in the outskirts of Damietta, on the Nile delta, that is no longer in existence, but that was, in medieval times, famous for its luxurious textiles (Wiet 1983).

5. A gold coin introduced by the Almoravids (Miles 1983).

8. innamā jā-nī ḏā l̥ḫabar la-ḏikar
   l-ajli mā qultuh lak min amri ṣ-ṣiġar
   wa-niṣaf lak fī ḏā l-ma'ānī ḫabar
   lā ġinā an tasma'uh qaṣur aw ṭāl

The following incident comes to mind,
only because of what I've confided about my youth,
so I'll tell you an anecdote on the subject,
which you shall hear, be it long or short:

9. kuntu wāqif bi-bābī ba'da l-'aṣar
   iḏ ra'ayt šaḫsan qad ḫaṭar wa-naẓar
   aššu kān hāḏāk šamsi kān aw qamar
   aw ḫumār kān aw ḥaqqi aw šuġal bāl

One afternoon, I was loitering at my door,
when I saw someone look at me, while passing by.
What was that? A sun or a moon?
Was it a drunkard's high, a reality, or a hallucination?

10. [raqbatan] šaṭṭah bayḍa miṯla l-quṭūn
    'aynan akḥal wa-ḥājiban maqrūn
    BON kulli l-milāḥ BON [BON] BON
    mā 'aẓunn an yurà la-hā [min] miṯāl

I beheld a slender neck, white as cotton;
a collyrium-dark eye, and an eyebrow joined to its twin.[6]
Good! Every kind of beauty! Good! Good! Good!
I don't believe anyone like her will ever be found.

11. wa-fī ḥadday-hā wardatan ka-l-ḥayā
    al-'ibādah dūn an tarā-hā riyā
    wa-sawālif turà šu'ā' al-ḍiyā
    sitta ṭal'ah bayn al-ridā wa-l-hilāl

On her cheeks lay roses like blushing modesty.
Without having seen her, Piety is mere Hypocrisy,
while her braids seemed like rays of light:
Six of them peeped out between her mantle and its pin.

12. [wa]-ḍuraysāt ka-'anna-hā l̥kāfūr
    wa-šufayfāt ka-'anna-hā z-za'rūr
    immā jinnīya kānat immā ḥūr
    wa-ḥalwah wa-kulli siḥran ḥalāl

She had charming little teeth, white as camphor,
and delightful little lips, red as hawthorn berries;
she was either a female jinni, or a houri;
she was Sweetness itself, and every kind of white magic.

13. qāl̥ī qalbī tamdī tarà ayn tadḫul
    wa-ta'ālaj fa-'immā 'an taḥṣul
    [aw] ta'arbaḍ fa-tuqtal aw taqtul
    qiṣṣatayn hī 'immā halāk aw wiṣāl

My heart told me: "Go and see where she enters,
and make a pass at her; you must either win her,
or quarrel; you must either be slain by her, or slay her.
You have only two alternatives: death or a love union."

14. qultu sittī nukūn ġulāmak qaṭ
    hāḏā 'unqī ḥud al-ḥabal wa-rbaṭ
    mawlatī kam tizan wa-kam taḫbaṭā
    rūḥī yazhaq fī 'amri hāḏā d-dalāl

I said: "Milady, I'll be your slave forever!
Here is my neck; take a rope and tie it.
How much will you pay for me? And beat me how much?
My soul is perishing on account of your coquetry."

15. qālat aḥsant akṯar niḥibbak anā
    lassu 'an kulli-mā ḏakarta ġinā
    qultu jīd hū fa-'ajjal amši bi-nā
    qālat aṣbar yabqà lak an taḥtāl

She replied: "Well spoken! I love you even more!
Everything you've mentioned must take place."
I answered: "That's great! Hurry then! Let's get it on!"
She responded: "Be patient! You must act with stealth!

16. zawjī ḫārij ba'd al-'išā la-l-mazad
    jī wa-lākin iyyāk yamayyaz-ka ḥad
    wa-lbas aṭmār wa-jubba w-ašmā tajad
    wa-kalāmak ġayyar ma'a l-aškāl

After the evening hour, my husband goes to Qur'ān school.
Come to me then, but beware lest anyone recognize you.
Wear rags, a hooded robe, whatever you can find,
and modify your speech, along with your appearance."

17. aš nuqūl lak baqayt ka-ḏā mabhūt
    w-aḥaḏ-nī faza' bi-ḥāl man yamūt

What can I say? I just remained tongue-tied;
I was gripped by terror, like a dying man,

---

6. The unibrow, or "Frida Kahlo look," was considered a sign of great beauty by medieval Arabs.

wa-qafaz qalbī qafza miṯla l-ḥūt wa-ḍarab bi-l-jināḥ bi-ḥāl PARṬĀL	my heart flip-flopped like a fish, and beat its wings like a sparrow.

18. wa-rajaʿ jismī kullu šuʿlat nār
wa-bi-ḥāl man ġaṭas fī māʾan ḥār
w-aš fī ḏā min ʿaẓīm lamma naṣfārā
law rajaʿ r‚ūḥī lī las kin-nasʾāl

My entire body turned into a firebrand;
it felt like one who plunges into hot water.
Is it so surprising that I turned pale?
I'd not have asked, had I had my wits about me.

19. qultu yā layta šiʿrī ʾaš naʿmalā
qumtu ʿammamtu rāsī bi-l-ḥanbal
wa-fataltuh bi-yaddī wa-ʿtadal
šay ʿalà šay šuklat banī zirwāl

I said: "If only I knew what to do."
I arose and wrapped my head in the rug on the bench,
which I coiled in my hand, till it was even,
section by section, after the fashion of the Banī Zirwāl.[7]

20. jāt la-ʿamrī malīḥ šayyan ʿaẓīm
law-lā mā tamma kullu fà t-taʿmīm
aġāṯ allāh wa-faḍla ʿan talṯīm
aš-šubaykah baš yuṣṭād as-SARDĀL

The bench-rug would have looked very elegant, indeed,
had I not used it all up in making my turban.
God help me! In order to fashion a veil as well,
I used the little net for catching sardines.

21. mandīl al-ḫubzi ṣār ʿalayyà qaṣīr
zidtu fīh maqṭaʿan jadīd min ḥaṣīr
wa-baqà lī ʿan al-awātiq katīr
wa-ḥarazt ar-rašam wa-jā fà š-šimāl

The bread-cloth proved to be far too short for me,
so I attached a piece of fresh rush matting to it,
but since too much of that was left over at my shoulders,
I sewed up the edge, so that it draped over my left.

22. ṯumma wallayt ḫārij li-bāb az-zuqāq
bi-dīk aṭ-ṭalʿah wa-ṭ-ṭiyāb ar-riqāq
law tarà-nī ḥāfi bi-lā ʾaqrāq
wa-r-rakīzah fī yad fī ʿawḍ agzāl

Then I went out to the gate of the alley,
dressed in that get up, and those elegant clothes.
If only you could have seen me barefoot, *sans* cork sandals,
with a grape-stake in my hand, instead of a pike,

23. ka-ṭ-ṭubayyab matà s-sijāj malbūs
wa-s-salīḥah li-ʿunqī ʿan burnūs
subḥān allāh! mā znam-kum al-andalūs!
taḍrabū l-būˌq wa-tatnazū bi-r-rijāl

Dressed like a folk doctor; a healer of wounds,
wearing a fleece around my neck by way of a burnoose!
Glory to God! How cunning you are, people of al-Andalus:
You blow the trumpet to make a mockery of men!

24. fī suwayʿah ḥaṣal lī ʿinda n-nās
min šamātah wa-ʿuqūbah akdās
qawm yuqūlū ḫruj tarà VEN VERÁS
w-uḫar yaḍrabū lī ba-l-injihāl

All at once, I suffered, at the hands of those people,
insults and torments, by the heap.
Some were saying: "Come out and see! Come out and see!"
While others beat their clay castanets in my face!

25. qultu jīd hū as-sāʿa ṣirnā milāḥ
lā ʿašīqah wa-lā ʿuqūlan ṣiḥāḥ
laʿan allāh man yaḫtayal ḏā l-muzāḥ
aḥnā nabqà li-ḏulli hawlā [s-sifāl]

I said: "This is great! Now we're in fine shape!
We've won no lady-friend, and have no sound mind left!
God curse the one who thought up this jest!
Here I'm left to be humiliated by this rabble!"

26. ṯumma ʾinnī huḏḏibtu ḏā l-aḫbār
wa-taraktu ṣ-ṣibā wa-l-istihtār
wa-btadayt min jadīd li-madḥ al-kibār
wa-naẓamtu l-jawāhir istirsāl

Then I mended my ways:
I gave up youthful folly and my wanton behavior,
and turned over a new leaf, in order to praise magnates,
fluently stringing the pearls of poetry together.

---

7. The manuscript (Gunzburg 1896: fol. 93), reads *banī zirbāl*, emended in Corriente (1989: 303, n. 8), where that author cites Ibn Ḥazm (1948: 463), to the effect that members of the Berber Banī Zirwāl tribe existed in al-Andalus.

27. wa-ḍamamt ad-dawā w-aḥaḍt al-qalam
    wa-jamaʿt aṯ-ṯanā wa-suqt al-ḥikam
    wa-nazal yaddī fà l-waraq wa-raqam
    wa- tamamtu wa-jā ʿamal ʿammāl

I grasped the inkwell; I seized the pen:
I gathered praise; I produced aphorisms,
my hand hit the page, and embroidered it;
I finished my poem, which proved to be a masterpiece!

28. fa-waṣaftu l-jalāl baytan bayt
    wa-l-maʿālī ʿalà ḍurūb sammayt
    wa-madaḥtu fa-kulli mā rawwayt
    ḥarajat lī maḥāsinu ʾirtijāl

I described majesty, strophe by strophe,
and extolled lofty virtues, in all their varieties,
as well as praising them, while the beauty of all
that I recited was produced by improvisation.

29. yā samāʾ al-jalāla yā zuhrī
    ya sanā-hā wa-l-kawbab ad-durrī
    lak makārim miṯla n-nujūm tasrī
    wa-ʾayādīk habbat ṣabā wa-šamāl

O heaven of excellence; O Zuhrī;
O heaven's brilliance, and its shining asterism,
yours are virtues that travel by night, like stars,
while your favors blow like the East and North winds.

30. wa-ʾiḍā hamma bi-l-faḍāyil siwāk
    wa-ʾarādū ʾan yabluġū-hā ka-ḍāk
    ṯumma ẓannū bi-ʾanna-hum ahnāk
    rūsu-hum minnuh fī makān an-naʿāl

Although others may aspire to win honors,
and wish to obtain them at that,
and eventually think they have attained their ambition,
their heads still remain at the lowly level of your sandals.

31. ya ʾajalla l-warà ʾiḍā qīl man
    balaġ al-waṣfi [min-ka] mā ʾamkan
    fī madāyiḥak jārat il-alsan
    wa-bi-ḍikrak tuṣarraf al-amṯāl

O loftiest of mankind, when one asks: "Who is the loftiest?"
Description of you has achieved all that is possible.
In praising you, tongues become confused,
whereas proverbs about you make their rounds among men.

32. ḍanna bīk aš-ṣaraf ḍanant anta bīh
    lam tujārà wa-lam tunāzaʿ fīh
    fa-ʾiḍā qāl aḥad wajad lak šabīh
    astawà ʿinduh al-hudà wa-ḍ-ḍalāl

Glory, to which you cling, clings to you.
You have no rival or competitor in it,
so that, if anyone claims to have found your equal,
then, truth and error are all the same to him.

33. ayyad allāh bi-saʿdak al-islām
    wa-ʾarat-ka surūrak al-ayyām
    mā staḥal aḍ-ḍiyā wa-qām aẓ-ẓalām
    wa-sarat an-nujūm wa-lāḥ al-hilāl

May God protect Islam through your good fortune,
and may Time show you manifold joys,
as long as light dims and darkness deepens,
stars travel by night, and the crescent moon shines.

(Gunzburg 1896: fols. 92–94; García Gómez 1972, I: 436–447; Corriente 1980: 561–575; 1984: 202–207, 344–345; 1989: 172–176, 302–303; 1995: 266–274).[8]

Commentary

In the first seven strophes of his thirty-three strophe long "*Zajal 87*" Ibn Quzmān's poetic persona looks back on his youth, from the vantage point of maturity, and offers us a portrait of the artist as a young man who is vain, frivolous, and empty-headed. From boyhood, he had grown up to be a strong, healthy, and physically attractive youth (strophe

---

8. Any editorial modifications are mine.

1), so concerned with his appearance, that he used to cut his hair fashionably, for which he became famous (strophe 2). Furthermore, he was a dandy, and attired himself in expensive robes, cloaks, and turbans (strophe 3). Add to this, that he ignored any and all advice (of the middle-class morality sort) offered by his well-intentioned friends and acquaintances, and lived, instead, merely to satisfy his appetite for fine clothes and good food, with no thought for the morrow (strophe 4). His character is thus portrayed as that of a vain and superficial young fop. Furthermore, he dwelt in an expensive little apartment (his bachelor's quarters) and, when the landlord raised his rent from one quarter to three-eighths of a *miṭqāl*, not only did he not object, but he actually declared his willingness to pay an even higher rent, should it have been demanded (strophe 5). His lodgings, he tells us with characteristic vanity, were extremely elegant, and provided a fine view of the surrounding countryside (strophe 6), but, and this appears to have been a key issue with him, the neighborhood had no pious men, or scholars of the Holy Law, living in it, but was, instead, conveniently and largely inhabited by pretty widows "without husbands" who used to come by to visit him at all hours, to satisfy certain needs of theirs that the poet evasively declines to specify while, at the same time, coyly drawing attention to them (strophe 7).

This *zajal*, like many others by Ibn Quzmān, is based on the principles of ring-composition and, inasmuch as its structural organization allows us to perceive some of its deeper levels of meaning, the present discussion will begin by concentrating on that circular dimension of the poem.[9]

Ring-Composition in "Zajal 87"

(1) Internal Structure of the Poem's Four Thematic Sections:

	A	1.	Poet grows up to be a physically attractive young man.
	B	2.	Poet is vain: He takes pride in his external appearance.
	C	3.	Poet is frivolous: He wears expensive, luxurious clothing.
I	D	4.	Poet ignores all advice offered by others. He lives only for the day.
	C'	5.	Poet is frivolous: He rents expensive lodgings.
	B'	6.	Poet is vain: He takes pride in the interior of his bachelor's quarters.
	A'	7.	Widows are physically attracted to grown up young Poet.

	E	8.	*Transition: Remembrance of youthful folly inspires Poet to tell a story about a former attempt to seduce a Lady.*

	F	9–10.	Lady looks at Poet. Her seductive appearance makes Poet doubt her true identity.
II	G	11–12.	Lady is seductively beautiful. She thus enslaves Poet.

9. For further instances of ring-composition in Ibn Quzmān, see Monroe (1979), (1985–1986), (1987), (1988a), (1996), (1997b), (2003), Article in press, Article forthcoming.

G' 13–14. Poet determines to seduce Lady. He offers to be her slave.

F 15–16. Lady instructs Poet. He must disguise his seductive appearance in order to deceive her Neighbors as to his true identity.

H 17–18. *Transition: Poet's intense erotic emotion paralyzes him both physically and mentally.*

I 19. Poet's intense emotion prevents him from recognizing Lady's intention to deceive him, so that he disguises his head grotesquely.

III J 20–21. Poet proceeds to disguise the rest of his body in a grotesque manner.

Ĵ 22–23. Poet appears in disguise on the street, looking grotesque.

Ī 24. Poet's disguise fails to prevent Neighbors from recognizing his intention to deceive them, so that he becomes a grotesque object of ridicule.

E' 25. *Transition: Failure of attempted seduction inspires Poet to recognize the vanity of his youthful folly.*

K 26. Poet returns to God. He composes praise-poetry for Patron. Poems are likened to strung pearls that shine. They will make Patron's name live forever.

L 27. Poet's composition is unrivalled.

M 28. Poet's entire composition is improvised, and thus spontaneous.

IV N 29. Patron's name is invoked. His virtues are eternal and universal.

N' 30. Patron's honor is unrivalled. His virtues are unique to him.

M' 31 Patron's full description is impossible, and thus unachievable through spontaneity.

L' 32. Patron's glory is unrivalled.

K' 33. God is asked by Poet to bring joy to Patron as long as celestial bodies shine, i. e., the hope is expressed that he will live in joy forever.

Not only is this *zajal* based on ring-composition, but it also contains a set of four thematic sections, each exhibiting its own internal ring-composition within the overall, circular structure of the entire poem. Like a complicated planetary system, the poem thus contains inner ring structures within the outer one. Of the four internal rings, the preceeding summary of strophes 1 to 7 constitutes the first. To restate the claims of the poet in circular terms, in strophe 1 he indicates that he grew up to be a physically attractive young man (A), whereas in 7 he implies that the pretty widows who lived in his neighborhood were physically attracted to him (A'). In strophe 2, he gives evidence of his vanity by mentioning the pride he took in his *external* appearance (specifically, his hairstyle), which people greatly admired (B), whereas in 6 he gives equal evidence of his vanity by boasting of the elegant *interior* of his bachelor's quarters, from which he could admire a fine view of the outdoors (B'). In strophe 3, he speaks of the frivolity with which he spent his money on expensive clothes (C), whereas in 5 he does the same by boasting of the high rent he paid for his lodgings (C'). In the center of this first set of rings (strophe 4), he declares that he used to ignore all advice offered to him, and that he lived only for the day, with no thought for the morrow (D), thereby indicating that he was formerly an improvident fool and, by implication, currently an unreliable narrator. This entire section of the poem further sets up an opposition between the superficial values to which the poet adheres, and the underlying criticism of those values that the reader is being encouraged to discover for himself. Put differently, the poem sets up a contrast between appearance (the speaker is handsome and elegant) and reality (he is vain and foolish), that the reader is indirectly being invited to consider.

Strophe 8 is transitional. In it the poet declares his intention of furnishing a specific anecdote designed to illustrate the frivolity of his youth. That anecdote involves an attempt by the poet to seduce a married woman who, however, manages to turn the tables on him. In turn, that anecdote constitutes a second thematic section within the poem. In strophes 9 to 10, the poet is loitering at the door of his house (presumably having nothing better to do, given the overall idleness of his youth) when a beautiful lady walks by and looks at him. Further on within the poem, it is implied that the lady is unveiled in public, since the speaker can see her neck, cheeks, mouth, and teeth (strophes 10:1, 11:1, 12:1–2). It is also implied that she is a blonde, since her braids, which are visible, are compared to rays of light (strophe 11:3). This detail is of some significance, insofar as blonds, in the Mediterranean context, were generally considered unreliable, deceitful, and prone to transmitting the evil eye. Not only is the lady blonde, but so is the poet, as he is quick to point out in many other *zajals*.[10] The present occasion is, therefore, an unusually dangerous encounter in which blond meets blonde. The lady is also characterized as employing Berber vocabulary (strophe 16:1: *mazad* 'Qur'ān school' from B **amzad* [Corriente 1997: 501]), while the poet disguises himself in a headdress of the type worn by the Berber tribe of the Banū Zirwāl, when visiting her (strophe 19:4), presumably in

---

10. See, for example, "*Zajal 20*," strophe 14, and "*Zajal 137*," strophe 10. As noted above, throughout the Mediterranean area, according to folk beliefs, redheaded or blond people were, and still are, considered unlucky and untrustworthy; in particular, they are believed to cast the evil eye, especially if their own are blue (Westermarck 1926, I: 419–421). The following passage from the medieval Spanish translation of the *Sirr al-asrār* reads like a perfect description of Ibn Quzmān's literary persona:

> Onde sabet que el que es muy aluo et muy ruuio, et demas zarco, es sennal de desuergonçado, et de traydor, et de fornicioso et de poco seso. Et podedes esto entender en los çiclaues [*siqlab* = 'Slav', a term used in al-Andalus to designate slaves imported from Northern Europe], que son de tal facion que todos son locos, et traydores et deuergonçados. Pues guardat uos de cada uno ruuio et zarco, et si ouiere con esto la fruente mucho ancha, et la baruiella pequenna, et las mexiellas grandes, et el cuerpo roxo, et cabellos muchos en la cabeça, guardat uos del commo uos guardariedes de la biuora mortal ['Whereby you should know, concerning anyone who is very tall, and very blond, and blue-eyed to boot, that this indicates that he is shameless; a traitor, a fornicator, and a man of little sense. You can observe this in the Slavs, who are so built that the entire lot of them are crazy, treacherous, and shameless. Therefore, beware of every blond and blue-eyed person and, if he also has a very broad forehead, a small chin, large cheeks, a red body, and much hair on his head, beware of him as you would beware of a deadly viper'], (Kasten 1957: 62).

There are, in the Arab world, very ancient precedents for the prejudice against blond people (Lewis 1970), who are naturally, ethnic non-Arabs, and therefore outsiders. Furthermore, the Devil is portrayed as redheaded, while, in the illuminated manuscripts of the *Maqāmāt* of al-Ḥarīrī, the trickster al-Sarūjī is often depicted as a redhead. Thus blondness, red hair, and blue eyes, whatever they may have to do with the actual appearance of Ibn Quzmān in real life, are qualities that, according to the medieval science of physiognomy, denote foolishness and treachery, and it is in the latter sense that they are being used literarily by the poet, to indicate the unreliable nature both of his persona and of that of the lady. For more on the evil eye, see Elworthy (1958), Maloney (1976), Di Stasi (1981), Dundes (1981).

order to blend in with, and thereby go unnoticed by, the residents of her neighborhood, which must, therefore, be a Berber one. Finally, the poet grasps a grape-stake in his hand instead of an *agzāl*, a kind of pike used by Berbers (strophe 22:4). The above are all indications that the lady is a Berber, that her husband is also a Berber, and that the poet will attempt to disguise himself as a Berber in order to pass unnoticed in her neighborhood when he goes to visit her, under cover of darkness, and in the absence of her husband. In turn, the implication that the lady is a Berber is important to our understanding of the poem, as we shall see in due course.

As the lady walks by the poet, she looks at him (strophe 9:2), an act that is in direct violation of a famous prophetic *ḥadīṯ* according to which members of the opposite sex are enjoined to avert their glances from one another lest they succumb to the lustful temptations of the flesh (Giffen 1971: 124–125; Bell 1979: 123–147). The lady's seductive appearance immediately causes the poet to wonder whether she is real, or merely a figment of his imagination. He thus entertains doubts about her true nature, and is reduced to uttering exclamations to express his wonderment over her incomparable beauty. Further details are provided concerning her features in strophes 11 and 12: Her cheeks are like roses, her braids are blond, her teeth are white as camphor, and her lips, red as hawthorn berries. In strophes 13 to 14 the poet, who is, by now, roasting over the red-hot coals of passion, determines to win the lady or die, and so, he addresses her by declaring himself to be her slave. To this, she replies (strophes 15–16) that she loves the poet even more than he loves her, whereupon the poet enthusiastically invites her to join him in amorous dalliance. The lady, however, prolongs and increases his ardor by instructing him to visit her that night, for a rendezvous scheduled to take place at a time when her husband will have gone off to his Qur'ān school. The lady further advises the poet to disguise himself and modify his voice, so that he will not be recognized by her neighbors.

Restated in circular terms, when, in strophes 9 to 10, the lady looks at the poet, her seductive glance and appearance cause him to entertain doubts as to her true identity (is she a female jinni or a houri?), (F), whereas in strophes 15 to 16 she instructs him to disguise his seductive appearance in order to deceive her neighbors with regard to his own true identity (F'). Then, in strophes 11 to 12 the lady is described as being so seductively beautiful that she enslaves the poet (G). In contrast to this, in strophes 13 to 14 the poet determines to seduce the lady by declaring himself her slave (G').

The thematic center of the entire poem coincides with two of its centrally located strophes, namely 17 and 18, and constitutes another transitional passage. In it, the poet declares that he was left tongue-tied, that he was overwhelmed by fear, that his heart beat uncontrollably, that his body was on fire, that he boiled, turned pale, and lost his mind. Put differently, the intensity of his passion caused him to lose his mind and, therefore, to act like the fool that he was.

The third thematic section of the poem under analysis spans strophes 19 to 24. The poet, whose intense emotion prevents him from realizing that the Berber lady's intention in inviting him to her house is not exactly to welcome a lover, but to turn the tables on her would-be seducer and, thus, teach him a lesson, begins to disguise himself by coiling a rug, of a kind used for covering benches, around his head, in imitation of Berber headgear (strophe 19). Then, he proceeds to improvise a grotesque costume that makes him look like a clown, and that contrasts sharply with the elegant clothes he normally delights in wearing. He puts on a *liṭām*, the veil with which Almoravid men covered their faces, improvising a small net for catching sardines (strophe 20); i. e., an item not likely to be found in landlocked Córdoba (this suggests the unreliability of the narrator). He then puts on a cloth for covering bread, but since it is too short, he adds a piece of rush matting, which then makes his headdress too long, so that he drapes the excess over his left shoulder (strophe 21). Dressed in this grotesque apparel, he goes to the gate of the alley in which his lady-love resides, barefoot and with a grape-stake in his hand, instead of the standard Berber *agzāl* ("pike") (strophe 22). The poet further describes himself as being dressed like a healer of wounds, with a sheepskin around his neck rather than the Berber burnoose, adding that the people of al-Andalus are quick to make a mockery of men (strophe 23), for the inhabitants of the neighborhood suddenly appear on the street, calling out to one another to come and see the extraordinary spectacle (no doubt having been alerted to the poet's imminent arrival by the Berber lady) and they then proceed to make a mockery of the poet (strophe 24).

In terms of ring-composition, this section may be outlined as follows: In strophe 19, the poet's intense passion prevents him from recognizing the lady's intention to deceive him, and so, he disguises his head in a grotesque costume (I), whereas in strophe 24 his disguise fails to prevent the lady's neighbors from recognizing his intention to deceive them, so that he becomes an object of ridicule himself (I'). Likewise, in strophes 20 to 21 the poet proceeds to disguise the rest of his body in a grotesque manner (J), whereas in stophes 22 to 23, he appears on the street, looking grotesque (J').

Strophe 25 is again transitional. In it, the poet recognizes his failure to win the lady, along with the fact that he lacks common sense (and is, therefore, a fool), so that he curses the lady (no courtly love here!) for having betrayed him to the rabble that is currently humiliating him. In circular terms, this strophe corresponds to strophe 8, which was also transitional. If in strophe 8 the remembrance of his youthful folly had induced the poet to begin the story about his attempt to seduce the Berber lady (E), in strophe 25, the failure of the poet's attempted seduction induces him to end his story, and to recognize the vanity of his youthful folly (E').

Strophes 26 to 33 constitute the fourth and last thematic section of the poem. In this section, the poet announces that, after his disastrous attempt at seducing the Berber lady, he mended his ways, abandoned his youthful folly and turned over a new leaf, by beginning to praise notables in verse (strophe 26). Grasping the inkwell and pen, he composed words of praise, embroidering the page with them (no oral composition here!), while his poem turned out to be a masterpiece (strophe 27). He described majesty, extolling and praising virtues, all through the art of improvisation (*irtijāl*) (here, oral composition is implied, thus contradicting the statement made in the previous strophe and, once again suggesting that the poet is either an unreliable narrator, or that he has not read Albert B. Lord's seminal work on oral-formulaic improvisation [Lord 2000]) (strophe 28). Then, the name of the patron, a certain unidentified Ibn al-Quraši al-Zuhrī is invoked, and described as a "heaven of excellence" and a "shining asterism," but since this individual's identity remains obscure, the words uttered in his praise would seem to be somewhat exaggerated (strophe 29). The poet then proceeds to indicate that no one can compare with al-Zuhrī in honor (strophe 30), that he is the loftiest of all mankind, and thus impossible to describe (strophe 31), that he has no rival in glory and, thus, no equal (strophe 32), and concludes by expressing the hope that God will protect Islam through the good fortune of the patron, and that Time will provide the latter with many joys as long as Time endures (strophe 33).

Restated in circular terms, in strophe 26, after his failed attempt to seduce the Berber lady, the poet claims to experience a desire to reform, and to return to godliness. He then composes a praise-poem for his patron. It is further stated that the lines of the poem are like strung pearls and, therefore, it is implied that they shine brilliantly, while it is also implied that they will make the patron's name live forever (K). In contrast, in strophe 33, God is asked, by the poet, to bring joy to the patron as long as the celestial bodies (the stars and moon) shine. Put differently, the hope is expressed that the patron will live in joy, if not forever, at very least till the end of Time (K'). Then, in strophe 27, it is stated that the poet's composition is an unrivalled masterpiece (L), whereas in strophe 32 the claim is made that the patron's glory is unrivalled (L'). In strophe 28 it is stated that the poet's entire composition is improvised, and thus spontaneous (M), whereas in strophe 31 it is claimed that the patron's full description is impossible, and thus unachievable through spontaneity (M'). In strophes 29 and 30, which constitute the very center of the ring-composition for this section, the poet, while invoking the patron's name, chooses to have things both ways, by stating that al-Zuhrī's virtues are *universal* (strophe 29, N), whereas his honor is declared to be unrivalled, and his virtues are simultaneously declared to be *exclusive* unto himself alone (strophe 30, N').

The four thematic sections of the poem that have been analyzed above, in turn exhibit an overall ring-structure: In the first section (strophes 1 to 7) the poet admires his own physical attributes and refined tastes. In this portrait of the poet, who is presented as a frivolous dandy, appearance (which is superficial) is stressed at the expense of reality (which is substantive), (A). In contrast, in the fourth and last thematic section (strophes 26 to 33) the poet admires the virtues and glories of his patron. In this portrait of the patron, presented by a frivolous dandy, (superficial) appearance is again stressed at the expense of (substantive) reality (A'). In the first transitional strophe (8), we are introduced to the story of how the poet and would-be trickster will eventually be tricked by the Berber lady (B), whereas, in the third transitional strophe (25), the story of how the poet and would-be trickster was tricked by the Berber lady is brought to a conclusion (B'). In the second thematic section (strophes 9 to 16) the poet attempts her seduction, while the idealized portrait of the fair lady is followed by a flirtatious dialogue in which she deceitfully invites the poet to an evening rendezvous (C), whereas in the third thematic section (strophes 18 to 24) the seduction is subverted by the lady, while the poet depicts his attempt to disguise himself in grotesque clothes for the rendezvous, but, upon arrival at her street, becomes an object of ridicule himself (C'). In both these sections we further have an interplay of appearance and reality: The poet fails to realize that the lady intends to deceive him, whereas his attempt to pass unrecognized among, and thereby deceive, the lady's neighbors, is a failure. Finally, two of the centrally located strophes of the poem (17 and 18) are transitional. In them the poet and would-be trickster falls victim to his passion, and loses his mind, thereby indicating that he is a fool and, thus, an unreliable narrator (D).

(2) External Structure of the Poem's Four Thematic Sections:

A   I   1–7.   Poet admires his own physical attributes and refined tastes. Portrait of Poet, presented as a frivolous dandy, stresses superficial Appearance over substantive Reality.

B   8.   *Transition: Poet-trickster will be tricked by Lady.*

C   II   9–16.   Seduction attempted by Poet. Idealized portrayal of Lady is followed by a flirtatious dialogue in which deceptive Lady invites Poet to an evening rendezvous. Lady's appearance and reality do not correspond (she looks sympathetic, but is not).

D   17–18. *Transition: Poet-Trickster falls victim to his passion, and loses his mind.*

C'   III 18–24. Seduction subverted by Lady. Grotesque portrayal of Poet on his way to rendezvous is followed by a scene in which he himself becomes a grotesque object of ridicule. Poet's appearance and reality do correspond (he looks like a fool, and is fooled).

B'   25.   *Transition. Poet-Trickster has been tricked by Lady.*

A'   IV   26–33. Poet admires the virtues and glories of his Patron. Portrait of Patron, presented by a frivolous Poet suggests superficial Appearance over substantive Reality.

The Poem Itself

In the first three sections of "*Zajal 87,*" Ibn Quzmān portrays his literary persona as being that of a vapid young dandy who attempts to seduce a married Berber woman with whom he falls in lust, but who turns the tables on him by luring him into her neighborhood, whose inhabitants she has forewarned of his imminent arrival, so that they lie in wait for him and reduce him to humiliation through their public mockery of him. When, in strophe 14, the poet declared his love to the lady by stating that he had become her slave, and she, a total stranger, replied in strophe 15:1 that she loved him even more, he should immediately have become suspicious of her intentions. Instead, he takes her words at face value, whereupon disaster ensues. The poet is, therefore, punished for his intention to commit adultery, a crime that, according to Islamic law, is punishable by death (Peters 2002).

Nor is the lady entirely guiltless. To begin, she violates the Islamic *ḥadīṯ* on averting the glance, by gazing at the poet as she passes by his door (strophe 9:2), thus indicating an interest in him. In light of her provocation, the punishment she metes out is, if not unjust, at least one which she has no moral authority to impose. In sum, the poet is an elegant if vain fool, and the lady is a beautiful if cruel and treacherous beloved. In both cases, the external appearance of the characters, which is attractive, is not in keeping with their internal reality, which is loathesome. The poet gets what he deserves at the hands of a lady who tricks him after having herself aroused and encouraged his passion for her. Insofar as this whole section of the poem involves trickery and deceit; a victim and a victimizer, it would not be far wrong to say that it is, in fact, a *maqāma* in verse, and that the cruel lady and hopeless lover of idealized Classical Arabic poetry have now been reduced to the level of trickster figures.

Ring-composition aside, other, equally meaningful correspondences may be detected within the poem under analysis. Thus, for example, section I corresponds to section III. In both these sections, clothes, which are meant to conceal, reveal instead, the true nature of the poet, namely that he is a dandy and a fool. Likewise, section II corresponds to section IV. In these two sections, words, which may be used to reveal, here conceal the true nature of human sentiments; namely that the lady is a trickster and, by implication, that the poet/panegyrist is insincere.

The poem also explores matters dealing with liminality. For example, in strophe 6, mention is made of a belvedere with a large door (*bāb*) from which the poet may contemplate the outdoors from within his home. Then, in strophe 9, he is loitering at the front door (*bāb*) of his house looking out at the street, where he sees the lady outdoors. In strophe 22, he goes to the gate (*bāb*) of the lady's alley looking for her, and finally, in strophe 24, her neighbors come out of the implied doors (*abwāb*) of their houses to look at (*ven, verás*) the poet. Like clothes then, doors too, reveal and conceal, all of which stresses the lack of correspondence existing between appearance and reality in this poem. Thus, in several ways, and like many other *zajal*s by Ibn Quzmān,[11] this one also exhibits a remarkable thematic coherence, not to speak of organic unity and careful, circular patterning on the level of themes.[12]

---

11. See n. 9, above.

12. For a recent attempt to deny the existence of organic unity in Arabic poetry, see Van Gelder (1982). In what amounts to an aberration within the general discipline of literary criticism, promoted and perpetuated largely by certain Arabists, Professor Van Gelder (not to mention his numerous predecessors and many followers), mistakenly assumes medieval Arabic rhetoricians to be identical, in their practice and goals, to modern literary critics. Nevertheless, medieval rhetoricians, unlike modern literary critics, were not engaged in the task of interpreting, or assigning meaning to literary texts. As a result, they were not concerned, in the case of poetry, with literary relationships that went beyond the individual line, and thus did not discuss them. Contrary to what Van Gelder assumes and asserts, this does not mean that poets were unaware

...../....

As in other poems by Ibn Quzmān, in this one we are also faced with an unworthy persona, who, despite his moral defects (he boasts of being a a dandy and a seducer of widows), feels qualified to praise a patron. In turn, this raises serious questions about the validity of the poet's praise, about the nature of any patron who would accept the praise of such a poet, etc. Thus, we are confronted with the figure of an unreliable narrator. When, in strophe 27, the poet informs us that he wrote down his words of praise for his patron al-Zuhrī with pen and paper, adding in strophe 28 that his praise was simultaneously produced through improvisation (*irtijāl*), we are left with nagging doubts about the speaker's veracity, and about the truth and sincerity of the panegyrical section of the poem. Is the praise directed at al-Zuhrī to be taken at face value, or is it the product of an unreliable narrator, and thus questionable? The panegyrical section of this *zajal*, which is only 8 strophes long, in a poem consisting of 33 strophes, appears to come as a distinct afterthought, whereas the poem's center, as we have noted, is occupied by a fool's failed attempt to seduce a lady.

On the subject of panegyric, the rhetorician Ibn Rašīq al-Qayrawānī (390/1000–456/1063, or 463/1071), distinguishes between such language as is appropriate for praising (or blaming) kings, secretaries, viziers, generals, and judges (in that descending order). He says:

> When the patron is a **king**, the poet need not be concerned over what he says about him, nor over how much he exaggerates in either praising or blaming him, *but if the patron is a subject, the poet should beware of exaggerating his rank for, if he does so, he will be like one who diminishes that rank.* Similarly, the poet should not fall short of what is deserved by the patron, nor bestow on one patron the attributes of another, thereby praising the secretary for his courage, and the judge for his anger and severity. This often happens in the case of contemporary poets, yet it is an error, unless an actual connection to the patron accompanies the praise, indicating the soundness of the poet's opinion on the subject. Likewise one should not praise a king for qualities pertaining to lesser leaders, even though such qualities are positive ones (Arabic text in Ibn Rašīq 1962, II: 129).

It is appropriate for the poet's intention in praising a **secretary** or **vizier** to coincide with what Qudāma[13] and others have recommended and, likewise, with qualities such as sound judgment, righteous presence of mind, extreme prudence, lack of indifference, depth of con-

---

...*/...*

of broader relationships going considerably beyond the line. Thus, the organic unity of individual poems cannot be established on the basis of rhetorical treatises, the main purpose of which was not to interpret poetry, but (1) to formulate the rules of poetic composition, and (2) to point out lapses therefrom. Organic unity must, instead, be teased out of the individual poems themselves. There is, therefore, a basic methodological flaw in the arguments proposed, and conclusions reached, by Van Gelder. No one, to the best of my knowledge, has ever actually analyzed a single Arabic poem in order to demonstrate that it lacks structural coherence or organic unity. All arguments to the effect that Arabic poems are incoherent are, instead, based on the fact that Arab rhetoricians do not discuss the subject of thematic coherence. The above are, therefore, mere arguments from absence and, as such, are invalid. To offer one simple analogy to this situation, how can that which is *not* said in Chemistry books be used to demonstrate a lack of coherence in the laws of Physics?

13. On the rhetorician Qudāma ibn Ja'far (d. 320/932, or 328/939, or 337/948), author of *Kitāb Naqd al-ši'r* ("The Book on Detecting the Faults in Poetry"), see Qudāma ibn Ja'far, Abū l-Faraj (1980), Bonebakker (1980).

cern for the Caliph, perseverance on his behalf in difficult situations, either by word, or by deed (Arabic text in Ibn Rašīq 1962, II: 134).

The most excellent virtues for which a **general** can be praised are generosity, courage, and their derivatives, such as high rank, boundless bravery, readiness to attack, and the like (Arabic text in Ibn Rašīq 1962, II: 135).

A poet should praise a **judge** for qualities consistent with justice and fair play; for making difficult decisions, where equity is concerned, and for rejecting facile ones; for taking from the powerful and giving to the weak; for treating the poor and the rich equally; for his kindly disposition, for his leniency, and for his independence of mind when imposing legal penalties and rejecting people's claims. Moreover, should the poet add mention of piety, self-restraint, and their like, to the above, he will attain the utmost limits of excellence. It is appropriate to apply the qualities of a **judge** to a ***ṣāḥib al-maẓālim***[14] but, *as far as anyone below these three ranks is concerned (not to mention that of Caliph), I see no way in which he can be praised*, yet if necessity should compel the poet to do so, let him praise each individual for his excellence in his particular profession, and for his knowledge in the kind of life he leads; let the poet stress attributes dependent upon such spiritual qualities as were mentioned by Qudāma, while if, to these are added accidental and physical qualities such as beauty, splendor, good character, ease of circumstances, and abundance of relatives, this would be excellent, despite the fact that Qudāma categorically refused to recognize and, instead, rejected the validity of, such qualities. Nonetheless, this is not right, for Qudāma should have recognized that praise of physical qualities is most honorable and appropriate. As far as his having rejecting such qualities is concerned, I do not think anyone will support him, or agree with him on the subject (Arabic text in Ibn Rašīq, 1962, II: 135).

From Ibn Rašīq's remarks, it becomes clear that men occupying different ranks in society should be praised for the specific qualities each is expected to manifest in his given rank. It is equally clear that, in "*Zajal 87*," Ibn Quzmān is violating all expectations by praising an obscure patron with language so lofty that its application to a king would be more suitable. According to S. A. Bonebakker, Qudāma ibn Jaʻfar had even argued that "a prayer to grant immortality to a ruler cannot be justified, since immortality in man is inconceivable" (Bonebakker 1980: 321a). Thus, when, in the last strophe of his poem, Ibn Quzmān declares to his patron:

> May God protect Islam through your good fortune,
> and may Time show you manifold joys,
> as long as light dims and darkness deepens,
> stars travel by night, and the crescent moon shines,

the poet is clearly treading on dangerous ground, for his praise overshoots its mark by some, and thus produces a comic, if not burlesque effect. Al-Zuhrī is, therefore, being damned (if not ridiculed) with excessively loud praise.

---

14. An official charged with investigating cases of injustice committed against individuals, to whom the latter could address their complaints in hope of redress (Nielsen 1991).

In this poem, there is a further subtlety worthy of note: Ibn Rašīq also makes the following statement:

> Contrary to what others are permitted to do, the poet is not allowed to admire himself, or to praise his own poetry, even if the latter is essentially perfect, and sounds excellent to its listener; all the more so, if it is, in fact, inferior to the poet's own opinion of it, as is the case with those who devote themselves to self-praise, and waste their entire lives doing so, yet never achieve any literary stature. God –Mighty and Exalted be He– said: "Do not praise yourselves" [*Qur'ān*, 53:32]. This is required, unless the poet wishes to arouse a desire [to reward the poet?] in the patron, or to intimidate him, in which case he may praise himself, and mention the excellence of his *qaṣīda*, for in that case it is allowable and permissible, as is apparent in the case of many poets in their poems, where they praise their own *qaṣīda*s (Arabic text in Ibn Rašīq 1963, I: 201).[15]

Praising his own poem is precisely what our poet does in strophe 27, where he declares it to be a masterpiece. Thus, if Ibn Rašīq is right, then the poet is actually attempting to extract a reward from al-Zuhrī by means of cupidity, or through intimidation, rather than from sincere and disinterested admiration. The poem is, thus, an inversion of its corresponding courtly genre, the panegyrical *qaṣīda*.

If the poet presents himself as a scoundrel and a sexual opportunist, the portrayal of the Berber woman is equally unflattering. It is she who deliberately arouses the poet, thus indicating that she is all too willing to betray her husband. Andalusīs, in fact, never ceased to wonder at their Berber rulers, whose men, contrary to Arab custom, wore the *liṯām*, whereas their womenfolk went about in public with their faces unveiled, as is the case in this poem. The poet's attempt to construct a *liṯām* for himself out of absurd odds and ends, and his care in carrying a grape-stake in his hand to mimic the *agzāl* borne by the Almoravids, are grotesque efforts to pass himself off as a Berber. In this respect, we are being offered the prejudiced view of Berbers held by sophisticated Andalusīs during the Almoravid period, namely that their women were all loose, and their menfolk all cuckolds, wittols, and pimps (Garulo 1999). Furthermore, by attempting to seduce a Berber woman, the poet is symbolically attempting to dishonor all Berber men. But later on, when he is mocked for his immoral intentions, his affront against the Berber nation is rendered ineffective, and it is his persona, an embodiment of anti-Berber prejudice, that is ultimately dishonored in the poem. Thus, Ibn Quzmān is not sharing the prevailing anti-Berber sentiment held by his countrymen but is, instead, actually condemning it. This is why his adventure is presented, ultimately, as a failure, so that the poem becomes a literary example of self-mockery.

As has been shown elsewhere (Monroe and Pettigrew 2003), Ibn Quzmān's slightly older contemporary, al-Saraqusṭī (d. 538/1143), leads us to the same conclusion in his "*Maqāma 41 (The Berbers)*" (al-Warāglī 1995: 385–392; Ferrando 1999: 222–226; Monroe 2002: 418–424). In it, the author has his fictional narrator al-Sā'ib ibn Tammām, who

---

15. I would like to thank Mr. Raymond K. Farrin for kindly alerting me to the existence of the passages by Ibn Rašīq quoted in this article.

is an Easterner and an Arab, appear on the beaches near Tangier, where he is waiting for passage to al-Andalus, about which he has heard marvelous reports, and whose impressively high cultural standards he deeply admires. The Arab speaker has just been in Tangier, whose Berber population, in sharp contrast, he despises with an intense prejudice reflecting that of the Andalusīs of the author's own, and earlier periods. While the speaker is on the beach, he sees a mysteriously veiled man who is addressing a crowd of Berbers. "He was jabbering to the natives, whom he could understand, in a language unintelligible to me. Then, he gestured toward me, and praised me to the skies before them" (al-Warāglī 1995: 386). Yet how can the speaker know that the stranger is praising him to the skies if he cannot understand the language in which he is doing so? Again, we seem to have an unreliable narrator. Eventually, the narrator, al-Sā'ib, recognizes the mysterious stranger as his persecutor, the master-rogue Abū Ḥabīb al-Sadūsī, also introduced as a purebred Arab, whom al-Sā'ib reproves for commingling with non-Arabs: "Have you gone to all the trouble of coming west, only to join non-Arabs with Arabs in a promiscuous friendship?" (al-Warāglī 1995: 386). On the recommendation of Abū Ḥabīb, who has won the confidence of the Berbers, the latter welcome al-Sā'ib into their midst, and regale him with their lavish hospitality. Al-Sā'ib, in turn, grudgingly allows himself to be persuaded to accept that hospitality, particularly the splendid meals he is served, while, at the same time, he constantly and ungratefully complains about the uncouth manners and barbaric customs of his Berber hosts.

One day, the Berbers get so drunk on a potent beverage called *anzīz* (which, according to al-Idrīsī, was manufactured and consumed by Maṣmūda Berbers in the south-west of Morocco), (Monroe 2002: 48–49), that they are all rendered unconscious. The point to be made here, is that al-Idrīsī is describing a custom peculiar to the Berber inhabitants of the region of Sūs, in the south-west of Morocco, namely that they drink *anzīz*, whereas the action being narrated in the *maqāma* under consideration purportedly takes place in the extreme north of that country, in Tangier. This geographic inconsistency suggests a further lack of narratorial reliability, designed to put us, as readers of the text, on our guard.

While the Berbers are asleep, Abū Ḥabīb proposes to al-Sā'ib that the two of them steal the Berbers' money and abscond with it. The ethnically prejudiced and ungrateful narrator tacitly agrees to go along with the plan. Abū Ḥabīb gathers all the money that he can, which he then proceeds to bury on the beach. Then he declares:

> No crime is committed, as long as one does not behave so stupidly as to get caught. May you survive until we meet again. Choose a road that is not my road and leave my company and group, for I plan to return to yonder Berber people, and then hunt you down, since I have left my honor in a splendid state among them, while imposing on you a heavy burden of betrayal (Arabic text in al-Warāglī 1995: 388–389).

Let us note that, all the time the Arabs are denigrating their Berber hosts, the text is actually revealing that the Berbers exhibit the single greatest virtue that Arab culture admires and recognizes, namely generosity and hospitality, especially when it is directed at the guest and stranger (Malti-Douglas 1985). Their only defect lies in trusting their

Arab guests, and in getting drunk when the latter are around. At the same time, the Arabs are guilty of the worst abomination recognized by Arab culture, namely the betrayal of the laws of hospitality, for it is the Arabs who are here portrayed as stealing from their hosts. Let us also note that, in this *maqāma*, there is no honor among thieves, since Abū Ḥabīb proceeds to betray al-Sā'ib, his all too willing partner in theft. Furthermore, al-Sā'ib had told us, from the very outset of the *maqāma*, that he had come down to the shores next to Tangier seeking passage to al-Andalus. These are the very shores in which his subsequent encounter with Abū Ḥabīb and the Berbers, his betrayal of Berber hospitality, and his own betrayal at the hands of Abū Ḥabīb, have taken place; these are the very shores from which al-Sā'ib has been advised by Abū Ḥabīb to escape if he would save his life from the avenging Berbers the latter threatens to unleash against him. In such circumstances, it is highly unlikely that al-Sā'ib would have remained for long in so dangerous an area, while waiting for passage to al-Andalus, thereby putting his life at risk. Hence, we have strong grounds to suspect that the story he is telling is a tall tale, told to deceive the listener into sympathizing with its teller's plight and, perhaps, even to pay for his passage to al-Andalus. The serious question thus arises, as to whether any of what the narrator has told us, actually ever took place. Such a conclusion is reinforced by the earlier inconsistency in the episode, according to which the narrator had simultaneously informed us (a) that the mysterious stranger he encountered was speaking in an unintelligible foreign tongue and (b), that in that same unintelligible tongue, he was praising the narrator to his Berber listeners. In other words, the agent-narrator is trying to hoodwink the reader, just as the rogue has tricked the agent-narrator. The narrator is thus, to put it bluntly, a liar and, therefore, any information proceeding from him is unreliable. This being the case, what are we to make of his praise of Andalusīs, and his scorn for Berbers, coming as it does from an Arab speaker?

Al-Saraqusṭī was himself an Andalusī, either of genuine Arab extraction, or one who passed himself off as being an Arab (from the tribe of Tamīm), and who not only served and praised Arab kings in Zaragoza and Almería, but lived to see the twilight of Arab dominion in al-Andalus, as power passed from the Andalusī Arabs to the Berber Almoravids. His narrator, who claims to be an Arab and despises Berbers, is also a liar. If we were to delve beneath the surface of the text, we might conclude that the author, as opposed to his character is, in this instance, commenting on the depravity of the times, when Arabs are utterly treacherous and without honor, and nobility can only be found among Berbers. He may also be implying that, although the Berbers may seem uncouth, barbaric, and generally uncivilized in comparison with Andalusī sophisticates, they are actually honest, generous, militarily powerful and, therefore, the only people capable of saving al-Andalus from the onslaught of the anachronistically termed Christian "Reconquista."[16] In

---

16. This noun is a neologism; it was not recorded by the *Real Academia de la Lengua Española* until the nineteenth century, and does not appear in any known medieval texts. The verb *reconquistar* was first used in the late eighteenth century by Leandro Fernández de Moratín (1760–1828) and Gaspar Melchor de Jovellanos (1744–1811), but was not recorded by the Real Academia until 1843. It designates (retroactively) the period between AD 722 (battle of Covadonga) and 1492 (fall of Granada), as if the 770 intervening years constituted one single, long, uninterrupted war, which it never was (Corominas and Pascual 1981, IV: 719a).

other words, the author is calling for a responsible national and foreign policy; he is pleading for the creation of a united front transcending narrow ethnic ties; he is calling for a strengthening of those cultural bonds provided by Islam, that unite Arabs and Berbers against their common Christian foe. Furthermore, all intelligent Arabs knew that without the support of the Berbers, the Arabs would never have conquered the Iberian Peninsula in the first place; without the Berbers, they would never have held it for three centuries of Umayyad rule and, as we now know with the benefit of retrospect, without the Berbers, they would never have continued to hold it for three more centuries. When the chips are down, the author seems to be asking his countrymen whether it is not better to be "a cameldriver in Africa rather than a swineherd in Castile." In sum, one should read the "*Maqāma* of the Berbers" not as an illustration of Andalusī anti-Berber prejudice shared by the author, but as an ironic critique of that same prejudice; a critique designed to exhort the author's contemporaries to rise above a divisive version of narrow ethnic solidarity that, precisely because it was not heeded, eventually proved fatal. This, in sum is exactly what Ibn Quzmān is also doing in his "*Zajal 87.*" In this sense, buffoonery can provide a valuable means for social criticism. Ibn Quzmān is not just a funny poet; instead he is addressing issues central to the survival of his world, and this is a very serious matter indeed.

Such a conclusion can be readily supported if we consider Ibn Quzmān's "*Zajal 90,*" studied in detail elsewhere (Monroe and Pettigrew 2003), and in which parallel conclusions can be reached. In "*Zajal 90,*" the poet finds himself in an establishment of ill-repute, where a Berber woman, who is both married and a prostitute, initiates an exchange with him, which leads to his going to bed with her. The following morning, when the poet refuses to pay for her services, he is beaten and humiliated by the other members of her establishment. With this disgraceful background to recommend him, the poet then proceeds to praise a patron, just as occurs in "*Zajal 87.*"

As long as the ʿAbbāsid caliphate was firmly in control of Arabs, it would seem that the literary genre enjoying the greatest prestige in Arabic was the *qaṣīda*, a type of poetry that could be either panegyrical, invective, or elegiac. By its very nature, the *qaṣīda* is a courtly genre, and its delivery constitutes an important courtly ritual. Its function is to uphold a specific ideal of rulership, and it (1) Either praises the ruler for living up to that ideal, while simultaneously reminding him of the ideal itself, (2) Chastizes him for not living up to the ideal, or (3) Mourns his death, while simultaneously reminding us of the ideal up to which he lived. Without a ruler and a court conversant with the Arabic language, to sustain it, both the ritual itself, along with its vehicle, the *qaṣīda,* are rendered meaningless.

Badīʿ al-Zamān al-Hamaḏānī (358/969–398/1008), the inventor of the *maqāma* genre, lived at a time when the Buwayhids, a Šīʿite and Persian dynasty (r. 320/932–454/1062), held effective military *power* over major areas of the Middle East, including Baghdad, the seat of the former Arab Empire, yet they ruled in the name of the Sunnī and Arab ʿAbbāsid caliphs, from whom they derived their spiritual *authority*. It would appear that the *maqāma* genre filled a vacuum produced when the *qaṣīda* was no longer viable, because military-based courts no longer enjoyed the sublime prestige formerly enjoyed by religious-based ones, and foreign rulers lacked the command of the Arabic language necessary to appreciate the *qaṣīda*. How could poets continue to eulogize mere secular rulers in the same terms in which they had formerly praised the religious aura of caliphs, and how would foreign, non-Arab rulers have understood them, had they attempted to do so?

In his *Collection of Histories*, the author al-Tanūḫī (328/940–383/994) implies precisely the above when he states:

> Raḍī [r. 322/934–329/940] had many merits, and was the last Caliph to do many things. He was the last to compose verse; to command the armies himself; to administer the finance; to preach from the pulpit on Fridays; to sit with companions and entertain courtiers; to maintain the practice of the original caliphate in the matter of establishment charges, gratuities, gifts, service, pensions, treasury, kitchen, wines, entertainments, officials, chamberlains, etc. (Arabic text in al-Tanūḫī n. d., I: 3; Eng. trans. in al-Tanūḫī 1922: 159).

Al-Tanūḫī goes on to put matters in terms of a moral and cultural decline, yet it should be noted that the Persian-speaking Buwayhids entered Baghdad in 334/945, only five years after the end of al-Raḍī's reign, and reduced the 'Abbāsids to the status of mere puppets. Therefore, the abandonment of established literary genres, and their replacement by new ones is, in reality, the result of a crisis in literary patronage brought about by the economic and political dismemberment of the Arab Empire, not to mention its fall into the hands of non-Arabic speaking rulers.

In the case of al-Andalus, which is what primarily concerns us here, let us note that al-Saraqusṭī was writing during the Almoravid age (448/1056–541/1147). The Almoravids were Berbers with little understanding either of the Arabic language or of the subtleties of its poetry. During their rule, the two greatest Andalusī poets were Ibn Ḥafāja (450/1058–533/1138), who abandoned the panegyric *qaṣīda* and adapted it to praise the beauties and mysteries of nature (Monroe 1973, al-Nowaihi 1993, Yaqub 1999, Garulo 1999, Liebhaber 2003), and Ibn Quzmān (d. 555/1160), who abandoned the Classical Arabic language altogether, to write mock panegyrics, not of sublime rulers, but of his everyday fellow citizens, in Colloquial Andalusī Arabic, and in a native, Ibero-Romance form, the *zajal*. This is one more indication, among many, that the panegyrical *qaṣīda* had ceased to be viable in al-Andalus, for lack of a courtly environment to sustain it (García Gómez 1945 and 1949, Garulo 1999).[17]

Al-Saraqusṭī was not only a *maqāma* writer, but also a poet, whose poetic production was collected into a *dīwān* now lost. It is significant, however, that of the ten poems by him, that are not included in his *maqāmāt*, and that have survived, five are love songs, while the remaining five, which are panegyrics, are all dedicated to princes from the pre-Almoravid period of the *mulūk al-ṭawā'if* (ca. 400/1010–483/1090).[18] If one excludes al-

---

17. The major center of literary patronage for poets under the *mulūk al-ṭawā'if* was the Seville of the 'Abbādids, particularly under the reign of al-Mu'tamid (r. 461/1069–484/1091), who was himself a poet. As García Gómez pointed out, after that king was deposed by the Almoravids, and literary patronage disappeared, the topos of "hatred of Seville" became a commonplace among disgruntled poets, whose productions were no longer appreciated in that city.

18. These surviving poems are collected, edited, and translated in Monroe (1997a): 31–37.

Saraqustī's non-literary, philological works (of which the dates are unknown and which are irrelevant to the present argument), and concentrates exclusively on his surviving poems, one notes that, from the period after the Almoravid conquest of al-Andalus (484/1091) only his *maqāmāt*, of which the poetry is rarely panegyrical, are extant. He too, clearly seems, after the Almoravid conquest, to have suffered from a crisis in patronage.

The *maqāma* does not deal primarily with rulers in their courts (when it does so, it is ironic, and not sincerely encomiastic); instead, it deals with society at large, which it views with a suspicious eye, providing us with a negative portrait of its pretensions, activities, and aspirations. If the *qaṣīda* is a genre for the consumption of insiders, privy to royal courts, the *maqāma* may be viewed as the literature of rejected and disgruntled outsiders no longer welcome at those courts (hatred of Seville), and who turn a critical eye on society at large. Finally, to take this argument one step farther, one suspects that, in the poetry of Ibn Quzmān, the praise-poem has either come to be influenced by the *maqāma*, from which it has acquired a clownish, ironic, and picaresque approach to society in general, along with a deceptive surface that, nonetheless, masks a very serious underlying purpose, or else, the very same social conditions that led to the rise of the *maqāma*, and its adoption and cultivation in al-Andalus, also brought about the radical changes introduced into the panegyrical *qaṣīda* by Ibn Quzmān and his predecessors.

Thanks to the genius of Ibn Quzmān, who was clearly a literate poet, despite the fact that he wrote in a colloquial dialect, the *zajal* which, in its seemingly oral prehistory, appears to have been as scurrilous as it was scandalous, thereby serving as a perfect vehicle for *hijāʾ*, was able to continue serving this important social function (albeit indirectly and ironically) in al-Andalus.

New Text, Old Theories: Oral and Improvisational Imperatives in Federico García Lorca's "Romance Sonámbulo"

Wifredo de Ràfols

Improvisation is the name of a comedy club I used to frequent in Los Angeles, where comedy routines were more often, well, routine than improvised. Only the most experienced comedians would chance speaking extemporaneously before an audience. Even when interacting with the public in apparently unique exchanges, the improvisational talent of these stand-ups obviously banked on a sizeable toolbox of one-liners, come-backs, and jokes. The truth is that it's not always easy to know the precise extent to which an ad-libber is winging it; only the ad-libber knows for sure how much depends on memory and how much is invented on the spot. The same might hold for the living tradition of *bertsolaritza*, except that its reverence of spontaneous invention –even to the point of abhorring the verbatim recitation of a single verse– assures us otherwise. This assurance is stronger when we witness the invention and stronger still when we know and have an opportunity to interact with the *bertsolari*.

In spite of these assurances, the distinction to be drawn between traditional and improvisational oral poetry is confounded by factors related to the originality of any given performance. The latter poetry is sometimes called "oral non-traditional poetry" because it is not based on a tradition of previous recitations, but this may not be the most suitable term, if only because the practice *is* traditional, at least in the sense that it is grounded on a longstanding custom of composing poetry on the spur of the moment. Originality is vital in improvisational poetry, but not normally of much concern in the oral traditional kind. Yet, when a bard simultaneously composes and performs a piece that is based on a formulaic system, a theme, and a story-pattern, how original is it? One way to speak of degrees of originality in oral poetry is to posit hypothetical extremes in a continuum that ranges from purely extemporaneous composition to wholly memorized delivery, with a composition created on the basis of traditional "building blocks" (formulas, themes, story-patterns) falling somewhere in between. Since *bertsolaritza* radically espouses spontaneity, let us place it, for the moment, toward the initial part of this continuum.

Oral poetry participates in a metaphysics of presence that requires the attendance of a listener and an authenticating speaker. To the extent that this speaker (or singer) delivers a verbal composition from memory –for example, a Spanish formulaic *romance* passed on from prior generations or from another locality– its authorship, in the modern sense, is subject to question. After all, the singer is most likely not the original author, even if the composition is in some way enhanced or impaired during oral transmission and is not based on a fixed text intended for verbatim recitation. The same cannot be said of *bertsolaritza* and other improvised poetry –like that practiced by *decimistas* in Cuba, Louisiana, Murcia, and the Canary Islands– which participates in what might be called a metaphysics of absolute presence; since here the audience is present at a one-time, unique event in which it is understood that the performer and the author are one and the same, the authenticity of the piece can hardly be questioned in the same manner. Moreover, as spectators and listeners of *bertsoak*, we witness not only an author who performs (or a performer who authors), but also the act of creating a singular work that is not founded on any particular antecedent – rather than the act of creating a new form of what may already be a multiform work. Thus, although originality is thought to be a Romantic notion that sprung from print-culture (Ong 1982: 133), it is by no means an alien concept in the art of *bertsolaritza* and other improvisational traditions. On the contrary, where the mnemonic imperative of orality in Europe was driven by duplication and dissemination –at a time when authorship (let alone copyright) was of little or no concern– the improvisational imperative of *bertsolaritza* and similar traditions already was driven by a protocentric will to celebrate the first and only instantiation of a work and to preserve the author-performer unity. This determination to hold creativity and authorship sacrosanct speaks to the etymological cores of both "originality" and "poetry" by insisting, on the one hand, on the value of innovation and, on the other, as much or more on the value of making (*poiesis*) as on the value of what is made. Much in the same way that post-copyright era authors become celebrities, *bertsolaritza* and similar traditions, probably since archaic times, have celebrated authors rather than works. This is to be expected, since the improvised oral utterance vanishes as soon as it is uttered, while the performer-composer remains to tell another tale.

The more skilled and experienced the *bertsolari*, the more prepared he or she is to deliver unprepared presentations and to win the *txapelketak*, or championship competitions. But the requirements of improvisation are not easily satisfied, since they entail, as my use of the words "prepared" and "unprepared" a moment ago predicted, certain inescapable contradictions. We need not recall the words of Lucretius, "*nihil posse creari de nihilo*," to realize that no *bertsolari* can invent *in vacuo*, on a *tabula rasa*, bereft of all knowledge. Usually the *bertsolari* has in mind some inkling of what to compose, perhaps the topic, general story, emotional thrust, or theme that will steer the invention, and is equipped with considerable information and insight about the language, culture, and poetics that will govern it. In these instances what is preordained is the prosodic formula, the topic, and the cultural context; what is not preordained is the exact manner in which these prescriptions will be filled. Gorka Aulestia concedes that "as soon as he chooses his melody, the *bertsolari* already knows what type of verse he will create, its various possibilities for poetic discourse, and the emotional tone that he will set with the melody" (1995: 22). The musical component may not be entirely original or improvised, even if the music is only incidental: "The accompanying melodies are usually popular and of older origin. Melody serves as the foundation of the *bertsolari*'s improvised poetry" (Aulestia 1995: 31). The same holds for other improvisational traditions, like that practiced by *decimistas*. At competitions, themes are assigned; the results might be called, to borrow a term from music, "variations on a theme."[1] In all of these restrictive senses, *bertsolaritza*, or the art of improvising sung verse, is not too far removed from oral traditional poetry in which a nonverbatim rendition of a work is recomposed by relying on building blocks. While the predeterminants of *bertsolaritza* do not seem to be either as numerous or as deeply encoded as those of oral traditional poetry –which may include prefabricated phrases, syntactical formulas, stock story-lines, epithets, and names of people and places from earlier versions– gauging the exact degree of inventiveness associated with any given composition-performance is beyond our ken. With respect to Aulestia's findings (1995), James W. Fernandez has noted that, since *bertsolari* compositions are relatively brief, "the underlying presence of guiding schema [might] be detected in a more detailed analysis of a significant sample" of verses (Fernandez 1996: 404). For the time being, however, I think we can surmise that *bertsolaritza* resides more toward the initial part of our originality continuum than does oral traditional poetry, and that its logic of improvisation entails a necessary and especially strong play between the foreseen (*provisus*) and the unforeseen (*improvisus*). In *bertsolaritza*, where more is intentionally unforeseen than in oral traditional poetry, this play is all the more likely to produce occasional linguistic, melodic, inflectional, or gestural accidents. Of these, the linguistic kind are the most apt to occur (or to be noticeable), since the prosodic and discursive requirements are the most stringent.

The extempore nature of the performance forbids emending these accidents, among which we might find, for example, an occasional ungrammatical utterance or a lack of causality in conveying a sequence of events. In addition, since the performing-composing consciousness is continually under pressure to provide the next word and to do so always within certain prosodic, topical, and cultural constraints, it is likely, at times, to tap the unconscious, in a manner not unrelated to that occasioned by a classic slip of the tongue. Since the use of parallel structures eases impromptu composition, it is likewise one of the features of improvisational poetry. The same holds for the use of end-stopped lines and stichomythia. To these etiological observations must be added a trait of *bertsolaritza* that

---

1. Zulaika (1985) points out that these contests now assume the aura of sporting events rather than artistic performances, which does not necessarily bode well for the art of *bertsolaritza*. The same is true of *decimista* competitions elsewhere, where scoring performances on numerical scales is anathema to the art of improvisation.

Xabier Amuriza and Jon Sarasua, Gasteiz, Basque Country, 1992. *Bertsolaritza* is close to a pure form of improvisation, in the strong, inherent relationship between the foreseen and unforeseen.
By permission of the Xenpelar Dokumentazio Zentroa, Donostia.

was put forward by Manuel de Lekuona in his seminal *Literatura oral vasca* (1935; rpt. 1964 and 1978). In contrasting the imagistic serenity of written poetry with the flurry of vivid images found in *bertsoak*, Lekuona put forward an analogy that may not have the same import now, after the development of motorized digital cameras, as it did when he proposed it, but its intended meaning is clear: the images of improvisation come rapidly, as though taken with an instant camera (1964: 22). This swiftness, which Lekuona notes is at times vertiginous, refers to the succession of images and concepts in the work. Indeed, improvised poetry is likely to contain more images per verse than poetry produced after calm forethought and careful revision. Lekuona suggests that this density is characterized by a relative abundance of elisions, by a notable absence of rhetorical and grammatical connectors (parataxis), by a certain laxity in obeying a logical or chronological order, and by an apparent lack of relatedness between some images and the subject matter (1964: 23). To these observations we must add another noted by Aulestia: ellipses, especially verb-omissions, are common (1995: 59–60). Yet, as anyone familiar with the Parry-Lord theory knows, many of these same features are symptomatic of any oral traditional poetry that does not rely on verbatim recitation, and even of some that do. This is because the pressure to produce the next word in real time is shared by traditional and improvisational oral poets alike, and, more peculiarly, because many of the same factors that ease pure improvisation also ease oral composition based on building blocks; in turn, some of these same factors ease memorization. Parataxis, for example, is a fairly constant feature straight across the originality continuum. Shunning repetition of set phrases, however, is characteristic of *bertsolaritza* and not of oral traditional poetry in general, whether partly improvised or wholly memorized – even if *bertsoak* sometimes include a refrain which the audience can repeat at the end with the *bertsolari* (Aulestia 1995: 33). Epithets, on the other hand, are more common in oral traditional poetry than in *bertsolaritza*. Irrespective of these important distinctions, it stands to reason that the more we move toward the left of our continuum, that is, toward *bertsolaritza* and a hypothetically pure improvisation, the more likely we are to encounter the accidents referred to earlier. Indeed, *bertsolaritza* adherents have words for such accidents, among them, *betelana* (a logical error in a *bertso*) and *poto egin* (erroneously repeating a rhyme within a verse). To be sure, what an orally improvised poem may lack in coherence and rationality is more than offset by the resonance and musicality which the prosodic requirements lend to it, and, especially, by the genuineness, daring, and immediacy associated with its spontaneous production, as well as by the somatic components that accompany it. Transcribed, the rhetorical, logical, and unconsciously derived imperfections of oral improvisational poetry may be read by some as blunders to be excused or oddities to be overlooked, but they also constitute the telltale marks, if not the hallmarks and the charm, of extemporized invention. Since we cannot penetrate the heart and mind of the improvisational artist to determine the exact manner in which the foreseen and the unforeseen coalesce to generate poetry, we can do no better than to learn to recognize those telltale marks and attempt to understand their significance.

As a discipline, oral performance criticism must embrace reiteration and improvisation as coagents of orally based thought.[2] With respect to improvisation, the author-per-

---

2. Walter J. Ong, in his influential *Orality and Literacy* (1982), goes far in establishing the elements of such a discipline, although he neglects improvisation in general and oral improvisational poetry in particular.

former unity and protocentrism of *bertsolaritza* –and similar improvisational traditions– provide fertile grounds for oral performance critics trained not only in anthropology and ethnography but also in literary criticism. When literary scholars record, transcribe, and study orally transmitted works, however, the scene of collection may be artificial (a scholar and a tape recorder), the resulting publications are perforce bound in visual rather than aural textuality, and the accompanying interpretations are likely to be the product of a hermeneutic process that is akin to scrutinizing a motion picture by studying the screenplay rather than by watching the movie. Moreover, when those of us who are trained in literary studies practice oral performance criticism, we are naturally inclined to borrow from the highly developed tenets of literary criticism; when we do so, we must be wary of using a typographic mindset to analyze the product of an oral one, bearing in mind that analysis is, in the first place, a construct favored by literate rather than oral cultures.

The reader will have guessed that I am about to risk doing the opposite, namely, to borrow from the tenets of oral performance criticism with a view to engaging, through an ostensibly oral mindset, a printed text – in particular, our Peninsula's most celebrated and studied poem of the twentieth century, Federico García Lorca's "Romance sonámbulo." In the process, I hope to show that literary criticism can benefit from applying orally based precepts to interpret and appreciate a typographic artifact. I will suggest neither that Lorca penned this renowned ballad in one fell swoop, in an impromptu fit of automatic writing, nor that he was in any way influenced by *bertsolaritza* or *decimistas* (in this respect, the regional influences of the Andalusian *cante jondo* and the Spanish *romance*, not nearly as author-centered or protocentric as *bertsolaritza*, cannot be discounted). An approach to Lorca's "Romance" that calls to mind the symptomatic features of orality and improvisation will prove useful for other reasons.

As with most artists, inspiration and craftsmanship were not always balanced impulses in Lorca, who was wont to produce some poems spontaneously and others after considerable effort.[3] We know that he relished reciting his poetry publicly in conferences and privately to friends, to whom he would sometimes give his scrawled verses, never to be read by him again – and never to be published.[4] Lorca loved the vocal moment more than the written page and, as his friend Jorge Guillén notes, looked for listeners rather than readers (1986: XLVII). "Nunca se recalcará bastante," writes Guillén, "que en Federico renacía el bardo anterior a la imprenta" (1986: xlv). However much Lorca's thinking may have been orally based, his published poetry is taken to have been composed by setting pen to paper and, accordingly, is judged and interpreted with a chirographic mindset, with critical eyes that are accustomed to deploying a wide gamut of literary rather than oral constructs. "Romance sonámbulo" is more than a case in point because, aside from the

---

3. Commenting on Lorca's work habits, Jorge Guillén notes that "hubo romances que fueron escritos de un golpe" (1986: lxiii); on the other hand, Lorca notes that one ballad, "Gitanillo apaleado," took him six weeks to write (García Lorca 1986: III, 884).

4. Lorca knew "Romance sonámbulo" and many other poems by heart; Rafael Alberti recalls that Lorca recited the ballad to him in a garden when they first met (Gibson 1989: 139).

Federico García Lorca. Lorca cherished the oral performance of his poetry, and sought listeners before readers. This demonstrates the still powerful influence of the oral tradition on the modern literary tradition.

accolades it has garnered, it bears the distinction of having been interpreted in countless ways, many of them mutually contradictory, by absolutist and relativist critics alike, with the result that the poem has turned into a resounding testament to indeterminacy and a veritable Rorschach test of our literary sensibilities. Our failure to appreciate the extent to which the poem participates in the time-honored tradition of oral performance, together with our unwavering determination to apply literary constructs to a work that, in my view, evokes orality and improvisation rather than literacy and premeditation, may well account for the broad disparity of the authoritative interpretations it has provoked, as well as for the intensity of certain ongoing quarrels about its intended meaning. The improvisational imperative typically gives rise to gaps that are filled in very differently by literary critics, who, more often than not, apply divergent generic biases and overriding literary principles which, when the gaps are filled accordingly, confirm, in each instance, that the biases and principles applied were the right ones (see Ràfols 1995: 366). Among the quarrels, we find elaborate arguments on both sides of the broad question of genre (is the poem narrative or lyrical or both?) and disputes about more specific issues like whether, at the beginning of the piece, the *gitana* is dead or alive. My proposing to take the Rorschach test with an ostensibly oral mindset will not resolve these quandaries –it may, in fact, add to them– but it should serve to explain how the poem fosters them and how orality admits, paradoxically, varying interpretations from different listeners. I say "paradoxically" because speech, unlike writing, is held to guarantee the full presence and integrity of meaning, since the speaker is present; in actuality, listeners may walk away with very different impressions of what was said, especially when what was said bears the peculiar stamps of orally based thought and improvisation. In our phonocentric attempt to appreciate Lorca's "Romance sonámbulo," let us, then, listen (García Lorca 1986: I, 400–403):

1   Verde que te quiero verde.
    Verde viento. Verdes ramas.
    El barco sobre la mar
    y el caballo en la montaña.
5   Con la sombra en la cintura
    ella sueña en su baranda,
    verde carne, pelo verde,
    con ojos de fría plata.
    Verde que te quiero verde.
10 Bajo la luna gitana,
    las cosas la están mirando
    y ella no puede mirarlas.
                    *
    Verde que te quiero verde.
    Grandes estrellas de escarcha,
15 vienen con el pez de sombra
    que abre el camino del alba.
    La higuera frota su viento
    con la lija de sus ramas,
    y el monte, gato garduño,
20 eriza sus pitas agrias.
    ¿Pero quién vendrá? ¿Y por dónde...?
    Ella sigue en su baranda,
    verde carne, pelo verde,
    soñando en la mar amarga.
                    *
25 Compadre, quiero cambiar
    mi caballo por su casa,
    mi montura por su espejo,
    mi cuchillo por su manta.
    Compadre, vengo sangrando,
30 desde los puertos de Cabra.
    Si yo pudiera, mocito,
    ese trato se cerraba.
    Pero yo ya no soy yo,
    ni mi casa es ya mi casa.
35 Compadre, quiero morir
    decentemente en mi cama.
    De acero, si puede ser,
    con las sábanas de holanda.
    ¿No ves la herida que tengo
40 desde el pecho a la garganta?
    Trescientas rosas morenas
    lleva tu pechera blanca.
    Tu sangre rezuma y huele
    alrededor de tu faja.

45 Pero yo ya no soy yo,
    ni mi casa es ya mi casa.
    Dejadme subir al menos
    hasta las altas barandas,
    ¡dejadme subir!, dejadme,
50 hasta las verdes barandas.
    Barandales de la luna
    por donde retumba el agua.
                    *
    Ya suben los dos compadres
    hacia las altas barandas.
55 Dejando un rastro de sangre.
    Dejando un rastro de lágrimas.
    Temblaban en los tejados
    farolillos de hojalata.
    Mil panderos de cristal,
60 herían la madrugada.
                    *
    Verde que te quiero verde,
    verde viento, verdes ramas.
    Los dos compadres subieron.
    El largo viento dejaba
65 en la boca un raro gusto
    de hiel, de menta y de albahaca.
    ¡Compadre! ¿Dónde está, dime?
    ¿Dónde está tu niña amarga?
    ¡Cuántas veces te esperó!
70 ¡Cuántas veces te esperara,
    cara fresca, negro pelo,
    en esta verde baranda!
                    *
    Sobre el rostro del aljibe
    se mecía la gitana.
75 Verde carne, pelo verde,
    con ojos de fría plata.
    Un carámbano de luna
    la sostiene sobre el agua.
    La noche se puso íntima
80 como una pequeña plaza.
    Guardias civiles borrachos
    en la puerta golpeaban.
    Verde que te quiero verde.
    Verde viento. Verdes ramas.
85 El barco sobre la mar.
    Y el caballo en la montaña.

The first source of bewilderment is the title, about which critics have hazarded an impressive assortment of interpretations, most of them related to determining just who in "Romance sonámbulo" is somnambulating. For Lázló András and others, it is the *gitana* who sleepwalks (1978: 186), to which Federico Bonaddio objects that there is an "absence of detail regarding her movement in sleep from one place to another" (1995: 387). This objection is moot for readers who feel that the girl drowned accidentally in the cistern while sleepwalking, before the poem begins. H. Ramsden, however, believes that she cast herself into the water "like a sleepwalker," lured by the moon and its reflection (1988: 28). In turn, this distinction between being a sleepwalker and acting like one is unimportant for readers who are sure that the girl committed suicide. One such reader, Juan Felipe García Santos, offers four interpretations of the title, the fourth of which –the one he prefers– being that "sonámbulo" alludes to events taking place at night, near dawn (1998: 89–90). Daniel Cárdenas believes that "sonámbulo" means "moribundo" (1973: 112), while Alan Smith speaks of a somnambulistic reorganization of narrative time, based not on cause and effect, but on an unconscious causality, typical of dreams, that is governed by symbolic attractions and contagions (1993: 69, 71). Similarly, Beverly J. DeLong-Tonelli feels that the title prepares the reader for an oneiric experience in which symbols are key, although this, in her view, leads to a sense of "timelessness" and lyricism rather than of reorganized narrative time (1971: 290, 294). Robert G. Havard, who believes that there is no sleepwalker in the ballad, sees the title as a virtual instruction to read the poem as a dream, which he does splendidly, by the light of Freud (1988: 196–202). For Bonaddio, the title word "sonámbulo" fuses two separate activities, since the *gitana* does the dreaming (thus, the sleeping), and the two *compadres* do the walking. Bonaddio further argues that female roles are linked to lyrical passages and male roles to narrative ones, which leads him to conclude that the title word "sonámbulo" also encapsulates "the fusion of lyric and narrative *romance* modes." This ingenious interpretation of the title word has the advantage of supporting his thesis of generic fusion (1995: 387–388), a perhaps unnecessary feat in the eyes of those who view the *romance* form as a hybrid of epic and lyric genres (Armistead 1994b: ix). All told, and setting aside still other interpretations of the title and what has been written about somnambulism in Lorca's poetry in general (see, for example, Aguirre 1975), answers to who is sleepwalking in "Romance sonámbulo" range from the *gitana* alone (either before or during the poem), to the *gitana* and the *compadres*, to the *mocito* alone, to no one, to the "poetdreamer," to the ballad itself. Each of these conflicting positions is argued more forcefully and elaborately than I can reflect here, and each is naturally entwined in interpretations of the piece as a whole, in ways that support those interpretations even as they are consequences of them.

My reluctance to embrace any of these explanations of the title is not based on qualms about their logic or hermeneutic circularity; instead I wonder about the wisdom of placing so much weight on two words which, given the orality of the piece, might have been set at the top of it as a literate afterthought, albeit a masterful one. "Title" is derived from the Latin *titulus*, meaning "superscription," "inscription," "label," concepts more germane to writing than to natural speech. In this respect, Ong reminds us that "written or printed representations of words can be labels; real, spoken words cannot be" (1982: 33). Titles are useful identifiers in books, indices, and catalogs, less so in oral poetry –especially the improvisational kind– although a title might have the effect of inclining the audience toward a particular kind of reception (DeLong-Tonelli is one Lorca critic who entertains this aural notion [1971: 290]; Havard's similar view is by contrast graphocentric, where the title is equivalent to an instruction to read, and thereby to ana-lyze, the poem in a particular way [1988: 202]). While a title like *La casa de Bernarda Alba* is a perfect octosyllabic with bountiful alliteration in *a*, "Romance sonámbulo" is not, nor does it enjoy any particular prosodic relationship (other than hypometry) with the poem it names. That relationship is instead purely descriptive, with respect to the first word, and probably more evocative than descriptive, with respect to the second – it has cer-tainly evoked a wide array of interpretations. While a title is essentially a parergual apparatus that may be viewed as residing both inside and outside the work (*ergon*), most typographic folk tend to view it as a constituent part of the work; some, like García Santos in his essay on Lorca's ballad, go so far as to suggest that the title is in the work even when the work bears no title: "El título es la palabra clave de un texto, porque el título nos da el *tema*. Tan importante es el título que, si un texto no lo tiene, la primera labor será ponerle un título [...]" (1998: 86). This chirographic fixation on titularity goes hand in hand with other exegetic chores, like settling on a theme with doctrinal con-tent and discovering a figurative key that cracks the text's code. Instead, in the realm of song, a title is more exergual than not, and I think we are safe to assume that the title was not the first thing on Lorca's mind when he began to compose the piece, nor, in musical terms, is it the first note that we hear when the ballad begins, nor, if we accept his claim that he had no idea of what happens in the poem (García Lorca 1986: III, 341), is the title likely to contain any key to unlocking its meaning.[5] On the contrary, the title seems to have had the effect of placing the ballad on many an analyst's couch, and of multiplying rather than limiting the number of interpretations. As an orally delivered exergual prompt, the title may simply have the effect of lifting us away from ordinary consciousness.

Bertsolariak might call the ballad's initial verse an error, for it is repeated often, it begins and ends with the same word, and it is identical to the first verse of a popular song that Juan Ramón Jiménez claims to have heard in his youth: "Verde que te quiero verde / del color de la aceituna / con el pelo derramado / y los ojos con la luna" (1959: 35). Irrespective of whether Lorca was familiar with these verses, and irrespective of whether he cited the first verse intentionally, Juan Ramón's claim (to my knowledge, no scholar

---

5. In addition to claiming that he did not know what happens in the poem, Lorca correctly predicted that it would con-tinue to give rise to shifting interpretations: "Siempre tendrá luces cambiantes, aun para el hombre que lo ha comunicado, que soy yo" (García Lorca 1986: III, 343).

has collected these four verses independently) enhances the oral dimension of the ballad even as it adds to the already wide-ranging views on the meanings of its first verse and the color green. Among other difficulties associated with the verse is determining the identities of the "yo" and "tú" in "te quiero."

The lack of graphic markers (quotation marks, dashes) that would help indicate which words are attributable to which speaker –especially during the perceptible dialogs in verses 25–52 and 67–73– is a reflection of the orality of the piece and the extent to which it flows from a single agent who may well be improvising, without pausing to specify who says what. Listeners fill in these voids automatically, aided by the somatic component of delivery and the inflections of the speaker, whereas readers must do a bit of deciphering, especially on a first reading, to determine who is speaking.[6] While there is some consensus about who speaks to whom in the dialogs (less so about their relationship to each other and to the *gitana*), one listener might decide that the often repeated "Verde que te quiero verde" is meant to be in quotes, as a phrase mentioned rather than used, while another might read it as voiced by one or more of the characters in the ballad or by the poetic I alone. András offers an interpretation of the asterisks between strophes (1978: 190); other graphically minded readers have suggested that a comma is needed between "Verde" and "que" – not the only proposal to dabble with punctuation in the poem. One scholar who has risked putting forward a phonocentric interpretation, at least of this verse, is Alan Smith, who suggests that "Verde que te quiero verde" vibrates sympathetically with "Verte que te quiero ver" (1993: 67).[7] This proposition is unlikely to find wide acceptance among typographic folk, notwithstanding Smith's reasoned arguments in favor of it. Havard suspects that the exceptional renown of what he rightly calls this "haunting verse" owes more to "subliminal than rational understanding," a suspicion that is subsequently upheld by his Freudian analysis of the poem (1988: 194). Some listeners might hear subliminally Jiménez's popular ballad or Smith's suggested echo, while others might visualize the beginning of Havard's attributions of oneiric projections or hear a surrealist call to dream; yet all must hear the sonority (seven of the eight syllables are in *e*) and anacoluthon-like ungrammaticality that signal this end-stopped line's orality.[8] Moreover, its epanalepsis (beginning and ending with "verde") is immediately compounded by the anadiplosis committed in the next elliptical and internally parallel verse, "Verde viento. Verdes ramas." The ensuing repetition of "verde" and of the entire verse "Verde que te quiero verde" throughout the ballad is cumulative, appearing in such a way that meanings develop from one recur-

---

6. This notion is in marked contrast with Havard's observation that "the ballad tradition, being oral, always took great care to introduce and distinguish between speakers" (1988: 202). But there are many exceptions to this rule, which should be modified to read "often," or even "sometimes," rather than "always."

7. In like manner, albeit for metaphorical rather than phonetic reasons, Cárdenas proposes that "Muerte que te quiero muerte" is equivalent (1973: 114).

8. The epanalepsis of the initial verse is akin to that found in the initial verses of several *romances,* as in the version of the death of King Ferdinand I that begins, "Doliente, estaba doliente" (C. Colin Smith 1969: 88).

rence to the next. This incremental repetition of the verse and the word, typical of oral poetry, produces in audition an effect of emotional intensification, which culminates at the end of the poem.[9] In my estimation, the ballad achieves its strongest emotional impact by traditionally oral means: the same four verses that tend to be associated enigmatically with life in the beginning are associated enigmatically with death in the end.

As to who speaks to whom in "te quiero," some readers posit that the girl speaks to the young man, others vice versa, others a combination of both (for example, that the girl is recalling what the young man used to say to her), and still others that, in the verse, the poetic I or Lorca himself (as a poet-dreamer) is expressing his desire, the object of which is erotic and perchance taboo, but not otherwise clearly defined within the poem. For my part, the initial verse (five occurrences, irregularly distributed), the couplet it forms with the second verse (as a couplet, three occurrences, irregularly distributed), and the quatrain it forms with the next three verses (as a quatrain, two occurrences), combine a feature that is symptomatic of improvisation (irregularity) with features that are symptomatic of ritual (repetition, especially of the quatrain or refrain that marks the beginning and end of the ballad as a ring composition).

Albert Bates Lord described three general divisions of oral poetry by genre: ritual, lyric, and narrative (1993: 863). Arguments about whether Lorca's piece is lyrical or narrative (or both) overlook the genre where the origins of oral poetry ought to be sought, namely, ritual, of which the refrain, in the context of our ballad, reflects two types: incantation and lament. Just as *bertsoak* sometimes contain a refrain which the audience can repeat at the end with the *bertsolari* (Aulestia 1995: 33), the audience can repeat Lorca's refrain, whose incantatory effects, as a resonant expression of desire that is designed to move rather than convince or explain, are compounded and woven throughout the ballad by way of twenty-four occurrences of "verde." The reiteration –epanalepsis and anadiplosis– contained within the initial couplet is typical of the way many *romances* begin (see note 8), where the repetition, as C. Colin Smith notes, "is intended simply to have an incantatory effect, lifting our minds from everyday reality [...]" (1969: 35). As we will see, the spellbinding sorrow cast by the refrain may not be apparent in the beginning of the ballad, but it should be more than apparent in the end.

The third and fourth verses ("El barco sobre la mar / y el caballo en la montaña") of the refrain constitute a parallelistic couplet whose orality further resides in ellipsis (no verbs), parataxis (conjunction only), and swiftly moving imagery (ship, sea, horse, mountain). Connecting its parallel structure with that of the previous verse leads to the possibility that "Verde viento" refers to the wind that propels the ship on the green sea, while

---

9. While critics have interpreted *verde* in dozens of ways (unripe orange, lime, olive, life, hope, desire, eroticism, nature, spring, youth, fertility, spirit, pain, sadness, death, despair, disillusionment, putrefied flesh, Salvador Dalí's complexion, and so on), whichever meanings we associate with it in the initial verses most likely will be compounded, if not radically transformed, by the time we hear the final ones. As with somnambulism and the moon, the color green in Lorca has merited concerted study – see, for example, Havard (1972).

"Verdes ramas" refers to branches on the mountain.[10] Notwithstanding this possibility, most readers construe the images of the third and fourth verses as symbols of femininity (the vessel on the sea) and virility (the horse on the mountain). Yet no great appreciation of symbolic logic is required to associate the first image with the girl and the second with the young man, since she, a "niña amarga," dreams on the sea ("soñando en la mar amarga") and he, apparently having just arrived from the "monte," speaks of his "caballo" and "montura." (Note that she dreams "on" and not "of" the sea, contrary to what Cobb writes [1983: 71].)[11] Any sense of propriety –the ship is on the sea, the horse is in the mountain, things are where they belong– felt at the beginning of the piece is quashed by the time these four verses are repeated at the end, at least for listeners who associate the girl with the ship on the sea and the young man with the horse on the mountain. For, by the end of the piece, these same listeners must associate the first image with that of a girl's body floating on the cistern, and the second with that of a horseman who was mortally wounded on the mountain. With these parallelistic associations in mind, a sensitive performer can hardly intone the couplet in the same way at the beginning as at the end of the piece; a pause to mark the difference and to emphasize the separation between ship and horse (or between the *gitana* and the *mocito*, one dead and the other death-stricken) is fitting, and is reflected in the text by the period that separates the two final verses – where none does so at the beginning of the ballad. Aside from its technically oral features, the quatrain, then, is also thematically oral: it is doubly ritualistic, as both incantation and lament.

Many interpretations of the fifth verse, "Con la sombra en la cintura," focus on various symbolic meanings of "sombra" (death, approaching dawn, suicide, and homosexuality) and neglect a more plain understanding of it as simply descriptive. When we consider its syntactically chiasmic relationship with the eighth verse, "con ojos de fría plata," which is repeated verbatim in verse 76 –when it appears that the girl is dead, floating on the water by the light of a probably crescent ("carámbano") moon– the shadow at her waist could well be that cast by her belly if she were heavy with child. As motifs, neither *cintura* nor pregnancy are alien to the oral tradition, which can be as explicit as "de la cintura abajo / como hombre y mujer se han" (C. Colin Smith 1969: 173) and "Ximena quedó preñada" (Díaz-Mas 1994: 115); nor is the death of a pregnant bride exceptional (Díaz-Mas 1994: 402). The advantage of hazarding this interpretation is that it requires no figurative maneuvering –the shadow at her waist is literally a shadow at her waist–

---

10. More than one critic (Cobb 1983: 71; Miller 1986: 17; Semprún 1974: 259) believes that the green branches are a phallic symbol, a reading which Havard and Semprún also apply to the fish and the fig tree (Havard 1988: 200). The green wind is more clearly erotic in another *Romancero gitano* ballad, "Preciosa y el aire," where Preciosa is pursued by the "viento-hombrón" who has asked her to let him lift her dress to see her, when a voice is heard to say, "¡Preciosa, corre, Preciosa, / que te coge el viento verde!" (García Lorca 1986: I, 396).

11. Lorca might have intended "soñando *con* la mar amarga" and avoided it because it would produce one syllable too many. I prefer to hear the preposition *en* as consistent with "ella sueña en su baranda," and with the notion that the waters of the cistern are comparable to the waters of the sea, as I will explain shortly. On *con* versus *en*, see Alonso (1973: 133).

and that it doubles the elegiac poignancy of the ballad as a ritualistic lament.[12] Next comes a problematic verse in which the *gitana* "dreams" on her veranda or balcony railing. The verse is problematic because some believe that, if she is dreaming, she must be alive, while others surmise that she is dead, taking the verb "to dream" and, therefore, "to sleep," as a conventional euphemism for death. I favor this latter view because it is more consistent with the adjacent verses: the couplet it forms with "verde carne, pelo verde" is repeated in verse 75, where the girl is apparently dead – in contrast with what she used to look like when alive, with her "cara fresca, negro pelo" (verse 71); "ojos de fría plata" certainly implies death; and the final two paratactic verses of this strophe ("las cosas la están mirando / y ella no puede mirarlas") likewise suggest death. The effectiveness of these last two verses cannot be underestimated: in this totalizing vision, under a personified gypsy moon, the surrounding objects are personified also, looking at someone who cannot look back. In a sense, the speaker empathizes with the scene and the surroundings to the point of melting away, as though what is seen in this purely visual strophe were brought to us by the things themselves rather than by a mediating subject.

Since time will not permit me to address ensuing verses individually, I want to continue in broader strokes, focusing on a few salient verses and, especially, on the ballad's motifs and oral features. With "las cosas la están mirando" fresh in our minds, in the subsequent strophe we hear more details about the environs, including the fig tree and the mountain, depicted in a paratactic quatrain that intensifies and makes patent the effect of the wind, even as it raises the dramatic tension. (There is no dearth of symbolist interpretations here either, including one which views the movement of the fig tree's branches as a "masturbatory action" and the cat fur and agaves as "erection motifs" [Havard 1988: 200; see also Semprún 1974: 259]). The anomalous "¿Pero quién vendrá? ¿Y por dónde …?" disrupts the lyrical flow of these surrealistic descriptions in a classically oral and audience-centered move that invokes narrativity, encloses a journey motif, and heightens our sense of anticipation. Disruptive and elliptical, the verse has an improvisational tone, as though the composer-performer were wondering aloud what will happen next. More importantly, the two questions imbue the whole panorama and, in particular, the veranda-as-look-out-point, with a sense of waiting – a sense that is confirmed later, in verses 69–72. As this second strophe ends, the *gitana* remains in her veranda, and the audience remains in suspense, wondering who will arrive.

The next strophe shifts abruptly to a dialog *in medias res*.[13] Here the listener is obliged to fill in many gaps – among them, the one between a drawn-out scene of waiting and, rather than an arrival or entrance, a sense of "he is already here and is speaking," without the usual "bien oiréis lo que dirá" or some such introductory remark. Listeners have

---

12. By itself, this interpretation neither reduces nor increases the possibility that the *gitana* drowned by suicide. If married, it reduces it; if unmarried, it increases it. On the Andalusian notion that suicide by drowning is the only respectable alternative for an unmarried pregnant woman, see Harris (1985: 91).

13. The ballad also begins and ends *in medias res*, as is often the case in oral, episodic narrative (Ong 1982: 144).

much to ponder. Is the interlocutor the one who was expected? Who is he? What is his relationship with the *gitana* and the *compadre*? Why is he bleeding? To be sure, this sort of leap from description to action *in medias res* is typical of the *fragmentismo* of Spanish ballads, which over time retain only the most significant and dramatic parts of the story. Normally, listeners fill in the rest, including who did what to whom, based on their recollections of history or previous versions of the ballad – unless their epic memories fail. Except that here there has never been any such collective memory or previous versions, nor anything to replace them except listeners' guesses about possible backgrounds to the story; all of this leads us to attribute the leap either to an improvisational impulse to move forward in recounting events, or to a willfully crafted imitation of balladic *fragmentismo*. Whichever is true, this third and most extensive strophe is also the one whose orality is most palpable, and not merely because it contains an unmarked dialog. The opening anaphoric quatrain, laden with images ("Compadre," "caballo," "casa," "montura," "espejo," "cuchillo," "manta"), is a formulaic exchange proposal whose contrasting imagery is not far removed from that noted in many traditional ballads, like "Fernán González y el Rey," where a swift medley of images linked to one person is contrasted with those linked to another ("vos con guantes olorosos | yo con los de acero claro; / vos con la gorra de fiesta, | yo con un casco afinado" [Díaz-Mas 1994: 128]). Much can be gathered about the sharp contrast between images linked to the *compadre* and images linked to the *mocito*, which, all told, reflect a longing on the part of the latter to change his lifestyle from a nomadic to sedentary one. The image of the *mocito* bleeding profusely as he travels is likewise traditionally agonistic (on the agonistic tone of oral poetry, see Ong 1982: 43–45), and is reminiscent of certain *romances*, like the Carolingian, "¡Oh Belerma!," where Durandarte arrives death-stricken, saying, "traigo grandes las heridas, / mucha sangre derramada" (C. Colin Smith 1969: 169) or the epic "Visión de don Pedro y el Reino perdido," where the king travels "tan tinto de sangre | que una brasa parescía" (Díaz-Mas 1994: 138). (This last epic *romance*, coincidentally, begins with images –wind, moon, fish– not unlike the initial images of "Romance sonámbulo": "Los vientos eran contrarios, | la luna estaba crescida, | los peces daban gemidos […]" [137]). Similarly formulaic is the twice repeated "Pero yo ya no soy yo / ni mi casa es ya mi casa," a parallelistic riddle that must remain unsolved until nearly the end of the ballad, when it is unraveled for listeners who gather that, when the *compadre* pronounced it, he had already discovered his lifeless daughter in the cistern, and was therefore distraught and no longer himself. This is the prevailing solution of the riddle, supported more strongly by textual evidence than, for example, Rupert Allen's contention that the *compadre*, as the *gitana*'s lover rather than father, is distraught because he has been betrayed by the *mocito* (1968: 342), or András's supposition that the *compadre* is distraught because the civil guards mentioned in the final strophe habitually come to the house to enjoy the *gitana*'s services, thus having turned the place into a bordello (1978: 192). In Miller's Jungian analysis, the *compadre* is only an archetypal projection of the *mocito* (the *gitana* is the *Anima* figure) and, since according to this view all three die in the end, the riddle means that "death is about to supplant [the *compadre*] as master of the house" (Miller 1986: 20). Whichever solution is correct, the larger point here is that "the riddle belongs in the oral world" (Ong 1982: 53).

The motif of wanting to die decently in bed is likewise time-honored in oral poetry, even in the detail of longing for "sábanas de holanda," an image echoed in *romances* like "Espinelo [Texto B]" ("Mandóle hacer la cama, | la cama de la enfermería: / le puso cinco almadraques, / sábanas de holanda fina" [Díaz-Mas 1994: 267]). Even more frequent in Spanish ballads and oral epics is the hyperbole of "Trescientas rosas morenas," akin to "trescientas cuerdas de plata" (Díaz-Mas 1994: 137), where the number 300 is a favorite in referring to large quantities of horses, knights, ladies in waiting, and so on (Díaz-Mas 1994: 99, 102, 185). The strophe ends with a plaintively repetitive last wish (a motif as ancient as poetry): let me at least go up, the *mocito* pleads, to the high veranda railings. Aside from the sonorous triple repetition of *dejadme* and *barandas/barandales*, these last six verses analeptically and proleptically serve to orient the listener with respect to the *gitana*'s whereabouts, and function also as a fixative that bonds several images: the veranda railings, the moon, and the color green hark back to her location in the initial strophe, while "barandas" and "barandales" extend the image of the formerly singular veranda railing, broadening our sense of the location; looking forward, the strophe's final verse, "por donde retumba el agua," brings the cistern into that expanded location –naturally at a high elevation, perhaps for purposes of irrigation– where the *gitana* will be found. In these final verses, then, the veranda railings and the cistern are associated with one and the same place.

The two men ascend to that place in the brief strophe that follows, which begins with the classic "ya suben" of oral epic descriptions (e.g., "ya lo llevan [...]," "ya tomaban [...]" [C. Colin Smith 1969: 162]). The parallelistic and elliptical couplet, "Dejando un rastro de sangre. / Dejando un rastro de lágrimas," is a vivid portrayal of anguish that is characteristic of oral genres (on gross physicality and orality, see Ong 1982: 44), which are not averse to juxtaposing blood and tears (for example Díaz-Mas 1994: 160). Obviously, the blood flows from the death-stricken *mocito*, the tears from the grief-stricken *compadre*. Some take the "Mil panderos de cristal" (note, again, the hyperbolic "Mil") to be a metaphor of rain, but the glass could easily be that of "farolillos" trembling in the wind. The emotional effect of the final quatrain is to raise the tension and rekindle our sense of anticipation as the men walk up to where we expect the *gitana* will be found.

The penultimate strophe repeats the opening incantation as the men arrive at their destination. Either coincidentally or perhaps as an unconscious impulse, the triple repetition, earlier, of the *mocito*'s plaintive "dejadme" now finds its third and final echo (the first two in "*Dejando* un rastro de sangre. / *Dejando* un rastro de lágrimas") in "El largo viento *dejaba* [...]." Among the more peculiar interpretations of these three verses (64–66) is one that views the "long wind" as a phallic symbol which, in the next verse, is introduced into the mouth, whereby the poet "has emphasized the homosexual nature of the imagery" (Cobb 1983: 72). I am perfectly content, instead, with a literal interpretation of these verses, which complete the sensorial dimensions of the ballad (sight, scent, sound, and, now, taste) in a manner that reflects a perhaps unconsciously derived consistency: the wind leaves the flavor of green things in the mouth. Moreover, given the *mocito*'s physical condition, the taste of bile in the mouth is not far-fetched, and the verses reflect the extent to which the poetic voice has interiorized, viscerally and empathetically, the character's sensations. The dialog is renewed as the *mocito*, presumably upon arriving at the "altas barandas," finds that the *gitana* is nowhere in sight. The conversation is again anaphoric and, while it does not reveal where the *gitana* might be, it confirms that this is the place where she would wait for the *mocito*, when her face was fresh and her hair was black – in contrast to her now greenish appearance. This confirmation comes doubly in "¡Cuántas veces te esperó! / ¡Cuántas veces te esperara […]," where "esperara" transmits the archaic value of the past tense (pluperfect or *pretérito indefinido*), frequent in oral epics and romances, and emphasizes that here is where the *gitana* would wait repeatedly and indefinitely for the *mocito* to arrive.

The final strophe is pithy and somber. Alongside the girl's floating body, the moon is reflected on the water, as if holding her there – an interpretation to which most critics subscribe, although, admittedly, it relies on liberal construals of *mecer* and *sostener*. Some readers attribute the girl's greenish countenance to moonlight reflecting on the veranda's foliage, while others view it simply as a surrealist device with multiple meanings. Then again, the algal waters of the cistern, normally used to collect rainwater, might account for the greenish coloration. The reaction to the moment of realization –here, finally, is the *gitana*, lifeless– for both the *mocito* and the audience is captured in the totalizing "La noche se puso íntima / como una pequeña plaza." The effect of this couplet, when orally and publicly delivered, is to lend a communal aspect to the ballad, linking the audience with the *compadres*, as though all of us were in a small public square where everyone knows all there is to know about everyone, and where the sad truth has just been revealed. The civil guards, drunken public servants, encroach on the scene and the ballad closes with its incantatory lament.

Of course we do not know everything there is to know about these characters. We probably know enough about them, however, to be riveted by the emotional implications of their condition and the situation, if not by the hypnotic effect of the ballad's incantatory repetitions and sheer aural power. The narrative component which conveys that condition is, as in oral genres, episodic and fragmentary, but this has not deterred some critics from imposing on it the kind of rigid pyramidical plot structure that belongs to print culture, where the climax is the moment when the girl is found dead in the cistern, and the dénouement is the moment when the civil guards arrive to arrest the protagonist. Actually, the guards might have come to investigate the girl's death, or for other reasons, and the ending does not, as any proper dénouement should, disentangle everything (Ong 1982: 149). Indeed, we do not know why or how the *mocito* was wounded, nor whether he is a smuggler, a murderer, or something else, nor whether he is wanted or pursued by the law or by anyone, nor whether he is betrothed or married to the *gitana*; we do not know how or why she died, nor, for certain, whether she is with child.

The list goes on. Nevertheless, if we accept my running commentary –which, whenever possible, conforms to literal rather than figurative interpretations– the ballad's central topic is subject to being expressed in fairly simple terms: a death-stricken lover arrives
to find his beloved dead in the place where she customarily awaited his return. This topic
is well within the realm of oral genres, where motifs like impossible love, journey, the
return of the hero, mortal wounds, last wishes, and death abound. Any number of building blocks might be used to develop the topic; the ones used in "Romance sonámbulo"
could be made to correspond with the six sections that are separated by asterisks in the
text. If so, the building blocks might be defined in general terms as descriptive (waiting),
anticipatory (suspense), dynamic (arrival), anticipatory (renewed suspense), protractive
(mystery), and revelatory (discovery). The point of these reductive comments is not to
explain away the ballad's structure or content in a few words; rather, it is to show the
extent to which it participates in a potentially improvisational and decidedly oral discourse.
This participation is sustained by the symptomatic features of orality I have been outlining, which are better appreciated when contrasted with other poetry from the same period, like the hypotactic and geometric constructions of Jorge Guillén (Ràfols 2005), to
which I will refer in a moment.

First, to recap those features, we have seen that "Romance sonámbulo" is densely formulaic, almost entirely paratactic, bearing few instances of enjambment and many of stichomythia (especially if we consider that *romances* can be written in 16-syllable lines divided into 8-syllable hemistiches with continuous assonance at the end of the lines). It contains
ungrammatical, elliptical, and verbless verses, and jumps from one scene to the next in
fragmentary fashion, shunning explanatory digressions and disregarding strict causality.
Its syntax is additive rather than subordinative, its approach totalizing and rhapsodic
rather than analytical. An empathetic and agonistic speaker deals with sundry concrete
images rather than abstract notions, and centers on communal rather than solipsistic
matters, intoning formulas that are closer to incantations and riddles than to syllogisms.
Swiftly moving from one image to the next and evoking motifs that echo earlier Spanish
oral genres, the speaker includes gross physical imagery (blood, tears, and bile) and
repeats the just-said in redundant rather than linear fashion, irregularly gilding the ballad
with an incantatory lament. True, the malleability of the text is such that it can be made
to conform to more than one generic principle, with varying degrees of success. Aside
from the generic biases of narrative and lyric which most critics have deployed, the bias
of drama has also been applied by Miller, who reads the ballad as an archetypal minidra-
ma that he divides into two acts and an epilogue (1986: 23). I submit that the bias of
orality is more aptly and productively applied to "Romance sonámbulo" than any one of
these biases, if only because it encompasses them and the bias of ritual as well.

My commentary is not meant to invalidate the many wonderful interpretations of
Lorca's most renowned ballad, the bulk of which operate on a symbolic plane. It could
well be, for example, that the civil guards represent the poet-dreamer's super-ego (Havard
1988: 203). Rather, my commentary is meant to stress the ballad's abundant oral fea-

tures and, having established them, to hazard an immediate, primordial interpretation, of the kind that orally-minded folk might derive from hearing it. Such an interpretation is more likely to rest on unembroidered, literal precepts than on carefully considered figurative ones –where every image threatens to be a symbol– and to accentuate emotional rather than intellectual aspects. At the very least, the text's oral and improvisational features belong on the ground floor of any approach to "Romance sonámbulo," after which we may marvel at the many hermeneutic stories that can be made to tower above it.

Nearly all of the symptomatic features of orality I have just outlined enjoy typographic opposites. Ironically, Guillén, who recognizes and esteems Lorca's innate orality, is the best modern example we have of a poet whose verses categorically belong to print culture. There is one feature of orality which I omitted: the old mnemonic and improvisational world of oral poetry is "warmly human" (Ong 1982: 167). A longstanding point of debate among Guillén detractors and apologists centers on the question of whether his prize-winning poetry is cold, even glacial. In my view, this perceived coldness is part and parcel of the hypotactic, abstract, analytical, objectively distanced, enjambment-laden verses that can only be produced in a post-literate world. While we know that Guillén assiduously and repeatedly revised many of his poems –as chirographic folk are wont to do– we do not know whether Lorca did the same with his "Romance sonámbulo." Given the deep sense in which his ballad participates in orality, however, we can surmise that it is more likely the product of impulse, unmediated passion, and improvisation than the product of a cerebral, circumspect, pen-and-paper effort. If, instead, he deliberately crafted this ballad to make it seem as though it was spontaneously improvised, he succeeded in that also, by giving us the most memorable and warmly human printed tribute to orality and to the living voice of poetry that modern Spanish letters offers.

Part III:

BERTSOLARIAK: HISTORIES

Bertsolaritza: Island or Archipelago?

GORKA AULESTIA

Introduction

When, some three years ago, I received an invitation from the *Euskal Herriko Bertsozale Elkartea* (Basque Country Association of *Bertsolaritza* Followers) to a meeting in Donostia (San Sebastián) with a view to organizing an international conference about *bertsolaritza* and similar phenomena, I didn't hesitate a moment in responding positively. I've always felt that any comparison between *bertsolaritza* and other expressions of popular oral poetry would be most beneficial for both the Basque Country and those other countries where forms of improvised oral poetry performed before a public had been maintained. Therefore I congratulate in advance the organizers of this International Symposium for the wonderful idea of gathering here this group of people, some of whom do not know each other personally. I'm convinced that these kinds of meetings, like ones held previously in the Canary Islands, Mexico, and the Basque Country will be to everyone's advantage. As regards Basques, we take heart from the motto of the bard José María Iparragirre, *"eman ta zabal zazu munduan frutua"* ("produce and scatter your fruit throughout the world"), which encourages us to share with others (both offering and receiving) the different experiences gleaned from the analysis of our respective fields of popular and oral literature.

The fact that *bertsolariak* ("versifiers") use *Euskara* (the Basque language) –the only surviving non-Indo European language in Western Europe– should not blind us to this mutual and enriching collaboration. It has always been the case that in the field of improvisational poetry (as in other areas) that which unites people is far greater than that which divides them. Consequently, during the preparation of my dissertation about *bertsolaritza* (1987) I added (thanks to the advice of Samuel Armistead) a chapter dedicated to "Phenomena Similar to *Bertsolaritza.*" Through its very novelty, this chapter –about the reality of improvisational poetry around the world– provoked interest elsewhere; for example, in an article by Joxean Agirre, where he remarked that, "in this jewel of a chapter the cases examined are the "*regueifa*" or improvisation of Galicia, improvised literary duels in Carta-gena, the old *trobadores* of Cuba, the "*payadores*" of Argentina and Chile, the duelists of Brazil, the bards of Yugoslavia, the African Bedouin women's improvised songs, and the Celtic bards of Wales" (Aguirre 1991: 49).

Here I will try to advance a little further into this wonderfully dense forest of popu-lar oral literature, comparing various milestones in the history of *bertsolaritza* with similar events in the rest of the world. As regards the nature of *bertsolaritza*, I will adopt a defini-tion that mostly centers on what is generally understood by the phenomenon: an oral style of Basque poetry where poets sing improvisations before an audience. As regards phenomena similar to *bertsolaritza*, I will mention some new cases while at the same time exploring in more detail others I have looked at elsewhere (Aulestia 1995). Furthermore, I will also take account of subsequently published interesting works such as *La teoría de la improvisación* ("The Theory of Improvisation") (1998) by the Cuban poet and improviser, Alexis Díaz-Pimienta.

Euskal Pizkunde (Basque Cultural Renaissance)

Aitzol's Political and Cultural Project (1927–36): Aitzol (1896–1936)

Between 1927 and 1936 José Mari Ariztimuño or "Aitzol" undertook a variety of cultur-al work (unusual in pre-Civil War Spain) in favor of a Basque cultural renaissance, as a judge of literary beauty and patron of many young Basque writers from that era. Among these writers was J. Zaitegi, who described this exceptional man's age group as "Aitzol's generation." And indeed, Aitzol was, without doubt, the key individual in the cultural life of the Basque Country between the mid 1920s and mid 1930s. Born on March 18, 1896 in Tolosa (Gipuzkoa), he was executed by Franco's troops on October 18, 1936, and later buried in a common grave (together with other Basque priests) next to the cemetery walls, although outside sacred ground, of the parish church in Hernani (Gipuzkoa).

From an early age he was preoccupied by the fate of "stateless nations," together with the recuperation of *Euskara* through potentially gaining co-official status in the Basque Country and thereby encouraging bilingualism. He thus personally traveled to Leu-ven/Louvain (Belgium) in 1927 to see first hand the problems that bilingualism raised. Ait-zol's project was not only cultural but also political, and he took an active interest in the emergence of new nations out of the fall of the Habsburg Empire after World War One (1914–18). Back home he always felt that the Basque language and literature (and espe-cially poetry) were intimately linked to achieving the self-determination, autonomy and independence of Euskadi (the Basque Country). These, he believed, were the best means through which a nation might attain its own identity.

---

1. In 1891 Iñarra won first prize for poetry in a competition organized by the *Euskal Festak* ("Basque Festivals") in Donostia competing, among others, with Txomin Agirre (1864–1920). His uncle's library was important in encouraging the literary vocation of the young Lekuona.

Aitzol (in the same way as José Mari Agirre, "Lizardi," and the majority of writers from that generation) believed that poets were providential figures in the resurgence of nations and the architects of lesser developed languages' survival; quite an extensive romantic idea throughout nineteenth-century Europe. He was, therefore, a fervent advocate of *"couleur locale romantique"* and promoting minority languages. This had also been the case of Frédéric Mistral (1830–1914), winner of the Nobel Prize for literature in 1904, who acquired a certain international prestige for a minority language –in this case Provençal– through the success of his work *Mirèio*. As a result, in 1930 (on the occasion of the hundredth anniversary of Mistral's birth) Orixe (Nicolás Ormaetxea) published a Basque version of *Mirèio* (Orixe 1930) at the request of Aitzol. He was at the same time well aware of the latest academic trends, such as an International Conference on Popular Art held in Prague in 1928, which was recalled in the verses of the *bertsolari* Basarri (Zubimendi 1935: 144):

Bertsolariak eman diote	Th *bertsolariak* have adorned
Txeko erriari gorantza;	the Czech people;
"Mireio" batek edergallutan	with a "Mireio"
yosia zuan Provenza.	full of Provençal grandeur.

However, in order to achieve the socio-political and cultural goals he desired it was not enough for Aitzol merely to translate a work, however distinguished its author was. What was needed was a Basque poet to write a grand Basque epic that would extol the Basque nation and make *Euskara* shine: Orixe (Aitzol's choice) duly completed *Euskaldunak* ("The Basques") in 1936, although it was not formally published until 1950 for reasons beyond his control (war, imprisonment, and so on).

Elsewhere, in 1930 the Bizkaian poet Lauaxeta (Esteban Urkiaga) won a prize for his poetry "Maitale Kutuna" ("Favorite Lover") in the First *Olerti Eguna* (Basque Poetry Day) held in Errenteria (Gipuzkoa); and in 1931 Lizardi won the same prize at the same event, this time held in Tolosa, for "Baso Itzal" ("Shady Forest"), from his 1930 poem, "Urte giroak ene begian" ("The Seasons of the Year Through My Eyes"). During the early years of *Pizkundea* (the Basque Cultural Renaissance) Aitzol advocated a refined poetry that would reach the quality and level of other European countries. However this influential (and at times domineering) judge, who as part of a jury had awarded prizes to the two aforementioned beautifully textured works, began to lose patience with (in his opinion) the disorientation of some Basque poets. In 1932 he condemned the poems of his two friends, Lizardi and Lauaxeta, for being too difficult to understand for most Basques, together with their closed and vanguard nature. This marked the beginning of a tense period of debate regarding the kind of poetry that should be created in Basque; namely, between writing a modern, conceptual and elitist verse that was difficult for most people to understand, or a kind of traditional narrative poetry that was close to the popular oral style of the *bertsolariak*.

In 1933, on the occasion of the Fourth Basque Poetry Day, held in Urretxu (Gipuzkoa) in honor of the bard Iparragirre, the jury awarded the main prize to the straightforward poem "Bost lore" ("Five Flowers") by Patxi Etxeberria. This was composed of a structure close to a *kopla zaharra* or traditional verse and esthetically very different from the winning poems in 1930 and 1931. Aitzol, in a 1933 article, harshly condemned his friends' difficult poetry, at the same time confessing his own guilt (1933: 1): "We have bored those who read about and love all things Basque with our difficult and incomprehensible verses . . . . I take full responsibility . . . . poets and most writers are going in the wrong direction."

And in 1934 he wrote about the theory of popular Basque poetry in "Euskal Olertikera berezia (estetika)" ("A Type of Special Basque Poetry (Aesthetics)"), where he defended the existence of a genuine aesthetic in traditional Basque literature. By now, his pessimism had reached its nadir, as was obvious from a letter written towards the end of 1934 to his friend, J. Zaitegi, then living in exile in Marneffe (Belgium) with other Jesuits expelled by the government of Spain's Second Republic (1931–36):

> With the *Euskara* we're coming up with now we're boring our readers. The books don't sell. We're creating an artificial literature. We don't know how to get into the soul of the people, and the people run away; what's happening is truly pitiful. *Euskara* is being spoken less and less; people are also reading less (Ariztimuño 1988: I, 65).

In 1935, after considering all the works published the previous year, he praised three: *Itz-lauz* ("In Prose") and *Umezurtz Olerkiak* ("Orphaned Poetries") by Lizardi, and *Barne Muinetan* ("In the Essence of the Interior") by Orixe. However, at the end of the day, he highlighted what in his opinion were the negative aspects of these works: "We can almost be assured that these three volumes, despite their undeniable literary value, will never manage to strengthen what is really important, *Euskara*. They lack that essential quality, originality and the genuineness of a fluid, easy and intelligible *Euskara*" (Ariztimuño 1935: 1).

By now he was close to abandoning those innovatory poets and encouraging instead the oral poetry of the *bertsolariak*, basing his new thought on Manuel Lekuona's *Literatura oral euskérica* ("Oral Literature in Basque") (1935). As such he actively contributed to organizing the "First *Bertsolari* Day" (or First National Championship), which took place on January 20, 1935, in Donostia's *"Poxpolin"* theater, and was officially planned by two associations: *"Euskaltzaleak"* (Friends of Basque) and *"Eusko Gaztedi"* (Basque Youth). Twenty *bertsolariak* took part and the winner was a young Basarri.

Manuel Lekuona (1894–1987)

This distinguished oralist and poet, who dedicated more than seventy years of his life to research, acquired an early interest in Basque culture through consulting the library of his uncle, the priest Miguel Antonio Iñarra (1864–1898), in his native town of Oiartzun (Gipuzkoa).[1] Lekuona worked in different genres –poetry, theatre and essays– publishing highly demanding academic works in the period 1918–1936. After 1939, in the immediate aftermath of the Spanish Civil War, he continued to research into and write about various dimensions of Basque culture (ethnography, art, history and so on), and eventually he would publish twelve volumes: *Idazlan Guztiak* ("Collected Writings") in 1984. He studied at the Gasteiz Seminary (Araba), being ordained a priest in 1916, and also taught Basque there until the outbreak of the Civil War in 1936. He was a clear devotee of *bertsolaritza* and even gave a talk on "Basque Metrics" at the seminary to inaugurate the 1918 academic year.

However, what really motivated him to study the field of oral literature and *bertsolaritza* were the derogatory words of a journalist from Donostia in a talk given in Oñati (Gipuzkoa), during the First Congress of *Eusko Ikaskuntza* (the Society of Basque Studies), held in September 1918. Specifically, the reporter contrasted German peasants in beer-halls, who listened to the beautiful poems of Goethe and Schiller, and Basque *baserritarrak* ("farmers"), who met in cider houses to listen to the nonsense of *bertsolariak*. As Lekuona confessed, "classifying our popular bards as nonsense hurt my soul. And I would say that from that moment on I conceived the objective and plan of devoting my time to defending *bertsolaritza*" (Manuel Lekuona 1984: VIII, 358).

After several years examining different expressions of oral literature, Lekuona gave one of his most important talks in September 1930 in Bergara (Gipuzkoa), at the Fifth Congress of *Eusko Ikaskuntza*. The title of the lecture was "Basque Oral Poetry" and it was divided into three parts: decorative poetry, "*Kopla Zaharrak*" ("Old Verses") and *bertsolaritza*. In this last section Lekuona's analysis advanced a theoretical perspective of the phenomenon which had important consequences for Basque literary creation. Its impact on Aitzol was especially striking and from that moment on he began to favor a kind of *bertsolaritza* different from that practiced in cider houses (at that time the only "universities" of *bertsolariak* such as Joxe Manuel Lujanbio, "Txirrita") that might serve his general cultural project. Indeed, Aitzol severly criticized these traditional *bertsolariak*: "What a shameful spectacle when on Saint Thomas' Day. . . . two *bertsolariak*, with terrible voices and an incredible conceptual coarseness, with an impudent turn of phrase and bad taste, and who sing badly timed verses that are more elastic than rubber, perform in the Bellas Artes theater!" (Ariztimuño 1930: 1).

The year 1935 was extremely important in the history of *bertsolaritza* for both the "First *Bertsolari* Day" and the publication of Lekuona's work, *Literatura oral euskérica* ("Oral Literature in Basque"). This book was the result of his general research up to that point and more specifically, the Bergara lecture. Lekuona also acknowledged the influence of *Le Style oral rhythmique et mnémotechnique chez les verbo-moteurs* ("Mnemonic and Rhythmic Oral Style Among People Who Speak a Lot") (1925) by the eminent oral expert and Sorbonne professor, Marcel Jousse (1886–1962). This work addressed, among other subjects, the language problems encountered in analyzing human gestures or expressions. Starting from childhood experiences and memories enlivened through orally communicated tales by his (illiterate but not uncultured) mother and grandmother, Jousse questioned the hegemony of our (essentially writing-based) culture which society attempted to impose on people as the only possible means of civilization. Putting to one side the dominant idealist philosophy of most French universities at that time, Jousse studied peasant socialization in great detail, playing down the importance of Greco-Roman culture, because that hid a richer and deeper cultural reality. This French Jesuit, an old First World War soldier, argued that human beings expressed themselves not only through the spoken word but also by bodily gestures, and especially through use of their hands. Furthermore, he contrasted his childhood experiences with Biblical passages and Homer's two epics, the *Iliad* and the *Odyssey*, coming to the conclusion that throughout these works set or stereotypical phrases and formulas existed that had been taken from popular oral tradition.

Although Lekuona already had years of experience and interest in the study of popular oral literature, Jousse's book marked an important landmark in shaping his thought. In addition to frequently mentioning the work, Lekuona also highlighted several points raised by the Sorbonne professor: the importance of memory in oral literature; the diverse sources used by Homer and Virgil, and the stylistic differences between these two classical Greco-Roman authors; the importance of rural village get-togethers where people sang and recited passages without previously reading them; and the citation of certain Biblical characters who stood out for their capacity to poetically improvise.

Lekuona's nephew, the poet and oralist Juan Mª Lekuona, summed up his uncle's life in the following way (1995a: 68–69):

> When faced with highlighting his most characteristic specialty, I would say that he was considered the *senior figure* of Basque oralists . . . . He enjoyed fieldwork. He knew like few others the living oral tradition and collective memory. Furthermore, he dedicated many years to studying local documentation, rummaging around in archives . . . . Manuel Lekuona taught us how to become learned through local ways but without losing a universal perspective. Our culture begins with that which is nearest to hand. Here the legacy Don Manuel bequeathed us becomes more specific as does the quiet message of his life and work.

Inazio Eizmendi, Basarri (1913–99)

Another of the figures that Aitzol counted on to undertake his cultural project was the young *bertsolari*, Basarri (Inazio Eizmendi). In 1935 Lekuona had come to support this project with his book and participation (as a jury member) in the "First *Bertsolari* Day" held in Donostia. At this same competition, a young twenty-two year old born in Errezil (Gipuzkoa), though living from the age of seven in Zarautz (Gipuzkoa), became the paradigmatic *bertsolari* for Aitzol and many nationalists, on being proclaimed champion of the contest. Txirrita, the elderly patriarch of traditional *bertsolaritza* –at the age of seventy five, weighing 260 pounds and dressed in the customary long black shirt– did not fit the image envisaged by Aitzol. What was needed was a *bertsolari* that would transform and reinvigorate the subjects and means of traditional *bertsolaritza*. In Juan Mª Lekuona's opinion (one of the best specialists in this literary form and well familiar with Basarri's work), he

Jose Manuel Lujanbio, "Txirrita" (center). Prior to the advent of public performances in squares, and later indoor competitions, *bertsolaritza* was typically practiced in cider houses, and its greatest exponent was Txirrita. By permission of *Sendoa*.

became not only a champion but a pioneer and leader of *bertsolaritza*'s innovative project that was marked by a new school, taking the form out of the cider houses and into the towns and squares (1992: 295): "When the "First *Bertsolari* Day" was held in 1935, Basarri didn't only win the prize, he took control, leading the new way of performing *bertsolaritza*. And later, for many years, he maintained this new way of performing *bertsolaritza*, more than anything else publicly and in front of an audience."

For several years thereafter, Basarri's contribution to Aitzol's general cultural project centered on descriptions of *bertsolaritza* in journals and newspapers. This new "school" didn't forsake *bertsolaritza*'s past and indeed, praised the work of Bilintx (Indalecio Bizkarrondo), Pedro Mª Otaño and Kepa Enbeita. However Basarri believed that cider house *bertsolaritza* (Udarregi, Errota and so forth) –whose principal exponent at that time was Txirrita– was finished. As a child, Basarri learned about *bertsolaritza* first-hand for the best *bertsolariak* of that era used to visit "Azken-Portu", his parents' bar in Zarautz. He later recalled that, even at a young age, he was aware that it needed an urgent overhaul (Eizmendi 1984: 158): "I was twelve when I realized this. We had a bar at home, and the most famous *bertsolariak* of the era sang there . . . . they chose the worst of all directions to their own detriment . . . .They scared off the listeners that they should have attracted with their awkward and cheap way of speaking."

Through voracious reading, culture played an important role within Basarri's *bertsolaritza* project. One had to break free of the time when *bertsolariak* didn't know how to read or write or (as in a minority of cases) they only knew how to read. Such was the case with Xenpelar (Francisco Petrirena), Txirrita and the vast majority of the nineteenth- and early twentieth-century Basque bards.[2] For that reason, the self-taught Basarri achieved sufficient education to become a journalist and radio announcer in Donostia, ultimately working in journalism for forty years, writing prolifically about traditional Basque sports and *bertsolaritza* in numerous journals and newspapers. He also wrote several books, six in verse and one of prose: *Atano III: bere edestia bertsotan* ("Atano III: His History in Verse") (1949); *Basarriren Bertso-Sorta* ("A Bouquet of Strophes by Basarri") (1950); *Kantari nator* ("My Songbook") (1960); *Laugarren Txinpartak* ("Four Books of Poetry") (1966); *Sortu zaizkidanak* ("My Creations") (1973); *Kezka giroan* ("A Time of Unease") (1983); *Bertsolaritzari buruz* ("About *Bertsolaritza*") (1984); and *Nere bordatxotik* ("From my Hut") (1992).[3]

With such a prodigious output, one might wonder at which school, high school or university Basarri studied in his youth. The following citation leaves no doubt regarding the cultural origins of this enlightened and groundbreaking bard in the new direction taken by *bertsolaritza*; as well as highlighting how lowly *bertsolaritza* was considered (Basarri, qtd. in Etxezarreta 1993: 209):

> "Basarri," unfortunately, is ignorant in both singing and music; incapable of reading the notes on a pentagram. Those who also believe me to be a cultured, educated man, an intellectual are wrong . . . . All those who read my work should know that "Basarri" only went to school until the age of eleven; that he was forced to abandon school after his first communion to attend to family needs . . . . He suffered terribly from the lowly and intolerable language that the old *bertsolariak* used in public. They didn't succeed in versifying but instead used to attack one another in coarse and impertinent ways. Drunkenness, theft and adultery were acceptable subjects. The sillier their remarks, the more the public applauded them. But respectable people, people who felt the same, moderately cultured people, kept well away from the *bertsolari*. He belonged to the lowest level of society. I've seen that there are those people who still believe that verse should be like that; that the *bertsolari* should be a kind of comedian, just there to make people laugh.

While many thought that the *bertsolari* was a comical figure whose sole purpose was to make people laugh, thereby making *bertsolaritza* a form of humor (in which Txirrita was the grand master), the young Basarri spent many hours shaping his project through

---

2. The *bertsolari* Juan José Alkain, "Udarregi" (1829–95), born in Usurbil (Gipuzkoa), found a way of getting around the problem: As he could neither read nor write, every time he improvised a strophe he made a mark on the old walls of the farm where he lived. When he realized there were a certain amount of marks, he turned to his friend, Jose Txiki, to write them down on paper. It was similar in Txirrita's case. As he couldn't write, his nephew, José Ramón Erauzkin, transcribed the verses that his uncle improvised.

3. There is also a lot of material about this *bertsolari* in the special collection published by Auspoa. See Eizmendi (1992), a 570-page book of verses.

gradually acquiring an education (Eizmendi 1984: 76). As opposed to the cicada ("Txir-rita" in *Euskara*), who spent whole evenings in cider houses, the "ant" of Zarautz assidu-ously worked to achieve his objectives, though even he recognized that, "in those days cider houses became the schools and academies of *bertsolaritza*" (Eizmendi 1984: 99). He tried to achieve a popular but elegant form of *Euskara*, following the trail laid down by Pedro Mari Otaño, without the dominant "purisms" and sought to overhaul the strophes and melodies; a Basque without so many Spanish borrowings (such as that of Udarregi, Txirrita, and others); more current affairs and interesting subjects that could attract a wider audience through use of the media (press and radio); and shorter performances to stop the public getting bored. As regards the strophes, they had to smoothly interlock avoiding "*bete lana*" or stuffing verses full of words without saying anything special. The *bertsolari* shouldn't just limit himself to carefully elaborating a final verse in order to gain the public's applause, but rather the final verse had to result in the culmination of a pre-viously well thought out and relevant verse, following the theme of a logical narration: "All that is waffle . . . . Good verses, splendid whole substantial verses are not made like that. From start to finish they're strong. Although its spice and wit emerge at the last moment, a verse made that way [in the waffling style] does not deserve applause" (Eiz-mendi 1984: 17).

As regards the rhyme and types of strophe –such as the *bederatzi puntukoa* (nine point verse; a strophe of fourteen verses and nine rhymes)– Basarri did not favor aggravating the situation by imposing this difficult strophe on *bertsolariak* in competitions. That would only put them in a fix and spoil the spectacle: "What most defeats us *bertsolariak* here is the point rule . . . . Imposing subjects and making the *bertsolariak* sing nine point verses opposite one another. One couldn't choose a better system to slow the *bertsolariak* down, to make them more nervous, and to weaken the festivals" (Eizmendi 1984: 21).

One of the central ideas of this project was undoubtedly his definition of the *bertsolari*. The Basque bard, according to Basarri, was merely a popular poet. This qualifying adjec-tive marked the difference and distinguished Basarri from a poet who wrote poetry with-out improvising and singing it before an audience. Here he entered into a debate with the renowned Bilbao poet, Gabriel Aresti, for whom the *bertsolari* was the best of all poets: "I can say only one thing to Basarri, that *bertsolariak* are poets too, rural poets . . . . unedu-cated poets, but in my opinion the best of all Basque poets, better than all poets" (Aresti 1986: 184). Basarri, however, disagreed and, although accepting the fact that *bertsolariak* might be closer to the people and of more value to *Euskara*, he believed Aresti's argument was akin to saying that miners made the best fishermen (Eizmendi 1984: 44).

Basarri dedicated his life to the development and diffusion of popular Basque culture, and especially of *bertsolaritza*. After suffering the consequences of being on the losing side in the Spanish Civil War (exile, imprisonment, and forced labor, for example), he was eventually able to continue performing as a *bertsolari* in the company of his friend, the three-time champion Uztapide (Manuel Olaizola). He also won the 1960 *txapelketa* (nation-al championship) and was runner-up in 1962. Then he decided to take no further part in these competitions, until, in 1968, he won (together with Fernando Aire, "Xalbador") an important competition organized by "Piensos Onena" in Donostia. He died just short of his eighty-sixth birthday, on November 4, 1999, and with his death the Basque Country lost one of its most accomplished *bertsolariak*.

The 1960s: Uztapide and Xalbador

Manuel Olaizola, Uztapide (1909–1983)

One can't appreciate Basarri's project without mentioning one of the most-loved (as a person for his naturalness) and appreciated (as an artist) *bertsolariak*: Uztapide. The Basarri-Uztapide duo was the first pair[4] that, during the most severe years of Spain's Franco dictatorship (the 1940s and 1950s), reinvigorated Basque culture. These Gipuzkoan *bertsolariak* traversed almost the entire Basque Country in a quarter of a century. Basarri himself later confirmed this hectic activity (Eizmendi 1984: 97): "Twenty odd years my friend "Uztapide" and I spent serving the Basque Country. Here and there without stopping."

At a time when using *Euskara* was only permitted in church, the presence of these two *bertsolariak* was also essential in the festivals of many towns. They were very different from one another, both as people and as artists. Possibly due to such great differences, when it came time to express their art, they were capable of forming an ideal duo, requested and appreciated in a number of towns. As a person Basarri was serious, whereas Uztapide was a mixture of the mischievous night-owl Txirrita (capable of spending the whole night drinking and improvising verses) and the loyal *baserritarra* or farmer committed to the chores of his farm. Three of his most important dialectic weapons were a fine sense of irony linked to a humor that never hurt anyone and an incisive intelligence. Throughout these years the former got more and more conservative, while latter always seemed more popular and closer to the young people. Basarri was better than Uztapide in rhythms and melodies (some of which he even created), while the latter preferred to use the *zortziko* (an eight-verse strophe) and the *hamarreko* (ten-verse strophe). Both, though, were exceptional *bertsolariak*: Uztapide won three national championships (1962, 1965 and 1967) and Basarri two (1935 and 1960). Performing as a duo, they complemented each other perfectly. Basarri was a kind of plough that prepared the land so that his colleague Uztapide could begin to sow it. Basarri was also careful, during competitions, to not sever his *partenaire*'s dialectic thread, and was always very careful with grammatical and rhetorical forms, being one of the *bertsolariak* who improvised the least incorrect verses in the modern history of the phenomenon. Uztapide's artistic qualities, on the other hand, were never as rhetorical, since their author was not as educated as Basarri. But when challenged, he could improvise a never-ending flow of verses and resembled the character *Martín Fierro*, from whom verses flowed like spring water (Hernández 1972: 30):

---

4. Later the Xalbador-Mattin (Mattin Treku) and Jon Lopategi-Jon Azpillaga pairings would emerge.

Cuando llego a abrir el pico,	When I open my mouth,
téngalo por cosa cierta,	take it as a sure thing,
sale un verso y en la puerta	a verse comes forth and, at the door,
ya asoma el otro al hocico.	the next one is about to come out.

While Basarri retired from national competitions at the age of forty-nine in 1962, Uztapide continued with other partners such as Manuel Lasarte and Lazkao Txiki (José Miguel Iztueta), until he was later forced to retire through illness.

Fernando Aire, Xalbador (1920–76)

The Spanish Civil War (1936–1939) and the subsequent dictatorship of Franco (1939–1975) undoubtedly interrupted Basque cultural life, condemning it to an icy, forty-year long winter. While *bertsolaritza* did not escape the terrible consequences of this awful storm, there were periods of calm. After almost a quarter of a century, national championships were resumed in the 1960s, a decade in which a new and different *bertsolari*, Xalbador (Fernando Aire) emerged in the national championships: fourth place in 1960; third in 1962 and 1965; and second in 1967, also achieving second place in the 1968 "Piensos Onena" competition in Donostia. In addition, he won four first prizes in the "Xenpelar Saria" competition of Errenteria (Gipuzkoa) (1972, 1973, 1975 and 1976) for his *bertso-paper-ak* or written verses, as well as similar awards in the "Mendaro Txirristaka" and "Donostiako Kutxa Saria" competitions. Xalbador was, without doubt, the best *bertsolari* from the northern Basque Country –declaring himself a *citoyen français* according to his passport, but a Basque at heart– and certainly one of the best bards in the history of *bertsolaritza*.

Born in the beautiful little town of Urepele (Nafarroa Beherea), on June 19, 1920, from an early age Fernando Aire showed signs of having a strong personality. He left school at the age of eleven and at sixteen took charge of his family's flock of sheep in the high mountains near his beloved shepherd's hut, to which he would later dedicate some of his most beautiful lyrical strophes; at the same age he ventured to improvise a strophe for the first time in front of a few people. When he was nineteen, and finally felt ready to perform in public, his start in *bertsolaritza* was curtailed by the outbreak of World War Two (1939–45) and his father's death. However, in Donibane-Lohitzun (Lapurdi) after the war he met Mattin, his "page," with whom he would form a thirty-year partnership.

Xalbador was an atypical *bertsolari* for a number of reasons: his use of a Basque dialect from Nafarroa Beherea, with which the vast majority of the people who heard him were not familiar; the novelty of melodies that were, until that time, unknown south of the Pyrenees; for the poetic delicacy and sensitivity that marked his verses; for the profundity of his thought; for the lyricism that emanated from many of his best verses; for his contribution in the strophic field with new rhythms, following Xenpelar's nineteenth-century example;[5] for his capacity to express the most trivial subjects in beautiful ways; for

---

5. For example, one might cite the long, eighteen-syllable (5+5+8) verse of his "Esperantzarik gabeko amodioa" ("Hopeless Love")

some of his improvised verses that would, without doubt, be included in the anthology of best verses; and finally, for the beauty of his written verses, some of which highlight a very high poetic level.[6]

Among his improvised verses, I would select three as perfect examples of his versifying ability: "Emazte il zanaren soñekoari" ("To Your Late Wife's Dress"), in the 1965 national *txapelketa*; "Bazkaria serbitu dizun neskatxari" ("To the Waitress Who Served You Lunch"), improvised in the 1967 *txapelketa* (*Bertsolari Txapelketa (1967–VI–11)* 1967: 71); and "Ohea" ("The Bed"), improvised in the same competition (1967: 119–20). These verses, such as that dedicated to his late wife's dress, demonstrate Xalbador's skill in conversing with objects as if they were living people (*Bertsolari Txapelketa 1965* 1965: 93–94):

Pentsa zazute alargun bat	Understand that a widower
ez daike izan urusa,	cannot be happy.
dolamen hunek, oi! ez dezala	Oh! I hope this sorrow
ainitz gehiago luza,	doesn't last much longer;
orai urte ziloan sartu	it was a year ago that we buried
andereñoaren gorputza,	the young wife's body in the tomb.
haren arropa hantzet dilindan	I sadly see her dress
penaz ikusten dut hutsa.	hanging there alone.
Geroztik nihaur ere nabila	Since then, I myself live
guzia beltzez jantzirik	dressed in strict mourning.
ez dut pentsatzen nigar eiteko	I think that my eyes
ene begiak hesterik,	can do no more but cry.
ez pentsa gero andre gaxoa,	Don't believe, poor wife,
baden munduan besterik	there's another woman in the world,
zure arropa berriz soinean	who on her body again
har dezaken emazterik.	could wear your clothes.

Another quality with which Xalbador surprised those listening was his ability to adapt to the required moment and place, sometimes using similes and metaphors; for example, in the following verse from a competition held in Donostia on January 6, 1962 (The Epiphany Festival) (*Errege eguneko bertso-sayoa* 1962: 89):

Egun Erregen eguna da ta	As today is the Epiphany Festival,
nik ere hartu indarra	I have also made the decision
nunbait ni ere Erregen gisa	to set out on the road,
bidean asi bearra,	as they [the Three Wise Men] did.

---

6. They can be found in at least three of the four *txapelketak*, published both in the *Auspoa* collection, *Bertsolari Txapelketa* nos. 22 (1963), 43 (1965) and 67 (1967)), and in his three books: *Ezin bertzean* ("Against One's Will"; 1969), *Herria gogoan* ("With the People in Mind"; 1981) and especially *Odolaren mintzoa* ("Blood Language"; 1976a). In the latter work, several of his written verses would be highlighted such as "Esperantzarik gabeko amodia" ("Hopeless Love"), "Jainkoa eta ni" ("God and I"), "Gure artzain etxolari" ("To Our Shepherd's Hut"), and "Ortzirale saindu batetako gogoetak eta otoitza" ("Good Friday Reflections and an Oration").

goizean etxetik erten eta	I left home this morning
abiatu naiz azkarra,	and I departed quickly;
gero Donostiren par-parean	later a star detained me
geldtu zeraut izarra.	very close to Donostia.

As the years passed, the admiration for the art of this shepherd grew and grew and his figure will always be remembered with affection and admiration among both friends and enthusiasts of *bertsolaritza*. His loyal friend and partner Mattin believed that, "there was no one equal to him in writing verses" (Treku 1977: 25), while the fine poet from Lapurdi, Jean Diharce or "Iratzeder," highlighted the reflective quality of his verses by observing that, "nowhere was there a *bertsolari* as profound as he" (Diharce 1984: 492). And the Bizkaian *bertsolari* Jon Lopategi highlighted the same quality, even dedicating his champion's *txapela* or beret, on December 17, 1989, in Donostia's Anoeta cycle track, to the Urepele shepherd (Aire 1976b):

Gauza sakonak asmatu eta	For the profound things devised
gauzak sakon adierazten,	and the intimate things expressed,
Urepeleko maixuagana	to the level of the Urepele *maestro*
ez gera inor irixten.	we could never reach.

Another devotee of Xalbador is the champion *bertsolari* Xabier Amuriza. In his first book of poetry, *Menditik Mundura* ("From the Mountain to the World"), he dedicated eight strophes to Xalbador, one of which (1977: 253) offered the following praise:

Beste munduko sinesmen finez	You often showed us
hots egin zenigun sarri;	your strong faith in the afterlife;
aitortzen dizut hori ez dela	I must confess to you that
niretzat hain kezkagarri.	that doesn't worry me so much.
Baldin badago ezin guk kendu	Since if something does exist we can't deny it
ez badago ezin jarri;	and if it doesn't exist, we can't create it;
baina egia balitz nahi nuke	but if it were true,
zure aurrean itzarri;	I'd want to wake up in front of you;
betikotasun osoa eman	so that we'd be looking at each other
dezagun beha elkarri.	for the rest of eternity.

The music world was also keen on working with him through choirs as well as individual voices.[7] That simple, self-taught shepherd who abandoned a French school, because he preferred to be an uneducated Basque than a civilized (but without *Euskara*) Frenchman, was posthumously proposed as a member of *Euskaltzaindia* or the Royal Academy of the Basque Language. Erramun Martikorena, another shepherd like him from Ipar-

---

7. Among the first group, I'd highlight Gotzon Aulestia's record, *Atako Bandan*, in which the song (composed of four mixed voices), "*Bertsolaria*" appears. The lyrics were composed by Joxe Martin Apalategi and the song was performed by the *Kresala* choir of Ondarroa (Bizkaia). Other singers such as Mikel Laboa, Anje Duhalde, and Txomin Artola, have performed Xalbador's poems.

ralde or the northern Basque Country, describes him with a warm voice and lyrics composed by the poet-singer Xabier Lete (Martikorena 1998):

Adixkide bat bazen orotan bihotzbera	Once upon a time, there was a very good friend,
poesiaren hegoek	whom poetry's wings
sentimentuzko bertsoek	and deeply felt verses
antzaldatzen zutena.	had transformed.
Plazetako kantari bakardadez josia	A public singer, weighed down by his solitude,
hitzen lihoa iruten	learnt through suffering
bere barnean irauten	to spin a yarn of words,
oinazez ikasia.	to take refuge inside himself.
Nun hago, zer larretan	Where are you? In which meadow?
Urepeleko artzaina,	shepherd from Urepel,
mendi hegaletan gora	who, climbing mountain slopes,
oroitzapen den gerora	escaped towards the future
ihesetan joan hintzana. (bis)	that is a memory. (Repeat)
Hesia urraturik libratu huen kanta	Breaking down the barriers you freed singing,
lotura guztietatik	wishing to feel free
gorputzaren mugetatik	of all restrictions,
aski sentitu nahirik.	of bodily limitations.
Azken hatsa huela bertsorik sakonena,	Your last breath was your most meaningful verse,
inoiz esan ezin diren	the most powerful shriek
estalitako egien	of hidden truths
ohiurik bortitzena.	that could never be told.

Xalbador died at the age of fifty-six on November 7, 1976. In a mass tribute held in his home village, with the dual pleasure of presenting his book, *Odolaren Mintzoa*, and the sounds of *Gernikako Arbola* this lyrical and melancholic *bertsolari* for whom the pain of his country, Euskal Herria, was transformed into an agonizing ballad, left us.

Two Distinguished Oral Experts in Basque Literature: Antonio Zavala and Juan Mª Lekuona

The list of people involved in the academic study of different popular Basque expressions (literature, song, folklore, ethnology and so on) is somewhat short. Some, though, do stand out (the majority of them ecclesiastics) such as Resurrección María de Azkue, Manuel Lekuona, Father Donostia, Jorge de Riezu, José Miguel de Barandiaran and Justo Mª Mokoroa. To this list another two names –Antonio Zavala and Juan Mª Lekuona– deserve to be added for a variety of reasons. Both were clerics, Gipuzkoans, full academic members of *Euskaltzaindia*, almost the same age and judges in the 1960, 1962, 1965, 1967, 1980 and 1982 *txapelketak*.

Antonio Zavala (1928–)

The Jesuit Antonio Zavala spent more than half a century researching and writing about popular Basque literature, publishing 283 volumes in his *Auspoa* collection. This tireless worker and born compiler, the authentic heart of the important *Auspoa* ("The Bellows") collection, realized the importance of preserving Basque popular oral literature, in all its diverse expressions (*bertsolaritza*, ballads, proverbs, tales and so on). The *Auspoa* collection is, moreover, a historical, anthropological and folkloric arsenal representing a centuries-old collective memory.

Zavala stands out for his painstaking skill as a compiler of the aforementioned collection; the quite unique and original methodology that he employed; the ease with which he communicated with normal people and the deep respect he showed to both people and diverse cultures; his loyalty to original texts; and finally, his universal quality. As a demonstration of this, one only need look at his *Bilbioteca de Narrativa Popular* ("A Library of Popular Narrative"). This is a special collection, where, without abandoning the rich source material of Basque popular literature, he also addresses different Spanish regions (La Rioja, Andalusia, Extremadura, León, Galicia, Asturias, Castile, Aragón, and Cantabria), in order to listen to, transcribe and publish the anonymous voices of diverse characters (shepherds, farmhands and beggars, for example), searching for material among numerous attics and store rooms. In twenty-five volumes (published in Spanish) he presents different rural ways of life narrated in the first-person by the characters, mainly old people, themselves.

Zavala, following the trail paved by Manuel Lekuona, was ahead of his time in emphasizing the importance of popular oral literature. From his first lecture in 1956,[8] to his 1999 speech at the University of Deusto (Bilbao), on being named an *Honoris Causa* Doctor, this atypical academic always maintained the need to consider popular literature in and of itself, without submitting it to the criteria of written literature. Similarly, he has also continuously argued for a revision of the evaluative criteria of literature which persist in academia. For he was acutely aware of acerbic views, like that of Francisque Michel (1857: 213), on Basque popular poetry: "One might perhaps ask if the Basques didn't have any popular poetry, like most other nations, how rather small and insignificant they would be. To be sure, they do not at all lack either ballads or verses; but these pieces do not present any characteristics that might warrant the name poetry."

Zavala disagreed with the age-old habit of considering popular oral literature as a literature of secondary importance. This was reflected in the lack of sensitivity on the part of the university world; the absence of oral literature, even in some of the most used guides to Basque literary history in the Basque Country; the dismissal of some of the oldest *bertsolariak*, demonstrated at the beginning of the twentieth century by intellectuals like

---

8. Given on September 15, 1956 in the Arantzazu Sanctuary (Gipuzkoa), and entitled "Bertso berri billa Euskalerrian zear" ("In Search of Popular Poetry Throughout the Basque Country") (Zavala 1996a).

the poet and academic member of *Euskaltzaindia*, Carmelo Etxegarai (1865–1925); and the scorn of educated figures in general for *bertsolaritza* due to the *Euskara* used by the likes of Udarregi, Txirrita, and Pello Errota. Zavala always championed the literary production of those *bertsolariak*, many of them illiterate, arguing that, "personally I am convinced of their literary excellence" (1996a: 37). Of his extensive bibliography on *bertsolaritza*, I would choose as a straightforward sample the book published in 1964, *Bosquejo de historia del bertsolarismo* ("A Summary of the History of *Bertsolaritza*").

Juan M[ª] Lekuona (1927–)

The name Lekuona was initially associated with popular oral literature through the work of Manuel Lekuona. And although at first Manuel's influence on his nephew, Juan M[ª], was obvious through the various expressions of this literature (*bertsolaritza*, verses, old songs, the playful choral aspect of oral poetry and so forth), the younger Lekuona soon began to shine in his own right. This was especially evident in his own written poetry that later, in 1991, won him the *"Premio Euskadi"* award (Juan M[ª] Lekuona 1990) and which I have analyzed elsewhere (Aulestia 1998). Here I want to describe the collaboration of one of the best Basque poets of the second half of the twentieth century with the world of oral literature, and more specifically, with *bertsolaritza*. I would contend that Professor Lekuona, throughout his long university teaching career, has analyzed aspects of popular oral poetry in a way no other Basque writer of his era could. Indeed, his position at the University of Deusto (Donostia campus) implied a kind of challenge in a field where unfortunately there scarcely existed adequate material. In an early article, for example, Juan M[ª] Lekuona highlighted the then lack of appropriate material in the field of oral literature (1978b: 59):

> There is a lack of guides and a general absence of appropriate didactic material about oral literature subjects. And as such, it remains symptomatic that two histories of Basque literature, those of L. Villasante and I. Sarasola (so important in other ways) do not directly examine oral literature, when in the Basque case the incidence of popular literature in written production is so definitive.

Teaching classes in oral literature, however, subsequently enabled Lekuona to fill those profound spaces that had impeded the development of normal university courses. And few teachers could have fulfilled this task with the required academic competence as this distinguished poet, who was so closely connected to popular oral literature by vocation, family tradition and complete dedication.

Juan M[ª] Lekuona began to publish poetry in 1950 while at the Gasteiz Seminary. In the 1960s he became well known for his participation in *bertsolaritza* competitions as a jury member. In 1962 he was named a corresponding member of *Euskaltzaindia* and in 1987 a full member, occupying the place left vacant by the death of his uncle, Manuel Lekuona, that same year. In 1988 Juan M[ª] Lekuona made his official entrance into the Royal Academy of the Basque Language in the city hall of Oiartzun, his home town, with a talk about semi-orality. He then occupied the post of vice-president in *Euskaltzaindia* for seven years (1989–96) and has also headed the commissions of written literature (1990–2003) and oral literature for more than a decade, working quietly but efficiently.

Between 1974 and 1976 he wrote several articles about *bertsolaritza* in Basque journals, together with prologues to books about individual *bertsolariak*.[9] In 1977 he received his first invitation to write about Basque literature, publishing the article "Literatura oral vasca" in the *Libro blanco del Euskara* ("The White Book about Basque"). However, it was his *Ahozko euskal literatura* ("Basque Oral Literature") (1982), which subsequently became a classic guide and essential volume in university teaching. This work is composed of fifteen chapters in which the author analyzes several genres of Basque popular literature. Seven of these are related to *bertsolaritza*; its history; the various stages of the phenomenon; improvised *bertsolaritza*; the varieties of improvised *bertsolaritza* performances (duels, floral games, competitions and so on); a description of four Basque bards: Bilintx, Iparragirre, Txirrita and Basarri; and an analysis of the distinct strophic models used by these artists. All this work, some of which had been previously published in both the journal *Jakin* (1980: nos. 14–15) and in Zavala's *A los 100 años de su muerte, Bilintx (1831–1876)* ("A Hundred Years after his Death, Bilintx (1831–1876)"), is still relevant today.[10] Among these I would highlight chapter nine, "Bertsolarien estrofa-motak hegoaldeko usarioan" ("Various Strophic Types of *Bertsolariak* in the Tradition of the Peninsular Basque Country"), where Lekuona enters the world of metrics and seems to be in his element. With the publication of this book, then, he finished one stage of his literary production to begin a second one.

Sixteen years later, and after retiring from the University of Deusto, Juan Mª Lekuona published *Ikaskuntzak euskal literaturaz (1974–1996)* ("Studies on Basque Literature 1974–1996"). This 670-page work includes thirty articles related to both oral and written Basque-language literature, with an emphasis on the former. After presenting the work in the Koldo Mitxelena Kulturgunea cultural center in Donostia, the author expressed one wish: "*Baliagarri izango ahal da*" ("That it might be of some use") and I believe that anyone involved in teaching Basque oral literature, as the immediate beneficiaries, appreciates this authentic literary jewel. With time, there will obviously be new contributions to the *bertsolaritza* phenomenon, but these two books will always be indispensable instruments for the study of Basque-language oral literature, and especially, *bertsolaritza*.

The 1980s

After the death of Franco on November 20, 1975 and the end of his dictatorship, there was an era of reform with a new constitution, a democratic parliament and political par-

---

9. For example, he wrote about Manuel Lasarte in *Zeruko Argia* (1975a); about Txirrita and Basarri in *Euskara* (1975b); Xalbador, in *Garaia* (1976) and by way of a prologue, about Uztapide (Juan Mª Lekuona 1974).

10. See, specifically, Zavala (1975a, 1975b, 1976, 1978a, 1980a, 1980b, 1982b, 1984, 1987, 1992, 1994 and 1995b). To these publications another two books of his related to the world of popular oral literature may be added: See Zavala (1995a and 1999).

ties, the 1979 Statute of Autonomy for the Basque Country, and a new General Law regarding the normalization of *Euskara* in 1982. The new political situation forced *bertso-lariak* into reconsidering the suitability of regularly using political subjects in *bertsolaritza* performances. Elsewhere, a new public made up especially of young people of both sexes burst onto the *bertsolaritza* scene and Basque public television (Euskal Telebista; ETB) also increasingly aided the development of this new awareness.

Xabier Amuriza: Txapelketak in 1980 and 1982

In the 1980s a new figure emerged in *bertsolaritza*: the Bizkaian Xabier Amuriza (1941–). He subsequently implemented a series of important changes, such as a questioning of the traditional axioms regarding *bertsolaritza*, the introduction of unified Basque, and the use of new melodies, which taken together implied a qualitative leap in the development of the phenomenon.

Among these new features, Amuriza called into question the maxim traditionally defended by Jules Moulier, "Oxobi" (1888–1958), Salaberry (1903–77), Basarri and others: namely, that the ability demonstrated by Basque bards was a gift from God and one could not acquire it through training or scholastic learning. For these individuals, it was one of nature's gifts, like the singing of birds: "God and only God. The bird doesn't study and it knows how to sing better than the best people schooled in singing. That bird has an instinct like that and God imparted all such instincts" (Moulier 1952: 316); or, in the words of Salaberry (1954: 70), "the gift of the *bertsolari* is . . . . God-given, like all other things that came forth from God's hand;" and according to Basarri (Eizmendi 1984: 99), "a *Bertsolari* must be born; his must have a special stamp; if he doesn't have that stamp, if he doesn't have that special something, all his effort will be of no avail at all."

Amuriza tried to demonstrate the opposite, arguing that (under normal linguistic conditions) the art of *bertsolaritza* was a problem of effort and learning like any other art; and indeed, this argument has been confirmed by the existence of more than eighty *bertsolaritza* schools throughout Euskal Herria today (Agirreazaldegi 2003). Amuriza was a pioneer in the preparation of learning material for these schools, which he undertook during a spell of more than seven years in prison in Zamora. Among this material three books stand out: *Hiztegi errimatua* ("A Rhyming Dictionary"), *Hitzaren kirol nazionala* ("The National Sport of Words") (1981) and *Zu ere bertsolari* ("You Also a *Bertsolari*") (1982); with the latter demonstrating the author's general objective: namely, that any Basque with a normal dominion of his or her language could become a *bertsolari*.

Another of Amuriza's innovations in the 1980 and 1982 *txapelketak* was his use of unified Basque. That said, this Bizkaian *bertsolari* also defended the use of his provincial dialect, whenever circumstances required it, as is apparent through his published work: the two-volume *Bizkaiko Bertsogintza* ("The Production of Verse in Bizkaia") (1995 and 1998); traditional Bizkaian verses he compiled which led to the CD *Vizcayatik... Bizkaiara* ("From Vizcaya to Bizkaia") (2001) by the group "Oskorri"; *Bizkaieraz bertsotan* ("Making Verse in Bizkaian") (1996); and a book about old verses, *Bizkaiko Kopla Zaharrak* ("Old Verses from

Bizkaia"), musically interpreted by both Joseba Tapia and in Oskorri's CD *Katuen Testamentua* ("Testament of the Cats") (1993). However, Amuriza, understanding that one has to perform in front of all Basques, has been a defender of *Euskara batua* (Unified Basque), a standardized form of the language that was created in the late 1960s. Indeed he tried to demonstrate that this kind of Basque, endorsed by *Euskaltzaindia*, was neither dry nor artificial.

The variety of melodies (some he created himself) was another important aspect of the change brought about during the 1980s. Not only did he win the champion's beret during these two competitions, he also obtained the prize given to the *bertsolari* who used the most new melodies. The dramatic quality of his verses, the beauty of his *Euskara*, his improvisational ability especially in individual tests, his ability to tackle serious subjects and his rich scale of rhetorical and poetic resources are the principal qualities which mapped out significant new terrain for *bertsolaritza*.

This enrichment of rhymes, rhythms, new melodies, and different approaches to the treatment of subjects also implied a profound reflection in the theorization of *bertsolaritza*, following the path established by other *bertsolariak* like Basarri and Xalbador.[11] It would, then, be impossible to comprehend the contemporary resurgence of *bertsolaritza* without taking account of Amuriza's contribution in the 1980 and 1982 *txapelketak*. This is a widely shared opinion, as demonstrated by the current champion, Andoni Egaña, who feels greatly indebted to the Bizkaian *bertsolari* (1994a: 62): "Xabier clearly taught us two things: to what level we might aspire and what steps had to be taken to get there. And for that not only me, but a whole generation of *bertsolariak* and devotees of *bertsolaritza* are indebted to him."

The 1990s

Andoni Egaña (1961–)

Just as the years go by, so *bertsolaritza* has evolved as an art and social phenomenon while still maintaining its essential elements. For example, one might define it in general terms as improvised, oral-style Basque poetry, which popular poets sing in front of an audience. One of the most influential representatives of contemporary *bertsolaritza* is Andoni Egaña, born in Zarautz (Gipuzkoa) in 1961. The versatile Egaña is a champion *bertsolari*, an award-winning writer, and a university lecturer. As such he has broken free of the boundaries of a traditional *bertsolari*. Yet he remains an artist that skillfully dominates the difficult techniques of *bertsolaritza*.

As a writer he has produced novels, short stories and essays with works such as: *Socratikoek ere badute ama* ("Socratic People Have a Mother Too"), a book of short stories written in 1989; *Aitaren batean* ("Immediately"), a collection of articles published in the

---

11. See Basarri (Eizmendi 1984) and the section, "Noiztik eta Nondik" in Xalbador's *Odolaren Mintzoa* (Aire 1976a: 23–70).

"*Zabalik*" section of the newspaper *El Diario Vasco* between 1988 and 1990; *Zaudete geldi pixka batean* ("Stop For a Little While") (1999); *Zozoak beleari* ("The Blackbird Said to the Crow") (1997), an epistolary essay written with Jon Sarasua; *Imanol Urbieta: Luzea da bidea* ("Imanol Urbieta: The Journey is Long") (2002); and the novel *Pausoa noiz luzatu* ("When to Take Another Step") (1998). He has contributed to newspapers and journals, while also working as a scriptwriter and television presenter for Basque public television, ETB; at the same time, he is the author of the CD *Tximeletak sabelean* ("Butterflies in the Stomach") (1994) in which he sings Basque verses.

As a lecturer he has participated in courses organized by both the (public) University of the Basque Country and the University of Deusto. In the latter talk, given in September 1995 as part of a series of lectures entitled "Gu geu bertsolari euskaldunok" ("We, the Basque *Bertsolariak*"), Egaña shared various aspects of his life through ten photographs: his childhood in Zarautz's "Salbatore Mitxelena" *ikastola* (a school where instruction is carried out in Basque), under the guidance of teachers like the writer Andu Lertxundi and the musician Imanol Urbieta; sad memories of the Franco regime's execution of ETA activists Juan Paredes Manot, "Txiki," and Angel Otegi, in September 1975; the gratification that Amuriza's victory in the 1980 *txapelketa* gave him; and his university studies in Basque Philology which he began in Donostia's EUTG university and finished at the UPV/EHU (University of the Basque Country) in Gasteiz. It was during these courses that he acquired his first theoretical impressions of *bertsolaritza*, under the initial guidance of the aforementioned Juan Mª Lekuona: "To a certain extent I am indebted to Juan Mari Lekuona for starting to make verses. In EUTG Juan Mari taught us oral literature; I enhanced my basic theoretical understandings with him" (Egaña, qtd. in Camino and Landa 1986: 41). His long, ten-year sojourn in Araba as a cultural official for the Gasteiz City Hall, and his return to Zarautz as husband and father, completed one part of this biographical overview. In the course of the talk, those present gradually acquired a better understanding of Egaña: shy by nature yet also hyperactive, with some two hundred *bertsolaritza* performances every year, and a consummate sportsman despite being a hardened smoker: "You know that my vice is cigars" (Egaña, qtd. in *Bertsolari Txapelketa Nagusia 93* 1994: 244).

As a *bertsolari* two facets about him stand out: that of the inexperienced young Andoni who was looking for his own identity, and that of the mature Egaña, respected for the well-earned prestige gained through winning three national competitions in 1993, 1997 and 2001; as well as being a finalist in those of 1986 and 1989. If, within the first facet, the personality of a shy young man stood out, in the second one can see the strong personality of a fighter in the combat of *bertsolaritza*: equipped with swift reflexes, the possessor of a sharp intelligence and a fine irony that becomes his best weapon in such didactic duels.

Egaña is a self-taught *bertsolari* who has deliberately reflected on this phenomenon. Yet he is also an eclectic bard who has known how to combine the influence of traditional *bertsolaritza* from the Urola valley of Gipuzkoa (Joxe Lizaso, J. Agirre "Oranda", Imanol

Lazkano, and so on) with the new contributions of a fairly close group of contrasting *bertsolariak* such as Sebastián Lizaso (Champion of Euskadi in 1989), Jon Sarasua, Anjel Mari Peñagarikano (Champion of Gipuzkoa in 1991), Iñaki Murua, Xabier Pérez or "Euzkitze," Mikel Mendizabal, and Mikel Tellería. Thanks to this synthesis, Egaña has managed to make his art of *bertsolaritza* easy to understand, both by old and young followers alike. His admiration for the subtle and humorous Gipuzkoan *bertsolari*, José Miguel Iztueta, "Lazkao-Txiki" (1926–93) is also well-known as was demonstrated when he dedicated to him his champion's beret in the 1993 championship. Egaña understands how to learn from different sources, thereby achieving a command of different skills and a very personal style.

As with many other *bertsolariak,* the bard of Zarautz is a man committed to Basque cultural development, as demonstrated with the verses he sang in Bilbao in honor of the poet Gabriel Aresti, echoing the Bilbao writer's poetry (*Euskal Herriko Bertsolari Txapelketa Nagusia 1986* 1987: 115):

Arestin asmo bikain zar hura	That splendid old intention of Aresti
da gure helburu berria,	is our new objective;
ia pittinka egiten degun	let's see if we can build bit by bit
euskal harrizko herria.	a rock solid Basque Country.

But Egaña is, above all else, an innovative *bertsolari*. If Basarri took *bertsolaritza* out of the cider houses and into the handball courts and Amuriza transferred it to the schools and *ikastolak,* Egaña has taken it into the university, where he originally learned the theoretical base of this artistic phenomenon. Among some of his proposals for change, Egaña has highlighted the need for a profound reworking of rhymes; and this desire to enrich the "warehouse of rhymes" is expressed in a nice seafaring simile (Egaña 1996b: 29): "I have the feeling that we are in a situation as if an anchor has been dropped."

In the five national competitions in which he's taken part (1986, 1989, 1993, 1997 and 2001), I would recommend the consideration of several poems: "*Artxandatik Bilbora begira*" ("Looking at Bilbao from Artxanda") (*Bertsolari Txapelketa 1986* 1987: 148); the initial greeting dedicated to women in general and to the *bertsolari* Maialen Lujanbio in particular (*Bertsolari Txapelketa Nagusia 97* 1998: 222); the strophe dedicated to the head ("*burua,*" *Bertsolari Txapelketa Nagusia 1997* 1998: 238); the pickpocket that tries to steal in the Seville "Expo 92" (*Bertsolari Txapelketa 1997* 1998: 305); the forty-five year-old teacher who falls in love with an eighteen year-old student (*Bertsolari Txapelketa 2001* 2002: 276–77); and a dialogue between two mothers who have lost their sons (one an *ertzaina* or Basque police officer assassinated by ETA and the other a member of this organization who was killed while trying to escape; *Bertsolari Txapelketa 2001* 2002: 301–03).

Egaña feels a part of that group of *bertsolariak* who are trying to adapt *bertsolaritza* to the modern age. One of the specific results of this reflection is the book, *The Art of Bertsolaritza* (Garzia, Sarasua and Egaña 2001), from which I would point out the following reflections: Intellectual experimentation is one of the most important aspects of contemporary *bertsolaritza*. The improvised *bertsolaritza* of the last twenty-five years has been full of texts which confirm the tendency of young *bertsolariak* like Amuriza, Egaña, and Jon Sarasua to experiment intellectually. For them, the poetic dimension is not the most imperative aspect of improvised *bertsolaritza* although it continues to be an important one. Body language and gestures are also significant resources. Contemporary *bertsolaritza* is characterized by its use of a large number of melodies, in contrast to the situation in the past. It is also marked by the quantity and quality of its performances, its improvisational authenticity, the presence of creative young people and its introduction into the educational system. As regards its organizational level, there is the Euskal Herriko Bertsozale Elkartea (Basque Country Association of *Bertsolaritza* Followers) with well over a thousand members. Its goals include generational transmission, documentation, research and organizing its expansion. Contemporary *bertsolaritza* has a number of *bertso eskolak* or *bertso* schools throughout the Basque Country and, since 1997, the Xenpelar Documentation Center. The Bertsozale Elkartea association maintains international relations through international meetings, for the moment in Spanish and Latin American circles. To conclude, then, those in charge of *bertsolaritza*'s contemporary organization are looking for a new theoretical framework for improvised *bertsolaritza*. Within this framework rhetoric will play an important role: "To analyze *bertsolaritza* as a rhetorical genre does not, in principle, imply dismissing its literary nature, however far this literary nature does not constitute an end in itself"(Garzia, Sarasua and Egaña 2001: 191).

To conclude this first section concerning Basque *bertsolaritza* and the *bertsolari* Egaña, I'll include here the strophe that Amuriza dedicated to him when he became champion for the second time in 1997 (*Bertsolari Txapelketa Nagusia 97* 1998: 317):

Lehendik txapeldun haundi hintzena	You, who before held the champion's beret
bigarrenakin hor hago;	appear now with your second;
txapela ere somatzen diat	I can even see that the beret
sekula ez bezain harro,	is prouder than ever,
hire buruan sentitzen baita	since on your head it feels
bera ere ederrago.	more beautiful too.

If Amuriza sung this on the occasion of Egaña's second *txapela* in 1997, what might he have sung after he won his third in 2001, thus achieving the mythical status of Uztapide?

Some Phenomena Similar to *Bertsolaritza*

On mentioning the comparison between *bertsolaritza* and other similar phenomena at the beginning of this article, I argued that there is more that unites than that which divides us, in spite of the unique dimension of Basque. *Bertsolaritza* is essentially improvised sung oral poetry and the ability to create it should not be the exclusive property of any one nation, aristocratic class, or language, however old it might be.

Since human beings began to inhabit the planet, they have been intimately connected to esthetic creation. In ancient times poetic declarations were sung and, often, improvised.

There is evidence of this in both the Greco-Roman and Celtic worlds: namely, the contest among the bards Menalcas and Dametas which appears in Virgil's *Eclogue III*; and the troubadour poetry of the Middle Ages. There is also evidence that this artistic phenomenon existed in seventeenth-century Nuremberg (Germany) and eighteenth-century Italian carnivals. That same century, a significant event, narrated by the celebrated writer from Gijón (Asturias), Gaspar Melchor de Jovellanos (1744–1811), took place in an Asturian festival: He recalls that once an archbishop visited an Asturian hermitage where girls were singing and dancing. This disturbed the archbishop's peaceful lunch and he ordered them to be quiet. However, a little later he was forced to listen to this improvised verse (qtd. in Zavala 1999: 85–87):

El señor obispo manda	His grace the Archbishop orders
que se acaben los cantares;	that all songs should be done away with;
primero se han de acabar	but first they should do away with
obispos y capellanes.	Bishops and Chaplains.

As can be clearly seen, the habit of singing improvised verses is very old and is not specific to any one place. There exist vestiges of this artistic expression today on all five continents: Asia (India, Thailand, Japan, Afghanistan, Indonesia and so on); Africa (Mauritania, Madagascar, and in the Sahara); Europe (the Basque Country, France, Spain, Greece, Turkey, Portugal, Cyprus, Crete, Russia, Wales, Croatia, Serbia, Bosnia, Albania, Kosovo and Italy – Sardinia, Sicily, Lazio, Tuscany). In Spain alone there is clear evidence of it in Galicia, the Canary Islands, the Balearic Islands (Mallorca, Menorca), Cartagena, Alpujarras (Almería and Granada), and so on. In the Americas, in the United States (Louisiana), Mexico, Panama, Puerto Rico, Argentina, Brazil, Chile, Uruguay, Colombia, Venezuela, Ecuador, Peru, the Dominican Republic, Cuba and so forth.

Cuba

In 1998 the Cuban poet and improviser Alexis Díaz-Pimienta published an interesting book that helps one understand in detail the improvisation of Cuban *decimistas*: *Teoría de la improvisación*. This work was the outcome of serious research, which tells the personal tale of an exceptional character who adopts various names: *repentista, rapsoda, trovero, payador, bertsolari, verseador, decimista*, and so on according to the country where this phenomenon of improvised and sung oral poetry takes place.

In this work I would highlight those chapters dedicated to the subject of pure and impure improvisation. The author begins with a concept of improvisation, defining it as, "the art of improvising verses, with different strophe forms and distinct music, with or without musical accompaniment" (Díaz-Pimienta 1998: 45). In the same way, he defines pure *repentismo* as "the 'total' improvisation of verses, a one hundred percent spontaneous creation, without the poet even resorting to memorized strophes, worked out beforehand" (Díaz-Pimienta 1998: 46). However, he also confesses that in impure *repentismo* strophes worked out beforehand, either wholly or partially, are used.

With the authority that his status as a distinguished *decimista* and poet gives him, the author shows his disagreement with the opinion of the renowned oralist Zumthor who argues that, "improvisation is never total: text produced in a performance is that way by virtue of cultural norms, even pre-established rules" (1991: 237). As an expert in the intricacies of this literary phenomenon, Díaz-Pimienta sincerely expresses his own opinion on this subject. If he accepts, to some extent at least, Professor Zumthor's opinion, he clearly states his disagreement about the oralist's complete denial of pure and total improvisation: "This is the first time . . . . that a *repentista* has publicly confessed that he, and his colleagues, do not always improvise. I wish to make clear that I do not subscribe to the *Zumthorian* thesis of a "never total" improvisation, I only say that in some determined performances some improvisers don't always improvise" (Díaz-Pimienta 1998: 231).

The great Cuban *decimistas*, like Indio Naborí (the most important current figure); an important female example, Tomasita Quiala or "*La alondra de Lisa*" ("The skylark of Lisa"); Raúl Herrera; and the author of the book himself are all figures that are increasingly known and recognized by followers of *bertsolaritza* in the Basque Country. They always use the *décima* (a strophe of ten octosyllabic verses with a consonantal rhyme, ABBA-ACC-DDC), and are accompanied by a lute (a twelve-stringed instrument) or a guitar.

Balearic Islands (Mallorca, Menorca)

Thanks to an article by Professor Eusebi Ayensa i Prat (1998?) one can add to this comparative study of the phenomenon of sung improvised oral poetry. Once again, linguistic (in this case Catalan and Greek) and geographical differences have not been an obstacle to establishing certain similarities between the *glosadores* of the Balearic Islands and the *pitàrides* of Cyprus, in spite of the distance which separates these Mediterranean islands.

The popular poets of the Balearic Islands, known by the name *glosadores*, are reminiscent of medieval troubadours and minstrels. *Glosadores* were very common in Mallorca and Menorca from the eighteenth century until the eve of the Spanish Civil War (1936–39). The outbreak of this war, coupled with its long duration, greatly harmed the development of this literary expression. The vast majority of these poets was illiterate and came from rural backgrounds. The subjects of their sung duels (as was to be expected) were related to traditional religious values, good habits and vices, love and so on. Although these challenges between members of different villages were frequent in the past, their social influence was minimal due to their rural origins. Even today, despite the fact that they perform on the radio and television in areas where most people speak Catalan, their public social impact and reception is minimal, if one compares them, for example, to the *bertsolariak* of Euskal Herria.[12] If one adds to this the fact that the vast majority of them are quite old, *glosa*'s future is not very promising. However, despite this, lately one can notice a resurgence of sorts, as is evident in the creation of the Asociaciò d'Amics de

---

12. According to a poll carried out by SIADECO, 21.6 percent of Basque-speakers said they didn't follow *bertsolaritza*; 78.3 percent said they followed *bertsolaritza* to some extent; and 15 percent of those said they were enthusiastic followers.

la Glosa ("The Association of *Glosa* Followers") and in the meetings that young and old *glosadores* undertake in Mallorca and Menorca.

The first written evidence of the *glosa* dates from the seventeenth century. In the Inquisition records, two characters, Jesus Christ and the Jew, appear as a means of entertainment, dueling through the improvisation of sung *glosadas*. In the document one sees how the Holy Office (Inquisition) had to condemn such a public performance because the Jew expressed a desire to kill Jesus. Such improvisational confrontations were held throughout the year in Mallorca, with the Saint Antonio Abad's day festival being especially important. Today, such performances generally take place in winter when agricultural chores are not so pressing. Such performances are held in closed spaces, such as bars, small theaters, and so on. Two or three *glosadores* compete by first greeting the public and then dialectically confronting one another through a verbal assault. Personal references, in which irony and criticism of an opponent's poetic capacity stand out, normally abound. The audience also plays an important role since they decide, to a great extent, the length of the performance. This has evolved with time; while in the past these poetic duels began at dusk and went on all night, nowadays they do not go beyond two or three hours.

As regards technical aspects one can see that generally, they are composed of heptasyllabic verses, introducing at the beginning of each verse an exclamation (the vowel *i*) thanks to which the *glosador* has a few seconds to prepare a new strophe. Elsewhere, the subject of the rhyme plays an important role as it is essential to the overall evaluation of the verse. Although one cannot talk in terms of clichéd rhymes, these improvisers try to avoid a "black" list of words that, because they are so infrequently used, make the swift creation of verses difficult. Finally, while in Menorca a guitar is always used, in Mallorca they both use a guitar and sometimes sing *a capella*.

Unfortunately, the number of *glosadores* that know how to improvise in an expert way is today very small, no more than a dozen. Most of them use stereotyped formulas that impede true improvisation.

Cyprus

Despite being two independent literary demonstrations, the Balearic *glosas* are quite similar to Cypriot *tsàtismes*. The custom of improvising verses is also very old on the island of Cyprus, since there are records of poetic competitions dating back to the sixteenth century. For example, in 1580 the cleric F. Etienne de Lusignan described the fondness of the Cypriots for this kind of poetic competition, as can be seen in the citation below. In this document one notices the presence of people from different social levels who sing, dance and attend improvised poetic competitions: "After lunch middle class people, as well as those of more humble status, always relax in their gardens, lovers of games and dances: and it is natural if one is inclined to poetry, which is nicely composed, without however possessing much artistic quality or rules." (qtd. in Ayensa i Prat 1998?: 83).

In Cyprus the violin, as a musical accompaniment, is never lacking. This makes it easier for the poets to sing; there is one set melody which means that often it becomes monotonous through repetition. On some occasions, the lute and the flute replace the violin. As regards the technical dimension, the folklorist K. Langullis has demonstrated the existence of clichéd rhymes that, together with the stereotyped plans, make up the formal base from which the poetic technique of the Cypriot improvisers is formed.

Conclusions

In the first instance, one should say that all these artistic expressions are phenomena related to oral literature or exponents of a popular poetry which are very old; a heritage that is still alive in some nations which has survived through many centuries. Obviously I am not referring here to written poetry but to that poetry which is improvised and sung before an audience and is bequeathed from the oral tradition. This is the creation of artists possessing great speed of thought, through which they quickly elaborate a strophe without having time to redo what they previously expressed. These artists create through improvisation and at the same time they improvise verses, they offer them to an audience. Ultimately the audience forms the *raison d'être* of their art.

The following description of an old *bertsolari* while he performs accurately captures many of the ideas discussed here: "With his tilted beret and hands behind his back, he's staring into space while searching for the right words amid a storm of words. He must immediately think up and sing, looking for the most beautiful expressions" ("Abestiak" 1986: 29). Respect for tradition, creation in performance and quality of improvisation are some of the goals which all artists of popular oral literature seek. One small incident which occurred during the National *Bertsolari* Championship in 2001 demonstrates improvisational quality: During a blackout caused by a power cut in the Anoeta cycle track (Donostia), Unai Iturriaga improvised a strophe comparing the breakdown to *coitus interruptus*, to the surprise of the thousands of spectators (*Bertsolari Txapelketa Nagusia 2001* 2002: 64).

Among the most outstanding differences that exist between *bertsolaritza* and other similar phenomena one might highlight the following: *Euskara* used as a national language by the Basque bards; the style of singing *a capella*, as opposed to the diversity of musical instruments which are used in other places; the seriousness and concentration of the *bertsolariak* who confine themselves to rapidly searching among the far reaches of their minds, as opposed to the expressiveness and diversity of gestures among *payadores*, *decimistas*, and so on; the variety and richness of Basque rhythms and melodies compared to their scarcity in several other artistic movements; the security and help afforded *bertsolariak*, as an infrastructure, by the Basque Country Association of *Bertsolaritza* Followers as opposed to the lack of institutional help for most of the other movements; the existence of more than eighty *bertsolaritza* schools scattered throughout the Basque Country compared with the listless life of some other movements, namely in Galicia (Agirreazaldegi 2002 and 2003: 54).

Yet these and other differences cannot and must not erode the common cultural treasure that underscores each one of these literary expressions. Meetings and conferences like the one we are holding today in Reno (Nevada) must oblige us to carry on looking for that millenarian wealth that is still hidden in the innermost reaches of our different nations' souls. "*Eman ta zabal zazu munduan frutua*" ("Produce and scatter your fruit throughout the world").

The Folk Arts of the *Maskarada* Performance

KEPA FERNÁNDEZ DE LARRINOA

Introduction

Zuberoa, or Soule in French, constitutes the easternmost Basque-speaking geographic area. It covers eight hundred and seven square kilometers which are traversed by the Uhaitza river. In Zuberoa there are thirty-five villages or communes, of which twenty-eight are considered to be mountainous. Around fifteen-thousand people live in this valley, among whom forty percent make their living mostly from farming and businesses direct-ly related to agricultural production, while about twenty-five percent are employed in industrial work (INSEE; Institut National de la Statisque et des Études Économiques, 1991: 182–195) On the whole, Zuberoa represents an essentially rural Pyrenean land-scape.

The present paper describes *Maskarada* traditional folk performances in Zuberoa, understanding them as a genuine Zuberoan folk genre. However, *Maskarada* performanc-es also share many similarities with other theatrical celebrations held during the winter period in both Mediterranean and Atlantic Europe (Alford 1928), as well as in North Africa (Hammoudi 1993). There is a further view of *Maskaradak* (plural) which sees them as the enactment and public exhibition of the most intricate traditional folk arts in Zuberoa. As such, even though there are a large range of folk arts involved in a *Maskara-da* performance, it is that of the dancers which has been given greatest significance, both in local discourse and in academic research.

As dancing does occupy an extremely strong place in rural Basque society, scholars have tended to examine many of its festivities by focusing primarily on the dances. As a result, a significant number of studies concerning traditional rural festivals have only addressed their dancing. Indeed, several festivals in the Basque Country are known sim-ply by the name of their associated dance. A similar process has occurred in Zuberoa, where the dancers and dances of *Maskarada* performances have come to represent the entire folk festival. This paper, however, demonstrates that the organization of a *Maskara-*

Entrance of performers at the Gotaine *Maskarada*, Zuberoa, 2000. The *gorriak* or red team, including the flag-bearer, are followed by the lord and lady, and accompanied by musicians. Photo by Lisa Corcostegui.

da is a complex social activity, where dancing is but one of many parts which make up the entire performance. Therefore, the use of analytical categories such as "dance-event" (Royce 1977) opens up wider possibilities to the study of folk performance in Zuberoa. Moreover, I would contend, studying *Maskarada* performances in terms of a "mask-event," "storytelling-event," or "song-event" is just as accurate as that of "dance-event."

Approaching *Maskarada* Performance from Anthropology

The word *Maskarada* implies a complex set of performing arts mainly carried out by young, generally unmarried men, who mask their faces, disguise their bodies, dance and recite grotesque and coarse speeches, and chant poetry, while visiting neighboring villages of the valley. Consequently, the study of the aesthetics involved in a *Maskarada* perform-ance is not an easy enterprise, because a number of circumstances take place at the same time. However, regarding verbal and visual imaginary, two main points should be empha-sized: on the one hand, images of prestige, authority and power seem to intensify before an audience; on the other, there is a playful, grotesque and ironic exhibition of images which are usually taken from everyday life and which are also drawn in such a way that

Audience participation in the Gotaine *Maskarada*, Zuberoa, 2000. Public participation at the end of the performance is an important element of the *Maskarada*. Photo by Lisa Corcostegui.

they come to depict a rather deviant scene of the quotidian experience (Fernández de Larrinoa 1997). A *Maskarada* performance, therefore, exhibits two key characteristics: (1) an intensification of hierarchical, authoritative political meaning and (2) a joyful enactment of insurgent cultural images or subversive social and political meaning; in other words, both a heightening and a transgression of cultural categories and social behavior are portrayed throughout the Zuberoan *Maskarada*.

Similarly, in terms of bodily expressions and patterns of action, a clear distinction has to be made between the different performers. For example, within the *Maskarada* one can differentiate between the *dantza* ("dance") movements of the *gorriak* (the red team, literally "the reds") and the *basa* ("rude," "wild," "untamed") movements of the *beltzak* (the black team, literally "the blacks"). Several scholars have pointed out that these two kinds of bodily expression should be interpreted as mutually opposing movements (Hérelle 1925; Caro Baroja 1965; Fourquet 1990; Garamendi 1991). As such, the members of the red team (the *gorriak*) dramatize an intensification of meaning, principally through their dancing; while the black team (the *beltzak*) attempts to subvert all meaning, primarily through their unrefined speech, use of obscenities, and uncontrolled bodily movements.

The characters comprising both the *gorriak* and *beltzak* enter the performance in a specific sequence: The *gorriak* are the first to emerge, initially through a group of dancers who represent five characters: a hobbyhorse; a cat-man; a flag-bearer; a man with a horse-mane stick; and a water-bearer. Secondly, there appear a lord and a lady; and thirdly, a male and female farm laborer. After these, in the fourth position, two blacksmiths emerge, and finally come the jesters. Then come the *beltzak*: four gypsies; four tinkers; two castrators; two knife-grinders and a doctor. These characters perform a series of well structured activities which are arranged in two main sections: one in the morning and the other in the afternoon. During the morning, a sort of "street ritualized theatre" takes place, where a number of households, as well as the authorities of the village where the *Maskarada* is being performed, are greeted and honored. After a lunch provided by the host villagers, the performers move into the *plaza* ("square") in order to enact a diversity of patterned sketches.

Units and Sequences in *Maskarada* Performance

The red group is composed of the *aitzindariak* ("the first ones" or "those who lead"); the *jauna* ("lord") and the *anderea* ("lady"); the *laboraria* ("male farm laborer") and the *laborarisa* ("female farm laborer"); the *marexalak* ("blacksmiths") and the *kukuileroak* ("jesters"). The black group is comprised of the *kereztuak* ("castrators"); *buhameak* ("gypsies"); the *kautereak* ("tinkers") and the *medizina* ("doctor").

GORRIAK	BELTZAK
aitzindariak (dancers) *entseinaria* (flag-bearer) *txerreroa* (man with horse-mane stick) *gathuzaina* (cat-man) *zamalzaina* (hobbyhorse) *kantiniersa* (water-bearer)	*kereztuak* (castrators) *nausia* (master) *mithila* (apprentice)
jauna eta anderea (lord and lady)	*buhameak* (gypsies) *buhame jauna* (gypsy king) *zilintzau* (bum) and two others
laboraria eta laborarisa (male and female farm laborer) *marexalak* (blacksmiths) (usually three)	*kautereak* (tinkers) *kabana handia* (big cabin) (the leader) *pitxu* ("fox"), *frupu*, and *pupu* *txorrotxak* (knife-grinders)
	nausia (master) *mithila* (apprentice)
kukuileroak (jesters) (three or more)	*medizina* (doctor)

The role of the *kukuileroak* ("jesters") is given to the youngest participants and their number may vary, but two or three is typical. *Kukuileroa* is a difficult word to translate. Etymologically, it derives from Latin and Garamendi connects these characters to the Medieval festivals of fools (Garamendi 1991: 137). Local sages hold that they are the lord's soldiers and during my fieldwork I was told that this role expresses youth. This idea is supported by the fact that the jesters are played by the youngest participants of the *Maskarada*.

The ritual action of these characters is developed through a predictable sequence of events which, as previously mentioned, take place in the morning and the afternoon. In the morning the troupe arrives in the host village where they are received by the *errezib-itzaileak* ("the receiving party"), a group of dancers from that village. Then the festival starts in earnest with music played by a *tabalaria* ("drummer"), a *txilaria* or *txiruralaria* ("piper"), and possibly also a *ttun-ttun* player ("string-drummer").

The specific act which starts the festival off is called *barrikada haustia* or the fall of the barricade. Members of the receiving party are the first to dance and it is they who, first individually and then collectively, commence the celebration. Then it is the turn of the *maskarakaiak*, members of the visiting *Maskarada*, to perform. First come members of the red group who, like the receiving party, dance first individually and then in a group. Their initial task consists of overcoming a small obstacle, made up of bottles of wine and named *barrikada* ("barricade"), which the hosts have placed in their path. The *aitzindariak* dancers are the first to cross the barricade, followed by the *entseinaria*, the *txerreroa*, the *gathuzaina*, the *zamalzaina*, and the *kantiniersa*. They are followed by the *jauna* and *anderea*, *laboraria* and *laborarisa*, the *marexalak*, and finally the *kukuileroak*. I have taken the above description from the *Maskaradak* I attended during 1992 and 1993, though variation is possible as Guilch-er has shown in his study of *Maskarada* choreography (Guilcher 1984).

Once the components of the *gorriak* clear the barricade it is the turn of the *beltzak* to do the same. They cross the barricade in their own particular way by running, shouting and shrieking. They then circle the red group and finally, fling themselves on top of one another. The end of performance thus comes to resemble a rugby scrum, with everyone huddled together. The *beltzak* perform in the following order: first come the *kereztuak*, who run around the *gorriak* while embracing each other and make a gesture as if to open the way. A short distance behind them appear the *buhameak*, the *kautereak* and the *medizina* in groups of two or three, and they likewise circle the red group while embracing one anoth-er. These last three groups, then, are those which throw themselves on the ground in a disorderly fashion. And they are followed by the *txorrotxak*, who walk across the barricade. As they walk, they sing a verse of greeting which ends when they reach the hosts who originally set up the barricade. At that point, cheers and shouts of jubilation are heard. After this initial performance all those present then mingle in conversation, while the bot-tles in the barricade are removed and opened to be offered around. At the same time, food is also served.

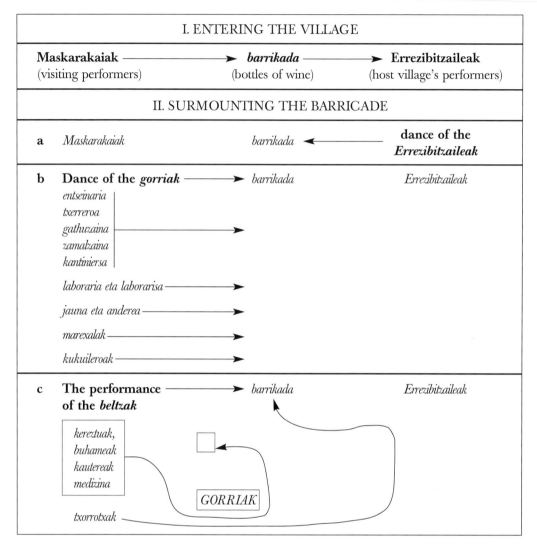

This same sequence is repeated throughout the morning, every time a barricade appears before the members of the *Maskarada*, and can happen several times en route from the entrance to the village up to the square. The final barricade awaits them here in the village square and is prepared by the local authorities. By the time they arrive in the square it is midday. Once the last barricade is cleared, the red and black members of the *Maskarada*, together with the authorities and inhabitants of the host village and other visitors, form a circle to dance *aitzina-phika* and *moneinak*, two versions of Basque dances called *jauziak* (literally meaning "jumps"). Once the dancing has concluded, the *Maskarada* performers are invited to have lunch. When the meal is over they gather again near the square where the afternoon ritual will be celebrated. Specifically, the troupe members line up to perform the *arribada* ("arrival") and enter the square that way. They then act out a series of scenes which I will summarize below.

Through the medium of dance, the *marexalak* shoe the *zamalzaina* and the presence of *kukuileroak* on stage revolves around the *zamalzaina*. The *aitzindariak* or leading dancers then perform the *lagabota* dance and next, the *kereztuak* appear. Their job consists of catching the *zamalzaina* and castrating him. It is understood that in this part of the performance the actors should speak in Occitan, the language of neighboring Béarn. For a long time, to be *Béarnais* by origin and a castrator by trade were synonymous in France, Spain and Portugal, because so many *bearnesak* (people from Béarn) used to make their living from traveling through southern Europe to castrate cattle. This in turn generated an image of the castrator who united nomadism or transhumance with ethnic origins and connotations (Arripe 1994). However, in the *Maskaradak* today, owing to lack of fluency in the language, many castrators mix Occitan expressions and words with French, Basque and Spanish. The use of Spanish expressions is a recent development, and a result of the fact that actors now not only have a better knowledge of Spanish than of Occitan, but are also aware of a significant number of Spanish Basque spectators in the audience. This changing language usage gives the actors new lines with which to improvise, as well as freshening up the performance with a modern touch which is missing from the traditional script.

The *txorrotxak* are then asked to sharpen the lord's sword and the action unfolds over the course of several scenes. Song, dance and ironic burlesque dialogue are used to act this out. In addition to this sequence the *txorrotxak* also introduce, through sung verses, the castrators, gypsies and tinkers when they appear onto the stage. The *aitzindariak* then perform the *bralia* dance and immediately afterwards, the *buhameak* appear. Their task is to read a *pheredikia* or sermon, performed by the *buhame jauna* or gypsy king. They conclude their performance with a sword dance which is exaggeratedly out of step and uncoordinated.

Once the leading dancers have performed the *godalet dantza* ("dance of the glass"), the *kautereak* act out the repairing of the pot which the lord has sent to be mended. While several tinkers set to repairing the pot, their leader, *kabana handia*, reads a speech to the audience in which he relates things which have happened in the world and in the village during the course of the year. The sharing out of the lord's payment for the repair of the pot gives rise to a dispute in which *pitxu* dies. The doctor is therefore called and to everyone's relief, he brings *pitxu* back to life.

The *Maskarada* closes with two events. Firstly, the actors come together to form a chorus and sing a song especially composed for the occasion. Secondly, they make a circle to dance *aitzina-phika* and *moneinak,* inviting all those who so wish to join in. After these dances, the *Maskarada* is officially concluded, but the festival continues in the village bar or bars.

SEQUENCE OF SCENES AFTER THE MIDDAY MEAL
(Field notes on the *Maskarada* of Altzürükü)

- *Arribada* and *aitzina phika* dances performed by the *aitzindariak*
- Verses of presentation by the knife-grinders
- Blacksmiths' performance
- *Lagabota* dance performed by the *aitzindariak*
- Verses of presentation by the knife-grinders
- Castrators' performance
- Knife-grinders' verses
- *Aitzina phika* dance performed by the *aitzindariak*
- Knife-grinders' performance
- *Braletik dantza haustea* dance performed by the *aitzindariak*
- Gypsies' performance and the gypsy king's speech
- Verses of presentation by the knife-grinders
- *Godalet dantza* performed by the *aitzindariak*
- Tinkers' performance and Big Cabin's speech
- *Maskarada* song sung by all members of the *Maskarada*
- *Jauziak* dance including all those present who so wish

Masks, Costumes and Roles in *Maskarada* Performance

Although the *gorriak* come to dramatize intensification of meaning through the use of several symbols and activities (mainly presented through dance), they also move through various other categories, for their costumes are made of human and animal attributes alike. On the other side, the *beltzak* display subversion of meaning primarily through their obscenities, unrefined speeches and the enactment of uncontrolled bodily movements. However, just as with the red team, the masks and disguises of the black team combine human and animal figures. The following is a brief description of the masks, costumes, roles and aesthetics which characterize the members of the *Maskaradak*.

As regards the *gorriak*, with the exception of the *jauna*, the *anderea*, the *laboraria* and the *laborarisa*, all members of the red team wear jackets whose designs echo a nineteenth-century military style. That said, colors, designs and ornaments change from village to village, from *Maskarada* to *Maskarada* within the same village, as well as from character to character. These costumes are usually made by local seamstresses, although today some villages prefer to borrow them from either *Zuberoako Zohardia* or *Aitzindariak*, two cultural associations founded to develop traditional Zuberoan dancing in the early 1970s and late 1980s, respectively.

Entseinaria wears a black beret, jacket and trousers, with a string band across his chest, and holds a flag which he swings while dancing. *Txerreroa* wears a red beret and jacket, but his trousers are black. He holds a stick to which the hair of a horse's mane has been attached. *Gathuzaina* wears a blue jacket, white beret and yellow trousers while holding long wooden shears which the dancer manipulates during the performance. *Zamalzaina*'s jacket is red, and he wears a *koha* ("crown") which is adorned with looking-glasses and feathers. Attached to his waist there is a wooden frame covered with white linen and carved in that frame is horse's head which the dancer grips during his performance. *Kantiniersa* is a dancer with a blue jacket and hat, but a red skirt. He also carries a small barrel.

These characters are the *aitzindaria* dancers and they all wear white dancing shoes and white breeches. These breeches are partially covered by gaiters which match the color of the trousers. The *entseinaria* is an exception to that rule since he does not wear breeches. The *marexalak* wear red berets and jackets, and black trousers, and carry a hammer and pliers, respectively. The *kukuileroak* wear white trousers and red jackets and berets, from which a tassel hangs. *Jauna* wears smart clothes with a string band across his chest, a tall hat, a sword around his waist and carries a stick. The *anderea* wears a white wedding dress today, but it used to be dark at the beginning of the century. The *laboraria* wears a black beret, jacket and trousers, while holding a goad and the *laborarisa* wears a black dress and scarf, as well as carrying a basket.

The members of the red team, particularly the *entseinaria, txorrotxa, gathuzaina, zamalzaina* and *kantiniera*, distinguish themselves from the rest of the *Maskarada* performers by means of their dancing expertise. During the performance, dancing takes center stage for the *arribada* and *barrikada haustea* sequences, or in the case of special choreography such as the *labagota, bralia, godalet-dantza* and *jauziak*. These are group dances and usually performed in a circle. Choreographies are composed of several foot movements known as *puntuak* and *entrexatak*, whose combination varies from village to village.

The aesthetics of the *beltzak* contrast radically with the colors, masks and disguises of the *gorriak*. Specifically, three peculiarities are inherent in the performance of the *beltzak*: In the first place, three types of colors predominate in the costumes: black for the clothing of the *kautereak*; brown for the *txorrotxak* and *kereztuak* and an abundance of bright colors for the *buhameak*. Secondly, the *beltzak* actors represent foreigners, or people passing temporarily through Zuberoa. The third distinguishing characteristic of this group is the way in which its ritual performance takes the form of chaotic bodily movements. And finally, the use of words plays a central role in their performance.

Among the *beltzak*, or *beltzeria* ("group of blacks") as they are sometimes referred to, there are various sub-groups: the *buhameak, kautereak, txorrotxak, kereztuak* and the *medizina*. However, toward the end of the nineteenth and beginning of the twentieth centuries, there existed a wider variety of characters within the *beltzak*. These included a barber, a pharmacist, a notary, a school teacher, and various other professionals who lived in the countryside and could not be identified as peasants (Herelle 1925: 30–40). From a local point of view, each of these sub-groups publicly reproduced a number of stereotypes, socio-cultural images, and pre-established definitions of their respective roles in society.

During the *Maskarada* parade the first members of the black group who appear are the *kereztuak* or castrators. Their role in the morning is limited to opening up the way for the entrance of the entire black group. The castrators' role during the afternoon is more substantial, and is related to a public exhibition of taming wildness, together with certain notions of gender which I have discussed elsewhere (see Fernández de Larrinoa 1997). Their afternoon performance, however, depicts other facets of social life not linked to gender, but demonstrating notions of socio-cultural identity and group belonging.

There are two castrators, who, throughout the performance, speak to each other, circle one another and demonstrate particular dance movements. As previously mentioned, these characters are migrant workers from Béarn, a neighboring geo-cultural area where *Béarnaise* (an Occitan dialect) is spoken. Here one should underscore the fact that the language they speak is a special type of Occitan, in other words incorporating a lot of French and Basque, so that the audience can understand their dialogue. This feature of the *Maskarada* demonstrates the human, linguistic, and cultural groups which border and compete with one another in Zuberoa. And the performance thus serves to highlight, in a jocular way, certain views about these groups' interrelations.

The *buhameak* or the gypsies follow the castrators. Generally, this group consists of four characters, whose most prominent member is the *buhame jauna* or gypsy king. They wear brightly colored clothing, shout loudly, and each carry a wooden sword with which a sort of rustic dance is performed at a certain point in the performance. The *buhameak* demonstrate their personality during the morning barricades by rolling around on the ground, causing mischief, taunting people, and chasing the local girls. The same type of behavior is on show during the afternoon, when these performers display a type of performance highly characteristic of peasant carnival celebrations. This variety of para-theatrical performance, termed a *pheredekia* or sermon, occurs in the following way: As the *buhame jauna* runs in a circle around the perimeter of the plaza, he declares out loud the advantages of his nomadic existence. Meanwhile, he is followed by the rest of the *tribe*, who display various attributes, ranging from laziness and ungratefulness to disorder and chaos. Below I reproduce in Basque with an English translation the *pheredekia* given by the *buhame jauna* of the *Maskarada* performed in Muskildi in 1987:

Agur, agur, herri huntako bizizailak; zaharrak eta gaztiak, ernaiak eta antziak, adardünak eta mañuak, paletak eta kükuak.	Good day to you, inhabitants of this village; both elderly and young, pregnant women and sterile ones too, those who have been cuckolded and those who haven't, quiet and boisterous.
Huna heben girela buhamiak. Ezagütü beharrez khüllu famatiak. Berahala düzie jakinen nun giren kurritiak bena lehenik nula giren batheiatiak.	Here we are the gypsies. You have to know who and how famous we are. Where we have been we'll tell you right now, but first come our Christian names.
Hau Dindo Tzarpategi gorri begiak, pattar tzintzürra, lüze barrabilak.	This is Dindo Tzarpategi, with red eyes, a throat like a mountain and big balls.

Ez dü horrek higatüko lana
nahiagoz lekatü bestek geinhatia.

Beste hau Ibrahim Abdalagoiti, beltz zankuak
lüze karrika beltza, eta nasaï zoriak.
Hazku zilo batetara zian urthuki bere amak
eta geroztik ez dü sekülan hunki hurrak;
ez dü segür zorik hastuari hunen ürinak

Eta hebentxo hau Atito Saskibü;
handi pantzoilla eta bürlüz errotak,
emaztea eta baltz jokiak
Horiek dira hunen lan handienak.

Eta hoien gibelian Maia Zankhasgora,
(Maiaaaaa! Maiaaaaa!).
Hau dügu Maia Zankhasgora, handi biesak,
bero zankhartia eta lodi azpiondua.
Ziberian ukhen dütü arrenküra handiak
Ilhortü zeikü eta geroztik handitü mustatxak,
Zeren üsü beitütü gaintitzen pilulak.
Bena zer koziniersa, zer apaïdiak

Üsü gozatzen dütügü saltsan sathorrak
eta gresilan aphotorruak.
Hargatik ezinago hun dütügü osagarriak
izana gatik gai oroz hartürik khakeriak.

Eta ni, Asma Koskabillanborda,
horik ene mithilak.
Ni errege famatia, ene espantiak bazter orotan
ezagütiak.

Mündü guzian hedatü dütügü lege berriak

haizü ebastiak eta aseskak;
üsü errutia, ahalez haitatüz besten habiak,
debakatürik lanak eta izerdiak,
txapelketak bezain nahi lukenka üztarriak.
Hola gira mündü guzian ezagütiak
eta orai düzue jakinen nun giren kurrutiak.

Izan gira Ziberian, han karruntatü ahanak.

Maïari lothü güne gaixtuan khandaluak
bertan gira lekhütü zinez flakatiak.

Poloniara eraman gütü ondotik gure bidajiak.
Han agürtü gütü Jaruselski jaunak.
Hunek üduri dü gure alhorretako khürtsuak
hartürik bezala ezin khakeginak.
Ohartü zeikü labamentu hun bat ziala behar
holako gizonak,

He'll never get tired,
as he doesn't know what work is.

This other one is Ibrahim Abdalagoiti, with dark legs,
a long black face and easy-going.
His mom threw him into a pile of shit
and he's not been near water since;
thus the scent doesn't come from his monkey.

And here is Atito Saskibü;
potbellied and bow-legged;
women and ball dances
are his biggest efforts.

And behind all these is Maia Zankhasgora.
(Maiaaaaa! Maiaaaaa!)
Here she is, Maia Zankhasgora, big teats,
hot between the legs and a roomy opening.
She suffered great pain in Siberia,
for she dried up and then grew a moustache,
which she already had as a consequence of using pills.
Nevertheless, what a cook she is and how we dine.

Often we enjoy mole in sauce
and grilled grass hoppers.
Equally good are our spirits,
and thus we empty our bowels every night.

And me, Asma Koskabillanborda,
these are my servants.
I'm a famous king, and throughout the world;
my greatness is known.

With us new laws have been propagated throughout the
world,
such as robbery and hard drinking;
often laying eggs, if possible in someone else's nest;
refraining from work and sweat;
planting our sausages in championship fashion.
Thus we are known throughout the world
and now you'll know where we tinkers have been.

We have been in Siberia where the soft part of our bodies
froze up.
In that awful place, Maia's opening closed up
and we all weakened.

Afterwards our journey took us to Poland.
There, Mr. Jaruselski welcomed us.
It seemed like, on trying the products of our land,
he couldn't shit.
We realized a guy like this needed a good cleaning out.

sakatü deïogü lindana eta kilo bat phipergorri.
Nahasirik biak laster zeitzo phartitü gizon horri
uzkerrak eta arrestakuak.

[So] we stuffed him with herbs and a kilo of chillies.
The mixture of both things broke him in two
with wind and gas.

Gero heltü gira Iranen, erosi beharrez
Maïari kaputxinak.
Han dira gizonak eta emaztiak tzarpatiak
oroek debekü ikhertzia salbü L'Ayatollak.
Huni gustatü zaitzo Maïaren bularrak
eta gük zerratü khanbera batetan biak;
ez dira han zahartü gure bi anjamiak
zeren Maïari ez zaitzo gustatü L'Ayatollaren
presentak.
Maïak behar dütü gü bezalako akherrak,
nahiago arrestelü gidarrak
ezinez tximaltü arrestelü xiriak.

Then we arrived in Iran, where we had to buy a veil for
Maia.
There women and men are segregated
and fooling around is not accepted, save for the Ayatollah.
He liked Maia's breasts
and we put them together in a room;
but our dangly bits didn't get old in that country
for Maia didn't like the Ayatollah's gifts.

She needs rams like us,
as she's got used to tough guys
and not tender ones.

Geroago Bengladeche, *quelle deche*, zer gosiak;

han buhameentzat lekhü mehiak,
hatia huntü dügü bertan hütsik zoruak
eta jo Inglaterra, ikhusteko zer zion Thatxerak
Atzeman deïogü moskua zorrotz, tzimaltürik
üzkü mathelak.
Eskentü deïotzogu gure gisako presentak
hebengo laboriaren phartez, lau ardi oso
trapatiak.

Later on we went to Bangladesh, what poverty, what a
famine;
a skinny country for a gypsy,
we left right away
and went to England to see what Thatcher had to say.
We found her iron well sharpened but her underwear
wrinkled.
We offered her our usual presents
and from some local farmers, four live sheep.

Beste kartiel hanitxetan ere gira korritiak:
Pakistan, Liban, Kurdistan, Afganistan herriak;
China, Conchinchina, Barrankilla, Harmakiña
kartielak deneta utzi dütügu gure zedarriak
eta bürratü ahala güntian güziak.
Gero Tchekoslovakian juntatü gira mündü
güziako buhamiak.
Hau ziren Landutx, Galthurutx, Arkutx eta
Kokutx anaiak;
Pandart, Pantzart, Xinfart eta Zankhart kusiak;
Hotzükü, Gatüzkü, Khotxüzkü eta Pitxerüzkü

We have traveled through other countries:
Pakistan, Lebanon, Kurdistan, Afghanistan;
also through China, Cochinchina, Barrankilla and
Harmakiña, where we left our mark
and removed those of others.
Finally, all the world's gypsies met in Czechoslovakia.

There were the Landuntx, Gathurutx, Arkutx, and the
Kokutx brothers;
the Pandart, Pantzart, Xinfart and Zankhart cousins;
the Hotüzkü, Gatüzkü, Khotxüzkü and Pitxerüzkü asekariak;
drunkards;

Jo, Jojo, Barjo eta Bedajo lau fripuak;
Aña, Maña, Mañaña, Betigaña ahizpak;
Spaghetti, Ravioli, Buitoni, Panzani,
Berluzkoni italianuak.
Thiratü dütügü han gaitzeko asiak
eta jüratü bethi ginela egonen buhamiak.

the four *fripus*, Jo, Jojo, Barjo and Bedajo;
the Aña, Maña, Mañaña, Betigaña sisters;
The Spaghetti, Ravioli, Buitoni, Panzani,
Berlusconi Italians.
We celebrated with a big drinking party
and took an oath to keep on being gypsies.

Gu gizon ikhasiak beigira eta elizan igantez
kurritiak badakigü,
sobera lüze direnian aphezen pheredikiak.
Bertan direla entzuten aharrausiak
Hortakoz hortan dütüt ütziko ene espantiak.

Because we are schooled people and churchgoers on
Sundays,
we know well that, when priests' sermons are too long,
the listeners yawn right away;
therefore I'll finish my stories here.

Hasteko hiru adelü horiekin, egüneko lanak:	With these three friends of mine, [here's] the day's business:
Lekatü behar dütügü Muskildiko tripot eta lukenkak.	We'll finish off the Muskildi blood sausages and pork sausages.
Hüstü herri huntako xahakuak eta barrikotak.	After that we'll empty this village's bota bags and wine barrels.
Eta hor ikhusten beitütüt ürrüxa zunbait argi begiak;	And from here I see several women looking shocked;
her deïet haien xerbütxüko direla buhamiak.	to whom I say, Gypsies are at your service.

According to local testimony, the fact that the gypsies' discourse contains extensive use of the pronouns *gü* ("we") and *ni* ("I") means that they are extremely eager to talk about themselves. It is interesting to note that the structure and content of this sermon does not vary from Sunday to Sunday for the different visits the group pays to various villages in Zuberoa.

This contrasts radically with the sermons of the *kautereak* or tinkers, in which new lines are written according to each village visited. In the morning, the tinkers' performance resembles that of the gypsies, although their respective costumes are different. The tinkers wear black trousers, overcoats, and hats decorated with duck-wing feathers, and they cover their faces with masks made of sheepskin and wool. There are four members of the tinkers group, each displaying short sentences expressing his opinions on various subjects across his back. Furthermore, each individual has a name and a sub-name. For example, *kabana handia* ("big cabin") or *kautere gehiena* ("principal tinker") is the group's chief. Then there are *fripu*, *pupu*, and *pitxu*; the latter fulfilling a largely transcendental role representing the spirit of the group. *Pitxu* performs in a costume decorated with the tail of a fox, the animal that most defines this character. He is clever, skilful, a cheat, sharp and always able to escape trouble in a graceful and triumphant way. During the afternoon performance, *kabana handia* recites (from a book) an ironic sermon relating the major events that have taken place in the village over the course of the previous year. At the same time his companions go about repairing a large cooking pot, typically belonging to the *jauna* or lord, which contains an exaggerated amount of holes. In the 1987 Muskildi *Maskarada*, for example, *kabana handia* read the following *pheredikia* or speech:

Arresti hun, herri huntako jenteak.	Good afternoon, people of this village.
Marmarka zirade heben kulloak,	We can see that some of you here are turbulent,
ostatua zerratu geroztik ez sobera kullu.	although since the bar was closed, much less so.
Pastorala eman geroztik ez apur fanfarru;	And since you performed a *Pastoral* you are rather arrogant;
etxetik espatzeko atzamaiten mila arrazu	you find any excuse to go out anytime and to go to parties anywhere.
Lanen egiteko, haatik, *on s'en fout*	But when the time to get some work done comes, "screw you,"
egun oroz balinbada ogi eta ardu.	so long as there's bread and wine every day.
Orai bazter orotan kurritü den kaute jenolia	Now I will introduce these tinkers to you
famatia presentatüko deiziet.	who have traveled throughout the entire world.
Hau Trastu, ostatüko nausia zen	This is Trastü, he used to run the bar,
bena ber denboraren askari haudiena beitzen,	but because he also drank the most,
bere emazteak dü kanporat ezarri.	his wife sent him away.

Hau Lanana Malibu, ez da sekülan eskontü,
ez emazerik
ernaltü, bena bai gizonak xikotü.
Beste hau Kortatü, heben sonü bordel batekin
aikü ertzotü.
Hau heben, Pitxu langile huna.
Eta ni horien oroen nausia, Kabana Handia.

Gizon oroek behar likie ni bezala eder, ni
bezala handi izan armada eginik Beyrouten.

Han ükenik *Légion d'Honneur* eta beste *pour*

Acte de bravoure, ara heltu niz etxerat.

Arrunt erranen dieziet zertara ginen hunat jinik:
SNCFeko nausiak beigütü
Muskildiera igorrik Ageretzian eta Karrikan
ez beitzien egiten ahal lo handirik.
Herri huntako bi *cheminots*ak greban dira eta
gara abantxü zerratürik.

San Antonioko *station de ski*an nausia
nigarrez hüstürik.
Negü huntako sosak oro zütiala galdürik.
Hanko nausia Harguindeguy *est à la maison.*
Beraz lanialat gira hunat hara,
eginik izan ez diren lanen egitera
eta gaizik eginik izan direnen zuzentzera.
Bena oroen gainetik trainen kontatzera
hura beita *cheminots*en lan handiena.
Eta badakiziela greban sartü aintzin
gure bi auther ez dues oker horiek zer dien egin?
Zübürralteko *viadu*an esküineko *rail*an
opilo handi bat, tian tiana ihurik ere ezin
desegin,
kaute jenolia hel ahal ez dadin.
Ah! Artetik ziek baitakizie siglen berri,
dudarik gabe badakizie SNCFek zer dian
erran nahi.
Nik erranen deiziet:
S-*ervice* N-*écesaire pour* C-*aser les* F-*aineants.*
Beste lankia handietan bezala lantegi hortan,
huherrenea haitatürik da nausi izateko
segür ez da urte zonbaitez gabe baratüko.
Bidajaren baliatzeko beste lanik ere hantü dügü.
*Crédit Agricole*ko coffre forte betatxatü;
eta lan horren egitian, coffre forte hori hütxirik,
zela ikusi dügü karrika tini hortan, oto eder bat
ezarri ziala.
Eta ber gizona ebaste hartaz ogendant ekarri
izan

This is Lanana Malibu, he never married,
never left any woman
pregnant, though he likes chasing after men.
This other one is Kortatü, he's gone mad after too much
music.
And this is Pitxu, a good worker.
And me, the master of all of them, Kabana Handia.

All men must look like me: handsome and,
like me, they must be something; I have fought as a soldier
in Beirut.

There I was decorated with the Legion of Honor and
another
for an act of bravery; afterwards I returned home.

Now I will tell you why we're here:
the SNCF [French Railroad Service] bosses sent us to
Muskildi because in the neighborhoods of Ageretzia and
Karrika nobody could get much sleep.
Two railroad workers from this village are on strike
and we're almost closed down for good.

The owner of the San Antonio ski resort is still crying.

He went bankrupt this winter.
That owner, Harguindeguy, is [now] staying at home.
So we the tinkers are here to work,
to do those jobs people never do
and to put right what is wrong.
But above all we are here to count trains,
because this is the hardest task for railroad workers.
And do you know what our two useless railroad workers
did before they went on strike?
They put a huge obstacle on the right-hand rail of the
Zübürralte viaduct, that not even a thunderbolt could
demolish,
so we tinkers couldn't come over.
Ah! From that stunt you know what the abbreviation means,
you no doubt know what SNCF stands for.

I will tell you:
A Necessary Service to Find Work for Slackers.
In this company, as in others,
the first one to be the boss
obviously won't retire for a long time to come.
To pay the expenses of our trip, we also took on another job.
We forced the safe of the *Crédit Agricole* bank;
but once we opened the safe, we realized it was already empty,
and we saw a fancy car parked outside the bank in that
little street.
So its owner was charged with the bank robbery

beita urruntürik izan da Mauletik Biarnola

> and sent far away from Maule to Béarn.

Paueko presuntegian ere bazterrak oro ikertü dütügü.

> We have also searched the prison of Pau.

Hanko bizizale zonbait beitzire lekükü,
sagü ziloak oro tapatü eta komitatiak ziukatü.
Hunat jin aitzin, Parisen güntian azken lanak.
Hanko *commissariat*etan bazütien arrenküra handiak.
Hamazortzi langilekin egin han behar zirenak
gurekin hartüz limak eta arraspak,
polizier horiek alde orotan beitzütien eginik
*Bravou*rak.

> As the residents there can testify,
> we covered all the mouse-holes and repaired the toilets.
> Before coming here our last job was in Paris.
> There was big trouble in the police station.
> Together with eighteen workers, we did what we had to do
> with files and sandpaper,
> [while] those policemen had to be very "brave" all over
> the place.

Parisen ginelarik ere izan gira ministro zonbaiten ikusten,
nahi beitgünean *fonctionarie* statütou üken.
Han Jacques Chirac eta Charles Pasquarekin mintzatü,
eta haiekin bazkaltü.
Kaka bezala mozkorrazi dütügü kurritü
gero Pasquaren otoan Pariseko karrikak dütügü kurritü.
Eta prefosta, han, heben bezain beste polizier beita,
lauak gütie arrestatü.
Charlesek izan behar dü *alcootest*eko baluian bukatü.
Eta hor *taux d'alcoolemie elevé* da agertü
Prefosta Pasquak amenda handi bat bildü dü
eta haiek ordain guri atzaman.
Hartüko zien lehen dezizionea izanen zela:
Taux d'alcool legal odolian hamar grama eta Erramaitia.
Le Pen-en etxaltiaren aitzinian
gure azken lanak izan dira
bere etxiaren beltzez pintatzia;
bere zurratü, geroztik da begi bakotx.

> While in Paris we also saw several ministers,
>
> for we wanted to be civil servants.
> There we spoke to Jacques Chirac and Charles Pasqua,
>
> and lunched together.
> We got them really drunk
> and then went for a ride through the streets of Paris in Pasqua's car.
> And of course, there, as there are as many policemen as here,
> the four of us got arrested.
> Charles had to pass the alcohol test.
>
> And here it was that a high alcohol level appeared.
> Of course Pasqua got an extremely heavy fine
> and instead, they took us away.
> The first decision they took was:
> Having ten grams of alcohol in the blood
> would be legal.
> Someone gave us Le Pen's address
> and our last job was
> to paint his house all black
> and punch him, which is why he's one-eyed.

Gure azken hitza: gizon horiekin bestaren egitea *c'est tout bon*,
bena ez balinbagira beren alde
attention de ne pas se faire pendre.

> Listen to our last words: To party with those people
> is all fine and well,
> but, if we're not on their side,
> be careful not to get left hanging.

Then at the end of the afternoon, the *medizina* or doctor arrives to heal *pitxu*, who, according to the storyline, has fallen ill due to eating too much. The doctor's behavior is intentionally grotesque and meant to be a parody of the act of healing. Indeed, the aim of practically all the *beltzak* is *erri egin arrazi* ("to mock") and for this group, irony, parody and exaggeration are recurring elements.

Closing the parade are the *txorrotxak* or knife-grinders. They play a dual role in the afternoon performance: Firstly, they perform a sketch in which they sharpen the lord's sword. Secondly, they recite verse to an audience that has witnessed the performances of the castrators, gypsies, and tinkers. In the morning, they also recite verse at each of the barricades they encounter on their way to the central *plaza* or square. For instance, here are the couplets sung by the *txorrotxak* when breaking through the first *barrikada* at the entrance of Muskildi:

Agur Muskildi eta muskidiar maitiak.	We salute Muskildi and its beloved villagers.
Irusik girade zien ikhustiaz.	We are glad to see you are fine.
Egin beitüzie Pastual Maskarada.	You have done a *Pastoral* and a *Maskarada*.
Lüzaz bizi dadin üskaldun üsantxa	Long live the Basque traditions!

The performance of the *Maskarada* finishes with a song especially composed for the occasion and sung by all the troupe members. In 1987 the *Maskarada* players of Muskildi chanted the following lyrics:

Lehenik Pastuala gero Maskarada;	First a *Pastoral* and now a *Maskarada*;
loaldi bat eginik Muskildi piztü da	after being asleep, Muskildi has awakened
erakuts xoko oroer zuberotar dela;	to show everyone and everywhere that it is Zuberoan;
zainetan dela bethi üskaldün odola.	that through its veins Basque blood has always run.
Herri baten bizia gazteen batarzüna;	The life of a village springs from the union of its youth;
jei honen errua da gure anaitarzüna	the cause of this feast is our brotherhood.
Denek batian dügü hartürik xedia	We have come to a strong decision
jokü zaharra berriz bizi araztia.	to give life again to the old play.
Agertzen dügü egün batera plazera	Today we exhibit our commitment,
jarraikiz üsaitxer mintzatüz üskara.	following upon the traditions and speaking Basque.
Zinez huts balizate gure izatia	Should our village lose the traditions,
herriak gal baleza bihar ohidüra.	without doubt there will be no identity for us.
Plazer handia dügü heben izatia	It has been a pleasure to be here,
zinez gozatü dügü zien batzarria.	really we have enjoyed your invitation.
Egün goxo bat zien iraganaztia	That you had a very good time with us,
hoi zen gure ametsa baita helbüria.	has been our dream and final aim.

Verbal Arts within *Maskarada* Performance

Several folklorists have approached the *Maskaradak* of Zuberoa by discussing their aesthetics and formal elements. Noticeably, they have focused primarily on the dances, the result being that an analysis of the activities carried out by the *beltzak* has largely been neglected. Similarly, the prominence given to dance has led to an over emphasis on the importance of the *aitzindariak* or lead dancers of the red group (for example, see Alford 1928, 1931a, 1931b, 1937; Urbeltz 1978, 1994; Guilcher 1984), while less attention has been paid to the study of the masks and verbal arts of the black team performers (Fourquet 1990; Truffaut 1986, 1988; Fernández de Larrinoa 1993b, 1999; Mozos 1985). As a result, the analysis of dance has come to represent that of the entire *Maskarada* performance. In other words, one aspect of the *Maskarada* (dance) has come to represent and define the whole event, thereby implying a sense of metonymy and reductionism. Similar

Zamalzaina (Hobbyhorse) at the *Maskarada* performed in Gotaine, Zuberoa, 2000. Perhaps the most emblematic character in the performance, the hobbyhorse has come to represent the *Maskarada* as an image on many kinds of souvenirs. Photo by Lisa Corcostegui.

metonymic images of the *Maskarada* also pervade posters, cards and other crafts designed for tourists who visit Zuberoa. In such souvenirs, particular images of the *Maskarada* have been selected to represent the province. These images might portray all five members of the *aitzindaria* group; a solo performer, most commonly the *zamalzaina* or hobbyhorse dancer; or the *aitzindaria* dancers performing the *godalet dantza* (the dance of the wine-glass). Thus both folklorists and craft sellers have projected a certain image of the *Maskaradak* and of Zuberoa, where the folk arts performed by the black team have little or no representation.

I previously remarked that within *Maskarada* performances several events are meant to be watched and others listened to. However, there are written messages as well. I will now give a brief account of the arts which characterize *Maskarada* performers within the black team and I would draw special attention to the speech, dialogue, song, and written sentences. Indeed, the verses sung by the knife-grinders, the speeches given by the gypsy king and big cabin, the short sentences written across the backs of the tinkers and the doctor, the dialogue between the castrators, *pitxu*'s improvised dialogues with the audience, together with his last will, are all performed by the black team.

Furthermore, during the *Maskarada* words are used in several contexts: Some, for example, are used in the form of *koplak* ("verses"); others as *oihuak* ("shouts") and tactless comments; while still others appear on the backs of the *maskarakaiak* (the members of the visiting *Maskarada*), constituting *grafitiak* ("graffiti"). The *txorrotxak* or knife-grinders sing verses, while the shouts, as they are composed of ugly or bad words, are the preserve of the *beltzeriak*. Graffiti are written across the backs of the *kautereak* or tinkers and the *medizina*.

The morning verses are sung in ritualized form. After the knife-grinders sing their verses, the barricade is broken down and for now the *errezibitzaileak* ("the receiving party") and the *maskarakaiak* are all mixed up together. Those who erected the barricade are bid farewell and thanked for the wonderful offering of food and drink, by means of the verses sung by the two knife-grinders. A special vote is taken among the young people of the village to select the two knife-grinders. They sing in duet style. One dominates, while the other plays a more unassuming role. In the dramatization of the game one is the *nausia* ("master") and the other the *mithila* ("apprentice"). They sing verses to the village in question, a particular house, well-known people, bars, the mayor, the priest and to one another.

During the morning barricades the black team's words are termed *oihuak*, because they repeatedly shout *ouha, ouha, ouha*. Moreover, they usually improvise conversations with the public by means of using or acting out tactless or bad words. The tinkers and the doctor wear graffiti across their backs and the subject-matter normally involves alcohol, sexual innuendo and parodying authority. As a result, they typically announce unacceptable behavior. The *medizina* also wears clothes covered in graffiti which involves self-parody, propagating images of the medical profession as pseudo-doctors or butchers. There are major differences in the spelling of this graffiti, both in the case of the pseudo-doctor and the tinkers, from town to town and *Maskarada* to *Maskarada*. The letters which get most mixed up between one another are *x/tch/ts/tx/tz, r/rr/(), t/th, ü/u, s/z, i/i, kh/k* and *ou/u*.

As with the morning activities, so the afternoon performance is also codified before the public. That is, afternoon activities are adapted to be performed before the public in a specific way. Words are especially important in the performances of the castrators and the knife-grinders, the gypsy king's sermon, the principal tinker's speech, *pitxu*'s last will and testament, the last song, and the songs performed by the knife-grinders to introduce each performance.

As I observed in the 1992 *Maskarada* in Altzürükü, the local people gave more importance to how well the castrators danced than how well they spoke or pronounced *Béarnaise* Occitan. Essentially, instead of this form of Occitan, the castrators spoke Basque to one another throughout the performance, with the exception of two or three sentences. Furthermore, as they knew that there were Spanish Basques in the audience, they also laced their dialogue with Spanish words.

The 1987 *Maskarada* in Muskildi, however, was different because here the castrators performed their dialogue in *Béarnaise* Occitan. Furthermore, normally the dialogue is stereotyped; that is, it is repeated from *Maskarada* to *Maskarada*. However, that year the Muskildi performers decided to renovate the traditional castrators' dialogue. With this objective in mind they introduced a specific event that had happened in the village by turning the strange story of a character named Aphalangai into a performance (see Fernández de Larrinoa 1993b: 149–151). That year a Muskildi native, Dominika Agergarai, told me that the castrators' language was not really *Béarnaise* Occitan. Muskildi, as Agergarai observed, was a long way from Béarn and its people didn't know Occitan at all. Consequently, in order to perform the castrators' roles the *Maskarada* organizers contacted a *Béarnais* person to help with their lines; yet although the castrators learnt the text by heart, they couldn't check the correct phonetic pronunciation very well. Therefore they had to use either Basque or French in their improvisation, as they didn't really know Occitan. Agergarai described her fellow townsmen's attempt to speak Occitan as bastardized French. That is, the Muskildi castrators spoke French with a hint of *Béarnaise* Occitan.

My third example comes from Eskiula. Eskiula is actually in Béarn, so the people there know Occitan. I followed the 1992 *Maskarada* in Eskiula very closely. Here the castrators' dialogue was very refined and brought a special sense of drama to the performance, unlike the case in Altzürükü. The castrators' dance occupied a smaller space in Eskiula, thereby giving the dialogue between the castrators greater importance. In the Eskiula *Maskarada* more importance was also given to the castrators' vernacular way of talking, because they knew there were *Béarnais* people in the audience. As a consequence, so that the castrators' performance would be really noteworthy, the castrators had to speak real *Béarnaise* Occitan. Moreover, so that the castrators' dialogue would be believable, beyond just speaking the language correctly, they also had to perform bodily movements and expressions very well. Maintaining these obligations, the Eskiula castrators brought more quality to the performance of the dialogue itself.

So far, then, we have seen three examples: Our first came from Altzürükü, where the castrators carefully performed the dance elements, but paid less attention to the linguistic, literary and dramatic quality of the text. The second came from Muskildi, where they wanted to inject some originality into the traditional text by adding several innovations. The third came from Eskiula, where they carefully prepared the drama and powerful language of the dialogue.

Pitxu takes part in the castrators' performance and his participation is very important, especially in a passage with the master castrator, in Occitan. They also speak Basque of course, mixing the two languages, as is the norm. And the performers also follow this established norm when they improvise. In this performance tangible personality-images are noticeable through the mentioning of several job-related attitudes. Normally the performers receive the castrators' dialogue from the previous *Maskarada*'s castrators. They get hold of the text in *Béarnaise* Occitan through contacting someone from Barkoxe (in Zuberoa, but right on the border with Béarn), Eskiula or another *Béarnaise* town, or through some other knowledgeable acquaintance. It is then customary for the castrators to rewrite the text by hand. On the day of the *Maskarada*, they can carry this text in their pockets, so that each one can remind themselves of it, usually quietly in some corner, before entering the square.

The knife-grinders' afternoon performance is to sharpen the lord of the *Maskarada*'s sword. Some of this activity is done while singing verses; another part in prose; another part through song, and others through dance, because they are different passages, and each one demands its own specialty. The knife-grinders' journey is expressed through dance. They sing a song while sharpening the lord's sword, and *say* verses to both the lord and each other. When singing or talking the knife-grinders speak Basque.

As with the castrators' performance, so *pitxu* also has a role in the knife-grinders' performance, as he must help the master knife-grinder to sharpen the lord's sword. Looking at the performance from a theatrical and cultural perspective, the knife-grinders' and castrators' performances are similar. Both display stereotyped social images, ideas and identities: laziness, skill in dealing with people, prudence, the importance of responsibility, and similar attributes or defects. In the knife-grinders' performance corporal movements are also important. The knife-grinders move around, normally in circles, as they sing verses and speak to one another. Dominika Agergarai prepared the 1993 Urdiñarbe knife-grinders. Through repetition the master knife-grinder told the apprentices over and over again that they had to make *cinema* throughout the performance.

Group movement and interaction are extremely important in the gypsies' performance so that it is credible and acceptable. When the young people of a village decide to organize a *Maskarada*, they perform in the squares of Zuberoa and beyond. The performances demand a sermon from the gypsies during the afternoon performance and in every square *buhame jauna* or the gypsy king proclaims the same sermon. On beginning to preach this sermon he must struggle against his fellow gypsies' shoving and opposing opinions. At this moment, as *buhame jauna* says something, his friends will often go against him by saying *"ez dük hala!"* ("It's not like that!"); *buhame jauna* then replies by shouting *"hala dük! hala dük!"* ("Yes, it is! Yes, it is!") to respond in a particularly strong way.

The sermons are divided into five parts: During the first part they greet the village. They next introduce themselves. Then *buhame jauna* explains how he was named king of all the gypsies. After this, they explain what the gypsies' profession is. Immediately afterwards, they confess that they are people from here and there –that is, that they are always traveling– by letting everyone know what villages and places they have been in. The gypsies' behavior is very stereotypical, and great importance is accorded the musical quality and phonetics of the sermon. This is very noticeable in the length and the rhyme of each section. It's also striking to hear, within the gypsy sermon, frank and open references to bodily holes and what they receive and emit.

Buhame jauna doesn't write the sermon but only performs it. He receives the text from someone else, normally from the previous year's *buhame jauna*. Once he has the sermon, he copies it in his own handwriting on a piece of paper and learns it by heart. He'll learn how to perform or change the text he's been given through repetition, though always under the guidance of the previous *buhame jauna* and the other visiting performers.

Five characters take part in the tinkers' performance: *kautere jauna* or the head tinker who is also known as *kabana handia* ("big cabin") or *gehiena* ("the principal one"), *fripu*, *pupu* and *pitxu*. *Kabana handia* carries a whip in one hand (to whip the others into doing some work) and in the other what appears to be a book. Reading from the book, he pronounces dubious stories and events. Lashing the whip, *kabana handia* wants the lord of the *Maskarada* to get on with things in the same way as the tinkers. Casting the sermon he is reading from the book to the four winds, he wants to make certain townspeople's misfortunes public knowledge.

Unlike the gypsies' case, the tinkers' sermon differs from village to village. The essence of the tinkers' sermon is to mention the most striking things that have happened throughout the year in the villages which they visit. As is the case with the gypsies, however, they do not come up with the text that they perform in the square. Instead, this is a task for another person or group of people. For example, the previous *Maskarada*'s tinkers might come up with the current *Maskarada*'s tinkers' sermon. The old tinkers take two things into account when composing the text that they must give to the new tinkers. On the one hand, the old tinkers look at the composition and style of their text, maintaining some rhetorical stanzas. On the other, they must find out what is worth criticizing, viable and funny in the villages that they visit, develop these ideas and include them in the sermon. Therefore they must talk to an informant in each village.

As the tinkers' sermons are very localized, they are hard to understand for outsiders. Only the villagers really understand the information spoken in the sermon and those who are not familiar with the local situation cannot follow all the irony that is expressed. As the aim of the sermon is not to be written down in the form of a book, when the chief tinker reads the sermon he sticks to specific rhythms and acoustics. The rhymes which are most widely used are the following: -ia, -tzeko, -ik, -tzen, -tü; the -ou ending is also common, as it is what one normally comes across when using French words. Curiously, the rhymes in French which end with -ou produce the most laughs.

The sermon ends by saying *amen*. Big cabin's sermon might be separated into different parts, with the initial one greeting the audience in the square and the village being visited. These greetings might use the formal rhetoric of official speeches, making this rhetoric itself appear funny. Secondly, they want to prove that they are traveling people. The allegory of the gypsies' and tinkers' sermon is explaining that traveling is an education. In the *Maskarada* taunting is done through such images, leaving it clear that many travelers are no more than idiots. As such, they want to demonstrate, through this kind of sermon, that the sense of what the gypsies and tinkers have studied on their travels is everyday things. Thirdly, each tinker introduces himself. Fourthly, they explain why they have come to Zuberoa. Lastly, the most striking things that have happened throughout the year in the village which is hosting the *Maskarada* are made fun of.

The tinkers' performance does not finish with the money paid for sharpening the lord's sword, because, just at the moment they are paid, *pitxu* dies and big cabin reads the deceased *pitxu*'s last will and testament. To round off the day, members of the visiting *Maskarada* come together to perform what is normally a new song, especially composed for the occasion.

Some Concluding Remarks

According to what recently performed texts demonstrate, the following characteristics are important when considering the *Maskarada*'s literary traits: First of all, the performers and creators of the text are not one and the same. Typically, previous performers show new ones how and *what* to perform (singing, speaking, shouting and so forth) in written form. Thus writing is an important characteristic in the *Maskarada*'s transmission. The tinkers', gypsies' and knife-grinders' verses are written down with the words being passed on from village to village and generation to generation. At least this has been the case until now. Moreover, during the morning barricade, the knife-grinders, although they create new verses, also write down and study them before singing them. The style of writing also differs greatly from village to village though in every village the same thing happens every year from *Maskarada* to *Maskarada*: namely, writing is more than just a method, for writing in French and the popular pronunciation that changes from place to place in Zuberoa are liberally mixed together at any given time, any given place and in any way throughout the text. Furthermore, the afternoon speeches of the black team are a parody or carnivalization of the rhetorical language used by civil and religious authorities, especially the rhetorical formulas of priests and notaries.

Within these verses and sermons some parts are repetitive and rhetorical. Others, however, are new; that is, they are improvised then and there. What is exposed in the verses and sermons is very revealing. Therefore what an actor principally has to bear in mind is the village being visited. To put it another way, looking at this phenomenon from a linguistic, social and communicative perspective, the community made up by the *Maskarada* is very small; in other words, a visiting team.

Basque Rap in the American West: *Bertsolariak*

Joxe Mallea-Olaetxe

Introduction

My parents were ordinary Basque farmers in Bizkaia and every winter two of their preferred pastimes were singing and telling stories to us, their children. As I remember, my
father had two favorite songs, "Gernikako Arbola" ("The Tree of Gernika") and "Behi
zaharraren bertsoak" ("Verses about the old cow"). The latter seemed especially funny to
us because it dealt with farm life, which as kids we could obviously relate to.

My mother favored romantic and tragic ballads, which I did not understand as well
as the animal stories. She often used to sing "Markesaren alaba" ("The daughter of the
marquis"), a tale of two lovers that was doomed from the start. But I think her favorite
verses were those exchanged between a mother and her son, who had just arrived home
after being abroad:

> The son returned with company, his bride no less. As a way of introducing her, he tells
> his mother that the woman was a lady from the French court. The mother reacts angri-
> ly and tells him that she does not want a French daughter-in-law. When he resists, the
> mother turns to the *mademoiselle*, still sitting on the mule she has ridden in on, and delivers
> this shocking verse, "Get off that mule so I can thrust this dagger into your heart."

We were young so our mother never explained the meaning of the stories; she would
just sing them and leave us wondering.

Psychologists must be right when they say that childhood experiences leave an indeli-
ble imprint on people, because singing and *bertsoak* have always moved me. As a result,
and somewhat automatically, in the 1980s I began videotaping *bertsolaritza* events throughout the American West. In particular, I tried to record the Kantari Eguna (Basque-Singing
Day) event in Gardnerville, Nevada, sponsored by the North American Basque Organization (NABO). I am a historian and initially I had no other motive than documenting
the Basque diaspora. However, one day in the year 2000, while talking to my *bertsolari*

friend and neighbor Jesus Goñi, without mincing his words he expressed his disenchant-ment at being a *bertsolari*. Speaking in Basque he told me:

> When other performers are invited to the [Basque] picnics, they are paid expenses and besides that, get some money. The woodchoppers, the weight-lifters, the dancers . . . . Those who are brought from the Old Country get even more. The thinking seems to be that we, *bertsolariak*, will perform for free. Sometimes we might get compensated a little, and we like that. We don't ask much, but at least they should pay our expenses . . . . No one seems to appreciate us *etxekuak* ["those who are familiar"].

I told Goñi that most Basque-Americans knew next to nothing of his ability as improvisational poet and, in fact, that there was little out there that they could turn to for information. No matter how great the verses might be, most of the audience couldn't even applaud, because they didn't understand them. I therefore suggested he get a translator.

Goñi seemed frustrated, but his allegations and diatribe made me keenly aware of a series of issues surrounding *bertsolaritza* in the American West. Indeed, I became newly sen-sitized to the issue and it was then that I decided to collect *bertsoak* in earnest, so that the art would not be lost for future generations. But how do you bridge the gap between *bert-soak* in Basque and an audience that is mostly English-speaking?

After some time the idea of a *bertso* anthology came to me. Initially, I envisioned a modest booklet of about one hundred pages that would reflect the lives of these bards and their art, but later I once again had that nagging thought about the language barri-er. Who would read such a book? Among Basque-Americans only a minority under-stands the language and even among those who appreciate *bertsoak*, few actually read books. By their very nature *bertsoak* are for listening, not reading. I therefore decided that the book would have to be bilingual;[1] therefore those who read the translation would at least get an idea of what *bertsolaritza* ("the art of verse improvising") was and what the singers were saying.

Almost immediately, it also occurred to me that with all the technology currently available, a book may not be the right medium. Indeed, I began to think that perhaps, I should be working on a video, CD, or DVD, I thought. However, for the time being I was committed to a book. I subsequently approached NABO (the North American Basque Organization) with the idea during their meeting in Mountain Home, Idaho, and the delegates accepted the project without opposition.[2]

---

1. Bilingual is one of my favorite words. The *bi* (which means two in Basque) is an obvious example of *Euskara*'s arcane and ancient influence on Indo-European cultures.

2. The book was published in September of 2003. Besides NABO, other major contributors were the Basque Gov-ernment, the Center for Basque Studies in Reno, the Basque clubs, and a host of their individual members. Sara Vélez, Managing Editor of the University of Nevada Press, Reno, edited and oversaw the project from start to finish, all pro-bono. "*Deneri milesker*" ("Many thanks to all"). The title is *Shooting from the Lip: Bertsolariak Ipar Amerikan: Improvised Basque Verse-Singing* and it can be ordered through NABO, the local Basque clubs, or by going to the NABO website.

The Popularity of Verse-Singing in the United States

Basques arrived in the American West centuries ago as colonists, explorers, and friars of the Spanish Empire; and later as miners and sheepherders during the previous century and half. One has to wonder how many verse-singing sessions might have taken place during this time in monasteries, *presidios*, mining and sheep camps, and boardinghouses, or at weddings and family gatherings. The further we go back in time so the number of monolingual Basques rises, therefore the more verse-singing we might reasonably expect to have taken place. These were, in many ways, rappers although ahead of their time.

I knew that during the 1880s and 1890s many *bertsoak* were published in the two Basque-language weekly newspapers printed in Los Angeles. *Escualdun Gaceta* pioneered the trade in 1885, although it only managed to publish three issues. Its editor, Martin Biskailuz, was a lawyer, and when the last number rolled off the presses he was annoyed by the poor reception for his newspaper (which had cost him $26 to print). In fact, he asked the readers outright: "*Nahi dusia* Escualdun Gazetak *segi desan ala es?*" ("Do you people want the *Escualdun Gaceta* to continue, yes or no?").[3]

J. P. Goytino's *California'ko Eskual Herria*, a four-page weekly, followed *Escualdun Gaceta* in 1893 and ran through 1898. It started publishing *bertsoak* in its fourth issue and continued to do so virtually until the very end. In the process, dozens of *bertsoak* appeared and were eagerly devoured by its readers. On several occasions an informal *bertsolari* contest took place within the pages of the newspaper; namely, verses published one week by one reader were answered in subsequent weeks by a new set of verses by another reader. These readers might come from any number of places between California and Mexico and their topics included immigration, the economy, sheepherding, culture, history, and so on.[4]

When I began this work I envisioned a quick and relatively easy project because the *bertsoak* I had in mind dated only from 1988 to the present. Moreover initially I was only interested in four *bertsolariak* –Jesus Arriada, Johnny Kurutxet, Martin Goikoetxea, and Jesus Goñi– as they were the principal individuals I had seen improvising and singing in the Basque picnics or festivals of the American West. To this list originally I would have added one other name, Patxi Txurruka of Reno, but he told me that his *bertsolari* days were over.

Once I immersed myself in the research, however, word spread that I was gathering *bertsoak* and I soon started receiving more information than I originally expected, including wads of typed verses and others sent by email. It soon became clear to me that California had been, and still is, the center of *bertsolaritza* in the United States. In the Golden State today you can find not only improvisers but *bertso-paperak*; that is, composed or written verses, a genre which is closer than *bertsolaritza* to poetry. Gratien Alfaro, Mattin Etxam-

---

3. *Escualdun Gazeta* (Los Angeles). Vol. 1. No. 3. 16 Jan. 1886: 1.

4. For the history of the Basques in the United States, there is no corpus written in Basque quite as extensive and important as this one. Goytino claimed that *California'ko Eskual Herria* was the only Basque newspaper in the world, yet many Basque libraries and institutions lack a copy of this outstanding publication.

endy, Charles Moustirats, Manes Kurutxet, Damatitt "Ximun" Bidaurreta, and Manex Pagola are some of poets who have composed such *bertso-paperak*. Alfaro is an improviser as well, but perhaps the master of them all was Pedro Juan Etchamendy, who died in 2002.

Incidentally, all the bards mentioned here are from the old kingdom of Nafarroa or Navarre, except Txurruka, who is Bizkaian. In addition, I know people in California, Nevada, and Idaho who are capable of standing in front of an audience and singing from memory a dozen strophes without missing a beat. Examples of such performers include Pete Salla of Winnemucca, Nevada, and Xabier Aldekoa (currently) of Boise, Idaho.

Thus I came to realize that Arriada, Goikoetxea, Kurutxet, and Goñi constituted, so to speak, the tip of the *bertso* iceberg in the American West. In sheep camps and *ostatuak* ("boardinghouses") throughout the western states, verses had been improvised and enjoyed by eager audiences for decades, yet we know almost nothing about this activity. With great relish, Goñi still recalls his sheepherder days in Idaho, when he and Jesus Urkidi, a Bizkaian bard, used to delight the audience in Rupert's Basque hotel. He added that Enpan, a Bizkaian herder, recorded some of the verses improvised during those years.

The *bertsolari* art is tremendously popular among the immigrant generation that grew up without TV and little radio. These people were used to generating their own entertainment, and every get-together was an occasion for enjoying food, wine, and song, whether *bertsoak* or just singing some of the numerous traditional ballads.

I was truly surprised at discovering that work of the caliber of Pedro Juan Etchamendy was little known and remained unpublished. I would imagine that most Basques outside southern California are totally unaware of Etchamendy's lifelong accomplishments. Although he was a pillar of the Basque community in the Barstow-Chino area, some of his fellow-*bertsolariak* didn't know about him either. In the process of writing my manuscript I often talked with the four *bertsolariak*, but none of them ever mentioned Etchamendy or indeed, any other bard. I found this both surprising and disturbing at the same time. The Basque community is very small, and most news travels fast through the grapevine, but when it comes to cultural information, there would appear to be a definite lag. This, it seems to me, is reflective of the fact that Basques don't advertise or promote their own culture enough, and they should.

Fortunately, Etchamendy's work will soon be published in Europe. The man was more than just a composer of *bertso-paperak* of course; he was a California dairyman dedicated to Basque culture in general, a composer and a player of several musical instruments. Indeed, for many years he and his accordion entertained a multitude of Southern California Basques and he was so popular in the area that Mike Bidart of Chino, California, dedicated a few verses that he wrote himself to Etchamendy and his accordion.

When Martxel Tillous of San Francisco sent me a sample of Etchamendy's poetry, I realized that he had a keen imagination and unmatched command of the language. I subsequently contacted Antonio Zavala, publisher of Auspoa *bertso* books in the Basque Country, and he encouraged me to submit a manuscript. While working on the Etchamendy project, I received unwavering support from Etchamendy's children, and as of June 2003 Zavala was already editing and type-setting the manuscript, which will include several tunes, some of which are Etchamendy's own.[5]

Bertsolariak Sing About Life

These Basque rappers sing first and foremost about what they know: their life experiences. Anyone who undertakes a study of *bertsolaritza* in the American West thus receives as a bonus an insider's view of the Basque diaspora. And for anyone interested in sheepherding and the sheepherder's life, *bertsolaritza* will give them a direct access to this world. Not far behind in the minds of these bards loom the Basque clubs, the picnics or festivals, and the old country. In short, listening to *bertsolariak* you get a glimpse of Basques in the United States delivered the way only an eyewitness and a performer can.

Arriada, Goikoetxea, Goñi, and Kurutxet are all now men in their fifties and sixties. Three were born in the Basque Country and came to the United States to herd sheep, while the fourth, Kurutxet, although born in California, actually grew up in the old country and herded sheep there. They were, then, all sheepherders once but no longer. For decades now living in urban environments has brought them into contact with American society, to the point that, culturally-speaking, although they might live in a mostly Basque ghetto, they are also thoroughly immersed in American society.

I use the term "Basque ghetto," for our bards still cling tenaciously to the culture of their youth in the Pyrenees. It is the culture, specifically of the waning years of the self-sufficient *baserri* (Basque farmstead), which they knew before they came to the United States and which remains frozen in time in their hearts and minds. Their Basque Country still consists of neat red and white farmsteads scattered throughout verdant valleys and hills; this, despite the fact that today only two percent of Basques are farmers, and eighty-five percent of the population live in urban areas.

At the same time, the Basque Country has undergone profound political, social, and cultural changes which Arriada, Goikoetxea, and Goñi missed, because they were living in the United States. Kurutxet's parents returned with him to Iparralde (the Northern Basque Country) when he was a few years old, and for all practical purposes he was raised in the same rural environment as his three fellow rappers.

In their youth, Goñi and Kurutxet dabbled for a time in contraband across the French-Spanish border, but neither bard sings much about such matters. When Kurutxet turned twenty, he decided to return to San Francisco, California, where today he owns a landscaping business, as does Arriada. After leaving the sheep business, Goñi joined the building boom in Reno, Nevada, and became a construction worker. Goikoetxea went to college to learn English and after several business ventures he currently owns a truck dealership in Rock Springs, Wyoming.

---

5. The Jesuit Antonio Zavala, through Auspoa, continues his remarkable mission of gathering *bertsoak* wherever in the world he finds them. He has already published several books on North American Basque verse singers, but I daresay, nothing comparable to P. J. Etchamendy's.

The basic principles governing the world of our bards remain firmly rooted to the Old Country-farming world. A farmer must work hard if he wants to be successful and respected by his peers. In other words, if you don't do manual labor you might be considered lazy. A 1992 exchange that took place in a Basque restaurant in Elko, Nevada, between Goñi and Goikoetxea is enlightening in this respect, for it centered on the fact that Goikoetxea sold trucks while Goñi was employed in the construction industry. Goñi started the charge:

Goñi

Gaurkoan bildu gerade ta	We are gathered here today, and
hemen entzun behar dezu,	now you must listen to me,
ondo jan d'edan eginez,	as long as you eat and drink well,
laneko inportik ez dizu;	you could care less about work;
zer langile zaren zeure itxurak	your very appearance tells clearly
ondo erakusten du.	what kind of worker you are.

Goikoetxea

Arrozoi hori franko txarra zan	Your argument was a very bad one
lagun bati esateko;	to direct to a friend:
nik zuri orain arrozoi bat	Now I, too, have one
badaukat'e emateko:	to give back to you.
maien zu're hor a'itu zera	I saw how you conducted yourself at the table,
ez zinan alperrik egoteko;	you were not idle, no;
zure ikustean hobea	you, too, look better fit for eating
laneko bainan jateko.	than for working.

Bertsolariak can be very blunt with each other, but they must also try to ignore any attacks and focus on out-singing the opponent. Goñi continued:

Goñi

Kristonak hasi zait orain	He has started giving me hell,
Wyoming'dik etorrita,	this fellow coming from Wyoming;
aspaldian kotxe saltzian dabil	he has been selling cars for a while,
lan gogorrak utzita.	after leaving all hard work behind.
Honen lanak errezak dira	Work is easy for this fellow,
batzuk engainatuta;	he fools a lot of people,
amerikano karruk saltzen ditu	by selling them American cars
japones motorra ezarrita.	that have Japanese engines.

Goikoetxea

Bertzek bezela lanean nik'e	Just like any other Joe,
pasatutzen det eguna,	I, too, spend my day working,

eta tratua eiteko nazu	and, when I am dealing [in trucks],
gizon zintzo ta biguna.	I am an honest and good-hearted person.
Jendia ongi tratatutzeko	I always treat people well,
beti det hizketa leguna,	with kind words;
prezio onean saltzen ditut-ta	I sell at a good price
jendeak erosi nahi duna.	the vehicles that people want to buy.

Goñi was clearly implying that Goikoetxea did not have to undertake the hard manual labor he was forced to do. A little later, Goñi stated that, if Goikoetxea had been a hard worker, he would have stayed in Europe, without realizing that his argument was hypocritical as he too was an immigrant. Undaunted by the charges and the public's reaction, Goikoetxea in his rebuttal directly confronted Goñi's old country-work ethics by singing, "what is wrong with working less and making a living?" As the two bards continued, the audience, including myself, felt for a while as if we had been transported back to our hometown taverns in the Basque Country – such was the evocative and creative power of these two rappers.

Jesus Goñi, Reno Basque Festival, 2001. Originally from Oronoz in Navarre, Goñi came to the United States as a sheepherder, and later moved into the construction industry. Throughout the summer, Basque communities of the American West celebrate picnics or festivals, at which several *bertsolariak* perform their art. Photo by Joseba Etxarri.

Ex-sheepherders still feel like immigrants, even after having lived most of their lives in the United States. During the picnics, *bertsolariak* are sometimes asked to sing about a tricky topic, such as whether they feel Basque or American. This is a real dilemma for them as they have to take sides between the old country and the reality of the American life they love. However, the bards usually manage to remain neutral quite effectively. As regards this issue, Gratien Alfaro delivered a particularly masterful strophe:

Eskual Herritik jin nintzan	I came from the Basque Country,
hiru hogoita hiruan,	in sixty-three [1963],
neguko lanbete inguruan	when winter chores were at their peak,
urtarrilaren hiruan;	on the third day of January:
geroztik hunat sortu lekua	Ever since then, I have always
beti atxiki dut goguan.	had my birthplace in mind.
Berriz sortu behar nuela	And then, I realized that
ikusi nuen orduan.	I needed to be born again.[6]

Life with the Sheep

For more than a century, sheepherding permeated the reality of Basque life in the American West, so it is no surprise that the bards always found in it a ready-made topic. As the pages of *California'ko Eskual Herria* demonstrate, sheep concerns were never too far from the bards who submitted *bertsoak* for publication in the newspaper. While most of those published were probably composed, we are fortunate enough to have sixteen powerful verses improvised in the 1920s by an unknown herder in California. These verses are truly remarkable, almost serving as an indictment of the whole Basque community in general. In one strophe, the herder-bard actually observed that sheepherding was detrimental to the Basque people, thus contradicting most of the extant literature on the subject. Below appear some selections from the sixteen *bertsoak*:[7]

Zer bizi trixtia den artzainen bizia!	What a sad life it is, a sheepherder's life!
Ni nihaur egoiten naiz arras harritia.	I myself wonder, I am totally astonished.
Hortan desegiten da eskualduneria,	That is where Basque people go to waste,
hala nola baitugu eskola handia.	which is to be expected, because we are so educated.

This bard may have had some education, and was apparently criticizing his countrymen, who were "so educated," that they had no other choice but to herd sheep. He was especially critical of urban-based Basques who took advantage of the sheepherders in their free time. When a "bearded" (the word he uses) sheepherder descended from the moun-

---

6. By "born again" Alfaro meant culturally, not spiritually.

7. I found these verses among some papers donated to the Basque Studies Program (now the Center for Basque Studies) at the University of Nevada, Reno, and entrusted to me by my good friend Eugene Azpeitia, a native of Irisarri (Behenafarroa). They appeared in the *Basque Studies Program Newsletter* 4–5 (May 1977). I have made some changes in punctuation, and the translation is mine.

tains, everybody knew he was coming with some money, and his countrymen pounced on him like birds of prey. Such sheepherders were quickly invited to have a drink in one of the Basque hotels, but after that the unfortunate ones were often expected to pay for all the others:

Orai bertze trago bat, prest dago barrara;	Now another drink, [the Basque in town] is ready at the bar;
Hura, gaiso artzainak, pagatu beharra,	Poor sheepherder, you must pay for it;
trago hunek luzian kartzen du adarra;	this drinking in the end brings consequences [for]
Dener oihuka daude, "Zaute edatera."	they are yelling at everybody, "Come and have a [drink."

And paying for the drinks was just the beginning:

Trago hau egin eta mus partidañoak;	After this drink we will play a few little games of *mus* [A Basque card game];
Harat bilduak dire herri guzikoak,	Everyone from town has already converged there,
han daude errabian, hartz eta otsoak;	where the bears and the wolves are raging.
Zer zafraldia duken gaur artzain gaisoak.	What a beating the poor sheepherder is going to get today!

In subsequent verses the *bertsolari* described how the hapless sheepherder was cheated by his own countrymen, who sent him back to the mountains *larrua ageri* ("showing his skin"), a metaphor for being penniless. In the last strophe, we are told that the bard improvised and sang these verses in the mountains in the presence of fellow herders. The lyrics are so powerful that, at night while thinking about his own experience, it would not be impossible to conceive of some herder losing sleep over such criticism. We don't know how the verses were recorded, but someone obviously took an interest and, miraculously, they survived.

Sheep camp verse-singing ended decades ago. Increasingly today, *bertsolariak* perform primarily at the many summer picnics and other events. Contrary to what some people predicted, these Basque picnics and the clubs that sponsor them have not gone into decline, but on the contrary, have increased considerably in the last decade alone. The main arena for *bertsolariak* in the United States, however, has been Kantari Eguna or Basque-Singing Day, organized annually by the Mendiko Euskaldunak club in Gardnerville, Nevada. The first and only formal *bertsolari* championship (*txapelketa*) in the United States –and perhaps in the Americas– took place there on April 23, 1988. Since then, instead of championships, the format of *bertsolari* performances has always been more informal. That said, you can never take the competition out of a *bertsolari* event.

You Cannot Take the Sheep Out of a Sheepherder

Gardnerville is surrounded by ranches and fields, and during Kantari Eguna it is almost a prerequisite that the *bertsolariak* sing something about sheepherding. After all, most of the adult audience that converges on the town for this event was once engaged in ranching and herding, and a few of them still are. In the 1991 Kantari Eguna the four rappers were given the following topic to sing about: Goñi is the sheep boss, Arriada the herder holding the lambs for docking, Kurutxet is a female lamb, and Goikoetxea is *ohotsa*, the buck lamb, who for obvious reasons resists being caught.

Goñi

Ardi nagusia, kezketan nago	I am the sheep boss and I worry.
artaldearen begira,	As I look at the herd of sheep,
bildots urruza xarmantak ditut	there are some nice looking she-lambs,
artaldean segira,	for the future of the herd,
baina artzaina hor ondotikan,	but the herder over there is chasing them,
oso zorrotzak baidira.	because they are very quick.
Ni nago ederrenak dotxobanian	I am afraid that the most beautiful ones
erreta jango baitira.	will be eaten roasted in the Dutch oven.

Arriada

Nagusi jauna, nere kejak orain	Boss man, I will start now
zuri erraitera niz hase;	by telling you of my complaints;
Hainbertze urte ardi lanean,	I have been a sheepherder for so many years,
eta e'nuzu gehio gazte.	and I am no longer a young man.
Nere burua harrepatzen dut	I am aware of my own capabilities,
egia erran, orain triste.	that is the sad truth, so please,
Bildots urruzak eta irikuak	you yourself must separate the she-lambs,
ezarri zuk, ahal ba'uzu, aparte.	from the male ones, if you can.

Kurutxet

Egun honetan ez naiz ni ere	On this day I myself am not
haintsu gisa ez atseginekin;	too happy either, as they seem to be;
Kamion hortarik urrun egoiteko	I am trying to stay away from that truck,
ez dakit zer egin.	but I do not know what to do.
E'nuke matantzan oraindikan deus egin,	I'd rather not go to the slaughterhouse yet,
eta gibeletikan ditut	but here both the sheepherder
artzaina eta Martin.	and Martin are chasing me.

Goikoetxea

Gauza xelebre esan beharra	A funny thing we must talk about
hemen esaten gera-ta,	and discuss here today, but
kasoik txarrena nik daukat eta.	my situation is the most difficult one,
Hok hemen emandako lata,	[for] these fellows do not leave me alone.
hor biltzen zeraten egunian	On the day the rest of you gather together,
ni han izango naiz falta;	I will certainly be missing,
Neri ez dezu harrapatuko,	and you will not catch me either
zu gizenegi zera-ta.	because you are too fat.

Goñi

Ardi nagusiak behar du orain	The boss man now must speak up
zerbait isetan mintzatu-ta.	ridiculing something.
Bat kapatzailea, bestea onduan,	The castrator and the man next to him,
elkarre daude hartuta.	are both in this together;
Nik artaldean autetsi ditut	I noticed that some very nice lambs
bildots eder batzuk falta.	are missing from the herd:
Hok herrian neskatan dabiltza	These two fellows sell my she-lambs,
nere bildots urruzak salduta.	and with the money they chase girls in town.

Arriada

Izanik ere nausia hemen,	Because the boss is here,
egia erraiteko gaitz baita.	it is difficult to tell the truth.
Berak dionez artaldetikan	According to him in the herd,
bildots zenbait daukala falta.	he noticed some lambs missing.
Anitz aldiz ere artzainak	Well, often the sheepherder
jar baitu anitz abanta.	has set up lots of perks for himself.
Nausi jauna bildots ohotsak	Dear boss man, please castrate
ahal bezain laster zikita.	the buck lambs as soon as possible.

The old sheepherder Arriada is giving orders to his boss, while taking a nonchalant attitude to his own job. He couldn't take such liberties in real life, but to a singer of verses almost everything is allowed.

Kurutxet

Gure nausiak ez du gure ez	I can see that our boss man
behar gabeko aitzaki.	does not want weak excuses,
Nik zer pentsatzen dudan ene baitan	[but] what I have in mind
hain segur honek ez daki.	this fellow most certainly does not know:
Zu eta artzain txar hau	You and this pathetic sheepherder of yours,
otoi, bistatikan parti.	please, get out of my sight;
Ni urus bizitzeko	for me to live happily,
Martin badut aski.	all I need is Martin.

Goikoetxea

Morroia dabil nere segika,	The hired hand is chasing me,
esperoan nagusia;	while the boss is waiting.
Hok bion arte kendu nahi dute	The two of them are collaborating
nere gustoko guzia;	to take away what I hold most dear.
Bai al dakizute nola	What do you guys know [about]
egin nahi deten bizia?	how I want to live my life?
Ukitu gabe utzi zaidazu,	Leave my body parts alone;
zabaldu nahi det hazia.	I want to spread my seed.

The casual listener cannot fail to detect a profound connection between humans and animals that is reflected in these verses. In photographs of the old sheep camps, the herder is rarely very far away from his animals. Jesus Goñi, after working for fifteen years of his life with sheep, one day made up his mind to leave this world and move to an urban environment. He subsequently described in song his final moments, at an Idaho sheep ranch. His girlfriend was waiting for him outside in a car, and he could not contain his excitement at embarking on such an adventure in a new world. Yet something still made him feel a little guilty:

Agur orain mendiari,	Now I bid good-bye to the mountain
agur ere artaldia;	and to the sheep band:
Urte askoren buruan	After so many years,
komeni zait ahaztutzia;	it is good that I forget them.
Arrantxo bazterrian daude	At a corner of the ranch,
zakurra eta zaldia;	I see the dog and the horse,
Karreteran espero ditut	while waiting for me on the road
neskatxa eta kotxia.	are the girl and the car.

Eye on the World

American *bertsolariak* are not educated people in the sense that a poet might be, but they are equally sensitive, emotional, and fully engaged. You don't become a verse-singer by isolating yourself or by being aloof, or by shutting your eyes and ears to reality. These rappers are by nature curious about the world and all the creatures that inhabit it, so let no one think that they only sing about sheep and immigration. Frequent topics they deal with include politics, the economy, emotional relationships, drinking and driving, gambling addiction, homosexuality, and the classic confrontation between the young woman and the old bachelor with money.

Other topics can be more unusual, such as the sheepherder with one girlfriend in Europe and another in Nevada, two best-friends in a leaky boat in the middle of the ocean (only one can be saved, so one must persuade the other to jump out), and a doctor who proscribes all the things his patient enjoys in life. The priest plays an important role in the Basque community and mocking him is also a favorite subject, such as the case of the priest during Prohibition who was caught with a truckload of wine. Of course, he was going to tell the policeman that he needed it for Mass, but what was his excuse for visiting the whorehouse? To save lost souls?

Bertsolariak are also especially attentive to everyday issues that affect the Basque community. These may involve the current Basque priest who is leaving and a new one coming; the anniversary of the Basque club; a wedding anniversary; or tributes to honor particular individuals who have served the community in various capacities, such as handball or dance instructors, cooks, boardinghouse managers, or club workers. On these occasions, the bards are proud to sing and carry the audience's voice.

Johnny Kurutxet, Kantari Eguna, Gardnerville, 2001. Born in San Francisco, California, Kurutxet was raised in Iparralde or the Northern Basque Country, returning to the United States as a young man. Kantari Eguna (Basque-Singing Day) remains the principal stage for US *bertsolariak*. Photo by Joseba Etxarri.

Bertsolari verses are an open window into the Basque peasant's soul, which is distinguished by its unaffected philosophy and deep sense of reality. During one *bertsolari* event, for example, the moderator asked Johnny Kurutxet what two things he wished God would grant him. In his response, Kurutxet did not sing about abstract notions of happiness, knowledge, freedom, or universal peace. He did not even ask for heaven:

Grazia baitu gaurko hau
atseginez galdatzeko,
nahiz denak ez direnez
eginak hen batendako.
Intentzione anitz banuke
egiaren erraiteko;
Hal're lehenik osasuna
hemen huntsa bizitzeko.

Sortuz geroz beti bada
bertze zerbaiten gutizia;
Alferra den batek beti
sosetik eskaseria.
Uros bizitzeko, Jeinkoa,
emadazu behar guzia.
Hortarik hemen kentzen badazu,
iduki zazu zeria.

This topic here has some humor
[and] I will gladly deal with it.
Even though not everyone
always agrees with the truth,
I have every intention
to tell it candidly:
First of all, therefore, I would want health,
so I can have a good life on earth.

Once a person is born, he/she
always desires one more thing,
and the person who is lazy
is always in need of money.
In order to live happily, dear God,
give me everything that I need,
and if you take that away from me,
you can keep your heaven.

Conclusion

Basque rap in the American West is also a mirror of the Basque Country in Europe. The Basques of Iparralde came from a more traditional setting than, say, their compatriots in Bizkaia, and this is one reason why there are more bards in California than in Idaho.[8] *Euskara* is the key to *bertsolaritza* and Iparralde Basques have maintained it more vigorously than Bizkaians. People from Iparralde can usually sing a dozen Basque songs without missing a beat, while Bizkaians can muster considerably fewer verses on average. Almost all those who sing songs during Kantari Eguna are from Iparralde, although Bizkaians are well represented whenever the impressive Boise choir Bihotzetik participates.

Finally, as regards the question of patriotism, old country Basques who read the verses of the American bards may be surprised to find numerous patriotic lines. The Basques of the diaspora may not belong to any political party, but when it comes to culture and other important issues affecting Euskal Herria today, they are united and vocal. And no one is more patriotic than the *bertsolariak*.

---

8. The overwhelming majority of the Basques in Idaho are of Bizkaian origin, while most in California have Iparralde or northern roots.

Bertsolariak and Writers: An Old Tale of Fathers and Sons[*]

JOSEBA ZULAIKA

The world of the *bertsolariak* is tied in my early experience mainly to one person: my father. A typical event I recall from my childhood was the sight of my father singing *bertsoak* from a book in the corner of the kitchen. This was after he had spent twelve hours working in a dusty marble quarry or, more likely, during the Sunday repose. I always imagined him as if belonging to another world – a preliterate culture of simple social forms in which speech was everything; neighbor relations marked the main social ethos; magical experiences were still told; accordion music colored the gaiety and sentimentality of fiestas and personal relations; and to which I could project a certain pre-political innocence. He was certainly not what I was: a schoolboy who wanted to be a writer. He was, at his best, a *bertsolari* but he could never be a writer. We lived in separate worlds. Or so I thought at the time. Much later, when I became a father myself, I began to realize how he must have felt about me and in fact, how close we were. Now that he is gone, I take the excuse of writing about the *bertsolari* culture in an attempt to understand his generation's mentality and experience.

From the Quarry to the Library, from *Bertso* to Writing

My father worked in a quarry twelve hours a day, six days a week, fifty-two weeks a year, and, for all I know, never entered a library in his life. I work and live in a library six days a week. He never perused a book and had no idea of what a catalog card was. It seems to me, however, that this is all I have done for decades. As such, we obviously belong to different worlds. That said, I have been told all my life how alike we are, despite my assumptions that his world was remote from mine.

There were no bookshops in our village but my father had acquired those *bertso* books somewhere –in fairs, in *bertso* competitions, from door to door booksellers– paper-

* An earlier version of this article appears as "Bertsolariak eta idazleak: aita-semearen arteko kondaira zaharra," in Joseba Zulaika (2003: 67–100).

backs with strophes lined up on each page, written by some *bertsolari* or, more likely, dictated to some *bertso* collector such as Antonio Zavala. He kept them all piled up on top of the big Phillips radio. On Sunday afternoons he would religiously follow reports of soccer games on this radio. In any other spare time he might put his glasses on and go to his library on top of the radio for the *bertso* books.

There were both happy *bertsoak* (such as the *koplak* "Betroi behei zaharrarenak") and sad *bertsoak* (such as that sung by a prisoner in order to extend his life); there were poetic ones (such as those of the *bertsolari* Lazkao Txiki) and dramatic ones (such as those of the *bertsolari* Lasarte); there were those –just a few– that celebrated some past event (such as the sad one about Saint Genevieve's life) and those –almost all– that referred to some everyday event. Some humorous *bertsoak* would elicit laughter, which father would be eager to share with whoever was present; other elegiac *bertsoak* would provoke tears. Laughter and tears, I can hardly remember him without them. He would take the appropriate melody and quietly hum the *bertsoak* from the book in his hands resting at the corner of the table. He didn't mind the fact that nobody would pay attention to his low-key singing. His song was likely to be the only background noise in the kitchen; there were no radios or televisions competing for the audience. He would sing one *bertso* after another until the six, ten or whatever number of strophes dedicated to the topic was completed. Then he would pick up another series of *bertsoak*, perhaps with the same melody, more likely changing the tune to adapt to the mood of the new song.

Besides reading *bertso* books, on rare occasions I also heard my father improvise songs in some tavern, usually after being challenged to it by another *bertsolari*. By the standards of professional *bertsolariak*, however, he was mediocre. On the first weekend after Easter there was a tradition of our extended family getting together at both father's and mother's farms; this used to be a signaled occasion for my father and uncles to sing *bertsoak*. He would also sing, I was told, during the yearly *fiesta* with his co-workers at the quarry. On very rare occasions he could also improvise at home and once, he sang at his oldest daughter's wedding. In his youth, following tradition, he had gone serenading from house to house on Saint Agatha's eve with a group of peers, singing praises to and humorous remarks about each household's members. Father loved to brag that in his youth he had been friends with the great champion *bertsolari* Uztapide. They both worked together as loggers and would sing *bertsoak* in their spare time. Uztapide urged him to start singing in public but he felt shy and not competent enough to do it. Later, the illiterate Uztapide became one of the greatest *bertsolariak* of all time. His voice was beautiful, his sense of the word precise, his measured irony penetrating, and his preferred themes were taken from ordinary life. He and his partner Basarri, the other giant *bertsolari* who was, unusually, a cultured man who could read and write, both toured every Basque town and village performing their *bertsoak*. During this time the public would frequently favor the 'humble' but graceful Uztapide, who would never engage himself in the kind of cultist and sermonizing song Basarri was capable of. Needless to say, Uztapide would always remain my father's idol. When in the 1950s and 1960s Uztapide had to travel somewhere

Manuel Olaizola, "Uztapide," and Iñaki (or Inazio) Eizmendi, "Basarri." In the 1940s and 1950s, their partnership –based on the contrast between the 'humble' Uztapide and the 'cultured' Basarri– rejuvenated *bertsolaritza* as they performed throughout the Basque Country.
By permission of *Sendoa*.

near our village, my father would volunteer to pick him up on his motorcycle (cars came much later in life). I was in a private religious school when Uztapide won the 1962 championship and my father came the next day to visit me with the front page news of the newspaper in his hand.

This love of *bertsolaritza* was my father's legacy to me throughout my entire childhood and I especially came to enjoy those kitchen-table *bertsoak*. At times, when he was not present, I might take the books myself and sing the songs. Later, after he retired in the late 1970s, when the daily newspapers and television had long conquered the image and noise backgrounds of every household, my father had much more time to become 'literate'. He read the daily newspapers, for example, although he could not help to do it communally by verbalizing whatever he was reading for the rest of us, even if he knew that we had read the news already. Literature per se, without the performance of the spoken word, would never be his mental universe.

In the meantime I had gone to college and writing had become my calling. My first publication was a book of poems. I vaguely assumed that my writing might have something to do with my father's love for oral verse, but I was also very aware that writing poetry was an entirely different exercise from what he was doing. He was a *bertsolari*, while I was a poet. Maybe he was also a poet and maybe my later ethnographic work was a type of *bertsolaritza* (the dean of Basque ethnographers, José Miguel de Barandiarán, used to compare his work, ironically, as one of "extracting stones from a quarry"), yet at the time there could hardly be a bridge between the two worlds.

Father sang his *bertsoak* for sheer pleasure. Now I wonder whether he was also engaged in something else. Wasn't this his way of opening up to us a window into his most subjective world? Cultures are about the transmission of knowledge and how we pass this knowledge gained from experience is always a tricky issue. Suddenly, that kitchen song has become most revelatory.

From the Kitchen to the Basement: Foosball, Pinball, and Playstations

In the generational transitions from fathers to sons and daughters, if during my childhood the kitchen was the main arena of interaction, now that I have children of my own I wonder what is the equivalent arena of cultural transmission in our home. Culture is in the end about teaching new generations the codes of behavior handed down from tradition and their learning, a task obviously filled with ambiguities and ambivalences. This has something to do with what my teacher Jim Fernandez once wrote about; namely, that gray area of human experience which he calls "the inchoate," and which he finds to be categorical and irreducible. Jim's career-long interest, so tied to this symposium's topic, has been the study of "the play of tropes in culture," as he subtitled his collection of *Persuasions and Performances* (1986). Pronominal metaphors, ritual scenarios, and verbal play are strategies he has long pursued to examine the vicissitudes of the cultural inchoate. High on his list of a culture's performative arenas are children's games as quintessential to the subject's attaining of a sense of identity. He examined Asturian children's games based on animal identities and argued persuasively for the decisive role of cultural metaphors and ritualized contexts of behavior in shaping culture. Furthermore, he situated the inchoate in an unlikely place – "the dark at the bottom of the stairs." In the Asturian houses studied by Jim, that dark at the bottom of the stairs was typically the stable – as an ethnographer, taken aback by the clouds of acrid animal smells, this was understood when the cattle herder showed him his treasure with arms opened in ecstatic praise, "*¡Qué hermosura!*" ("What beauty!").

From the ethnographer's holistic approach, verbal and ritual games share a culture's performative contexts. As regards games and the space at the bottom of the stairs, there is a basement in my house. This is the space that my ten-year-old son is likely to remember in the future if he ever reflects on the collision course between his world and that of his parents. For it is in the basement that he finds pleasure for hours while playing videogames. And in the basement there is another major experience my son and I share for hours: watching sports on TV. Whether it is football or the NBA, these are our favorite moments together.

But there is something else at the bottom of the stairs that is almost as revelatory as my father singing *bertsoak* in my childhood. There was a pinball machine that one of my colleagues, Bill Douglass, gave to another colleague, Carmelo Urza, who in turn passed it down to me once his kids went to college and he needed to make room in his own basement. The only problem was that it didn't work and I was lucky to exchange it for a brand new foosball table. I used to love playing pinball during my Bilbao student years, and in my childhood playing the village tavern's foosball was an expensive treat. I was, therefore, happy to bring home the foosball table with which my kids and I were going to enjoy playing. I soon realized, however, that there was no way they'd play such an archaic game with me; that is, until something else happened: after three years of going skiing, my son decided he had had enough of it. He knew I was not happy about this and he had to find a ploy to make sure that I was still friends with him. "Daddy, let's play foosball," he said at one point to my great surprise. In effect, he had to do something as extraordinary as venturing into my dinosaur world by playing foosball, something he hadn't done in two years, in order to tell me that we were still friends. My elation at beating and being beaten by him at foosball subsequently reaffirmed how true his assumption was. This might seem rather irrelevant but the foosball communication signaled a major reinforcement of the father/son relationship. It just points out how tenuous the generational transmission link can be.

This brings me back to my father's song in the corner of the kitchen. My son is learning basic math and basic literary skills under my supervision, and I shouldn't be threatened by his knowledge. However, my illiterate parents were faced with a historical change in that, for the first time in the family's history, their children were being schooled – we could read, write, and speak Spanish fluently, and we were obtaining the skills to learn and travel on our own. They were happy for us and there was nothing they wanted more than our education. Still, what was going to bridge the gulf between their world and ours?

I remember my mother asking me about it and not being altogether happy with the somewhat disdainful reply she got from me. Beyond her native Basque, she had not even been able to speak Spanish. My father had been taken to a town near Bilbao during his adolescence in order to learn Spanish. He had also mastered the four basic arithmetical operations. The apex of his scholarly knowledge revolved, therefore, around how to find cubic squares of the large beautiful marble stones he and his workers would extract from the quarry – he had to multiply the height, width and depth of the quadrangular stone by the specific stone's weight. But there was a sense in which father's true intimate experience and knowledge had more to do with his singing of *bertsoak*. His song must have been animated by the presence of a gulf between his world and ours. The pleasure of that verbal art, the imaginative world evoked by those strophes, the emotional continuity brought about by that song – what else must have made him more at home with himself and his family? It was in that song that he was best portrayed and therefore, that should have been able to bridge any distance.

I used to blame my father for our lack of communication, which surely had to be the result of his ignorance –it is the father who is supposed to know, not the son– and of his belonging to another world so different from mine. Then my time to have a child arrived and now I am lucky to have a foosball table in the dark at the bottom of the stairs. If my son could at least think of me, with all my readings and writings, as an old fashioned *bertsolari* who needed poetry at the end of the day, I would feel safe. What I am increasingly afraid of, however, is that his world might become so "post-script" (Foley 2002) that he might find mine even more antiquated than I found my own father's, and thus refuse to have anything to do with it. If at some point I might have thought that the communication between father and myself was non-existent because of his lack of formal education, the sobering discovery that foosball can turn into a last resort to connect with my son is surely a corrective.

My son doesn't hear me sing *bertsoak* at home (although I try that as well when we go together for long road trips). He sees me read instead. And I wonder whether my reading is for him, as my father's singing was for me, merely a gesture indicating an obsolete world that won't be his. Will he ever have a clue as to how important reading and writing has been for me? If the problem of how we pass knowledge across generations appeared particularly acute in the transition from illiteracy to literacy (when the very codes for processing knowledge were themselves transformed), isn't there a similar gulf between my world of literacy and my son's world of computer animation? Isn't he going to feel, as I did of my father, that my imaginative world and my entire culture is an altogether foreign country for him?

Words and Silence

It hardly needs to be emphasized that the central register of my father's generation's mentality was oral. Their sense of communication, identity, norms, and community hinged fundamentally on the centrality of the word. Reading, thinking, communicating, and praying were for them primarily oral processes that needed to be verbalized and spoken. With the exception of a few letters my father and I exchanged while I was a teenage seminarian (we even swapped some written *bertsoak*), our communication was always face-to-face. Still, if I were asked whether there was a lot of verbal communication between father and me, the answer would be no. We must have spent many hours together when I visited home and when we went to places together; we must have spoken about something or other, but hardly ever about anything thematic that had something to do with our world-view or our experience. If I were to be asked about his opinions on anything, I probably would not have a clue. Still, the idea that we might have needed to communicate more, so common nowadays, would have been totally strange to him. There was really nothing more necessary than the fact that we needed to communicate to each other. We were happy to be in each other's presence and the talk didn't seem to have any other purpose but that reassurance. As a result, there was never a sense that there were unspoken things which we needed to tell each other. If he lived in an oral universe, this surely did not mean that we were expected to speak all the time. Indeed, the opposite was perhaps the case in that he had a clear sense of the limits of language. This common-sense wisdom forced a sense of taboo on communicating too much, particularly about private issues, and, contrary to the assumption that speaking one's mind is always good all the time, the value posited on "keeping things inside," as a means to avoid the hubristic dangers of showing off and imposing one's own opinions that may go along with over-communication, was also important.

Still, there was no lack of knowledge about each other's states of mind. This is the type of knowledge that in Basque is termed *ezagutu* (in French "*connaitre*," in Spanish "*conocer*") as opposed to *jakin* ("*savoir*," "*saber*"). We did not need to utter a word to "know" each other's moods. This communication by silent presence was most limited in moments of crisis. But the assumption that the pathos of life cannot always be orally articulated was taken as a given by him. After all, my father had experienced the death of five of his children (I had no sense of this enormity until I had a child of my own). And as a reminder, the brother who had inherited his father's farmstead had literally died of grief two weeks after the death of his own ten-year-old son. My father took him to see games during those two weeks to distract him from his sorrow but to no avail. As I found about this later in life, I kept asking my father about his brother's death, and he became impatient with my insistence; I was trying to find some explanation where there was nothing but grief; I was turning into a conversation what should only elicit silence. My assumption that everything could be known or at least talked about was humbug. His brother simply could not share the enormity of his grief; caught unaware of how much he needed his son for his own life, he could not communicate this. It was a kind of secret he took to the grave and should therefore be left unspoken.

The linguistic economy of oral culture is far apart from the tragicomic approach of the writer who is likely to seek and dwell in deliberate experience in order to write about it. Take someone like Unamuno, for example, in his famous essay on the "Tragic Sense of Life"; someone provoked by the unsolvable dilemmas between reason and faith, or by the political nostalgia of an imperial Spain that had lost its dominions in 1898. There is no shame for the writer in communicating everything and in assuming that his God-like freedom allows him to opine on anything.

The idea that non-communication of certain sorts is needed in situations of hierarchical difference (such as those between the sacred and profane contexts, or between generational distances, or between speech and the unconscious) is one that I, as writer, tend to forget, but my father, as a primarily oral man, seemed to assume firmly. Now that I have a son and a daughter of my own I am more receptive to his wisdom. There is a lot I cannot and should not "say" to them. The best communication regarding the sacred or aesthetic or tragic aspects of experience –practically everything that is of importance in life– is perhaps best left silent. And yet that is what we most want our children to know about. The reason for such taboo is that, "Communication is undesirable, not because of fear, but because communication would somehow alter the nature of the ideas" (Bateson and Bateson 1988: 80). These are the moments of silence that can only be broken by prayer or song. Thus my father never talked to us about the grief of his children's death; he just sang *bertsoak* at the kitchen table, laughing and shedding tears, making it all understandable and bearable.

Writing as Seduction: The Powers of Promising

Uztapide and Basarri were the two prominent *bertsolariak* in the 1950s. My father was close friends with Uztapide, but it was Basarri, the only *bertsolari* who could write at the time, who reported on a religious "promise" my father had made in his regular column, "Nere bodatxotik," for the *Aranzazu* magazine. I found this article while researching for this paper. None of my brothers and sisters knew about this page-long story ever being written about my father by Basarri. It was one of those things that my father would prefer to have left unspoken. Only a writer son would dwell on such things.

Basarri wrote that the occasion of my father's promise was his grief for an incurably sick daughter in constant excruciating pain. He asked that either she be cured or else die to spare her the intolerable pain, and that "if that cross was removed from the family," in Basarri's words, "then he would erect another cross in memory of the event." Soon afterwards she died and my father, as promised, erected a five-meter high, two-and-a-half-meter wide marble stone cross on top of Otaerre hill where his quarry was located.

The nature of such a "promise" is a good starting point to distinguish the ways in which language is used in a predominantly oral culture versus that same use in a predominantly written culture. The preliterate person invokes the linguistic power of promising in order to bow to the larger circumstances that he/she cannot control, and as a way to fend off sorrow and uncertainty. Thus the word is used to carry out a final deliberation, make a contract, reach a decision, and impose some sort of permanence and redemption on human endeavors. Yet promising can be a starkly different affair in a predominantly literary culture. For the writer, for whom the world is essentially a text, everything is a sign and its meaning is indeterminate until the writer ascribes one to it. In modern times the sign itself disintegrates under various interpretive perspectives. As Barthes observed regarding such disintegration, "the goal today is to empty the sign and infinitely to postpone its object" (1986: 148). Thus writing easily becomes a self-referential play of seduction in which the author is typically engaged in "writing to seduce and seducing to write about it" (Ràfols 1997). Unlike the situation of a person of "the word," for whom language is his or her main conduit, identity, resource and knowledge, for the writer/seducer the word may become a field of self-referential indeterminacy. The person who relies on the word for his or her identity and primary communication cannot use the word as if it were a tool of seduction by means of promises and self-referential utterances. The oral speaker assumes that the word has a reality of its own in various social and personal contexts, whereas the performer of the word in a context of seductive play knows that it is nothing but talk; in the classic case of Don Juan, a promise of marriage means nothing more than a verbal act with no necessary link to its being fulfilled in real life (Felman 1983). The writer similarly knows that his written word is nothing but text, with no need to take its relationship to the actual world as anything but speculative and non-committal.

We might think of seductive promises as essentially verbal performances, rather than written texts. But the fixation of the text has more to do precisely, not with the event of speaking itself, but with the 'said', "where we understand by the "said" of speaking that intentional exteriorization constitutive of the aim of discourse" (Ricoeur 1971: 532). The textual nature of a promise springs from such "intentional exteriorization" by means of a verbal utterance. This helps explain why the semiotics of Zorrilla's Don Juan, as shown by de Ràfols, are essentially those of a writer. His arts of verbal persuasion are formidable, but he does it with the help of writing and by infusing his speech with the indeterminacy that characterizes writing. In Ràfols's words, "writing is at the core of Don Juan's will to conquer and seduce: it is the means by which he publicizes his powers (the posters), one of the means by which he seduces (the letter), and the immediate end for which he executes his designs (the catalog)" (1997: 254). For all his world of action and deception, in the end Don Juan is primarily a captive of "the culture of writing."

One of the features of the writer's transformation is that he/she becomes a "name." Don Juan can even forfeit the pronoun "I" to speak of himself in the third person. Writing allows him to use his real or fictional subjectivity as an example for others. In the end it won't really matter whether his exploits were real or fictional; what will matter will be text itself and what it shows about the logic of promises. Don Juan rebels against his father's logocentric authority, against the dictatorship of the committed word. He uses speech not as a literal text but as a field of pleasure. He wants the power of promising not in order to fulfill a promise but in order to break it. This shows not the logic of commitment but language's logic of self-reference.

Compare the writer's seductive "I promise" to that of my father's religious "promise" in an oral context. Both are promises, yet their intentional nature could not be more

apart. The writer's donjuanesque promise is closer to lying since he uses language's deceptive properties with the goal of obtaining a desired result, regardless of the truth of the
statement; Don Juan promises marriage left and right in order to seduce and gain
women's consent. His great trick is precisely the self-referentiality of language by which
words don't necessarily have to have a referent in the real world. The religious promise
of a converted or desperate person is just the opposite: its main goal is precisely to rule
out such linguistic indeterminacy in an act that aims at being anything but arbitrary and
deceptive. Such religious promises are premised on sacramental literalness and permanence, not on the self-referential playing that is intrinsic to other forms of speech underlying humor, irony, allegory, or metaphor. A question we might, then, raise is whether Don
Juan, and in general the person who relies on the culture of writing, is capable of an entirely religious type of literal promise; or, inversely, whether the oral person is ever allowed
to use language deceptively in the manner a writer can.

Don Juan's hell consists of the fact that not even he can any longer believe in his own
promises. It is fun to play with language performatively and take advantage of its semantic duplicity, but once the speaker is deprived of the literal use of words he or she is also
deprived of a basic function of language. This is the fixed meaning of words and cultural conventions that are so economic for a face-to-face communication, crucial to the oral
contexts of family life and relationships of friendship and trust. The writer's Derridean
premise that there is nothing outside the text lends to the conclusion that there is no other
rule to be obeyed beyond language itself. Any promise, therefore, is nothing but a linguistic
act. As a writer I understand this well; I even wrote an entire book on the history of the
Guggenheim Bilbao Museum from the viewpoint of "the chronicle of a seduction." And I
believe that a good politician or a good therapist needs to take advantage of such linguistic ambiguity and arbitrariness. What, then, of the promise my father made? Would
I be able to make a promise of that sort? Of course I would, a million times I would, if
my child was suffering from an incurable pain; not as the result of religious belief, but
because I would imperiously need to believe that language, as if by magic, could indeed
effect the world and change the unchangeable.

Could my father, on the other hand, be captive to the deceptions of the culture of
writing? The capacity for promising and lying are intrinsic to any speaker. Yet, to the
extent that he relied on mere orality to think and communicate, he should have been
immune to the writer's all too common seductions. There was of course one major exception in which he could use language playfully and analogically: *bertsolaritza*. While singing
bertsoak he could pretend to be or to do anything, to lie humorously and even become anybody else's experience and song. But there was no danger that such exercises in song
would deprive him from the literal strictures of his day to day use of language. In no way
was he in danger of falling into the delusional aspects of my all too literary world. Yes,
he could use language performatively and for mere pleasure, but he would mark the step
into this context of *bertsoak* and humor by a clear demeanor of shyness or postured brava-
do while singing a song or telling a story. In a culture of writing, on the other hand, the

distinctions between language as seduction and performance, and language as plain commitment or truth, can be far more obscure. Just consider our dependence on the media for our information on world affairs, or the inevitability of having to place our retirement investments in the stock market, or the pressure in academia to follow the latest intellectual fashion. The success of such "bubbles" relies largely on the aberration inherent to language's powers of promising.

All of this brings us to the ironic reality that the culture of writing is at once far more knowledgeable, but in the end also far more deceiving and ignorant, than the culture of the word. This is precisely the stuff of Socratic irony, Socrates being, as we all know, the one who refused to write. Considered to be the wisest of the Greeks, Socrates is the one whose knowledge was essentially an apology of his ignorance. Ignorance mistaken for knowledge is what Socrates thought to be the natural state of people's minds. His own famed Socratic irony consisted in the fact that he, the exemplar of virtue, insisted that he did not know what virtue was nor could he teach it. There are obviously complex layers of irony built into this Socratic attitude, and at least two quite different types of knowledge (the systematic one that produces certainty, of which Socrates knows nothing, and the fallible one of ethical truth of which Socrates can have some claim to knowing), matters which are beyond this analysis (Nehamas 1998). What concerns us here is that, in the old enmity between speech and writing, Socrates took a decidedly negative approach to writing. In Socrates' story, as recounted by Plato, "those who acquire it [writing] will cease to exercise their memory and become forgetful; they will rely on writing to bring things to their remembrance by external signs instead of on their own interior resources" (qtd. in Ràfols 1997: 258). As this quote points out, what really mattered to Socrates were the "internal resources," that is, how to live. The puzzle about Socrates is how he managed to live as he did; his accomplishment was that, by means of self-creation, he established a new art of living that would later become the paradigm of truth for authors such as Montaigne, Nietzsche, Kierkegaard, or Foucault. And he did it not by writing, but essentially by becoming silent – which reminds us of the previously discussed wisdom of non-communication in certain contexts.

Types of Reading and Writing

In the transition from my parents' generation to my own generation's mental world, the main difference had something to do with the centrality of reading and writing in our culture. My father also read his *bertso* books and the daily newspapers in the kitchen. He sought enjoyment in singing the *bertsoak* and information in the newspapers; but he could not read the *bertsoak* without singing them, nor could he read the news without vocalizing it. For him, then, reading was thus basically performative and public, and not a means of schooling or instruction, or the search for an argument or a theory, or indeed a tool for the care and transformation of his own self.

For the people of my generation, reading and writing were the first skills we learned and practiced in childhood. The long compulsory years of schooling forced into our lives a "career" orientation; reading and writing were the gateway and the very substance of the learning required to advance in such a lifelong career. Besides fostering our professional selves, our most intimate selves also depended largely on the pleasures and challenges of reading and writing. Those of us sent to religious schools and seminaries, for example, soon found out that so-called "spiritual reading" was an integral part of the school's curriculum. Reading was about providing the self with exemplary lessons taken from historical figures. Wasn't Saint Ignatius of Loyola converted by reading biographies of saints? And didn't Quixote forge his character by reading chivalry books? The religious orders knew all too well how to turn reading into a disciplinary tool that promised spiritual enlightenment. My father was never asked anything of this sort.

People of my generation tried hard to access the pleasures of reading either by venturing into the texts of world literature or those of religious tradition. Self-transformation was the expected reward. If there were illuminations of some sort out there, whether profane or sacred, we believed they would be attainable while trying our best to experience them through reading. For some of us, whose only access to higher education had been possible on the condition that we surrender ourselves to a religious order, spiritual reading became a source of intense jouissance while expectant of complete conversions in pursuit of sainthood. The stakes were so high that there could be no middle ground: there would be either glorious plenitude or spectacular failure. One or the other was going to be decided by our response to the texts that were implacable witnesses to our lives.

In such a context of sacramental Catholicism, reading was far from mere play. Our spiritual lives, not to mention our very sanity, were at stake. But such education in radical reading was going to lead some of us into other extremes of reading. What happened was that, as we began to study philosophy, so we ended up reading other texts with the same passionate commitment to self-transformation. Suddenly the Baroque religiosity of an Italian religious order was being mixed, say, with the hyperbolic atheism of Nietzsche's Zarathustra. What a culture shock! Suddenly Dostoevsky's godless Ivan Karamazov was as lovable as his spiritual brother Aliosha, and reading Freud's essays on sexuality not only broke a taboo but led us to discover an ocean that was all too real to be left unspoken. Reading was to blame for this earthquake. There was no more risky affair than reading. Indeed, the same absolutism of reading we had experienced with religious desire led us into the extremism of libertarian ideals in our personal, religious and political lives. Just as the sculptor Oteiza discovered that the statue had for him turned into "a sacrament" which could completely replace religious transcendence, so something of the sort happened to us with reading and writing: they had become the only avenues to personal salvation.

Thus suddenly reading and writing were the only fields of struggle in which philosophical and ethical truths were to be fought out. What we were to believe and to value, indeed who we were to be, was pivotally decided by those readings. As a substitute for the tragicomic religious apocalypse we had undergone, new types of reading and writing were going to become our true anvil of self-transformation, the arena in which we were going to challenge any mythology and establish our own truth, the precipice from which we could stare at the abyss of freedom. My first book of poems was a rewriting of the myth of paradise entitled "Adam's unfinished poem." Writing was allowing me to rebel against the myth of paradise that the book of Genesis had forced upon me. In my version nobody expelled Adam from paradise; he himself decided to leave in search of new territories and unexplored perspectives. My rebellion against the Adamic myth was of course yet another recreation of that same myth, and one more validation of its deep psychological truth.

All of this took place while I was working as a porter in the fracture clinic of London's old Charing Cross Hospital, one hundred yards away from Trafalgar Square. Stripped of all the texts that had informed my experience throughout my adolescence, the exuberance of freedom was soon drowned by the darkness of depression. While reflecting on the wreckage my life had become, I thought of my loving father and the abysmal distance I had created between us. He would never be able to understand the hell I had sunk into, I thought in self-pity. I envied him for not having to experience the misfortune I had brought upon myself by becoming vulnerable to those readings and by being forced to rewrite my own version of Adam's fall from paradise.

I had become a subjective ghost totally dependent on reading and writing. Yes, there was the pride of liberty – the pride of Milton's fallen angel. I had written myself out of Adam's righteous paradise but I was soon invoking Milton's and Blake's and Kierkegaard's mythologies as my own territory. Suddenly everything was phantasmagoria and existential doubt. Suddenly I was left with the inconsistent vagaries of writing as my only companion. Could I make it an inhabitable universe for myself? I returned to Plato's view of writing as a kind of shadow. Gone was the redemptive quality of human suffering. All I could do was look at the world and write about its arbitrary signs and meanings. My voice had been reduced to that of an impotent solitary pen. Truth had been downgraded to a series of interpretive plays. I had fallen captive to the monster of writing.

My Father's Texts

In his old age my grandfather could still recite all the questions and answers of the catechism he had learnt by heart before he was ten. That had been his entire schooling. My father's education was much the same, except that in his early twenties he was taken to the town of Alonsotegui, near the industrial capital of Bilbao, to learn Spanish and the four math operations. This was an exceptional qualification for a young Basque rural boy at the time. He had no romantic view of the *baserri* farmstead lifestyle of his parents and was happy to move away from it to help as a servant in his uncle's house near Bilbao.

To the extent that his daily life was framed in a preliterate world, my father's relationship to texts was basically defined by a sense of their inaccessibility. Texts, writing, literacy, and law all belonged to the world of the Castilian language and he barely mastered the rudimentary knowledge of Spanish, although it did give him a huge advantage in life.

Yet essentially Castilian was not his world and he felt awkward in it. A visit to the doctor, the lawyer, the pharmacy, the bank, or the hospital was a visit to the Spanish-speaking world. Even his boss, from the provincial capital San Sebastian, would speak to him in Spanish. Consequently, signing a contract, calculating the square meters of each stone block, or making the weekly report on the output –in other words his job-related texts– were all in Spanish and therefore belonged to a foreign place. And if the market was dominated by the Castilian language, then the political world was even more so.

Migrancy, diaspora, and homelessness are nowadays fashionable topics in cultural studies. We tend to think that this is the lot of our contemporary world as opposed to the static peasant lifestyle of our parents. The reality is that the experience of my father's generation –living in the most peasant, Basque, orally-based traditional of cultures in the midst of the most industrial, Spanish and globalized world– might have been in a sense more diasporic and homeless than anything my generation has experienced. Their transitions from rural to urban, from peasant to industrial, from Basque to Spanish, from village to nation and from oral to written worldviews were as radical as any cultural transition could be. In the case of my father, his time spent in Alonsotegui had been his only instructional period, his university. Recently, while doing fieldwork in Bilbao, I decided to visit Alonsotegui – a small mining town with basic apartment houses crowded across both sides of a narrow road with heavy traffic. As I walked through the town imagining the grim exile of my young father, a shy stuttering man trying to learn Castilian and desperately in search of escaping his *baserri* ("farmstead") world, I was overcome by an awareness of the "homelessness" he must have experienced there between his peasant worldview and Bilbao's larger industrial world.

His weekend job consisted of selling tickets behind the window at the movie theater that belonged to his uncle. Those tickets were his main texts. They were tickets to a world of visual animation that he must have felt was so removed from the world of his own parents on the *baserri*. His parents, and even he himself when younger, had experienced a world of witchcraft that was still part of peasant lives during the first decades of the twentieth century. Yet the movies then came along to replace them. My father, much like myself thirty years later, must have felt so removed from his parents' world of illiteracy. He was living now near industrial Bilbao, speaking Spanish, seeing the heavy smoke from the chimneys across the Bizkaian sky, visiting the urban center and its ebullient red-light district. How could he explain to them what a blast furnace, a train, a movie were? Exiled from the bucolic landscape of his natal *baserri*, he sold tickets to a brave new world beyond the narrow confines of his parents' universe of face-to-face oral communication.

The uncle from Alonsotegui had a prosperous business in Mexico and for a while my father entertained the prospect of migrating there to work for him. Yet it was not to be, on the basis that my father was unschooled. Such unfulfilled life opportunity accompanied him for the rest of his life as an alternative imaginary map that he would have been happy to travel. Instead, he had to return to his rural roots and its peasant economy, with hunting as the main weekend pleasure and *bertso* singing as the basic verbal play.

In the end he could not escape his rural world. For two years he worked as a servant in a remote *baserri*. Then he became a logger, one of the few industries in *baserri* society.

There was no political consciousness in such a peasant society. My father was of course a Spanish citizen, a marginal condition in his life that could be all but forgotten except for the fact that he was legally obliged to do military service for the nation-state. However, by making the most of his poor skills in speaking Spanish and by exaggerating his stuttering, through the mediation of a priest, he managed to evade his military duties, an exemption that was extended during the bloody Spanish civil war (1936–1939). The same ignorance of Spanish and verbal deficiency that made his citizenship trivial had saved him from the citizen's main duty – military service.

Hunting and *bertso*-singing were in general the two main male passions and texts of my father's rural generation. Hunting provides a complex semiotics of its own in which words, maps, or anything fixed by writing is remarkable by its absence. It is an activity in which the primary sensorial experience of smell, touch, and visual traces predominate, and talking is anathema. Hunting provides a text in which typically the main carrier of information is an animal scent caught by the dog's sense of smell, which subsequently gets translated into barking, the meaning and direction of which has to then be guessed and interpreted by the hunter. This is the least fixable, visual, readable, rule-governed information one can get. It is a type of communication that remains for the most part indexical without reaching the level of symbolicity typical of fixed words, images, or grammatical rules. In order to trace and guess animal behavior, it has to function at the level of preverbal animal communication. Still, it is a text that gets deeply engraved in the body of the hunter. Traditionally hunters were vulnerable to being visited by the errant priest of legend, Mateo Txistu, who, as punishment for having abandoned mass to go hunting with his dog, had been condemned to an endless wandering. The ritualized confrontation with the beast in a context imagined as one of life or death elicits intense body reactions. By conquering the beast the hunter affirms the superiority of human culture and society.

That was my father's primary culture and those were his elusive texts. However, in the middle of this textual poverty there was something else: there was the art of *bertsolaritza*. This was the world of his friend Uztapide, of the after-meal *bertsoak* among brothers and friends, and, in my childhood, of the texts sung in the corner of the kitchen. Such quiet song was the only escape into the world of literacy and art. His children were all being schooled and we were likely to wonder at his ignorance, yet he could still sing. He too had an imaginative world of his own to which the *bertsoak* were just a window, a place in which laughter and emotion were pivotal. This song was the compendium of his life, distilled from the *baserri* safety of his childhood, the difficulties of his life as a young man, the experiences and failures of his trip to Alonsotegui, the hardships and pleasures of work and family life, and the pathos of dead children. He had to sing that song. Whether anyone would listen to it or not was secondary. Everything was all right as long as he could sing that song.

Conclusion: The Ethnographer as *Bertsolari*

As I started to write poetry in my adolescence, father's kitchen singing became an increasingly remote and odd activity for me. I saw it as completely unrelated to the world of literature and philosophy I became immersed in. But as I moved into anthropology and began to write ethnography, I soon perceived the singular relevance of *bertsolaritza* to understand traditional Basque culture. During my graduate years, nothing regarding my work interested my mentor, Jim Fernandez, more than the *bertsolariak*. Still, I chose the study of Basque political violence as my dissertation topic. I wanted to know the real reasons behind the tragedy. And what did I discover? I found that the *bertsolari*'s way of performing could be a perfect model with which to understand the political activist. The impromptu quality of the activist, its unpredictability and improvisation, could be modeled after the *bertsolari*; the mentality of action was intimately related to the ideology of *hitza* ("the word") with its insistence on literalness, economy of expression, and commitment. The political activist's performance surely ascribed to the "rapid-fire association and composition" that characterized the singer of tales according to Albert Lord (1960). We might say that the *bertsolari*'s texts, unlike those of a formal politician, are non-fixed, informal, and momentary. The *bertsolaritza* dictum that "the end is the beginning" has a counterpart in the way the political activist projects his course of action by drawing energy from anticipation of the end. If *bertso* texts generate expressive power from ellipsis and from disrupting ordinary causal links, as Manuel de Lekuona (1935) showed in his masterful work, so then, the activist also behaves by not explaining his actions. What both the *bertsolari* and the political activist do is to impose "an argument of images" (Fernandez 1986a), that is, an argument based not on abstract links and logical inferences but on a juxtaposition of vivid images bound together by the formal frame of a rhymed song.

Not only could the activist be modeled after the *bertsolari*, but even more, as stated in the Prologue to my book, I came to the conclusion that: "this ethnography resembles the script of an epic poem in which the literalness of the plot is a literary convention for the poet's song on men's honors and shames. In this respect is not the work of an 'expert' searching for a 'solution' to the Basque problem; its goals are closer to the poet's attempts to turn into a song what is self-generating and incomprehensible in human experience" (Zulaika 1988: xxviii). It never occurred to me to ask myself where I learned that, in the end, human experience could only be adequately expressed by the *bertsolari*'s deep song. And it is only now that I realize I must have learnt it from the preliterate *bertsolari* of my childhood singing in the corner of the kitchen.

But did I ever learn anything from him? I always thought I did not, since all he did was sing *bertsoak* by himself. And then, after all the schooling and all the research, one day I came to the conclusion that all I wanted for my writing was that it be something akin to the work of a *bertsolari*. In the end, as recognized by the Cuban poet Indio Naborí (pseud. Jesús Orta Ruiz) in relation to his own father (Orta Ruiz 2000: 35), I was –I am– simply repeating my father's kitchen song.

And so it goes, this old tale of fathers turned *bertsolariak* and sons turned writers. Whether in sung *bertsoak* or written texts, and regardless of the latest inscription or technology, it is the poet we all look for to translate sense experience –darkness, solitude, joy, humor– into words; or, even better, into the incantatory, prophetic, shared festival of words that is a *bertso* song. Such a song ultimately is based on a language that, in Benjamin's words, longs for the "messianic idea of a universal history" which goes beyond the multiplicity of languages and the plurality of histories. This world beyond translation and which is human communicability per se, "is a history celebrated as a festival," whose language "is free prose, a prose which has broken the chains of writing" (Benjamin qtd. in Agamben 1995: 17–18). And it is only by overcoming the bonds of writing –technology, theory, seduction– that sons can understand the redemptive immediacy of their father's kitchen song.

Part IV:

NEW THEORIES ON *BERTSOLARIAK*

Formulas in the Mind: A Preliminary Examination to Determine if Oral Formulaic Theory May Be Applied to the Basque Case[1]

Linda White

In an earlier article (White 2001) I broached the subject of Basque orality in relationship to Basque nationalism. The scope of that discussion allowed only a cursory examination of the form and structure of the art of *bertsolaritza* imbedded in information about the state of *Euskara*, the Basque language, and the relationship between the language and the nationalist movement. At this time, I would like to select some ideas espoused in the broader field of orality studies with an eye to the process of the creation of *bertsoak* (the verses extemporaneously sung by the *bertsolari* or Basque troubadour) in an attempt to identify whether or not formulaic theories can be applied to the Basque art.[2]

---

1. I would like to thank John Miles Foley for his insights, which assisted me greatly in focusing the conclusions of this article. I would also like to thank Joxerra Garzia, Andoni Egaña, Jon Sarasua, and Xabier Paia for inviting me to participate in the 2003 conference "Ahozko Inprobisazioa Munduan" ("Oral Improvisation in the World") and allowing me the opportunity to discuss these ideas with other scholars and with *bertsolariak*.

2. There are surprising similarities between the nature of Basque *bertsoak* and some of the verses created within the African oral tradition. Finnegan describes funeral verses from East Africa: "In a number of cases, too, there is clear evidence of the kind of simultaneous composition/performance described by Lord for Yugoslav poets. One instance –the *nyati-ti* "lyre" song of the Luo of East Africa– is described by Anyumba (1964). Here the composer/performer builds on common and known themes to create a new and unique composition of his own. The most common context for his performance is a funeral when he is expected to deliver laments" (Finnegan 1990: 248). The composer sits and drinks and sings while admirers drop pennies in his plate. His laments are partly musical but contain stock phrases. He also includes the names of relatives of the dead and adds details about his family, and he elaborates on incidents in the life of the deceased. Finnegan continues: "In the absence of a strong epic tradition, however, the great African form seems to be the panegyric. Praise poetry is a developed and specialist genre in most of the traditional states of Africa and one that is logically often regarded as the most highly valued and specialized of their poetic genres. In this poetry incidents in the hero's life are depicted, but in general the chronological element is relatively undeveloped, and the style is laudatory rather than narrative. It thus differs from epic poetry in its tone and intention, as well as in length: the number of lines in African panegyric poetry is generally to be reckoned in –at most– hundreds rather than the thousands of much epic poetry" (1990: 250). This praise poetry brings to mind the verses sung for different families on St. Ageda's day by *bertsolariak*. There is also an element of payment involved there, as well, as the families reward the *bertsolari(ak)* involved in the performance.

In his *Theory of Oral Composition*, Foley provides thumbnail sketches of different approaches to oral theory. Radlov speaks of "idea-parts" and "defines the singer's art in terms of how idiomatically and even artistically he handles" the "recitation-parts" (Foley 1988: 12). Krauss speaks of "Klichés" used by the singer in order to compose fluently and add to his repertoire. Thus a *guslar* puts the Klichés in order when composing a song of unfamiliar subject matter (Foley 1988: 13). Van Gennep also explains the phenomenon in terms of juxtaposition of clichés. The nature of the clichés is fixed. Only the order of placement can vary (Foley 1988: 13).

In *bertsolaritza* we cannot explain the phenomenon in terms of multiformity, where entire lines can be substituted by others in the retelling of an old tale. The tales are contemporary, dealing with modern topics which are assigned moments prior to the performance, and the repetition of lines, indeed, of words, would be judged a fault in Basque *bertsoak*. According to Duggan (1990: 84), "there has been general agreement that any group of words bounded on either side by a natural pause or caesura and repeated in substantially the same form (allowing for inversions, paradigmatic variations and a few other admissible modifications) should be counted as a formula."

Do such groupings exist within the verses of the *bertsolariak*? There are two ways to examine such a possibility. One would be by reviewing the verses of one *bertsolari* to see if such groupings exist within the work of a single artist. Duggan did something similar when he used a computer-aided method to determine repetitions within separate poems (1990: 88). In his opinion, "by confining the examination of each poem's formulas to those which can be distinguished through a scrutiny of the poem itself, we are at least assured of working with phrases which possessed an identity as formulas in the mind of the poet who uttered them" (Duggan 1990: 89). The other way to search for groupings would be to examine the verses of several *bertsolariak* for the existence of any groupings they might have in common. Duggan felt a comparison of poems would entail great difficulty owing to disparate orthographies and dialects. The same could be said of the separate works of the Basque *bertsolariak*.

Bertsolariak, and Basque scholars who study them, believe that each verse is unique and no patterns are repeated or followed. This is the general wisdom regarding *bertsolaritza*. However, no one has actually examined the verses for such patterns. Perhaps the nature of *Euskara* provides groupings of meanings, rather than groupings of words. The post-position nature of the Basque language and the frequent use of affixes, often multiple affixes, can imbue what appears (or is considered) to be a single word with a group of meanings which is often represented in other languages by groups of words. Would an examination of Basque *bertsoak* reveal any patterns of this nature?

Mini-Methodology and Results

In an effort to discover whether the Basque *bertso* demonstrates any formulaic qualities, I examined the *bertsoak* created by two *bertsolariak* as transcribed in the collection entitled *Bapatean 97*.

In order to explore this idea, I examined the transcribed verses of *bertsolariak* in a regular performance (as opposed to a championship or *txapelketa*). I felt that this would provide the closest model, since the performances were recorded and the verses were then transcribed for publication. Furthermore, no written revisions would occur in these verses. I chose two *bertsolariak* who were performing and whose verses were recorded and transcribed in the *Bapatean* series.[3]

In his conclusion to *Immanent Art*, Foley relates the tale of the *guslar* Bajgorić who uses the modern name of a village (Markovac) in his song and describes it as "accursed" (*kleti*), a descriptor that hardly seems appropriate since the village was named after a Serbian hero (Foley 1991: 244–245). The *guslar* maintained that the line had to be sung that way. Foley points out that the *guslar*'s motivation is one of aesthetics, not a desire to emulate the literary rules and textual manipulations to which we have become accustomed in a society of the written word.

In the Basque case, the *bertsolari* is also more concerned with the aesthetics of the creation than with other factors, although naturally great care is taken to be as accurate as possible with facts within the limitations of the verse itself. If a *bertsolari*'s topic is a historical one, for example, the historical facts of the case are certainly important, but should the structure of the verse require some abbreviation of the tale, the inclusion of the all the facts is not the *bertsolari*'s primary concern. That is, in all cases, the *bertsolari* is charged with creating an aesthetically pleasing *bertso*, and the judges of the competitions are looking for aesthetic qualities, not a recitation of facts.

Foley's "retailoring" of Iser's critical method known as Receptionalist theory can be applied easily to the Basque phenomenon, or to put it more accurately, the experience of *bertsolaritza* is a superb demonstration of the validity of the theory as Foley reinvents it:

> Receptionalism offers . . . . a direct and powerful way to come to terms with the dynamism of the oral traditional work. With certain adjustments in the critical parameters, we can take advantage of its focus on reader / audience participation and co-creation of the experienced work and correspondingly deemphasize the literary, post-traditional values and assumptions that have become so much a part of our unconscious critical heritage (Foley 1991: 42–43).

The phrase, "audience participation and co-creation of the experienced work," is exactly what Aulestia is discussing when he says the audience is a necessary part of the *bertsolari*'s art. The words take on vibrant meaning as you sit with an audience that is com-

---

3. One of the people who did the recording provides us with an example of the dedication and humor involved in an undertaking of this sort. The existence of the automobile means that fans of *bertsolaritza* can travel to many competitions, often two or three in the same weekend. As recorder Josu Goikoetxea relates in the *Bapatean 97* volume, "every weekend there will be one or two sessions, and there I go in my old car, the tape recorder tucked into my green backpack, most often with a headache from my hangover stabbing me between the ears . . . . I'll leave there at two a.m., if all goes well, and return home at three a.m. The next day, let's suppose it's Sunday, there's another session in the afternoon; I grab a greasy cup of coffee in a friend's tavern and once again in my old car –the radio doesn't work–, I'm on the road again . . . . I'll get home around nine p.m." (*Bapatean 97* 1998: 7).

plicit in the *bertsolari*'s performance to the extent that it sings the closing lines of the *bertso* along with the *bertsolari* as he or she extemporaneously creates them.

The nature of the *bertso* is part of the reason an audience can perform this feat. The content of the verse leads the audience to expect a certain outcome, and the demands imposed by the melody provide not only a potential outcome but in some cases, when the content strongly indicates the conclusion, even an inevitable outcome.

In the oral traditional genres discussed by Parry, Lord, Foley, and others, repetition of certain elements of the story provide contextual clues to the listener. However, in the Basque case, the story is different every time, new and fresh, with no historical context for the listener to refer to. Even in the structure of the verses, repetition is frowned upon and a performer can lose points for repeating a word (much less a phrase). Under these circumstances, there must be other characteristics of the *bertso* that allows audience complicity to the extent that listeners can co-create the *bertso* contemporaneously with the *bertsolari*.

Seeking these characteristics, my attention was captured by Dorson's somewhat contradictory statement in *Folklore and Fakelore* (1976: 135): "If an oral poem or recital is the unique production of one mind, it will represent a creative energy and artistic imagination of a different order from the efforts applied to transmitting a piece previously heard and known, in whole or in part. Improvisation involves re-creation, no original creation." Upon closer examination, the contradictory nature of this statement revolves around his use of the word "improvisation" to refer to the retelling of a previously heard tale or song.[4] The Basque *bertso* does not appear to involve re-creation. When the word "improvisational" is used in conjunction with *bertsolaritza*, the speaker is referring to the extemporaneous creative activity that produces an original *bertso*.

However, is a *bertso* "the unique production of one mind"? That appears to be the question of the moment. How can an audience co-create the final lines of some *bertsoak* if the creation is completely unique? Lord spoke of the audience reacting actively to the oral performance, and also of the affect these reactions have on the performer. When the performer's creation is formulaic, both the audience's reaction and the performer's next line may be anticipated (Lord 1960; Renoir 1986: 104). Can this be turned around to imply that if an audience can anticipate the performer's next line, there is then *de facto* an element of formularity in the performance itself?

Each *bertso* is created around a different topic, and the words appear to be unique in each case, within the confines of a shared language. What are the other factors vital to the creation of a *bertso*? The melody is a vital factor, and it imposes constraints upon the language with regard to rhythms and rhymes. Hadjú describes the importance of melody in Samoyed epic songs in two theses (1980: 95):

---

4. Dorson's discussion of Oral Literature and Oral Traditional Literature are pertinent to another Basque form, the oral folktale, which has been studied in great detail by José Miguel de Barandiarán. Transcriptions of selected folktales have been translated and published in English in Barandiarán (1991).

1. In Yurak folk poetry melody has a very important role: it is the invariant (constant) part of the song, while the words of a song live only together with melody. Without melody and rhythm they have no aesthetic value.

2. This principle appears in such a way, that words of a versline being shorter than melody-curves are to be modified, adjusted to the melodic curve. For the lines to reach the set length, to be adjusted to the melody, glides, expletive syllables and meaningless particles may be added to the word-endings or even inserted between syllables, or some words already uttered may be chanted anew.

Melody is equally important in *bertsoak*, albeit with some variations on the theses above. In the Basque *bertso*, it can also be said the melody is the constant part of the song. I would hesitate to say that the words have no aesthetic value without the melody, but my hesitancy most likely stems from my own acculturation to a society of written letters. Modern *bertsoak* are recorded, transcribed, and published in written form, and thus the orality of the *bertso* begins to cross the line into written territory. However, in the experiential environment of a performance, it can certainly be said that the words would not exist without the framework of the melody.

With regard to the second thesis point, the *bertsolari* is required to construct the verbal context in such a way as to fit the notes of the melody. Glides and meaningless particles are not allowed, and repetitions are considered a major error. However, in both instances, the Yurak and the Basque, the melody rules the creation of the verse.

But could there be more? Could the language itself be assisting the *bertsolari* and the audience at the moment of co-creation? And could these factors of melody and language conspire to create "formulas of the mind"?

Gesemann defined and illustrated the "composition-scheme" of the South Slavic improviser. This scheme consisted of a narrative structure with a beginning, middle and end which could be used by the improviser as a guide for placement of verses (Foley 1988: 14). Within *bertsolaritza*, the artist is not placing verses within the structure of an existing story or historical tale, at least, not in the same sense as those who passed on the oral epics. Yet structure is provided in various ways. The *gaijartzaile* or "theme-prompter" presents the *bertsolari* with a scenario around which verses will be created.

In addition, although a *bertsolari* extemporizes verses on a topic supplied at the moment of creation, each *bertso* is required to demonstrate a certain amount of narrative structure. An example of such a topic illustrates the setting provided by the *gaijartzaile*. In a performance held in Ordizia, Gipuzkoa, on January 1, 1997, *gaijartzailea* Joserra Garzia gave the following assignment to J. Agirre and Murua, two of the *bertsolariak* competing against each other (*Bapatean 97* 1998: 43):

> Hi Murua lehen artzain hintzen, orain ertzain. Artzaintzatik ezin bizi, eta hirira alde egin huen denak han utzita. Trafikoa zuzentzen jarri haute; trafiko handia dagoen momentuan han hago trafikoa zuzentzen, eta mendian utzitako hire artzain-txakurra etorri zaik eta botak miazkatzen hasi.

Andoni Egaña and Maialen Lujanbio, National *Bertsolaritza* Championship, Donostia, Basque Country, 2001. In the closing stages of the major championship, the two leading participants face one another in a final round of challenges. Photo by Gorka Salmeron. By permission of *Bertsolari Aldizkaria*.

You, Murua, used to be a shepherd, now you're a policeman. Unable to make a living as a shepherd, you left everything behind and fled to the city. They put you to directing traffic; there you are directing traffic at a moment when the traffic is heavy, and your sheepdog that you left on the mountain comes to you and starts licking you.

The *bertso* must make sense by itself. It should have a strong ending line or "punch line." Furthermore, it should contribute to the overall story of the finished product. Often two *bertsolariak* are creating *bertsoak* in alternating order, replying to the *bertso* created by the previous performer. The best verses will clearly relate to what the other *bertsolari* is singing, and all the *bertsoak* together should form a whole that tells a story or completes an argument. The judges at competitions take all these factors into account when they are scoring a performance.

Although the lyrics composed by the *bertsolari* are endlessly varied, each verse has a structure required by the melody that is imposed upon the performer immediately prior to the initiation of the creation of verses. In the case of the sheepdog scenario above, along with the topic, the melody "Salbatoreko ermitan" is also imposed. That melody has the rhythm and rhyme pattern known as *zortziko nagusia* or "the big eight." The *bertsolari* knows at once that the verse will contain eight lines alternating ten and eight syllables each with the rhyme occurring on the shorter line, and the last line in the verse will be sung twice (making the verse look like a nine-line verse).

Various melodies are employed in this fashion; all of them well known to the *bertso-lariak* and the audience, and each one requires definite meter and rhyme patterns. The number of melodies used for this purpose seems overwhelming to a non-native. Howev-er, they represent a lifetime of cultural accumulation and, in the case of some *bertsolariak*, they are studied in *bertsolari* schools or workshops where aspiring artists practice the required melodies. A quick glance at the four-volume set entitled *Bertso doinutegia* ("A *bertso* melody book") reveals that there are 266 melodies that have the "big eight" rhythm and rhyme pattern. These melodies also have original lyrics attached to them, and in the orig-inal lyric, if a line was repeated, that is a clue to the *bertsolari* that the corresponding new lyric that fits the notes of the repeated line should also be repeated in the new extempo-raneous verse.

How *Bertsolariak* Learn the Art

With all this talk of rhythm and rhyme and how a *bertso* is created, it might be instruc-tive to examine one of the methods for training young *bertsolariak*. Xabier Amuriza's *Zu ere bertsolari* ("You Also a *Bertsolari*") provides much insight to the process and, as a by-prod-uct, to the structural creation of a *bertso*. In the search for "formulas of the mind," no greater research tool can be found than this step by step guide to creating *bertsoak*.

The first step is choosing a melody (Amuriza 1982: 12). Since the accepted norm is one syllable per note of melody, this selection will govern the rhythm or syllable count of each line of the *bertso*. The second step is rhyme (Amuriza 1982: 13–14). Amuriza's book instructs the learner to pick a word and build a list of rhyming words from which a per-former can choose a few to use in the *bertso*. Rhyme is addressed several times in the book, but more in the form of exercises than in theory. Students practice placing rhymes in the appropriate location when mentally outlining a verse. The third step is rhythm (Amuriza 1982: 17) or the need to build a preliminary thought or phrase into a *bertso* with the correct number of lines, each containing the required number of syllables that will fit the melody chosen in step one.

On pages 34 and 35 of his method, Amuriza provides four groups of words and phrases to be studied or memorized by the student. These groups contain:
1. One-syllable words.
2. Two-syllable words.
3. Words of three or more syllables.
4. Adverbs that can be used to finish or fill in a line.

The emphasis where these lists are concerned is syllable count, being able to select quickly from groups of words that will ensure the proper rhythm.

More lists are provided on pages 97 through 102. The first consists of common words that appear in more than one form. For example, if a *bertsolari* wants to say "you all" (*zuek*), but needs three syllables instead of two, this list offers the variation, *zeroiek*. Next, a group of suffixes is provided with variations that allow a *bertsolari* flexibility again with syllables, such as the two and three syllable varieties of *tako / tarako* and *bera / behera* ("downwards") and also with rhyme, in the case of pairings such as *antz* / *untz* and *antza* / *untza* ("towards"). A list of suggestions is similarly offered for lengthening or shortening verb forms as needed. A performer can use *genuen* or *genun*, *dakien* or *dakin*, *nintzateke* or *nintzake*, to comply with the required number of syllables per line. Also provided are lists of synonyms and like words that can be memorized and used in different circumstances.

After examining these methods, can we say that *bertsolariak* use formulas in the construction of their verses? The need for formulaic work for the *bertsolari* is clearly stronger in the area of rhythm than in rhyme or story content. Formulaic theory in other oral literatures is generally concerned with content, with pieces of a story, or with phrases that are combined to create a new telling or singing of a tale. If we stretch the definition of formula to include not only content but also the process of fulfilling a required rhythm, then we might be able to say that *bertsolariak* do employ "formulas of the mind" when creating extemporaneous verses, even though these formulas are not phrases that are memorized or repeated to build a story. In other words, the *process* of fleshing out a melody with the requisite number of syllables might be a formula, albeit an unconscious one, employed by the *bertsolariak* in the making of *bertsoak*. The next question is whether or not this process is apparent in the verse itself.

An Abbreviated Study of Thirty-Six *Bertsoak*

For the purpose of this brief study, I examined thirty-six *bertsoak* created in performance by two *bertsolariak*, J. Aguirre and Murua, during events held in 1997. The lyrics of those *bertsoak* were recorded, transcribed, and published a year later in the volume *Bapatean 97*. Twenty of the verses were created by Aguirre (Appendix 1) and sixteen by Murua (Appendix 2).

Having discussed the emphasis placed on rhythm in the *bertsolari* training method, I confess I did not count syllables to verify that each verse completes the required rhythm since errors of this type are not at all common. I take it on faith that these experienced *bertsolariak* have complied with the rhythmic demands of the melodies used for their verses. My examination of these *bertsoak* was limited to the rhyme patterns in an attempt to uncover any words or phrases that might demonstrate favoritism on the part of the performer or a tendency to repeat certain words or phrases from verse to verse.

Of the twenty verses by J. Aguirre, eleven employed the same part of speech when forming rhymes. Nouns were used in four *bertsoak*, verbs were used in three, the inessive case was used in three, and adjectives were used in one (See Figure 1). Of the sixteen verses by Murua, eight employed the same part of speech or grammatical case or element when forming rhymes. Nouns were used to make the rhymes in three *bertsoak*, verbs were used in two, the inessive case was used in two *bertsoak*, and the end of clause marker -*teko* was used in one verse (See Figure 2). Thus, out of thirty-six *bertsoak*, nineteen (or fifty-three percent) rely on the use of one part of speech or grammatical case or element in order to make the rhyme. And if we examine the *bertsoak* from the point of view of rhyming pairs, as opposed to complete verses, we find seventy-six possible rhyming pairs, and fifty of them (or sixty-six percent) match with regard to part of speech or grammatical case or element. This increases to fifty-one instances (or sixty-seven percent) if we use the final rhyme as our starting point and work up to the first rhyme in each *bertso*.

This examination of rhyme showcases the elements of *Euskara* that make versifying easier than in some other languages. Its postpositional nature means that any group of nouns can be made to rhyme, and nouns that share a single final syllable can become very strong or rich rhymes when suffixes and postposition markers are added, as seen in J. Aguirre's rhymes in *-kea*, recorded in *Bapatean 97* (1998: 44):

nekea	noun	[exhaustion + singular nominative marker}
ta kea	noun	[fervor + singular nominative marker]
trukea	noun	[exchange + singular nominative marker]
pakea	noun	[peace + singular nominative marker]

Conclusions

I did not find any favoritism with regard to specific bare words or phrases. However, there was obvious favoritism shown toward certain grammatical cases and parts of speech. In the small sample examined here, nouns, verbs, and the inessive case were the clear favorites for use in rhyming.

There was no evidence in the *bertsoak* of groups of words "bounded on either side by a natural pause," as described by Duggan, unless of course we take into account the line break after each rhyme; but this was not necessarily what Duggan intended by his description. Furthermore, in *bertsolaritza*, there are no recognizable "idea parts," no "kliches" to be manipulated into a new form, at least not in the sense defined by Radlov, Krauss or van Gennep.

Due to the nature of the Basque language, a case could be made that the postpositional structure of the language serves as an oral formulaic guide with regard to rhyme, keeping in mind that these one, two, and three syllable similarities are not what others in the field intend when they speak of oral formulas. However, an even stronger case can be made for labeling as a formula the *process* of fulfilling the rhythmic requirements of a *bertso*.

Figure 1: Use of Like Parts of Speech or Grammatical Elements in Aguirre's Rhymes

p. 44	nekea	noun
	ta kea	noun
	trukea	noun
	pakea	noun
p. 55	uzteak	noun
	besteak	noun
	ikusteak	noun

(*bertso* was six lines long, with three rhymes)

p. 55	jartzea	verbal noun
	hartzea	verbal noun
	hiltzea	verbal noun

(*bertso* was six lines long, with three rhymes)

p. 256	dana	verb used as noun
	erdibana	verb used as noun
	emana	verb used as noun
	dana	verb used as noun

p. 166	dendu	verb
	ematen du	verb
	mantendu	verb
	bazendu	verb

p. 167	datozkio	verb (with NORI)
	zaizkio	verb (with NORI)
	dizkio	verb (with NORI)
	gaizkio	verb (with NORI)

p. 256	prenda	verb
	ertenda	verb
	egoten-da	verb and causative
	izaten-da	verb and causative

p. 258	ilean	inessive
	zailean	inessive
	ipumasailean	inessive
	sailean	inessive

p. 259	azkenian	inessive
	lanian	inessive
	egonian	inessive
	zanian	inessive
p. 259	ahotan	inessive
	gehiotan	inessive
	frankotan	inessive
	galtzekotan	inessive

p. 260	bajua	adjective
	atajua	adjective
	flojua	adjective
	jua	adjective

Figure 2: Use of Like Parts of Speech or Grammatical Elements in Murua's Rhymes

p. 44	dena	noun (made from verb)
	nabarmena	noun
	sena	noun
	nintzena	noun (made from verb)
p. 82	gazteak	noun
	besteak	noun
	tristeak	noun
	uzteak	noun
p. 115	jokoak	noun
	mutikoak	noun
	mokoak	noun
	hegoak	noun
	bezelakoak	noun
p. 44	aditu	verb
	jarraitu	verb
	aurkitu	verb
	zaitu	verb
p. 83	irizten	verb
	pizten	verb
	sinisten	verb
	iristen	verb
p. 66	jaietan	inessive
	besoetan	inessive
	bertan	inessive
	ametsetan	inessive
p. 231	barrenean	inessive
	aldamenean	inessive
	gehienean	inessive
	lanean	inessive
p. 231	eusteko	end of clause marker (oración final)
	gorpuzteko	end of clause marker (oración final)
	hasteko	end of clause marker (oración final)
	aberasteko	end of clause marker (oración final)

Appendix 1: Analysis of J. Aguirre *bertsoak* from *Bapatean 97*

p. 40 rhymes in -ik (J. Agirre)

aitamenik	partitive
dut nik	pronoun
kemenik	partitive
hemendik	ablative
oraindik	adverb (based on ablative)

p. 43 rhymes in -on (J. Agirre)

dagon	verb
egon	verb
on	adjective
konpon	idiomatic expression based on verb

p. 44 rhymes in -eta, -ata (J. Agirre)

beteta	adverb
det-eta	verb and causative
aukera-ta	verb and causative
aterata	adverb

p. 44 rhymes in -kea (J. Agirre)

nekea	noun
ta kea	noun
trukea	noun
pakea	noun

p. 45 rhymes in -ela (J. Agirre)

zatozela	subordination marker
bezela	adverb
zitezela	subordination marker
bestela	adverb

p. 55 rhymes in -ztu, -xtu (J. Agirre)

ez du	verb
laztu	verb
juxtu	adverb

(*bertso* was six lines long, with three rhymes)

p. 55 rhymes in -steak, -zteak (J. Agirre)

uzteak	noun
besteak	noun
ikusteak	noun

(*bertso* was six lines long, with three rhymes)

p. 55 rhymes in -tzea (J. Agirre)

jartzea	verbal noun
hartzea	verbal noun
hiltzea	verbal noun

(*bertso* was six lines long, with three rhymes)

p. 165 rhymes in -te (J. Agirre)

daukate	verb
digute	verb
bate	adverb (shortened form of batere)
diote	verb

p. 166 rhymes in endu (J. Agirre)

dendu	verb
ematen du	verb
mantendu	verb
bazendu	verb

p. 167 rhymes in -zkio (J. Agirre)

datozkio	verb (with NORI)
zaizkio	verb (with NORI)
dizkio	verb (with NORI)
gaizkio	verb (with NORI)

p. 168 rhymes in -asua, -osua (J. Agirre)

erasua	noun
arazua	noun
peligrosua	adjective
goxua	adjective

p. 256 rhymes in -enda (J. Agirre)

prenda	verb
ertenda	verb
egoten-da	verb and causative
izaten-da	verb and causative

p. 256 rhymes in -nik (J. Agirre)

nik	pronoun
azkenik	adverb
eramanik	adverb ending
diranik	negative subordinate marker

p. 256 rhymes in -ana (J. Agirre)

dana	verb used as noun
erdibana	verb used as noun
emana	verb used as noun
dana	verb used as noun

p. 258 rhymes in -ilean (J. Agirre)

ilean	inessive
zailean	inessive
ipumasailean	inessive
sailean	inessive

p. 259 rhymes in -nian (J. Agirre)

azkenian	inessive
lanian	inessive
egonian	inessive
zanian	inessive

p. 259 rhymes in -otan (J. Agirre)

ahotan	inessive
gehiotan	inessive
frankotan	inessive
galtzekotan	inessive

p. 260 rhymes in -jua (J. Agirre)

bajua	adjective
atajua	adjective
flojua	adjective
jua	adjective

p. 260 rhymes in -ola (J. Agirre)

ajola	noun
nagola	verb and subordinate marker
zegola	verb and subordinate marker
odola	noun

Apendix 2: Analysis of Murua *bertsoak* from *Bapatean 97*

p. 44 rhymes in -ena (Murua)

dena	noun (made from verb)
nabarmena	noun
sena	noun
nintzena	noun (made from verb)

p. 44 rhymes in -itu (Murua)

aditu	verb
jarraitu	verb
aurkitu	verb
zaitu	verb

p. 45 rhymes in assonance A / E (Murua)

jotake	adverb
kalte	adverb
aparte	adverb
didate	verb

p. 45 rhymes in -ana (Murua)

emana	noun (made from verb)
laztana	adjective
lana	noun
dijoana	noun (made from verb)

p. 65 rhymes in -ela (Murua)

nobela	noun
epela	noun
papela	noun
nauela	verb with subordinate marker

p. 66 rhymes in -etan (with one weak -tan) (Murua)

jaietan	inessive
besoetan	inessive
bertan	inessive
ametsetan	inessive

p. 66 rhymes in -ira (Murua)

dirdira	noun
Gabirira	allative
dira	verb
begira	noun

p. 82 rhymes in -steak/-zteak (Murua)

gazteak	noun
besteak	noun
tristeak	noun
uzteak	noun

p. 82 rhymes in -ina (Murua)

adina	noun
imajina	noun
sorgina	noun
bagina	verb

p. 83 rhymes in -izten / -isten (Murua)

irizten	verb
pizten	verb
sinisten	verb
iristen	verb

p. 115 rhymes in -oak (-koak / -goak) (Murua)

jokoak	noun
mutikoak	noun
mokoak	noun
hegoak	noun
bezelakoak	noun

p. 116 rhymes in -ori (Murua)

zori	noun
erori	verb
tori	verb
txori	noun
hori	pronoun

p. 116 rhymes in -ala (Murua)

makala	adjective
tamala	adverb
hegala	noun
berehala	adverb
gerala	verb and subordinate marker

p. 231 rhymes in -nean (Murua)

barrenean	inessive
aldamenean	inessive
gehienean	inessive
lanean	inessive

p. 231 rhymes in -steko (Murua)

eusteko	end of clause marker (oración final)
gorpuzteko	end of clause marker (oración final)
hasteko	end of clause marker (oración final)
aberasteko	end of clause marker (oración final)

p. 232 rhymes assonant a/o and -ago (Murua)

akabo	adverb
oparo	adverb
sakonago	comparative
dago	verb

A Theoretical Framework for Improvised *Bertsolaritza*[1]

Joxerra Garzia

Introduction

To date, and almost without exception, *bertsolaritza* has been considered a sub-genre of Basque popular literature. However, the term "Basque popular literature" is a form of pigeon-holing anything that does not fit into the classification of written literature. Basque popular literature is thus identified by the heterogeneity of genres and expressions which it displays.

As regards the heterogeneity of artistic work, the level of orality in Basque popular literature varies greatly from one manifestation to another. The fact that Basque popular literature is "essentially oral" clearly does not, however, mean that only oral literature is popular. In colloquial use, both meanings are often interchangeable. Even Juan Mari Lekuona, one of the principal figures in the study of the subject, called his work the "Classification of Basque Oral Literature." It is clear, however, given that their production and reception are in written form, genres such as popular novels or autobiographies are only oral in regard to the communicative strategies used; that is, in their structure. There are also written manifestations which are produced orally: street theatre, *pastorales*, probably many pieces of ornamental poetry and, of course, nearly all anthologies of both traditional and modern songs. There is also great heterogeneity in the aesthetic meaning (literary, artistic) among all the manifestations of Basque popular literature. Idioms and, to a great extent, proverbs, also derive solely and exclusively from the linguistic competence of the speakers, without any conscious awareness of their aesthetic value.

Given such a heterogeneous panorama, it is clearly almost impossible to establish a single valid method of analysis for all manifestations of Basque popular literature. Yet there is a need to draw up a suitable theoretical framework as the methodologies in use

---

1. An earlier version of this article appears as Section IV in Garzia, Sarasua and Egaña (2001).

are plainly inadequate in explaining so specific a phenomenon as the improvised oral art of the *bertsolariak*. It was this inability of current theories to describe, in a thorough manner, the reality of improvised *bertsolaritza* which persuaded us to draw up a theoretical framework, rather than any predilection for a specific theoretical school. Consequently, our book (Garzia, Sarasua and Egaña 2001) attempts to provide a thorough explanation of improvised *bertsolaritza* and a first step to drawing up a suitable method for its analysis, given the fact that current analytical models are so inadequate in explaining its extemporary nature.[2] And this is precisely why we do not analyze non-improvised *bertsolaritza*; not because we consider this unimportant, but rather, because we believe it to be a radically different genre and, as such, requiring another analytical method.

However it may have come about, the reality is that, throughout the twentieth century, *bertsolaritza* underwent a progressive and radical change. Although the name remained the same, *bertsolaritza*, at the beginning of the twentieth century, had little to do with that at the end. And far from being a superficial change, the transformation affected practically every aspect of the artistic activity. To cite one such change, written *bertsolaritza* (the most important format at the beginning of the century) gradually ceded primacy to the improvised form. Thus, at the end of the century, it was the person improvising their *bertsoak* before the public that was seen as the true *bertsolari*.

In the aforementioned work, then, we propose a new theoretical framework, which will allow us –we trust– to analyze and research this phenomenon of improvised *bertsolaritza* in a more suitable manner. That said, the novelty of the theoretical framework we suggest is relative, as it fundamentally deals with an adaptation of the canons of classical rhetoric, up-dated with the hindsight of different contemporary pragmatic approaches. Its novelty is, therefore, not so much in the theoretical framework in itself, but more in its application to a phenomenon, which, to date, has been exclusively studied from the perspective of written poetry.[3]

The Dead-End Analysis of Oral Art in Terms of Written Poetics

In studies of *bertsolaritza*, it is not difficult to find references to the specificity of the art form, especially regarding its oral and improvised character. Despite these and other statements, what tends to happen in such studies, according to Rainer Friedrich's criticism (and quoting Albert Lord in reference to Homeric rhetoric) is that,

> after proclaiming their belief in the oral Homer, Homerists would proceed to interpret Homer applying the canon of traditional literary criticism. This prompted Lord to warn

---

2. On the lack of accuracy in the current frameworks and the need of "rethinking some of our most basic assumptions about poetic communication," among more recent works, see Foley (2002), Raible (1996), and Díaz Pimienta (1998). See also Lord (1960), Finnegan (1977; rpt. 1992) and Ong (1982).

3. For excellent attempts that employ this approach, see esp. Foley (2002) on Tibetan Paper-Singers, North American Slam Poets, South African Praise-poets, the South Slavic oral epic, and improvised poetry in the Hispanic tradition (Díaz Pimienta 1998).

that unless Homerists were willing "to understand oral poetics" and "learn from the experience of other oral traditional poetries . . . . *oral* is only an empty label and *traditionally* devoid of sense. Together they form merely a façade behind which scholarship can continue to apply the poetics of written literature (1991: 22).

Effectively, despite abundant statements to the effect that the oral and improvised character of *bertsolaritza* is important, the fact is that most studies of the subject have been carried out from the perspective of the theory of written poetics. And the result is always the same: the improvised *bertso* is rarely deemed to be of artistic value and consequently the majority of improvised *bertsoak* are, judged from the viewpoint of written poetry, seen to be of a low poetic level.

Text as a Pretext

The most radical posture in this respect is that of Matías Mujika, who, in a libel (as he himself terms it), which appeared on the internet in the fall of 1997, uses just one *bertso* to trash Basque culture as a whole. Mujika starts, with no explanation, by introducing the *bertso* in question (or more precisely, its translation into Spanish):

Una paloma blanca se me ha acercado	A white dove came to me
esta mañana al amanecer.	this morning at dawn.
¡Qué alegría me han producido,	What joy these words
queridos señores, sus palabras!	gave me, dear sirs!
Y yo ahora estoy ante ustedes	And now I stand before you
lleno de contento.	full of happiness.
Lo primero, buenos oyentes,	Firstly, dear listeners,
buenos días a todos de corazón.	good day to you.

This suffices to justify a general denigration of *bertsolaritza* as a whole and, by association, all Basque literary work and culture. In conclusion Mujika claims it is impossible that pieces of this nature could, in any way, arouse esthetic pleasure: "fundamental, physiological, direct and honest joy does not exist. It is pure pantomime."

Mujika's position may seem extreme, but it is in no way unusual, and reflects a general tendency to judge and analyze works of oral art within the parameters of written culture. Thus by ignoring oralists' contributions, the theory of speaking performance, pragmatics and the new rhetoric that has analyzed oral communication, one can easily come to the same conclusion as Mujika did. Indeed, if one demands of the improvised *bertso* something that it does not pretend to be or to have, the result can hardly be otherwise. However, by exploring beyond the limits imposed by relying on an analysis from the perspective of written culture alone, one can find improvised *bertsoak*, which, poetically, do have poetic quality. I am, however, straying from the point and, in any case, most improvised *bertsoak* do not stand up to such a test.

For example, returning to the *bertso* quoted by Mujika, one must recognize, that, poetically speaking, it is nothing special. According to the principal axiom of written poetry, any text capable of producing poetic emotion in the recipient must have poetic value in the text (namely, it is a text that encompasses some intensity of poetic-rhetorical resources). If we accept this axiom and apply it to improvised oral *bertsolaritza*, one can only conclude that Mujika's observation is accurate. However, to deduce that the "fundamental, physiological, direct and honest joy" that this *bertso* arouses is a "pantomime" implies a great leap of logic. And Mujika's theory is clearly unable fully to explain the emotion the text might have produced. I, on the other hand, having passionately perceived –and continued to perceive– the emotion that similar *bertso* texts have produced, can only conclude that the theory of poetics is inadequate for the analysis of improvised *bertsolaritza*.

The analysis of improvised *bertsolaritza* from the perspective of written literature and poetic theory has two main consequences: It reduces the improvised *bertso* to mere text; that is, it ignores the prosodic, paralinguistic, extra-linguistic and musical aspects of the pieces in play in a *bertso*, uprooting it from the *context* in which and for which it was created, while not considering the *bertso* as a whole. And it adulterates the very purpose of improvised *bertso*, judging it from a perspective of literary beauty which the improviser does not pretend to achieve. The aim of the improvising *bertsolari* is not necessarily to produce texts of grand poetic quality, although, if this does occur, the satisfaction is double.

What, then, are the objectives which *bertsolariak* set for themselves? Jon Sarasua has made it quite clear. For him, the questions are: how do you approach the performance, where do you start from, how do you surprise the listeners, where are you going, how do you perceive the world of your listeners and what do you have to do to reach them? To this end, you do not have to sing collected *bertsoak*; it is the performance as a whole that matters (see Garzia 1998).

The Text in Context: Co-Text and Situation

There is nothing strange in this statement. After all, the essential peculiarity of improvised *bertsolaritza* lies in the fact that the construction of *bertsoak* –their emission and their reception– are carried out at the same time, in a place which is physically shared between oral artist and audience. The text, which in written literature is practically the only link between creator and recipient, is but one more element that *bertsolariak* have at their disposal in order to achieve the end-result of inducing emotion among the listeners. Indeed, the importance of the text in improvised *bertsolaritza* is inversely proportional to the degree of cohesion of the context shared between *bertsolari* and audience.

The different textual strategies have been meticulously identified, analyzed and catalogued. However, non-textual elements (which are of such importance in improvisation) have been very little studied to date, at least in the analysis of improvised *bertsolaritza*. Here the imbalance is clear; namely, the concept of "context," in which the totality of all non-textual elements of the *bertso* is included, turns out to be too generic to be applied.

Thus, given the aforementioned concerns, one might now introduce some methodological pointers which will allow a better definition of the analysis. Here the word "text" is used to designate the transcribable part of the *bertso*, although in doing so, one must discard other accepted definitions in fields such as the Text Sciences. Moreover, here "context" is understood as the totality of non-textual elements which improvised *bertsolaritza* involves. Finally, I differentiate, within this context, two components: the "co-text" and the "situation," which can be described in the following manner:[4]

CONTEXT

Co-Text	**Situation**
Bertso	Performance
Intervention	Place, date
Performance	Motive
Corpus of *bertsoak*	Participants:
Shared references	Presenter
(values, beliefs)	*Bertsolariak*
	Public
	Listeners

The contextual factors (both co-textual and situational) are a prime source of resources for the improvising *bertsolari*. Therefore to exclude or minimize these factors is to misunderstand the very nature of the object one is trying to analyze. Indeed, contextual elements are crucial in any communicative act and indeed they are even in those formats where transmitter and recipient are more distant in time and space (as in written literature, for example). The difference with improvised *bertsolaritza*, however, is in the concentration of these factors. Unlike other communication types, transmitter and recipient form part of the situation; in other words, they are immersed in it. A performance is unrepeatable and allusions to the different situational elements only strengthen the bond between *bertsolari* and listeners, creating positive feed-back for the artist.

a) Co-textual factors

The level of cohesion in the co-text is a key factor in the creation of an improvised *bertso* and this is how, as will be seen, good criteria can be established for the suitable periodization of improvised *bertsolaritza*. Unlike in the case of the situation, the level with which the *bertsolari* and the audience enjoy a shared context changes according to a number of historical, social, cultural and educational variables. In specific socio-historical circumstances the (unshared) totality of values and references of the *bertsolari* and the listener tend to be insignificant. In such cases, then, the (shared) referential worlds of the *bertsolari* and the audience almost totally coincide. One might term this homogenous-context *bertsolaritza*. At the other extreme, however, there are occasions in which shared references are much less. In such cases one might then talk about heterogeneous-context *bertsolaritza*. In general, the more homogenous the co-text, the less text the *bertsolari* needs in order to arouse emotion in her/his audience:

---

4. For a more detailed exposition of this and other aspects of the theoretical framework, see Garzia (2000a).

When the public is homogenous, it is much easier to improvise *bertsoak*, at least in a certain sense. What this is saying is that there are strongly shared feelings, and it is sufficient for just one of these to touch the heart and/or the soul of the people. The *bertso* has many elements, some merely technical, such as meter and rhyme. But, in the final analysis, what is important is sparking emotions. And emotions can be aroused with the mere mention of a feeling that you know is strongly shared; you do not need any elaborate devices to achieve your aim (Jon Sarasua, qtd. in Garzia 1998: 50).

The principal factors that determine the level of homogeneity or contextual cohesion are (1) The socio-political-cultural situation: Limiting ourselves to the recent history of *bertsolaritza*, it is clear (and a number of *bertsolariak* have repeatedly pointed this out) that during Franco's dictatorship the collective nature of *bertsolaritza* (*bertsolariak*, the public and others) was strongly cohesive, unlike the case today. In this sense it is often said that, "improvising *bertsoak* in Franco's time was easier –or cozier– than it is today"; (2) The size of the audience: To put it simply, the greater the number of people present, the more homogeneity; and (3) The level of academic education of both the *bertsolariak* and their public: The greater the educational level, the greater the variety of references and, consequently, there is less homogeneity.

These are not, of course, fixed, immutable factors. This is what Jon Sarasua means when he compares *bertsolaritza* under the dictatorship with the present:

What has happened to our current *bertsolariak*? Well, that homogeneity of *bertsolaritza*'s public has been broken and not only because the historical circumstances have changed. Due to our determination and efforts to renew *bertsolaritza*, many new people have entered its world. Our public is more pluralistic than ever. Among our listeners there are political nuances to suit all tastes; there are young and old listeners; there are university graduates; people from the country and from the city . . . . We now have a public or, rather, several publics. Before, we did not. Before, *bertsolariak* improvised for the people (Sarasua, qtd. in Garzia 1998: 50).

Taking into account that improvised *bertsolaritza* prior to 1960 was reduced to anecdotes and a few *bertsoak*, one might regard everything which happened before this date as the *prehistory* of improvised *bertsolaritza*. Thereafter, from 1960 onwards and within the *history* of *bertsolaritza*, one can distinguish two great periods:

(i) Homogeneous co-text bertsolaritza *(1960–1979)*: Specifically, the *bertsolaritza* of survival (1960–1973), with Basarri (Ignacio Eizmendi) and Uztapide (Manuel Olaizola) as the principal references, and the *bertsolaritza* of resistance (1973–1979), with Jon Lopategi and Jon Azpillaga as the prime exponents. Other famous *bertsolariak* of this time included Lazkao Txiki (José Miguel Iztueta), Xalbador (Fernando Aire), Manuel Lasarte, Joxe Lizaso, Joxe Agirre, Imanol Lazkano, Joaquín Mitxelena, José Luis Gorrotxategi, Mattin (Mattin Treku), Txomin Garmendia and Mikel Arozamena, among others.

(ii) Heterogeneos co-text bertsolaritza *(1980–2000)*: Specifically, the *bertsolaritza* of renewal (1980–1990), with Xabier Amuriza as its chief exponent. The *bertsolariak* of the previous period still had a role to play, but, with the change encouraged by Amuriza, a new

generation of oral improvisational artists emerged in the Basque Country to lead the next phase: the recent *bertsomania* phase (1991–1998). With the generation led by Andoni Egaña, *bertsolaritza* broke into the communication media, particularly television, creating previously unthinkable audience levels. Other notable *bertsolariak* included Sebastian Lizaso, Anjel Mari Peñagarikano, Jon Sarasua, and Euzkitze (Xabier Pérez); and now we have multipolar *bertsolaritza* (1998– ?). The presence of women among the elite of *bertsolaritza* now is normal. Maialen Lujanbio, Igor Elortza, Unai Iturriaga and Jesus Mari Irazu are the most notable names of the new generation, the evolution of whom is yet to be seen.

Even taking into account these different periods, each one represents a differentiated type of *bertsolaritza*, if only because both the homogeneity of the co-text, as well as the kind of *bertsolaritza* that each period developed, have to be considered as poles along a single continuum which can be represented in the following manner:

Table 1: *Bertsolaritza* according to homogeneity of co-text

Homogeneous co-text	Heterogeneous co-text
– Abundance of values and references, strongly & intimately shared	– Scarcity of values and references, strongly & intimately shared
– Possibility of inducing emotion on mere mention of references	– Difficulty in inducing emotion on mere mention of references
– The audience is perceived as "The People"	– The audience as the audience: Diversified public
– Relative importance of the text:	
– Few textual resources	– Greater textual intensity:
– Short *bertsoak*	– Greater textual intensity
– Formulaic style	– Long *bertsoak*
– Synthetic *bertsolaritza*, not analytical: Absence of distancing.	– Relativization of the formulae
	– Analytical-critical *bertsolaritza*: Distancing.

A good example of homogenous-context *bertsolaritza* is the *bertso* improvised in the 1962 championship by Uztapide (the champion *bertsolari* in 1962, 1965 and 1967). The topic of his performance, given him by the organizers, was "mother." This was his first *bertso* (*Bertsolari Txapelketa 1962–XII–30* 1963: 145):

Hauxe da lan polita	Nice theme here
orain neregana	given to me now
alboko lagunendik	from my companion
etorri zaidana.	it has come.
Bertsoak bota behar	We have to sing
dira hiru bana	three *bertsoak* each,

Estitxu Arozena, Estitxu Fernandez and Amaia Telletxea, Young *Bertsolari* Day, Bera, Basque Country, 1993. One of the principal changes to have taken place in contemporary *bertsolaritza* is the increasing presence of women. By permission of the Xenpelar Dokumentazio Zentroa, Donostia.

hortan emango nuke	about this I could say
nik nahitasun dana:	anything I wanted:
beste ze-esanik ez da	but there's nothing left to say
esatian "ama."	on saying "mother."

Clearly, the mere text itself would not easily excite anybody; nor would the *bertso*-poem, sung in its entirety to the audience, if it had not been for the fact that "mother" was one of the values most strongly shared by the *bertsolari* and the listeners. In fact, this was a tremendously important archetype in the Basque popular imagination. In reality, Uztapide only had to mention the theme imposed and he would generate shared pathos with the audience. As can be seen, he used the remaining syllables to refer to various elements in the communicational situation. The mother about whom Uztapide was singing was any mother, "mother" as an archetype and a value strongly shared by all there present. Nowadays, however, no *bertsolari* would dare use the strategy that Uztapide used. Yet does this mean that we can discredit the *bertso* or dismiss the emotion produced that day as pantomime or farce? For a more sophisticated *bertso* text would not have produced such emotion. As such, this was an excellent *bertso*, even though, according to the protocols of the theory of written poetry, it might not appear so.

Let us now consider a similar theme, but within the heterogeneous co-text. In the 1980 championship, the topic "father" was presented to Xabier Amuriza, considered by many to be the father of current *bertsolaritza* (*Bertsolari Txapelketa Nagusia (Donostia, 1980-1-6)* 1980: 141):

Aita izena kanta beharrak	On having to sing the name of my father,
jarri dit bihotza bero,	my heart burned,
aukera eder hau izango zenik	this fine opportunity never
ez nuen asko espero;	occurred to me before;
preso nengoen Zamoran eta	when I was a prisoner in Zamora
han gelditu ia ero,	almost driven crazy,
joan nintzen ta bertan nengola	there I was
aita hil zitzaidan gero,	when my own father died,
nahiago nuke edozer baino	there's nothing I would wish for more
hemen bizirik balego.	than to have him here alive.

And that was just how it happened: Amuriza's father had died while the *bertsolari* was in the Zamora penitentiary. But that was not all. Amuriza knew perfectly well that to spark the emotions of his audience, the mere mention of the word, "father" was not sufficient. Something more was needed and this extra quality implied more rhetorical elaboration. In the first place, he discarded the idea of the archetype and presented his own father. This kind of thinking (or greater rhetorical elaboration) requires a *bertso* which is more ample (*hamarreko handia*) and the melody is also a rhetorical resource. Amuriza had composed his own airs and he employed one of these, the one that he knew would best fit the register in which he wished to perform.

In the second *bertso*, perhaps the best in the series, he addressed more deeply the figure of his father, declaring that his relationship with him went beyond that of merely father and son. For his father was also his teacher, instilling in him a love for *bertsolaritza*. In this way, Amuriza united his personal and sentimental past with the present improvisation, both in place and in time (*Bertsolari Txapelketa Nagusia (Donostia, 1980-1-6)* 1980: 141):

Aita nuen nik umoretsua,	I had a father with a great sense of humor
inoiz geza ta gazia,	never sad or bitter,
harek agertu zidan bidea	he showed me the way
baitzen bertsoz ikasia;	as he knew about *bertsolaritza*;
oi, nere aita, nire egunak	oh, dear father, my days
ere aurrera doaz ia,	are catching up on me too,
baina zugandik hartua baitut	but given my debt to you
bertsotarako grazia,	for my *bertso* skills
nik egingo dut arbola haundi	I will make a great tree
zuk emandako hazia.	from the seed you gave me.

In the third and final *bertso* the formulaic strategy reappeared. Although it was directed at his father, he also directly involved the listeners, inviting them to applaud him. The
principal strategy of the *bertso* was thus its direct connection to the situation of the session
(*Bertsolari Txapelketa Nagusia (Donostia, 1980–1–6)* 1980: 141):

Gai hau kolpera jarriko zenik	As I have touched on this theme
ia ametsa dirudi;	it's almost like a dream;
baserri hartan izan genduen	in that farmhouse we lived
hainbat harri eta euria;	so much hail and rain;
zu, aita, zinen hain on niretzat,	you, father, who were so good to me,
ez gogorra, baizik guri;	not hard, but soft;
Euskalerria nola dagoen	now that the Basque Country
orain Donostin ageri,	is here in Donostia [San Sebastián]
niri jotako txalo guztiak	all the applause I'm getting
bidaltzen dizkizut zuri.	I send to you.

Another of Amuriza's great skills is apparent in this last *bertso*: namely, his capacity
for drama and masterly weaving together of the context in which the performance was
taking place, together with the fiction he was improvising on the spot. Who would the
public applaud at the end of the session? The *bertsolari*? His father? Both? This moment
was, whichever the case, one of the most emotional of the whole final. This last *bertso* was,
however, the weakest (from a mere textual viewpoint) of the three. Regarding rhetorical
strategy, however, though not the best, it was the most effective.

As can be seen both in the case of Uztapide, with the mother theme, and that of
Amuriza, with the father topic, they handled the same elements: text, co-text, and situation. What differed was the management of these elements and the relative importance
given to them in the improvised communication as a whole.

It should be remembered, however, that the situational cohesion can, whatever the historical situation may be, re-establish the communicative homogeneity. Even when Basque
society was suffering from severe social divisions (during the last decade of the twentieth
century), and when politico-ideological confrontation was clearly reflected among *bertsolaritza* audiences (including among the *bertsolariak* themselves), those performances that were
most free and informal (without presenter, prompts or a specific public) were the ones
which did not need texts of great poetic intensity. It was enough to mention or point out,
at an opportune moment, the situational elements in order to arouse the desired emotional
reaction among the listeners.

Improvised *bertsoak* at these kinds of events are not easily transplantable to the mass
media, as they are then stripped of the situational references from which their powerful
communicative elements and emotions originate. With a few exceptions, they are thus
totally anodyne (re)productions for those perceiving the event, through the communication medium and outside the situation in which and for which the *bertsoak* were created in
the first place. Even though a television show can go some way to recreating the atmos-
phere of *bertsolaritza* by showing images of *bertsolariak* making fun of, for example, a well-

Xabier Amuriza, performing at the 1983 Day of the *Bertsolari*, Donostia, Basque Country. Amuriza was the most influential *bertsolari* of his generation, and is considered by many to be the father of contemporary *bertsolaritza*. By permission of *Sendoa*.

known Basque chef, the viewer will find it very difficult to share in the *bertso*'s hilarity originally produced at the live event. And it is this shared emotion, during a live event, between oral artist and listeners under the same roof, which can never be replicated by a video or other means of recording.

I should say in passing that the tendency –in one way natural and understandable– for the media to prioritize those *bertsoak* with greater textual punch results in a certain distortion. The TV soccer viewer, used to seeing repetitions of the best moments of play in matches, may become bored in the stadium itself because of a lack of intensity in the game. In the same way, "second hand listeners" (those who hear *bertsoak* on the radio or TV) expect and demand a high level of intensity (and textual excellence) from each *bertso* performed. Most probably, on attending *bertsolaritza* in person such listeners would be frustrated, particularly if the performance were a free or post-prandial event.

Although it is not a sufficiently analyzed theme, the nature of the discursive unit of each *bertso* appears to wane considerably in these kinds of events. Not having a pre-determined number of *bertsoak* to improvise to, the *bertsolari* tends to go for a longer discursive unit, often sacrificing the strength of each improvised piece. Even so, as has been said before, the mode of production involved in the improvised *bertso* is such that it always conserves the character of the discursive unit that the *bertsolari* has had to construct. Underlining the central importance of the situational elements in the most informal formats of *bertsolaritza* performance does not reduce the importance that these have in the other performances. The *bertsoak* of Uztapide and Amuriza cited above were improvised in the most formal of existing formats (the championships) but which, as has been observed, are full of referential situations. As in almost all communication, the situational cohesion works as a continuum.

Taking those criteria of assessment for improvised *bertsoak* used by the juries in championships, one can only conclude that the use of situational strategies by *bertsolariak* in championships is indicative of poor creativity. The *bertsolari*, as they say, has to "stick to" the topic on which it has been her or his luck to improvise, and to develop it with cohesion and coherence. Everything else is to "get away from the point." This perspective, which fortunately appears to have been amended in the assessment criteria drawn up for the 2001 championship, reflects clearly the extent to which written poetry has been the predominant framework for analysis in improvised *bertsolaritza*. Indeed, "sticking to the point" is nothing more than "sticking to the mere text" and situational references, rather than "getting off the point" ("getting off the text"), which is only a punishable offence for those who consider improvised *bertsolaritza* from the reductionist perspective of written poetry.

There are certainly people who claim that Uztapide's *bertso* on the mother was one of scant value, given that, as we have seen, his principal argument was the cut and dried mention of the imposed theme; and that the discursive development to get to that point was no more than an accumulation of situational references. In other words, Uztapide did not develop the topic. It goes without saying that I do not share this view. In improvised *bertsolaritza*, the situational references, if pertinent and efficacious, have the same category and value as textual arguments.

Uztapide improvised that *bertso* in the 1962 championship, and thirty years later, the polemic resurfaced. In the 1997 championship, Unai Iturriaga and Jon Maia (both young men) verbally dueled in an improvised oral confrontation (*hamarreko txikia*) over the following theme: "You are two girls and you have always been very close in friendship. Now, you are beginning to realize that yours is something more than just being good friends."

Iturriaga opened the confrontation, making it clear that he was going to treat the topic with total normality (*Bertsolari Txapelketa Nagusia 97* 1998: 279):

Eskolatik batera	Together to school
gabiltz pausuz-pausu,	we always went,
toki beretan topo	in the same places
egin dugu usu.	we often ran into one another.
Baina zerbait arraro	But something strange
darabilgu, aizu!	is happening to us, hey!
Lagun gisa gehiago	Just as a friend,
neri ez eman musu,	don't kiss me any more,
titi-muturrak tente	you make my nipples
jartzen dizkidazu.	stand up erect.

On hearing this, there were murmurs and giggles from the audience. Some (though not most) had reacted to the theme as a joke. It was then the turn of Maia (*Bertsolari Txapelketa Nagusia 97* 1998: 279):

Batetik muxua ta	A kiss here,
bestetik fereka,	a caress there,
berotzen ari gara	we're working ourselves up
gu biok uneka:	very quickly:
ni ez naiz harrituko	I'm not surprised by it,
normala da eta.	because it's perfectly normal.
Gaia esandakoan	Just the mention of the topic
hara zer iseka!	and you people jeered!
Ez dakit zertan hasi	I really don't see
zareten barreka!	what the fuss is all about!

This provoked a serious reaction from the public, some of whom declared that it deserved punishment from the jury, as it had strayed from the theme. Part of the jury thought the same and Maia got 17.5 points compared to 20 for Iturriaga's *bertso*. It goes without saying that I do not agree at all. In my opinion, Maia's situational "happening" (the audience's reaction to the original *bertso*) was at least as brilliant as Iturriaga's textual "happening" (with his reference to nipples). The text, I would contend, is but one of the elements the *bertsolari* has at her/his disposal in carrying out the labor of rhetoric, and denying the improviser the possibility of exploiting the situational elements is to transform radically the very nature of *bertsolaritza*.

Lately, a species of "specialized" events have been organized; events with a plot or monographic performances (for example, erotica, black humor, alternative youth culture, or rockers). This kind of performance is usually organized by younger *bertsolariak* in smaller premises and with a select public. Although it is a recent phenomenon, I believe that behind such initiatives is a desire by the *bertsolariak* to develop themes and styles for a wider, more heterogeneous public.

Enchantment by, but a Lack of Charm in, Oralist Theory

I mentioned above that when *bertsolaritza* is analyzed, its oral character is often ignored. Here I have tried to demonstrate how this kind of (less rigorous) approach results in misinterpretation. Given the inability of written poetry to describe *bertsolaritza*, some analysts have thus tried to invoke oralist theory as the only valid method for its analysis. By "oralist theory" here, I understand the general research derived directly or indirectly from Homeric studies, the origin of which goes back to 1928 and the work of Milman Parry. Oralist approaches (in more or less orthodox fashion) have subsequently counted on the support of scholars from a wide range of disciplines, the most outstanding of which being Adam Parry, Lord, Notopoulos, Havelock, Ong, Zumthor, Finnegan and Foley. Regarding studies of Basque popular literature, the most direct and influential reference is undoubtedly Walter J. Ong, whose work has been repeatedly quoted and paraphrased by almost all scholars. Next to Ong, and also from the French anthropological tradition, Marcel Jousse enjoys great standing, particularly through Ives Beaupérin, a disciple of the great French anthropologist.

The enchantment induced by oralist theory for anyone, who, coming from a written tradition, discovers it for the first time is understandable. This discovery is also essential and beneficial in that it illustrates the existence and differentiated character of orality. Beyond this discovery, however, orality theory is an insufficient instrument in our research for several reasons, some of which I will now address.

In the first place, and as several authors have shown, the opposition between orality and writing is not as radical as oralist theorists would have it: "The differences between oral and literate expression, although considerable, are not so profound as is widely assumed" (Kirk 1976: 69). Indeed, "there is no clear-cut line between oral and written literature, and when one tries to differentiate between them –as has often been attempted– it becomes clear that there are constants overlaps" (Finnegan 1977; rpt. 1992: 2). From my research in improvised *bertsolaritza*, I can only endorse this idea. Orality and writing are not two mutually exclusive realities, as the oralists would have it. Rather, they live together, at least in modern societies, in continuous interaction.

The presentation of orality and writing as a black and white duality is inadequate when one subjects an object to concrete study. As Scheunemann (1996: 81) points out:

> The construction –primary orality, written and print culture, secondary orality– takes on an almost biblical configuration. I am afraid, that –apart from the narrow focus of the description of the age of secondary orality– it is precisely this configuration which causes particular weaknesses in the formula.

Apart from this quasi-biblical character of the oralist theory in general, it should also be pointed out that its application to different manifestations of oral literature has been carried out many times without reference to the specificity of each one:

> So we encounter concepts of orality and literacy which have been worked out in *too rigid a fashion* and polarized in the form of ideal types which inevitably adds to the despair of everyone who tries to apply the set of categories to any concrete work or area of study. There is also no doubt that the qualities and effects ascribed to the different modes of cultural expression –whether the wisdom of the storyteller in oral cultures or the emergence of individualism and nationalism as a consequence of writing– very often remain global assumptions lacking contextual investigation which might disclose the range of other factors which, along with dominant communicative forms, give shape to cultural study (Scheunemann 1996: 81).

Effectively, the theory of orality, at least in the canonical formulations of Notopoulos and Ong, establishes a radical distinction between the oral and written modes of production. One can, then, argue that, as a consequence of oral thinking or the mental process deriving thereof, oral expressions are necessarily:

- Accumulative rather than subordinate
- Accumulative rather than analytical
- Superfluous or verbose
- Conservative and traditionalist
- Close to the essence of the human world
- Tones of anguish
- Empathetic and participatory rather than objectively distant
- Homeostatic
- Situational rather than abstract

If one were to try, as I have done, to see how these nine features are reflected in current improvised *bertsolaritza*, one would soon give up: effectively, one would come to the same conclusion G.S. Kirk found in Homer; namely, that "the oral epic, at least at the unmatched level of Homer, can display some of the supposedly distinctive subtleties of written poetry" (1976: 69). Therefore, if in the previous section the relevance of oral strategies in certain written texts was highlighted, here we see some oral texts that can be ascribed a similar subtlety to that of written poetry. This, evidently, does not mean that the achievement of such subtlety is the be-all and end-all of oral literature. Rather, it just means that one cannot discard out of hand the possibility that such poetic excellence might be expressed in oral texts; a feasibility rejected, it would seem, by oral theorists.

When written poetics criteria are applied to oral literature, written poetry is, Notopoulos denounces, a kind of Procustean bed in which oral literature rarely comes up to scratch. At the other extreme, strictly applied oral theory turns out to be too small a bed. This is what happens, according to Rainer Friedrich (1991: 24), when oral theory is applied to Homeric art: "Here it is well to remember that the notorious Procustes was the happy owner of two beds. Could it be that an oral poetics, when applied to the Homeric epic, has the effect of Procustes' short bed?"

The same thing happens, I believe (although for different reasons) when one uses oralist theory as the only instrument for analyzing *bertsolaritza*, at least for current improvised *bertsolaritza*. Here space precludes examining the extent to which each and every one of the characteristics which Ong attributes to oral expression actually comes up to (his) expectations. I can only say that, taking it to its ultimate consequences, oralist theory presents a reductionist perspective of improvised *bertsolaritza*. Why is this so? Some of the reasons include:

a) Formulas in present-day *bertsolaritza*

Improvised *bertsolaritza* is no longer "accumulative rather than analytical." According to Ong the accumulative, rather than analytical, character of oral expression stems from the creation of texts based on a formulaic procedure; namely, according to oralist theory, the oral poet composes her/his pieces based on pre-designed units which Ong refers to as "formulae" and Parry (1932: 31) as, "a group of words which is regularly employed under the same metrical conditions to express a given essential idea." Obviously the improvising *bertsolari* manipulates previously created units to fit into a given metrical structure. Jon Sarasua, for example, has acknowledged this, although he does not use the expression "formula," but the more metaphorical "snippets." Whatever the case, the contemporary *bertsolari* does not have a repertory of closed formulae, given that the variety of themes covered makes such a repertory unfeasible. In fact, using a repertory of formulae is only relevant when the communicative situation is archetypal (*bertsoak* of greetings or funeral rites, for example) or the theme or role is imposed.

As explained elsewhere (Garzia, Sarasua and Egaña 2001: 62–65), the themes or roles that *bertsolariak* have to deal with are not at all archetypal. The fundamental thing about *bertsolariak* is not their formulaic repertory, then, but rather their capacity to continually create new formulae; for example, the ability to fit any cognitive content, however new or complex, within the most common metrical structures, currently those of 5–5/8 syllables and 7/6. Part of this work may be carried out prior to the improvisation, but it is mostly done by means of improvisation (See Garzia, Sarasua and Egaña 2001: 81–133).

Understood like this, the formulaic nature of *bertsolaritza* does not, in any way, impede its analysis and, in fact, aids it. In reality, the task of the improvising *bertsolari* is basically one of a double formulaic skill. On the one hand, one has to be able to improvise convincing and suitable formulae as one goes along. Secondly, the *bertsolari* has to manage astutely the rhetoric of the formulae that have been previously mentally constructed. The prior and conscious construction of formulae to be used seconds or minutes later in sung improvisation is, perhaps, one of the distinguishing aspects of current *bertsolaritza*, with respect to that practiced in the past. Another is the rhetorical use the modern *bertsolari* makes of these more-or-less pre-constructed formulae.

As regards this last aspect, as in so many others, the case of Xabier Amuriza is paradigmatic. Far from using formulae as mere technique to help express platitudinous situations or values, Amuriza charges them with a great sense of poetry and rhetoric. As such, the formulae acquire great communicative importance in the *bertsoak* and are used to reinforce ideas and content which are in no way platitudinous or commonplace. His solo performances, when the event is totally, as it were, under his control, are as a result outstanding. In the 1980 championship final, when it was his luck to have the theme "*bihotzean min dut*" ("my heart aches"), Amuriza improvised three *bertsoak*, the first two of which I reproduce below.

We have seen how *bertsolariak* are accustomed to placing the key of their rhetorical strategy, the most coherent reason they have been able to think up, at the very end. And it is precisely here that Amuriza placed his formulae, which were full of expressive force. The formula is frequently a direct appeal to the public (*Bertsolari Txapelketa Nagusia (Donostia, 1980–1–6)* 1980: 36):

Sentimentua sartu zitzaidan	Emotions entered
bihotzeraino umetan,	my heart as a child,
geroztik hainbat gauza mingarri	since then I've seen so much suffering
ikusi mundu honetan.	in this world.

Euskalerriaz batera nago	My heart goes out to
bihotz barneko penetan;	to that of the Basque Country;
anaiak alkar hartu ezinik,	we can't be brothers,
etsaiak su eta ketan,	as the enemy beats us black and blue,
esan dudana gezurra bada	if what I say is a lie,
urka nazazue bertan. (bis).	hang me here and now (repeat).

At other times, there is an emotional reinforcement of something previously said (*Bertsolari Txapelketa Nagusia (Donostia, 1980–1–6)* 1980: 36):

Sentimentua nola dugun guk	Our emotions are like
haize hotzeko orbela,	leaves in the cold wind,
mingainetikan bihotz barnera	from the tongue to the bottom of the heart
doa herriko kordela;	runs the thread of our people;
esperantza dut zerbait hoberik	I like to think that better times
bearbada datorrela,	are perhaps coming,
mundu hontara sortu zen bati	that which has come into this world
bizitzea ere zor dela;	deserves a life as well;
bihur bekizkit hesteak harri	may my guts turn to stone
hori ez bada horrela (bis).	if this is not true.

These last two lines of the *bertso* could well have been prepared by Amuriza before the start of the championship as they are applicable to any theme with an epic or tragedy in mind. Their function is not to develop the theme but rather to reinforce what has been stated beforehand. However this, far from being a deficiency, is perhaps Amuriza's greatest virtue, for it involves (among other qualities) the conscious use of rhetorical strategies. So Amuriza makes maximum use of the most typically oral resources, adapting them to the new expressive needs.

Another example of modern formulaic use, applied in this case to a much more playful and less serious theme, is the following *bertso* by Andoni Egaña, improvised in one of those new-style exercises or assignments; in this case, each *bertsolari* had to imagine what the infancy of the other was like. One of the other artists was Mañukorta, a *bertsolari* whose public image is that of the eternal bachelor with a natural sense of humor which does not exactly come from formal schooling (*Bapatean 97* 1998: 101):

Mañu eskolan ikusten det nik	I can see Mañu at school now
sarri ezin erantzunda:	unable to answer the questions:
eme ta *a*, *ma*; *eme* ta *i*, *mi*;	*em* and *a*, *ma*; *em* and *i*, *mi*;
letzen ikasi nahi zun-da.	as Mañu wanted to study
Eme ta *i*, *mi*; *eme* ta *o*, *mo*;	*em* and *i*, *mi*; *em* and *o*, *mo*;
arrotz zitzaion burrunda;	it all sounded strange;
mu bakarrikan ikasi zuen	the only one he learned was *mu*,
etxeko behiei entzunda.	having listened to the cows at home.

Evidently, in order to improvise this *bertso*, Andoni Egaña would have had to experiment with the names of the letters beforehand, trying to fit them into groups of five syllables. There is no problem whatsoever in accepting the formulaic character of this kind of *bertso*, always remembering that the nature and the management of these newly-coined formulae are radically different from what oralist theory says about them. To mention an obvious dimension, for example, the analytical skill of the *bertso* in question is undeniable.

b) Intellectual experimentation

Ong denies the capacity for intellectual experimentation in oral expression. This is why he states that oral expressions are conservative and traditional. However, as has been seen in some of the *bertsoak* cited here, intellectual experimentation is one of the key aspects of contemporary *bertsolaritza*. Indeed, the corpus of improvised *bertsolaritza* from the past twenty years is full of pieces which testify to the capacity of modern *bertsolariak* for intellectual experimentation. One example here will suffice (*Bapatean 98* 1999: 118):

Sarasua

Baina bizitzak zentzu gutxi du,	But life has little meaning,
gero eta gutxiago,	less so as time goes by,
ni neuz aparte beste Jainkorik	if, apart from the God in me
inon ere ez badago.	there is no other.

Egaña

Aspaldi baten galdera entzun nun,	This one I heard before,
aho dotore batetik,	from a wordsmith,
ia bizitzak existitzen dun	it is whether life exists
heriotzaren aurretik.	before death.

Sarasua

Ondorio bat aterea det,	I've come to a conclusion,
Platon maitea, adizu:	dear Plato, listen up:
zuk hitz gehiago dakizu baina	you know a lot more words,
nik bezain gutxi dakizu.	but are just as ignorant as me.

Egaña

Ni erdi tonto bilakatu nau	You have turned me into a halfwit;
ondo erantzun ezinak,	I don't have a good answer;
ta zu jakintsu bihurtu zaitu	you, however, have been made wise
duda eta jakinminak.	by doubts and a thirst for knowledge.

c) Distancing

Stating that oral expressions cannot be "objectively separable" or are inseparably "homeostatic" is the same as denying any possibility of the distancing of the artist from such utterances of oral art. Without distancing there is neither personal style nor literature as such. In fact, it is this distancing that is precisely the principal feature of today's improvised *bertsolaritza*.

When Egaña won his first national championship, he had to play the part of a father who had lost his young son and only child through illness. In contrast to the dead child's mother (played by Jon Enbeita), who found some consolation in her religious faith, the father (Egaña) was afflicted with all kinds of doubt (*Bertsolari Txapelketa Nagusia 1993* 1994: 223):

Bizitzaren merkatua	Life is but a market place;
nago neka-nekatua;	I can't go on;
ez zen handia, inola ere,	it wasn't so great,
haurran pekatua.	the child's sin.
Zein puta degun patua;	Fate is a damned joke;
gure ume sagratua	our adorable child,
lotan al zeunden, ene Jaungoiko	were you sleeping when it happened
madarikatua?	damned God?

This was the *bertso* that started the improvised oral confrontation. And this was Egaña's third and last *bertso* (*Bertsolari Txapelketa Nagusia 1993* 1994: 223):

Sinismentsu dago ama,	The mother persists in her faith,
haurra lurpean etzana;	the child lies buried below;
nola arraio kendu digute	Why the hell did you take
hain haurtxo otsana?	our innocent child?
Hossana eta hossana,	"Hosana, hosana"
hainbat alditan esana!	how many times they intoned!
Damu bat daukat: garai batean	I have one regret: at one time
fededun izana!	being a believer!

This questioning of religious faith demonstrates that *bertsolaritza* is not devoid of thoughts unthinkable (or unutterable) only a few decades ago. In similar fashion, there follow two *bertsoak* improvised by Sarasua and Egaña at a dinner in Arantza (Navarre) in 1992. Egaña was defending the need to continue singing until the listeners told them to stop. Sarasua, in turn, was trying to finish the session as soon as possible. Sarasua sang first (*Bapatean 92* 1993: 216):

Honek jarraitu egin nahi luke	He would like to go on;
ene, hau da martingala!	my, what a to-do here!
Aitortzen dizut azken-aurreko	I'm telling you:
nere bertsoa dedala.	This is my last *bertso* but one.
Ta honek berriz eman nahi luke	And he would like to carry on,
oraindik joku zabala,	dragging out the contest.
hau begiratuz gaur erizten dut	When I see him, now I'm confirmed
lehen beldur nintzen bezala,	in what I feared from the beginning:

Jon Sarasua, Nevada, United States, 2003. Jon Sarasua is an example of the modern *bertsolari*, combining his art form with a career as a university professor.
By permission of *Bertsolari Aldizkaria*.

bertsolaria ta prostitute	That the *bertsolari* and the prostitute
antzerakoak dirala.	are similar.
Sarasuaren aldetik dator	You see that Sarasua
ez dakit zenbat atake,	doesn't stop attacking me:
errez salduko naizela eta	Maybe he thinks
hor ari zaigu jo ta ke;	I'm easily bribed.
lantegi honek berekin dauka	In this art of ours,
hainbat izerdi ta neke,	there is sweat and tears;
bertsoalriek ta prostitutek	both *bertsolariak* and prostitutes
sufritzen dakite fuerte,	know what suffering is,
baina gustora dauden unean	but they also have moments
gozatu egiten dute.	of great satisfaction.

In 1994, Egaña improvised the following *bersto* on the presumed suicide of the cyclist, Luis Ocaña, in Aretxabaleta (Gipuzkoa). This *bertso* is also a good example of the strategic complexity of *bertsoak* with five rhymes *(Bapatean 94* 1995: 216):

Geure buruen txontxongillo ta	At times we are
sarri besteren titere,	but a replica of ourselves;
ustez antuxun ginanak ere	at others, puppets
bihurtzen gara titare;	pulled by the whims of others;
Luis Ocaña hor joana zaigu	Luis Ocaña has left us
isilik bezin suabe:	discretely saying nothing:
pistola bat parez pare,	a pistol to the temple,
zigilurik jarri gabe,	the safety catch off,
ez lore ta ez aldare;	not a flower, not an altar;
baina inortxo ez asaldatu,	but let nobody be scandalized,
egin zazute mesede,	do me this favor,
askatasunak mugarik ez du	freedom has no limits
heriotz orduan ere.	not even at the moment of death.

Here, by way of conclusion, I would argue that the distancing which oral theory regards as exclusive to written literature is the prime characteristic of the improvised *bertsolaritza* that has been practiced since the 1980s: a distancing with respect to co-textual values, untouchable to date, but also in regard to situational elements, as we saw in the improvised oral confrontation between Iturriaga and Maia on the theme of lesbian friends.

Improvised Bertsolaritza as a Rhetorical Genre

From what we have dealt with up to now, we can deduce that improvised *bertsolaritza* is a genre which is oral; sung; improvised; and not specifically literary (in that its aim is to arouse specific emotions amongst the audience), but still close to literature (namely, it is capable of producing texts subject to literary analysis). This last feature makes *bertsolaritza* a genre closer to rhetoric than to literature, following Aristotle's definition of rhetoric as, "the faculty for considering, in each case, what is possible in order to persuade" (1971: I, 2, 1355, 25–26).[5] Two millennia have gone by since Aristotle formulated this definition of rhetoric and his concept –of rhetoric and persuasion being one and the same– might seem strange to today's reader. This is especially so, given that the accepted meanings of both terms have changed so radically over this long period; namely, in its use as an adjective, "rhetorical" has come to mean "empty and misleading verbosity," while the word "persuasion" is today almost exclusively used in the sphere of advertising and propaganda.

George A. Kennedy, perhaps the most prestigious researcher of classical rhetoric as art of persuasion, offers a much more descriptive notion of rhetoric than that of Aristotle:

> *Rhetorike* in Greek specifically denotes the civic art of public speaking as it developed in delib-
> erative assemblies, law courts and other formal occasions under constitutional government

---

5. See also Plato [Platon], *Gorgias*, (1972: 361): "If I do not understand incorrectly, you say that rhetoric is skill of persuasion and that all its activity is to that end."

in the Greek cities, especially the Athenian democracy. As such, it is a specific cultural sub-set of a more general concept of the power of words and their potential to affect a situa-tion in which they are used or received (1994: 3).

As is well-known, there are three rhetorical genres according to the aim and type of persuasion employed in each case: judicial, deliberative and epideictic. The judicial and deliberative genres were clearly practical and were used to practice a type of direct per-suasion in the currently accepted sense of the word. The idea was to win over the audi-ence to the orator's theses which, in the case of the judicial genre, dealt with past events and, in the deliberative genre, with future themes. In the epideictic genre, on the other hand, "persuasion" has a different meaning: "Perhaps epideictic rhetoric is best regarded as any discourse that does not aim at a specific *action* but is intended to influence the val-ues and beliefs of the audience" (Kennedy 1994: 4).

I previously stated that the main aim of the *bertsolari* is to "arouse emotions" among the listeners. Perhaps this is not the best description of *bertsolaritza*, but it should suffice to recall Jon Sarasua's words which illustrate that to "arouse emotions" and "to influence values and beliefs" in the audience are two sides of the same coin: "This is the question: how to approach the performance, where to start, how to surprise the audience, where the argument is going, how you perceive the world of your listeners and what you do to become involved therein" (Sarasua, qtd. in Garzia 1998: 61).

If there remains any doubt about the pertinence of improvised *bertsolaritza* belonging to the epideictic genre of rhetoric, below I cite a description of the same theme by Chaïm Perelman, the main driving force behind the reinstatement of rhetoric in the middle of the twentieth century:

> It is to do with a funeral eulogy or an elegy of a city before the citizens, with a theme bereft of current usage, as in the praise of a virtue or a divinity while the listeners, according to the experts, only play the part of mere spectators. After listening to the orator, they do noth-ing more than applaud and leave. These discourses were, as well, a select attraction in those festivals where people from one place or more regularly met. And the most obvious result was to make the author of these verses famous (Perelman and Olbrechts-Tyteca 1958; rpt. 1976: 63).

It seems undeniable that improvised *bertsolaritza*, by its nature and aims, fits in better with this description than with any other literary genre, oral or written.

It remains to be seen, however, if the epideictic genre of rhetoric turns out to be a bed of Procrustes; namely, too short for improvised *bertsolaritza*. In other words, would not the assimilation of *bertsolaritza* into the genre of rhetoric impede the appreciation of a literary excellence, which, in some cases, the *bertsolari* achieves? The analysis of *bertsolaritza* as a genre of rhetoric does not have to involve the uprooting, in principle, of its literary char-acter, even though this character does not constitute an end in itself. As Perelman (Perel-man and Olbrechts-Tyteca 1958; rpt. 1976: 67) further clarifies:

It is in the epideictic that all the procedures of literary art are admissible, given that it makes possible all that enhances the communion between artist and audience. It is the only genre which makes one think immediately of literature, the only one which could be comparable to the libretto of a cantata, which thus is most likely to become recitative, to become rhetorical, in the pejorative and habitual sense of the word.

I would thus argue that it is rhetoric, and more specifically its genre, which is the natural framework for a full understanding of the phenomenon of improvised *bertsolaritza*. That said, the assimilation of *bertsolaritza* into this rhetorical genre should not be mechanistic. Rather, we should endeavor to fit rhetorical doctrine to the differentiated characteristics of improvised *bertsolaritza*, which, unlike other manifestations of epideictic rhetoric, is a sung and improvised genre. We can, therefore, refine our definition offered at the beginning of this section, stating that *bertsolaritza is a rhetorical genre of an epideictic, oral, sung and improvised nature*.

Bertsolaritza and the Five Canons of Rhetoric

Classical rhetoric, more than a purely theoretical construction, is a critical and meticulous description of the mechanisms and procedures of the orators of the time. As I have stated, I am not trying to apply these instruments and procedures in a mechanistic way to improvised *bertsolaritza*. It is more a case of constructing our own critical description, from the direct observation of the tasks undertaken by today's *bertsolariak*. It is here that classical rhetoric can offer us a methodology which has proved to be fruitful and efficacious. However, "the study of rhetoric, most seem to agree, is essentially the study of rhetoric's five canons . . . . They provide a structure that allows rhetors and rhetoricians to analyze and study separately the various parts of a complete rhetorical system" (Reynolds 1993: 2).

These five canons (also called parts, faculties, functions, categories or divisions) of rhetoric are generally known by their Latin names:
- *Inventio*. The search for and creation of suitable arguments.
- *Dispositio*. Articulation of the arguments in a suitable order. Structuring of the discourse.
- *Elocutio*. Suitable formulation of the arguments.
- *Memoria*. Retention in the memory of the suitably ordered and formulated arguments; the discourses were prepared to be put down into writing, and they had to be memorized as such.
- *Actio/Pronuntiatio*. The realization of the discourse, performance.

These five canons of classical rhetoric make up a first-class analytical model, the validity of which has lasted to this day: "In classical rhetoric, the canons represented the process followed by rhetors as they composed pieces of discourse . . . . In modern rhetoric, they represent the aspect of composing which work together in a recursive, synergistic, mutually dependent relationship" (Reynolds 1993: 2). As regards its application to *bertsolaritza*, it is better to interpret the five canons just as they were understood in antiquity, as they allow us to analyze the process that *bertsolariak* follow when they compose pieces for discourse; in other words, when they improvise their *bertsoak* and establish differences between this and the creative process of other genres.

From the critical description of the mechanisms for the construction of the improvised *bertso*, outlined by Garzia, Sarasua and Egaña (2001: 81–133), it follows that the *bertsolari*, on improvising the *bertso*, carries out (more or less consciously) the five tasks corresponding to the five canons of rhetoric. Here it was also pointed out that, for the improviser, each *bertso* is a "rhetorical piece" which (s)he has to organize suitably. The *bertsolari* faces each *bertso* as if it were an independent discourse, even though it may, at times, form part of a longer discursive unit (a performance or a whole event). Whatever the case, each *bertso* makes up an independent discursive unit and it is in each *bertso* that we have to look for and analyze which elements from each of the five canons of rhetoric are adopted in improvised *bertsolaritza*.

A Final Point

The voices raised about the progressive impoverishment of discourse are many (see, for example, Crystal 2001 and Morris 2000). Such impoverishment is not inseparable or inevitable but is due, in fact, to a flagrant lack of rhetorical-discursive ability. Compounding the decline of the nuclear family as a conversational school is the manifest inability of the education system to remedy the lack of rhetorical-discursive ability among young people. Elsewhere (Garzia, Sarasua and Egaña 2001), as regards a regression to hieroglyphics in SMS, mention has been made of several symptoms of this rhetorical and communicative inability. I do not wish to leave unmentioned, however, another symptom of this same ailment which afflicts us: namely, the appearance, in chat and e-mail texts, of a more informal register than in the so-called emoticon. By means of these caricature-like graphic symbols, we are trying to make up for the lack of appropriate rhetorical strategies. Discourse in itself is not capable of arousing emotion in the recipient. It needs a pointer in each paragraph to indicate what the intended reaction of the transmitter is, as in those mediocre TV sitcoms where canned laughter prompts the viewer when to force a smile and when to guffaw.

Unlike this communicative dysfunction which we suffer from, the rhetoric skill of the *bertsolari* consists precisely of improvising a structured oral discourse in a matter of seconds. This is a skill which is highly valuable in ambits other than *bertsolaritza*, such as in the new ways of connecting people through cutting-edge technology. In the art of *bertsolaritza*, the Basque school system has an unbeatable instrument for encouraging rhetorical skills. To ignore it would be a terrible mistake, in these times when, it is said, communication is the key to almost everything and to opening almost every door.

Present-Day *Bertsolaritza*: Reality and Challenges[1]

Jon Sarasua

The Socio-Cultural Reality of Present-Day *Bertsolaritza*

The Basque-Speaking Community

Bertsolaritza is a cultural expression within *Euskaldun* ("Basque-speaking") culture. To understand *bertsolaritza*, then, one must first comprehend the socio-cultural reality of *Euskaldunak* or Basque-speakers. This is a 600,000-strong linguistic community spread over four provinces in the Spanish State and three in the French Republic, in which the total population is about three million. They are, therefore, a community of speakers forming a minority in their native land.

It is also a linguistic community with a long history. The latest research in a number of disciplines confirms its pre-Indo-European origin and current data shows it to be one of the oldest linguistic communities in Europe and the world. In order fully to understand the current socio-cultural reality of *Euskaldun* culture it is also important to be aware of the key steps in its historical evolution; in other words, the key moments, events and activities involved in resisting the disappearance of its roots. It is also important to note its adaptation through time to a myriad of epochs, invasions, empires and other contexts, and ultimately its ability to retain a specific identity. Such perspectives also influence the way in which *bertsolaritza* faces its future, as they reappear in a continual struggle to assure the *Euskaldun* linguistic community its own future as a cultural identity.

So *bertsolaritza* has had a remarkable trajectory of survival and adaptation in a relatively small cultural community, but it still faces a number of serious challenges for the future. I would emphasize that this is a challenge of survival, for, in some areas, it is on the point of extinction and seriously threatened by new forms of cultural and linguistic

---

1. An earlier version of this article appears as Section I in Garzia, Sarasua and Egaña (2001).

uniformity. It is a challenge, nevertheless, which the wide spectrum of people who support the art are taking on more and more in a campaigning and entertaining sense than in a negative or dramatic one.

The Socio-cultural Relevance of Bertsolaritza *within the Basque-Speaking Community*

Bertsolaritza is a living art form within the cultural activity of the Basque language. Sociological analysis carried out in 1993 demonstrates the reality of *bertsolaritza* and of its place in the *Euskaldun* linguistic community: specifically, 15 percent of Basque speakers classed themselves as great lovers of *bertsolaritza*, 35 percent said they were enthusiasts and 28 percent stated that they were attracted to the artistic activity in some way – a total of 78 percent. Even taking account of the fact that the study was carried out at an especially popular moment in the history of *bertsolaritza*, it is still useful as a barometer indicating the widespread social acceptance of this artistic activity. Indeed, this same study concludes that the passion for *bertsolaritza* reflected in the survey can be represented by three concentric circles, at the center of which is a strong nucleus guaranteeing the active involvement of subsequent generations of people (the *bertsolariak* or improvisers themselves, together with theme-prompters, critics, judges, teachers, organizers, and enthusiasts) and therefore the future of this particular expression of oral culture.

This solidity of what *bertsolaritza* actually means within Basque-speaking society is not due to chance. On the one hand, it has a historical foundation, given that *bertsolaritza* has played an important role in Basque cultural activity through the ages. On the other it is also due to the efforts of a renewal carried out over the past twenty years by the *bertsolariak* themselves and a socio-cultural strategy in which a whole generation of *bertsolariak*, *aficionados* and organizers have collectively guided the artistic activity over the past twelve years.

Bertsolaritza *Today*

Bertsolaritza is currently developing in a number of ways and in various fields. Below I outline a general perspective of these fields in order to appreciate better it as a current sociocultural phenomenon. First of all, we can divide present-day *bertsolaritza* into five principal manifestations:
- As a spectacle or public performance
- As a contest or championship
- As a group entertainment activity at an informal level in *bertsolaritza* workshops or schools
- As regards its intrinsic content and as a pedagogical exercise in statutory schooling
- As a sub-genre in the media

As a Spectacle or Public Performance: The most important or central manifestation of contemporary *bertsolaritza* is its expression as a cultural spectacle. This occurs both in open and closed arenas with some 1,200 contracted performances every year. These events have different levels of rules and regulations, and range from performances in large metropolitan cinemas or theaters to those in the smaller town squares, village halls, and *frontones* ("*pelota* or Basque handball courts"), typically in the program of local *fiestas*. Furthermore, recitals also take place as post-prandial entertainment in restaurants, cider houses and gastronomic societies. The organizers of these performances contract a minimum of two and a maximum of eight *bertsolariak* out of a pool of about one hundred practicing artists (although there are a regular twenty or so who are more often called up). The age of the *bertsolariak* ranges from twenty-one (Maialen Lujanbio) to sixty-nine (Joxe Agirre) and the nucleus is made up of a generation aged between thirty and forty-five at the time of writing.

Table 1: *Bertsolaritza* Events Organized in the Year 2000

PROVINCES	Festivals	Free recital	Post-prandial	Contests	Conferences	Other events	Special format	Championships	Educational	Others	Total
GIPUZKOA	80	147	241	15	9	31	88	3	16	18	648
BIZKAIA	62	66	60	8	1	14	55	24	5	2	297
NAVARRE	11	22	57	4	0	12	7	8	1	0	122
ARABA	9	6	15	6	2	3	8	3	3	0	55
IPARRALDEA	8	15	26	2	0	10	7	2	19	1	90
TOTAL	170	256	399	35	12	70	165	40	44	21	1,212

A number of events within this first section –namely the public performance of *bertsoak* ("verses")– can be differentiated:
- Recitals (sung performances) directed by a theme-prompter (*gai-jartzailea*) who decides the topic(s) on which the *bertsolariak* have to improvise. These spectacles take place in theaters, *frontones* or in the open air.
- Free recitals by two or three *bertsolariak* who decide themselves on what to perform, with no recourse to a theme-prompter.
- Dinner-table recitals or post-prandial performances in a street-party style (namely, so-called "popular" lunches or dinners) organized expressly for such events.
- Complementary performances at other events such as funerals, inaugurations, weddings, political events, tributes, and social occasions.
- Novel formats such as *bertso-trama* ("*bertso*-plot"), an improvised performance on a theatrical quasi-script which the theme-prompter introduces, and experimental monographic performances on one theme with a single *bertsolari*.

Contests and Championships: Public competitions between *bertsolariak*, where the improvisers compete before a jury which grants prizes based on points (the champion being presented with a large *txapela* or Basque beret), are a particularly important manifestation of the art. These contests are held among different age groups (from infants and young people to adults), and at area and provincial levels. They culminate in the All Euskal Herria Championships, held every four years.

Group Entertainment at an Informal Level: Bertsolaritza *Workshops and Schools:* Yet another expression of *bertsolaritza* is its use as entertainment, oral literary fun in the *bertso-eskolak* ("workshop-schools") at the local level or among groups of friends. A more informal tradition is the performance of *bertsolaritza* in cider houses, taverns and farmhouses. Such performances are generally organized today by groups of friends and *aficionados*. They form, without doubt, the most spontaneous expression of *bertsolaritza* and should provide new generations of talent from which future artists will come.

The Content and Practice of Bertsolaritza *in Compulsory Education:* The pedagogical aspects of *bertsolaritza* were first introduced into the classroom at the beginning of the 1980s. Although not completely integrated into the school system, it has gone from strength to strength in the last fifteen years as a complementary element in both primary and secondary education. Although it does not exist in its own right as a school subject, it is studied for its intrinsic content and as a complement to language and literature.

There have been two decades of experimentation in this field. Some projects have been organized by teachers on their own initiative and others by teachers specifically involved in co-ordination within the Federation of *Ikastolak* (schools where instruction is carried out in Basque). A considerable amount of teaching material has already been published (both in ad hoc booklets and on cassette, or as course content and complementary exercises in language texts). At present, several new pedagogical projects are being developed on the potential contribution of *bertsolaritza* to school education. These projects focus, above all, on redressing shortfalls in linguistic acuity (particularly at the oral level) among school-age children. It is still too early to assess comprehensively the potential contribution of *bertsolaritza* to primary and secondary education, and how it might be more fully integrated into the Core Curriculum. However, several dimensions of its potential educational value might be outlined:

a) The development of personal skills. A positive attitude towards, and ability for, improvisation encourages self confidence, self-esteem and a creative personal outlook. Improvisation also aids communicative organizational skills, through a more effective handling of variable factors in communication, such as perceiving certain determining characteristics in the recipient, experience in, and the management of, feedback, and a greater general awareness of important conditioning factors stemming from particular surroundings. Such skills are, further, enhanced through the development and treatment of informational content in terms of its potential entertainment aspect (humor, irony, satire, and so on); and strategies for impacting the sensibility of the listener together with aesthetic aspects of the formulation, such as sounds, rhymes, rhythms. Furthermore, improvisation encourages an ability to relate to others through an inherent cooperative approach at the core of the dialectic in *bertsolaritza*. Finally, it unquestionably aids the development of memory, specifically as a result of engagement in a common cultural heritage through participation in sung memory.

b) The engagement of pupils with their cultural heritage. Understanding oral improvisation as a universal cultural expression develops certain human faculties. Furthermore, such engagement promotes an awareness of a living Basque cultural reality and enhances the prospects for participation in such activity, while at the same time encouraging an engagement in *Euskaldun* cultural heritage via sung memory. Finally, one might underscore the complementary use of *bertsolaritza*'s cultural heritage as a means of getting closer to the events, different points of view, and other aspects of Basque history.

c) The complementary enhancement of linguistic competence as additional training in both resources for oral expression and the entertainment dimension of the language.

d) The complementary enhancement of musical competence. This is the consequence of a necessary familiarization with the heritage of Basque melodies contained in *bertsolaritza*'s wide-ranging repertoire, together with a development of certain capacities for song through these same melodies.

As a Sub-Genre in the Media: *Bertsolaritza* also operates as a sub-genre in the audio-visual media as a result of its dissemination through television and radio programs. These are weekly programs which mainly use recorded compilations of improvisational performances, and are accompanied by discussions and comment. This activity is already quite well established on the radio, where *bertsoak* have been broadcast for more than thirty years. Television began to experiment with *bertsolaritza* ten years ago. Nowadays, the weekly *bertsolaritza* show *Hitzetik Hortzera* is a classic program on Basque television.

Achieving a Balance among the Challenges Facing *Bertsolaritza*

Some Revealing Features

The contemporary development of *bertsolaritza* has, as a cultural expression, certain features which contrast sharply with some of the main tendencies of mass culture. Here I will examine some of these features I believe to be especially significant.

The Total Absence of Mass Reproduction: A large part of consuming what we term "culture" is based on certain reproductions. Typical cultural products such as books, records, videos, and films, as well as other products which function using the new communications technology, are based (at an increasingly global level and with fewer and fewer barriers) on the reproduction of some original creation. Moreover, they are normally produced at a great distance, in a different context, and at another time. Cultural creation fashioned live before a public is somewhat different yet even in such expression, in most cases there is still a certain degree of reproduction. For example, while a live song never sounds exactly the same as on its previous airing, this does not stop it from being the umpteenth reproduction of a piece created at another time. And the same thing happens in stage art.

Bertsolaritza is –and herein lays both its value and its limitations– one of those rare cultural expressions before a public which is not based on any form of mass production. A *bertsolari*'s performance stands out precisely for not reproducing any previously produced ad hoc creation. Indeed, the act of improvisation itself and the total originality of every time and place underpin such performances. Creation in *bertsolaritza* is unrepeatable. It is the capacity for mental poise and the ability to create in response to a fleeting moment

Sebastian Lizaso, Iñaki Murua, Andoni Egaña, Jon Maia, Anjel Mari Peñagarikano, Millan Telleria, and the *gai-jartzaile* or theme-prompter, Lazaro Azkune (seated), 1995. All the *bertsolariak* stand before the audience at both the beginning and the end of a performance, as if to emphasize their recognition of the public, and so that they, too, may be recognized.
By permission of the Xenpelar Dokumentazio Zentroa, Donostia.

that stamps character on this creation. It is in that inexorable fleetingness or recess of the improviser's mind that the *bertso* acquires sense and meaning, wherein is discovered the banality of the straw and the sublime quality of the grain.

Public Participation and the Vital Importance of Feedback: Previously, I set out the various expressions of *bertsolaritza*: as a public spectacle, a group entertainment activity, an educational activity, and a sub-genre in the media. It is not difficult to imagine a highly participatory element to *bertsolaritza* when considering it as group entertainment or an educational activity. Yet it is also important to underline the special participatory character of *bertsolaritza* in its expression as a public spectacle.

In fact, a public performance by *bertsolariak* in a town square, theater or *pelota* court, is one in which public feedback plays a very important role. The importance of the public response or feedback is self-evident in any public spectacle. However, when this spectacle is based on improvisation, on the unrepeatable nature of the time and place, the relationship between creator and public acquires a special importance. In the case of *bertsolaritza* the reaction of the public –its eyes, applause, laughter, and silences– is tremendously significant for the improviser. In other words, spectators influence the creative stream itself as a consequence of its improvised nature.

This confers on the *bertsolari*'s performance a high degree of public participation in its eventual outcome and the response of the public has a considerable influence on the development of the creation. After all, the general context in a *bertso* recital is an essentially creative element.

The Nature of Live Performance in a Public Area and Group Participation: Bertsolaritza, in common with many other cultural expressions, operates principally as a live event requiring the public to attend and participate in a collective act. In contemporary mass culture a large part of cultural consumption is conducted individually and in private. It is in individual houses, and in solitude, when the majority of products of what we call "culture" (such as books, records, videos and web pages) are digested. It is true that new technologies have opened up the scope for inter-communication and mitigate the effects of a one-way flow of the contents which are transmitted. However, it is important to recognize that the vast majority of the cultural products consumed by modern-day western citizens are done so at one remove, in private and with little chance of collective participation and interaction.

Like many other art forms performed on stage, *bertsolaritza* gets people out into public spaces. For the enthusiast, attendance at a performance involves two basic dimensions: leaving home to go to a town square, *pelota* court or theater and participating in a manner which is, to a certain extent, interactive and germane to the development of the improvisation. This latter dimension is an act which itself entails the subtle sensation of participating in a collective event together with other members of the public. This collective participation is even more marked in a postprandial recital, where a lunch or dinner is specially organized in order to listen to two *bertsolariak*. Here the collective sense of participation is even greater. Indeed, this live, collective and public element is inherent in *bertsolaritza*, providing a favorable environment in which reciprocity between creator and audience is possible as well as being a key element for the improvised creation of the *bertsolari*.

The Integrated Nature of the Audience: A *bertsolaritza* audience is not made up of an easily-defined age-group or a particular type of *Euskaldun*. It embraces a cross-section of the Basque cultural community and, at any given performance, the public will probably reflect quite a wide range of ages, cultural sophistication, occupations and so on.

This contrasts, to a certain extent, with a general tendency in cultural consumption towards the fragmentation of the public. Therefore those people, who, for example, might listen to a certain type of teenage music, the followers of a particular rock group and those who attend the opera are fairly well-defined and generally far removed from each other. In general, every cultural expression, indeed every individual group or artist has, to a large extent, a definite audience profile. This does not necessarily mean that there is no room for a wide range of types, but normally this is not the case within the main body of the audience. However there are some cultural expressions, such as the cinema, where the cross-generational and cross-class nature of the audience is self-evident.

In the case of *bertsolaritza*, it has gone from being an almost exclusively rural expression to being a cultural offering which has developed more recently in an industrial or post-industrial society. Curiously, it would seem that singing for the community, as a response to some type of popular or community-based need, still makes some sense within the Basque-speaking population. And there would not seem to be so great a division by age, class or social status as exist in other types of performance or cultural consumption. In many *bertsolaritza* performances the audience make-up suggests a certain sense of community or *fiesta* in a symbolic encounter where people of all types participate. This is something which varies from place from place and which would be necessary to qualify, given that we live in a society in transition and in tension between many tendencies, but it is an element which is still, to a certain degree, valid in *bertsolaritza*.

Accessibility of the Bertsolari: *Economic Self-Sufficiency and Modesty*: In *bertsolaritza* the creator or artist is more or less an ordinary person belonging to the social environment in which (s)he performs. Such artists don't acquire any special social or economic status, nor are they especially physically, symbolically or economically distanced from their natural environment. The *bertsolari* elite, at the moment, consists of two teachers, three students, an electrician, a journalist, a salesman, a university professor, a farm laborer and only the occasional individual whose principal source of income (excluding students) is the performance of *bertsoak*. This makes *bertsolaritza* an economically modest activity which self-regulates its supply and demand without any external intervention and therefore with zero dependence on commercial agents or public sponsorship.

This implies a large degree of social accessibility on the part of *bertsolariak* – an accessibility which is both economic and personal. To give an example, the most prestigious *bertsolari* enjoys, on the one hand, a social prestige comparable to that of the Basque Country's best writer or musician, but on the other (s)he is accessible to any person who cares to call and ask her/him to sing at their wedding, or to propose a charity recital for an *ikastola*, or some other popular body or movement. This availability or easy access is a legacy which the present-day *bertsolariak* maintain, although for some of them this can sometimes mean a furious rate of public performances. Indeed, some *bertsolariak* take part in between one-hundred fifty and two-hundred performances a year. All this makes the *bertsolari* a curious figure who stands somewhere between enjoying a general camaraderie with the public and attaining media stardom.

What Does the Bertsolari Sing About?

One of the key factors in the social response which *bertsolaritza* arouses in a modern society, such as the Basque-speaking one, is the fact that the *bertsolari* employs form and content which connect with a wide cross-section of the audience. After all, this is a public which is primarily urban, stemming from an industrial society with university-educated and widely traveled youth. As such, it is a wide and changing audience. What does the *bertsolari* sing about which allows, with a degree of success, some connection to this contemporary audience?

In principle at least, (s)he addresses every aspect of social and personal life. This is one of the important points in the topicality of *bertsolaritza*: the *bertsolari* sings about life. It is not just the fact that no facet of life escapes their attention, but rather that *bertsolariak* make an express effort to regard every aspect of life worth singing about or dealing with through improvisation.

Obviously, many aspects do escape consideration. If the subject matter is of little interest for the times or represents a subconscious taboo in the society of the day, then the same is true in *bertsoak*. But all those areas which, to put it bluntly, are discussed at the kitchen table, in the bar or on radio talk shows, can also be dealt with in the performance of the *bertsolariak*. Indeed one might say that subjects which receive little or no attention in many everyday circles often surface in *bertsolaritza*, due to an eagerness and zeal for new subjects and approaches among *bertsolariak* in recent years.

A List of Subjects Employed in the Final of the Most Recent Championship: Below I list some of the themes which improvised verse singing in Basque has recently addressed in both its confrontation format and by individual *bertsolariak* responding to theme-prompters. I do not attempt to transcribe the whole theme proposed, as it often has a longer formulation with a giving out of parts in imaginary or concrete situations. Rather, I will limit myself to providing key references to the themes: Social customs regarding alcohol; NGOs and co-operative development; matrimony or couples and the division of labor; problems related to university education in Basque; a mother-daughter relationship regarding nights out; the reaction to being in Cuba; father-son relationships; the dispute between a mayor and a rock group; pacifists; spatial aeronautics; organic cooking; the life of missionaries; the viability of village schools; father-daughter relationship over a letter; immigration and Basque culture; Himalayan mountaineering; retirement and free time; the political conflicts in Euskal Herria and Ireland; the representation of Christmas; a relationship between lesbians; a port-a-potty; the relationship between Saint Peter and a recent death; an operation for phimosis; the circus and an accident; sheep-farming; the thirty-five-hour working week; cancer and a cure; models and obesity; the memory of war; and pick-pocketing and corruption.

Bertsolaritza is a type of alternative communication circuit where (sometimes ironically, at other times humorously or poetically) national, state, local and international current affairs are ruminated on. The bovine association of the verb ruminate is suggestive in this context, for a cow regurgitates unchewed grass previously introduced into its stomach and then quietly masticates it, only to gulp it down once again, now mixed with its own juices. The average modern western citizen gulps down mass-media information to a saturation point and the inability to digest all that information is one of the characteristics of (post)-modern man. *Bertsolaritza* affords a small opportunity to ruminate on part of that information in a humorous, personal or poetic way, and through an artistic, participatory and collective activity.

One might question the intellectual value of the *bertsolari*'s improvisation on a topic of the day or a universal question. It could be argued that it is very insignificant, given that such an intellectual contribution requires learned scientific treatises or long literary works. There are, however, those who see significant contributions in improvisation. Whatever the case, the *bertsolariak* ruminate on and mix, via poetic and entertaining extemporization, various strands of information which they introduce, entertain themselves with and, when they get it right, cause others to be entertained.

The contribution of *bertsolariak*, if indeed they do contribute anything to such subjects, is found precisely in this mixture; namely, a mixture of levels involving the consideration of current social, political, sexual, cultural and local affairs together with references to the situation of their audience, all impregnated with personal allusions and posited against the messages of their fellow improvisers. It is in that blend of levels (such as the juxtaposition of a comment about sheep-cloning with a remark about the theme-prompter's ears, the incongruity of talking about a death or the ETA truce, alongside a remark about a companion's emotions) wherein the originality of the improvisation operates, and where, from time to time, memorable pieces arise.

In this alternative circuit of rumination on social and personal information, the *bertsolari* plays a role somewhere between the social and the poetic, between leader and fool, between columnist and satirical newspaper cartoonist, while at the same time remaining an ordinary member of her or his social milieu. *Bertsolaritza* performances (exceeding a thousand a year), significant audience numbers, and the inherent complicity in this type of communication all go to make the *bertsolari* an important figure of reference regarding social opinion within the Basque-speaking community.

Achieving a Balance among the Challenges: What Are Roots For?

The wide-ranging group of people that form the driving force behind *bertsolaritza* has had, during the last two decades, some intuitively derived guidelines which have served to steer the art form through various challenges presented by the modern age. These intuitive guidelines have, moreover, given *bertsolaritza* a dynamic balance with which to develop in modern culture without leaving behind any of its fundamental nature. These can be summarized in the following way:

An Appreciation of What is of Value in One's Own Tradition: Previously, I noted some of the more revealing features of *bertsolaritza*: the absence of mass-production; its participatory nature; the vital importance of feedback; its direct, collective sense; and the popular and accessible nature of the artist. These features can be, and often are, understood as valuable by the protagonists of this cultural expression. Indeed they are values, modest ones perhaps, of the cultural phenomenon that is *bertsolaritza*. They are values which mass culture might, some day, wish to recover. Or perhaps not. Whatever the case, people interested in the development of *bertsolaritza* ask themselves if these worthwhile features come anywhere near what should be that collection of human activities which our society labels as culture, or if they contribute anything to humanizing cultural activity. A critical view of mass culture tells us that the commercialized society of spectacle only sees in a positive light those end-products which can move or be moved at great speed, even if they make no sense or are lacking in content. Using the concepts of this criticism, one might say that the agents of *bertsolaritza* continually ask themselves if the art form, while perhaps not capable of circulating at great speed, makes any sense or transmits any content.

It could be argued that, if the answer is yes, then the people involved in *bertsolaritza* have decided to lend it speed to allow this cultural expression to circulate in contemporary society. Not the standard speed of circulation of the fleetingly successful goods of modern culture, but rather the speed with which those people involved dare to advance. Speed, in the end, is necessary to survive, live and develop; survive and live, that is, in the spectacular commercial society that it perhaps criticizes, but in which modern *bertsolaritza* is inevitably involved.

Choosing to Live, not just to Survive: This approach, embraced by the world of *bertsolaritza*, does not consist of judging all the options implied by mass culture to be contemptible nor in believing that all its own "idyllic" features should unquestionably be preserved. That has not been the attitude underlying the survival of the Basque language and its culture into this millennium. With such closed-minded attitudes in the face of the new, surely neither *Euskara* nor *bertsolaritza* would be alive today. Rather, they have both opted to live in the world of the present and of the future.

Is it possible to establish a balance between operating among such dominant tendencies and conditioning factors while still remaining true to oneself? Where is the balance between adaptation and identity? These are never-ending questions which always arise in the case of deep-rooted minority cultural realities. The answer to the question about a point of balance between adaptation and identity throws up an interesting intuitive solution: namely, the creative outlook. The key to facing up to this difficult balancing act is the creative tension that emanates from a love of the tradition in question and an opening up to the present. And it would appear that *bertsolaritza* intuitively understands it in this way.

Ultimately, the aforementioned significant features (together with many other aspects) form a valuable legacy that the *bertsolaritza* cultural heritage has inherited and which this association has chosen to adopt, develop and modernize. Development and modernization, however, imply adapting and changing in order to continue making sense and grow (though not an unfeeling growth) within a changing cultural panorama made up of manifold influences and challenges.

Daring to evolve: *Bertsolariak*, and in general all those involved in the movement, have opted for trying out new spaces and forms, for getting into television and seeking out dimensions hitherto unknown to *bertsolaritza*. However, this has given rise to certain contradictions, dangers and distortions. The predominant approach has been to remain alert to these distortions. For example, *bertsolaritza*'s entry into television, with a weekly anthology program which enjoys a considerable audience, has been a major force for boosting interest in the art form. However, *bertsolaritza* is aware that it operates in a similar way to nuclear energy: namely, that there are many risks involved if its use is not correctly managed. For example, viewers might make television the principal medium for regulating the prestige and renewal of the *bertsolariak*. Similarly, a reliance on media dissemination might lead to changing perceptions of *bertsolaritza* according to the conditioning factors under which this audio-visual medium operates in making its compilations; or that the most interesting features of *bertsolaritza*, such as its direct communication, essential feedback and collective or participatory nature lose their importance. Without doubt, such risks are many and worrying.

While remaining aware of these dangers, however, those involved in *bertsolaritza* seem to believe that this is the important battlefield. They have placed their trust in continuing with *bertsolaritza* and facing up to the changes that new trends generate while maintaining and developing even more deeply the essence of sung improvisation with all its demands of simplicity, starkness and authenticity in improvisation. And despite the many doubts and contradictions, one could argue that the reality of *bertsolaritza* in 2005 is interesting and vigorous at all its different levels: the quantity and quality of performances, an authenticity in the improvisation itself as well as its organizational level, a continuing social acceptance, the regeneration of young improvisers and the introduction of the phenomenon into schools.

Three Keys to Future Development

How can we continue to develop what is the essence of *bertsolaritza* –an expression of improvised singing– within the mass culture of the twenty-first century? How does one maintain, adapt and improve on its social acceptance and its cultural, intellectual and entertainment value in Basque society?

The *bertsolaritza* movement is looking for and experimenting with answers to such questions and some of these are worth consideration. In particular, three distinct elements associated with the development of *bertsolaritza* in its current socio-cultural context stand out: attitudes of self-confidence, a determination to maintain transmission from generation to generation, and organizational self-management.

Attitudes of Self-Confidence: Self-confidence is a necessary attitude in the improviser, the extempore poet, and the *bertsolari*. Improvisation in general or extempore art as a metaphor for an attitude to and of life is a fascinating theme, although space precludes exploring it further here. The *bertsolari* creates *bertsoak*; (s)he improvises. Yet the people who sponsor or encourage *bertsolaritza* are also, in a way, creating the artistic activity. They are improvising the route maps for this cultural heritage on a road dominated by mass culture. It would seem a good idea to take this road, and to some extent we already have, with that confident attitude of the improviser; a self-confidence evident at a number of levels. This is well illustrated in the following excerpt from my presentation at the Sixth Latin-American *Décima* and Improvised Verse Festival:

> A self-confident attitude about what we are and what we want to be. A self-confidence despite the difficult but vital challenge facing our language and Basque culture in general . . . . A self-confident attitude to *bertsolaritza* where we do not have any great external references to copy or guide us . . . . Self-confidence in the face of political pressures from different directions, within this long and hard political and social situation which our people are

currently going through and which also influences our creators in their cultural projects . . . . Self-confidence in the face of members of the literary intelligentsia who point the finger at us for hypertrophy in oracy or mediocrity in written work. An attitude of self-esteem in the face of an oral art appearing to be something unusual or abnormal (not part of the surrounding norm) compared to the powerful cultures that envelope our own, wherein we believe we do not have to imitate canons and mechanisms of others, although they might be stronger in their power to expand. An attitude, in the final analysis, of confidence in that which serves us as persons and creators, and in those values which we intuitively share with that oral art we have inherited . . . . Self-confidence in the face of the dangers and distortions which plague our means of transmission and communication (television, new technologies, new formats). This confidence transforms itself into a belief that we can face and deal with these dangers and that it is worth taking risks in forging ahead, being quite aware that what we are talking about here is not conservation, but creation; the question is not one of surviving, but of living. And it is through creating and living that we make sense of and give sense to our tradition (Sarasua 2000).

Transmission from Generation to Generation: The *bertsolaritza* movement, having made a significant mark during these past twenty years, has come down firmly in favor of promoting the transmission of the oral tradition from generation to generation. Indeed, the encouragement of this transmission has been especially close to the heart of all *bertsolaritza* promoters and enthusiasts.

As a result, the on-going work during these two decades has involved the introduction of *bertsolaritza* into schools, together with the specific creation of workshop-schools for new *bertsolariak*. Above all, special attention has been given to promoting up-and-coming young people who show promise. This has also lead to the consolidation of a youth following which sees *bertsolariak* (some as young as themselves) articulating their own worries and likes. As such we can safely conclude that the seed sown is now bearing fruit.

The generation gap is a common element in all cultural expressions and *bertsolaritza* is certainly not free of the phenomenon. Nevertheless, in the case of *bertsolaritza*, transmission prevails over rupture. *Bertsolariak* of all ages have to share the same stage, the same controversies and co-operate in the communal improvisation. As a result, the experience of older improvisers is of great value to the younger artists. And among the *bertsolariak* there is patent respect for veterans of the art who act as a reference for their younger counterparts. Furthermore, among these improvisers there is an interesting fluidity of intergenerational communication.

Organizational Self-Management: The Bertsozale Elkartea: The key organization which has made all this possible, as well as a great deal of the reality described here, is the Bertsozale Elkartea ("The Association of Friends of *Bertsolaritza*"). This is the principal body that has coordinated the development of bertsolaritza at multiple levels.

In 1986 the *bertsolaritza* movement opted to organize itself in a self-managed way. Since then, it has worked to create a participatory organization which has brought together everyone wishing to contribute to this cultural project. In general terms one might classi-

Miren Artetxe and Xabier Paia, performing at the 1996 School *Bertsolaritza* Championship. In contemporary Basque society, there are now special *bertsolaritza* schools designed to encourage the art form, and its pedagogical benefits are increasingly being recognized.
By permission of the Ikastolen Elkartea.

fy this as a socio-cultural project that consists of laying the foundations for the future of *bertsolaritza*.

General Characteristics of the Organization: The Bertsozale Elkartea has seventeen-hundred members, most of whom are individuals. Almost all the *bertsolariak* and other active members in the world of *bertsolaritza* belong to the association. The Bertsozale Elkartea is decentralized throughout the Basque Country, with an associated federation in each of the historic territories. The association thus brings together those active in the expression of the oral art (*bertsolariak*, writers of *bertsoak*, theme-prompters, juries, teachers, organizers, aficionados) in order to map out collectively strategies and organize activities in a number of areas: the creation and management of the Archive Center, negotiations with the media and public administration, the organization of championships and other special events, and the monitoring and co-ordination of schools, research, publications, international relations and so on.

During the last fifteen years, little by little, a cultural project has been developed and the foundations have been established to enable great strides to be made in a clear and purposeful manner. This project, essentially the work of the organization, is based on three fundamental elements: the transmission of the art from generation to generation, the effective management of its growth, and the related activities of archiving and research. It has also been acutely aware of the need to emphasize an all-embracing territorial reality, with the aim of developing these three aspects throughout the Basque-speaking territories and without leaving aside those areas where the language and its culture might be going through a critical moment.

Since the creation of the organization in 1986 it was quite clear that it was not simply an association of *bertsolariak*. A large part of the organizational impetus of the association has come from people who are not oral artists as such but aficionados of *bertsolaritza*. This being the case from a qualitative point of view, it is even more so from a quantitative perspective: of the aforementioned seventeen-hundred members, about two-hundred are practicing *bertsolariak*, with around twenty of these forming what might be termed the top artists. However, at its inception it was perceived as an association of *bertsolariak* alone and even its name, the Bertsolari Elkartea ("The Association of *Bertsolariak*"), seemed to indicate as such. To put an end to the disjuncture between name and reality, in 1996 the title was changed to the Bertsozale Elkartea ("The Association of Friends of *Bertsolaritza*").

Bertsogintza *and* Bertsolaritza*: Artistic and Organizational Aspects*

Two aspects in the trajectory of the *bertsolaritza* movement have been particularly important. *Bertsogintza* refers to the artistic activity of the *bertsolariak* which they produce and develop as creators. This aspect relates directly to the *bertsolariak* themselves, who develop it as free creators and not subject to any organizational interests. As a result, the Bertsozale Elkartea does not play a part at this creative level and nor does it intrude in matters which are solely of concern to the circle of *bertsolariak*. Fortunately, *bertsolaritza*, in its public expression, is an economic activity which is self-regulated. Consequently it neither needs nor longs for big grants and so does not depend on organizations in order to achieve public patronage. This means that the trajectory of their artistic activity is quite natural and spontaneous, guided more by internal (artistic) mechanisms than by the interventions of external bodies.

The term *bertsolaritza* is used here to designate, in broader terms, the cultural project being encouraged around this creative oral activity. This socio-cultural project consists (among other functions) of guaranteeing the transmission of the art, investigating its contribution to schooling, establishing fields for research into it, encouraging forms of getting its message across, general coordination, deciding on a policy of dissemination and extending international relations.

This cultural project is coordinated by the Bertsozale Elkartea and, during the last fifteen years, has gradually taken shape through a series of trials, arguments, deliberations, crises and important achievements. It is, therefore, a project that has been fermenting step by step, in a highly participatory way and with contributions from the different Basque geographical areas. It is, in short, a project with a decidedly long-term vision.

The Foundations of Bertsolaritza as a Cultural Project

That original impetus to encourage *bertsolaritza* during the initial years of the organization has, little by little, solidified into a project based on the three fundamental pillars highlighted above: transmission, dissemination and archiving/research. There is, though, another key dimension to the general socio-cultural project of *bertsolaritza*: territoriality.

By way of conclusion, let us briefly examine these key elements which make up the work of the Bertsozale Elkartea:

Transmission: There are two areas which are crucial in the transmission of *bertsolaritza* to new generations: the role of *bertsolaritza* in primary and secondary schools, and the *bertsolaritza* workshops. As such, a key task of the Bertsozale Elkartea is to examine the contribution of the art in the compulsory school sector and develop materials and teaching programs to aid its incorporation. Furthermore, *bertsolaritza* schools are spreading throughout the Basque Country and their coordination is also a major undertaking, as these school-workshops and groups effectively form the social base of the whole *bertsolaritza* movement.

Dissemination: The aim here is to encourage the dissemination of *bertsolaritza* in a balanced manner. That is, the association has been careful to avoid promoting *bertsolaritza* in old-fashioned way or with the attitude that, "the more the better." Rather, it has sought to advance it in a sustainable manner. In order to achieve this a number of different approaches have been adopted, paying special attention to any presence *bertsolaritza* might have in the media, encouraging it throughout different geographical areas by organizing special events, championships, publications and, in general, all initiatives regarding its dissemination and promotion.

Archiving and Research: The third pillar consists of encouraging the keeping of records and promoting research. This involves the systematic collection of improvised oral creation, and concomitantly, the support of academic research in the field. The star resource here is the Xenpelar Archive Center, which, in its ten years of existence, has had three professionals working exclusively to document some 20,745 records in storage and retrieval systems. Xenpelar makes a special point of collecting improvised *bertsoak* from throughout the Basque Country. Although not all the collections are complete, the collating of material has been undertaken in a systematic way and the center is gradually becoming a focus for all and any kind of documented records on improvised singing. The strategy of the Bertsozale Elkartea for the past ten years has been, with a great deal of organizational and budgetary effort, to create and maintain the Xenpelar Center. Moreover, since 1997 a number of Basque public administration authorities have also participated in its financing by means of agreements signed with the Bertsozale Elkartea. This center also serves as a platform for establishing relations and cooperation with other centers around the world and shares experiences and records about oral literary culture and improvisation from many different traditions. Besides Xenpelar, this third pillar of the Bertsozale Elkartea project is involved in drawing up a general policy for research into *bertsolaritza*. Seminars and symposia (such as *Bertsolamintza*) are organized as well as participation in a number of university forums, summer courses and so on.

The Sense of Territoriality: The territory of *bertsolaritza* is delimited only by *Euskara*. From its inception the Bertsozale Elkartea has been a decentralized association which is currently constituted into a federation of territorial associations. There is, then, a federated association in each of the historic Basque territories: Bizkaia, Araba, Navarre, Iparralde (the northern Basque Country) and Gipuzkoa. Territoriality is an important dimension of the organization, not only because it is decentralized, but also in those very aims of its work in the three fundamental pillars. As a result, the Bertsozale Elkartea targets its special efforts and impetus in those areas where the health of *Euskara* and, therefore, of *bertsolaritza*, shows signs of most weakness.

The Process of Creating Improvised *Bertsoak*[1]

Andoni Egaña

Introduction

Improvised verse is, as its name indicates, an act of improvisation. "Improvise" is a verb which is often used in a perjorative sense in contemporary society; namely, as the last recourse of those who are unable to plan or build on what might have been planned; it is a last minute "everyone for themselves" desperation, the result of which is always imperfect and ephemeral. A positive interpretation, however, abounds in the sporting context, when competitors are capable of improvising a move here or a strike there, or coaches can solve a problem on the spot due to their capacity and genius for improvisation.

As far as *bertsolariak* ("versifiers") are concerned, the act of improvisation has nothing to do with either of these phenomena. The *bertsolari* ("versifier") does not improvise for lack of ability to plan; nor because (s)he is necessarily an extremely talented person. For the *bertsolari*, improvisation is a way of expressing her/his ideas and feelings, a cultural manifestation which goes way back in time and is part of the cultural heritage which the *bertsolari* has been immersed in since childhood. For *bertsolariak*, improvisation is a pre-established framework of entertainment wherein their relationship with both themselves and their surroundings can be resolved dialectically.

The improvised *bertso* ("verse") has something magical about it and, although it is not actually magic, to a certain extent this is what the public expects; waiting expectantly for the white rabbit to appear, knowing full well that the top hat does not have a false bottom, unless it is the linguistic and dialectic skill of the *bertsolari*. Improvising *bertsoak* ("verses"), however, is neither trickery nor necessarily the fruit of an extraordinary genius.

It may seem paradoxical, but improvisation for the *bertsolariak* is very much a thought-out act. They have continuously lived out and practiced situations analogous to those they

---

1. An earlier version of this article appears as Section III in Garzia, Sarasua and Egaña (2001).

Xabier Arriaga, "Txiplas," Araba and Bizkaia Championship, Zaldibar, Basque Country, 1998. The public waits expectantly for the *bertsolari* to, metaphorically speaking, magically pull a white rabbit out of the hat with the improvisation. By permission of the Xenpelar Dokumentazio Zentroa, Donostia.

may have to face, at any given moment, on the stage of their extempore art. They have learnt to work the oral and mental skills of this art form within the rules of improvised *bertsolaritza* (the given musical airs, rhyme, meter, and so on) in such a way that the restrictions are nothing more than an aid to improvise more freely. They have become used to soaking up whatever may, at some time later, opportunely come in handy for the moment of improvisation.

It is a labor of management and logistics where the idea is to keep the store well filled and then put everything in order so that, at the right moment, the most complete and attractive presentation can be given. Pure improvisation does not exist; nobody improvises anything starting from scratch. So where does the beauty of improvised *bertsolaritza* lie? It comes from the fact that it is one of the few cultural expressions wherein the moment of artistic creation and that of its exposition to the public are one and the same. The *bertsolari* improvises and, as (s)he does, the public listens.

When the interspersing of certain English words into everyday conversation was the fashion, the term "performance" caught our attention quite powerfully. We thought that this must be something very unusual or innovative, until we realized that it was no more than what we, improvising *bertsolariak*, had been doing for years and years.

Formal Aspects

To construct an improvised *bertso* there are a number of formal aspects to be considered. The *bertso* consists of a *sung, rhymed and measured* discourse. Thus, independently of the content of such discourse, the *air*, the *rhyme*, and the *meter* are inseparable elements of improvised *bertso* singing. One might say that anyone who can sing and construct a *bertso* with the chosen meter and rhyme has the minimum skills of an improvising *bertsolari*; but this is just the technical aspect of the profession. The quality of the *bertso* depends on the dialectic, rhetorical and poetic values of the constructed verse.

The Melodies

Unlike other improvisers (Cubans, Mexicans, Mallorcans, Colombians, and so on) the improvising *bertsolari* always performs without musical accompaniment; but her/his discourse is always a sung one. The melodies used are generally traditional airs, the majority which are of anonymous origin. However, *bertsolariak* also use modern ones composed by Basque or foreign songwriters whose compositions have coincided with the meter normally used for improvisation, or airs composed by musicians at the specific request of the *bertsolariak* themselves. Thus, there are three sources which the *bertsolari* uses as a supply store: traditional melodies; modern melodies coincidental in meter; and expressly commissioned melodies. Regarding the number of existing melodies, Juanito Dorronsoro, the main researcher on this theme, has managed to collect an admirable 2,775 tunes, although the truth is that the actual number of airs used in public performances is much less, with each period using those melodies that are fashionable or popular at the time.

Given that there is no musical accompaniment whatsoever, the voice of the *bertsolari* is primordial in communicating the content of the discourse. Up to the mid-twentieth century, it was a necessary condition for the *bertsolari* to have both a potent and graceful voice, so as to be easily heard in any public space. With the advent of the microphone, however, this requisite became a secondary consideration. Nowadays, more than having a potent or perfectly modulated voice, it is more important for the *bertsolari* to be capable of singing in a way that is in harmony with the subject matter of the moment. The success or failure of the communicative act thus depends more on the choice of a suitable melody than on the quality of the *bertsolari*'s voice.

Among the aforementioned 2,775 melodies, some are more suitable for transmitting the feelings associated with an epic poem; others are more suitable for narration; still others are pertinent to drama; and others to the purely descriptive. The pertinent choice of melody is an important factor in the successful communication of this art.

Meter

Bertsolariak compose their *bertsoak* accommodating them to a definite meter or, to be more exact, meters. However, the *bertsolari* never spends time counting syllables while improvising. This would be extremely hard work and, moreover, a waste of time. The *bertsolari* knows perfectly well to which meter the melody chosen to improvise on belongs. If (s)he sings without forcing the melody, it is clear that the artist is complying with the rules regarding the pertinent number of syllables. If, on the other hand, the tune is forced by cutting it short or prolonging it, it is clear that the rules of meter for the verse in question are not being complied with.

The question of *meter* is one the biggest headaches facing the improviser. Though melody and rhyme are questions of maxima and minima (one can sing or rhyme badly, very badly, acceptably well, well or sublimely), there are no variations acceptable or allowable regarding the meter. It is either correct or incorrect with no gray area in between, although there are a few melodies where the usual 7/6 has evolved into 8/6 through usage.

Moreover, it is meter that is the most difficult element facing the *bertsolari* when preparing for a performance. While rhyme, melodies, lexicon and even content of distinct subject matter may be ciphered and stored with the aim of retrieval at a future opportune moment, the *bertsolari* always has to accommodate them to the meter. And, although constant use and practice provides great self-confidence, the act of improvisation is always given to metrical slip-ups which mark any composition, no matter how ingenious it may be. The meters most used in *bertsolaritza* are known as *Zortziko Handia* and *Zortziko Txikia*:
(i) *Zortziko Handia*

$$
\begin{array}{r}
\text{- - - - - - - - - -10} \\
\text{- - - - - - - - 8 A} \\
\text{- - - - - - - - - -10} \\
\text{- - - - - - - - 8 A} \\
\text{- - - - - - - - - - 10} \\
\text{- - - - - - - - 8 A} \\
\text{- - - - - - - - - 10} \\
\text{- - - - - - - - 8 A}
\end{array}
$$

The *Zortziko Handia* is, therefore, a composition of four *puntuak* in which the odd lines have ten syllables and the even ones eight; it is these even lines, moreover, that have to rhyme with each other, and the rhyming is always of the same family. Here, the coincidence in the use of the eighth syllable by improvisers from other cultures is especially striking. Those from the Las Alpujarras region of Granada in southern Spain, for example, together with those from the Canary Islands and Cuba, improvise in *décimas*, which, as is well known, are ten verses of eight syllables each.

(ii) *Zortziko Txikia*

In the *Zortziko Txikia* the structure of four *puntuak* transcribed in eight lines is kept, as is the rule of rhyming at the end of the even lines, but the number of syllables in each verse is modified. Given the fewer syllables and the more compact discourse, this type of meter and its corresponding melodies are more given to humorous situations of pure dialectic, and less to the epic or dramatic discourses, although this last observation is by no means an absolute rule:

```
- - - - - - - 7
- - - - - - 6 A
- - - - - - - 7
- - - - - - 6 A
- - - - - - - 7
- - - - - - 6 A
- - - - - - - 7
- - - - - - 6 A
```

There also exist more recently created meters, often by *bertsolariak* themselves with the aim of winning a championship; although this is even more complicated. One might say that the greater the number of *puntuak*, so the greater the number of rhyming words. Yet the danger of falling, without a safety net, is also greater, as is the chance of success if the *bertso* is rounded off in a victorious manner. And, not only that, but it is also a response to a modern tendency, wherein the improviser needs sufficient textual terrain in order to demonstrate her/his originality, the complexity of the argument, and the distance from the proposed theme. Today, the context being less agglutinative than before, it is the text which bears the weight of communicative success to the greatest extent. And this is why the trend is for texts to get longer.

Except occasionally (as we will see later), the *puntu* is always from the same group (A) and always has consonance. The difficulty lies, therefore, in finding the right number of words which rhyme together, without repetition. If the rhyming word or foot is repeated, it is said that the *bertsolari* has committed *poto*, the technical error most penalised by both the public and the jury.

Rhyme

For many, rhyme is the formal quid of a *bertso*. Without rhyme there is no *bertso*. If we rhyme (though the quality may not be excessively rich) we are constructing a *bertso*. The rhyme (*puntu*), as we have seen, is always from the same family or group and its level of consonance is greatly valued. For example, we can appreciate that *burua* ("head") rhymes with *ordua* ("hour" or "time"), but this consonance is relative, limited as it is to the last two syllable-vowels of each word and, thus, regarded as a poor rhyme. *Elizan* ("in the church") and *gerizan* ("sheltered"), however, make up a better quality of rhyming; because the suffix (-an) and the preceding fricative (z-) rhyme, as does the vowel preceding this fricative (-i-) and even the vowel forming the first syllable in each word. (-e-). So, from the classical perspective of distinguishing between rich and poor rhymes based on their consonance, I would argue that, "bur*ua* / ord*ua*" is a poor rhyme, whereas "*elizan / gerizan*," on the other hand, is a rhyme of quality.

Nevertheless, the level or quality of consonance is not the only factor when considering rhyme. Perhaps rhyme is an aspect beyond the merely formal for the improviser when (s)he is constructing a *bertso*. It may seem that both meter and rhyme are technical difficulties, formal laws to be abided by and which restrict the *bertsolari*; and indeed they are. But this does not mean that the improviser could construct better texts, with improved content, greater reasoning and so on if (s)he did not have such constraints. Moreover, due to force of habit and mental training, what is a restriction for a non-improviser is an advantage for the improviser. The improviser creates using these rules. And the *bertsolari* feels more comfortable when constructing her or his discourse corseted by the rules of the game than within a vacuum created by a total lack of norms.

So the *bertsolari*, in one sense, never says what (s)he wants to say but rather what is permitted by the meter and the rhyming words which the artist has stored and can, at the opportune moment, retrieve. No *bertsolari* utters what they want to say at the same time as rhyming and using a meter, though there are *bertsolariak* who rhyme and use meter and, at times of great lucidity, come close to it. From this perspective, rhymes are not poor or rich only as regards their level of consonance. On starting to construct a *bertso*, the improviser tries to pertinently choose the final rhyming word *(azken puntua)* with which they are going to wind up the discourse. This is because the artist has to find, in that mental store, others of the same rhyming family and have, on the tip of their tongue, a sufficient reserve of suitable responses on the theme that has been proposed.

Moreover *puntuak*, apart from being formally poor, okay, or rich, are also elements which are related to the very discourse itself. The *bertsolari* fits the content of what (s)he is going to say around the available rhyming words. Thus, the work of storing, ordering and retrieval in the memory of such elements is primordial. *Bertsolariak* may have any number of words from this or that group in their heads. For example, they may have twenty terms ending in -*ina*. But if they have them stored in a disorderly fashion, they cannot use them in the most effective way for one type of discourse or another.

Take, for example, the aforementioned ending -*ina*; here are twenty words that have this ending: *sorgina* ("witch") *egina* ("done"), *ahalegina* ("attempt"), *grina* ("passion"), *ezina* ("impossibility"), *panpina* ("doll"), *zina* ("oath," "promise"), *osina* ("nettle"), *kriskitina* ("crackle"), *okina* ("baker"), *jakina* ("evident"), *bina* ("two each"), *zezina* ("dried meat," "jerky"), *erregina* ("queen"), *mina* ("pain"), *arina* ("light"), *dotrina* ("doctrine"), *irina* ("flour"), *latina* ("Latin"), and *pinpirina* ("coquette").

Here, then, in principle at least, there appears to be more than a sufficient number of rhyming words available for any given meter, that, as we have seen, mostly only four or five rhyming words are used, as the use of a composition with nine is extremely rare. It is also true that, with this number of rhyming terminations, nearly everything, if not everything, can be said. However, the quality of the composition is greater when the rhyming words used are optimum to the theme which is being sung.

As a result, an efficiently ordered group of *puntuak* will result in a more exact and effective discourse. And the aforementioned "*totus revolutus*" requires ordering. All *bertsolariak* carry out this mental ordering in a personal way, either consciously or unconsciously. And every *bertsolari* has their ordered place for a rhyming word, although with time this may change, either because some have been forgotten or because those rhyming words most used in one period are not those used in another. Therefore, a form of ordering, though not the only one or necessarily the best, may consist of several factors: the frequency of use; the polyvalent nature of certain word-rhymes; a division into grammatical categories; greater or lesser levels of consonance; or loan words from other languages. If we take into account all the above-mentioned factors, the mental ordering of the rhyming words in each group may be seen in the form of a daisy in which we store the most used words, and those of greatest polyvalence, at the central nucleus. Then we arrange the rest of the words on different petals according to, for example, their semantic or grammatical value or to their origin.

An example, then, of such mental ordering with a group of words ending in -*ina* might be the following:

1. grina, ahalegina, egina, ezina, atsegina ("pleasure," "joy").
2. panpina, erregina, sorgina, krabelina ("carnation"), pinpirina.
3. arina, duina ("honorable," "worthy"), fina ("fine", "smoothe," "subtle").
4. dotrina, latina, jakina.
5. zina, osina, zezina.
6. liftina ("face-lift"), puentina ("bungee-jumping"), pierzina ("piercing").
7. mina, samina ("bitterness"), sumina ("anger").
8. kriskitina, irina, okina.

Through such mental ordering the improviser knows that the most used and polyvalent rhyming words are those in group 1; group 2 has a series of substantives which are very easy to associate with adjectives; group 3 contains only adjectives; 4 has words of the same semantic field; 5 of words with a great consonance among them; and on petal 6 there are loan words from other languages (Spanish, English, and so on). From this ordering what the *bertsolari* does is to combine words alternatively from one petal with those from another. So one might start, for example, using *mina* from petal 7, then continue with *puentina* from petal 6 and *jakina* from 4, and finally, *atsegina* and *egina* from petal 1.

The ordering of the rhyming words imparts a methodological and practical advantage. It is methodological because, on combining words from different grammatical categories, the oral structures needed to finish using them will be different and will give the constructed text more life. It will thus ensure variety and avoid monotonous discourse. It is practical because it makes it easier not to repeat a rhyming word. Remember, this is one of the technical faults (*poto*) most penalized by both the public in general and, more particularly, by juries in contests. *Poto* is simply the repetition of a rhyming word in the same *bertso* (in the same discursive unit). Given that in *bertsolaritza* all *puntuak* derive from the same family (A), the skill of the *bertsolari* consists of looking for as many words as possible from this group, but without repeating any of them. *Poto* can occur due to either simple carelessness or insufficiently fast reflexes to be able to come up with, in a split-second, the appropriate rhyming word from that mental store that every *bertsolari* carries around with her/him. Therefore an improviser's ordering (like that outlined above) minimizes the risk of carelessness and facilitates the coming to mind of those pre-fixed *puntuak*.

The Principal Strategy in the Construction of the Improvised *Bertso*

A sung *bertso* lasts for approximately between twenty seconds (*kopla*) and one minute (*bederatzi puntukoa*), though this can always vary somewhat, depending on the *bertsolari*. For both the transmitter and the recipient, then, these are small doses of discourse in time. Both identify the *bertso* as the unit of discourse. In other words, in each *bertso* of approximately forty seconds, the transmitter has to be able to create a text which is self-sufficient and which manages to connect with the heart and soul of the recipient with its grace, depth, brilliant dialectic deduction, and so on.

The principal way the *bertsolari* carries out her or his art is through the mode of improvised oral confrontation or a verbal duel with another improviser. One defends their role or person with their own arguments and tries to rebut those of the opponent. In strict turn, they exchange a set of three, four, six or ten *bertsoak* in order to achieve a more plausible argument than the opponent. Each *bertso*, however, stands on its own as a complete discursive unit.

When the *bertsolari* sings alone on a given theme, the same thing happens. If the artist sings three *bertsoak*, for example, it is important to maintain the common thread of the discourse in such a way that one *bertso* does not contradict the content of the previous one. Even so, it is the individual *bertso* that has to be perceived by both creator and the listener as the principal discursive unit.

General Strategy: The Sting in the Tail

The essence of the problem lies in how the artist can manage, in forty seconds, to attract the attention of the recipient and keep the listener glued to the *bertso*. To this end, the *bertsolari* has a basic strategy which is used in a systematic way: namlely, to think up the end first.

It may seem a cliché, but maybe not. How many times have we witnessed discourses of various kinds where there has been no connection with the audience because the content transmitted was not organized in a suitable form? The *bertsolari*, on hearing a proposed theme, turns on her or his mental machinery. And this is carried out within parameters that are very close to those of classical rhetoric (see Garzia, Sarasua and Egaña 2001: 135-235). *Bertsolariak* think about what they are going to say and intuitively plan in which order they are going to say it, keeping the most potent and elaborate verbal strategy for the end. The artist starts to sing and, as (s)he goes along, tries to express the subject matter in as poetic, dramatic, epic or whatever form seems most fitting for the situation. All this is supported by memory, to ensure that the oral punch line at the end (thought up at the beginning) has not been forgotten and that the content is transmitted to the audience with the greatest impact.

This fundamental strategy in keeping what was thought up at the beginning for the final discourse gives the artist two advantages:

(a) Methodological. If the *bertsolari* knows, from the start, where and how the *bertso* is going to end, the path that must be followed to get there is that much clearer.

(b) Communicative. A well rounded discourse is synonymous with success in any performance. It is better to start weakly and finish off reasonably well than the other way round. Moreover, the audience perceives the *bertso* in an inverse manner to that in which the *bertsolari* conceives it. After all, the artist knows how the *bertso* is going to end but the audience only hear it, logically, from the beginning. They are waiting, expectantly and anxiously, for the end. It is not magic but they feel like it is. Any co-incidence between the attention of the transmitter and the recipient should be avoided. The *bertsolari*'s mind, on opening her or his mouth, is focused on the final lines of the *bertso*, while the audience is concentrating on the first words uttered by the artist. This is why they are so joyfully surprised when the *bertsolari* constructs a text that rises in crescendo to a potent finishing touch; in other words, when she or he delivers the sharp punch line thought up before even uttering a word.

Methodologically the *bertsolari*, in the few seconds elapsing between the theme being proposed and the recital of the discourse, thinks out a rational ideological and verbal plan and chooses a melody and fits the plan around the chosen meter and melody. Alternatively, the artist chooses a melody from a specific paradigm, as (s)he has fitted the plan to a concrete number of syllables. Indeed, this is always the first step. The *bertsolari* has already constructed the plan for the end of the *bertso* and has fitted it around a specific number of syllables.

A Practical Example: "The Dilemna of Designer Drugs"

Let us take the case of the following topic: "A good friend of yours has offered you some pills which will guarantee you a better performance on many fronts. You are hesitating about taking them." This was proposed to Aitor Mendiluze at a festival in Elgoibar (Gipuzkoa) in 1997. His task was to construct three *bertsoak* by himself. We will now look at the process of this creation for the first *bertso*.

Aitor, on hearing the proposed theme, looked for an argument which reflected his own opinion about designer drugs. The first argument to *enter his head* was the following: "*hobetuko naiz, baina neu izan gabe*" ("I would be better, but I would not be me"). He then mentally fitted this idea and sentence around a meter of 10/8 syllables:

Hobetuko naiz, baina orduan	10	I would be better,
ni izan gabe, ordea.	8 A.	but I would not be me.

Here one should remember that, on fitting the argument around this number and arrangement of syllables, Aitor had other potential ways of expressing the same idea. For example:

Hobetuko naiz baina tamalez	10	I would be better,
neu izateai utzita.	8 A	but I would not be me.

or

| Hobetuko naiz baina orduan | 10 | I would be better, |
| ni neroni izan gabe. | 8 A | but I would not be me. |

He had many other alternatives to choose from linguistically, but Aitor chose what he did for its overall impact. He also knew that a group of words end-rhyming in *-ea* had a sufficient and suitable lexicon to construct a discourse which would take him and his *bertsoak* to the successful conclusion that he had decided upon at the start. Had he had a different intuition, he would have had to change the formulation and adopt one of the other alternative *bertso* lines. Therefore Aitor found his thesis-argument, fit it around a specific metrical formula and fashioned the phrase in such a way that the final *puntu* would give him room to maneuver with enough rhyming words. Moreover, he chose the melody he was going to use on the basis of the meter to which the final *puntu* and the type of subject matter to be transmitted were molded.

Some fifteen or twenty seconds passed since the theme was proposed. The public waited in anticipation, not knowing what might be going on inside Aitor's head during this time. He then started to sing, knowing where he had to get to and how. He knew that he had to look for rhyming words in his mental store and what path he had to follow until reaching the final, which of course he had thought up at the start.

However, half a second before starting to sing and in a moment of inspirational lucidity, Aitor remembered the word *hobea* ("better"). This would serve him well in maintaining the common thread of the argument in the final sentence. And then he started to sing, "*Ene laguna ...*" ("My friend ..."). From this moment on, all his discourse, until reaching the previously worked out end-part, would be pure improvisation:

```
          Ene laguna- - - - - 10
          - - - - - - - - 8 A
          - - - - - - - - - - 10
          - - - - - - - 8 A
          - - - - - - - - - 10
          - - - - - - - 8 A
          - - - - - - - 8 A
          - - - - - - - 8 A
          - - - - - - - - - 10
          - - - - - hobea 8 A
          hobetuko naiz baina orduan 10
          ni izan gabe ordea. 8 A
```

Here, the part of the discourse constructed by Aitor *before* starting to sing approximates to the words that appear; while that part of the *bertso* constructed *while* he was actually singing corresponds to those sections marked with discontinuous lines.

Aitor knew what he was going to sing at the end. However, to arrive at that point he had to construct the greater part of the discourse in such a way that the final *puntu* made sense and had the maximum impact. In order to do this, he searched his storage-retrieval system or "daisy" of rhyming words and found the word *noblea* ("honest"). This worked for him and he started to sing:

Ene laguna uste zintudan,	My friend, I believed you
jatorra eta noblea.	to be faithful and honest.

The audience remained expectant. Aitor had opted to talk directly to an imaginary friend of his who had suggested taking the tablets. What would he decide to do? In which direction would he go? Aitor knew, of course, but the public did not. At most they could only make a guess. The next rhyming word which Aitor retrieved from his store was *gordea* ("hidden"). It was not a bad choice and came in useful to continue constructing the discourse:

Ene laguna uste zintudan	My friend, I believed you
jatorra eta noblea.	to be faithful and honest.
Zuk ere alde ilun, triste bat	Apparently you, too,
nonbait bazendun gordea.	have a hidden, sad side.

He thus found a way to express the contradiction in which he had been placed in the *bertso*, constructing it with the chosen meter and rhyming style. He had a close friend he thought to be faithful and honest but this friend had a dark side. And now he was telling him just that! The expectation of the public was growing all the time; yes, he explained the contradiction to his friend, but what now? What decision would Aitor take?

The next rhyming word taken from the store was *dotorea* ("nice"). Given that this word carries with it a great dose of value-judgment, this is exactly what the artist began to transmit: "Egin didazun eskeintza ez da uste bezain dotorea." ("What you're offering me is not as nice as it might appear").

Ene laguna uste zintudan	My friend, I believed you
jatorra eta noblea	to be faithful and honest.
Zuk ere alde ilun, triste bat	Apparently you, too,
nonbait zenukan gordea.	have a hidden, sad side.
Egin didazun eskeintza ez da	What you're offering me
uste bezain dotorea.	is not as nice as it might appear.

By now the artist had set out the initial contradiction and made a value-judgment. The next step, then, was to reinforce this by example. And so, once again searching for the rhyming word, he came up with *umorea* ("mood") and *doblea* ("double"); two words that would suit him very well in the logic of his discourse. He thus sang, "Emango dit umorea" ("It will improve my mood") and then, "ta abildade doblea" ("and double my skills").

As a result, he managed to arrive at a place he had initially thought up for the ending. He was doing fine, having expressed up to this point the following ideas:

1. I thought you were an honest and faithful friend.
2. But even you have a dark, hidden side.

3. Your offer is not as nice as it might appear.

4. It will put me in a better mood.

5. And I will increase my skills two-fold.

Aitor, then, had constructed a coherent and interesting discourse. Nobody knew exactly how it was going to end, though, except the improviser. Here it is worth remembering that a *bertsolari*'s memory is honed to retain the idea initially thought up; and despite the fact that a lot of mental energy is expended during the pure improvisation (recalling and retrieving the best rhyming words, placing them in suitable meter, trying not to commit any linguistic error, and so on), a *bertsolari* still remembers the oral segment thought up forty seconds beforehand (in our case here, "*hobetuko naiz baina orduan neu izan gabe, ordea*").

Returning to Aitor, then, he knew that if he could manage to get to this point, success in connecting with the audience was assured. He also remembered that he has reserved the rhyming word *hobea* (better) for hooking onto the final point of the argument. Only the last *puntu* was left to construct, and it was this *hobea* which would provide him with the opportunity. He therefore sang:

Hartu ezkero izan naiteke	Once taken, I would be
naizena baino hobea.	better than I am.

And thus the discourse was coming to an end. He told his friend that he thought him loyal, but that he had a dark, hidden side. The offer was not as great as it might have seemed. It would put him in a different state of mind and double his skills, and if he took the drug, he would be better than he really was.

What the public had heard up to now is the following:

Ene laguna uste zintudan	My friend, I believed you
jatorra eta noblea.	to be faithful and honest.
Zuk ere alde ilun triste bat	Apparently you, too,
nonbait zeneukan gordea.	have a hidden, sad side.
Egin didazun eskeintza ez da	What you're offering me
uste bezain dotorea.	is not as nice as it might appear.
Emango dit umorea	It will improve my mood
ta abildade doblea.	and double my skills.
Hartu ezkero izan naiteke	Once taken, I would be
naizena baino hobea.	better than I am.
- - - - - - - - - - 10 A	
- - - - - - - - 8 A	

At this point, of course, the audience knew only that part of the discourse that the creator had improvised while singing the actual *bertso*; and not that part of the discourse that had previously been thought up (though, here, the privileged reader does). As a result, when Aitor concluded with, "*hobetuko naiz, baina orduan ni izan gabe, ordea*" ("I would be better, but I would not be me") the act of connecting with the people reached its climax.

A Number of Exceptions

Thinking up the end and starting at the beginning is, therefore, the most usual formula that the improviser has when faced with the construction of a *bertso*. The improvising *bertsolari* looks for the final argument and, adhering to a plan very close to that of classical rhetoric, continues along the road to the end. Yet it does not always have to be like this, for there are some exceptions to this way of doing things. Such exceptions are usually the result of what might be termed either internal or external conditions.

As regards internal conditions, the first exception to the previously outlined general strategy refers to a situation when the improviser finds it impossible to find any idea or argument in a reasonable period of time. The artist has to improvise alone or in improvised oral confrontation with another *bertsolari* on a topic proposed by the theme-prompter. Seconds pass and the improviser just cannot find a reasonable idea, due to lack of skill, concentration or whatever. Time is running out and the public are impatient. The *bertsolari* is not capable of finding new ideas nor even of repeating old, already used, ones. Time ticks on and, although there is no rule about the number of seconds allowed before answering, the improviser knows (s)he has to start. In this situation the *bertsolari* has no end, but must start! Therefore it is a case where the usual strategy does not operate or a kind of a leap in the dark; in other words, starting without having a clear idea where one is going.

This is a situation in which all of us, as improvisers, have found ourselves on more than one occasion. The public does not, of course, realize that the improviser has started without a concrete idea about how the *bertso* is going to end and will try to construct it sufficiently well to cover up this serious fault. Nevertheless, it is very difficult to come out with flying colors in these conditions. Trying to build something without any plans always is. Here the improvisation is without doubt "pure," yet not out of choice. Rather, it is due to the failure (through lack of skill or for whatever reason) to hit on a final line before starting the *bertso*.

Another exception to the aforementioned strategy occurs when one's memory fails. The improviser has thought up the end and has begun to sing in accordance with the rhyme of this final line. The artist knows this and is relatively comfortable. Then, in a split-second, (s)he realises that (s)he does not remember what had been constructed for the final only a few seconds before. The *bertsolari* tries to recall it but it is not that easy when you are concentrating on the construction of a *bertso*. If the forgotten line is not recovered very soon, the artist will be obliged to improvise the ending too. This would be a shame because the initial seconds creating a good end-argument will be wasted and now a last-second improvisation will have to be employed. Furthermore, it will not be at all easy to achieve one of the same quality as the first. This is ultimately a situation where the usual strategy breaks down.

I have thus outlined two cases in the construction of atypical *bertsoak* where the usual equilibrium between the "thought-up" and "improvised" parts is broken for different reasons. Yet such a rupture always favors the "improvised" part, so, in both cases, due to conditions of an internal nature –pertaining to the *bertsolariak*, themselves– there is more improvisation than in the *bertsoak* constructed following the usual strategy.

The contrary case can, however, also apply. Namely, the *bertsolari* constructs the *bertso* thinking holistically and hardly improvising the delivery at all. This can occur in several situations: greeting ceremonies, presentations, and *bertsoak* of praise, for example. In general terms we can say it occurs in those cases where there is sufficient time to "think up" everything. This might be the case of a young *bertsolari*, who, through lack of self-confidence, "thinks up" the whole *bertso* before starting to sing. Or it might even happen to the professional in an event (a mass, a meeting, a tribute, and so on) in which there is more than enough time to construct one or more entire *bertsoak* before appearing before the public.

In such cases, the "thought up part" is infinitely greater than the "improvised part". And this is how it is perceived by the public. Logically, the quality of the *bertso* should be that much greater, although paradoxically as it may seem, the risks are also that much greater. The *bertsolari*, who, instead of improvising a *bertso* as (s)he goes along, instead constructs it in her or his mind's eye and then reproduces it in sung form, is taking big risks. During the moment of the performance, the mental effort is limited to remembering what has been thought up and the slightest slip-up in memory may bring the entire *bertso* crashing down. This is because the improviser is not concentrating on resolving the small problems which crop up all the time. As a general rule, and as typically imparted advice, it is often said that the best *bertso* is that made up as one goes along, improvising it as it is being sung.

As regards external conditions, one of the most traditional formulations is that of "*puntuari erantzun*," which we might term an "imposed start-up." It is, from the perspective of constructing a *bertso*, a completely different form from any other. And although the public may not perceive it as such, the improviser certainly does. In this form, the theme-prompter starts a *bertso* and the *bertsolari* has to finish it. As such, both the proposed theme and the *puntu* to be used are set by someone else and, to make matters worse, the response has to be immediate and pertinent to the subject matter of the theme, both in its form and in its rhyming. As a result, the *bertsolari* does not have sufficient time to think about the final *puntu*, as well as starting to answer the question or suggestion thrown at her or him, and having to carry on and on; and to finish in the most coherent manner possible! In such a format there are no valid strategies and here, too, improvisation is the purest of any branch of *bertsolaritza*.

Another very common format is the "running rhymes" (*puntuka*), where a *bertso* is constructed between two or more singers, in such a way that each sings a *puntu* alternatively. Given that the discursive unity is constructed between two or more individuals, and that one never knows what the other is going to say, once again there is no single, valid strategy. What counts here are one's reflexes and capacity for pure improvisation.

Consequently, either through a lack of ability in that moment, or because of the demands of a different "format" (or for whatever other reason), we may once again find ourselves faced with *bertsoak* not constructed according to the usual strategy. Moreover, and to show more clearly what that strategy consists of, I have highlighted *bertsoak* sung by *bertsolariak* alone. Yet in the oral improvisation by *bertsolariak*, as in other analogous phenomena in oral improvisation, it is the improvised oral confrontation that is the most genuine and frequently performed manifestation.

The Soul of *Berstsolaritza*: Improvised Oral Confrontation

In improvised oral confrontations, one *bertsolari* faces another and they weave a performance of a greater or lesser number of *bertsoak* between the two of them. It might be that the improvisers have no theme-prompter as such, so the two have to generate the discourse themselves, taking into account the circumstances of the place where they are performing, the day, the audience, the characteristics of each *bertsolari*, and so on. Or it is possible that a theme-prompter imposes a role for each, in which case, each will have to find the optimum arguments to defend her or his characterization at the same time as attacking the "opponent." In the improvised oral confrontation format, the above-described principal strategy does not vary at all: the improviser thinks up her or his argument, keeps it in mind for the end and starts singing from the beginning. Thus, the construction of the *bertso* is carried out in a manner identical to that of the *bertsolari* singing alone.

In improvised oral confrontation, however, the skilful management of the available time for the improvisation plays a primordial role. When singing solo, the improviser thinks up the end-piece in the least number of seconds possible and then starts to sing. And once a *bertso* is sung, (s)he immediately does the same: namely, thinks up the end and starts to sing; and so on, successively. Moreover, the argumental thread of the discourse is uniquely that of the solo *bertsolari*, obliging the artist to be that much more coherent in what is sung and what is going to be sung. Improvised oral confrontation, however, is a matter of two people and, as such, with both improvisers singing alternatively, we have two variables, which, up to now, have not been considered: the arguments of the rival and the available time to think, while the rival sings their *bertso*.

In improvised oral confrontation, obviously, the improviser has to respond to what the rival has said. An improviser who does not respond to a well-constructed argument of a rival is not defending the role taken on, or the imposed character, very successfully. That said, it is not enough just to defend oneself; at the same time, one also has to go on the attack. To do this, one usually has a sufficient number of seconds to prepare such a tactic, thinking up the response while it is the rival's turn to sing their *bertso*.

I have used the term "thinking up" and this is the on-the-spot reality. Wasting precious seconds not thinking at all is not a good strategy. However, nor is it a good strategy to devise an argument while listening and assimilating the rival's *bertso*, and pertinently responding with what may have been prepared seconds before, independently of the content of the rival's *bertso*! In many cases, a halfway formula is adopted, with a response to the opponent and adding the argument thought up while the rival sings.

General Strategic Possibilities in Improvised Oral Confrontation

The format of improvised oral confrontation in defending, attacking, devising an argument and responding to the rival's *bertso* at the same time is not an easy format. In general, there are three forms of approaching the problem:

A. Devise an argument while the rival sings and performs, independently of what this rival might say.

B. Wait and listen until the whole of the rival's *bertso*-discourse is over and then, in a very short time, respond to it.

C. Devise an argument while the rival sings, listen to their argument, and opt for mixing what was devised with a response to the rival.

Formula A has the big drawback that the thread of the improvised oral confrontation may be lost. If we only say what we want to say, without reference to the rival's line of argument, the discourse can break up. In *bertsolaritza*, improvised oral confrontation is, deep down, and though it may seem the opposite, an act of co-operation. In other words, it is difficult to perform a great work of oral art if the other *bertsolari* performs badly. This formula, then, has the advantage that at least we present our arguments with clarity.

Formula B has the disadvantage of there being little time to prepare the response. Moreover, when the rival's argument turns out to be weak or faulty and as a result, not susceptible to an answer, we are obliged to depend on our own argument, with the added difficulty of having to do so in a precipitate manner. And, if we just limit ourselves to responding to the rival's *bertso*, we are not contributing much of our own thinking to the improvised oral confrontation. In other words, the verbal battle always takes place in the opponent's field.

In any case, one can always fall back on thinking up an argument before hearing out the rival's *bertso* but then discard it completely in order to respond to it more pertinently, even though this may mean some loss in terms of quality or brilliance. One well-known *bertsolari* complained about the way another –known for his unusual form of argumentation– performed in improvised oral confrontation. The latter would wander from the point or look for any *sui generis* argument, pertinent or not. As a result, the former concluded that, "to sing three *bertsoak* with him, one has to think of six!" Effectively, he was referring to the three thought up while the other was singing and another three *bertsoak* –the sung ones– on listening to the rival's arguments. However, this is the formula which facilitates a greater level of improvised oral confrontation. When two improvisers get entangled in a dialectic where there is a brilliant response to a well–constructed argument, improvised oral confrontation is at its best in terms of quality.

Formula C is perhaps the most commonly used one. Not only are the lines thought up in anticipation not sung as such, but the *bertsolari* does not wait until the rival's *bertso* is finished. In effect, both strategies are combined. While the rival sings, some form of argument is being thought up and then, depending on what the rival has delivered, the reply involves what has been previously thought up; yet combining it with some form of mini-

response at the beginning of the *bertso*. For the public at large, formula C is most similar to B. For the expert or performer, however, it is nothing more than a cleverly disguised form of formula A.

Which formula is the best? That is difficult to answer. The purest, without doubt, is formula B. However, it has the drawback that rarely do two improvisers get to perform an improvised oral confrontation with this schema (assuming that the performer who starts always does so with formula A, as (s)he does not initially have to respond to anyone). A schema of the type A-B-B-B-B-B would be ideal, but difficult to respond to with only one *bertso* and this, in turn, is more difficult to follow with an argued reply, and so on.

Although there is no one completely valid strategy for all occasions, I would venture to recommend one. In an improvised oral confrontation which has to be sung and, say, there are four *bertsoak* for each performer, it would be quite balanced if one *bertso* was type A, another C and a couple in B. We would thus be assured that our own argumentation be heard with A, while with B we are able to respond to the rival's arguments and C allows us to do a little of both. However, it might be just as easily balanced with two As and two Bs or one A and three Bs. As I mentioned previously, there is no one, single strategy.

The most difficult choice, on taking part in improvised oral confrontation, is to decide on the opportune moment to use A or B. Imagine we have a brilliant idea that has occurred to us while the rival is singing, but the rival's idea has also been brilliant. This obliges us to respond with another idea and discard the first. A brilliant *bertso* thus ends up not being used and it is quite possible that there will never be another occasion to use it. On such occasions, when we have the aforementioned brilliant idea, but the rival does not oblige us to respond in a different manner, then we may introduce A. However, the decision has to be taken in a split-second and the improviser does not always opt for the best solution.

As regards improvised oral confrontation, then, I have employed much technical detail. The reality, though, is that the improviser never works strictly along the lines of A, B or C highlighted above, nor with any theoretical "script." Instead, (s)he acts according to instinct, to the dialectical skills available, and recallable lexicons at the time. Moreover, this species of dissection of the act of improvised oral confrontation applies more to those improvised oral confrontation*s* with a set theme (championships, festivals, and so on) than for those without a proposed topic.

Improvised Oral Confrontations without an Imposed Theme

In those improvised oral confrontations without an imposed theme, the two improvisers take the stage to weave together a performance on a theme not imposed from the outside. The extempore artists, themselves, have to "look for" different topics of improvised oral confrontation according to the place, the day, the reason for the event and the characteristics of the audience. It is in this modality that the work of co-operation of an improvised sung oral confrontation can best be appreciated. After stepping down from the stage, one will not hear a *bertoslari* commenting that (s)he had performed well. Whether sung badly or well or managing to transmit the message or not, it is done as a team. Either both do well or neither does.

For a good performance it is important for both *bertsolariak* to pre-arrange a route to follow for the next half or three-quarters of an hour of the performance. They talk with each other and fix a schema. For example, we'll start talking about the town, then we can talk about the Saint's day and then we can introduce the current municipal problems affecting the listeners. Then, changing the melody, we might go on to the political situation, have a go at each other and, finally, changing the air again, one will send the other up about their approaching wedding day. Such a schema, evidently, can vary from place to place and *bertsolari* to *bertsolari*. The more experienced the *bertsolari*, given the great number of engagements and performances, the less time they may have to construct a minimum schema and, at times, they may go up on stage without an idea in their head as to how to start. Only their skills and experience give them the wherewithal to be able to make it up as they go along.

The division of functions between *bertsolariak* is normally primordial. That is, one of them will take the responsibility for putting up arguments for improvised oral confrontation: looking for themes, opening up new ideas, and changing the melody. The other tries to follow the "script" and sticking to it, its theme, its arguments and its airs, tries to respond accordingly and to the best of her or his ability, always remembering that the most arduous work is that of his companion.

Experience comes into play a lot here. Maybe there are no themes, but there are always motives for singing. It is a question of keeping one's eyes well-peeled and ears well-tuned. Knowing what theme to bring up, when the public is enjoying this or that theme, when a theme has spent itself and when to move on, when to get stuck in to a companion so that the joint effort will be that much better, are all key elements here; in other words, one must know a lot more than just merely how to construct a *bertso*. In these collaborative improvised oral confrontations, then, the discursive value of each *bertso* loses importance. It is the performance, itself, in its totality (a half hour, three quarters of an hour, or sometimes a whole hour) that is important. That is why a *bertsolari* might even "sacrifice" the quality of a *bertso* in order to keep focused on the way ahead in order to achieve an end-result.

Part V:

THE MUSIC OF *BERTSOLARITZA*

Bertsolaritza and its Musical Foundations: Some Observations

Israel J. Katz

There is no question that Basque improvised oral poetry (*bertsolaritza*) has, since its inception, been inextricably linked with music. The earliest *bertsoak* (verses) were modeled on traditional airs, as were the *bertso-paperak* (verses contributed by learned poets that were printed on loose sheets and widely circulated throughout the Basque Country). Thus, while traditional and popular tunes served as vehicles for disseminating oral poetry, they also inspired literary creativity. These precious loose sheets that have come into our possession have provided us with fleeting glimpses of the past, ranging from personal thoughts and depictions of situations occurring in daily life to vivid descriptions of historical events; all embedded in verse, and whose messages and images bear significance for the time they were written. While we cannot link any of these documents to specific melodies, we might be able to distinguish specific genres of songs and dances from their stanzaic structures and metrical scansions.

Bertsolaritza's principal aim was to preserve the Basque language (*Euskara*). By the turn of the nineteenth century, when it had begun to surface as a cultural movement, nothing was yet known of its music.[1] More than a century would pass before the *bertso-paperak*

---

1. Recognized as a vibrant cultural movement emanating from the Basque provinces, *bertsolaritza* (*bertsolarismo* in Spanish) has earned its rightful place among the diverse regional performing traditions of the Iberian Peninsular, where music plays an essential role. As such it has been accorded an entry in the newly published *Diccionario de la Música Española e Hispanoamericana*. Its author, S. Bikandi Belandia, who describes *bertsolaritza* as "la manifestación más característica de la literatura vasca de transmisión oral" (1999: 218), discusses its principle categories, historical development (by epochs), components (formal characteristics, rhyme and accent, and rhythm and meter), and improvisation. I am indebted to Bikandi's concise entry, from which I gleaned information concerning its historical background. For additional studies devoted to *bertsolaritza*, I recommend those authored by Aulestia (1990 and 1995), J. R. García (2001), Sarasusa (2000), and Zavala (1996b and 1996c). The most recent contribution to date, concerning the processes and intricacies involved in improvised verse making, is that of Garzia, Sarasua and Egaña (2001).

texts were systematically collected and transcribed,[2] followed later by the collection and transcription of melodies to which they were sung. Meanwhile, during the early decades of the 1800s, *bertsolaritza* had enjoyed marked activities, predominantly in rural and agricultural areas. It was a time when traditional music throughout the Basque countryside was still unknown to Continental European ears, and only those outsiders who were fortunate enough to journey to the Basque-speaking region were able to hear some of the most cherished genres of song, rendered in their pristine manner and to view local traditional dances performed with their costumed and stylized choreography. What little we know about Basque music during the decades before the close of the first Carlist War,[3] in 1839, can be found in Wilhelm Freiherr von Humboldt's (1767–1835) unedited *Colectánea lingüística*, which contains twenty-five melodies (including *zortziko*s and drinking songs) that he collected during his last visit to the Basque Country in the Spring of 1801, for the purpose of studying *Euskara*.[4] Humboldt, I should mention, served as both the Prussian Minister of Education and Prussian Ambassador in Rome, and furthermore was the founder of Berlin University.

A second and important source was the collection of Basque dances (Iztueta y Echeberría 1824; 2nd ed. 1826; rpt. 1927), published in San Sebastián in 1824, which included their history and manner of execution. Its collector was the Basque writer and dance instructor, Juan Ignacio de Iztueta (1767–1845). As an astute folklorist, he took heed of the activities of his European counterparts, who, at that time, were collecting and preserving traditional songs and dances as purely nationalistic endeavors. More important than Humboldt's collection, Itzueta's second edition, published in 1826, is recognized in Spain as the very first serious *cancionero* containing traditional music – among whose fifty-two melodies, thirty-one are linked to specific dances. Iztueta sought the assistance of Pedro Albéniz to make the musical transcriptions.[5] It is noteworthy that nine of the *zortziko*

---

2. Antonio Zavala's contribution to the present volume, which was distributed to the Symposium's participants, is a fascinating discussion of his life-long involvement in collecting and studying this literary genre. His twenty-five books deal not only with his collected prose and versified texts, including hundreds that were dictated to him, but also with biographies and memoirs of noted *bertsolariak* based on personal interviews, together with testimonies from numerous elderly informants.

3. Among his many interesting and varied projects, Antonio Zavala (1928–) has for long studied *bertso-paperak* relating to the Carlist Wars (1833–39 and 1873–76 respectively). At the *Coloquio* concerning traditional song, held in Reus (Tarragona) in 1990, he focused on a manuscript of fifteen strophes pertaining to the famous battle of Andoain (south of San Sebastían) that took place on September 14, 1837 and which resulted in some eight hundred fatalities. As a specimen of the style of popular poetry circulating at the time, Zavala came across numerous other examples relating to this and other contemporary battles.

4. According to Rey García (2001:159), Humboldt's unedited *Colectánea*, otherwise referred to as "Papeles de Humboldt," was originally housed in the Preussische Staatsbibliothek. The original manuscript can be found at the Biblioteka Jagiellonska in Krákow University (Poland). The Eresbil Archive in Errenteria (Gipuzkoa) has a microfilmed copy of its musical notations. Humboldt kept a diary of his visit, which was translated by Telesforo de Aranzadi (1922 and 1923).

5. His full name was Pedro Pérez de Albéniz y Basanta (1795–1855), an extraordinary pianist, prolific composer and pedagogue. After his family settled in San Sebastián in 1805, he was chosen, at the age of ten, to occupy the position of organist at the parochial church of San Vicente. The reputation of this young and gifted musician came to the attention of Iztueta through the organist Juan Manuel de Larrarte from the parish church in Hernani (Gipuzkoa), who along with others sang the songs that Pedro was asked to transcribe. He also ordered their placement in the second edition (Itzueta 1826: preface, 3). Shortly after its publication, he left for Paris to further his musical studies.

tunes notated in this collection –tunes that were originally transcribed in 6/8 meter– were later re-transcribed in 5/8 meter in the 1927 edition by José Antonio de San Sebastián, more familiarly known as Padre Donostia.[6] It was Iztueta's intention that his collection would serve as an instructional guide for teaching his fellow countrymen the traditional dances and their accompanying melodies.

The epoch between the first and second Carlist Wars (1840s–1870s), which exhibited increased activity over a wider geographic area, was considered the Golden Age of *bertsolaritza*. Included among the *bertsolariak* ("versifiers") were some of the most distinguished literary figures, whose *bertso-paperak* served as models for refining the language and enriching the rhyme. Still without concrete musical examples, those few that we do possess can be found in the song anthologies of Jean-Dominique-Julien Sallaberry (fl. second half of the 19th cent.),[7] who collected them primarily in the French Basque provinces.

It was during the third epoch (1876 to 1935) that *bertsolaritza* became urbanized. Industrialism, together with an ever increasing yearning for national identity and the literary currents that encouraged it, form its basis. This epoch, which began with a surge in social and political consciousness, ended on a surprisingly sad note. Following the grand *bertsolari txapelketak* or championship competitions that were held in San Sebastián on January 1, 1935 and again in 1936,[8] the scheduled ensuing competition was suspended because of the Spanish Civil War (which officially broke out on July 18, 1936). Not only the curtailment of the competitions, but through further drastic injunctions issued by the Franco regime:

> the Basque language was outlawed, as was any demonstration of Basque culture . . . . Basque music became synonymous with resistance: the Basque choral group Eresokinka sang throughout the world,[9] and the dance group Dindirri performed throughout the Basque lands, flouting the silence imposed upon them . . . . For twenty-four years, despite the official cultural blackout, versifiers continued improvising in secret and in isolated villages . . . . [And] months [before the reinstated 1960 competition] with the birth of the Euskadi Ta Askatasuna (ETA 'Basque Nation and Freedom'), a secret armed group that fought the Spanish dictatorship for Basque independence, versifiers reappeared in public as Basques,

---

6. Much has been written about the *zortziko*, whose varied connotations in musicological and literary circles have at times proven controversial, particularly among musicologists with regard to its origins and evolution. The Basque dance *zortziko* and the polemic concerning its asymmetric 5/8 [3+2/8] meter are aptly discussed by Preciado (1969: 222–229) and most recently by Gaizka Barandiaran (2002).

7. An illustrious lawyer from Mauleón (Maule in Basque) in Soule (Zuberoa) in the French Basque Country, whose *Chants populaires du Pays Basque* (1870) was highly praised among French Basques.

8. It was Manuel Lekuona's (1984–1987) *Aozko Literatura* or *Literatura oral vasca* (1935; rpt. 1978), considered the pioneering work devoted to the art of *bertsolaritza*, that led to the first championship competition. Aulestia's article (included in these proceedings) concerning Lekuona's distinguished achievements.

9. Decades before these concerts, there was an ever-growing appreciation for Basque choral works. For this important chapter in Basque music, see Murua Iñurritegui (1992). Even today concert halls throughout the Iberian Peninsula and the major cultural centers of Europe are filled to capacity when Basque choral groups perform works from their native repertoire.

[reclaiming] their identity, and versifying championships took place in 1962, 1965, and 1967 (Laborde, 2000: 315).[10]

Still, from this third epoch, we possess some 2,500 specimens of traditional Basque songs thanks to the early efforts of José Antonio Santesteban Arizmendi (1835–1906),[11] Charles [Marie Anne] Bordes (1863–1909),[12] José Manterola Beldarrain (1849–1884),[13] and the later extraordinary collections of Resurrección María de Azkue Aberasturi (1864–1961),[14] and José Antonio de Donostia (1886–1956).[15] Rodney Gallop (1901–1948), an ardent admirer of Basque culture, included many songs, together with harmonizations, in his widely scattered publications.[16] Taken together, their collective corpus of songs and dance tunes, gathered during varied excursions to villages and towns throughout the Basque Country, was, for the most part, familiar to *bertsolariak*, who resided in or who had traveled through those localities.[17]

---

10. Until 1960, when the third competition was reinstated, there was still very little published musical documentation relating specifically to these competitions. The material from the 1935 and 1936 competitions, as I am given to understand, is still unedited and in a precarious state.

11. A composer and organist who not only followed the profession of his father, José Juan Santesteban (1809–1884), but also shared his interest in Basque folk music. His *Aires populares vascongados* (1862–70), containing eighty-one traditional melodies arranged for voice and piano, was awarded a prize at the 1876 Exposition in Vienna.

12. A French composer and musicologist. He was a student of César Franck and co-founder, with Vincent d'Indy and Alexandre Guilmant, of the Schola Cantorum (Paris, 1894). He was commissioned by the French Minister of Education to assemble a collection of early Basque songs and dances, which he undertook in the French Basque provinces from 1887 to 1889, working mainly in Zuberoa (Soule). Many of his Basque musical works were published under the imprint Archive de la Tradition Basque and he was among the first to study seriously Basque folk music.

13. A Basque folklorist, director of the journal *Euskal-Erria* (which he founded in 1880) and, prior to his death, he served as the director of the Biblioteca Municipal (Municipal Library) in San Sebastián. His three-volume *Cancionero vasco* (1877–80) contains only twelve traditional melodies, which he copied from earlier collections.

14. A musical folklorist, composer, philologist, priest, and experienced seafarer. A fervent champion of the Basque language, he was associated with the *Academia de la Lengua Vasca* (*Euskaltzaindia*) from its founding in 1919 until his death. Inspired by the publications and compositions of Charles Bordes, his early musical creations were based on Basque tunes. In the years prior to 1910 he began to collect folk music throughout the Basque Country. By 1912 he had amassed some 2,000 melodies (representing song, dance, and instrumental genres). Among his major contributions to Basque folk music and folk literature are his eleven-fascicle, two-volume *Cancionero popular vasco,* containing 1,001 songs (Bilbao: Euskaltzaindia, 1922–1925), and the four-volume *Euskalerriaren Yakintza. Literatura popular del País Vasco* (1935–1947; rpt. 1959), in which he added an additional 109 songs.

15. Pseud. for José Gonzalo Zualaika y Arregui. A musicologist, composer, organist, and priest. According to Riezu (1984: 168), Donostia's widely known *Euskal Eres-Sorta* (1919) "se redactó con criterio estético y no etnológico. Pero en las canciones publicadas en la revista *Gure Herria* de Bayona nos dio con superabundancia, cuanto se puede pedir al etnomusicólogo."

16. An English-born diplomat and scholar of folk music, Gallop spent the greater part of his visits to the Basque Country collecting folksongs, primarily in the French Basque provinces. His small collections of harmonized Basque songs were published by the Musée Basque (Bayonne) and in various Basque and British periodicals. As an ardent admirer of the Basques, he introduced their culture to the English-speaking public with his quasi-ethnographic study *A Book of the Basques* (1930; rpt. 1970).

17. Riezu's chronological survey (1948) of Basque *cancioneros*, beginning with the first collected by Iztueta and those of the aforementioned collectors, is an important document for its inclusion of such lesser known folklorists as Augustin Chaho (1811–1858), Jean Duvoisin (1810–1891), the Irish-born Antoine d'Abbadie (1810–1897), Mme. de La Villéhélio (nee Julie Adrienne Carricaburu; 1827–1998), to whom Riezu attributes the first true anthology of Basque songs, the Parisian-born Julien Vinson (1843–1926), Christopher Duffer (1888–1922) and his collaborator Jean Barber 1875–1931), who used the pseudonym Nehor. In a later article (1984) Riezu presents some very interesting anecdotes and facts concerning these figures, including a section concerning "el origen de la canción popular vasca."

The two epochs that followed established the solid foundation which present-day *bert-solaritza* enjoys. The first, the so-called fifth epoch (1935–1968), constituted the period of its rebirth despite the hardships imposed by the Franco regime. Following the movement of Basque society, its activities found greater and more adept audiences in urban and industrial settings. *Euskaltzaindia* (The Academy of Basque Letters) reinstated the third *Txapelketa* (national championship) in 1960, and again in 1962, 1965, and 1967. Stricter rules for competition were imposed, *bertso-paperak* were showing signs of decline, the media was expressing more interest in live performances, and the quality of improvisations rose to a higher level than that achieved previously. It was also during this epoch that the *bert-so eskolak* (*bertso* schools) were established, wherein they followed a formalized curriculum to teach the technical aspects of this popular and traditional art. The second, so-called present epoch commencing in 1968, has witnessed the complete urbanization of *bertsolar-itza* and a more intensified social awareness of Basque culture, language, and independence, particularly after the demise of Franco's dictatorship in 1975 (see Garzia, Sarasua and Egaña 2001: 26–29).

A fact we should bear in mind about traditional Basque music is that song took precedence over dance and the purely instrumental genres.[18] This preference has persisted until the present day[19] and thus by its very nature, *bertsolaritza* belongs to the category of vocal music. Its association with traditional dance, however, derives from the appeal for specific dance tunes, whose characteristic meters served to enhance the dramatic impact of their improvisations, by the *bertsolariak*. Yet, strangely enough, *bertsolaritza* maintained its distance from instrumental accompaniment.

And inasmuch as we know very little about the musical foundations of *bertsolaritza* prior to the nineteenth century, we may gain some insights from some fundamental facts about early Basque music.[20] The most distinct feature of Basque song is its syllabic style. One only has to search through any of the afore-cited collections to confirm how ingrained this style is in the Basque musical psyche. Its roots point northward to France and perhaps even further north into the European continent. From the north there came the Gregorian liturgy, with its chants and strophic hymns, to which the Basques, as devout Catholics, were exposed for countless generations. Padre Donostia (1954: 2197) claimed that French church music was the dominant stream for the Basques during the

---

18. For important surveys and studies on Basque dance. see G. Barandiaran (1963–1969); Preciado (1969: 229–236); Jorda (1978); Murua Iñurritegui (1992); and Ramos and Jimeno Jurío (1992). Concerning instruments and instrumental genres, see Barrenetxea Gutiérrez (1975) and Donostia (1948 and 1952).

19. Even Arana Martija, in his lecture addressing the problems of Basque music at the opening session of the 1976 Musikaste –the week-long celebration honoring Basque composers– affirmed that "la principal manifestación del Pueblo Vasco en música ha sido la relacionada con el canto. El bertsolari y el kantari han sido el núcleo de la musicalidad [vasca]" (1984: 79).

20. I have long considered Preciado's "Folklore vasco" (1969) an important overview of Basque folk music. Other condensed outlines can be found in the dictionary entries of Donostia (1954), J.M. de Barandiarán (1980) and Laborde (2000 and 2001).

seventeenth and eighteenth centuries. Yet the prominent Basque folklorist Resurrección María de Azkue was uncertain as to when the Basques began to sing religious songs in their churches, believing that this took place at the beginning of the eighteenth century, when religious *villancicos* were introduced.[21] For many centuries French and foreign pilgrims passed through the Basque Country on their way to Santiago de Compostela singing penitential and other hymn-like songs, many of which were most likely absorbed by the Basques. Most influential were the French *cantiques*, which were adapted to the Basque language and which became increasingly abundant in the French Basque repertory (Donostia 1954: 2197). Utilizing Gregorian and earlier musical landmarks, Jesús María de Leizaola, in his study on Basque poetry (1969: 265–267), believed that the music of the Basque strophes –which maintained a close relationship to Basque *romances*– employed archaic features that displayed a general affinity to earlier religious music from the ninth century. To him, Basque music appeared to be much closer to the forms of the fourth to the seventh centuries.

Music and poetry are so highly regarded in Basque life that there is not a single chore, observance or event, spanning from the cradle to the grave, where songs and poems are absent, and even dances for joyous and festive occasions. Attesting to the Basques' natural ability to improvise, Óscar Camps y Soler (1837–1899?), an Egyptian-born composer and musicologist who settled in Spain during the early 1860s and who spent many years in the Spanish Basque provinces, wrote in 1871 (1871:1):

> Es asombrosa la facilidad con que algunos aldeanos vascos improvisan, por espacio de horas enteras, canciones sobre temas obligados. Muchas veces se desafían en este ejercicio, empezando una estrofa por el mismo verso con que otro ha terminado la anterior. El tema suele ser propuesto por cualquiera de los asistentes, y a pesar de ser la mayor parte de las veces insípido y sencillo, es admirable oír la multitud de argucias, gracejos y sutilezas que salen de esas rústicas bocas, con una facilidad y una espontaneidad que suponen de hecho predisposiciones especiales para esta clase de ejercicios.[22]

> The ease with which some Basque villagers improvise songs, hour after hour, on previously agreed-upon topics, is astounding. Often they will challenge each other in such a contest, by beginning a strophe with the same verse that another singer has just used to end a previous strophe. The theme usually is proposed by any one of the singers present and, despite being insipid and simple in most cased, it is admirable to hear the many subtleties and witty saying that are uttered by those rustic singers, with an ease and spontaneity, which, in fact, imply a special predisposition for this sort of activity.

---

21. Mentioned by Preciado (1969: 215), who did not reveal Azkue's source.

22. [Camps's note:] "Entre los canteros suelen abundar los *versularis*. Gastan un palo generalmente largo, sobre el cual apoyan el brazo, y en mitad de la calle, e uno en frente del otro, y rodeados de numerosos oyentes, suelen verificar su *desafíos*, que son la mayor parte de las veces improvisados." [Among the singers there are usually many *bertsolaris*. They carry a long stick, on which they rest their arms, and standing in the middle of the street, one facing another, and surrounded by many listeners, they will versify their *desafíos* (challenges), which, in most cases, are improvised.]

Throughout the Basque Country, *bertsolariak* were highly regarded for their improvisational skills. In his classic study, *A Book of the Basques* (1930: 135), Rodney Gallop, quoting from Joseph Nogaret, a respected authority on the French Basques, tells us that there were once old homeless women, "living on public charity, who wandered from home to home and from village to village, gossiping to all about events that happened at different places. They composed poems of an infinite number of stanzas, and sang them to audiences which used to gather round during the long winter nights."

Following a lecture he gave before the Royal Music Association in 1934, Gallop was asked if Basque male and female peasants, like those in Portugal, exchanged extemporaneous verses across adjacent fields. Gallop replied that he had not witnessed such performances, but affirmed that, whereas Portuguese men and women also participated in oral verse competitions, he only witnessed solo improvisations. However, with regard to the Basque country, he recalled having heard "a couple sitting together at an inn, or at competitions, [extemporizing on a given] theme, such as the life of an agriculturist *versus* that of a sailor" (1934–1935: 78).

When the Irish scholar and inveterate foot-traveler Walter Starkie undertook his fourth pilgrimage to Santiago de Compostela in 1954, it was in Pamplona that his Basque friends convinced him to travel along the northern Basque route, one which hitherto he had not explored. Thus heading directly northward, he ultimately reached the frontier town of Fuenterrabía (Hondarribia), where, to his good fortune, he was invited by a local Basque farmer to attend a social gathering at an old farmhouse on the slopes of Mount Jaizkibel. Among the attendees were two minstrels –an accordionist and a saxophonist– who performed music hall and jazz selections, interpolating, at times, humorous anecdotes about smuggling and black marketing, along with occasional traditional Basque songs. After additional musical selections, a young *bertsolari* improvised verses in honor of Starkie's visit. According to Starkie's description of the event (1957: 168), the *bertsolari* continued to sing other songs with a "tragic expressive face [that] gave to each . . . . an added significance . . . . and that [the *bertsolari*] had an uncanny power of [suddenly] changing [his facial] expression . . . . from melancholy to wild, unrestrained gaiety, and in that mood he would utter any mad thought that came into his head."

There are undoubtedly countless instances such as these concerning the figure of the rustic *bertsolari* that have been recorded in popular and scholarly publications during the past century, and perhaps earlier. Still, little attention has been paid to these singular poets, who, during the course of their sedentary or itinerant lives, practiced an art that was not encumbered by the stringent rules to which their later professional counterparts were subjected at the various levels of competitive *bertsolaritza*; that such a class of rustic poets existed is reason enough to explore their trajectory as harbingers of an art that was to evolve in present-day *bertsolaritza*.[23]

---

23. With regard to Nogaret's aforementioned description of the old itinerant women, Garzia, Sarasua and Egaña (2001: 19–20) point to the *Fuero* (Ancient Charter) for Vizcaya (Bizkaia), written in 1452, whose Title 8, Law I, concerns improvisations sung by shameful and agitating women, whose couplets were rendered in an infamous and libelous manner. It is suggested that, "in all probability, [these women] can be regarded as the direct ancestors of modern-day bertsolaris."

What differentiated these early *bertsolariak* from the homespun ballad singers from other linguistic regions of the Iberian peninsula (Castile, Catalonia, Galicia, and Portugal), who perpetuated a venerable poetic tradition (the *romancero*),[24] is that the *bertsolariak* were the sole creators of their verses, which, unless written down or recorded, were immediately lost to oblivion, as were the countless tunes and ditties to which they were sung. Their customary venues were homes, taverns, the village square, local *romerías* and festive gatherings, where, if not the central focal point of entertainment, their spontaneous creations were always appreciated for their appropriateness to the occasion. For the more adept and experienced *bertsolariak* there were local *desafíos* ("challenges"), *lore jokoak* or *juegos florales* ("poetry contests"), *jaialdiak* ("special festivals"), and, much later, for the professional competitors, regional competitions which provided greater visibility and fame as they forged ahead to the grand *txapelketa*. In all, the competitions ranged from informal gatherings to the most highly regulated in terms of artistic competence and temperament. Among the foremost *bertsolariak*, who advanced to the highest category, including those who emerged as victors, were many who were illiterate.

Soon after its creation in 1985, the *Euskal Herriko Bertsolari Elkartea* (Association of *Bertsolariak* from the Basque Country) began a project aimed at preserving *bertso doinua* ("bertso tunes") that were rendered at the varied regional and national competitions. The Association's first volume, published in 1995 under the direction of Joanito Dorronsoro,[25] contains two-hundred ninety-nine tunes ordered alphabetically according to their initial verses,[26] alongside which are the initial letters (enclosed in parenthesis) of the Basque provinces in which they were collected. The entire volume contains *bertsoak* belonging to the *zortziko txikia*, the most common stanzaic type. Its verse structure consists of four *puntuak* ("rhymes"), each containing thirteen syllables divided in two lines (*lerroak*) of seven and six syllables, respectively. Many of the volume's traditional melodies that conform to this structure include examples from earlier collections such as those of Azkue, Bordes, Donostia, Manterola, Riezu, Sallaberry, Santesteban, and so on, as well as the more current popular melodies that were taken from recent periodicals and anthologies of poetry relating directly to *bertsolaritza*. Dorronsoro even included *bertso* tunes which he transcribed from recordings and cassettes of live and private performances.

Of the volume's two-hundred ninety-nine notated *bertso* tunes[27] only two-hundred seventy-three subscribe to the *zortziko txikia* structure, whose melody phrases are aligned, one under the other, in accordance with the *lerroa* divisions of their respective *puntuak*. Inasmuch as Dorronsoro has limited his analyses of the tunes in this volume to three musical parameters: formal structure (*egitura*), ceasura (*etena*), and mode (*tonua*), I would like to focus on

---

24. Ballads were rendered primarily in octosyllabic, and occasionally in hexasyllabic hemistichs, each pair rhyming in assonance, and sung as quatrain or distich strophes of indeterminate lengths, adding here and there their own variants to the traditional verses and tunes that were passed down orally from previous generations.25. The project's chief researcher, who had already begun (around 1980) to compile melodies from published song anthologies, collections of folk music, *bertso* books which contained musical examples, recordings, and cassettes, and the more current recorded materials issued by Basque songwriters since 1960. More than two thousand melodies have been added since 1995.

26. From «Abade bat bizi zan» in Azkue (1922–1925, rpt. 1968, 1990: no. 597), through «Gezurretan ari ziran» in Etxaniz (1967: no. 38).

27. Spread over three-hundred one pages, musical notations are missing on pages 30 and 292.

Piarres Bordazarre, "Etxahun-Iruri." Etxahun-Iruri did much to revive and extend the oral tradition in Iparralde, the north or French Basque Country, in the twentieth century.
By permission of *Sendoa*.

three randomly selected examples to illustrate the extent to which his collection of melodies can be utilized for future comparative studies.[28]

The first (Ex. 1), «Frailek erein omen du» (Dorronsoro 1995: 284), is a nineteenth-century festive song taken from Padre Donostia's *Euskal Eres-Sorta* (1919: no. 90). It was collected in the village of Arano (situated in the northwestern part of the province of Navarre) and comprises, according to Dorronsoro, an AABA structure rendered in the Minor mode. While his structural analysis is based primarily on the level of the *puntuak*, his alignment of the tune's constituent melody phrases ignores the bipartite *lerro* division, thus diminishing its value as a comparative tool for seeking out similar structures among the few thousand tunes he has already amassed. By applying the hemistichal divisions utilized in ballad analysis, a more accurate accounting of the constituent melody phrases of Example 1 would read ABAB CBA'D. Dorronsoro's designation 'A' for the final two phrases is misleading, since the latter cadential phrase ends on the tune's *finalis* g. One should consult Appendix I*a*, wherein Dorronsoro's designation AABA occurs seventy-three times, whereas there is only one instance of the hemistichal verses ABAB CBA'D.

---

28. I am most grateful to Joseba Zulaika for providing me with a photocopy of Dorronsoro's initial volume, together with several compact disks containing *bertsoak* from various *txapelketak* and those sung by noted *bertsolariak*. Regrettably, the disks did not contain a single example that bore even the slightest resemblance to the tunes notated and transcribed tunes in Dorronsoro's volume.

Example 1: «Frailek erein omen du»

Inasmuch as Example 1 is in the Minor mode, its plagal form has been overlooked by Dorronsoro. Its *ambitus* spans a Minor 7th. Note also its ascending and descending intervals from the schematic below. One should not misconstrue the encircled descending pattern g-f-sharp-d as a transposed version of what G. Barandiaran alludes to as "a typical Basque cadence" from a cradle song (1980: 242, Ex. 4):

Another example can be found in Donostia (1919: no 28):[29]

Ben - ta - ra nu - a   hen - ta - tik   na - tor ben - tan da ne - re   go - gu - a.

The second (Ex. 2) «Agiz Samigeletako» (Dorronsoro 1995: 13), rendered by the *bertsolari* Orixe [pseud. Nikolas Ormaetxea], a Gipuzkoan by birth and Navarrese by adoption, was copied from his published collection *Euskaldunak: Los Vascos* (1950; rpt. 1976: 45). Here, Dorronsoro analyses the musical strophe as A^1A^2BD [*sic* A^1A^2BC],[30] for which I suggest the more accurate delineation ABAC DEFB. Here it is obvious that he has differentiated the cadential phrases of 'A¹' and 'A².' However, in terms of my nomenclature, one will readily see that melody phrases B and C serve as distinct cadential units, and the B reappears again as the *bertso*'s final cadential phrase. Moreover, while Dorronsoro's modal analysis indicates Major, here again he ignored its plagal form. Notice how the melody hovers around the *finalis* a̲, within the *ambitus* of an octave. Melody phrases D and E lend a sparkling aura of contrast, wending its way to e̲' at phrase D's mid-point, and returning as the cadential tone of 'E.' Phrase F comprises a descending octatonic scale (e̲'-d̲'-b̲-[a̲]-g-sharp-f-sharp-e̲) leading directly to the final cadential phrase.

In Appendix I*a*, Dorronsoro's AABD strophe occurs in thirty-eight instances, whereas my suggested ABAC DEFB designation appears only once (1995: 45). Appendices I*a-c* express a three-fold presentation of the formal structures in Dorronsoro's initial volume: *a*) comprising a comparative overview between Dorronsoro's analysis by *puntu* and the hemistichal by *lerro*, ignoring the exponential signs (') and (") which indicate melodic variants; *b*) illustrating a break-down of Dorronsoro's basic formal schemes according to their variant nomenclatures. Thus, for the aforementioned AABD (App. I*a*), whose occurrence in thirty-eight instances represents fourteen percent of the total collection, its breakdown in Appendix I*b* shows that it remains the same in seventeen instances, but that its variant form A^1A^2BD accounts for twenty-one examples, each of which yields 6.2 and 7.7 percent, respectively. Appendix I*c* represents the structural breakdown by hemistichs, whose comparison with Dorronsoro's nomenclature can be seen by viewing their respective page numbers. It also bears additional information, particularly in items 2) concerning quatrain strophes, 3) presenting a more accurate depiction of variant melody phrases, 4) singling out tune variants or versions which share the same text, 6) identifying 'circular tunes" and 7) tunes that appear to be modulatory.

---

29. Oddly enough, among the 393 musical examples in Donostia (1919), only this one bears the cited cadence. In Dorronsoro's volume, it can found in the cadential phrases of his first and third *puntuak* (1995: 49), in the final cadence (1995: 155–157), in the concluding cadences of the second and fourth *puntuak* (1995: 223), at the conclusion of his second *puntu* (1995: 278), and the concluding *puntu* (1995: 291).

30. Since the letter C is not in the Basque alphabet, A1A2BD should read A1A2BC. This substitution should hold for the entirety of Dorronsoro's collection.

Example 2: «Agiz Samigeletako»

Example 3, «Bertsoak entzuteko» (Dorronsoro 1995: 159) from the province of Gipuzkoa, is a transcription of the competing *bertso* sung during the 1989 *txapelketa* (in San Sebastián) by the noted *bertsolari* Sebastian Lizaso. Dorronsoro's analysis ABDB [*sic* ABCB] for the musical strophe is incorrect. It should read ABAB, since its constituent phrases comprise repeated quatrain strophes (ABCD ABCD) that typify ballad tunes. Although the tones utilized in this rollicking 6/8 melody form a Dorian hexachord (g-a-b-flat-c'-d'-e'), there is no question that the tune belongs to the Major mode, whose *finalis* f Lizaso has totally ignored. Singing the tune as notated, one will readily sense its strong Major modality. Its conclusion on the 3rd degree (a) places it in the class of 'circular' tunes. It is an excellent device for generating successive *bertsoak,* whereupon the sole performer or the competitor, while singing the final *bertso,* may seize the musical moment by concluding on the actual cadential tone.

Referring again to Appendix I*a,* ABDB yields thirty-one occurrences, whereas the repeated quatrain strophe ABCD has eleven structural counterparts (Dorronsoro 1995: 26, 36, 75, 118, 159, 194, 208, 227, 240, 250 and 256).

Example 3: «Bertsoak entzuteko»

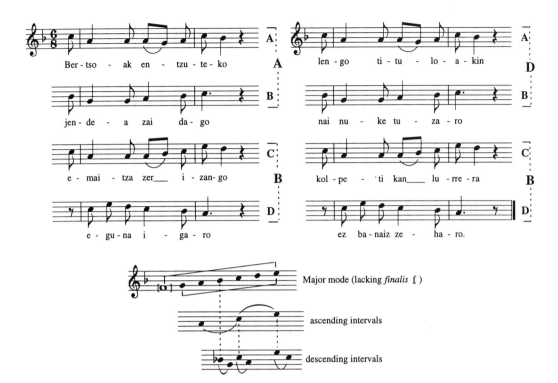

As seen from the preceding comments, Dorronsoro's brief analyses lack refinement regarding formal structure and mode. Of the modes employed throughout the initial volume, one can see their distribution in Appendix II (see below), where they range from Major and Minor tetrachords, pentachords, and hexachords to Minor and Major, plus their plagal forms. Interestingly, one will also find examples in the Dorian, Lydian, and Mixolydian modes. The Major mode and its plagal form accounts for 157 examples or forty-seven percent of the tunes; the Minor mode and its plagal form for 96 examples, or thirty-five percent of the entire collection.

Many interesting facts can also be gleaned from metrical analyses of the entire corpus, delineating, as well, those particular rhythmic patterns which enhance the melodic character of certain tunes. Appendix III indicates the breakdown of meters, wherein duple meter predominates over triple, that is, in 103 over 36 examples, representing 38.5 percent and thirteen percent, respectively, for the entire collection. Compound duple meter occurs in 48 instances, or 17.5 percent of the collection. What appear to be *zortzikos* in their traditional 5/8 meter includes 27 examples (or ten percent of the collection). The remaining tunes in 5/8 differ greatly from the *zortziko* meter. The tunes rendered in mixed meters are either strict or non-strict in their respective notations.

To fully appreciate the distributions discussed in the aforementioned Appendixes, one would have to include the remaining examples from Dorronsoro's extended collection to draw more meaningful conclusions.

Turning now to the *bertsoaldi* (the singular competitive performances between *bertso-lariak*), I would like to present three transcriptions of partial renditions from two distinct levels of competition, the first two (national) taken from a compact disk of the 2002 *Txapelketa*, and the third (local) from a phonogram disk produced by Manuel García Matos (1912–1974), one of Spain's most distinguished musicologists and renowned collector of folk music.

In the following transcriptions, one should take particular notice of the meter, a strong sense of which is one of the primary requisites in *bertsolaritza*. Manuel Lekuona stressed its importance for the rendering of *bertsoak*, noting "that the *bertsolari* is practically incapable of improvising without the help of a melody" (qtd. in Garzia, Sarasua and Egaña 2001: 24). Inasmuch as I have not been able to identify the sources of the tunes employed in the foregoing transcriptions, they each appear to display a traditional character. For each, I have limited my comments to its most pertinent elements.

In Example 4, *bertsolari* I, responding to the theme, "you have parked the car and here is the tow truck taking it away," and the metrical pattern (*hamarreko txikia*) imposed by the theme prompter (*gai-jartzailea*), chose a melody in triple meter (3/8) conforming to the plagal Minor mode (*finalis* g). Note that the 6th degree (f or f-sharp) is missing. The *hamarreko txikia* is actually a *zortziko txikia*, to which an additional *puntu* is added. *Bertsolari* II's adherence to the same melodic scheme exhibits embellishments in the cadential portions of melody phrases A', C, E, G and D. He also alters the concluding tones of phrases A (not in initial phrase of his second *bertso*) and F'. Notice also the variant readings of phrases B' and F', as well as his pitch fluctuations (encircled) in phrases C and E.

Example 4: «Kalean tokirik ez»[31]

31. Transcribed from the compact disk containing *bertsoaldi* from the 2002 *txapelketa* (*i.e.*, track 2, beginning at the elapsed time of 9:00 minutes).

Example 4 (cont.):

An *etena* (caesura) figures prominently at the conclusion of all the melody phrases, except that of the penultimate (G). Phrases E and F provide a transition of contrast between the initial (ABCD) and final (ABGD) phrases. An alternative interpretation points to a possible tripartite ABA' form, wherein bipartite phrases E and F serve again as the contrasting element "B," enclosed by what appears to be two quatrain strophes (whose phrases C and G are totally unrelated). Phrase (G) displays a unique melodic ascent to e', followed by a meandering octaval descent to e (the lower 5th degree), furnishing, like phrases E and F, an additional element of contrast. Its concluding tones a-g-sharp-e recall the "typical Basque cadence," albeit here, functioning as a half-cadence, it progresses convincingly and without pause to D:[32]

Kalean tokirik ez	No place in the street
ta nenbilen hestu;	and I was anxious;
lekutxu bat hala ere	but finally a small space,
hor bazegon justu.	there it was, just there.
Grua zalea horra	But there you also have the tow truck
ondatzeko prestu;	ready to ruin everything.
nere autoa hartu	You took my car
duzu zure esku.	in your possession.
Zu gorroto zaitunak	Whoever hates you
pekaturik eztu.	doesn't commit a sin.
Donostira bisita	A visit to San Sebastián,
etzan lenengua;	it wasn't for the first time.
kuidado gehiagokin	You better take more care
izan urrengua.	next time you come.
Hor bazegoan nunahi	You had ample
horrentzat lekua,	space to park,
baino gaizki zegon ta	but you chose the wrong spot
etorri da grua.	and the tow truck had come.
Azpi-azpitik lotu	I hitched from the base
ta berakin nua	and I'm taking it with me.
Lekurik eztagola	Everybody knows
denek dakitena,	that there is no parking place.
ta horra grua nunahi	And there you have the tow truck
ta noiznahi irtena.	everywhere and at all times.
Hartu behar trena.	Now I must take the train.
Nola izan zitezke	How could you be
hain astakirtena.	such an ass.
Zu egin zintuenak	I feel pity
emanten dit pena.	for the one who gave birth to you.

---

32. Again, I am indebted to Professor Zulaika for this and the remaining translations.

Leku gutxi daukagu	We don't have much space
Donosti hestuan.	in narrow San Sebastián.
Ta kalea pasatzen	And this guy was barely
hau justu-justuan.	passing through.
Gero utzi du berak	Then he left the car
nahi zuen lekuan;	wherever he felt like.
Karneta re ez dakit	I don't know where
nun atera zuan.	he got his driver's license.
Urrena Donostira	Next time [you visit] San Sebastián
etorri astuan.	come on a donkey.

Example 5 is a transcription of the first two of three *bertsoak* rendered by the esteemed *bertsolari* Abel Enbeita according to the verse structure of the *zortziko handia*. Its rhyming lines of verse comprise four *puntuak* of 18 syllables each. In response to the stipulated theme, "the fisherman husband's boat arrives from the sea, but the husband is missing," he has chosen a somewhat somber tune, in the natural Minor mode (*finalis* <u>d</u>) which suits the customary division of 10 and 8 syllables, respectively. Moreover, a traditional performance demands that the initial 10 syllables be broken up into bi-phrasal units of five syllables each.

Here, however, one hears the required *etena* between each of the subdivided syllables in the penultimate melody phrase of the first *bertso*, and in the first, third, and fifth melody phrases of the second. Melody phrases C and D constitute the contrasting element of this seemingly repetitious tune. Only in D' (in the second *bertso*) does the *bertsolari* ascend, but momentarily, to the octave (<u>d'</u>), its only occurrence in the entire rendition. Figuring prominently throughout is the lower <u>c-sharp</u> of phrase B which, after leaping immediately to <u>f</u> (a leap of a diminished 4th), proceeds somewhat haltingly to the *finalis*. The most interesting feature of this example concerns the rhythmic and metric fluctuations that vary considerably between the same melody phrases of the first and second *bertsoak*. From a melodic standpoint, the singer assures us of his total familiarity with the tune. The rhythmic discrepancies and pronounced metric changes, however, are due to his articulation of the improvised *bertso* texts.[33] Only in two instances is the melo-rhythmic line preserved intact (see second phrase B of *bertso* I, and the last phrase B of *bertso* II). Through his renditions, the *bertsolari* has taken extreme care to honor the five-syllable sub phrases of the 10-syllable lines.

---

33. This is probably what Laborde was trying to convey when he wrote that, a "*Bertsulari* must sing in a throat voice and a declamatory manner, so that the words can be understood. The syllabic character of the singing is indispensable for this purpose" (2000: 314).

Example 5: «Gogoratzen naiz ezteguetan»[34]

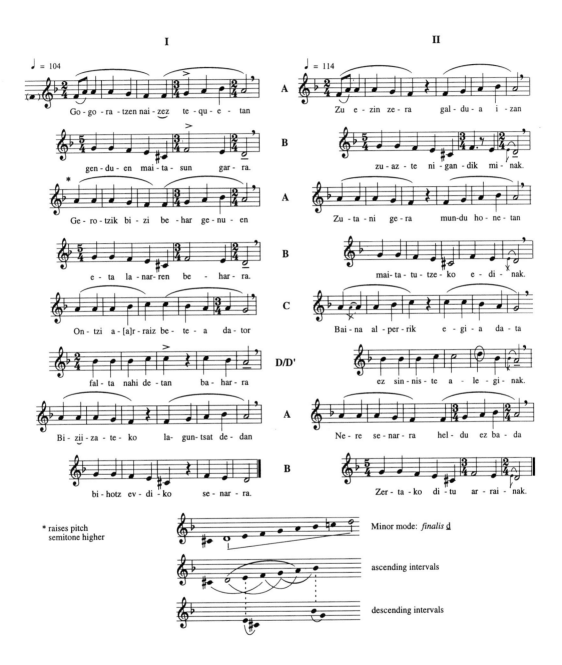

34. Transcribed from the same compact disk (track 2, beginning at the elapsed time 5:08).

Gogoratzen naiz ezteguetan	I remember what passionate love
genduen maitasun garra.	we made during our honeymoon.
Geroztik bizi behar genuen	Later we had to live
eta lanaren beharra.	and we needed work.
Ontzia arraiz betea dator.	The boat is arriving full of fish.
Falta nahi detan bakarra:	The only one I want is missing:
bizi izateko laguntzat dedan	the one friend I have to continue living;
bihotz erdiko senarra.	the husband from the midst of my heart.
Zu ezin zera galdua izan.	You cannot be lost!
Zoazte nigandik minak.	Sorrow! Depart from me!
Zu ta ni gera mundu honetan	You and I were born in this world
maitatuzeko eginak.	to love each other.
Baina alperrik egia data	But it is in vain, for it is true,
ez siniste aleginak.	these attempts to disbelief.
Nere senarra heldu ez bada	If my husband did not come home,
zertako ditut arrainak	why do I need the fish?

The final musical transcription (Ex. 6) offers an example of what appears to be a *kopla* –a traditional Basque tune whose text consists of two *puntuak*– sung alternately by two *bertsolariak* in the informal context of a *bertso desafío* ("*bertso* challenge"). This fine specimen, recorded in the province of Bizkaia (at an undisclosed location), was obtained from Manuel García Matos's *Anthology of Spanish Folklore Music* (1960; Side 8, band 5), issued by Hispavox.

The tune, which aptly suits the verse structure of the *zortziko handia* genre, may have been initiated by the first *bertsolari* or, like the theme "feelings of loneliness expressed by shepherds," mutually agreed upon by both. Here the chosen *kopla* comprises a quatrain strophe (ABAC), wherein melody phrases A accompany the subdivided 10-syllable lines; B and C, the adjoining 8-syllable lines.

A scalar arrangement of the tune's constituent tones exhibits a Major-[Dorian] hexachord, implying an overlapping dual modality (based on *finalis* c). Moreover, each of its melody phrases exhibit uniquely characteristic elements. Phrase A, a simple descending-ascending Major triad (g-e-c-e-g) which concludes on f, contrasts beautifully with melody phrase B's constricted downward arch (f-e-flat-f-g) and with C's descending pattern, wherein the Minor 3rd (e-flat) plays a prominent cadential role. While the Major-[Dorian] modal designation might be considered misleading, it bears some validity, particularly with regard to melody phrase C's hexatonic descent (a-f-e-flat-d-c) to the *finalis*. The triple-metered measures interspersed in each strophe rendition reflect the respective articulations of each *bertsolari*.

Example 6: «Ene Iñaki, beti zabilzu»

E - ne I - na - ki, be - ti zal - bil - zu zeu - re ar - di - en at - zi - an.

Men-di ho - ne-tan la - gun-ta - su - nik zeu - pe ez de - zu al - di - an.

An auditor's response: Ederki! Bota helok honeri!

Ze-u-re mai - ti - a be - gi - ra da - go, sa - ri as - ko - tan a - ti - an,

e - ne I - na - ki, o - rain men-di - tik, noi - ze - tor - ri - ko za - i - an.

E - ne I - na - ki, it - xi - ein do - zuz, ar - dik ba - kar - rik men - di - an,

Mai - te - txu - re - kin e - go - nei - te - ko ber - be - tan be - re et - xi - an.

Auditor's response: Iuju! Hori dok esta!

O - ra-in Mai - te - txu, i - ku - si - e - gaz I - na - ki zeu - re aur - ri - an,

Zeu - re bi - ho - tza o - so jau - zi da I - na - ki zu - re on - du - an.

Auditor's response: Ederki! Taba'at ha-Mitosim!

Major-[Dorian] hexachord: *finalis* ç

ascending intervals

descending intervals

Ene Iñaki, beti zabilzu	Dear Iñaki, you are always
zeure ardien atzian.	tending your sheep.
Mendi honetan laguntasunik	On this mountain you hardly
zeupe ez dezu aldian	have any companionship.
(Erdeki! Bota heiok honeri!)	(Wonderful! Answer that one!)
Zeure maitia begira dago	Your beloved is frequently
sari askotan atian.	looking out from the door.
Ene Iñaki, orain menditik	Dear Iñaki, wondering when
noiz etorriko zarian.	you will come from the mountain.
Ene Iñaki, itxi ein dozuz	Dear Iñaki, you've left the sheep
ardik bakarrik mendian;	alone on the mountain;
maitetxurekin egon eiteko	to keep talking with Maitetxu
berbetan bere etxian	at her home.
(Iuju! Hori dok eta!)	(Wow! That's a good one!)
Orain Maitetxu ikusiegaz	Now Maitetxu, when you saw
Iñaki zeure aurrian,	Iñaki in front of you,
zeure bihotza oso jauzi da	your heart fell completely
Iñaki zure onduan	at Iñaki's feet.
(Ederki!)	(Wonderful!)

The previously transcribed *bertsoak* from Dorronsoro's (1995) collection (Exs. 1–3) and those transcribed from compact disks and phonogram recordings (Exs. 4–6) each constitute a "discursive unit," wherein their respective melodies have served to enhance their "unitary discursive character."

Among the Basques, *bertsolaritza* has, since its inception, served as a unique communicative art. The earliest *bertsolariak* functioned somewhat like minstrels, whose spontaneous verbal and sung recitations enriched the level of social discourse at varied gatherings, occasions, and events. In time, as their artistry achieved regional and national recognition, they developed a preference for poetic genres and metric structures that became so quintessentially Basque, that they further distinguished themselves from those practiced by their Balearic, Canarian, Castilian, Murcian, and Galician counterparts.

Maximiano Trapero, in the summary he appended to his paper "Improvised Oral Poetry in Spain" (2003), points to three general types of oral poetry in Spain: a) the narrative (the *romancero*), b) the lyric (emanating from *cancionero* poetry), and c) oral improvised poetry ("which neither exists throughout the country nor shares [with the others] such a well-known disseminated history"). Among the varied Spanish traditions adhering to the characteristic octosyllabic verse, Trapero stresses the metric differences he encountered in the,

> Galician *quarteta* (quatrain) or four-line stanza (known there as the *regueifa*), in the Murcian and Alpujarran *quintilla* or five-line stanza (known there as the *trovo*), in the Balearan *octavilla* or eight-line stanza (known there as the *glosat*), in the Canarian *décima* or ten-line stanza

(known there as the *punto cubano*)[35] and [in] the wide variety of strophic combinations known in the Basque country by the term *bertsolaritza* (2003).

Bertsolaritza may also distinguish itself as a tradition that has relied mainly on the practice of contrafaction, namely, all its improvised verses have been modeled, for the most part, on traditional, popular (meaning current), or newly created songs. Its sung texts are rendered syllabically, following a stylistic tradition to which the Basques have adhered for centuries. Each chosen tune, or *doinu*, governs the meter and rhythm of the desired or imposed verse structure and sometimes even a text that has for long been associated with a traditional tune has much to do with its choice. One example of this is the case of a traditional tune associated with a well-known nursery rhyme that was used by a *bertsolari*, who, at a competition was instructed to create a poem in which he must play the role of a parent who reads a bed time story to his child (Garzia, Sarasua and Egaña 2001: 187–188). And, we are also told that the manner in which the artist sings the tune is a factor which determines the success of his rendition.

Joanito Dorronsoro deserves our utmost gratitude for identifying the sources of the *bertso* tunes he has collected to date and for preserving this unique corpus in his on-going series of publications. Inasmuch as it has been my intention to share some observations concerning *bertsolaritza* and its musical foundations within the context of Basque traditional music, there is presently sufficient musical, musicological, and contextual material, particularly for specialists conversant in *Euskara,* to undertake a much-needed in-depth study of this most fascinating poetic tradition.

---

35. Here I should like to call attention to Trapero (1994b) in which one will find two articles centering on the musical analysis of the *décima*: N. Fernando's study (289–309) of the *décima* in Mexico and Rodríguez Ramírez's analysis (341–359) of melodic models in the Canarian *décimas*. Furthermore, a most interesting observation about the the Canarian *décima* and its links with formal aspects originating from early Arabic poetry can be found in L.Siemens Hernández's contribution (361–367).

Appendix I*a*: Formal structure (Comparative) (*Zortziko txikias*)

A. According to Dorronsoro
(per *puntu*):

AAAA	4	
AABA	73	(20%)
AABB	10	(4%)
AABD	38	(14%)
ABAB	17	(6%)
ABAD	6	(2%)
ABBB	2	
ABDA	6	
ABDB	31	(11%)
ABDD	3	
ABDE	<u>83</u>	(30%)
	273	

B. According to hemistical
(*lerro*) **divisions**

AAAA BCAA		1
AABB ACDE		1
AABC DEBC		2
AABC DEFG		2
ABAA ABCD		1

*ABAB ABAB		1
ABAB ACAC		1
ABAB CBAB		1
ABAB CBAD		1
ABAB CBDE		1
ABAB CCDE		1
ABAB CDAB	(12%)	33
ABAB CDCB		1
ABAB CDCD		2
ABAB CDEB		2
ABAB CDEF	(3%)	9
ABAB DCAB		1
*ABAC ABAC		3
ABAC DAAC		1
ABAC DBAC		1
ABAC DBEC		1
ABAC DBEF		2
ABAC DDAC		2
ABAC DDAE		1
ABAC DDEF		1
ABAC DEAC	(10%)	28
ABAC DEAF	(2%)	6
ABAC DEDF		4
ABAC DEFB		1
ABAC DEFC		4
ABAC DEFG	(6%)	16
ABAC EFGH		1
ABAD EEFG		1
ABAD EFAG		1

ABBC DEDE		1
ABBC DEFG		1
*ABCA ABCA		1
ABCB CDAB		1
ABCB DEDC		1
ABCB DEDF		1
ADCB DEFG		1
*ABCD ABCD	(4%)	11
ABCD ABED		1
ABCD ABEF		3
ABCD AEFG		3
ABCD CECD		1
ABCD EBCD	(2%)	6
ABCD EBFG		2
ABCD EECD		1
ABCD EFAB		2
ABCD EFAG		3
ABCD EFCD	(6%)	17
ABCD EFCG		2
ABCD EFED		1
ABCD EFEG		4
ABCD EFFG		1
ABCD EFGA		1
ABCD EFGB		1
ABCD EFGD	(4%)	10
ABCD EFGF		1
ABCD EFGH	(21%)	<u>57</u>
		273

Appendix I*b*: Formal structure (according to Dorronsoro) (*Zortziko txikias*)

AAAA:178
AAA^2A^1: 135
$A^1A^2A^1A^2$: 39
$A^1A^2A^3A^4$: 162

AABA: 28, 29, 35, 38, 46, 49,
57, 77, 84–86, 101, 119,
125, 141, 145, 151, 164,
175, 191–92, 201, 203,
207, 207, 224–25, 229,
234, 236, 275–76, 280,
284, 296
(**Total** 33 = 12%)
$AABA^2$: 92, 136, 152, 188,
299, 300
A^1A^2BA:10
$A^1A^2BA^2$: 1, 11 12, 40–41, 47,
51, 71, 76, 78, 82–83, 91,
94, 110, 115, 131,
142,183, 213, 233, 235,
259, 263–64, 279
(**Total** 26 = 9.5%)
$A^1A^2BA^3$: 55, 137, 173, 202,
235, 301

AABB: 122
AAB^1B^2: 24, 104, 109, 133,
237, 288
$A^1A^2B^1B^2$: 16, 80, 155

AABD: 6, 9, 62, 74, 88, 90, 102
120, 123, 150, 159, 168,
190, 245, 249, 257, 272
(**Total** 17 = 6.2 %)
A^1A^2BD: 5, 13, 44, 48, 52, 60,
67, 93, 149, 157, 169, 177,
187, 197–98, 218, 247,
254–55, 287, 290
(**Total** 21 = 7.7%)

ABAB: 20, 26, 36, 45, 75, 96,
118, 194, 208, 219, 240,
256 (**Total** 12 = 4%)
$A^1B^2AB^1$::161
ABA^2B: 215, 289
AB^1AB^2 : 227, 250

ABAD : 15, 21, 138, 230–31
A^1BA^2D: 258

$AB^1B^2B^1$: 106
$AB^1B^2B^3$: 105

ABDA: 8, 252
A^1BDA^2: 56, 58, 107, 260

ABDB: 3–4, 7, 18, 32, 54, 61,
108, 112, 116, 179, 184,
205–06, 214, 223, 241,
244, 261–62, 273, 278,
297
(**Total** 23 = 8%)

AB^1DB^2: 99, 121, 129, 144,
239
$ABDB^2$: 69, 146, 181

ABDD: 43
ABD^1D^2: 87, 114

ABDE: 2, 21, 25, 34, 37, 42, 50,
53, 59, 63, 65–66, 70, 73,
79, 81, 89, 95, 98, 100,
103, 111, 117, 124,
126–28, 130, 134, 139–40,
147, 153–54, 156, 158,
160, 163, 165–67, 170–72,
180, 182, 185–86, 189,
193, 195–96, 199, 204,
209–12, 216–17, 220–22,
226, 228, 232, 238,
242–43, 246, 248, 251,
253, 265–68, 277–78,
281–83, 285, 291
(**Total** 81= 30%)

Appendix Ic: Formal structure (hemistichal) (*Zortziko txikias*)

1) The tunes are numbered according the their respective pages in Dorronsoro's volume.
2) An asterisk (*) designates repeated quatrain strophes.
3) The exponential signs ' and " denote variant melody phrases.
4) Tunes enclosed in parenthesis ( ) are variants or versions which share the same texts.
5) Structures indicated with bold letters designate two or more examples.
6) A number followed by a raised zero (°) represents a 'circular' tune.
7) Tunes that appear to be modulatory (‡)

AAʼAAʼ BCAAʼ: 38
AAʼ BBʼ ACDE: 15

AABC DEBC: 54
AAʼBC DEBC: 61
AABC DEFG: 160
AAʼBC DEFG: 127°

ABAʼAʼʼ ABCD: 31

*ABAB ABAB: 178
ABAB ACAC: 264
ABAB AʼCDE: (123, see 120–22 and 124)
ABAB' CB"ABʼ: 49
ABAB CBAʼD: 284
ABAʼB CBDE: 232
ABABʼ CCDE: 187
ABAB CDAB: 12, (28–29), 35, 46, 57, (77, see 78), (84–85, see 86), 101‡, 119, 125, 141, (145, see 144, 146 and 47), (151,see 150), 175, 191, 207, 234, 236, 274°–75, 299 (**Total** 23 = 8%)
ABAʼB CDAB: (86, see 84–85), 164
ABAB CDAʼB: 152, 188, 249
ABAB CDABʼ: (51°, see 52), 203, 298
ABABʼ CDABʼ: 110, 229
ABABʼ CDCBʼ: 24
ABAB CDCD: (122, see 120–21 and 123–24)
ABAB CDCDʼ: 104°
ABAB CDEB: 192
ABABʼ CDEBʼʼ: 52°
ABAB CDEF: 6, 9, 74, 90, 102, (150, see 151), (190, see 189), 288, 300 (**Total** 9 = 3%)
ABAʼB DCAB: 164

*ABAC ABAC: 39, 45, 219
ABAC DAʼAʼʼC: 161
ABAC DBAC: 88°
ABAʼC DBEC: 3
ABAC DBEF: 245

ABAC DBʼEF: 290
ABAC DDʼAʼC: (83°, see 82°), 285
ABAʼC DDAʼʼE: (63, see 62)
ABAC DDʼEF : 44
ABAC DEAC: (11, see 10), 41°, 76, (78, see 77), (82°, see 83°), 94, 131, 142, 179, 183, 201, 213, 224–25, 233, 261, (279–80) (**Total** 18 = 6.5%)
ABAʼC DEAC: 91, 259
ABAʼC DEAʼC: 40, 47
ABAC DEAʼC: 1, 55, 115, 214
ABAC DEAʼC': 202, 296
ABAC DEAF: (10, see 11), 71, 173, 235, 263, 301
ABAC DEDF: (80, see 81), 109. 133
ABAC DEDʼF: 237
ABAC DEFB: 13
ABAC DEFC: 93, 105, (157°, see 155°–56°), 226
ABAC DEFG: 5°, 48°, 60, (67), 134, 149, 177, (198, see 199), 218ᵃ, 247, 254–55, 270, 276 (**Total** 14 = 5%)
ABAʼC DEFG: 34, 287
ABAʼC EFGH: 37°

ABAʼD EEFG: 169°
ABAD EFAG: 92

ABBʼC DEDE: 87°
ABBC DEFG: 137

*ABCAʼ ABCAʼ: (96, see 95)

ABCBʼ CʼDAB: 117
ABCB DEDC: 281
ABCB DEDF: 222
ABCBʼ DEFG: 134

*ABCD ABCD: (26, see 25), 36, 75, 118, 159, 194, 208, 227, 240, 250°, 256 (**Total** 11 = 04%)

ABCD ABED: (231, see 230)
ABCD ABEF: 138, (230)
ABCD AʼBEF: 242
ABCD AʼEFG: 162°, 258
ABCD AEFG: 73
ABCD CECD: (106, see 107)
ABCD EBCD: (20, see 21) 262, 289, 297
ABCD EBʼCD: 168
ABCD EBCʼDʼ: 108
ABCD EBFG: 172°, 228
ABCD EECD: 206
ABCD EFAB: 8, (252, see 253)
ABCD EFAG: 56, 107, 260
ABCD EFCD: 4?, 7, 32°, 112, (124, see 120–23), 184, 205, 209, 215, 223, 241, 244, 257, 273 (**Total** 14 = 05%)
ABCD EFCDʼ: 18, 204, 278
ABCD EFCG: (146, see 145 and 147), 181
ABCD EFED: (155, see 156–57)
ABCD EFEG: 16, (43°‡, see 42), (81, see 80), 114
ABCD EFFG: 221
ABCD EFGA: 268
ABCD EFGBʼ: 126
ABCD EFGD: (42, see 43), (62°, see 63), (95, see 96), 116, (120, see 121–24), 129°, (144, see146–47), 212°, 239 (**Total** 9 = 3%)
ABCD EFGDʼ: (156, see 155 and 157)
ABCD EFGFʼ: 50
ABCD EFGH: 2°, (21‡, see 20) 59°, 65–66, 69–70, 79, 89, 98, 103, 111, (121, see 120 and 122–24), 128°, 130, 139–40, (147, see 146), 153–54, 158, 163, 165°–67°, 171, 180, 182, (185–86), (189, see 190), 193, 195°, 196°–97, (199, see 198), 210–11, 216–17, 220, 238, 243, 246, 248°, 251, (253, see 252), 265°–67, 271–72, 277, 282–83, 291, 294 (**Total** 55 = 20%)
ABCD EFGH: 10

Appendix II: Mode

Undecided: 104, 133

Minor tetrachord: 38
Minor tetrachord, plus *subsemi-finalis*: 279

Minor pentachord: 178, 194, 219, 262
Minor pentachord, plus *subsemi–finalis*: 28, 39
Minor pentachord, plus *subsemi–finalis*: 64, 224

Major pentachord: 113, 288
Major pentachord, plus *subsemi–finalis*: 118

Minor hexachord: 78, 83, 95 (e-f-g-a-b-**c'**), 106, 169 (f-sharp-g-a-b-c-sharp'-**d'**), 206, 208, 221, 231, 256, 264 (a-b-flat-c'-d'-d'-e-**f**), 265, 274 (f-sharp-g-a-b-c–sharp'-**d'**), 276 (f-sharp-g-a–b-c-sharp'-**d'**)
(**Total** 14 = 5%)

Major hexachord: 180, 184, 226, 246, 281
Major hexachord, plus *subfinalis*: 278

Minor: 1, 3, 10, 19–20, 22, 26, 33, 40, 42–43, 45–46, 53, 57, 65, 69, 89, 91–92, 100, 110, 125–26, 132, 134, 139, 143, 145, 149–50, 152, 155, 158–59, 162, 165, 177, 179, 181, 185–86, 193, 199, 205, 207, 233, 244, 257, 268, 277, 290, 294, 297
(**Total** 54 = 20%)

Minor (plagal): 7, 31–32, 35–37, 60, 67, 70, 77, 87, 102, 108, 116, 121, 124, 127, 142, 153, 156–57, 172–73, 182, 188, 203 (missing e-flat), 204, 210–11, 235, 238, 251, 253, 261, 267, 270, 275, 284, 286, 293, 300–1
(**Total** 42 = 15%)

Major: 8, 9, 11, 24, 25, 34, 41, 44 48, 51–52, 55, 59, 62, 68, 75–76, 80–81, 94, 101, 103, 107, 115, 119–20, 130, 135, 136–38, 146–48, 154, 159 (missing *finalis* g), 161, 166–68, 170–71, 174–75, 183, 189, 192, 195, 198, 202, 209, 212. 214–17, 220, 222, 225, 227, 232, 236, 241, 243,245, 247–49, 252, 255, 258, 260, 265, 271–72, 276, 278, 282–83, 287, 295–96, 298–99
(**Total** 81 = 30%)

Major: 2 (d-e-f-g-a-b-**c'**), 15 ([**f**]–g-a-b-flat-c'-**d'**), 17 (lacks *finalis*), 96 (a-b-flat-c'-d'-e'-**f**), 51 (d-e-f-g-a-b-**c'**), 88 (d-e-f-g-a-b-**c'**)
(**Total** 6 = 2%)

Major (plagal): 5, 12–14, 16, 18 (lacks 2nd degree), 21 (with a two-phrase intro in another key), 23, 27, 29, 47, 49–50, \54, 56, 58, 61, 63, 66, 71–74, 79, 82, 93, 97–98, 105, 109, 111, 114, 122–23, 128–29, 131, 140–41, 144, 151, 160, 163–64, 176, 187,190–91, 196–97, 200–01, 218, 223, 228–30, 234, 237, 239–40, 242, 254, 259, 266, 273, 280, 285, 289, 291
(**Total** 70 = 26%)

Dorian: 84
Dorian w/ b-flat: 6, 85–86, 99, 112, 117, 250, 263, 269
(**Total** 9 = 3%)

Lydian: 4 (d-e-**f**-g-a-b-flat)

Mixolydian: 90
Mixolydian, with *subsemifinalis*: 213

Appendix III: Meter

Free meter (*parlando rubato*): 25, 64, 165, 248

Duple meter

2/8: 208, 237

2/4: 4, 12–14, 18, 20, 24, 26, 28, 34, 36, 40, 42, 49, 54–55, 57, 70–71, 84–87, 92, 94, 102, 104–05, 108–10, 119–24, 132,134, 140, 155–57, 167–68, 171, 175, 181, 183, 188–89, 198, 201, 204, 206, 213–14, 216, 226, 231–32, 238, 247, 253–54, 267, 270, 273, 275, 278, 280, 284, 293, 300
(**Total** 73 = 27%)

4/4: 15, 37, 52, 95–97, 107,117, 127, 133, 139, 148, 162–63, 202, 207, 209, 211, 215, 221, 222, 229, 239–40, 242, 249–50, 277
(**Total** 28 = 10%)

Triple meter

3/8: 31, 63, 69, 101, 114, 138, 145, 158, 233–34, 283
(**Total** 11 = 4%)

3/4: 1, 10–11, 16, 44, 47, 56, 60, 66, 78, 82, 89, 111, 114, 118, 128, 137, 180, 185, 236, 244, 271, 276, 279, 298
(**Total** 25 = 9%)

Compound duple

6/8: 6, 19, 61–62, 88, 91, 93, 99, 106, 113, 116, 125, 136, 146, 149, 152, 159–60, 169, 178–79, 184, 187, 190–92, 200, 203, 205, 212, 219–20, 225, 227–28, 230, 241, 245, 252, 256–57, 259, 261, 264, 281, 288
(**Total** 46 = 17%)

6/4: 76
12/8: 147

Compound triple

9/8: 9, 38, 218, 260, 274

Zortzikos (5/8=3+2/8): 2, 8, 17, 43, 45, 65, 67–68, 79, 100, 144, 153–54, 166, 170, 172, 172, 210, 217, 255, 265–66, 282, 290, 294–95, 299
(**Total** 27 = 10%)

5/8: 35, 41, 48, 50, 58–59, 90, 98, 112, 126,129, 177, 224, 235, 243, 246, 251, 258, 285, 301
(**Total** 20 = 7%)

5/4: 272

Other meters

1/4: 81
7/4: 77
10/8: 22

Mixed meters:

2/4 3/4: 46

3/4 2/4 4/4: 3
3/4 2/4 5/8: 7
3/4 2/4: 223
3/4 4/4: 141

2/4 5/8 7/8 (non strict): 74
2/4 3/4 (non strict): 29, 80
3/4 2/4 (non strict): 33, 75
3/4 4/4 (non strict): 73
6/8 + 2/4 (non strict): 135, 174
6/8 9/8 (non strict): 27
6/8 3/4 (non strict): 3

Bibliography

"Abestiak." *Habe* 93 (1986): 29.

Abrahams, Roger D. *Deep down in the Jungle: Negro Narrative from the Streets of Philadelphia.* 1st rev. ed. Chicago: Aldine, 1963.

Agamben, Giorgio. *The Idea of Prose.* Albany: State University of New York Press, 1995.

Agirre, Joxean. "Gorka Aulestiaren tesi doktorala, bertsolaritz lan sistematikoa." *Egin* March 1, 1991: 49.

Agirreazaldegi, Ainhoa. "Euskal Herriko Bertso Eskolak." *Bertsolari* 48 (2002): 1–48.

——. "80 Bertso eskola baino gehiago daude Euskal Herrian." *Gara* Feb. 26, 2003: 54.

Aguergaray, Arnaud. *Des Pastorales Basques.* Diss. Université de Toulouse, 1992.

Aguirre, José María. "El sonambulismo en Federico García Lorca." *Federico García Lorca.* Ed. Ildefonso-Manuel Gil. Madrid: Taurus, 1975. 97–119.

Aire, Fernando [pseud. Xalbador]. *Odolaren Mintzoa.* Tolosa: Auspoa, 1976a.

——. Audiocassette. No. 3. K15. Donostia: Elkar, 1976b.

Alford, Violet. "The Basque Mascarade." *Folk-Lore* 39 (1928): 68–90.

——. "Dance and Song in two Pyrenean Valleys." *The Musical Quarterly* (1931a): 248–258.

——. "Ensayo sobre los orígenes de la *Maskarada* de Zuberoa." *Revista Internacional de Estudios Vascos* 12 (1931b): 373–396.

——. *Pyrenean Festivals: Calendar, customs, music and magic, drama and dance.* London: Chatto & Windus, 1937.

——. *The Hobby Horse and Other Animal Masks.* 1937. Rpt. London: Merlin, 1978.

Allen, Rupert. "An Analysis of Narrative and Symbol in Lorca's 'Romance sonámbulo.'" *Hispanic Review* 36.4 (1968): 338–352.

Alonso, José M. "Más sobre el 'Romance sonámbulo' de García Lorca." *Proceedings of the Pacific Northwest Conference on Foreign Languages, May 4–5, 1973.* Corvalis, Oreg.: Oregon State University, 1973. 130–145.

Alvarez, Pedro, and Eneida Bustamante. *Cancionero popular de Liébana.* Vol. 1. Torrelavega: Artes Gráficas Quinzañas, 1992.

Amades, Joan. *Cançoner.* Vol. 2. *Folklore de Catalunya.* Barcelona: Selecta, 1951.

Amuriza, Xabier. *Menditik mundura.* Bilbao: Printzen, 1977.

——. *Hiztegi errimatua.* Zamudio: AEK, 1981a.

——. *Hitzaren kirol nazionala*. Zamudio: AEK, 1981b.

——. *Zu ere bertsolari*. Donostia: Elkar, 1982.

——. *Bizkaiko Bertsogintza*. Bilbao: Tinkoketa; Bizkaiko Diputazio Forala, 1995. Rpt. Bilbao: Bizkaiko Bertsozale Elkartea; AEK; Zenbat Gara, 1998.

——. *Bizkaieraz bertsotan*. Donostia: Euskal Herriko Bertsozale Elkartea, 1996.

——. *Bizkaiko Kopla Zaharrak*. CD. KD 540. Donostia: Elkarlanean, 1999.

András, Lázló. "El caso de la gitana sonámbula." *Actas del Simposio Internacional de Estudios Hispánicos (Budapest, 18–19 de agosto de 1976)*. Ed. Mátyás Horányi. Budapest: Akadémiai Kiadó, 1978. 181–194.

Arana [Martija], José Antonio. "Problemas de la música vasca." *Cuadernos de Sección. Música* 1 (1984): 73–82.

Aranzadi, Telesforo de. Trans., "Diario del viaje vasco de 1801 de G. de Humboldt." *Revista Internacional de Estudios Vascos* 13 (1922): 614–658 and 14 (1923): 205–250.

——. "Los vascos o apuntaciones sobre un viaje por el País Vasco en la primavera de 1801." *Revista Internacional de Estudios Vascos* 14 (1923): 376–400 and 15 (1924): 83–127, 262–305, and 391–445. Rpt. as *Los vascos. Apuntaciones sobre un viaje por el País Vasco en la primavera del año 1801*. San Sebastián: Auñamendi, 1975.

Revista Internacional de Estudios Vascos 14 (1923). 376–400 and 15 (1924), 83–127, 262–305, 391–445. Rpt. as *Los vascos. Apuntaciones sobre un viaje por el País Vasco en la primavera del año 1801*. San Sebastián: Auñamendi, 1975.

Aresti, Gabriel. *Artikuluak. Hitzaldiak. Gutunak*. No.10. Bilbao: Bizkaiko Foru Aldundia; Susa, 1986.

Aretz, Isabel. *Costumbres tradicionales argentinas*. Buenos Aires: Raigal, 1954.

Arias Arguelles-Meres, Luis. *La Nueva España* Jan. 31, 2003: 31.

Aristotoles [Aristotle]. *Retórica* [*Rhetoric*]. Trans. Antonio Tovar. Madrid: Instituto de Estudios Políticos, 1971. Rpt. 1990.

Ariztimuño, José Mari [pseud. Aitzol]. "Desaparecerá el bertsolari." *Euzkadi* May 6, 1930: 1.

——. "Antziñako oituren piztutzea." *El Día* Feb. 5, 1933: 1.

——. "Euskal olertikera berezia (estetika)." *Yakintza* 10 (1934): 343–55.

——. "Balance literario euskeldun de 1934." *Euzkadi* Jan. 6, 1935: 1.

——. *Idazlan Guztiak*. Vol. 1. Donostia: Erein, 1988.

Armistead, Samuel G. *The Spanish Tradition in Louisiana*. Vol. 1. *Isleño Folkliterature*. Musical transcriptions by Israel J. Katz. Newark, Del.: «Juan de la Cuesta», 1992.

——. "Judeo-Spanish Traditional Poetry in the United States." *Sephardim in the Americas: Studies in Culture and History*. Ed. Martin A. Cohen and Abraham J. Peck. Tuscaloosa: University of Alabama Press, 1993. 357–377.

——. "La poesía oral improvisada en la tradición hispánica." *La décima popular en la tradición hispánica. Actas del simposio internacional sobre la décima (Las Palmas, 17–22 de diciembre 1992)*. Ed. Maximiano Trapero. Las Palmas de Gran Canaria: Universidad de Las Palmas de Gran Canaria; Cabildo Insular de Gran Canaria, 1994a. 41–69.

———. "Estudio preliminar." *Romancero*. Ed. Paloma Díaz-Mas. Barcelona: Crítica, 1994b. ix–xxi.

———. "Los estudios sobre la poesía improvisada antes de la décima." *El libro de la décima. La poesía improvisada en el Mundo Hispánico*. Ed. Maximiano Trapero. Las Palmas de Gran Canaria: Universidad de Las Palmas de Gran Canaria, 1996. 15–34.

———. "Ibn Hafsūn, ʿUmar." *Medieval Iberia: An Enciclopedia*. Ed. E. Michael Gerli. New York: Routledge, 2003. 412–413.

Armistead, Samuel G., and James T. Monroe. "A New Version of *La Morica de Antequera*." *La Corónica* 12.2 (1983–1984): 228–240.

Armistead, Samuel G., and Joseph H. Silverman. *Tres calas en el romancero sefardí (Rodas, Jerusalén, Estados Unidos)*. Madrid: Castalia, 1979.

———. *En torno al romancero sefardí (Hispanismo y balcanismo de la tradición judeo-española)*. Madrid: Seminario Menéndez Pidal, 1982.

Arripe, René. *Les Crestadous*. Pau: Presses de Covedi, 1994.

Aulestia, Gorka. *Bertsolarismo*. Bilbao: Bizkaiko Foru Aldundia, 1990.

———. *Improvisational Poetry from the Basque Country*. Trans. Lisa Corcostegui and Linda White. Reno, Las Vegas and London: University of Nevada Press, 1995.

———. "Un siglo de literatura vasca (IV, a)." *Sancho el Sabio* 9 (1998): 30–46.

———. "*Bertsolaritza*: Island or Archipelago?" Old Songs, New Theories: A Symposium on Oral Improvisational Poetry. Center for Basque Studies, University of Nevada, Reno, May 16–17, 2003.

Ayape, Humbelino. *Las tardes de la Bardena*. 4 vols. Oiartzun: Sendoa, 1994.

Ayensa i Prat, Eusebi. "Glosat i 'tsàtisma': una aproximació al fenomen del combat poètic a Xipre i a les Balears." *Randa* (Catal. Curial) 40 (1998?): 81–94.

Azkue Aberasturi, Resurrección María de. *Cancionero popular vasco*. 11 notebooks in 2 vols. Bilbao: Euskaltzaindia, 1922–1925. 2nd ed. with prologue by Manuel de Lekuona. 2 vols. Bilbao: Biblioteca de la Gran Enciclopedia Vasca, 1968. 3rd ed. With prologue by José Antonio Arana Martija. 2 vols. Bilbao: Euskaltzaindia, 1990.

———. *Euskalerriaren Yakintza. Literatura popular del País Vasco*. Madrid: Espasa-Calpe, 1935–1947. Rpt. 1959.

Bapatean 92. Donostia: Euskal Herriko Bertsozale Elkartea, 1993.

Bapatean 94. Donostia: Euskal Herriko Bertsozale Elkartea, 1995.

Bapatean 97. Donostia: Euskal Herriko Bertsozale Elkartea, 1998.

Bapatean 98. Donostia: Euskal Herriko Bertsozale Elkartea, 1999.

Barandiaran, Gaizka. *Danzas de Euskal Erri*. 3 vols. San Sebastián: Auñamendi, 1963–1969.

———. "Zortziko." *Diccionario de la Música Española y Hispanoamericana*. Vol. 10. Madrid: Sociedad General de Autores y Editores, 2002. 1193–1195.

Barandiarán, José Miguel de. "Basque Music." *The New Grove Dictionary of Music and Musicians*. Ed. Stanley Sadie. Vol. 2. London: Macmillan, 1980. 242–246.

———. *A View from the Witch's Cave*. Trans. Linda White. Reno: University of Nevada Press, 1991.

Barrenetxea Gutiérrez, José Mariano. *Nuestros instrumentos musicales*. Bilbao: Caja de Ahorros Vizcaína, 1975.

Barthes, Roland. *The Rustle of Language*. New York: Hill and Wang, 1986.

Bar-Yosef, Amatzia. "Traditional Rural Style Under a Process of Change: The Singing Style of the Ḥaddāy, Palestinian Folk Poet-Singers." *Asian Music* 29.2 (1998): 57–82.

Bateson, Gregory, and Mary Catherine Bateson. *Angels Fear: An Investigation into the Nature and Meaning of the Sacred*. London: Rider, 1988.

Bauman, Richard. *Verbal Art as Performance*. Prospect Heights, Ill.: Waveland Press, 1977.

Bell, Joseph Norment, *Love Theory in Later Ḥanbalite Islam*. Albany: State University of New York Press, 1979.

Bender, Mark. *Plum and Bamboo: China's Suzhou Chantefable Tradition*. Voices in Performance and Text. Urbana: University of Illinois Press, 2003. E-companion at www.oraltradition.org.

Bertsolari Txapelketa (1962–XII–30). Auspoa 22. Tolosa: Auspoa, 1963.

Bertsolari Txapelketa (1965–I–1). Auspoa 43. Tolosa: Auspoa, 1965.

Bertsolari Txapelketa (1967–VI–11). Auspoa 67. Tolosa: Auspoa, 1967.

Bertsolari Txapelketa Nagusia (Donostia, 1980–I–6). Auspoa 141. Tolosa: Auspoa, 1980.

Bertsolari Txapelketa Nagusia 1993. Donostia: Euskal Herriko Bertsolari Elkartea; Elkar, 1994.

Bertsolari Txapelketa Nagusia 1997. Donostia: Euskal Herriko Bertsozale Elkartea; Elkarlanean, 1998.

Bertsolari Txapelketa Nagusia 2001. Donostia: Euskal Herriko Bertsozale Elkartea; Andoain: Bertsolari Liburuak, 2002.

Bevan, Anthony Ashley. Ed., *The Naqāʾiḍ of Jarīr and al-Farazdaq*. 3 vols. Leiden: E. J. Brill, 1905.

Bikandi Belandia, Sabin. "Bertsolarismo." *Diccionario de la Música Española y Hispanoamericana*. Vol. 2. Madrid: Sociedad General de Autores y Editores, 1999. 218–222.

Blanco, Domingo. "La poesía oral improvisada en Galicia. Las *regueifas.*" *Actas del VI Encuentro-Festival Iberoamericano de la Décima y el Verso Improvisado (Las Palmas de Gran Canaria, del 6 al 11 de octubre de 1998)*. Vol. 1. *Estudios*. Ed. Maximiano Trapero, Eladio Santana Martel and Carmen Márquez Montes. Las Palmas de Gran Canaria: Universidad de Las Palmas de Gran Canaria; ACADE, 2000. 339–352.

Blecua, Alberto. Ed., *Juan Ruiz. Arcipreste de Hita. Libro de buen amor*. Madrid: Cátedra, 1992.

Bonaddio, Federico. "Lorca's 'Romance sonámbulo': The Desirability of Non-Disclosure." *Bulletin of Hispanic Studies* 72.4 (1995): 385–401.

Bonebakker, Seeger A. "Irtidjāl." *The Encylopaedia of Islam*. Ed. H.A.R. Gibb et al. New ed. Vol. 4 Leiden: Brill, 1978. 80–81.

———. "Ḳudāma." *The Encyclopaedia of Islam.* 2nd ed.Vol. 5. Leiden: E. J. Brill, 1980. 318–322.

Bonmattí Limorte, Casimiro. "El trovo del Campo de Cartagena (Murcia)." *Actas del VI Encuentro-Festival Iberoamericano de la Décima y el Verso Improvisado (Las Palmas de Gran Canaria, del 6 al 11 de octubre de 1998).* Vol. 1. *Estudios.* Ed. Maximiano Trapero, Eladio Santana Martel and Carmen Márquez Montes. Las Palmas de Gran Canaria: Universidad de Las Palmas de Gran Canaria; ACADE, 2000. 371–392.

Bonner, John Tyler. *The Evolution of Culture in Animals and Men.* Princeton: Princeton University Press, 1980.

Borges, Jorge Luis. *Aspectos de la literatura gauchesca.* Montevideo: «Número», 1950.

Borges de Castro, António. *Cantigas ao Desafio.* Oporto: Edição do Autor, 1983.

Bossy, Michel-André. Ed. and trans., *Medieval Debate Poetry: Vernacular Works.* New York: Garland Publishing, 1987.

Bradbury, Nancy Mason. *Writing Aloud: Storytelling in Late Medieval England.* Urbana: University of Illinois Press, 1998.

———. "Traditional Referentiality: The Aesthetic Power of Oral Traditional Structures." *Teaching Oral Traditions.* Ed. John Miles Foley. New York: Modern Language Association, 1998. 136–45.

Braga, Theóphilo. *Cantos Populares do Archipélago Açoriano.* Oporto: Livraria Nacional, 1868.

Brann, Ross. "Judah Halevi." *The Literature of al-Andalus.* Ed. María Rosa Menocal, Raymond P. Scheindlin and Michael Sells. Cambridge: Cambridge University Press, 2000. 265–81.

Brogan, T.V.F. "Inspiration." *The New Princeton Encyclopedia of Poetry and Poetics.* Ed. Alex Preminger and T. V. F. Brogan. Princeton, N.J.: Princeton University Press, 1993. 609–10.

Brooks, Elaine S. "The Word is the Sword: A Study of Language, Themes, and Rhyme in Fifteenth-Century «*Cancionero*» Poetry." Diss. University of California, Davis, 1990.

Caballero Barriopedro, Jesús. *¡Buen pie para una cuarteta! (Historias de Brihuela).* Madrid: Compañía Literaria, 1996.

Caldevila, Alfredo, and Antonio Zavala. *Una vida en los Picos de Europa.* Biblioteca de Narrativa Popular 15. Oiartzun: Sendoa, 1999.

Câmara Cascudo, Luis da. *Literatura Oral no Brasil.* 2nd ed. Rio de Janeiro: José Olympio, 1978.

Camino, Iñaki, and Josu Landa. "Bakoitzak bere era pertsonala finkatzea duk garrantzitsua." *Argia* Nov. 21, 1986: 41.

Camps y Soler, Óscar. "La música del pueblo vascongado, su poesía y sus costumbres (fragmentos de una obra inédita)." *La España Musical* 6.258 (1871): 1–2.

Canales, Maria Cristina, and Jane Frances Morrissey. Eds. and trans., *Gracias, Matiox, Thanks, Hermano Pedro: A Trilingual Anthology of Guatemalan Oral Tradition.* A.B. Lord Studies in Oral Tradition 12. New York: Garland, 1996.

Cárdenas, Daniel L. "Otra interpretación de 'Romance sonámbulo.'" *Explicación de Textos Literarios* 1–2 (1973): 111–118.

Caro, Rodrigo. *Días geniales o lúdicos.* Ed. Jean-Pierre Etienvre. 2 vols. Madrid: Espasa-Calpe, 1978.

Caro Baroja, Julio. *La vida rural en Vera de Bidasoa (Navarra).* Madrid: Consejo Superior de Investigación Científica, 1944.

———. *El Carnaval. Análisis histórico-cultural.* Madrid: Taurus, 1965.

Carré Alvarellos, Leandro. *Diccionario galego-castelán.* 3rd ed. A Coruña: Roel, 1951.

Carrizo, Juan Alfonso. *Cancionero popular de Salta.* Buenos Aires: Baiocco, 1933.

Carvalho-Neto, Paulo de. *Diccionario del folklore ecuatoriano.* Quito: Casa de la Cultura Ecuatoriana, 1964a.

———. *Antología del folklore ecuatoriano.* Quito: Editorial Universitaria, 1964b.

Casaverde, Janet. "La *copleada en rueda* y la improvisación en el noroeste argentino." *Actas del VI Encuentro-Festival Iberoamericano de la Décima y el Verso Improvisado (Las Palmas de Gran Canaria, del 6 al 11 de octubre de 1998).* Vol. 1. *Estudios.* Ed. Maximiano Trapero, Eladio Santana Martel and Carmen Márquez Montes. Las Palmas de Gran Canaria: Universidad de Las Palmas de Gran Canaria; ACADE, 2000. 393–400.

Chao Gejin. *Minority Oral Traditions in China.* Special issue of *Oral Tradition,* 2001.

Chas Aguión, Antonio. *Preguntas y respuestas en la poesía cancioneril castellana.* Madrid: Fundación Universitaria Española, 2000.

Chávez Franco, Modesto. *Crónicas del Guayaquil antiguo.* Guayaquil: Imprenta y Talleres Municipales, 1930.

Checa, Francisco. "El trovo alpujarreño, sedante en una tierra de dolor." *El trovo en el festival de música tradicional de La Alpujarra: 1982–1991.* Ed. José Criado and Francisco Ramos Moya. Sevilla: Centro de Documentación Musical de Andalucía, 1992. 271–281.

Christian Jr., William A. "Trovas y comparsas del Alto Nansa." *Publicaciones del Instituto de Etnografía y Folklore "Hoyos Sáinz"* 4 (1972): 243–428 and 7 (1975): 151–169.

———. *Person and God in a Spanish Valley.* Rev. ed. Princeton: Princeton University Press, 1989.

———. *Trovas y comparsas del Alto Nansa.* 2nd ed. Santander: Aula de Etnografía de la Universidad de Cantabria, 1998.

———. "Verso improvisado en las montañas occidentales de Cantabria." *Actas del VI Encuentro-Festival Iberoamericano de la Décima y el Verso Improvisado (Las Palmas de Gran Canaria, del 6 al 11 de octubre de 1998).* Vol. 1. *Estudios.* Ed. Maximiano Trapero, Eladio Santana Martel and Carmen Márquez Montes. Las Palmas de Gran Canaria: Universidad de Las Palmas de Gran Canaria; ACADE, 2000. 405–418.

Clotelle Clarke, Dorothy C. "Sobre la espinela." *Revista de Filología Española* 23 (1936): 293–304.

Cobb, Carl W. *Federico García Lorca.* New York: Twayne, 1967.

———. *Lorca's "Romancero Gitano"*. Jackson: University Press of Mississippi, 1983.

Cole, Peter. Trans., *Selected Poems of Shmuel HaNagid*. Princeton: Princeton University Press, 1996.

Contreras Oyarzún, Constantino. "El arte tradicional de la décima. Raíz hispana y fronda chilena." *Actas del VI Encuentro-Festival Iberoamericano de la Décima y el Verso Improvisado (Las Palmas de Gran Canaria, del 6 al 11 de octubre de 1998)*. Vol. 1. *Estudios*. Ed. Maximiano Trapero, Eladio Santana Martel and Carmen Márquez Montes. Las Palmas de Gran Canaria: Universidad de Las Palmas de Gran Canaria; ACADE, 2000. 189–199.

Córdova Iturregui, Félix. "Los trovadores puertorriqueños. Algunas consideraciones sobre el arte de la improvisación." *La décima popular en la tradición hispánica. Actas del simposio internacional sobre la décima (Las Palmas, 17–22 de diciembre 1992)*. Ed. Maximiano Trapero. Las Palmas de Gran Canaria: Universidad de Las Palmas de Gran Canaria; Cabildo Insular de Gran Canaria, 1994. 73–85.

Corominas, Joan, and José A. Pascual. *Diccionario crítico etimológico castellano e hispánico*. 6 vols. Madrid: Gredos, 1980–1991.

Corriente, Federico. Ed. and trans., *Gramática, métrica y texto del cancionero hispanoárabe de Aban Quzmán*. Madrid: Instituto Hispano-Árabe de Cultura, 1980.

———. Trans., *Ibn Quzman. El cancionero hispanoárabe*. Madrid: Editora Nacional, 1984.

———. Trans., *Ibn Quzmān. Cancionero andalusí*. Madrid: Hiperión, 1989.

———. Ed., *El cancionero hispano-árabe de Aban Quzmán de Córdoba (m. 555/1160) "Iṣābat al-aġrāḍ fī ḏikr al-a'rāḍ"*. Cairo: Majlis al-A'là li-l-Ṭaqāfa, 1995.

———. *A Dictionary of Andalusi Arabic*. Leiden, New York and Köln: E. J. Brill, 1997.

———. *Diccionario de arabismos y voces afines en iberromance*. Madrid: Gredos, 1999.

Cossío, José María de. "Cantares de Boda." *Boletín de la Biblioteca Menéndez Pelayo* (1928): 225–231 and (1930): 309–311.

———. "Noticia de Don Manuel de la Cuesta y sus versos." *Boletín de la Biblioteca Menéndez y Pelayo*. Homenaje a Miguel Artigas. 2 (1932): 446–537.

———. *Cantares cazurros*. Madrid: Talleres Espasa Calpe, 1942.

———. "La décima antes de Espinel." *Revista de Filología Española* 28 (1944): 428–454.

———. *Rutas literarias de la Montaña*. Santander: Diputación Provincial, 1960.

———. *Estudios sobre escritores montañeses*. 3 vols. Santander: Instituto de Literatura José María de Pereda; Institución Cultural de Cantabria, 1973.

Cossío, José María de, and Tomás Maza Solano. *Romancero popular de la Montaña. Colección de romances tradicionales*. 2 vols. Santander: Sociedad de Menéndez y Pelayo, 1933–1934.

Costa Fontes, Manuel da. *Romanceiro Português dos Estados Unidos*. Vol. 1. *Nova Inglaterra*. Coimbra: Universidade, 1980.

———. *Romanceiro da Província de Trás-os-Montes*. 2 vols. Coimbra: Universidade, 1987.

———. "The Study of the Ballad and Other Portuguese Folk Traditions in North America." *Canadian Ethnic Studies* 23.3 (1991): 119–139.

Covarrubias, Sebastián de. *Tesoro de la lengua castellana o española*. Ed. Martín de Riquer. Barcelona: S. A. Horta, 1943.

Crawford, J. P. Wickersham. "*Echarse pullas*: A Popular Form of *Tenzone*." *Romanic Review* 6 (1915): 150–164.

Crespo Pozo, José S. *Contribución a un vocabulario castellano-gallego*. Madrid: Revista "Estudios," 1963.

Criado, José. *De trovo con Candiota (1985–1987)*. Sevilla: Centro de Documentación Musical de Andalucía, 1993.

———. "La décima popular en La Alpujarra." *La décima popular en la tradición hispánica. Actas del simposio internacional sobre la décima (Las Palmas, 17–22 de diciembre 1992)*. Ed. Maximiano Trapero. Las Palmas de Gran Canaria: Universidad de Las Palmas de Gran Canaria; Cabildo Insular de Gran Canaria, 1994. 201–216.

Criado, José, and Francisco Ramos Moya. Eds., *El trovo en el festival de música tradicional de La Alpujarra: 1982–1991*. Sevilla: Centro de Documentación Musical de Andalucía, 1992.

Crystal, David. *Language and the Internet*. Cambridge: Cambridge University Press, 2001.

Cuesta, Daniel, and Antonio Zavala. *En la Montaña de León*. Biblioteca de Narrativa Popular 13. Oiartzun: Sendoa, 1996.

Cummins, John G. "Methods and Conventions in Poetic Debate." *Hispanic Review* 31 (1963): 307–23.

———. "The Survival in the Spanish *Cancioneros* of the Form and Themes of Provençal and Old French Poetic Debates." *Bulletin of Hispanic Studies* 42 (1965): 9–17.

Dannemann, Manuel. "Poesía juglaresca en América Latina, setecientos años después." *Actas del VI Encuentro-Festival Iberoamericano de la Décima y el Verso Improvisado (Las Palmas de Gran Canaria, del 6 al 11 de octubre de 1998)*. Vol. 1. *Estudios*. Ed. Maximiano Trapero, Eladio Santana Martel and Carmen Márquez Montes. Las Palmas de Gran Canaria: Universidad de Las Palmas de Gran Canaria; ACADE, 2000. 39–50.

DeLong-Tonelli, Beverly J. "The Lyric Dimension in Lorca's 'Romance sonámbulo.'" *Romance Notes* 12.2 (1971): 289–295.

Díaz-Mas, Paloma. Ed., *Romancero*. Barcelona: Crítica, 1994.

Díaz-Pimienta, Alexis. "Apuntes para el estudio del repentismo en Cuba." *La décima popular en Iberoamérica (Memorias del II Festival iberoamericano de la décima)*. Veracruz: Instituto Veracruzano de Cultura, 1995. 239–252.

———. *La teoría de la Improvisación. Primeras páginas para el estudio del repentismo*. Prologue Maximiano Trapero. Oiartzun: Sendoa, 1998.

———. "La décima improvisada." *La décima. Su historia, su geografía, sus manifestaciones*. Ed. Maximiano Trapero. La Laguna: Centro de la Cultura Popular Canaria; Câmara Municipal de Évora, 2001. 101–128.

Diharce, Jean [pseud. Iratzeder]. *Biziaren Olerkia*. Bilbao: Gero, 1984.

Di Stasi, Lawrence. *Mal Occhio [evil eye]: The Underside of Vision*. San Francisco: North Point Press, 1981.

Dölz-Blackburn, Inés. *Origen y desarrollo de la poesía tradicional y popular chilena desde la Conquista hasta el presente*. Santiago: Editorial Nascimento, 1984.

Donostia, José Antonio de. [pseud. José Gonzalo Zulaika y Arregui]. *Euskal Eres-Sorta. Cancionero vasco*. Madrid: Unión Musical Española, 1919.

———. "Instrumentos musicales de trabajo en el País Vasco." *Anuario Musical* 3 (1948): 3–49.

———. "Instrumentos musicales populares vasco." *Anuario Musical* 7 (1952): 3–49.

———. "Vasconia." *Diccionario de la Música Labor*. Ed. Joquín Pena and Higinio Anglés. Vol. 2. Barcelona: Labor, 1954. 2196–2202.

———. "Folk Music: Basque." *Grove's Dictionary of Music and Musicians*. Ed. Eric Bloom. 5th ed. Vol.3. London: Macmillan, 1954. 193–198.

Dorronsoro, Joanito. Ed., *Bertso doinutegia*. 4 vols. Donostia: Euskal Herriko Bertsolari Elkartea, 1995.

Dorson, Richard M. *Folklore and Fakelore: Essays Toward a Discipline of Folk Studies*. Cambridge, Mass. and London: Harvard University Press, 1976.

Dozy, Reinhart. *Spanish Islam*. Trans. Francis Griffin Stokes. New York: Duffield, 1913.

Dozy, Reinhart, and W. H. Engelmann. *Glossaire des mots espagnols et portugais dérivés de l'arabe*. 2nd ed. Leiden: E. J. Brill, 1869.

DuBois, Thomas A. *Finnish Folk Poetry and the* Kalevala. New York: Garland, 1995.

Duggan, Joseph J. "Formulaic Language and Mode of Creation." *Oral-Formulaic Theory: A Folklore Casebook*. Ed. John Miles Foley. New York & London: Garland, 1990. 83–108.

Dundes, Alan. "Projection in Folklore." *Interpreting Folklore*. Ed. Alan Dundes. Bloomington: Indiana University Press, 1980. 33–61.

———. Ed., *The Evil Eye: A Folklore Casebook*. New York: Garland Publishers, 1981.

———. *Fables of the Ancients? Folklore in the Qur'an*. Lanham, Md.: Rowman & Littlefield, 2003.

Dunn, Charles W., and Edward T. Byrnes. Eds., *Middle English Literature*. New York: Harcourt, Brace, Jovanovich, 1973.

Durand, José. "Romances y corridos de los *Doce Pares de Francia*." *El Romancero hoy. Nuevas fronteras*. Ed. Antonio Sánchez Romeralo et al. Madrid: Cátedra-Seminario Menéndez Pidal, 1979. 159–179.

Dutton, Brian, and Joaquín González Cuenca. Eds., *Cancionero de Juan Alfonso de Baena*. Madrid: Visor, 1993.

Egaña, Andoni. *Socratikoek ere badute ama*. Donostia: Erein, 1989.

———. *Aitaren batean*. Donostia: Elkar, 1990.

———. "1984.eko Errege Egunez." *Bertsolari* 16 (1994a): 61–64.

———. *Tximeletak sabelean*. CD. IZ-425. N.p.: IZ, 1994b.

———. "Características generales del bertsolarismo." IV Festival iberoamericano de la décima. Veracruz, Mexico, 1996a.

———. "Bertsolariak ez du nahi duena esaten, errimek esaten uzten diotena baizik." Interview. *Euskaldunon Egunkaria* July 2, 1996b. 29.

———. *Pausoa noiz luzatu.* Irun: Euskalgintza Elkarlanean Fundazioa; Alberdania, 1998.

———. *Zaudete geldi pixka batean.* Donostia: Elkar, 1999.

———. *Imanol Urbieta. Luzea da bidea.* Amorebieta-Etxano: Ibaizabal, 2002.

Egaña, Andoni, and Jon Sarasua. *Zozoak beleari.* Irun: Alberdania, 1997.

Eizmendi, Ignacio/Inazio/Iñaki [pseud. Basarri]. *Atano III: bere edestia bertsotan.* Zarauz: Icharopena, 1949.

———. *Basarriren Bertso-Sorta.* Zarautz: Itxaropena, 1950.

———. *Kantari nator.* Zarautz: Itxaropena, 1960.

———. *Laugarren Txinpartak.* Tolosa: Auspoa, 1966.

———. *Sortu zaizkidanak.* Tolosa: Auspoa, 1973.

———. *Kezka giroan.* Tolosa: Auspoa, 1983.

———. *Bertsolaritzari buruz.* Tolosa: Auspoa, 1984.

———. *Nere bordatxotik.* Auspoaren Sail Nagusiak 2. Tolosa: Auspoa, 1992.

Elliot, Robert C. *The Power of Satire: Magic, Ritual, Art.* Princeton: Princeton University Press, 1960.

Elworthy, Frederick Thomas. *The Evil Eye: An Account of This Ancient and Widespread Superstition.* New York: Julian Press, 1958.

Erdely, Stephen. *Music of Southslavic Epics from the Bihać Region of Bosnia.* New York: Garland, 1995.

Errege eguneko bertso-sayoa. Auspoa 10. Tolosa: Auspoa, 1962.

Escabí, Pedro C. *Estudio etnográfico de la cultura popular de Puerto Rico. Morovis. Vista parcial del folklore de Puerto Rico.* San Juan: Universidad de Puerto Rico, 1970.

Escabí, Pedro C., and Elsa M. Escabí. *Vista parcial del folklore. La décima. Estudio etnográfico de la cultura popular de Puerto Rico.* San Juan: Universidad de Puerto Rico, 1976.

Espinel, Vicente. *Diversas rimas.* Ed. and intro. Alberto Navarro González and Pilar Navarro Velasco. Salamanca: Ediciones de la Universidad de Salamanca, 1980.

Espinosa, Francisco. "Folklore salvadoreño." *La Revista Americana de Buenos Aires* 9.126 (1934): 126–136.

Estornés Zubizarreta, Idoia. "Apuntes sobre la sociedad guipuzcoana a través del *Guipuzcoaco provinciaren condaira* de Juan Ignacio de Iztueta." *Revista Internacional de Estudios Vascos* 33.1 (1988): 159–169.

Etxaniz, Nemesio. *Lur Berri Bila.* San Sebastián: Izara, 1967.

Etxezarreta, Jesús Mª. *Bertsolarien desafioak. Guduak eta Txapelketak.* Auspoa 10. Tolosa: Auspoa, 1993.

Euskal Herriko Bertsolari Txapelketa Nagusia 1986. Donostia: Elkar, 1987.

Feijóo, Samuel. Ed., *La décima popular*. La Habana: Biblioteca del Capitolio Nacional, 1961.

Felman, Soshana. *The Literary Speech Act*. Ithaca: Cornell University Press, 1983.

Fernandez, James W. "Poetry in Motion: Being Moved by Amusement, Mockery and Mortality in the Asturian Mountains." *New Literary History* 8 (1976–1977): 459–483. Rpt. in James W. Fernandez. *Persuasions and Performances: The Play of Tropes in Culture*. Bloomington: Indiana University Press, 1986: 73–102.

——. *Bwiti: An Ethnography of the Religious Imagination in Africa*. Princeton: Princeton University Press, 1982.

——. *Persuasions and Performances. The Play of Tropes in Culture*. Bloomington: Indiana University Press, 1986a.

——. "The Argument of Images and the Experience of Returning to the Whole." *The Anthropology of Experience*. Ed. Victor W. Turner and Edward M. Bruner. Urbana: University of Illinois Press, 1986b. 159–187.

——. "Response to Roger Keesing: Exotic Readings of Cultural Texts." *Current Anthropology* 30. 3 (1989): 459–479.

——. Rev. of *Improvisational Poetry from the Basque Country* by Gorka Aulestia. *Anthropological Linguistics* 38 (1996): 403–404.

——. "On Trees of Knowledge of Self and Other in Culture: Models for the Moral Imagination." *The Social Life of Trees*. Ed. Laura Rival and Maurice Bloch. Oxford and New York: Berg, 1998. 81–110.

Fernández, Xoaquín Lorenzo. *Cantigueiro popular da Limia Baixa*. Vigo: Galaxia, 1973.

Fernández de Larrinoa, Kepa. "Notes et reflexions autour de l'organisation et de l'experience festive dans un village du Pays de Soule." Fête et Identité de la Ville: Journées d'Étude de la Société d'Ethnologie Française. Musée National des Arts et Traditions Populaires, Paris, February 25–26, 1993a.

——. *Nekazal Gizartea eta Antzerki Herrikoia Pirinioetako Haran Batean*. San Sebastián: Sociedad de Estudios Vascos, 1993b.

——. *Mujer, ritual y fiesta*. Pamplona: Pamiela, 1997.

——. "Zuberoako Maskaradak izeneko antzerkiaren herri literatura." *Euskera*. Bilbao: Real Academia de la Lengua Vasca, 1999. 267–282.

Fernández Manzano, Reinaldo et al. "El trovo en la Alpujarra." *El trovo en el festival de música tradicional de La Alpujarra, 1982–1991*. Ed. José Criado and Francisco Ramos Moya. Sevilla: Centro de Documentación Musical de Andalucía, 1992. 25–61.

Ferrando, Ignacio. *Las sesiones del Zaragocí. Relatos picarescos (maqāmāt) del siglo XII*. Zaragoza: Prensas Universitarias de Zaragoza, 1999.

Finnegan, Ruth H. *Oral Poetry*. Cambridge: Cambridge University Press, 1977. Rpt. 1992.

——. Ed., *A World Treasury of Oral Poetry*. Bloomington: Indiana University Press, 1978.

——. "What is Oral Literature Anyway? Comments in the Light of Some African and Other Comparative Material." *Oral-Formulaic Theory: A Folklore Casebook*. Ed. John Miles Foley. New York & London: Garland, 1990. 243–288.

Fitz Stephen, William. *Norman London*. Trans. H. E. Butler. New York: Italica Press, 1990.

Foley, John Miles. *Oral-Formulaic Theory and Research: An Introduction and Annotated Bibliography*. New York: Garland, 1985.

——. *The Theory of Oral Composition: History and Methodology*. Bloomington and Indianapolis: Indiana University Press, 1988. Rpt. 1992.

——. Ed., *Oral-Formulaic Theory: A Folklore Casebook*. New York & London: Garland, 1990a.

——. *Traditional Oral Epic: The Odyssey, Beowulf, and the Serbo-Croatian Return Song*. Berkeley and Los Angeles: University of California Press, 1990b. Rpt. 1993.

——. *Immanent Art: From Structure to Meaning in Traditional Oral Epic*. Bloomington and Indianapolis: Indiana University Press, 1991.

——. "Word-Power, Performance, and Tradition." *Journal of American Folklore* 105 (1992): 275–301.

——. *The Singer of Tales in Performance*. Bloomington: Indiana University Press, 1995.

——. Ed., *Teaching Oral Traditions*. New York: Modern Language Association, 1998.

——. *Homer's Traditional Art*. University Park: Pennsylvania State University Press, 1999.

——. *How To Read an Oral Poem*. Urbana: University of Illinois Press, 2002. E-companion at www.oraltradition.org/hrop.

——. "How Genres Leak in Traditional Verse." *Unlocking the Wordhord: Anglo-Saxon Studies in Memory of Edward B. Irving, Jr*. Ed. Mark C. Amodio and Katherine O'Brien O'Keeffe. Toronto: University of Toronto Press, 2003. 76–108.

——. Ed. and trans., *The Wedding of Mustajbey's Son Bećirbey*, sung by Halil Bajgorić. Folklore Fellows Communications. Helsinki: Finnish Literature Society, 2004. E-companion at www.oraltradition.org/performances/zbm.

Fourquet, François. "La Mascarade d'Ordiarp." *Bulletin du Musée Basque. Bayonne* 129 (1990): 101–156.

Fraile Gil, José Manuel. *El Valle de Polaciones (Cantábria)*. CD. Madrid: Tecnosaga, 1997.

Friedrich, Rainer. "The Problem of an Oral Poetics." *Oralité et littérature/Orality and Literature*. Proc. of XI Cong. of the Intl. Compar. Lit. Assn. Paris: 1985. Rpt. New York: Peter Lang, 1991. 19–28.

Fuente, Alfredo de la. *El payador en la cultura nacional*. Buenos Aires: Corregidor, 1986.

Gallop, Rodney. *A Book of the Basques*. London: Macmillan, 1930. Rpt. Reno: University of Nevada Press, 1970.

——. "The Development of Folk-Song in Portugal and the Basque Country." *Proceedings of the Royal Musical Association* 61 (1934–1935): 61–80.

——. *Los vascos*. Trans. Isabel Gil Ramades. Madrid: Ediciones Castilla, 1948.

Garamendi, Mª Arene. *El teatro popular vasco. Semiótica de la representación*. Vitoria: Seminario Julio de Urkijo, 1991.

García, José Ramón. "El bertsolarismo del siglo XIX al XXI."*Historia de la literatura vasca*. Ed. Patricio Urquizu. Madrid: UNED, 2001. 403–479.

García, Juan Francisco. "Formas de la música folklórica dominicana." *Boletín del Folklore Dominicano* (Santo Domingo) 1.1 (June 1946): 10–14.

García, Manuel Jesús Javier. "La junta (Del natural)." *Boletín del Folklore Dominicano* (Santo Domingo). 1.1 (June 1946): 34–43.

García Cotorruelo, Emilia. *Estudio sobre el habla de Cartagena y su comarca.* Madrid: Real Academia Española, 1959.

García Fernández, Rosa. Personal interview by William A. Christian Jr. Uznayo, July 17, 1999.

García Gómez, E. "Un eclipse de la poesía en Sevilla. La época almorávide." *Al-Andalus* 10 (1945): 285–343.

———. "Nuevos testimonios del 'odio a Sevilla' de los poetas musulmanes." *Al-Andalus* 14 (1949): 143–148.

———. *Todo Ben Quzmān.* 3 vols. Madrid: Gredos, 1972.

García Lorca, Federico. *Obras completas.* Ed. Arturo del Hoyo. 3 vols. Madrid: Aguilar, 1986.

García Matos, Manuel. *Antologia del folklore musical de España.* Madrid: Hispavox, 1960.

García Santos, Juan Felipe. "El 'Romance sonámbulo'. ¿Un romance de ciego?" *El comentario de textos. Universidad de Málaga.* Ed. Inés Carrasco and Guadalupe Fernández Ariza. Málaga: Universidad de Málaga, 1998. 85–90.

Garulo, Teresa. "En torno a Granada. Reflexiones sobre la poesía en la época almorávide." *Qurṭuba* 4 (1999): 73–96.

Garzia, Joxerra. *Jon Sarasua Bertso-Ispiluan Barrena.* Irun: Alberdania, 1998.

———. "Gaur egungo bertsolarien baliabide poetiko-erretorikoak. Marko teorikoa eta aplikazio didaktikoa." Diss. Euskal Herriko Unibertsitatea-Universidad del País Vasco (Leioa), 2000a.

———. "Texto, contexto y situación en la poética de los bertsolaris." *Actas del VI Encuentro-Festival Iberoamericano de la Décima y el Verso Improvisado (Las Palmas de Gran Canaria, del 6 al 11 de octubre de 1998)* Vol. 1. *Estudios.* Ed. Maximiano Trapero, Eladio Santana Martel and Carmen Márquez Montes. Las Palmas de Gran Canaria: Universidad de Las Palmas de Gran Canaria; ACADE, 2000b. 429–438.

Garzia, Joxerra, Jon Sarasua and Andoni Egaña. *The Art of Bertsolaritza: Improvised Basque Verse Singing.* [Spanish version. *El arte del bertsolarismo. Realidad y claves de la improvisación oral vasca*]. Donostia: Bertsozale Elkartea; Andoain: Bertsolari Liburuak, 2001.

Gibson, Ian. *Federico García Lorca: A Life.* New York: Pantheon, 1989.

Giffen, Lois Anita. *Theory of Profane Love among the Arabs: The Development of the Genre.* New York: New York University Press, 1971.

Gomarín Guirado, Fernando. *Cancionero secreto de Cantabria.* Santander: Universidad de Cantabria, 1989.

Gómez de Tudanca, Rafael. *Semblanza y obra de José María de Cossío.* Santander: Sociedad Menéndez y Pelayo, 2000.

Gómez Lombraña, Luis. Personal interview by William A. Christian Jr. Salceda, July 17, 1999.

González Ortega, Manuel. *Vida y décimas de Juan Betancort*. Prologue Maximiano Trapero. Las Palmas de Gran Canaria: Viceconsejería de Cultura y Deportes del Gobierno de Canarias; Ayuntamiento de Tuineje, 1994.

Gorostiaga, Juan. *Antología de poesía popular vasca*. San Sebastián: Biblioteca Vascongada de los Amigos del País, 1955.

Guanche, Jesús. "Aspectos geográficos y cartográficos de la décima popular cubana." *La décima popular en la tradición hispánica. Actas del simposio internacional sobre la décima (Las Palmas, 17–22 de diciembre 1992)*. Ed. Maximiano Trapero. Las Palmas de Gran Canaria: Universidad de Las Palmas de Gran Canaria; Cabildo Insular de Gran Canaria, 1994. 257–264.

Guerrero Cárpena, Ismael. "Santos Vega y Poca Ropa: Payadores rioplatenses." *Boletín de la Academia Argentina de Letras*. 15.57 (1946): 637–669.

Guilcher, Jean-Michel. *La tradition de danse en Béarn et Pays Basque Français*. Paris: Éditions de la Maison des Sciences de l'Homme, 1984.

Guillén, Jorge. Prólogo. *Obras completas*. By Federico García Lorca. Ed. Arturo del Hoyo. Vol. 1. Madrid: Aguilar, 1986. xv–lxxxiv.

Güiraldes, Ricardo. *Don Segundo Sombra*. Buenos Aires: Proa, 1926. Rpt. Madrid: ALLCA XX, 1988. English version. Trans. Patricia Owen Steiner. Pittsburgh: University of Pittsburgh Press, 1995.

Gunzburg, David de. *Le divan d'Ibn Guzman*. Facs. I. Berlin: S. Calvary & Co., 1896.

Gutiérrez, Bernardo, and Francisco Arteaga. José Luis Teixe, guitar. *Puntos cubanos: Bernardo y el Gomero: Dos grandes versadores mano a mano*. Audiocassette. La Victoria de Acentejo, Tenerife: Estudios de Grabaciones "Acentejo," 1992. (TF 728–92).

Haboucha, Reginetta. "Folklore and Traditional Literature of the Judeo-Spanish Speakers." *The Sephardic and Oriental Jewish Heritage*. Ed. Issachar Ben-Ami. Jerusalem: Hebrew University Press, 1982. 571–588.

Hajdú, Péter. "Text and Melody in Samoyed Epic Songs." *Genre, Structure and Reproduction in Oral Literature*. Ed. Lauri Honko and Vilmos Voigt. Budapest: Akadémiai Kiadó, 1980. 95–96.

Hammoudi, Abdellah. *The Victim and its Masks: An Essay on Sacrifice and Masquerade in the Maghreb*. Chicago: University of Chicago Press, 1993.

Haring, Lee. *African Oral Traditions*. Special issue of *Oral Tradition*, 1994.

Harris, Derek. "Green Death: An Analysis of the Symbolism of the Colour Green in Lorca's Poetry." *Readings in Spanish and Portuguese Poetry for Geoffrey Connell*. Ed. Nicholas G. Round and Gareth D. Walters. Glasgow: University of Glasgow, Dept. of Hispanic Studies, 1985. 80–97.

Havard, Robert G. "The Symbolic Ambivalence of *Green* in García Lorca and Dylan Thomas." *The Modern Language Review* 67 (1972): 810–819.

———. *From Romanticism to Surrealism. Seven Spanish Poets.* Cardiff: University of Wales Press, 1988.

Haydar, Adnan. "The Development of Lebanese *Zajal*: Genre, Meter, and Verbal Duel." *Oral Tradition* 4 (1989): 189–212.

Hérelle, Georges. *Le Théâtre comique.* Paris: Champion, 1925.

Hernández, José. *Martín Fierro.* Buenos Aires: Ekin, 1972. 6th ed. Ed. Horacio Jorge Becco. Buenos Aires: Huemul, 1979.

Hernández, Miguel Ángel. *Décimas de José Hernández Negrín (Décimas de La Gomera).* Santa Cruz de Tenerife: Centro de la Cultura Popular Canaria, 1994.

Hernández Menéndez, Mayra. Ed., *La luz de tus diez estrellas (Memorias del V Encuentro-Festival Iberoamericano de la Décima).* La Habana: Editorial Letras Cubanas, 1999.

Herskovits, Melville J., and Frances S. Herskovits. *Suriname Folk-Lore.* New York: AMS Press, 1969.

Hidalgo, Laura. *Décimas esmeraldeñas.* Madrid: Visor, 1990. Rpt. Quito: Libresa, 1995.

Hockett, Charles. "The Origin of Speech." *Scientific American* 203.2 (1960): 88–111.

Hockett, Charles, and Robert Ascher. "The Human Revolution." *Current Anthropology* 5.3 (1964): 135–147.

Holmes, Urban T. *A History of Old French Literature.* New York: Russell & Russell, 1962.

Honko, Lauri. *Textualising the Siri Epic.* Folklore Fellows Communications 264. Helsinki: Finnish Literature Society, 1998.

———. Ed., *Textualization of Oral Epics.* Berlin and New York: Mouton de Gruyter, 2000.

———., et al. Eds. and trans. *The Siri Epic as Performed by Gopala Naika.* Folklore Fellows Communications 265–66. Helsinki: Finnish Literature Society, 1998.

Horace. *Satires, Epistles, and Ars Poetica.* Ed. and trans. H. Rushton Fairclough. London and Cambridge, Mass.: William Heinemann-Harvard University Press, 1970.

———. *The Satires.* Ed. Edward P. Morris. Norman: University of Oklahoma Press, 1974.

Hymes, Dell. "Breakthrough into Performance." *Folkore Performance and Communication.* Ed. Dan Ben-Amos and Kenneth S. Goldstein. The Hague: Mouton, 1975.11–74.

———. "Ways of Speaking." *Explorations in the Ethnography of Speaking.* Ed. Richard Bauman and Joel Sherzer. 2nd ed. Cambridge: Cambridge University Press, 1989. 433–51.

———. "Ethnopoetics, Oral-Formulaic Theory, and Editing Texts." *Oral Tradition* 9 (1994): 330–70.

Ibn Bassām. *Kitāb al-Ḏafīra fī maḥāsin ahl al-jazīra.* Ed. Iḥsān ʿAbbās. 8 vols. Beirut: Dār al-Ṯaqāfa, 1978.

Ibn Ḥayyān. *al-Muqtabas V.* Ed. Pedro Chalmeta et al. Madrid: Instituto Hispano-Árabe de Cultura, 1979.

Ibn Ḥazm. *Jamharat Ansāb al-ʿarab.* Ed. É. Lévi-Provençal. Cairo: Dār al-Maʿārif, 1948.

Ibn Rašīq. *Al-ʿUmda fī Maḥāsin al-šiʿr wa-ʾādābi-hi wa-naqdi-hi.* 3rd ed. 2 vols. Muḥammad Muḥyī l-Dīn ʿAbd al-Ḥamād. Cairo: al-Saʿāda, 1963.

"Improvisation." *The New Grove Dictionary of Music and Musicians.* Ed. Stanley Sadie. 2nd ed. Vol. 12. New York: Grove, 2001. 96ff.

I.N.S.E.E. Institut National de la Statisque et des Études Économiques. Report. 1991.

Irigary, Angel. Ed. and trans., *Poesías populares de los Vascos.* 2 vols. San Sebastian: Editorial Auñamendi, 1962 [transl. of ch. 11 of Francisque Michel, *Le Pays basque.* Paris: Libraire de Firmin Didot, 1857].

Itztueta y Echeberría, Juna Ignacio de. *Guipuzcoa'ko dantza gogoangarrien condaira edo historia beren soñu zar, eta itz neurtu edo versoaquin. Baita berac ongul dantzatzeco iracaste edo instruccioae ere.* San Sebastián: Ignacio Ramón Baroja, 1824. 2nd ed. as *Euscaldun anciña ancinaco ta are lendabicico etorquien dantza on iritci pozcarre gaitzic gabecoen soñu gogoangarriac beren itz neurtu edo versoaquin.* San Sebastián: Ignacio Ramón Baroja, 1826. Rpt. as *Guipuzkoako Dantzak.* Introduction by J.A. Donostia. San Sebastián: Eusko-Ikaskuntzaren Argitaldiak; La Sociedad de Estudios Vascos, 1927.

Jacobson, Roman. "Closing Statement: Linguistics and Poetics." *Style in Language.* Ed. T. Sebeok. Cambridge: Cambridge University Press, 1960. 350–377.

Jacquement, Marco. "Conflict." *Key Terms in Language and Culture.* Ed. Alessandro Duranti. Oxford: Blackwell, 2001. 37–40.

Jaffee, Martin. *Torah in the Mouth: Writing and Oral Tradition in Palestinian Judaism 200 BCE-400 CE.* Oxford: Oxford University Press, 2001.

Jarne, Hilario. *Junto al fogaril de Atares.* 3 vols. Oiartzun: Sendoa: 1995.

Jiménez, Juan Ramón. *El romance, río de la lengua española.* Puerto Rico: Universidad de Puerto Rico, 1959.

Jiménez de Báez, Ivette. *La décima popular en Puerto Rico.* Xalapa: Universidad Veracruzana, 1964.

———. "Décimas y decimales en México y Puerto Rico. Variedad y tradición." *Estudios de folklore y literatura dedicados a Mercedes Díaz Roig.* México: El Colegio de México; Centro de Estudios Lingüísticos y Literarios, 1992. 467–491.

———. "Décimas y glosas mexicanas. Entre lo oral y lo escrito." *La décima popular en la tradición hispánica. Actas del simposio internacional sobre la décima (Las Palmas, 17–22 de diciembre 1992).* Ed. Maximiano Trapero. Las Palmas de Gran Canaria: Universidad de Las Palmas de Gran Canaria; Cabildo Insular de Gran Canaria, 1994. 87–109.

Johnson, John William, et al. *Oral Epics from Africa: Vibrant Voices from a Vast Continent.* Bloomington: Indiana University Press, 1997.

Jorda, Enrique. "Notas sobre la danza vasca." *De canciones, danzas y músicos del País vasco.* Bilbao: La Gran Enciclopedia Vasca, 1978. 81–95.

Jousse, Marcel. *Le Style oral rhythmique et mnémotechnique chez les verbo-moteurs.* Paris: Gabriel Beauchesne, 1925.

Kasten, Lloyd A. Ed., *Poridat de las poridades.* Madrid: S. Aguirre Torre, 1957.

Kay, Matthew W. *The Index of the Milman Parry Collection, 1933–1935: Heroic Songs, Conversations, and Stories.* New York: Garland, 1995.

Kelber, Werner H. *The Oral and the Written Gospel: The Hermeneutics of Speaking and Writing in the Synoptic Tradition, Mark, Paul, and Q.* Rev. ed. Bloomington: Indiana University Press, 1997.

Kennedy, George A. *A New History of Classical Rhetoric.* Princeton: Princeton University Press, 1994.

Kirk, G. S. *Homer and Oral Tradition.* Cambridge: Cambridge University Press, 1976.

Kroeber, Karl. *Retelling/Rereading: The Fate of Story Telling in Modern Times.* New Brunswick: Rutgers Press, 1990.

Laborde, Denis. "Basque Music." *The Garland Encyclopedia of World Music.* Vol. 5. *Europe.* Ed. Timothy Rice et al. New York: Garland, 2000. 309–317.

———. "Basque Music." *The New Revised Grove Dictionary of Music and Musicians.* Ed. Stanley Sadie. London: Macmillan, 2001. 846–849.

Labrador Herratz, José J. *Poesía dialogada medieval.* Madrid: Maisal, 1974.

La décima popular en Iberoamérica (Memorias del II festival iberoamericano de la décima). Veracruz: Instituto Veracruzano de Cultura, 1995.

Lakoff, George, and Mark Johnson. *Philosophy in the Flesh: The Embodied Mind and its Challenge to Western Thought.* New York: Basic Books, 1999.

Laval, Ramón A. *Contribución al folklore de Carahue (Chile).* Madrid: Victoriano Suárez, 1916.

Lecuona, Manuel. *Literatura oral vasca.* 3rd ed. San Sebastián: Auñamendi, 1965.

LeGentil, Pierre. *La poésie lyrique espagnol et portuguaise a la fin du moyen âge.* 2 vols. Rennes: Plihon, 1949–1952.

Leite de Vasconcellos, José. *Tradições Populares de Portugal.* Oporto: Clavel, 1882.

———. *Tradições Populares de Portugal.* Ed. Manuel Viegas Guerreiro. 2nd ed. Lisboa: Imprensa Nacional-Casa da Moeda, 1987.

Leizaola, Jesús María de. *Los romances vascos (Üskal - khantoriak) y sus relaciones con reliquias literarias de la prehistoria.* Bilblioteca de Cultura Vasca 66. Buenos Aires: Editorial Vasca «Ekin», 1969.

Lekuona, Juan Mª. "Atari gisa." *Lengo egunak gogoan.* Vol. 1. Tolosa: Auspoa, 1974: 11–20.

———. "Manuel Lasarteren gordaiura." *Zeruko Argia* 663 (1975a): 8.

———. "Txirrita eta Basarri: bi belaunaldien arteko tenka." *Euskara* 20 (1975b): 333–339.

———. "Xalbadorren ekarriaz." *Garaia* 12 (1976): 38–39.

———. "Literatura oral vasca." *El libro blanco del Euskara.* Bilbao: Elkar, 1977. 155–178.

———. "Bilintxen bertsogintza." *A los 100 años de su muerte. Bilintx (1831–1876).* Ed. Antonio Zavala. Gasteiz: Eset, 1978a. 166–185

———. "Literatura oral vasca." *Cultura Vasca.* Vol. 2. Zarauz: Erein, 1978b. 59–109.

———. "Bertsolariak historian. Sailkapen saioa." *Jakin* 14–15 (1980a): 6–15.

———. "Jendaurreko bertsolaritza." *Jakin* 14–15 (1980b): 99–113.

———. *Ahozko euskal literatura.* Donostia: Erein, 1982a.

———. "Bertsolarien estrofa-motak hegoaldeko usarioan." *Euskara* 27 (1982b): 333–349.

——. "Uztapideren bapateko bertsolaritza." *Oiartzun* 14 (1984): 25–27.

——. "Iparragirre eta Bertsolaritza." *Iparragirre*. Bilbo: Euskaltzaindia, 1987. 109–133.

——. *Mimodramak eta ikonoak*. Donostia: Erein, 1990.

——. "Basarriren bertsolari proiektua." *Iker* 6. Bilbao: Euskaltzaindia, 1992. 283–296.

——. "Euskal estrofez." *Euskara* 39 (1994): 1187–1219.

——. *Manuel Lekuona Etxabeguren*. Donostia: Eusko Ikaskuntza, 1995a.

——. "Erretorikaren ildotik." *Bertsolari* 20 (1995b): 44–51.

——. *Ikaskuntzak euskal literaturaz (1974–1996)*. Donostia: Deustuko Unibertsitatea, 1998.

——. *Oiartzungo Kantutegia*. Oiartzun: Oiartzungo Udala, 1999.

Lekuona, Manuel de. *Literatura oral vasca*. San Sebastián: Colección Kardaberaz, 1935. Rpt. 1964; San Sebastián: Editorial Auñamendi, 1965. Rpt. 1978.

——. *Idazlan Guztiak*. 12 vols. Donostia: Gipuzkoako Foru Aldundia, 1984.

Levin, Samuel R. *The Semantics of Metaphor*. Baltimore: Johns Hopkins University Press, 1977.

——. *Metaphoric Worlds: Conceptions of a Romantic Nature*. New Haven: Yale University Press, 1988.

Lewis, Bernard. *Race and Color in Islam*. New York: Harper & Row, 1970.

Leyva, Waldo. "Movimiento actual en favor de la décima y del verso improvisado." *La décima. Su historia, su geografía, sus manifestaciones*. Ed. Maximiano Trapero. La Laguna: Centro de la Cultura Popular Canaria; Câmara Municipal de Évora, 2001. 197–240.

Liebhaber, Samuel. "Al-Shanfarā and the 'Mountain Poem' of Ibn Khafāja: Some Observations on Patterns of Intertextuality." *Journal of Arabic Literature* 34 (2003): 107–121.

Lima, Paolo. "O Estado da Décima no Sul de Portugal e a sua Contribuição para a História Oral." *Actas del VI Encuentro-Festival Iberoamericano de la Décima y el Verso Improvisado (Las Palmas de Gran Canaria, del 6 al 11 de octubre de 1998)*. Vol. 1. *Estudios*. Ed. Maximiano Trapero, Eladio Santana Martel and Carmen Márquez Montes. Las Palmas de Gran Canaria: Universidad de Las Palmas de Gran Canaria; ACADE, 2000. 215–226.

——. "A décima e o improviso en Portugal." *La décima. Su historia, su geografía, sus manifestaciones*. Ed. Maximiano Trapero. La Laguna: Centro de la Cultura Popular Canaria; Câmara Municipal de Évora, 2001. 153–178.

Linares Savio, María Teresa. "Funciones y realizaciones de la décima con la música con que se canta en Cuba." *La décima popular en la tradición hispánica. Actas del simposio internacional sobre la décima (Las Palmas, 17–22 de diciembre 1992)*. Ed. Maximiano Trapero. Las Palmas de Gran Canaria: Universidad de Las Palmas de Gran Canaria; Cabildo Insular de Gran Canaria, 1994. 111–132.

——. "La décima como 'viajera peninsular' y su regreso aplatanado." *La décima popular en Iberoamérica (Memorias del II festival iberoamericano de la décima)*. Veracruz: Instituto Veracruzano de Cultura, 1995. 93–106.

———. "Hipótesis sobre el origen de las tonadas de punto cubano." *La luz de tus diez estrellas (Memorias del V Encuentro-Festival Iberoamericano de la Décima).* Ed. Mayra Hernández Menéndez. La Habana: Editorial Letras Cubanas, 1999a.159–166.

———. *El punto cubano.* Santiago de Cuba: Ediciones de Oriente, 1999b.

———. "La décima cantada."*La décima. Su historia, su geografía, sus manifestaciones.* Ed. Maximiano Trapero. La Laguna: Centro de la Cultura Popular Canaria; Câmara Municipal de Évora, 2001. 129–152.

Lisón, Carmelo. "Arte verbal y estructura social en Galicia." *Perfiles simbólico-morales de la cultura gallega.* Madrid: Alkal, 1974. 49–69.

List, George. *Music and Poetry in a Colombian Village: A Tri-Cultural Heritage.* Bloomington: Indiana University Press, 1983.

Lopes, Frederico [alias João Ilhéu]. *Ilha Terceira. Notas Etnográficas.* Angra do Heroísmo: Instituto da Ilha Terceira, 1980.

López de Osornio, Mario A. *Oro nativo. Tradiciones bonaerenses, poesía popular y antología del payador de la pampa.* Buenos Aires: «El Ateneo», 1945.

López Lemus, Virgilio. *La décima. Panorama breve de la décima cubana.* La Habana: Editorial Academia, 1995a.

———. "Poesía y oralidad en la tradición cubana." *La décima popular en Iberoamérica (Memorias del II festival iberoamericano de la décima).*Veracruz: Instituto Veracruzano de Cultura, 1995b. 77–92.

———. *Décima e identidad. Siglos XVIII y XIX.* La Habana: Editorial Academia, 1997.

———. *La décima constante. Las tradiciones oral y escrita.* La Habana: Fundación Fernando Ortiz, 1999.

———. "Décima y oralidad en la tradición cubana." *Actas del VI Encuentro-Festival Iberoamericano de la Décima y el Verso Improvisado (Las Palmas de Gran Canaria, del 6 al 11 de octubre de 1998).* Vol. 1. *Estudios.* Ed. Maximiano Trapero, Eladio Santana Martel and Carmen Márquez Montes. Las Palmas de Gran Canaria: Universidad de Las Palmas de Gran Canaria; ACADE, 2000. 237–250.

———. "La décima culta." *La décima. Su historia, su geografía, sus manifestaciones.* Ed. Maximiano Trapero. La Laguna: Centro de la Cultura Popular Canaria; Câmara Municipal de Évora, 2001. 41–60.

———. *La décima renacentista y barroca.* La Habana: Pablo de la Torriente Editorial, 2003.

López Lemus, Virgilio, and Maximiano Trapero. "Geografía actual de la décima." *La décima. Su historia, su geografía, sus manifestaciones.* Ed. Maximiano Trapero. La Laguna: Centro de la Cultura Popular Canaria; Câmara Municipal de Évora, 2001. 179–196.

López Linage, Javier. *Antropología de la reciprocidad cotidiana. Supervivencia y trabajo en una comunidad cántabra.* Madrid: Ministerio de Agricultura; Servicio de Publicaciones Agrarias, 1978.

Lord, Albert Bates. *The Singer of Tales.* Cambridge, Mass.: Harvard University Press, 1960. Rpt. New York: Atheneum, 1968. 2nd ed. Ed. Stephen Mitchell and Gregory Nagy. Cambridge, Mass.: Harvard University Press, 2000. With audio/video CD.

———. "Oral Poetry." *The New Princeton Encyclopedia of Poetry and Poetics.* Ed. Alex Preminger and T. V. F. Brogan. Princeton, NJ: Princeton University Press, 1993. 863–866.

Lugones, Leopoldo. *El payador.* Buenos Aires: Otero, 1916.

Lukin, Borís V. "Testimonios sobre la poesía popular cubana del segundo tercio del siglo XIX." *Revista de la Universidad de Oriente* (Santiago) 31 (1978): 61–80.

Lurie, Yuval. "Geniuses and Metaphors." *Journal of Aesthetics and Art Criticism* 49.1 (1991): 225–233.

Machado, José E. *Cancionero popular venezolano.* 2nd ed. Caracas: L. Puig Ros & Parra Almenar, 1922.

———. *Cancionero popular venezolano. Cantares y corridos, galerones y glosas.* Caracas: "El Cojo," 1926a.

———. *El gaucho y el llanero.* Caracas: Vargas, 1926b.

Mallea-Olaetxe, Joxe. *Shooting from the Lip: Bertsolariak Ipar Amerikan: Improvised Basque Verse-Singing.* Reno: North American Basque Organization, 2003.

Maloney, Clarence. Ed., *The Evil Eye.* New York: Columbia University Press, 1976.

Malti-Douglas, Fedwa. *Structures of Avarice: The Bukhalā' in Medieval Arabic Literature.* Leiden: E. J. Brill, 1985.

Manterola Beldarrain, José de. *Cancionero vasco. Poesías en lengua euskara reunidas en colección, ordenadas en series, y acompañadas de traducciones castellanas, juicios críticos, noticias biográficas de los autores y observaciones filológicos y gramaticales.* 3 vols. Published as 9 vols. in 3 parts. San Sebastián: Juan Osés, 1877–1880.

Martikorena, Erramun. "Xalbadorren heriotzan." By Xabier Lete. *Olerkiaren oihartzuna.* CD. Donostia: Elkarlanean, 1998.

Martín Teixé, José Luis. *Las décimas de doña Pancha.* Mazo, La Palma: Ayuntamiento de la Villa de Mazo, 1992.

———. "La décima en Canarias: los verseadores." *La luz de tus diez estrellas (Memorias del V Encuentro-Festival Iberoamericano de la Décima).* Ed. Mayra Hernández Menéndez. La Habana: Editorial Letras Cubanas, 1999. 247–250.

Martín Teixé, José Luis, and Mario Luis López Isla. *La leyenda de Cuquillo. El poeta isleño de Mazo y Cabaiguán.* Santa Cruz de Tenerife: Centro de la Cultura Popular Canaria, 1994.

McCarthy, William B. *The Ballad Matrix.* Bloomington: Indiana University Press, 1990.

———. "Oral Theory and Epic Studies." *Choice* 39.1 (September 2001): 61–75.

McCurdy, J. Fredric. "Prophets and Prophecy." *Jewish Encyclopaedia.* Vol. 10. New York: Funk & Wagnalls, 1906–1907. 213.

Mendoza, Vicente T. *Glosas y décimas de México.* México: Fondo de Cultura Económica, 1957.

Menéndez Pidal, Ramón. "Elena y María." *Revista de Filología Española* 1 (1914): 52–118.

———. "Los cantores épicos yugoslavos y los occidentales. El *Mio Cid* y dos refundidores primitivos." *Boletín de la Real Academia de Buenas Letras de Barcelona* 31 (1965–1966): 195–225.

Michel, Francisque. *Le Pays basque.* Paris: Libraire de Firmin Didot, 1857.

Michelena, Luis. *Historia de la literatura vasca.* Madrid: Minotauro, 1960.

Miles, G. C. "Dīnār." *The Encyclopaedia of Islam.* 2nd ed. Vol. 2. E. J. Brill: Leiden, 1983. 297–299.

Millares, Luis, and Agustín Millares. *Léxico de Gran Canaria.* Las Palmas: «El Diario», 1926.

Miller, Norman C. "'Romance sonámbulo', an Archetypal Drama." *Hispanic Journal* 7.2 (1986): 17–24.

Miner, Earl. "Poetic Competitions." *New Princeton Encylopedia of Poetry and Poetics.* Ed. Alexander Preminger and T.V.F. Brogan. Princeton: Princeton University Press, 1993. 925–27.

Monroe, James T. "Oral Composition in pre-Islamic Poetry: The Problem of Authenticity." *Journal of Arabic Literature* 3 (1972): 1–53.

———. "Hispano-Arabic Poetry During the Almoravid Period: Theory and Practice." *Viator* 4 (1973): 65–98.

———. "Prolegomena to the Study of Ibn Quzmān: The Poet As Jongleur." *El Romancero hoy. Historia, comparatismo, bibliografía crítica.* Ed. Samuel G. Armistead, Diego Catalán and Antonio Sánchez Romeralo. Madrid: Gredos, 1979. 78–128.

———. "Prolegómenos al estudio de Ibn Quzmān. El poeta como bufón." *Nueva Revista de Filología Hispánica* 34 (1985–1986). 769–799.

———. "Wanton Poets and Would-be Paleographers (Prolegomena to Ibn Quzmān's *Zajal* No. 10)." *La Corónica* 16 (1987): 1–42.

———. "Salmà, el toro abigarrado, la doncella medrosa, Ka'b al-Aḥbār y el conocimiento del árabe de don Juan Manuel. Prolegómenos al *Zéjel Núm. 148* de Ibn Quzmān." *Nueva Revista de Filología Hispánica* 36 (1988a): 853–878.

———. "Ibn Quzmān on *I'rāb*: A *zéjel de juglaría* in Arab Spain?" *Hispanic Studies in Honor of Joseph H. Silverman.* Ed. Joseph V. Ricapito. Newark, Del.: Juan de la Cuesta, 1988b. 45–56.

———. "Maimonides on the Mozarabic Lyric (A Note on the *Muwaššaḥa*)." *La Corónica* 17 (1988–1989): 18–32.

———. "Which Came First, the *Zajal* or the *Muwaššaḥa*? Some Evidence for the Oral Origins of Hispano-Arabic Strophic Poetry." *Oral Tradition* 4.1–2 (1989): 38–63.

———. "The Underside of Arabic Panegyric: Ibn Quzmān's (Unfinished?) *Zajal No. 84.*" *Al-Qanṭara* 17 (1996): 79–115.

———. "Al-Saraqusṭī, Ibn al-Aštarkūwī: Andalusī Lexicographer, Poet, and Author of *al-Maqāmāt al-Luzūmīya.*" *Journal of Arabic Literature* 28 (1997a): 1–37.

———. "The Striptease That Was Blamed on Abū Bakr's Naughty Son: Was Father Being Shamed, or Was the Poet Having Fun? (Ibn Quzmān's *Zajal No. 133*)." *Homoeroticism in Classical Arabic Literature*. Ed. J. W. Wright Jr. and Everett K. Rowson. New York: Columbia University Press, 1997b. 94–139.

———. *Al-Maqāmāt al-luzūmīyah by Abū l-Ṣāhir Muḥammad ibn Yūsuf al-Tamīmī al-Saraqusṭī ibn al- Aštarkūwī (d. 538/1143), Translated with a Preliminary Study*. Leiden: E. J. Brill, 2002.

———. *Ibn Quzmān's 'Zajal 118': An Andalusī 'Ode to the Onion'*. (In press).

———. "The *Zajal* within the *Zajal*: Ibn Quzmān's '*Zajal No. 20*." (Forthcoming).

Monroe, James T., and Mark F. Pettigrew. "The Decline of Courtly Patronage and the Appearance of New Genres in Arabic Literature: The Case of the *Zajal*, the *Maqāma*, and the Shadow Play." *Journal of Arabic Literature* 34 (2003): 138–177.

Morante, Antonio [pseud. Quintana]. Personal interview by William A. Christian Jr. La Laguna, Jan. 24, 1998

Morante, Aurora. Personal interview by William A. Christian Jr. Uznayo, July 17, 1999.

Morínigo, Marcos A. *Diccionario manual de americanismos*. Buenos Aires: Muchnik, 1966.

Morris, Steve. *Perfect E-mail*. London: Random House Business Books, 2000.

Motta, Leonardo. *Cantadores*. Rio de Janeiro: A. J. de Castilho, 1921.

Moulier, Jules [pseud. Oxobi] "Pertxularien dohain-eginbideak." *Gure Herria* 24.5 (1952): 316–318.

Mouzo Pagán, Rogelio. *"El Minero" Manuel García Tortosa (Troveros de la tierra)*. La Unión, Murcia: Dirección General de Cultura de la Comunidad Autónoma de Murcia; Ayuntamiento de La Unión, 1966.

———. *Calle del trovero Castillo. Textos en homenaje al Trovero José Castillo Rodríguez*. La Unión, Murcia: Dirección General de Cultura de la Comunidad Autónoma de Murcia y Ayuntamiento de La Unión, 1995.

Mozos, Iñaki. *Ihauteriak Euskal Literaturan*. San Sebastián: Sociedad de Estudios Vascos, 1985.

Munar, Felip. *Manual del bon glosador. Tècniques, exercicis i glosades*. Palma de Mallorca: Edicions Documenta Balear, 2001.

Murua Iñurritegui, Ángel. "País vasco." *Tradición y danza en España*. Ed. Norberto A. Albaladejo Imbernón. Madrid: Consejería de Cultura, Comunidad de Madrid, 1992. 329–354.

Nagore Ferrer, María. *La revolución coral. Estudio sobre la Sociedad Coral de Bilbao y el movimiento coral europeo (1800–1936)*. Madrid: ICCMU, 2001.

Napier, John Russell. *Hands*. Rev. Russell Tuttle. Princeton: Princeton University Press, 1993.

Narváez, Isidro. Personal interview by William A. Christian Jr. San Sebastián de Garabandal, 1969.

Nava López, E. Fernando. "La décima cantada en México: algunos aspectos musicológicos." *La décima popular en la tradición hispánica. Actas del simposio internacional sobre la décima*

(Las Palmas, 17–22 de diciembre 1992). Ed. Maximiano Trapero. Las Palmas de Gran Canaria: Universidad de Las Palmas de Gran Canaria; Cabildo Insular de Gran Canaria, 1994. 289–309.

Nehamas, Alexander. *The Art of Living: Socratic Reflections from Plato to Foucault*. Berkeley: University of California Press, 1998.

Niditch, Susan. "Oral Register in the Biblical Libretto: Towards a Biblical Poetic." *Oral Tradition* 10 (1995): 387–408.

———. *Oral World and Written Word: Ancient Israelite Literature*. Louisville: Westminster John Knox Press, 1996.

Nielsen, J. S. "Maẓālim." *The Encyclopaedia of Islam*. 2nd ed. Vol. 6. E. J. Brill: Leiden, 1991. 933–945.

Noda Gómez, Talio. *Décimas de Severo*. Santa Cruz de Tenerife: Centro de Cultura Popular Canaria, 1993.

al-Nowaihi, Magda M. *The Poetry of Ibn Khafājah: A Literary Analysis*. Studies in Arabic Literature 16. Leiden: E. J. Brill: 1993.

O'Keeffe, Katherine O'Brien. "Diction, Variation, the Formula." *A Beowulf Handbook*. Ed. Robert E. Bjork and John D. Niles. Lincoln: University of Nebraska Press, 1997. 85–104.

Olaizola, Manuel [pseud. Uztapide]. *Lengo egunak gogoan*. Tolosa: Ausposa, 1975.

Olivera-Williams, María Rosa. *La poesía gauchesca de Bartolomé Hidalgo a José Hernandez. Respuesta estética y condicionamiento social*. Xalapa: Universidad Veracruzana, 1986.

Ong, Walter J. *Fighting for Life: Contest, Sexuality, and Consciousness*. Ithaca, NY: Cornell University Press, 1981.

———. *Orality and Literacy: The Technologizing of the Word*. London: Methuen, 1982.

———. "African Talking Drums and Oral Noetics." *Oral-Formulaic Theory: A Folklore Casebook*. Ed. John Miles Foley. New York & London: Garland, 1990.109–135.

Opie, Iona, and Peter Opie. *The Lore and Language of Schoolchildren*. Oxford: Oxford University Press, 1959.

Opland, Jeff. *Xhosa Oral Poets and Poetry*. Cape Town: David Philip, 1998.

Ormaetxea, Nicolás [pseud. Orixe]. *Mireio*. Bilbao: Verdes, 1930.

———. *Euskaldunak. Los vascos*. Bilbao: Auñamendi, 1950. Rpt. Donostia: Auñamendi, 1976.

Orta Ruiz, Jesús [Indio Naborí, pseud.]. *Décima y folclor*. La Habana: Ediciones Unión. 1980.

———. *El jardín de las espinelas*. Sevilla: Junta de Andalucía, Consejería de Cultura, 1991.

———. "Influencia canaria en la cubanización de nuestra poesía." *La luz de tus diez estrellas (Memorias del V Encuentro-Festival Iberoamericano de la Décima)*. Ed. Mayra Hernández Menéndez. La Habana: Editorial Letras Cubanas, 1999. 46–51.

———. "Autobiografía de un improvisador." *Actas del VI Encuentro-Festival Iberoamericano de la Décima y el Verso Improvisado (Las Palmas de Gran Canaria, del 6 al 11 de octubre de 1998)*.

Vol. 2. *Textos*. Ed. Maximiano Trapero, Eladio Santana Martel and Carmen Márquez Montes. Las Palmas de Gran Canaria: Universidad de Las Palmas de Gran Canaria; ACADE, 2000. 27–35.

Orta Ruiz, Jesús [Indio Naborí, pseud.], and Maximiano Trapero. "Origen de la décima." *La décima. Su historia, su geografía, sus manifestaciones*. Ed. Maximiano Trapero. La Laguna: Centro de la Cultura Popular Canaria; Câmara Municipal de Évora, 2001. 15–40.

Orta Ruiz, Jesús [Indio Naborí, pseud.], and Ángel Valiente. *Décimas para la historia. La controversia del siglo en verso improvisado*. Edición y prólogo de Maximiano Trapero. La Laguna: Centro de la Cultura Popular Canaria, 1997.

Oskorri. *Katuen Testamentua*. CD. KD 369. Bilbao: Elkar, 1993.

———. *Vizcayatik …Bizkaiara*. CD. KD 597. Donostia: Elkarlanean, 2001.

Otero Pedrayo, Ramón. *Historia de Galicia*. 3 vols. Madrid: Akal, 1979–1980.

Paden, William D. Ed. and trans., *The Medieval Pastourelle*. 2 vols. New York: Garland Publishing, 1987.

Paredes, Américo. "The *décima* on the Texas-Mexican Border: Folksong as an Adjunct to Legend." *Journal of the Folklore Institute* 3.2 (1966): 154–167.

Parks, Ward. *Verbal Dueling in Heroic Narrative: The Homeric and Old English Traditions*. Princeton: Princeton University Press, 1990.

Parry, Milman. "Studies in the Epic: Technique of Oral Verse-Making II. The Homeric Language as the Language of Oral Poetry." *Harvard Studies in Classical Philology* 43 (1932): 1–50.

Parsons, Elsie Clews. *Folk-lore from the Cape Verde Islands*. 2 vols. New York: American Folk-Lore Society, 1923.

Payá Ruiz, Xavier. Personal communication to William A. Christian Jr. Reno, May 16, 2003.

Pedrosa, José Manuel. *Cancionero de las montañas de Liébana (Cantabria)*. Santander: Fundación Centro de Documentación Etnográfica de Cantabria, 1999.

———. "Historia e historias de la canción improvisada." *Actas del VI Encuentro-Festival Iberoamericano de la Décima y el Verso Improvisado (Las Palmas de Gran Canaria, del 6 al 11 de octubre de 1998)*. Vol. 1. *Estudios*. Ed. Maximiano Trapero, Eladio Santana Martel and Carmen Márquez Montes. Las Palmas de Gran Canaria: Universidad de Las Palmas de Gran Canaria; ACADE, 2000a. 95–108.

———. "La poesía improvisada en la tradición vasca y la universal." *Antonio Zavalaren ohoretan. Herri Literaturaz gogoeta*. Bilbao: Universidad de Deusto, 2000b. 49–68.

———. "Las *bombas*: Un género de canción y de danza en las tradiciones mexicana y panhispánica." *Revista de Literatura Popular* 1 (2001): 157–187.

Pellat, Charles. "Hidjā." *The Encylopaedia of Islam*. New Edition. Vol. 3. Leiden: Brill, 1971. 352–55.

Peña, Justo. *El pastor del páramo*. 2 vols. Tolosa: Auspoa; Oiartzun: Sendoa, 1995.

Pereda, José María de. "De cómo se celebran todavía las bodas en cierta comarca montañesa, enclavada en un repliegue de lo más enriscado de la cordillera cantábrico." *Homenaje a Menéndez y Pelayo en el año vigésimo de su profesorado.* Madrid: Librería General de Victoriano Suárez, 1899. 941–946.

Pereira de Brito, Maria Filomena A. S. Carvalho. Rev. of *Ilha Terceira: Notas Etnográficas* by Federico Lopes. *Revista Portuguesa de Filologia* 18 (1980–1986): 733–737.

Perelman, Chaïm, and Lucie Olbrechts-Tyteca. *Traité de l'argumentation: La nouvelle rhétorique.* Bruxelles: Editions de l'Université de Bruxelles, 1958. Rpt. Bruxelles: Editions de l'Institut de Sociologie, 1976.

Pérez, Irvan. Personal interview by Samuel G. Armistead. Poydras, Louisiana, March 27, 1976.

Pérez Ballesteros, José. *Cancionero popular gallego*, vol. 1. Vol. 3. of Biblioteca de las Tradiciones Populares Españoles. Ed. by Antonio Machado y Alvarez. Madrid: Fernando Fé, 1885.

———. *Cancionero popular gallego.* 2 vols. Madrid: Akal, 1979.

Pérez Priego, Miguel Ángel. "Debates poéticos en la Edad Media." *Diccionario de Literatura Española e Hispanoamericana.* Ed. Ricardo Gullón. Vol. 1. Madrid: Alianza, 1993. 427–428.

Pérez Vidal, José. "La décima popular." *Revista de Dialectología y Tradiciones Populares* 21.3–4 (1965): 314–341.

Peters, Rudolph. "Zinā." *The Encyclopaedia of Islam.* 2nd ed. Vol. 11. E. J. Brill: Leiden, 2002. 509–510.

Pihel, Erik. "A Furified Freestyle: Homer and Hip Hop." *Oral Tradition* 11 (1996): 249–69.

Platon [Plato]. *Gorgias. Obras Completas.* Trans. María Araujo et al. Intro. J.A. Miguez. Madrid: Aguilar, 1972.

Preciado, Dionisio. "Folklore vasco." *Folklore Español.* Madrid: Stadium, 1969. 210–238.

Qudāma ibn Jaʿfar, Abū l-Faraj. *Kitāb Naqd al-šiʿr.* Ed. Muḥammad ʿAbd al-Munʿim Ṣafāja. Beirut: Dār al-Kutub al-ʿIlmīya, 1980.

Rábago, María. Personal interview by William A. Christian Jr. La Laguna, Jan. 24, 1998.

Ràfols, Wifredo de. "On the Genre of 'Espacio (3 estrofas)': The Camouflaged Verses." *Hispanic Review* 63.3 (1995): 363–385.

———. "Writing to Seduce and Seducing to Write about It: Graphocentrism in Don Juan Tenorio." *Revista Hispánica Moderna* 50 (1997): 253–264.

———. "Del cubismo a las circunstancias. El motivo de la mesa en dos momentos de la trayectoria poética de Jorge Guillén: 'Naturaleza viva' y 'A nivel.'" *Bulletin of Hispanic Studies* 82.1 (2005): 45–58.

Raible, Wolfgang. "Orality, Literacy, and Modern Media." *Orality, Literacy and Modern Media.* Ed. Dietrich Scheunemann. Columbia, SC: Camden House, 1996. 17–27.

Ramos, Jesús, and José María Jimeno Jurío. "Navarra." *Tradición y danza en España*. Ed. Norberto A. Albaladejo Imbernón. Madrid: Consejería de Cultura, Comunidad de Madrid, 1992. 279–295.

Ramsden, Herbert. *Lorca's "Romancero Gitano"*. Manchester and New York: Manchester University Press, 1988.

Randolph, Vance. "Nakedness in Ozark Folk Belief." *Journal of American Folklore* 66 (1953): 333–339.

Reichert, Victor E. Trans., *The Taḥkemoni of Judah al-Ḥarizi*. 2 vols. Jerusalem: Raphael Haim Cohen, 1965–1973.

Reichl, Karl. *Turkic Oral Epic Poetry: Traditions, Forms, Poetic Structures*. A.B. Lord Studies in Oral Tradition 7. New York: Garland, 1992.

Reimer, Bennet, and Jeffrey E. Wright. Eds., *On the Nature of Musical Experience*. Evanston, Ill.: The Center for the Study of Education and the Musical Experience, School of Music, Northwestern University, 1992.

Renoir, Alain. "Oral-Formulaic Rhetoric and the Interpretation of Written Texts." *Oral Tradition in Literature*. Ed. John Miles Foley. Columbia: University of Missouri Press, 1986. 103–135.

Rey García, Emilio. *Los libros de música tradicional en España*. Madrid: ÆDOM, 2001.

Reynolds, John Frederick. "Memory Issues in Composition Studies." *Rhetorical Memory and Delivery: Classical Concepts for Contemporary Composition and Communication*. Ed. J.F. Reynolds. London: Lawrence Erlbaum Associates, 1993. 1–15.

Ricoeur, Paul. "The Model of the Text: Meaningful Action Considered as Text." *Social Research* 38 (1971): 529–562.

Riezu, Jorge de. "I. El cancionero vasco y sus artífices." *Flor de canciones populares vascas*. Buenos Aires: Editorial Vasca «Ekin», 1948. 11–23.

———. "El cancionero vasco." *Cuadernos de Sección: Música* 1 (1984): 163–170.

Riquer, Martín de. *La lírica de los trovadores*. 3 vols. Barcelona: Escuela de Filología, 1948.

———. *Los cantares de gesta franceses*. Madrid: Gredos, 1952.

Roca, Ángel. *Historia del trovo (1865–1975)*. Cartagena; La Unión: n.p., 2000.

Rodrigues Lapa, Manuel. *Cantigas d'escarnho e de mal dizer*. 2nd rev. ed. Vigo: Editorial Galaxia., 1970.

Rodríguez Ramírez, Jesús–Mario. "Modelos melódicos en la décima canaria." *La décima popular en la tradición hispánica. Actas del simposio internacional sobre la décima (Las Palmas, 17–22 de diciembre 1992)*. Ed. Maximiano Trapero. Las Palmas de Gran Canaria: Universidad de Las Palmas de Gran Canaria; Cabildo Insular de Gran Canaria, 1994. 341–359.

Rodríguez San Juan, Antonio, and Antonio Zavala. *En la Reserva del Saja*. Biblioteca de Narrativa Popular 21. Oiartzun: Sendoa, 2000.

Romeu Figueras, José. "El canto dialogado en la canción popular. Los cantares a desafío." *Anuario Musical* 3 (1948): 133–161.

Rorty, Richard. "Unfamiliar Noises: Hesse and Davidson on Metaphor." *Proceedings of the Aristotelian Society* Supp. 61 (1987): 283–296.

———. *Contingency, Irony and Solidarity*. Cambridge: Cambridge University Press, 1989.

Royce, Anya Peterson. *The Anthropology of Dance*. Bloomington: Indiana University Press, 1977.

Rugarcía, Juan, and Antonio Zavala. *En la ribera del Cares*. Biblioteca de Narrativa Popular 11. Oiartzun: Sendoa, 1996.

Ruiz Fernández, María Jesús. "Poesía e improvisación en el folclore de Gibraltar (Cádiz)." *Actas del VI Encuentro-Festival Iberoamericano de la Décima y el Verso Improvisado (Las Palmas de Gran Canaria, del 6 al 11 de octubre de 1998)*. Vol. 1. *Estudios*. Ed. Maximiano Trapero, Eladio Santana Martel and Carmen Márquez Montes. Las Palmas de Gran Canaria: Universidad de Las Palmas de Gran Canaria; ACADE, 2000. 457–472.

Russo, Joseph A. "Oral Style as Performance Style in Homer's *Odyssey*: Should we read Homer differently after Parry?" *Comparative Research on Oral Traditions: A Memorial for Milman Parry*. Ed. John Miles Foley. Columbus, OH: Slavica, 1987. 549–565.

Salaberry, Etienne. "Eskualdun seme gehienaz edo Eskualdun seme bertsulariaz." *Gure Herria* 26.2 (1954): 69–74.

Sallaberry, Jean-Dominique-Julien. *Chants populaires du Pays Basque*. Bayonne: Lamaignére, 1870.

Sánchez Rodilla, Manuel Cascón. *El País* 30 Jan. 2003.

Sánchez Vicente, Xuan Xose. *La Nueva España* 10 Feb. 2003.

Santa Cruz, Nicomedes. *La décima en el Perú*. Lima: Instituto de Estudios Peruanos, 1982.

Santamaría, Francisco J. *Diccionario general de americanismos*. 3 vols. Mexico City: Pedro Robredo, 1942.

Santana Henríquez, Germán. "Épea pteróeta 'palabras aladas'. El fenómeno de la oralidad desde Homero." *Actas del VI Encuentro-Festival Iberoamericano de la Décima y el Verso Improvisado (Las Palmas de Gran Canaria, del 6 al 11 de octubre de 1998)*. Vol.1. *Estudios*. Ed. Maximiano Trapero, Eladio Santana Martel and Carmen Márquez Montes. Las Palmas de Gran Canaria: Universidad de Las Palmas de Gran Canaria; ACADE, 2000. 109–116.

Santesteban Arizmendi, José Antonio. *Aires populares vascongados*. San Sebastián: Almacén de Música, 1862–70.

Sarasua, Jon. "El bertsolarismo vasco. Deasfío de la improvisación en la cultura moderna." *Actas del VI Encuentro-Festival Iberoamericano de la Décima y el Verso Improvisado (Las Palmas de Gran Canaria, del 6 al 11 de octubre de 1998)* Vol. 1. *Estudios*. Ed. Maximiano Trapero, Eladio Santana Martel and Carmen Márquez Montes Las Palmas de Gran Canaria: Universidad de Las Palmas de Gran Canaria; ACADE, 2000. 473–480.

Sawyer, R. Keith. *Pretend Play as Improvisation: Conversation in the Preschool Classroom*. Mahwah, NJ: Erlbaum, 1997.

Sbait, Dirgham H. "The Improvised-Sung Folk Poetry of the Palestinians." Diss. University of Washington, 1982.

———. "Palestinian Improvised-Sung Poetry: The Genres of *Hidā* and *Qarrādī̆*: Performance and Transmission." *Oral Tradition* 4 (1989): 213–35.

Sbert i Garau, Miquel. "La poesía improvisada en Baleares. Els glosadors." *Actas del VI Encuentro-Festival Iberoamericano de la Décima y el Verso Improvisado (Las Palmas de Gran Canaria, del 6 al 11 de octubre de 1998)* Vol. 1. *Estudios*. Ed. Maximiano Trapero, Eladio Santana Martel and Carmen Márquez Montes. Las Palmas de Gran Canaria: Universidad de Las Palmas de Gran Canaria; ACADE, 2000. 481–492.

Scheunemann, Dietrich. "Collecting Shells in the Age of Technological Reproduction: On Storytelling, Writing and the Film." *Orality, Literacy and Modern Media*. Ed. Dietrich Scheunemann. Columbia, SC: Camden House, 1996. 79–95.

Schirmann, Jefim. "The Function of the Hebrew Poet in Medieval Spain." *Jewish Social Studies* 16 (1954): 235–52.

Schmid, Beatrice et al. Eds., *"Sala de pasatiempo." Textos judeoespañoles de Salónica*. Preface by Samuel G. Armistead. Basel: Romanisches Seminar der Universität, 2003.

Schmid, Walter. *Der Wortschatz des «Cancionero de Baena»*. Bern: A. Francke, 1951.

Seibel, Beatriz. *El cantar del payador*. Buenos Aires: Ediciones del Sol; Biblioteca de Cultura Popular, 1988.

Semprún Donahue, Moraima de. "Nuevos indicios en la interpretación de 'Romance sonámbulo'." *Cuadernos Americanos* 194 (1974): 257–260.

Serbo-Croatian Heroic Songs (Srpskohrvatske junačke pjesme) (SCHS). Ed. and trans. Milman Parry, Albert Lord, and David Bynum. Cambridge, Mass. and Belgrade: Harvard University Press and the Serbian Academy of Sciences. Vols. 1–2, 3–4, 6, 14 (1953–).

Siemens Hernández, Lotear. "Antecedentes de la forma musical de la décima y observaciones históricas sobre su empleo en Canarias." *La décima popular en la tradición hispánica. Actas del simposio internacional sobre la décima (Las Palmas, 17–22 de diciembre 1992)*. Ed. Maximiano Trapero. Las Palmas de Gran Canaria: Universidad de Las Palmas de Gran Canaria; Cabildo Insular de Gran Canaria, 1994. 361–367.

Simmons, Merle E. *A Bibliography of the 'Romance' and Related Forms in Spanish America*. Bloomington: Indiana University Press, 1963.

Slater, Candace. *Stories on a String: The Brazilian «Literatura de Cordel»*. 2nd ed. Berkeley and Los Angeles: University of California Press, 1989.

Smith, Alan. "Cómo se anda en un sueño. El 'Romance sonámbulo' de Federico García Lorca." *Revista Hispánica Moderna* 46.1 (1993): 65–72.

Smith, C. Colin. Ed., *Spanish Ballads*. Oxford: Pergamon Press, 1969.

Sowayan, Saad Abdullah. *Nabati Poetry: The Oral Poetry of Arabia*. Berkeley and Los Angeles: University of California Press, 1985.

——. "'Tonight My Gun is Loaded'': Poetic Dueling in Arabia." *Oral Tradition* 4.1–2 (1989): 151–73.

Starkie, Walter F. *The Road to Santiago: Pilgrims of St. James.* New York: E.P. Dutton, 1957.

Steinschneider, Moritz. "Rangstreit-Literatur: Ein Beitrag zur vergleichenden Literatur- und Kultur- geschichte." *Sizungsberichte der Philosophich-Historischen Klasse der Kaiserlichen Akademie der Wissenschaften* (Vienna). 155. IV Abhandlung (1908): 1–87.

Suárez López, Jesús. *Nueva colección de Romances 1987–1994.* Oviedo and Madrid: Silva Asturiana, 1997.

——. *Cuentos del Siglo de oro en la tradición oral de Asturias.* Gijon: Museo del Pueblo de Asturias, 1998.

Suassuna, Ariano. "Coletânea da Poesia Popular Nordestina: Romances do Ciclo Heróico." *DECA: Revista do Departamento de Extensão Cultural e Artística* (Recife) 6.5 (1962): 11–27.

——. "Notas sobre o Romanceiro Popular do Nordeste." *Seleta em Prosa e Verso.* Ed. Silviano Santiago. Rio de Janeiro: José Olympio, 1974. 162–190.

Taboada Chivite, Xesús. *Etnografía galega.* Vigo: Galaxia, 1972.

al-Tanūḫī. *Kitab Jāmi' al-tawārīf.* Ed. D. S. Margliouth. 2 vols. Cairo: Maṭba'at Amīn Hindīya, n.d.

——. *The Table-Talk of a Mesopotamian Judge.* Trans. D. S. Margoliouth. London: The Royal Asiatic Society, 1922.

Thesiger, Wilfred. *Arabian Sands.* New York: Penguin, 1980.

Toribio, Laura. Personal interview by William A. Christian Jr. Sarceda, May 11, 2003.

Torner, Eduardo M. *Lírica Hispánica.* Madrid: Castalia, 1966.

Trapero, Maximiano. *Lírica tradicional canaria.* Las Palmas: «Biblioteca Básica Canaria», 1990.

——. "El romancero y la décima juntos y enfrentados en la tradición de Canarias." *La décima popular en la tradición hispánica. Actas del simposio internacional sobre la décima (Las Palmas, 17–22 de diciembre 1992).* Ed. Maximiano Trapero. Las Palmas de Gran Canaria: Universidad de Las Palmas de Gran Canaria; Cabildo Insular de Gran Canaria, 1994a.141–174.

——. Ed., *La décima popular en la tradición hispánica. Actas del Simposio Internacional (Las Palmas, 17–22 de diciembre 1992).* Las Palmas de Gran Canaria: Universidad de Las Palmas, 1994b.

——. Ed., *El libro de la décima. La poesía improvisada en el Mundo Hispánico.* Las Palmas de Gran Canaria: Universidad de Las Palmas de Gran Canaria, 1996.

——. "Un campeonato de bertsolaris." *La Provincia* (Las Palmas de Gran Canaria) Jan. 1, 1998: 37.

——. "Vicente Espinel, la décima espinela y lo que de ellos dicen los decimistas." *Actas del VI Encuentro-Festival Iberoamericano de la Décima y el Verso Improvisado (Las Palmas de Gran Canaria, del 6 al 11 de octubre de 1998).* Vol. 1. *Estudios.* Ed. Maximiano Trapero, Eladio Santana Martel and Carmen Márquez Montes. Las Palmas de Gran Canaria: Universidad de Las Palmas de Gran Canaria; ACADE, 2000. 117–137.

———. "La décima popular en la tradición hispánica." *La décima. Su historia, su geografía, sus manifestaciones*. Ed. Maximiano Trapero. La Laguna: Centro de la Cultura Popular Canaria; Câmara Municipal de Évora, 2001a. 61–100.

———. Ed., *La décima. Su historia, su geografía, sus manifestaciones*. La Laguna: Centro de la Cultura Popular Canaria; Câmara Municipal de Évora, 2001b.

———. "Improvised Oral Poetry in Spain." Old Songs, New Theories: A Symposium on Oral Improvisational Poetry. Center for Basque Studies, University of Nevada, Reno, May 16–17, 2003.

Trapero, Maximiano, Eladio Santana Martel and Carmen Márquez Montes. Eds., *Actas del VI Encuentro-Festival Iberoamericano de la Décima y el Verso Improvisado (Las Palmas de Gran Canaria, del 6 al 11 de octubre de 1998)*. 2 vols. Las Palmas de Gran Canaria: Universidad de Las Palmas de Gran Canaria; ACADE, 2000.

Trapero, Maximiano, and Alexis Díaz-Pimienta. "Glosario de la décima y de la improvisación poética." *La décima. Su historia, su geografía, sus manifestaciones*. Ed. Maximiano Trapero. La Laguna: Centro de la Cultura Popular Canaria; Câmara Municipal de Évora, 2001. 249–264.

Treku, Mattin [pseud. Mattin]. "Nere garaiko bertso-jartzailerik onena." *Deia* Nov. 6, 1977. 25.

Truffaut, Thierry. "Essai de classification des carnavals ruraux basques en 1983 et 1984." *Dantzariak* 33 (1986): 8–48.

———. "Apports des carnavals ruraux en Pays Basque pour l'étude de la mythologie: Le cas du Basa-Jaun." *Cuadernos de Sección de Folklore* 6. San Sebastián: Sociedad de Estudios Vascos, 1988. 69–81.

Urbeltz Navarro, Juan Antonio. *Dantzak. Notas sobre las danzas tradicionales de los vascos*. Bilbao: Caja Laboral de Bilbao, 1978.

———. *Bailar el caos*. Pamplona: Pamiela, 1994.

Usandivaras, Julio Díaz, and Julio Carlos Díaz Usandivaras. *Folklore y tradición. Antología argentina*. Buenos Aires: Raigal, 1953.

Valenciano, Ana. "Memoria, innovación y censura colectiva en la tradición oral. Épica yugoslava *versus* Romancero hispánico." *Estudios de folklore y literatura dedicados a Mercedes Díaz Roig*. Ed. Beatriz Garza Cuarón and Yvette Jiménez de Báez. Mexico City: El Colegio de México, 1992. 33–40.

Van Gelder, Geert Jan H. *Beyond the Line: Classical Arabic Literary Critics on the Coherence and Unity of the Poem*. Leiden: E. J. Brill, 1982.

———. *The Bad and the Ugly: Attitudes toward Invective Poetry (Hidjā') in Classical Arabic Literature*. Leiden: E. J. Brill, 1988.

Vejo Velarde, Eloy. *Memorias de un emigrante*. Santander: Artes Gráficas Resma, 1976.

Viegas Guerreiro, Manuel. *Para a História da Literatura Popular Portuguesa*. [Lisbon]: Instituto de Cultura Portuguesa, 1978.

Villasante, Luis. *Historia de la literatura vasca*. Bilbao: Sendo, 1961.

Walther, Hans. *Das streitgedicht in der Lateinishcen Literatur des Mittelalters*. München: Beck, 1920.

al-Warāglī, Ḥasan. *Al-Maqāmāt al-luzūmīya, taʾlīf Abū l-Ṭhir Muḥammad ibn Yūsuf al-Saraqusṭī*. Rabat: Manšūrāt ʿUkāẓ, 1995.

Ward, Donald J. "On the Poets and Poetry of the Indo-Europeans." *Journal of Indo-European Studies* 1.2 (1973a): 127–144.

———. "Scherz- und Spottlieder." *Handbuch des Volksliedes*. Ed. Rolf Wilhelm Brednich et al. Vol. 1. Munich: Wilhelm Fink, 1973b. 691–735.

Webber, Ruth House. "Hispanic Oral Literature: Accomplishments and Perspectives," *Oral-Formulaic Theory: A Folklore Casebook*. Ed. John Miles Foley. New York & London: Garland, 1990. 169–188.

Westermarck, Edward A. *Ritual and Belief in Morocco*. 2 vols. London: Macmillan, 1926.

White, Linda. "Orality and Basque Nationalism: Dancing with the Devil or Waltzing into the Future?" *Oral Tradition* 16.1 (2001): 3–28.

Wiet, Gaston. "Dabīḳ." *The Encyclopaedia of Islam*. 2nd ed. Vol. 2. E. J. Brill: Leiden, 1983. 72–73.

Wittgenstein, Ludwig. *Lectures and Conversations on Aesthetics, Psychology and Religious Belief*. Ed. C. Barr. Oxford: Basil Blackwell, 1966.

Wolf, Fernando J., and Conrado Hofmann. Eds., *Primavera y flor de romances*. 2 vols. Berlin: A. Asher, 1856.

Ya'ari, Ehud, and Ina Friedman. "Curses in Verses: Unusual Fighting Words." *The Atlantic* (February 1991): 22–26.

Yaqub, Nadia. "Some of Us Must Depart: An Intertextual Reading of the Mountain Poem by Ibn Khafājah." *Journal of Arabic Literature* 30 (1999): 240–255.

Ysursa, John M. *Basque Dance*. Boise: Tamarack Books, 1995.

Zabala, Abel. "Funciones del canto improvisado en Argentina y Uruguay." *Actas del VI Encuentro-Festival Iberoamericano de la Décima y el Verso Improvisado (Las Palmas de Gran Canaria, del 6 al 11 de octubre de 1998)*. Vol. 1. *Estudios*. Ed. Maximiano Trapero, Eladio Santana Martel and Carmen Márquez Montes. Las Palmas de Gran Canaria: Universidad de Las Palmas de Gran Canaria; ACADE, 2000. 273–288.

Zaballa, Indalecio [pseud. Masio], and Antonio Zavala. *La última trova*. Biblioteca de Narrativa Popular 1. Oiartzun: Sendoa, 1993.

Zárate, Manuel F., and Dora Pérez de Zárate. *La décima y la copla en Panamá*. Panama City: «La Estrella de Panamá», 1953.

Zavala [Zabala], Antonio. *Pello Errotaren bizitza bere alabak kontatua*. Tolosa: Auspoa, 1963.

———. *Bosquejo de Historia del Bertsolarismo*. San Sebastián: Auñamendi, 1964.

———. "El cancionero vasco de las guerras carlistas." *Actes del Colloqui sobre cançó tradicional (Reus, setembre 1990).* Montserrat: Diputació de Tarragona, 1994. 455–464.

———. "Bertso berri billa Euskalerrian zear." *Auspoaren Auspoa* 1.238 (1996a): 21–40.

———. "Bosquejo de historia del bersolarismo." *Auspoaren Auspoa* 1 (1996b): 109–254.

———. "El bersolarismo." *Auspoaren Auspoa* 1 (1996c): 255–282.

———. *Oinez eta jakin miñez II.* Oiartzun: Auspoa; Sendoa, 1999.

———. "El conocimiento del idioma como base y fundamento de la improvisación en verso." *Actas del VI Encuentro-Festival Iberoamericano de la Décima y el Verso Improvisado (Las Palmas de Gran Canaria, del 6 al 11 de octubre de 1998).* Vol. 1. *Estudios.* Ed. Maximiano Trapero, Eladio Santana Martel and Carmen Márquez Montes. Las Palmas de Gran Canaria: Universidad de Las Palmas de Gran Canaria; ACADE, 2000. 493–497.

———. Address. Old Songs, New Theories: A Symposium on Oral Improvisational Poetry. Center for Basque Studies, University of Nevada, Reno, May 16–17, 2003.

Zemke, John. "General Hispanic Traditions." *Teaching Oral Traditions.* Ed. John Miles Foley. New York: Modern Language Association, 1998. 202–15.

Zipes, Jack. "Revisiting Benjamin's 'The Story Teller': Reviving the Past to Move Forward." *Happily Ever After: Fairy Tales, Children and the Culture Industry.* New York: Routledge, 1997. 129–142.

———. *Sticks and Stones: The Troublesome Success of Children's Literature from Slovenly Peter to Harry Potter.* New York: Routledge, 2001.

Zubimendi, Joseba. "Lenengo bertsolari eguna." *Yakintza* 3 (1935): 141–154.

———. "Bigarren bertsolari eguna." *Yakintza* 4 (1936): 141–158.

Zulaika, Joseba. *Bertsolarien jokoa eta jolasa.* Donostia: La Primitiva Casa Baroja, 1985.

———. *Basque Violence: Metaphor and Sacrament.* Reno: University of Nevada Press, 1988.

———. *Bertsolaritza bi saio.* Andoain: Bertsolari liburuak, 2003.

Zumthor, Paul. *Introducción a la poesía oral.* Madrid: Taurus Humanidades, 1991.

Zwettler, Michael. *The Oral Tradition of Classical Arabic Poetry: Its Character and Implications.* Columbus: Ohio State University Press, 1978.

Index

poetics as model for oral tradition, 282–83; intersection of written and oral media, 72–73; promise in, 252–57; text as pretext in *bertsolaritza*, 283–84

Literatura oral euskérica ("Oral Literature in Basque"), 186, 187

"Literatura oral vasca," 199, 345n

"Lizardi" (Agirre, José Mari), 185–86

Lizaso, Joxe, 286

Lizaso, Sebastián, *fig.*91, 203, 287, *fig.*310, 354

Lopategi, Jon, 195, 286

López Linage, Javier, 131n

Lorca, Federico García, 11, 161–79

Lord, Albert Bates: East African funeral verses, 265n; ethnographer as *bertsolari*, 260; Homeric rhetoric, 282–83; improvisation, 85n; oral-formulaic improvisation, 149; oralist theory, 293; prophetic speech, 83; repetition in *bertsolaritza*, 268; southern Slavic popular epic poetry, 46–47, 67, 78

lore jokoak ("poetry contests"), 348

Lourenço, 89–90

Loyola (Loiola), Spain, 15–16, 256

Lujanbio, Joxe Manuel ("Txirrita"), 20–22, 187, *fig.*189, 190, 192, 199n

Lujanbio, Maialen, 203, *fig.*270, 287

Lusignan, F. Etienne de, 207

lute, 206, 207

Lydian mode, 355

lyric poems, 50–51, 76–77, *fig.*76

Mabinogion, 70

Madariaga, Bautista, *fig.*99

Mahabharata, 70

Maia, Jon, 292–93, *fig.*310

Maimonides, Moses, 138–39

"Maitale Kutuna" ("Favorite Lover"), 185

Major mode, 353, 354, 355, 362

malagueña trovera, 57

male poetic genres, 76–77

Mallea-Olaetxe, Joxe, 11–12, 231–44, 429

Mallorca, *glosadores* of, 59, 206–7

Manterola Beldarrain, José de, 346

Manual (Munar, Felip), 59

Mañukorta, 297

maqāma, 151, 155–59

"Maqāma 41" (The Berbers), 155

marexalak ("blacksmiths"), *Maskarada* performances, 212–17

Marín, José María, 57

"Markesaran alaba" ("The daughter of the marquis"), 231

Martikorena, Erramun, 195–96

Martín Fierro, 37–39, 48, 192

Maskarada of Muskildi (1987), 218–24, 227–28

Maskarada performances: anthropological survey of, 210–12; costumes, 216–18; generally, 11, 209–10; masks, 216–17; public participation in, *fig.*211; roles, 212–15, 217–24; units and sequences in, 210–16; verbals arts, 224–30

maskarakaiak, 226

Massada legends (Israel), 115

mass media, 290–91, 309–10

Mattin, 193, 195

Mayan contemporary oral tradition, 72

mayordomas (wedding versifiers), 131

Maza Solano, Tomás, 121

media events, *fig.*69

medizina ("doctor"), *Maskarada* performances, 212–16, 223, 226

Meetings-Festivals, 62

melismas, 58

melodies. *See also* singing *bertsoak*, 52–53, 268–71, 325, 362

memoria, 303

"memorial poetry," 51

Memory of Past Days, The, 20

memory, of *bertsolariak*, 308, 334, 335

Mendiko Euskaldunak club, 239

Mendiluze, Aitor, 331–34

List of Contributors

Samuel G. Armistead (Ph.D., Princeton University) is Professor of Spanish Literature at the University of California, Davis. His fields of specialization are Medieval Spanish, Comparative Literature, and Hispanic Folk Literature. His research has been supported by grants and fellowships from ACLS, Amado, Guggenheim, NEH, Littauer, and NSF. Honors include Fellow of the Medieval Academy of America and of the American Folklore Society, Honorary Member of the Asociación Hispánica de Literatura Medieval (Alcalá de Henares) and UC Davis Faculty Research Lecturer (1998). He has published widely on medieval and oral literature, including *Judeo-Spanish Ballads from Oral Tradition: Epic Ballads (Folk Literature of the Sephardic Jews)* Vol. 2 (1986); *The Hispanic Ballad Today: History, Comparativism, Critical Bibliography* (S. Armistead et al., eds., 1979). He is currently writing a series on the traditional literature of the Sephardic Jews and is co-editing a series on the Portuguese traditional romances from the Azores Islands.

Gorka Aulestia was professor of Basque Literature at the Universidad de Deusto from 1989 until his retirement in 2000. He was also professor of Basque Literature in the Basque American Consortium in San Sebastián. He has been a member of Euskaltzaindia (the Royal Academy of the Basque Language) since 1996, and an editor of the journal *Sancho El Sabio*. He obtained a Ph.D. in Basque Studies (Language and Literature) at the University of Nevada, Reno in 1987. His publications include *Basque-English Dictionary* (1989), *English-Basque Dictionary* (with Linda White, 1990), *Erbesteko Euskal Literaturaren Antologia* (1992), *Improvisational Poetry from the Basque Country* (1995), and *The Basque Poetic Tradition* (2000).

William A. Christian Jr. is an independent scholar who writes mainly about religion in Spain and southern Europe. His approach combines insights from history, anthropology, and sociology. His central concern has been the relationship of individuals and groups with the saints, Mary, and God. His studies involve fieldwork in contemporary communities and archival work covering the medieval and early modern periods. His works include *Person and God in a Spanish Valley* (1972), *Trovas y Comparsas del Alto Nansa* (1972; rev. ed., 1998), and *Visionaries: the Spanish Republic and the Reign of Christ* (1999).

Andoni Egaña is a *bertsolari* who studied Basque at the University of the Basque Country (Gasteiz), and has won the last three National *Bertsolaritza* Championships in 1993,

1997 and 2001. He writes articles and television scripts on *bertsolaritza*, and has written several books, including children's stories and a novel. He is the co-author (with Joxerra Garzia and Jon Sarasua) of *The Art of Bertsolaritza: Improvised Basque Verse Singing* (2001).

James W. Fernandez is Professor Emeritus of Anthropology and of Social Sciences at the University of Chicago and has taught at Princeton, Dartmouth and Smith College. He has done ethnographic research in Africa and is presently working in northern Spain and Atlantic Fringe Europe on regionalism, shifting lifeways (from agro-pastoralism to mining to reindustrialization) and on revitalization processes. Although he retired in June 2000, he continues to teach. His publications include: *Persuasions and Performances: The Play of Tropes in Culture* (1986); (ed.) *Beyond Metaphor: The Theory of Tropes in Anthropology* (1991); (with Mary Taylor Huber, eds.) *Ironic Practice.* (2001).

Kepa Fernández de Larrinoa received a Ph.D. from the London School of Economics and Political Science. He is Profesor Titular de Universidad in the Department of Philosophy of Values and Social Anthropology, University of the Basque Country. From 1995–1998, he served as chairman of the Ethnography-Anthropology Department at Eusko Ikaskuntza (the Basque Studies Society). His publications include: (ed.), *Fronteras y puentes culturales: danza tradicional e identidad social* (1998); (ed.) *Invitación al estudio de la danza tradicional en el País Vasco* (1998); *Mujer, ritual y fiesta: género, antropología y teatro de carnaval en la sociedad rural pirenaica* (1997).

John Miles Foley is a specialist in comparative oral traditions. He serves as Curators' Professor of Classical Studies and English, as W.H. Byler Distinguished Chair in the Humanities, and as the founding Director of the Center for Studies in Oral Tradition at the University of Missouri-Columbia. His publications include *Traditional Oral Epic* (1990), *The Singer of Tales in Performance* (1995), and *Homer's Traditional Art* (1999). He has received awards and fellowships from the NEH, the Guggenheim Foundation, the American Council of Learned Societies, the Fulbright Commission, and other organizations.

Joxerra Garzia received a Ph.D. in Audiovisual Communication and Advertising, with a dissertation on *bertsolariak*. He produced a radio program on the subject for the Basque public radio station, Euskadi Irratia, and later created, directed and hosted the TV program "Hitzetik Hortzera" on the Basque-language public television station, Euskal Telebista 1. A *bertsolari* himself, he frequently judges *bertsolaritza* championships, and currently lectures on advertising at the University of the Basque Country. He is the co-author (with Andoni Egaña and Jon Sarasua) of *The Art of Bertsolaritza: Improvised Basque Verse Singing* (2001).

Israel J. Katz, a former Guggenheim Fellow (Spain, 1975–76), has been a Research Associate at the University of California at Santa Cruz and Davis since 1982, funded by the NEH. He specializes in the music of the Mediterranean region, with an emphasis on the medieval and traditional music of Spain, especially the ballad traditions of the Sephardic Jews. His awards include grants from the Rockefeller Foundation, Ford Foundation, Canada Council, American Philosophical Society, and a Council for Research and Humanities Award. His publications include *Judeo-Spanish Traditional Ballads from Jerusalem* (1972–75); and, with Samuel G. Armistead and Joseph H. Silverman, the series *Folk Literature of the Sephardic Jews* (1986–).

Joxe Mallea-Olaetxe received degrees in History from the University of Nebraska, Lincoln, and the University of Nevada, Reno. He has taught Basque language and history classes at the University of Nevada, Reno and the Truckee Meadows Community College, where he is currently employed. His extensive ongoing research interests focus on Basques during the time of the Spanish Colonies (especially Bishop Zumarraga in the sixteenth century) and in the American West, and in particular, sheepherder arborglyphs and *bertsoak*. His publications include *The Power of Nothing: The Life and Adventures of Ignacio "Idaho" Urrutia* (2000), *Speaking Through the Aspens: Basque Tree Carvings in California and Nevada* (2000), *Shooting From the Lip: Bertsolariak Ipar Amerikan: Improvised Basque Verse Singing* (in English and Basque, 2003), and *Pedro Juan Etxamendy, Californiako Bertsolaria* (ed. and intro., in Basque, 2003).

James T. Monroe (Ph.D., Harvard University) is a specialist in Arabic literature who teaches in the Departments of Comparative Literature and Near Eastern Studies, University of California, Berkeley. He works in the areas of lyric poetry, the Middle Ages, and East-West relations with particular interest in the importance of the Arab contribution to Spanish civilization. His publications on Arabic literature, with special emphasis on its Hispano-Arabic component, include *Ten Hispano-Arabic Strophic Songs in the Modern Oral Tradition: Music and Texts* (1989), with Benjamin M. Liu, and *The Art of Badi az-Zaman al-Hamadhani as Picaresque Narrative* (1985).

Wifredo de Ràfols, associate professor and graduate director in Spanish at the University of Nevada, Reno, received his M.A. from the Johns Hopkins University and Ph.D. from the University of California, Davis. He has delivered numerous conference papers in the United States and Europe and published widely within his area of specialization – 19th- and 20th-century Spanish literature. His publications examine works by Zorrilla, Galdós, Valle-Inclán, Jiménez, Jorge Guillén, and Lorca. His general research interests include hermeneutics, artificial reading, and bias studies.

Jon Sarasua is a *bertsolari* who received a Ph.D. in Basque Philology, and currently teaches the History of Thought at the Mondragon University in the Basque Country. He has published many popular articles, as well as co-authoring a book with Andoni Egaña on modern *bertsolaritza*: *Zozoak beleari* (1997). He is also the co-author (with Joxerra Garzia and Andoni Egaña) of *The Art of Bertsolaritza: Improvised Basque Verse Singing* (2001).

Maximiano Trapero is Professor of Spanish Philology at the University of Las Palmas de Gran Canaria. His research has centered on the fields of semantics, *El campo semántico 'deporte'* (1979), the lexicon of place names, *Para una teoría lingüística de la toponimia* (1995), *Diccionario de toponimia canaria*, with a prologue by Eugenio Coseriu (1999), and traditional poetry, as well as Hispanic improvised poetry. He is Vice President of the Asociación Iberoamericana de la Décima y el Verso Improvisado, and he directed the Encounter-Festival of Improvised Poetry in Las Palmas in 1992 and 1998, resulting in the publications *El libro de la décima* (1996) and *Actas del VI Encuentro-Festival Iberoamericano de la Décima y el Verso Improvisado* (2000).

Linda White received a Ph.D. in Basque Studies (Language and Literature) from the University of Nevada, Reno, and is Associate Professor at the Center for Basque Studies. Her current research is focused on the effect of nationalism on Basque women's lives as reflected in Laura Mintegi's *Nerea eta biok*. Other interests include genre fiction in Basque literature, the new women writers, Basque women who write in Spanish, and *bertsolaritza* and oral literature. Her awards include the Mousel-Feltner Award for Excellence in Research and/or Creative Activity (University of Nevada, Reno, 2000) and an induction into the Basque Hall of Fame by the Society of Basque Studies in America (1993). Her publications include *Basque-English English-Basque Dictionary* (with Gorka Aulestia, 1992), *English-Basque Dictionary* (with Gorka Aulestia, 1990), and several translations for the Basque Book Series.

Antonio Zavala was born in Tolosa, Gipuzkoa, and completed his early education in the Colegio del Sagrado Corazón and the Colegio de los Escolapios de Tolosa. He later entered the Jesuit Order in 1945, and his ecclesiastical studies were completed in Loyola, Oña, Javier, and Gandía. He began research on *bertsolariak* in 1954, and created the Colección Auspoa in 1961, in which he has authored over three hundred titles.

John Zemke is an Associate Professor of Romance Languages at the University of Missouri in Columbia. His main area of research is Hispanic oral traditions, particularly Judeo-Spanish literature. His publications include *Critical Approaches to the Proverbios Morales of Shem Tov de Carrión: An Annotated Bibliography* (1997), and he is the editor of the "Regimiento de la vida" (Salonica, 1564) by Moses ben Baruch Almosnino.

Joseba Zulaika received a Ph.D. in Anthropology from Princeton University, and is currently Director of the Center for Basque Studies, University of Nevada, Reno. His research topics include Basque culture and politics, various traditional occupations (fishermen, hunters, farmers), and theories of symbolism, ritual and discourse. He teaches a course on Basque Storytellers and Troubadours and is the author, among other works, of *Basque Violence: Metaphor and Sacrament* (1988) and *Bertsolariaren jokoa eta jolasa* (1985).